D1501327

DATA FOR BETTER LIVES

WORLD BANK GROUP

ISSN, ISBN, e-ISBN, and DOI:

Softcover
ISSN: 0163-5085
ISBN: 978-1-4648-1600-0
e-ISBN: 978-1-4648-1601-7
DOI: 10.1596/978-1-4648-1600-0

Hardcover
ISSN: 0163-5085
ISBN: 978-1-4648-1607-9
DOI: 10.1596/978-1-4648-1607-9

Cover design: Dania Kibbi, Base Three Studio

Cover illustration: Mijke Coebergh

Interior design: George Kokkinidis, Design Language, Brooklyn, New York, with updates and additional figure design by Dania Kibbi, Base Three Studio

Library of Congress Control Number: 2021935945

Contents

Boxes

Figures

Maps

Tables

Foreword

Data governance is the subject of intense debate in advanced economies and increasingly among large emerging markets. And yet many complex policy questions remain unanswered. In response, *World Development Report 2021: Data for Better Lives* surveys the emerging landscape and provides policy makers with a framework for thinking through the issues, opportunities, and trade-offs. One thing is clear: the perspective of lower-income countries has so far been largely absent from these global debates and urgently needs to be heard.

Data are a double-edged sword. On the one hand, they offer tremendous potential to create value by improving programs and policies, driving economies, and empowering citizens. On the other hand, data accumulation can lead to a concentration of economic and political power, raising the possibility that data may be misused in ways that harm citizens. Data are a resource that can be used and reused repeatedly to create more and more value, but there is a problem—the more data are reused, the higher is the risk of abuse.

It is hard to imagine a more dramatic example of these opportunities and tensions than the COVID-19 pandemic. Countries around the world have moved swiftly to repurpose mobile phone records to monitor the spread of the virus. But at the same time, they have struggled to balance this benefit against privacy concerns and the risk of misuse.

Beyond pandemic times, the statistical capacity to produce and effectively use core economic and social data is limited. Many poor countries are unable to accurately track public finances, report on external debt, or monitor their development goals. Without such data, the ability to hold governments accountable and track progress withers.

Data governance arrangements to facilitate greater use of data while safeguarding against misuse remain in their infancy. The legal and regulatory frameworks for data are inadequate in lower-income countries, which all too often have gaps in critical safeguards as well as shortages of data-sharing measures. There, the data systems and infrastructure that enable interoperability and allow data to flow to more users are incomplete; less than 20 percent of low- and middle-income countries have modern data infrastructure such as colocation data centers and direct access to cloud computing facilities. Even where nascent data systems and governance frameworks exist, a lack of institutions with the requisite administrative capacity, decision-making autonomy, and financial resources holds back their effective implementation and enforcement.

To address these concerns, *World Development Report 2021* calls for a new social contract for data—one that enables the use and reuse of data to create economic and social *value*, promotes *equitable* opportunities to benefit from data, and fosters citizens' *trust* that they will not be harmed by misuse of the data they provide. However, in seeking such a social contract, lower-income countries are too often disadvantaged because they lack the infrastructure and skills to capture data and turn them into value; the scale and agency to participate equitably in global data markets and their governance; and the institutional and regulatory frameworks to create trust in data systems.

Forging a new social contract for data is a pressing domestic policy priority that will require strengthening national data systems and engaging all stakeholders at the national level. Because of the global scale of data, some of the most challenging aspects of the social contract also call for closer international cooperation to harmonize regulations and coordinate policies—bilaterally, regionally, and globally. Critical areas for international engagement include reform of international taxation rights for data-driven businesses, World Trade Organization arrangements for trade in data-enabled services, regional collaboration on the development of data infrastructure, international harmonization of technical standards to support interoperability, and bilateral collaboration on law enforcement and antitrust regulation.

The World Bank stands ready to support its client countries on this important and challenging agenda. The findings of this *World Development Report* will shape support for client countries by identifying where public and private sector investments are the most critical, defining a rich program for policy reform and technical assistance, and highlighting areas in which global initiatives can help to convene and facilitate cross-border cooperation.

Realizing the full value of data will depend on a substantial commitment and effort, and it will be difficult. But the cost of failure is a world of missed opportunities and greater inequities.

David R. Malpass
President
The World Bank Group

Acknowledgments

This year's *World Development Report* (WDR) was prepared by a team led by directors Robert Cull, Vivien Foster, and Dean Jolliffe. Malarvizhi Veerappan served as report manager and as a member of the Report's leadership. The core team was composed of Jaffar Al-Rikabi, Adele Moukheibir Barzelay, Miriam Bruhn, Rong Chen, Niccolò Comini, Samuel Paul Fraiberger, Craig Hammer, Talip Kilic, Jan Loeprick, Daniel G. Mahler, Michael Minges, Martin Molinuevo, Nancy Morrison, David Newhouse, Sara Nyman, Vincent Francis Ricciardi III, David Satola, Dorothe Singer, Philip Wollburg, and Bilal Zia, together with research analysts Kenneth Zaul Moreno Sermeno, Nikkie Pacheco, and Elizabeth Salazar. Selome Missael Paulos provided the team with administrative support.

Davida Louise Connon, Hai-Anh H. Dang, Cem Dener, Lucas Kitzmüller, Aspasea Mckenna, and David Medine were members of the extended team. Rory Macmillan and Zia Mehrabi provided input as expert consultants. The Report was sponsored by the World Bank's Development Economics Vice Presidency and was prepared in close partnership with the Infrastructure Vice Presidency. Overall guidance was provided by Carmen M. Reinhart, Chief Economist, and Aart Kraay, Deputy Chief Economist. The team is especially grateful for the support and guidance provided by Makhtar Diop, who was at that time Vice President, Infrastructure, and Haishan Fu, Director, Data Group. The team is also appreciative of the comments and suggestions from Mari E. Pangestu, Managing Director, Development Policy and Partnerships. In the early months of the Report's preparation, Pinelopi Goldberg, then Chief Economist, provided guidance as well.

The team received suggestions from an advisory panel of high-level government officials, representatives of national statistical agencies and competition authorities, and private sector leaders: Anil Arora (Chief Statistician of Canada), Ola Awad (President, Palestinian Central Bureau of Statistics), Dr. Long Chen (Director, Luohan Academy, representing Alibaba Group), Neil Jackson (Chief Statistician, Foreign, Commonwealth and Development Office of the UK), Kersti Kaljulaid (President, Republic of Estonia), Francis W. Kariuki (Director-General, Competition Authority of Kenya), Zia Khan (Senior Vice President, Innovation, The Rockefeller Foundation), Ming Maa (President, Grab), Joyce Murray (Minister, Digital Government, Canada), Nandan Nilekani (Cofounder, Infosys, and architect of India's Data Empowerment and Protection Architecture), Regina Opondo (Community Director, Kounkuey Design Initiative), Sandra Quijada Javer (Director, National Institute of Statistics of Chile), Haleema Saeed (Director General, International Relations, Palestinian Central Bureau of Statistics), Julio A. Santaella (President, National Institute of Statistics and Geography of Mexico), Pravin Srivastava (Secretary and Chief Statistician of India), Kecuk Suhariyanto (Chief Statistician, BPS Statistics Indonesia), David Tudor (Group General Counsel, Prosus Group), Rodger Voorhies (President, Global Growth and Opportunity Division, Bill & Melinda Gates Foundation), Sheila Warren (Head, Blockchain and Data Policy, World Economic Forum), and Biratu Yigezu (Director, CSA Ethiopia). The team also received guidance from a technical board of leading academics: Emmanuelle Auriol (Research Faculty, University of Toulouse), Marshall Burke (Associate Professor, Stanford University), Luciano Floridi (Faculty, University of Oxford), Jan Kramer (Faculty and Chair, Internet and Telecommunications Business, University of Passau), Jacques Kremer (President, WorldWide Advisors, Inc.), Bruno Liebhaber (Director General, Centre on

Regulation in Europe), Fernando Perini (Senior Program Specialist, International Development Research Centre), John Pullinger (President, International Association for Official Statistics), Anna Scherbina (Associate Professor, Brandeis University), and Tommaso Valetti (Faculty, Imperial College London). The team valued their advice and found it very useful. Finally, Shaida Badiee, Oliver Chinganya, Johannes Jutting, Stephen MacFeely, Angela Me, and Claire Melamed provided specialized reviews of chapter 9. However, the views expressed in the Report do not necessarily reflect those of these advisers and reviewers.

The team would also like to thank the following World Bank staff, who were members of the "BrainsTrust," for their guidance during preparation of the Report: Luis Alberto Andres, João Pedro Azevedo, Andrea Barone, Kathleen Beegle, Tania Begazo, Jerome Bezzina, Calogero Carletto, Andrew L. Dabalen, Vyjayanti Desai, Marianne Fay, Michael Ferrantino, Marelize Gorgens, Mary Hallward-Driemeier, Kimberly D. Johns, Tim Kelly, Saki Kumagai, Daniel Lederman, William F. Maloney, Fredesvinda F. Montes Herraiz, James Neumann, Umar Serajuddin, Sharada Srinivasan, Davide Strusani, and Paolo Verme. Background and related research, along with dissemination, are being generously supported by the KDI School of Public Policy and Management (KDIS) Partnership Trust Fund, World Bank's Knowledge for Change Program (KCP, a multidonor trust fund), and the United States Agency for International Development.

The team drew on the analysis, research, and literature reviews of researchers and specialists from across the world. In addition, the team would like to thank the following for feedback and helpful discussions: Susan Ariel Aaronson, Ali Abbas, Moctar Aboubacar, Karina Acosta, Sonia Ahmand, Sabina Alkire, Noam Angrist, Belinda Archibong, Kaushik Basu, Vitoria Beard, Theresa Beltramo, Willem Buiter, Mayra Buvinic, Tsenguunjav Byambasuren, Anupam Chander, Anindya Chatterjee, Nancy Chau, Katie Clancy, Julie Crowley, Shanta Devarajan, Gary Fields, Avi Goldfarb, Zihan Hu, Yingyi Jin, Ravi Kanbur, Carlos Lopez, Bentley MacLeod, Chelsea Madryga, Annabella Ng, Jose Antonio Ocampo, Kevin O'Neil, Ariel Ortiz-Bobea, Brian Park, Michael Pisa, Maria Poli, Cristian Pop-Eleches, Christian Reimsbach Kounatze, Elettra Ronchi, Benjamin David Roseth, Phet Sayo, Heba Shams, Harman Sing Dhodi, Jenna Slotin, Michael Stanger, Joseph Stiglitz, Eric Swanson, Aberash Tariku, Jim Tebrake, Jeni Tennison, Anh Phuock Thien Nguyen, Kathryn Toure, Miguel Urquiola, Eric Verhoogen, Stefaan G. Verhulst, Sonali Vyas, and Yue Wang.

The following World Bank colleagues provided insightful comments, feedback, collaboration, and support: Rabah Arezki, Audrey Ariss, Angela Armstrong, Aziz Atamanov, Natalia Baal, Prospere R. Backiny-Yetna, Guadalupe Bedoya, Kathleen Beegle, Abdoullahi Beidou, Moussa Blimpo, Hana Brixi, Niklas Buehren, Greta L. Bull, Maurizio Bussolo, Cesar Calderon, Yu Cao, Greg Chen, Louise Cord, Paul Andres Corral Rodas, Jose Cuesta, Conrad Daly, Richard Damania, Olivia D'Aoust, Francesca Daverio, Zelalem Yilma Debebe, Asli Demirgüç-Kunt, Francesca de Nicola, Tami Ann Dokken, Mark Dutz, Alison Evans, Pablo Fajnzylber, Deon P. Filmer, Juliane Fries, Isis Gaddis, Emilia Galiano, Roberta V. Gatti, Tina George, Alejandro Medina Giopp, Chorching Goh, Lesly Goh, Markus Goldstein, Tania Gomez, Aparajita Goyal, Caren Grown, Boutheina Guermazi, Afef Haddad, Daniel Halim, Stephane Hallegatte, Nagaraja Harshadeep, Kristen Himelein, Johannes G. Hoogeveen, Chyi-Yun Huang, Elisabeth Huybens, Roumeen Islam, Ergys Islamaj, Ann-Sofie Jespersen, Anna Kalashyan, Woubet Kassa, Faruk Khan, Young Eun Kim, Soo Min Ko, Florence Kondylis, Ayhan Kose, Holly Krambeck, Megumi Kubota, Christoph Lakner, Somik Lall, Adriana Legovini, Norman Loayza, Nancy Lozano Gracia, Morgan Sofia Lucey, Cathrine Machingauta, Andrew D. Mason, Aaditya Mattoo, Anna Metz, Frederic Meunier, Sveta Milusheva, Miriam Muller, Mamta Murthi, James Neumann, Rochelle Glenene O'Hagan, Sandie Okoro, Madalina Papahagi, Utz Johann Pape, Elizaveta Perova, Tobias Pfutze, Martin Raiser, Laura Ralston, Martin Rama, Pooja Rao, Vijayendra Rao, Sheila Reszapi, Mark Roberts, Denis Robitaille, Carlos Rodriguez-Castelan, Dan Oliver Rogger, Clelia Rontoyanni, Rosemary Rop, Karla Viviana Saavedra Betancourt, Arisha Salman, Tara Sarma, Pierre Sauve, Marc Tobias Schiffbauer, Ethel Sennhauser, Gabriel Sensenbrenner, Fatima Shah, Parmesh Shah, Nurlina Shaharuddin, Siddharth Sharma, Brian William Stacy, Clara Stinshoff,

Prachi Tadsare, Daria Taglioni, Jomo Tariku, Jeff Thindwa, Hans Timmer, Margaret Triyana, Tea Trumbic, Vladimir Tsirkunov, Andrew Whitby, Mark Williams, Quentin Wodon, Keong Min Yoon, and Albert G. Zeufack.

Nancy Morrison provided developmental guidance in drafting the Report, which was edited by Sabra Ledent and proofread by Gwenda Larsen and Catherine Farley. Robert Zimmermann verified the Report's extensive citations. Dania Kibbi, Base Three Studio, was the principal graphic designer. Special thanks go to Stephen Pazdan, who coordinated and oversaw production of the Report; Mark McClure, who provided assistance; and the World Bank's Formal Publishing Program. The team would also like to thank Mary C. Fisk, who coordinated multiple translations of the overview and main messages; Bouchra Belfqih and her team in Translation and Interpretation, who worked patiently on the translations; Patricia Katayama, who oversaw the overall publication process; and Deb Barker and Yaneisy Martinez, who managed the printing and electronic conversions of the Report and its many ancillary products. Naureen Aziz, Mark Felsenthal, Chisako Fukuda, David Mariano, and Mikael Reventar developed the communications and engagement strategy. Monique Pelloux Patron provided the team with resource management support. The team would also like to thank Maria Alyanak, Marcelo Buitron, Gabriela Calderon Motta, Maria del Camino Hurtado, and Alejandra Ramon for their help with coordination.

Beyond Words studio designed and developed the WDR 2021 website (http://wdr2021.world bank.org) and data stories. The team comprised Kate Ashton, Rebecca Conroy, Jamie Gilman, Chris Hankins, Ceri Jones, Becca Muir, Richard Pullinger, Duncan Swain, and Lucy Swan. The illustrations for the website were created by Elisabetta Calabritto. Maarten Lambrechts and Adrianus Willem Tulp developed the website's data stories. Emmanuel Cosmas Maliganya, Vidhya Nagarajan, Balaji Natarajan, Somu Sinthamani, Anushka Thewarapperuma, and Roula Yazigi contributed to website development and dissemination.

This Report draws on background papers prepared by Meaza Abraham, Rodrigo Barajas, Noelia Carreras, Anupam Chander, Sandeep Chandy, Yuan Fang, Martina Francesca Ferracane, Angelina Fisher (New York University), Dayoung Park, Sharada Srinivasan, Clara Stinshoff, Thomas Streinz (New York University), Erik van der Marel, Dereje Wolde, Isabel Yu, and the WDR team. Federico Cardenas Chacon, Nicolas Conserva, Lillyana Sophia Daza Jaller, Paris Gkartzonikasm, New Doe Kaledzi, Olga Kuzmina, Aliaksandra Tyhrytskaya, and Yasmin Zand provided support for the data collection and research required for the Global Data Regulation Survey prepared for this Report.

Contributors to the special-feature spotlights in the Report are Diana Jimena Arango, Anna-Maria Bogdanova, Martin Brocklehurst, Libby Hepburn, Haruna Kashiwase, Stephen MacFeely, Angela Me, Sveta Milusheva, Vijayendra Rao, David Rogers, Evis Rucaj, Sven Schade, Lea Shanley, Rubena Sukaj, Vladimir Tsirkunov, Mariana Varese, and Divyanshi Wadhwa. The team would also like to thank the World Bank colleagues who helped organize and facilitate consultations and advised on translations: Jaffar Al-Rikabi, Adele Moukheibir Barzelay, Rong Chen, Candyce Da Cruz Rocha, Nicole El Hajj, Vivien Foster, and Jevgenijs Steinbuks.

The WDR team consulted policy makers, international organizations, civil society organizations, private sector companies, development partners, academics, research institutions, as well as the offices of the World Bank's Executive Directors and Bank colleagues. This year's *World Development Report* faced the additional challenge of the COVID-19 pandemic, which made it impossible to conduct the usual face-to-face consultation meetings. Nonetheless, the team was able to turn this into an advantage because virtual consultation events enabled much wider participation by hundreds of stakeholders. Due to travel restrictions, the team conducted consultations using a digital format and partner networks, thereby allowing more people with diverse backgrounds to participate. Some of the events focused on regional and targeted stakeholder consultations in multiple languages, allowing hard-to-reach organizations to join the discussion. Interactions with core contributing units to the *World Development Report* as part of ongoing debates in certain areas such as taxes leveraged wider consultations taking place on these related issues. Team members also drew heavily on their own experiences and interactions with the many data professionals, statisticians, data scientists, civil society organizations, and policy makers working in often difficult conditions to use data to achieve development outcomes.

The consultations were launched in October 2019 with a high-level roundtable—a side event of the World Bank's annual meetings—and continued until October 2020. The team also conducted a series of bilateral consultations from April through June 2020 with the national statistical offices of Canada, Chile, Ethiopia, India, Indonesia, Mexico, the United Kingdom, and West Bank and Gaza. The team thanks the organizers of the many events that brought together a wide variety of stakeholders, including government officials, civil society organizations, academic institutions, the private sector, and international organizations. The organizers were Germany's Federal Ministry for Economic Cooperation and Development (BMZ) and Deutsche Gesellschaft für Internationale Zusammenarbeit (GIZ); Canada's International Development Research Centre (IDRC), which organized consultations across Africa, Asia, and Latin America and the Caribbean in French, Spanish, and English; the Global Partnership for Sustainable Development Data (GPSDD); the GW Elliott School of International Affairs; Columbia and Cornell Universities; the Mastercard Advocacy Center of Excellence; A. T. Kearney's Global Business Policy Council; the Fletcher School of Law and Diplomacy's Institute for Business in the Global Context at Tufts University; Committee for the Coordination of Statistical Activities (CCSA); United Nations World Data Forum (UNWDF); Organisation for Economic Co-operation and Development's Development Assistance Committee (DAC); Global Data Barometer; and the Open Gov Hub.

The team organized and held a dedicated consultation event for civil society members and several bilateral consultations with technology firms, platform-based businesses, internet exchange points, payment industries, and cybersecurity firms in the private sector. They included Alibaba, Amazon, CADE (Brazilian competition authority), De Novo, Facebook, Google, LinkedIn, Lori Systems (Kenya), Mastercard, Power2SME (India), and UA-IX (Ukranian Internet Exchange Point). The team also reached out for guidance on specific topics from experts based in institutions that included Aelex Legal (law firm, Abuja, Nigeria), Atlantic Council (think tank), DataPrivacy.Com.Br (São Paulo, Brazil), Georgetown University, Hamu and Company (law firm, Lagos, Nigeria), Hogan Lovells (privacy and cybersecurity law firm), Hunton Andrews Kurth (global privacy and cybersecurity law firm), Interswitch (Lagos, Nigeria), New York University, Organisation for Economic Co-operation and Development, Oxford Internet Institute, Rockefeller Foundation, the United Nations Conference on Trade and Development (UNCTAD), the University of Southern California, and WilmerHale (data and cybersecurity law firm). Detailed information about all consultations and contributors can be found at https://www.worldbank.org/en/publication/wdr2021/consultations.

The team is grateful as well to the many World Bank colleagues who provided written comments during the formal Bank-wide review process. Those comments proved to be invaluable at a crucial stage in the Report's production.

The team apologizes to any individuals or organizations inadvertently omitted from this list and expresses its gratitude to all who contributed to this Report, including those whose names may not appear here. The team members would also like to thank their families for their support throughout the preparation of this Report.

Abbreviations

A4AI	Alliance for Affordable Internet
AI	artificial intelligence
AIS	automatic identification system
APEC	Asia-Pacific Economic Cooperation
API	application programming interface
ARPU	average revenue per user
ASEAN	Association of Southeast Asian Nations
ATAF	African Tax Administration Forum
ATI	access to information
BEPS	OECD/G20 Inclusive Framework on Base Erosion and Profit Shifting
BRICS	Brazil, Russian Federation, India, China, South Africa
B2B	business to business
B2C	business to consumer
B2G	business to government
CDR	call detail record
CPTPP	Comprehensive and Progressive Agreement for Trans-Pacific Partnership
CSIRT	Computer Security Incident Response Team
CSO	civil society organization
DEPA	Digital Economy Partnership Agreement
DLT	distributed ledger technology
DPA	data protection authority
DTA	Digital Trade Agreement
EITI	Extractive Industries Transparency Initiative
EU	European Union
FAIR	findability, accessibility, interoperability, and reuse
FAO	Food and Agriculture Organization
FCS	fragile and conflict-affected situations
FRAND	fair, reasonable, and non-discriminatory
GATS	General Agreement on Trade in Services
GDP	gross domestic product
GDPR	General Data Protection Regulation (EU)
GHG	greenhouse gas
GIS	geographic information system
GNI	gross national income
GPS	global positioning system
G2B	government to business
G2C	government to consumer
G2G	government to government
HAPS	high-altitude platform station
ICT	information and communication technology
ILO	International Labour Organization
IMF	International Monetary Fund
INDS	integrated national data system

IoT	Internet of Things
IP	Internet Protocol
IPRs	intellectual property rights
IRB	Institutional Review Board
ISO	International Organization for Standardization
ISP	internet service provider
IT	information technology
ITU	International Telecommunication Union (UN)
IUCN	International Union for Conservation of Nature
IXP	internet exchange point
KIXP	Kenya Internet Exchange Point
LEO	low Earth orbiting
LSMS	Living Standards Measurement Study
M&E	monitoring and evaluation
ML	machine learning
MLAT	mutual legal assistance treaty
MNE	multinational enterprise
MNO	mobile network operator
MPA	Marine Protected Area
MSMEs	micro, small, and medium enterprises
NGO	nongovernmental organization
NIC	news flow indices of corruption
NPDR	Non-Personal Data Regulation (EU)
NSDS	National Strategies for the Development of Statistics
NSO	national statistical office
ODbL	Open Database License
OECD	Organisation for Economic Co-operation and Development
OGP	Open Government Partnership
ONS	Office for National Statistics (UK)
PARIS21	Partnership in Statistics for Development in the 21st Century
PIMS	personal information management system
PPP	public-private partnership
PTA	preferential trade agreement
RADD	Radar Alerts for Detecting Deforestation
SCC	standard contractual clause
SDGs	Sustainable Development Goals
SINTyS	National Tax and Social Identification System (Argentina)
SMEs	small and medium enterprises
SPI	Statistical Performance Indicators
SSO	standard setting organization
TFP	total factor productivity
TVWS	TV white space
UN	United Nations
UNCITRAL	United Nations Commission on International Trade Law
UNDP	United Nations Development Programme
UNEP	United Nations Environment Programme
UNICEF	United Nations Children's Fund
USITC	United States International Trade Commission
USMCA	United States–Mexico–Canada Agreement
USSD	unstructured supplementary service data
VAT	value added tax
WFP	World Food Programme
WHO	World Health Organization

OVERVIEW

"

You can have data without information, but you cannot have information without data.

—Daniel Keys Moran, computer programmer
and science fiction author

Data, which are growing at an unprecedented rate, are becoming an integral part of the daily lives of most people everywhere. But how does that matter for the more than 700 million people living in extreme poverty? Is the explosion in the new types and uses of data improving their lives? Or will poor people and poor countries be left behind, creating a widening gap between those who reap the benefits of this new data-driven world and those who do not?

The innovations resulting from the creative new uses of data could prove to be one of the most life-changing events of this era for everyone. Like many general-purpose technologies such as the steam engine and electricity, the transformations emerging from the data revolution could touch all aspects of societies and economies. But such sweeping changes are not automatic. The productivity value of the steam engine and electricity was realized decades after they were first introduced. The delay occurred not because people did not recognize the importance of these innovations—sooner or later everyone did—but because the new manufacturing systems needed for these innovations to realize their economic potential could not take shape overnight. Just as electricity itself did not result in economic development, data alone will not improve well-being. Data can improve social and economic outcomes, but only if they are used systematically in ways that create information that generates insights that improve lives.

This Report aims to answer two fundamental questions. First, how can data better advance development objectives? Second, what kind of data governance arrangements are needed to support the generation and use of data in a safe, ethical, and secure way while also delivering value equitably?

One important message of this Report is that simply gathering more data is not the answer. Significant data shortfalls, particularly in poor countries, do exist, but the aim of this Report is to shift the focus toward *using data more effectively to improve development outcomes*, particularly for poor people in poor countries.

Advancing development objectives through data

Part I of this Report develops a conceptual framework that links data to development through three institutional pathways (figure O.1). The middle pathway is the use of data by governments and international organizations to support evidence-based policy making and improved service delivery. The top pathway is the use of data by civil society to monitor the effects of government policies and by individuals to enable them to monitor and access public and commercial services. The bottom pathway is the use of data by private firms in the production process—use that fuels their own growth as well as wider economic growth. One implication of the conceptual framework is that data alone cannot solve development problems: people (in society, governments, and firms) are the central actors transforming data into useful information that can improve livelihoods and lives.[1] Alongside capital, land, and labor, data are also an input to the development objectives that emerge along all three pathways. But, unlike capital, land, and labor, using data once does not diminish its value. Data that were initially collected with one intention can be reused for a completely different purpose (chapter 1).

Figure O.1 How data can support development: A theory of change

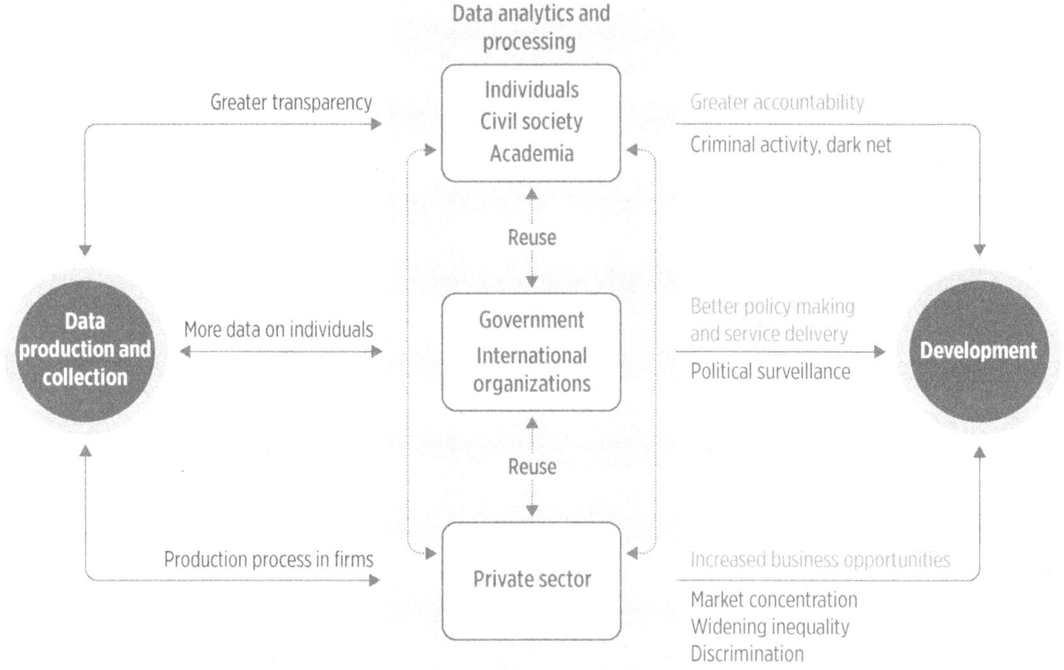

Data analytics and processing

Individuals Civil society Academia

Greater transparency

Greater accountability

Criminal activity, dark net

Reuse

Data production and collection

More data on individuals

Government International organizations

Better policy making and service delivery

Political surveillance

Development

Reuse

Production process in firms

Private sector

Increased business opportunities

Market concentration
Widening inequality
Discrimination

Source: WDR 2021 team.

Note: Positive impacts are shown in green; negative impacts are shown in red.

Disseminating, exchanging, and sharing data to enhance data reuse and repurposing

Because the potential of data to serve a productive use is essentially limitless, enabling the reuse and repurposing of data is critical if data are to lead to better lives. It is thus a central aspect of the conceptual framework. Figure O.1 uses two-way arrows to depict these flows. The two-way arrow between the private sector and government/international organizations indicates the reuse and repurposing of data originally collected for commercial purposes for public policy, and vice versa. Similarly, the two-way arrow between individuals/civil society/academia and government/international organizations indicates data being exchanged and reused by those parties. The final two-way arrows reflect the use of private sector data and data-driven applications by individuals/civil society/academia and the use of data and analysis generated by individuals/civil society/academia by firms. In practice, however, those holding data may be unwilling to exchange data. They may have concerns about data protection and security or the need to capture returns on investments in collecting data.

Or they may hope to gain market power from accumulating data to capture economies of scale or obtain any other kind of political or competitive advantage from hoarding them.

The phrase "sharing and reuse" is shorthand used in this Report for all the types of transactions and exchanges of data that permit reuse, from government open data initiatives for sharing data to market-based transactions for data involving private firms. In theory, defining clear economic property rights over data should enable data to be traded widely on markets. But in practice, the extent of the data trade (beyond the market for advertising) has been limited by competing claims on ownership, tensions between the wide dissemination of data and incentives to accumulate more data for private commercial gain, and difficulties in assessing the quality and accuracy of data.

Each of the three pathways illustrated in figure O.1 shows how data can improve lives, but those same pathways create openings for data to be used in ways that harm people. Through the government pathway, data can be abused for political ends, such as politically motivated surveillance or discrimination along lines of ethnicity, religion, race, gender, disability status, or sexual orientation. In the pathway running through individuals, there is the potential for cyber-criminals to inflict considerable harm by stealing and manipulating sensitive information. The "dark net" is a vast parallel network of hidden websites that provides an underground digital platform for a wide array of criminal activities, facilitating illegal trade in drugs, counterfeit currency, stolen goods, credit card numbers, forged papers, firearms, and human organs. Similarly, through the private sector pathway, examples of harmful use include, among other things, the exploitation of information about consumer preferences and behavior to engage in aggressive or manipulative marketing techniques based on microtargeting of persuasive messages or to apply algorithms that facilitate collusion among market players.[2]

Unlocking data for the public good and safeguarding against misuses: Some COVID-19 examples

Many countries have used data to control the COVID-19 pandemic. This use includes tracking people's locations to better understand mobility patterns during lockdowns or to aid in disease contact tracing. Using call detail records (CDRs) from March through May 2020 aggregated to mask individual-level data, policy makers in The Gambia were able to review maps showing the movement of people across administrative boundaries (map O.1). These maps helped them understand the extent to which lockdowns were succeeding in reducing movement

and allowed them to identify the factors linked to lockdown compliance and noncompliance and plan accordingly. Meanwhile, the government of Israel approved emergency regulations in March 2020 to allow the individual-level data collected from cell-phones to be used to track people and then, through contact tracing, to curtail the spread of COVID-19.

CDRs were not created to aid public policy making or to allow the government to track the movements of individuals, but they are an example of data being reused and repurposed (flowing in the vertical channels in figure O.1). In Israel, these data were being collected before the pandemic, but they could be accessed only for national security purposes.[3]

These early efforts at repurposing CDRs to track infected individuals seemed to have a positive effect. In The Gambia, the maps helped reveal that the lockdown disproportionally affected poorer districts, indicating a need for relief and recovery efforts to target these areas. In Israel, analysis of the cellular data suggested their use led to identification of more than one-third of all of the country's coronavirus cases in the early weeks of the pandemic (more than 5,500 of the 16,200 people who had contracted the disease), possibly contributing to Israel's exceptionally low initial rates of coronavirus infections and deaths.

This new use of CDR data to track large parts of the population of Israel sparked debate and pushback over concerns about the potential misuse of the data by government. In Israel, many lawmakers raised privacy concerns, and the Supreme Court eventually

Map O.1 Use of aggregated cellphone records to track mobility week by week during COVID-19 lockdowns in The Gambia, March–May 2020

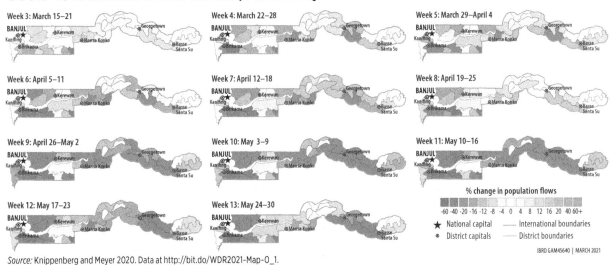

Source: Knippenberg and Meyer 2020. Data at http://bit.do/WDR2021-Map-O_1.

Note: Blue shades indicate outflow of people; green shades indicate inflow of people. A nationwide lockdown was imposed on March 22, 2020. Data were gathered using call detail records.

halted the program. The Court ruled in late April 2020 that the government must legislate the use of cell-phone tracking and that "a suitable alternative, compatible with the principles of privacy, must be found."[4]

Many of the themes of this Report are illustrated in this example. The sharing and reuse of private sector CDR data with public authorities created social *value* by supporting the control of COVID-19 infections, thereby saving lives. At the same time, this transfer of data raised fundamental concerns about *trust*, with citizens concerned that their CDR data could then be repurposed by government officials for other unintended and potentially harmful purposes beyond public health. Issues of *equity* were also at stake. Whereas in a high-income country like Israel smartphone penetration was 93 percent, in a low-income country like The Gambia smartphone penetration was only 75 percent. In each case, that minority of the population lacking a smartphone was unable to generate CDR data and would not necessarily benefit directly from the public health protection afforded by contact tracing.

These examples also illustrate a key conundrum. The potential benefits that people realize in the form of improved policies and service delivery may increase rapidly as more data, especially personal data, are shared and reused—but the risks of data being misused increase as well. These potential benefits depend on data being disseminated or exchanged between parties. But parties must *trust* the systems, regulations, and institutions that underlie the security of such exchanges to willingly engage in them.

How can people trust that their data will be protected and that they will share in the value that data can produce? The mounting nature of such concerns suggests the need for a new social contract around data—that is, an agreement among all participants in the process of creating, reusing, and sharing data that fosters trust that they will not be harmed from exchanging data and that part of the value created by data will accrue equitably (figure O.2). The idea that societies engage in these sort of agreements, or social contracts, has existed for centuries, often linked to the writing of philosophers such as Thomas Hobbes, John Locke, and Jean-Jacques Rousseau.

Legal systems, and governance more generally, can be viewed as instruments for establishing, facilitating, and enforcing social contracts. Persuading parties to abide by the rules of a social contract is not an easy task and will hinge on ensuring that the benefits from using data are shared in an equitable way—that is, everyone has something to gain. In this process, lower-income countries are too often disadvantaged, lacking, as they often do, the infrastructure and skills to capture data and turn them into value; the institutional and regulatory frameworks to create trust in data systems; and the scale and agency to participate equitably in global data markets and their governance.

With data reshaping our lives, our societies, and the world more generally, social contracts for data are needed both nationally and internationally, especially because of the cross-border nature of data transactions and flows. Spotlight 8.1 extends this idea of a social contract to the international realm, calling for a global consensus to ensure that data are safeguarded as a global public good and as a resource to achieve equitable and sustainable development.

The untapped potential of data; the evolving legal, regulatory, and governance frameworks for data generation, use, and reuse; the importance of country context (history, culture, governance, and political economy) in shaping appropriate frameworks; the role of technical capabilities for making the most of data safely; and the need for trust and more equitable sharing of the value of data—all these are the themes at the core of this *World Development Report*.

Part I of the Report begins by describing in more detail the potential development impact of data collected for public purposes—*public intent data* (chapter 2); data collected by the private sector as part of routine business processes—*private intent data* (chapter 3); and the synergies that arise from the joint use of different types of data (chapter 4). This distinction between public intent and private intent data is used

Figure O.2 A social contract for data founded on value, trust, and equity

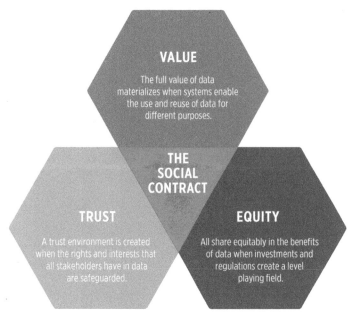

VALUE
The full value of data materializes when systems enable the use and reuse of data for different purposes.

THE SOCIAL CONTRACT

TRUST
A trust environment is created when the rights and interests that all stakeholders have in data are safeguarded.

EQUITY
All share equitably in the benefits of data when investments and regulations create a level playing field.

Source: WDR 2021 team.

regardless of who collected the data or the methods used to gather the data (such as customer surveys, accounting records, or digital transactions).

Public intent data can improve service delivery, targeting, accountability, and empowerment

Public intent data hold great potential for designing, executing, and evaluating public programs and policy (chapter 2). Because public intent data are a prerequisite for many government functions, government agencies are the primary producers of these data by means of censuses, administrative data collection, and more. Citizens, civil society organizations, nongovernmental organizations, academic institutions, and international organizations contribute critically to the production of public intent data using surveys, crowdsourcing platforms, and other means.

These kinds of data can lead to better lives through three main pathways: first, by improving policy making and service delivery; second, by prioritizing scarce resources and targeting them to reach marginalized populations and areas; and third, by holding government accountable and empowering individuals to make better choices through more information and knowledge.

An example from Nigeria illustrates the power of public intent data to improve and target service delivery. The 2015 National Water Supply and Sanitation Survey commissioned by Nigeria's government gathered data from households, water points, water schemes, and public facilities, including schools and health facilities. These data revealed that 130 million Nigerians (or more than two-thirds of the population at that time) did not meet the standard for sanitation set out by the Millennium Development Goals and that inadequate access to clean water was especially an issue for poor households and in certain geographical areas (map O.2).[5] In response to the findings from the report based on these data, President Muhammadu Buhari declared a state of emergency in the sector and launched the National Action Plan for the Revitalization of Nigeria's Water, Sanitation and Hygiene (WASH) Sector.[6]

The higher the quality of the data (in terms of features such as timeliness, accuracy, and resolution), the greater is their potential to generate value for development. Yet a variety of factors prevent countries—particularly low-income ones—from realizing greater value from data for the public good. These impediments include lack of resources, technical capacity, data governance, and demand for data-informed decision-making. The World Bank's Statistical Performance Indicators, released as part of this

Map O.2 Highly refined data pinpointed areas of Nigeria that needed better sanitation

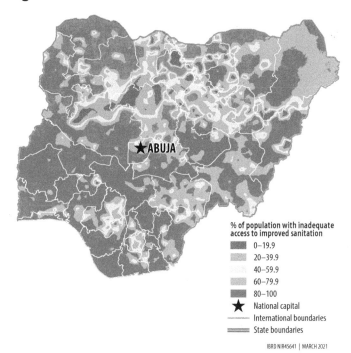

% of population with inadequate access to improved sanitation
- 0–19.9
- 20–39.9
- 40–59.9
- 60–79.9
- 80–100
- ★ National capital
- International boundaries
- State boundaries

IBRD NIR45641 | MARCH 2021

Source: World Bank 2017. Data at http://bit.do/WDR2021-Map-O_2.

Note: Geographic hotspots of inadequate access to improved sanitation are shown from the least severe (■) to the most severe (■) in terms of the percentage of the population in that area that meets an international benchmark for sanitation.

Report, identify gaps in the availability, quality, and usability of public intent data across 174 countries, focusing on features related to the timeliness, granularity, interoperability, and accessibility of those data.[7]

Unleashing the full potential of public intent data requires high-level prioritization of data in the policy process. Governments would then prioritize the production of high-quality data and the open and transparent use of data for decision-making. Transparency and reliability of official statistics can help build trust in government actions. A lack of transparency, such as not revealing a country's debt burden, can have harmful economic consequences and damage the public's trust in government (see spotlight 1.2). Fulfilling the potential of data requires long-term, stable financing of data; investments in statistical and technical capacity; and laws conducive to safe data production and reuse. Other areas that must be addressed include low levels of data literacy affecting the demand for data, policy makers' lack of incentives for and interest in using data, low trust in the quality of public intent data, and lack of infrastructure for accessing and using the data. These investments and initiatives rely on one another, and so failure to succeed in one area jeopardizes the overall value that data can bring to development. Effective use of data can generate more demand for data, thereby justifying investments to produce more, and higher-quality, data.

Private intent data can fuel growth and boost development

Data collected and curated by the private sector for commercial purposes also hold great potential to spur development (chapter 3). Innovations in the use and application of data by businesses are creating tremendous economic value by enhancing data-driven decision-making and reducing transaction costs. A 2011 study of 179 large firms in the United States indicated that firms adopting data-driven decision-making increased their productivity by 5–6 percent relative to what would be expected in view of their other investments and use of information technology.[8]

Although data are in many ways an input to the production process of firms, much of the recent explosion of new data has come about as a by-product of economic activity, such as digitization of firm operations, mobile phone usage by individuals, digital transactions, and social media interactions. These data are collected at high frequency and can provide detailed information on individuals, businesses, economic outcomes, and phenomena. They not only enhance the economic efficiency of the firms themselves, but also offer potential to be repurposed for public policy needs such as COVID-19 tracking. For example, financial services providers are increasingly adopting alternative credit scoring techniques to solve the long-standing issue of lack of data on potential borrowers (or more specifically, asymmetric information) in banking. These techniques take advantage of users' digital footprints to assess creditworthiness for those who otherwise lack documentation. Two prominent examples of this approach are Lenddo, which operates in the Philippines, and Cignifi, which operates in Africa, Asia, and Latin America.

But these trends also come with new risks that must be addressed to ensure that the data-driven economy raises social welfare. Concerns are growing about excessive data collection, insufficient governance of data held by private firms, and inadequate protection of personal data. Many of these concerns revolve around the misuse of personal data. Such misuses include the failure of firms to properly protect the financial information of clients—exposing them to theft of funds or identity—or firms' engagement in unauthorized use of, or failure to protect, individuals' confidential health or location data.

Many of the processes through which firms create value with their data are driven by algorithms and machine learning. In these models, algorithms determine, among other things, what information, products, or services individuals are exposed to and at what price; what insurance packages they are offered; whether their loan applications are approved; what jobs they qualify for; and what medical advice they receive.

All these types of activities have the potential to significantly improve economic efficiency. For example, by consuming more data types and extracting relevant information from seemingly unrelated patterns, machine learning could generate credit scores for more individuals with greater precision. However, if the data fed into the machine learning embed discriminatory assumptions, machine learning will amplify that discrimination, not only producing harmful results, but also magnifying them.[9] This point brings to mind the decades-old data science adage "garbage in–garbage out," meaning that a data processing system such as machine learning is no better than the data it is given to process.[10] But there is a deeper concern: the output from machine learning is typically opaque and changes frequently as new data enter the system. Almost by design, it creates a rule that is not transparent, and so identifying discriminatory elements of the algorithm can be technically very challenging.

Often, data-driven markets exhibit positive network externalities, leading to increasing returns to scale and a propensity for a few large firms to dominate. The result can be the exclusion of smaller or more traditional firms to the detriment of local entrepreneurship, with possible risks for consumer welfare. These effects may be exacerbated in developing markets, where entrants find it harder to raise start-up capital and where there is limited human capital in data sciences. To counteract this, policy makers can address the underlying constraints to achieving scale, such as geoblocking (restricting access to internet content based on the user's geographical location) or lack of harmonization of data policies across countries. They can ensure that sector regulations and government support schemes provide a level playing field for all firms.

Combining and repurposing data can deepen their development impact

Combining and repurposing different types of data can enhance the impacts of data on development (chapter 4). Development problems are complex, spanning economic, cultural, environmental, demographic, and many other factors. Policy design based on data covering only one factor will be incomplete, and sometimes ill-advised. Combining different types of data can fill data gaps and offer new perspectives on development problems.

As one example, public intent household surveys, which gather extensive data on living standards, consumption, income, and expenditures, are the basis for estimating national poverty rates in most countries. Because the survey instrument is so extensive and time-consuming to administer, the samples tend to be relatively small. Estimates of poverty are usually statistically valid for a nation and at some slightly finer level of geographic stratification, but rarely are such household surveys designed to provide the refined profiles of poverty that would allow policies to mitigate poverty to target the village level or lower. Meanwhile, for decades high-resolution poverty maps have been produced by estimating a model of poverty from survey data and then mapping this model onto census data, allowing an estimate of poverty for every household in the census data. A problem with this approach is that census data are available only once a decade (and in many poorer countries even less frequently).

Modifications of this approach have replaced population census data with CDR data or various types of remote sensing data (typically from satellites, but also from drones). This repurposing of CDR or satellite data can provide greater resolution and timelier maps of poverty. For example, using only household survey data the government of Tanzania was able to profile the level of poverty across only 20 regions of the country's mainland. Once the household survey data were combined with satellite imagery data, it became possible to estimate poverty for each of the country's 169 districts (map O.3). Combining the two data sources increased the resolution of the poverty picture by eightfold with essentially no loss of precision. Other examples of this innovative analysis are occurring in some of the world's most data-deficient environments such as Afghanistan and Rwanda, offering solutions to pressing data gaps.[11]

Examples of other ways of repurposing data include using online media and user-generated content to map water/flood events in real time for water management and food security and combining

Map O.3 Combining satellite imagery with household survey data increases the resolution of the poverty map of Tanzania

a. Poverty map using the Household Budget Survey (20 regions)

b. Poverty map combining the data in panel a with satellite imagery (169 districts)

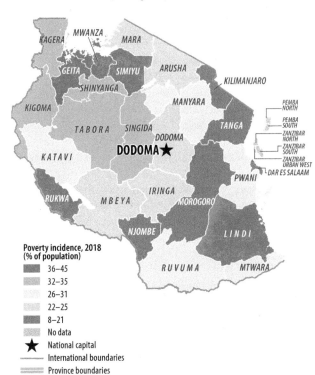

Poverty incidence, 2018 (% of population)
- 36–45
- 32–35
- 26–31
- 22–25
- 8–21
- No data
- ★ National capital
- ——— International boundaries
- ═══ Province boundaries

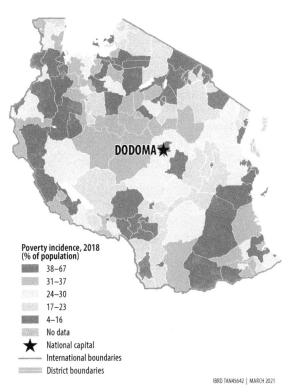

Poverty incidence, 2018 (% of population)
- 38–67
- 31–37
- 24–30
- 17–23
- 4–16
- No data
- ★ National capital
- ——— International boundaries
- ═══ District boundaries

IBRD TAN45642 | MARCH 2021

Source: World Bank 2019. Data at http://bit.do/WDR2021-Map-O_3.

satellite imagery data from public and private sources to monitor crop yields and forecast malnutrition.[12] Similarly, many examples in this Report highlight the potential for repurposing data to improve programs, policies, and outcomes in areas such as monitoring public health (including the spread of disease), managing crisis response and resource allocation, ensuring road safety in transport and transit, and monitoring illegal fishing and deforestation.

Novel ways to create and use data enable civil society to hold governments accountable for policies and to better monitor corruption.[13] For example, utilizing crowdsourced data and web scraping (extracting data from websites), social media discussion boards are emerging as ways in which local leaders can act against corrupt officials and receive real-time feedback on the impact of anticorruption policies. The "I paid a bribe" online initiative launched in 2011 by the Janaagraha Centre for Citizenship and Democracy in India has developed into one of the largest crowdsourced anticorruption platforms in the world. This tool collects citizens' reports of corrupt behavior and merges them with geospatial data to highlight problem areas. In doing so, it empowers individuals, civil society, and governments to fight corrupt behavior.

To encourage more efforts to repurpose and combine data sources, this Report describes ways in which donors, governments, and companies could invest in the people, partnerships, and research needed to leverage these new data sources for public benefit. Low-income countries should emphasize policy initiatives and investments in building the data skills of analysts and decision-makers; expanding tertiary education to encompass data science and analytics; promoting partnerships with universities and private companies in higher-income countries; strengthening the data literacy of senior government leadership; creating institutional environments that encourage the use of sophisticated data and evidence in policy making; and revamping national statistical offices to perform nontraditional roles with private intent data.

Aligning data governance with the social contract

A well-designed data governance framework allows countries to capture the full economic and social value of both public intent and private intent data and leverages synergies between them. This involves creating trust in the integrity of the data system, while ensuring that the benefits of data are equitably shared. Such a framework is the tangible expression of a country's social contract around data.

Part II of this Report describes these building blocks of data governance, which can deliver the potential benefits of data while safeguarding against harmful outcomes (figure O.3). These building blocks include data infrastructure policies (chapter 5); policies, laws, and regulations around data (chapter 6); related economic policies (chapter 7); and data governance institutions (chapter 8).

Although much of data governance is domestic in focus, an efficient and equitable resolution of many data governance challenges is possible only with international collaboration. Bilateral efforts are needed to manage cross-border spillovers of antitrust decisions and to join forces to combat cybercrime. Multilateral cooperation is essential to address global free-rider problems (such as data protectionism or tax evasion in data-enabled services) and to reduce transaction costs through harmonization of legal and technical standards for data protection and interoperability. At the same time, regional collaboration can help amplify the voice of low- and middle-income countries in global data governance negotiations and help realize scale economies in the development of data infrastructure.

Improving data infrastructure helps ensure equitable access for poor people in poor countries

The digital character of modern data calls for digital infrastructure—a prerequisite for collecting, exchanging, storing, processing, and distributing data (chapter 5). Yet the availability of such infrastructure is marked by inequity both within and between countries. Because the social and economic value of data infrastructure rises steeply as more and more citizens are connected, universal service policies have long existed to promote service rollout. In recognition of the transformative opportunities that broadband connectivity presents for both individuals and nations, the United Nations Broadband Commission has committed the international community to reaching 75 percent broadband-internet user penetration by 2025.[14]

That said, efforts to move toward universal access face fundamental challenges. First, because of the continual technological innovation in mobile technology service, coverage is a moving target. Whereas in 2018, 92 percent of the world's population lived within range of a 3G signal (offering speeds of 40 megabytes per second), that share dropped to 80 percent for 4G technology (providing faster speeds of 400 megabytes per second, which are needed for more sophisticated smartphone applications that can promote development). The recent commercial launch of 5G technology (reaching speeds of 1,000

Figure O.3 Data governance layers at the national and international levels

		National	International
	**Infrastructure policies**	• **Universal coverage** of broadband networks • **Domestic infrastructure** to exchange, store, and process data	• **Global technical standards** for compatibility of hardware and software • **Regional collaboration** on data infrastructure to achieve scale
	**Laws and regulations**	• **Safeguards** to secure and protect data from the threat of misuse • **Enablers** to facilitate data sharing among different stakeholders	• **Cybersecurity conventions** for collaboration on tackling cybercrime • **Interoperability standards** to facilitate data exchanges across borders
	Economic policies	• **Antitrust** for data platform businesses • **Trade** in data-enabled services • **Taxation** of data platform businesses	• **International tax treaties** to allocate taxation rights across countries • **Global trade agreements** on cross-border trade in data-enabled services
	**Institutions**	• **Government** entities to oversee, regulate, and secure data • **Other stakeholders** to set standards and increase data access and reuse	• **International organizations** to support collaboration on data governance and promote standardization • **Cooperation** on cross-border regulatory spillovers and enforcement issues

Source: WDR 2021 team.

megabytes per second) in a handful of leading-edge markets risks leaving the low-income countries even further behind. Policy makers can hasten technological upgrades by creating a supportive environment for private sector investment in the underpinning fiber-optic networks, while introducing more effective management of critical spectrum resources. Sharing infrastructure can also greatly reduce the cost of upgrades. Yet a careful balance must be struck between promoting competition in broadband provision wherever possible and encouraging cooperation between service providers in market segments where demand is too limited to support more than one infrastructure network.

The second challenge is that a substantial majority of the 40 percent of the world's population who do not use data services live within range of a broadband signal. Of people living in low- and middle-income countries who do not access the internet, more than two-thirds stated in a survey that they do not know what the internet is or how to use it, indicating that digital literacy is a major issue.[15] Affordability is also a factor in low- and middle-income countries, where the cost of an entry-level smartphone represents about 80 percent of monthly income of the bottom

20 percent of households.[16] Relatively high taxes and duties further contribute to this expense.[17] As costs come down in response to innovation, competitive pressures, and sound government policy, uptake in use of the internet will likely increase. Yet even among those who do use the internet, consumption of data services stands at just 0.2 gigabytes per capita per month, a fraction of what this Report estimates may be needed to perform basic social and economic functions online.

A third challenge in expanding connectivity is its potential impact on global warming. The climate impacts of increased connectivity present a set of complicated trade-offs. In 2018 the electricity needed to support data infrastructure was equal to approximately 1 percent of global consumption—a significant draw with environmental consequences. But because of reliance on renewable energy–supported data infrastructure and increasing energy efficiencies, greenhouse gas emissions linked to data infrastructure are disproportionately lower than for other sectors. Furthermore, access to data infrastructure can have significant positive climatic effects as illustrated by the massive reduction in travel and increase in videoconferencing during COVID-19 (spotlight 5.2).

Map O.4 Data infrastructure is not yet widespread across all parts of the world

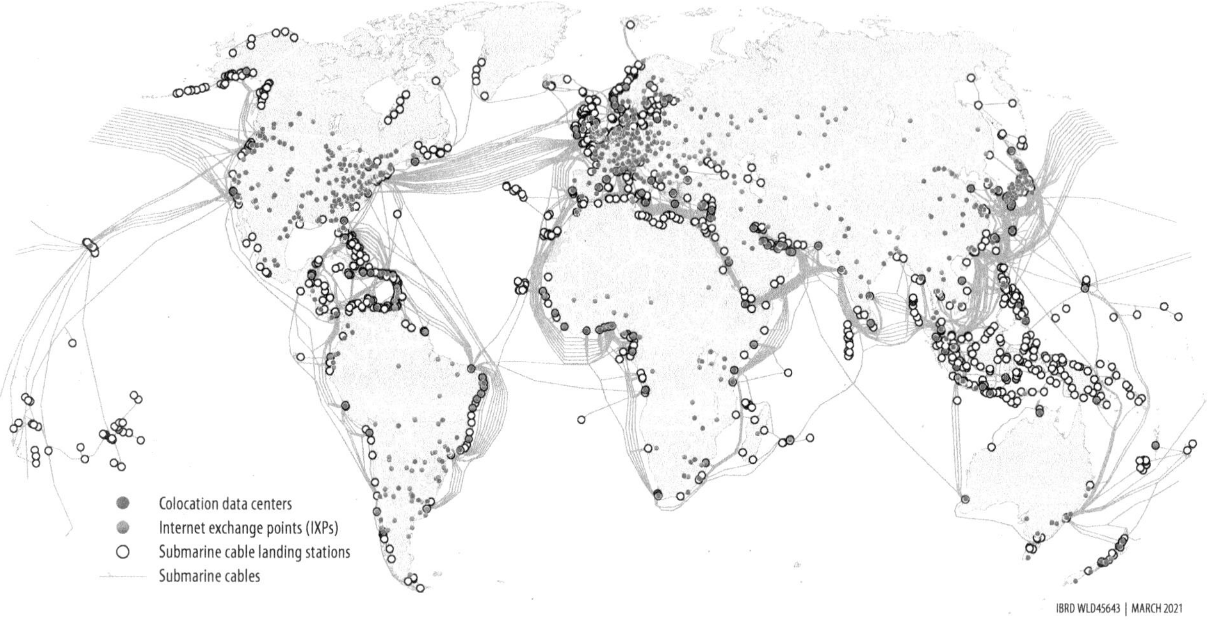

Colocation data centers
Internet exchange points (IXPs)
Submarine cable landing stations
Submarine cables

IBRD WLD45643 | MARCH 2021

Sources: PeeringDB, Interconnection Database, https://www.peeringdb.com/; PCH Packet Clearing House, Packet Clearing House Report on Internet Exchange Point Locations (database), accessed December 14, 2020, https://www.pch.net/ixp/summary; TeleGeography, Submarine Cables (database), https://www.submarinecablemap.com/. Data at http://bit.do/WDR2021-Map-O_4.

Full participation in the data-driven economy entails not only connecting individual citizens but also developing adequate data infrastructure at the national level. For the most part, low- and middle-income countries lack domestic facilities to allow their own locally generated data to be exchanged (via internet exchange points, IXPs), stored (at colocation data centers), and processed (on cloud platforms)—see map O.4. Instead, many continue to depend on overseas facilities, requiring them to transfer large volumes of data in and out of the country—for which they pay a substantial penalty in terms of slower speed and higher prices.

Policy makers can do much to improve access to data infrastructure progressively. This process begins by encouraging the creation of domestic IXPs and then fostering a suitable investment climate for colocation data centers. In these centers, popular internet content can be stored locally, and access to overseas cloud infrastructure can be facilitated through the provision of on-ramps. Such facilities can be shared at the regional level, where suitable fiber-optic connectivity exists between countries and there is adequate regulatory harmonization. Because of the extremely high standards of reliability required for data infrastructure, as well as concerns about the carbon footprint of data, the ideal private sector investment climate should provide for reliable, clean, low-cost electricity, natural cooling, and negligible disaster risk—conditions that are not always readily met in low- and middle-income countries.

Data laws and regulations can help create an environment of trust

Trust in data transactions can be supported through a robust legal and regulatory framework encompassing both *safeguards* and *enablers* (chapter 6). The establishment of such a framework remains a work in progress across all country income groups (figure O.4).

Safeguards promote trust in data transactions by avoiding or limiting harm arising from the misuse of data. A fundamental prerequisite for trust in data systems is cybersecurity. Achieving adequate cybersecurity calls for creating a legal framework that obliges data controllers and processors to adopt technical systems to secure data.[18] To date, only a small minority of low- and middle-income countries have adopted adequate legal frameworks for cybersecurity. Kenya's new Data Protection Act stands out as a good example of comprehensive cybersecurity provisions.

Creation of an adequate legal framework for data protection is also critical. Such a framework should clearly differentiate between personal data (data that identify the individual) and nonpersonal data

(data that do not contain any personally identifiable information). Among middle-income countries, Mauritius is notable as having relatively well-developed safeguards for personal data. Indeed, it has distinguished itself as one of the first Sub-Saharan African countries to ratify the Council of Europe's Convention 108+ for the Protection of Individuals with Regard to the Processing of Personal Data.[19]

The protection of personal data is grounded in international human rights law, which requires that the interests of the data subject be adequately safeguarded *before* enabling any kind of data transaction.[20] This protection is usually achieved by compelling the subjects of data to provide some form of explicit consent for use of the data. But is such consent meaningful? Evidence indicates that it would take the average person 76 days a year to thoroughly read the numerous disclosure documents soliciting his or her consent to each website and application visited![21] This finding suggests the need to strengthen the legal obligations for data service providers to act in the best interest of the customers whose data are being used.

Because of the less sensitive nature of nonpersonal data, they can for the most part be adequately protected through intellectual property rights, allowing some balancing of interests between data protection and data reuse. However, this Report finds that most low-income countries surveyed do not have intellectual property rights in place for private intent data.

Complicating matters further, the distinction between personal data and nonpersonal data is becoming increasingly blurred. This blurring arises from the widespread mixing and processing of different data sources using sophisticated algorithms that may render nonpersonal data (such as from mobile phones) personally identifiable, or at least make it possible to identify specific social groups.

Enablers facilitate access to and reuse of data within and among stakeholder groups to ensure that the full social and economic value of data can be captured. The nature and extent of provisions to support data sharing differ markedly across public intent and private intent data. Significant efforts have been made around the world to safely disclose public intent data through open data policies (encouraging proactive publication of government data), together with access to information legislation (giving citizens a legally enforceable right to compel disclosure). For real impact, however, open data policies must be supported by a consistent protocol for classifying sensitive data, combined with interoperable technical standards, machine readable formats, and open licensing to facilitate subsequent reuse.

Figure O.4 The legal and regulatory framework for data governance remains a work in progress across all country income groupings

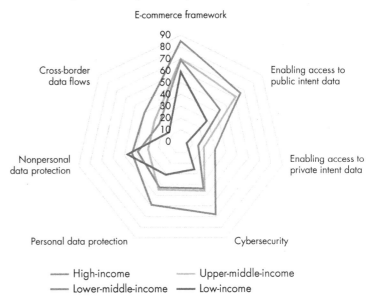

Source: WDR 2021 team, based on Global Data Regulation Survey conducted exclusively for this Report (https://microdata.worldbank.org/index.php/catalog/3866). Data at http://bit.do/WDR2021-Fig-O_4.

Note: The figure depicts the percentage of good practice laws and regulatory measures in place for countries covered by the survey in each country income group.

Governments have much less influence when it comes to disclosure of private intent data. Sharing of such data may serve as a remedy for the concentration of market power, such as in the Arab Republic of Egypt, where a merger between two major ride-hailing applications was made conditional on their sharing driver and rider information with smaller competitors. In other contexts, private intent data may also be critical for addressing important public policy challenges, such as the use of mobile phone records for contact tracing to control the spread of COVID-19. And yet relatively little attention has been paid so far to the possibility of incentivizing the exchange of private intent data through measures such as open licensing, data portability, and various types of data partnerships. Some countries—notably France—have nonetheless enacted legislation mandating the sharing of private sector data deemed to be in the public interest.[22]

Aligning data regulation with economic policy objectives can support the creation of value

Data play a central role in rapidly expanding platform-based business models. For example, search engines collect data on users' site visits, which they can sell to marketing companies so they can target advertisements more precisely. These platform-based business models are becoming increasingly important in low- and middle-income countries. The design of legal and regulatory frameworks for data has a real impact on the buoyancy of data-driven businesses and requires difficult policy balances. Providing access to essential sources of market data, for example, may be critical for promoting competition among platform businesses, but it also may affect incentives for investment and innovation in data-driven businesses. Again, regulations designed to protect personal data may restrict cross-border data flows and materially affect a country's competitive edge in the burgeoning trade of data-enabled services (chapter 7).

Competition and antitrust policy. Competition policy plays a critical role in ensuring that the value created by platform-based business models is equitably shared by producers and consumers. The presence of economies of scale in data collection externalities that increase the value of networks as more participants join platforms may lead to rapid accumulation of market power. Addressing such market dominance calls for two complementary strategies.

First, in countries that have sufficient capacity to enforce antitrust regulation, ex post antitrust enforcement should be applied—albeit with any adaptations

that may be needed to address the challenges posed by data-driven businesses. For example, the standard test of market dominance—overpricing by a market leader—may not be meaningful in sectors where platforms routinely provide consumer services for free. However, even though several landmark antitrust cases involving platform businesses have emerged in middle-income countries, such as Egypt, India, and Mexico, this Report finds that not a single low-income country has completed such a case, despite the presence of the same globally dominant firms in these markets.

Second, in parallel with antitrust efforts, ex ante regulatory measures to make essential data accessible to rival firms and new entrants also merit serious consideration, as does empowering consumers to switch among competing providers by mandating full portability of their personal data. Care should always be taken to verify that access to data is critical for competition and does not unduly affect incentives for innovation in data-driven businesses.

Trade policy. Platform-based businesses also open up new avenues for international trade, entailing substantial cross-border flows of data (figure O.5). A country's regulatory framework for personal data protection has a material impact on participation in such trade,

Figure O.5 Since 1990, the global trade in data-driven services has grown exponentially and now constitutes half of trade in services

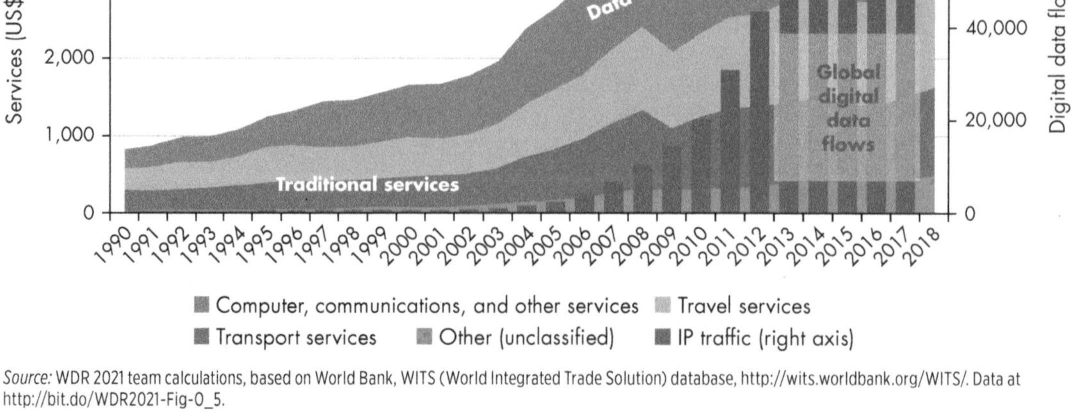

Source: WDR 2021 team calculations, based on World Bank, WITS (World Integrated Trade Solution) database, http://wits.worldbank.org/WITS/. Data at http://bit.do/WDR2021-Fig-O_5.

Note: IP = Internet Protocol; PB = petabytes.

creating some tension between trust and value creation. Countries have adopted a variety of approaches for dealing with this. Some, notably the federal jurisdiction in the United States, permit open data flows based on private sector standards, with limited government involvement. Others, such as China, Nigeria, the Russian Federation, and Vietnam, apply more stringent regulatory requirements, requiring copies of certain personal data to be stored domestically (data localization) and state authorization for many international exchanges. In between are countries (including members of the European Union and others such as Argentina and South Africa) that make cross-border transfers of personal data conditional on whether the partner trading country offers an adequate data protection regime. This Report finds that a combination of well-defined domestic personal data protection measures with relative ease of cross-border movements appears to offer the most favorable environment for international trade in data-enabled services.[23]

Tax policy. Even though data-driven transactions are creating more economic activity, the governments of low- and middle-income countries are struggling to share equitably in this value by mobilizing the associated tax revenues. For indirect taxes (such as value added taxes), the revenue rights are clearly allocated to the country in which the final sales are made. However, the administrative capacity to capture this revenue is typically lacking. Estimates for East Asian countries suggest that losses to fiscal revenues could amount to as much as 1 percent of the gross domestic product (GDP) by 2030.[24] As for direct taxes (such as corporate taxes), agreed-on international rules are lacking for allocating rights to tax businesses that operate in markets without any physical presence. In the absence of such a consensus, an increasing number of countries have been resorting to the application of ad hoc digital service taxes as a compensatory measure.

Sound institutions and governance can improve the development impact of data

If institutions do not function well, policies and laws and regulations are unlikely to be implemented or enforced effectively, and infrastructure will not deliver on its potential. An effective institutional framework for data governance must fulfill several critical functions, such as setting policy objectives, developing supporting rules and standards, enforcing compliance with such regulations, and continually improving governance through learning and evaluation (chapter 8). For example, Uruguay's creation of a lead agency close to the Office of the President and acting with a whole-of-government perspective has been critical in driving the country's successful e-government reforms since 2007.

Although there is no one-size-fits-all approach for governments seeking to create robust institutional arrangements for data governance, certain institutional design characteristics are of universal importance. Institutions should be formally mandated, sufficiently resourced, and have the technical capacity needed to effectively undertake their functions in a coordinated manner across the whole of government. The main institutional actors within this framework often include data governance entities, data protection authorities, and cybersecurity agencies, as well as new types of institutions such as data trusts—accountability-oriented data intermediaries allowing individuals to pool their legal rights over data and assign them to trustees with explicit fiduciary duties. Institutional independence and functional autonomy may be critical in some cases to shield data governance institutions from undue political or commercial influence. Behavioral and cultural norms and political economy constraints often stymie reform efforts, creating implementation gaps, especially in low- and middle-income countries. Change management, collaborative leadership, and a culture of performance and incentives can help institutions overcome barriers to implementation and coordination and effectively perform their roles and responsibilities.

To maximize buy-in from all participants in the data governance ecosystem, including society more broadly, data management must be socially inclusive and perceived as legitimate. Legitimacy is enhanced when governments manage and use data in a transparent manner and are subject to meaningful systems of accountability. Nongovernmental actors and emerging mechanisms such as data intermediaries can play an important role in the ecosystem by helping governments and end users responsibly share and use data to better harness their development value, while safeguarding against the risks of misuse or abuse. Engaging with stakeholders, across society and internationally, in a collaborative and transparent manner will foster trust and legitimacy and strengthen the social contract around data use. For example, the Association of Southeast Asian Nations (ASEAN) has adopted a regional Framework on Digital Data Governance, which helps coordinate members' data governance arrangements with a view toward interoperability.

Moving toward an integrated national data system

A well-functioning data governance framework ensures that infrastructure, laws, economic policies, and institutions work together to support the use of data in a way that aligns with each society's values, while protecting individuals' rights over use of their data. This framework defines the rules, and associated compliance mechanisms, for how data can be safely shared, used, and reused by all stakeholders.

Part III of this Report concludes with an aspirational vision of an integrated national data system (INDS) that can deliver on the promise of producing high-quality data and then making data open in a way that they are both protected and accessible to be shared and reused by all stakeholders (chapter 9). The aspirational INDS works seamlessly with the governance structure. If the governance framework can be viewed as creating and enforcing the "rules of the road," the INDS can be seen as the "network of highways" that connect all users, ensuring safe passage of data to and from destinations.

The INDS is built on an intentional, whole-of-government, multistakeholder approach to data governance. It explicitly builds data production, protection, exchange, and use into planning and decision-making across government entities and actively *integrates* the various stakeholders from civil society, the public sector, and the private sector into the data life cycle and into the governance structures of the system.[25]

A well-functioning system requires people to produce, process, and manage high-quality data; people to populate the institutions that safeguard and protect the data against misuse; and people to draft, oversee, and implement data strategies, policies, and regulations. The system also needs people to hold the public and private sectors accountable and people capable of using data from the production process of private firms to improve policies in the public sector. All this requires robust data literacy so that a wide cross section of people benefit from an INDS.

For a sound INDS, institutions and actors must also have the right incentives to produce, protect, and share data, and funding must be sufficient to implement the infrastructure and institutions needed for the system to function well. Finally, a culture of data use helps foster a high-quality supply of data and stimulate the demand for data-informed decision-making without which the national data system is not sustainable.

When government agencies, civil society, academia, and the private sector securely take part in a national data system, the potential uses of data expand and so does the potential impact on development. In fact, the more integrated the system and the more participants involved, the higher is the potential return. If two participants safely exchange data, data can flow in two directions. If three participants exchange data, data can flow in six directions, and with four participants, in 12 directions. As data are reused and repurposed, these connections will increase rapidly. Higher degrees of integration require close coordination and shared governance between participants, but such integration is otherwise compatible with a decentralized data architecture. The system is designed to ensure that data flow freely and safely—not remain in one place.

Even though most countries are far away from the aspirational goal of a well-functioning data system, setting sights on this target can provide countries with guidance on the next steps in developing such a system. How countries move toward this vision of an INDS will depend on their current capacity and the parameters of the social contract for data. There is no singular blueprint for how to build an INDS. Instead, this Report proposes a maturity model to help assess progress. Countries in the initial stages are likely to benefit the most from establishing the fundamentals for an integrated national data system. This includes developing policies and strategies aimed at better data governance, strengthening the technical capacity for data production and use of government agencies and the national statistical office, and promoting data literacy through education and training. With the fundamentals in place, governments can work on initiating and systemizing data flows across and between the participants in the national data system. This requires policies and standards that ensure the consistency and interoperability of data and institutions and infrastructure to enable the secure exchange of data that mitigates privacy risks. At advanced levels of data maturity, the goal is to optimize the system through shared data governance and collaboration between the various stakeholders from government, international organizations, civil society, and the private sector.

The structure of this system will differ from country to country, reflecting local norms for the safe reuse and sharing of data. Nonetheless, certain common attributes are needed to realize the development gains from reusing and sharing data. A well-functioning data system defines and establishes

Figure O.6 What happens in an integrated national data system?

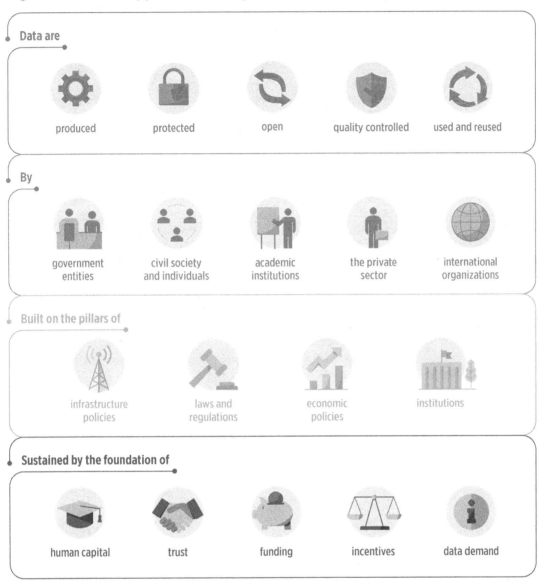

Data are

produced · protected · open · quality controlled · used and reused

By

government entities · civil society and individuals · academic institutions · the private sector · international organizations

Built on the pillars of

infrastructure policies · laws and regulations · economic policies · institutions

Sustained by the foundation of

human capital · trust · funding · incentives · data demand

Source: WDR 2021 team.

the authority and responsibility for data production, flow, and use in a nation. This system would build on the infrastructure, policies, laws and regulations, and institutions discussed here; integrate the many sources of data; and connect all the stakeholders (figure O.6).

For many countries, a system in which high-quality data flow and are used safely among various participants remains a distant vision. A low-income country suffering from high levels of poverty, fragility, and poor governance may struggle to produce even the most fundamental data, let alone set up

a whole-of-government, multistakeholder approach to data governance. Yet keeping this vision in sight matters for all countries, even those struggling the most with data, because it can serve as a guide in making decisions on how to develop their data systems (box O.1).

Coalescing around a common understanding of a new social contract for data—one built on trust to produce value from data that are equitably distributed—and finding the right blueprint for building an integrated national data system—one that unleashes the value of data to improve lives through

Box O.1 Toward an integrated national data system: Country examples

Important steps in the right direction. Many countries have adopted important initiatives that embody aspects of what is envisioned in an integrated national data system. South Africa's Department of Planning, Monitoring and Evaluation has developed a system that includes the data produced by citizens who monitor the performance of government programs. In Chile, civil society participation is mandated by the 2011 Law on Associations and Citizen Participation in Public Management, and the national statistical office has put in place a civil society council. The inclusion of multiple stakeholders in a national data system encourages sustainability and helps ensure that all participants have an opportunity to access and benefit from it. The Nepal Data Literacy Program, established in 2019, comprises a 100-hour modular, customizable pedagogy to support both technical skills building and efforts to enhance a culture of data use among Nepalis. The program is now partnering with Kathmandu University School of Management (KUSOM) to incorporate data literacy toolkits into the university programs and develop a data-driven course that will be free to other institutions and thousands of students.

A fully realized vision. In Estonia, the government has set up a national data system to safely manage citizens' personal data for use by government agencies and participating businesses. X-Road is an open-source data exchange layer solution that allows linked public and private databases to automatically share information, ensuring confidentiality, integrity, and interoperability between data exchange parties. It combines a technical solution (enabling technical architecture and a series of protocols) with a governance solution (the once-only principle enshrined in national law that obliges public sector agencies to refrain from duplicating data requests). Under this system, citizens have to supply government agencies and participating businesses with their information only once. It is then automatically transmitted to other participating entities. X-Road's cryptography protocols also enhance transparency because they log entries into the system and give individuals detailed insights into who is sharing their data and for what purposes.

The X-Road arrangement both builds on and enhances Estonia's social contract on data by providing trust, equity, and value. Its transparency engenders trust. Its national scope, available to all, promotes equity. Its ease and comprehensiveness provide value. To work well, this digital data system depends on some "analogue" components. Cooperation is fostered between government and the private sector and between components of infrastructure. Change management is built into the entire system, from its foundations in national law (and the social contract) to its design, uptake, and upkeep. A culture of trust and sharing (data sharing) is encouraged.

---

creative, innovative applications by a widening array of users—are highly aspirational goals. Achieving these goals will require significant changes in how data are produced, managed, protected, shared, and used. Making these changes will be difficult and will depend on substantial commitment and effort, but the cost of failing to change is a world faced with greater inequities and many missed opportunities.

Notes

1. Chapter 1 reviews definitions of data and describes how the term *data* is used in this Report.
2. Amnesty International (2019); Zuboff (2019).
3. Scheer and Cohen (2020).
4. Scheer and Cohen (2020).
5. World Bank (2017).
6. FMWR (2018).
7. World Bank, Statistical Performance Indicators (database), http://documents.worldbank.org/curated/en/815721616086786412/Measuring-the-Statistical-Performance-of-Countries-An-Overview-of-Updates-to-the-World-Bank-Statistical-Capacity-Index.
8. Brynjolfsson, Hitt, and Kim (2011).
9. For an extensive discussion of this problem and many other concerns about machine learning, see O'Neil (2017).
10. For an early reference to "garbage in–garbage out" in the statistical literature, see Parzen (1964).
11. Aiken et al. (2020).
12. Burke and Lobell (2017); Osgood-Zimmerman et al. (2018).
13. An early illustration of how data can be used to improve accountability for public expenditure can be found in a study of the use of education budgets in Uganda by Reinikka and Svensson (2001).
14. See Broadband Commission for Sustainable Development, International Telecommunication Union, "Target 3: Connectivity" (accessed October 31, 2020), https://broadbandcommission.org/Pages/targets/Target-3.aspx.
15. Chen (2021). Analysis is based on Access Survey 2017–18 data collected by Research ICT Africa in 22

low- and middle-income countries across Africa, Asia, and Latin America.

16. GSMA (2019).

17. World Bank analysis of World Trade Organization ad valorem duties for "Telephones for cellular networks 'mobile telephones' or for other wireless networks" (Harmonized System code 851712).

18. ITU et al. (2018).

19. COE (2018).

20. Safeguards for personal data are grounded in a human rights framework based on international law. These safeguards have their origin in the establishment of the "rule of law" with the expression of individual rights in the Enlightenment and were codified in international law after World War II. They were further refined in the context of analog data in the 1970s and 1980s with the Fair Information Practices, the Council of Europe's 1981 Convention for the Protection of Individuals with regard to Automatic Processing of Personal Data (Convention 108), and the first guidelines issued by the Organisation for Economic Co-operation and Development (OECD). The OECD guidelines and Convention 108 were updated in the digital context after launch of the World Wide Web in 1995 and continue to evolve.

21. Madrigal (2012).

22. OECD (2019).

23. Ferracane and van der Marel (2021).

24. Al-Rikabi and Loeprick (forthcoming).

25. An integrated national data system does not imply that all data are integrated in a national database. Instead, various participants are integrated in a system in which data are safely flowing and used. This is akin to a national statistical system in the sense that an ensemble of participants jointly collects, protects, processes, and disseminates official statistics. But unlike in the national statistical system, the scope of an integrated national data system goes well beyond official statistics; it requires an intentional approach to governing the participants and their roles.

References

Aiken, Emily L., Guadalupe Bedoya, Aidan Coville, and Joshua E. Blumenstock. 2020. "Targeting Development Aid with Machine Learning and Mobile Phone Data: Evidence from an Anti-Poverty Intervention in Afghanistan." In COMPASS '20: Proceedings of the 3rd ACM SIGCAS Conference on Computing and Sustainable Societies, 310–11. New York: Association for Computing Machinery.

Al-Rikabi, Jaffar, and Jan Loeprick. Forthcoming. "Simulating Potential Tax Revenues from Data-Driven Platform Businesses in East Asia." WDR 2021 background paper, World Bank, Washington, DC.

Amnesty International. 2019. "Surveillance Giants: How the Business Model of Google and Facebook Threatens Human Rights." Report POL 30/1404/2019, Amnesty International, London. https://www.amnesty.org/en/documents/document/?indexNumber=pol30%2f1404%2f2019&language=en.

Brynjolfsson, Erik, Lorin M. Hitt, and Heekyung Hellen Kim. 2011. "Strength in Numbers: How Does Data-Driven Decisionmaking Affect Firm Performance?" SSRN Scholarly Paper ID 1819486, Social Science Research Network, Rochester, NY. doi.org/10.2139/ssrn.1819486.

Burke, Marshall, and David Lobell. 2017. "Satellite-Based Assessment of Yield Variation and Its Determinants in Smallholder African Systems." PNAS, Proceedings of the National Academy of Sciences 114 (9): 2189–94. doi.org/10.1073/pnas.1616919114.

Chen, Rong. 2021. "A Demand-Side View of Mobile Internet Adoption in the Global South." Policy Research Working Paper 9590, World Bank, Washington, DC. http://documents.worldbank.org/curated/en/492871616350929155/A-Demand-Side-View-of-Mobile-Internet-Adoption-in-the-Global-South.

COE (Council of Europe). 2018. "Convention 108+: Convention for the Protection of Individuals with Regard to the Processing of Personal Data." COE, Strasbourg. https://rm.coe.int/convention-108-convention-for-the-protection-of-individuals-with-regar/16808b36f1.

Ferracane, Martina Francesca, and Erik Leendert van der Marel. 2021. "Regulating Personal Data: Data Models and Digital Services Trade." Policy Research Working Paper 9596, World Bank, Washington, DC. http://documents.worldbank.org/curated/en/890741616533448170/Regulating-Personal-Data-Data-Models-and-Digital-Services-Trade.

FMWR (Federal Ministry of Water Resources, Nigeria). 2018. "National Action Plan for Revitalization of the WASH Sector." FMWR, Abuja.

GSMA (GSM Association). 2019. "Connected Society: State of Mobile Internet Connectivity 2019." GSMA, London. https://www.gsma.com/mobilefordevelopment/resources/the-state-of-mobile-internet-connectivity-report-2019/.

ITU (International Telecommunication Union), World Bank, ComSec (Commonwealth Secretariat), CTO (Commonwealth Telecommunications Organisation), and NATO (Cooperative Cyber Defence Centre of Excellence, North Atlantic Treaty Organization). 2018. "Guide to Developing a National Cybersecurity Strategy: Strategic Engagement in Cybersecurity." ITU, Geneva. https://www.itu.int/pub/D-STR-CYB_GUIDE.01-2018.

Knippenberg, Erwin, and Moritz Meyer. 2020. "The Hidden Potential of Mobile Phone Data: Insights on COVID-19 in The Gambia." Data Blog (blog). September 10, 2020. https://blogs.worldbank.org/opendata/hidden-potential-mobile-phone-data-insights-covid-19-gambia.

Madrigal, Alexis C. 2012. "Reading the Privacy Policies You Encounter in a Year Would Take 76 Work Days." Atlantic, March 1, 2012. https://www.theatlantic.com/technology/archive/2012/03/reading-the-privacy-policies-you-encounter-in-a-year-would-take-76-work-days/253851/.

OECD (Organisation for Economic Co-operation and Development). 2019. Enhancing Access to and Sharing of Data: Reconciling Risks and Benefits for Data Re-Use across Societies. Paris: OECD. https://www.oecd-ilibrary.org/science-and-technology/enhancing-access-to-and-sharing-of-data_276aaca8-en.

O'Neil, Cathy. 2017. Weapons of Math Destruction: How Big Data Increases Inequality and Threatens Democracy. New York: Broadway Books.

Osgood-Zimmerman, Aaron, Anoushka I. Millear, Rebecca W. Stubbs, Chloe Shields, Brandon V. Pickering, Lucas Earl, Nicholas Graetz, et al. 2018. "Mapping Child Growth Failure in Africa between 2000 and 2015." *Nature* 555 (7694): 41–47. doi.org/10.1038/nature25760.

Parzen, Emanuel. 1964. "Review of Smoothing, Forecasting and Prediction of Discrete Time Series, by Robert Goodell Brown." *Journal of the American Statistical Association* 59 (307): 973–74. doi.org/10.2307/2283122.

Reinikka, Ritva, and Jakob Svensson. 2001 "Explaining Leakage of Public Funds." Policy Research Working Paper 2709, World Bank, Washington, DC.

Scheer, Steven, and Tova Cohen. 2020. "Israel Extends Coronavirus Cell Phone Surveillance by Three Weeks." *Emerging Markets* (blog), May 5, 2020. https://www.reuters.com/article/us-health-coronavirus-israel-surveillanc/israel-extends-coronavirus-cell-phone-surveillance-by-three-weeks-idUSKBN22H11I.

World Bank. 2017. *A Wake Up Call: Nigeria Water Supply, Sanitation, and Hygiene Poverty Diagnostic.* WASH Poverty Diagnostic Series. Washington, DC: World Bank. https://openknowledge.worldbank.org/handle/10986/27703.

World Bank. 2019. "Tanzania, Mainland Poverty Assessment 2019: Executive Summary." World Bank, Washington, DC. https://www.worldbank.org/en/country/tanzania/publication/tanzanias-path-to-poverty-reduction-and-pro-poor-growth.

Zuboff, Shoshana. 2019. *The Age of Surveillance Capitalism: The Fight for a Human Future at the New Frontier of Power.* New York: PublicAffairs. https://www.hbs.edu/faculty/Pages/item.aspx?num=56791.

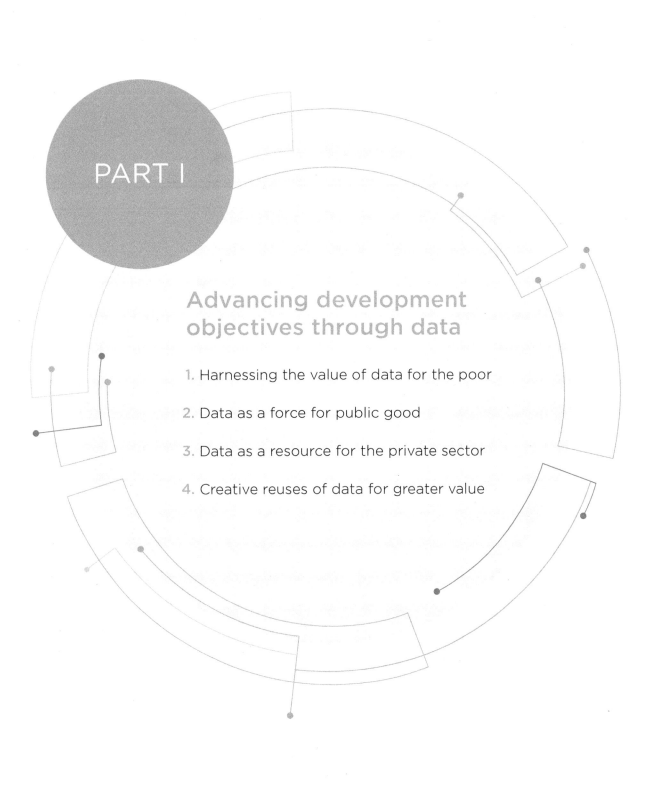

PART I

Advancing development objectives through data

1. Harnessing the value of data for the poor

2. Data as a force for public good

3. Data as a resource for the private sector

4. Creative reuses of data for greater value

CHAPTER

1

Harnessing the value of data for the poor

Main messages

1. Data can improve people's lives in many ways. However, economic and political factors typically prevent benefits from being shared equitably.

2. The value of data for development is largely untapped. Realizing data's full value entails repeatedly reusing and repurposing data in creative ways to promote economic and social development.

3. The challenge is to develop a trust environment that safeguards against harmful misuse of data as they are exchanged between parties and enables data to be created, reused, and repurposed.

4. A strong data governance framework, composed of appropriate policies, laws, regulations, and institutions, is needed to ensure that the full value of data is realized and shared safely and equitably.

The untapped potential of data to serve development objectives

At the turn of the nineteenth century, English sociologist Seebohm Rowntree interviewed a sample of families with the aim of better understanding the poverty experienced not only by those he interviewed, but also by everyone in the town of York.[1] The findings from this work changed preconceptions by revealing that poverty was pervasive outside of London and by demonstrating that people cycled in and out of poverty over the course of their lives.

How to turn data into information and information into insights that can help the poor is at the heart of this Report (see box 1.1 on the use here of the term *data*). In the twenty-first century, data possess the power to be truly life-changing. Most of the new and fascinating ways in which data affect the lives of many of us worldwide are linked to people being able

---

Box 1.1 What this Report means by *data*

The term *data* is difficult to define. It has meant different things at different times, and in different disciplines. Originally simply defined as facts, the term slowly came to mean facts as they related to mathematical representations. Despite the changing nature of data, most people would not have thought of things such as pictures, sounds, or words as data even as recently as a few decades ago. But times have changed, and major advances in computing power, together with innovative thinking, have resulted in, for example, radiomics, the science of converting medical images into data that, once structured and analyzed, can help improve a patient's diagnosis and prognosis.[a] Similarly, sound can now be digitized and analyzed to, for example, explore and better understand the galaxies.[b] And the growing field of text analytics converts words (such as keywords from Google searches) into structured data that help us better understand many social phenomena.[c] Because the evolving definition of data stems simply from technological advances in computing and creative thinking, it is challenging to provide a specific description of data that would not soon seem archaic or anachronistic.

In very general terms, Carrière-Swallow and Haksar point out that "data can be quantitative or qualitative in nature, and may be stored on analog (that is, paper, stone tablets) or digital media."[d] This view conforms with how this Report uses the term. Indeed, some data are still collected on paper in many countries. Processing these data—digitizing them and entering them in a spreadsheet or database—allows them to be more easily analyzed, but a digital format is not necessarily an attribute of data.

The Organisation for Economic Co-operation and Development (OECD) states broadly that data are "characteristics or information, usually numerical, that are collected through observation." More specifically, data are "the physical representation of information in a manner suitable for communication, interpretation, or processing by human beings or by automatic means."[e] Although this description aligns fairly well with how the term is used in this Report, a few distinctions are worth noting. Here, data are sometimes collected through observation, though they need not be. Data can be the result of digital transactions or simply by-products of our daily digital lives. Also, in this Report, data are not synonymous with information. Rather, data must be processed, structured, and analyzed to be converted into information. This semantic distinction between data and information emphasizes the critical role of improved data management, literacy, and analysis for extracting information, and creating value, from data.

An expansive description of data that resonates well with how the term is used in this Report is provided by the UK National Data Strategy:

> When we refer to data, we mean information about people, things and systems. . . . Data about people can include personal data, such as basic contact details, records generated through interaction with services or the web, or information about their physical characteristics (biometrics)—and it can also extend to population-level data, such as demographics. Data can also be about systems and infrastructure, such as administrative records about businesses and public services. Data is increasingly used to describe location, such as geospatial reference details, and the environment we live in, such as data about biodiversity or the weather. It can also refer to the information generated by the burgeoning web of sensors that make up the Internet of Things.[f]

a. Gillies, Kinahan, and Hricak (2015); Yala et al. (2021).
b. See, for example, Leighton and Petculescu (2016).
c. See, for example, Stephens-Davidowitz (2017).
d. Carrière-Swallow and Haksar (2019, 17).
e. Organisation for Economic Co-operation and Development (OECD), "Glossary of Statistical Terms: Data," OECD Statistics Portal, https://stats .oecd.org/glossary/detail.asp?ID=532.
f. See "What We Mean by Data" (DCMS 2020).

to extract greater value from data. Indeed, the data produced by people can be used in innovative ways to help them, but one does not have to be the producer or user of data to benefit from the data revolution. In fact, the data often collected from a small sample of people can help shape policy to improve the lives of a vastly larger population, whether they were part of the sample or not—just as Seebohm Rowntree revealed in his pioneering efforts. But for such approaches to work, the samples must be truly representative of the population, including the poor and other marginalized groups. And yet both traditional censuses and sample surveys, as well as new data sources captured by the private sector, may fail to fully cover the most disadvantaged groups.

An important attribute of data is that using them does not diminish their value to be reused for some other purpose—data are inexhaustible. But reusing or repurposing data typically requires well-functioning data systems that facilitate the safe flow of data in formats that make the data valuable to many users. These systems, however, typically do not function well in many low- and middle-income countries.

Moreover, data have a dark side. Making data accessible to more users and creating systems that facilitate their reuse also opens the door for data to be misused in ways that can harm individuals or development objectives. With lives becoming increasingly intertwined in the digital world, each day brings new concerns about protecting personal data; misinformation; and attacks on software, networks, and data systems.

Well-functioning data systems thus balance the need to *safeguard* against outcomes that harm people, while simultaneously *enabling* the potential for data to improve lives. This Report returns often to the need to strike this balance between safeguarding and enabling.

The findings and recommendations in this Report are drawn from an extensive array of material, including academic research, international development agency reports, commercial experiences, and a series of consultations with innovators and stakeholders in the data world. Although this Report reinforces and builds on findings from *World Development Report 2016: Digital Dividends*,[2] the World Bank report *Information and Communications for Development 2018: Data-Driven Development*,[3] and many reports on digital technology, this Report differs by focusing on how data themselves, rather than the adoption of digital technology, can improve the lives of poor people.[4]

World Development Reports often synthesize established findings from analytical work and research, but the issues and content surrounding data are evolving rapidly. Many of the topics covered continue to be widely debated in rich and poor countries alike. Consensus has yet to emerge, and research is at an early stage, particularly on how these issues affect low- and middle-income countries. The goal, therefore, is not to be overly prescriptive, but to develop frameworks to help policy makers and countries think through the trade-offs and adopt a balanced approach to developing both safeguards and enablers. Countries should make the most of data, but safely, and as appropriate for their social, political, and economic context.

The growing literature on data over the last few years is largely written from a high-income country perspective.[5] This Report therefore sets out to fill the large gap in the literature on the effects of data on poor people and poor countries.

A brief history of data

Many of the themes of this Report were emerging even in the earliest days of data collection and use. For millennia, people have been collecting data. The oldest censuses date back to at least 2000–1000 BCE to ancient Egypt, Greece, and China, who enumerated people, livestock, and food items.[6] The Romans fielded a census of men and their possessions every five years—a practice referenced in the Christian Bible.[7]

Over the long history of data collection, the type of data collected and the ways data have been used have changed as societies' priorities, values, power structures, and government objectives have changed.[8] Record keepers in the Incan Empire between 1400 and 1500 CE counted people, dwellings, llamas, marriages, and potential army recruits.[9] Rulers and administrators gave priority to counting sources of wealth and power considered of strategic importance (the data were kept secret from the public). They collected information first and foremost on property for taxation and men for military recruitment and labor force purposes, as well as enumerating newly conquered peoples and territories. With little reason to believe that the data being collected were meant to improve lives, distrust was widespread—it was not uncommon for citizens to resist being counted or having their possessions counted.[10]

The ascent of Enlightenment ideals in eighteenth-century Europe, with their emphasis on objective scientific inquiry, brought a shift in attitudes toward the role of data in society—from simply counting and registering phenomena to describing and understanding living conditions for society as a whole.[11] During this era, and under the influence of the leading

Figure 1.1 The share of people counted in a census grew from about 1 in 10 in 1850 to 9 in 10 today

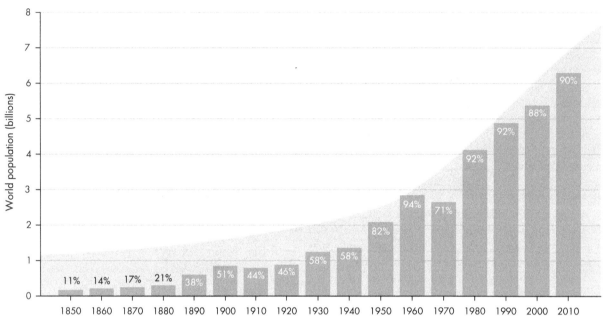

Source: Whitby 2020. Data at http://bit.do/WDR2021-Fig-1_1.

Note: The shaded area represents the world's population; the bars indicate the percentage of the population that was enumerated each decade.

intellectuals of the day, notions of the rule of law (and accountability of states) evolved, a social contract between the individual and the state coalesced, and the Declaration of the Rights of Man and of the Citizen emerged.[12] These became the foundational elements of the current discussions of a social contract for data based on human rights (see chapter 6).

Starting in the late eighteenth century, governments of the emerging nation-states in Europe and North America established statistical agencies to publish official statistics on the state of the nation and to inform public discourse. European nations began systematically conducting full-fledged population censuses, and a decennial national census became a provision of the US Constitution. By the end of the nineteenth century, half of the world's population had been enumerated in censuses (figure 1.1).[13]

These advances also led to some of the innovations in statistics and social science research methods that enabled the rise of the sample survey. The earliest examples of sampling date back to the late seventeenth and early eighteenth centuries, but they lacked the theoretical foundations to justify the method.[14] Sampling remained highly controversial throughout the nineteenth century, but methodological advances, especially the concept of random sample selection,

led to its gradual acceptance in the early twentieth century. A series of influential articles in the 1930s, 1940s, and 1950s filled the holes in the theoretical foundations of survey sampling around the same time that sampling frames with universal coverage became available.[15] Sample surveys grew enormously popular, especially in the United States, quickly covering a wide range of topics.

Modern geospatial data systems developed along a similar timeline. Building on the much older science of cartography, this type of data is rooted in the thematic maps of the eighteenth and nineteenth centuries. Its goal was to relate geography to other types of information.[16] A prominent early application was the spatial mapping of disease outbreaks—for example, of yellow fever in New York City at the end of the eighteenth century and especially of cholera in British and other European municipalities during the pandemics of the nineteenth century.[17] Most prominent among those is the map of London by physician John Snow. During the 1854 cholera outbreak, Snow plotted cholera-related deaths in London together with the city's water pumps, identifying a high concentration of cases close to a pump on Broad Street and deducing that water from this pump was causing infections (map 1.1). New cases in the area stopped almost entirely once the pump had been removed.[18] Since the advent of Snow's map, innovations in printing and computer technology as well as the rise of remote sensing have made geospatial data and their applications versatile and ubiquitous.[19]

With the digital revolution, the types and scope of data have changed dramatically, and the volume of data collected has grown exponentially. In this new landscape, private sector actors are playing an increasingly larger role in data collection through platform-based business models in which data are collected passively as a by-product of business processes. Digital platforms have also expanded the opportunities for citizens to collect data, which often occurs when governments fail to collect data (see spotlight 1.1). Examples include Utunzi, a platform that allows individuals and organizations to report and document violence against LGBTQI individuals,[20] and various platforms that allow users to report air pollution levels, deforestation, and other location-specific environmental data to raise awareness and spur action.

The foundational origins of data protection laws can be linked to the Enlightenment era. Although there is a clear arc from these historical concepts of rights governing interactions between the state and the individual to principles guiding data protection, most policies guiding data regulation are very modern (see chapter 6). The principles of data protection can trace their immediate roots to the US Fair Information Practice Principles developed in the 1970s and that formed the basis for the 1980 OECD (Organisation for Economic Co-operation and Development) Guidelines (revised in 2013).[21] Similarly, the basic substantive rights and obligations in the European Union's General Data Protection Regulation, reflected first in its 1995 Directive on the Protection of Personal Data, trace their roots to the OECD Guidelines.[22]

A data typology

Although data can be used to improve development outcomes, the challenges differ across data types. To help readers conceptualize these data types and better understand those challenges, this Report sorts data types using a two-dimensional framework (table 1.1). In the first dimension, data are classified based on whether the original *intent* was for public or commercial purposes. Both new and traditional types of data collected for commercial purposes are called *private intent data*. Data originally collected for public purposes are called *public intent data*, regardless of the collection instrument or the entity that manages

Map 1.1 John Snow's innovative mapping of the cholera epidemic in London in 1854 revolutionized tracing of the disease

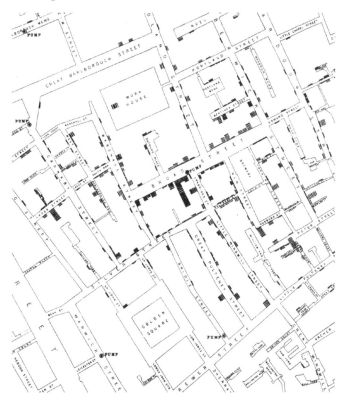

Source: Ball 2009. Map segment reproduced from John Snow, *On the Mode of Communication of Cholera,* 2nd ed. (London: John Churchill, 1855).

Note: The solid black rectangles of various sizes represent deaths from cholera.

the data. Public intent data tend to be collected purposefully with a view toward representativeness. By contrast, private intent data are self-selecting in that they cover only users of cellphones and the internet, for example, and collection of these data may be more incidental.

The second dimension distinguishes between "traditional" and "new" data collection methods. Public intent data are typically associated with traditional data types such as censuses and surveys, although newer sources of data (such as from satellite imaging or e-government platforms) have become more prevalent. By design, traditional data collection efforts by governments are for public purposes and are used to inform policy making. But because the collection of public data via traditional methods tends to be relatively costly,[23] surveys are conducted infrequently,[24] and they often lack the granularity necessary to make meaningful inferences about subpopulations of interest. Meanwhile, traditional public intent data offer important advantages over new private intent data

Table 1.1 Examples of data types based on original intent and collection methods

Data collection methods and tools	Public intent data	Private intent data
Traditional	Census, national accounts, household surveys, enterprise surveys, labor force surveys, surveys of personal finance, administrative records	Any survey conducted by private entities, including public opinion surveys deployed by private entities; administrative data from company financial accounts
New	Location data from satellite imaging, digital identification, facial recognition from public cameras, public procurement data from e-government platforms	Just-in-time digital data on individual behavior/choices from digital platforms in the private sector

Source: WDR 2021 team.

in terms of their coverage of the population—and thus their potential to benefit more people—and their format, which makes them amenable to inferential analytics by researchers and government officials.

Private intent data are often associated with new sources of data produced using digital tools and applications that are growing rapidly. Compared with traditional public intent data, new private data sources offer greatly improved timeliness, frequency, and granularity of data, but they may not be representative in coverage. New private intent data can contribute significantly to addressing public sector development challenges. Private intent data collected through cellphones, internet usage, satellites, remote sensors, and other sources provide information about individuals and geographic locations that traditional surveys simply cannot.

Any simple framework used to classify data types carries limitations. Although much public intent data have long been collected using traditional methods, those methods are being updated and adapted. The new methods will increasingly supplement or replace traditional methods, and so the traditional–new differentiation in table 1.1 is likely to evolve. The distinction between public and private stewardship of data also may not be a salient one in some cases. For example, citizen-generated data—data that people or their organizations produce to directly monitor, demand, or drive change on issues that affect them—can be produced through crowdsourcing mechanisms or citizen reporting initiatives, and such data are often organized and managed by civil society groups. The data may reside with a private entity, but they are clearly collected for public purposes.

Although data gathered through new methods for private purposes offer tremendous potential to improve timeliness and detail through massive sample size, they are not a panacea for the shortcomings

of public intent data collected using more traditional methods. For one thing, private firms have little incentive to curate their data for sharing, and thus these data are not readily amenable for public use. A potentially more difficult challenge is coverage. Data collected for public policy purposes are almost always designed to represent the relevant current population (such as individuals, firms, health facilities, students, or schools). However, survey designers face challenges in meeting the representativeness objective in terms of both coverage (such as underrepresentation of slum inhabitants, top earners, or informal enterprises) and timeliness (due to delays in data processing). By contrast, collectors of private intent data rarely need or have an interest in full population coverage; they focus much more on specific subgroups (such as consumers and suppliers). Thus, even though sample sizes can be massive and very timely, they can provide only partial reflections of the population. A study from the United Kingdom examined data from a variety of social media platforms and found that none was representative of the population, particularly underrepresenting the elderly, the less well educated, and lower-income people.[25]

Public policies and programs need to be informed by data that represent the relevant population. For this reason, private intent data should not be viewed as a substitute for public intent data in understanding the scope of many development problems (box 1.2). That said, the joint use of public intent data collected using traditional methods and newer sources of private intent data offers interesting opportunities to reap significantly more value added than the isolated use of one kind of data or the other. A key theme of this Report is that *governments should take advantage of complementarities between new and traditional data to confront development challenges.* For example, because the majority of the world's poor live in rural areas and derive

Box 1.2 Innovation in traditional surveys: A COVID-19 example in Brazil

A prime example of the importance of traditional surveys and their potential for innovation comes from Brazil. In May 2020, it was one of the first countries to complete nationally representative surveys to produce data on the prevalence of COVID-19.[a] Fieldworkers clad in personal protective equipment conducted a serology test on randomly selected household members. This test detects the presence of antibodies in the blood as a response to a specific infection, such as COVID-19—that is, it detects the body's immune response to the infection caused by the virus rather than the virus itself. While waiting for the results of the test, the fieldworkers administered a brief questionnaire to collect sociodemographic data and asked the tested household member whether she or he was experiencing symptoms associated with COVID-19.[b] Asking questions about symptoms enabled the research team to estimate rates of asymptomatic infection. Sociodemographic questions, especially those about work and travel outside the home, enabled the team to measure how much a household member adhered to social distancing guidelines.

The test results were conveyed to the household member before the fieldworkers left the dwelling, and information on positive tests was sent to health authorities to help them track the spread of the virus. In May, 25,025 interviews in 133 "sentinel cities" were completed in the baseline survey. Cities were chosen because of their primacy in the local region as hubs of commerce and services for surrounding urban and rural areas. The survey was conducted three more times, the most recent round in late August 2020. Multiple survey rounds enabled researchers and public health officials to track the spread of the virus over time by region.

At least two findings based on these serology tests and the interviews are striking. First, COVID-19 infections were far more prevalent than had been recorded. Overall seroprevalence—the share of the population that tested positive for the pathogen—for the 90 cities with a sample size of 200 or greater was 1.4 percent in the baseline survey. Extrapolating this figure to the full population of these cities, who represent 25 percent of the country's population, produced an estimate of 760,000 cases, compared with the 104,782 cases reported for those cities in official statistics as of May 13, 2020. In the fourth round of the survey in August, the seroprevalence rate had climbed to 3.8 percent.[c]

Second, there was a remarkably wide regional variation in seroprevalence around the 1.4 percent national average, ranging from less than 1 percent in most cities in the South and Center-West regions to 25 percent in the city of Breves in the Amazon (North region). Eleven of the 15 cities with the highest seroprevalence were in the North. The six cities with highest seroprevalence were located along a 2,000-kilometer stretch of the Amazon River. Beyond geography, seroprevalence varied across ethnic groups and was highest among indigenous populations (3.7 percent in the baseline survey). Understanding the scope of the overall problem and identifying regions and populations with the most pressing needs would not have been possible without population-based surveys. These data also provided information on the effectiveness (or lack thereof) of approaches adopted to combat the spread of the disease.

Broad support for investigating something as important and urgent as the prevalence of COVID-19 might have been expected, and yet opposition sprang up in some quarters. For example, in some areas sample size was suppressed by the rapid spread of disinformation through social media that characterized the interviewers as "swindlers," or even as part of a plot to spread the virus. In 27 cities, interviewers were arrested, and in eight cities the tests were destroyed by the local police force.[d] Overall, however, the example illustrates the importance of population-based surveys (and public intent data in general) for understanding the scope and nature of disease spread.

a. Hallal, Hartwig, et al. (2020). Brazil is the only country in Latin America to complete a national survey.
b. Hallal, Horta, et al. (2020).
c. UFPEL (2020).
d. Hallal, Hartwig, et al. (2020).

their livelihoods from the land, measuring agricultural productivity is central to policies and programs to eliminate extreme poverty. Yet recent research has shown that agricultural productivity, specifically crop yield, is poorly measured with traditional survey approaches that rely on farmer-reported information on crop production and land areas.[26] When sample surveys rely instead on objective measurement methods, the resulting data not only accurately capture crop yields at surveyed locations, but also can be used to inform and develop remote sensing models that combine data from surveys and satellites to provide highly localized crop yield estimates across entire regions and countries beyond the locations in which sample surveys are conducted.[27]

Both public intent and private intent data have advantages and disadvantages and pose distinct challenges in terms of reuse and exchange to achieve development objectives. But because public intent and private intent data have inherent complementarities, they can be used jointly to bolster development. A ministry of health would be able to issue better public policy if it could connect its health data with that of other ministries such as education, labor, and planning, as well as with that of health providers, whether public or private, around the country. A private firm would be able to operate more effectively if it could link its data with other sources of information, such as satellite data on population density and socioeconomic data on wealth and well-being.

Combining the two types of data could advance evidence-based policy through more precise and timely official statistics that are produced more cheaply, while preserving the representativeness characteristic of public intent data. For example, building on the well-established infrastructure for socioeconomic surveys conducted by governments,

satellite data and call detail records from mobile phones offer new opportunities for updating poverty estimates for small areas more frequently. More generally, the high frequency of data collected for commercial purposes holds promise for producing better estimates of current socioeconomic conditions when large-scale, costly surveys such as censuses or integrated household surveys such as those of the World Bank's Living Standards Measurement Study are infrequent. Real-time data on prices, nighttime lights, or trade flows could be used to help "nowcast" (that is, generate an estimate for the current time based on data collected with a lag in time) macroeconomic data to avoid lags in availability.

The economics of data and political economy issues

The potential to extract further value from the proliferation of data is significant because data are inexhaustible or "nonrival"—that is, a person's call detail records, location history, internet usage, and medical records, among other things, can be used repeatedly by firms and governments for different purposes without depleting them.[28] This finding is illustrated by the data life cycle (figure 1.2), which depicts the potential circularity of data use, reuse, and

Figure 1.2 **The data life cycle**

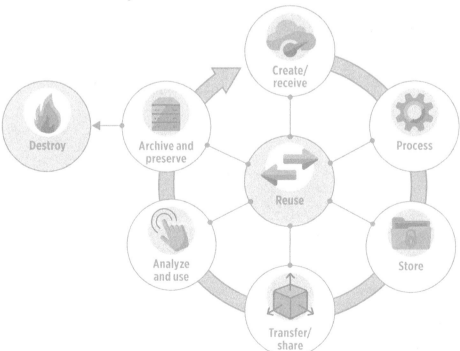

Source: WDR 2021 team.

repurposing, as long as data can be made safely accessible across a wide array of users and unless explicit steps are taken to destroy the data.

Because of the nonrival character of data and the implications for their limitless reuse, it is inherently difficult to place an economic value on data, although many attempts have been made to do so. The diverse approaches taken range from a cost-based methodology that adds up different components of the information value chain;[29] to approaches that directly quantify the economic benefits that data yield by improving efficiency, reducing transaction costs, or expanding markets;[30] to estimates based on the stock market value of data-intensive companies and related acquisition transactions.[31] Although all of these approaches agree on the high value of data, the partial nature of these estimates, together with the heterogeneity of the approaches, prevent any definitive conclusion.

In view of today's increasingly sophisticated application of machine learning and artificial intelligence to drive data-based innovations, it is quite conceivable that the economic value of unanticipated secondary uses of data may far exceed the value of the primary use of data—that is, the use for which they were originally collected. These characteristics raise the prospect of serious underinvestment in data collection from a social perspective because the entities bearing the cost of data collection will not necessarily be the ones capturing its full economic value.

At the same time, data are not a pure public good because they are excludable, allowing the entity that originally collects and holds the data to prevent others from accessing them. Examples abound across the public sector of the unwillingness of data holders to share data with other government entities and the public. In the private sector, firms may not want to sell or exchange their data with others, perhaps because governments and firms lack the capacity to share or exchange their data in a safe manner, or more simply because of a lack of incentives (or legal requirements) to make the data available. In some cases, reuse and sharing of data may cede informational advantages to competing firms in the private sector or rival entities in the public sector. Although the excludability of data suggests that they could readily be traded on markets, other economic characteristics complicate this classical approach to addressing allocation issues (see box 1.3).

A fundamental reason for the lack of incentives to share, sell, or exchange data is the considerable economies of scale that accrue to holding data and the associated economic or political power that they bring to the data holder. Although the returns to the first few bits of data are essentially zero, there is a point past which the returns from additional data, and from improvements in the systems supporting these data, are substantial and increasing until they ultimately level off.[32] For example, in the field of artificial intelligence the size of datasets is a critical determinant of the accuracy of predictive algorithms.[33] Modern deep-learning techniques, with their complex models, have an even more voracious appetite for large datasets than traditional machine learning, and they may not begin to experience diminishing returns until they incorporate much larger scales with datasets containing tens or hundreds of millions of data points.

In addition to economies of scale, data are characterized by economies of scope because combining different types of related datasets can yield insights that otherwise would have been unavailable from one type of data alone. Similarly, weak and seemingly very tangential relations can be identified through machine learning techniques with larger and larger volumes of data. For example, Google's search engine data may be used to evaluate the effectiveness of advertising on YouTube, which is also owned by Google.[34] Social media can also track users' behavior to then build very detailed advertising profiles.

Imbalances in information sharing, concentrations of power, and equity concerns: A dark side of data

Such strong economies of scale and scope in data, and the resulting assemblage of valuable information by some actors at the potential expense of those who are excluded from the transaction, may lead to a concentration of power—economic or political—in the hands of those with privileged access to large volumes of data.[35] In the private sector, market forces are likely to lead to data agglomeration and market concentration in data-driven businesses, which may preclude entry by small firms and eventually create conditions for the abuse of market power. Today, the firms that control the greatest agglomerations of data are among the world's largest. The concentration of personal information in a handful of companies raises concerns about market power and discrimination. A key theme throughout this Report is balancing the gains in efficiency that new data bring with such equity concerns. On the government side, data agglomeration may lead to a concentration of personal information, which can be used to amass and maintain political power, discourage dissent, and even discriminate against some population segments. Measures that limit and

Box 1.3 The challenges of trading data through markets

From an economic perspective, it seems plausible that access to data is best solved by first defining clear economic property rights over data and then allowing parties to trade in data. However, the limited nascent economic literature on this subject suggests that for two reasons these propositions are not as straightforward as they may initially seem.

First, legal and economic challenges confound the definition of property rights over data. A central issue is the ambiguity involved in allocating property rights between the data subject and the data collector, each of which has some legitimate claim to be the "data owner." Present legal frameworks such as the European Union's General Data Protection Regulation allocate certain specific rights to the data subject, implicitly leaving residual rights to the data collector as a purely de facto property right.[a] Typically, a greater degree of data protection will benefit the data owner to the detriment of other potential data users and vice versa. This finding suggests that there is an economically optimal level of data protection. However, without efficient allocation of property rights, this social welfare–maximizing outcome will not be attained.[b]

The large synergies and complementarities that arise across different types of data (economies of scope) raise the concern that fragmented ownership patterns will prevent them from being realized, whether through strategic behavior or through technical barriers such as lack of interoperability. However, the classic trade-off between the static objective of making data widely available to maximize economic value and the dynamic objective of preserving incentives for further data to be collected[c] has weakened considerably with the advent of digital data that are often collected without cost as a by-product of other economic activities.

Second, although private bilateral market exchanges of data are well established in certain niches (specifically, trading personal data to target advertising), there are as of today no open multilateral markets for data, and many attempts to create such data markets have failed.[d] Because data are one of many experience goods that are difficult to evaluate in advance in areas such as price and quality, an important challenge is how data providers can convey information about the quality of their data before providing access.[e]

In practice, data provenance has become the main means of signaling the quality and accuracy of data, relying on the reputation of the original source. However, the metadata needed to establish provenance may themselves be subject to legal restrictions in areas such as privacy, and data sellers may have strategic incentives to conceal or manipulate such information. The theoretical literature demonstrates that the institutional mechanisms currently available for trade in data have led to a sharp trade-off between the feasible scale of a data market and the ability to verify the quality of the data traded.[f] Data may be traded via markets on a much larger scale in the future, but legal and institutional adaptations will be crucial to address challenges regarding data property rights and quality.

a. Duch-Brown, Martens, and Mueller-Langer (2017).
b. Duch-Brown, Martens, and Mueller-Langer (2017).
c. Duch-Brown, Martens, and Mueller-Langer (2017).
d. Koutroumpis, Leiponen, and Thomas (2020).
e. This is known as the Arrow Information Paradox (Arrow 1962).
f. Koutroumpis, Leiponen, and Thomas (2020).

neutralize this kind of dominance founded on the control of data need to be central to any data governance framework.

Because reliable statistics can expose poor policy decisions and performance, dilute power, and increase public scrutiny and pressure on governments, vested interests can be expected to intervene to distort decisions about the collection, reuse, and sharing of data. And indeed this Report finds strong associations among country statistical performance, independence of national statistical offices, and freedom of the press, controlling for country size and income level (chapter 2). The patterns indicate that a free and empowered press is a critical check

on government power and an important facilitator of statistical independence and data transparency.

Alternative data sources can provide a check on political influences when the accuracy or impartiality of official statistics is in question. For example, online prices obtained through web scraping have been used to construct daily price indexes in multiple countries, providing a comparison with official inflation figures. Researchers found that from 2007 to 2011, when Argentina reported an average annual inflation rate of 8 percent, online data indicated that the rate exceeded 20 percent.[36] The higher figure was consistent with inflation expectations from household surveys conducted at the time and similar to estimates of some provincial governments and local economists. Because online price data were available outside the country, efforts by Argentina's government to discourage local economists from collecting these data independently were largely ineffective. These practices were halted in 2015 as Argentina took steps to reaffirm its commitment to the transparency and reliability of official data through its National Institute of Statistics and Censuses (INDEC). Similar disparities between official inflation statistics and those obtained from online prices have recently emerged in Turkey.[37]

Governments can pose broader challenges to the use of nonofficial data sources. For example, Tanzania's 2018 amendment to its 2015 Statistics Act threatened members of civil society groups that published independent statistical information with imprisonment. Approval of the National Bureau of Statistics was required to publish such information, and publishing statistics that "invalidate, distort or discredit" official statistics was deemed a criminal offense. These provisions were subsequently amended amid international pressure.[38]

Finally, the transparency and reliability of official statistics can have important macroeconomic implications. At a time when public debt levels are exploding from pandemic-related spending (see spotlight 1.2), governments may be less than forthcoming with data on the public debt, potentially enabling them to overborrow and hide debts from both citizens and creditors, at least for a while. Eventually, however, that strategy can have negative repercussions. For example, in Mozambique three state-backed companies took on in 2013 and 2014 more than US$2 billion in government-guaranteed debt, equivalent to about 13 percent of the gross domestic product (GDP).[39] Roughly US$1.2 billion of it was borrowed without being disclosed to parliament and the public. The country's access to international credit markets was severely curtailed after the hidden loans were revealed in 2016. To rehabilitate its reputation, the government has undertaken a complex reform package to foster greater transparency and improve governance and anticorruption frameworks.[40]

Data for development: A conceptual framework

This Report poses two fundamental questions. How can data better advance development objectives? And what kind of data governance arrangements are needed to support the generation and use of data in a safe, ethical, and secure way while also delivering value equitably? The first part of this Report identifies the multiple pathways through which data can support or inhibit the development process, relying on the conceptual framework presented in this chapter, together with concrete illustrations and examples from recent experience in less developed and emerging countries.

Three pathways by which data can support development

Data can contribute to development by improving the lives of the poor through multiple pathways. The conceptual framework that guides this Report focuses on three such horizontal pathways (figure 1.3). The middle pathway is data generated by or received by governments and international organizations to support program administration, service delivery, and evidence-based policy making (see chapter 2). The top pathway is data created and used by civil society and academia to monitor and analyze the effects of government programs and policies and by individuals to empower and enable them to access public and commercial services tailored to their needs. The bottom pathway is data generated by private firms. These data can be a factor of production that fuels firm and economic growth. But data also can be part of production processes in other ways (as an intermediate input, an output, or a by-product) and can be mobilized and repurposed to support development objectives (see chapters 3 and 4).

In figure 1.3, two-way arrows link data production and collection with the three groups of actors in the center of the figure. These arrows indicate that data do not merely flow to the actors. They also must be collected with purpose, and data processing and analytics by those actors provide important feedback about what data should be produced and collected going forward. The rectangle that encapsulates the actors indicates their centrality in processing and analyzing data to provide insights that lead to better lives and better development outcomes. Among these three pathways, data can be shared and exchanged flowing vertically across public, private, and civil society channels for further impact on development. Data collected for use in one of these pathways can be accessed and repurposed for a different use through other pathways or by other data users.

Government and international organizations. At a basic level, data enable governments to understand the impact of policies and improve program administration and service delivery. For traditional data types such as household and firm surveys, national accounts, and administrative data, governments (or agents authorized by governments) have been central to collection efforts. They have collected data typically

Figure 1.3 Three pathways along which data can foster development

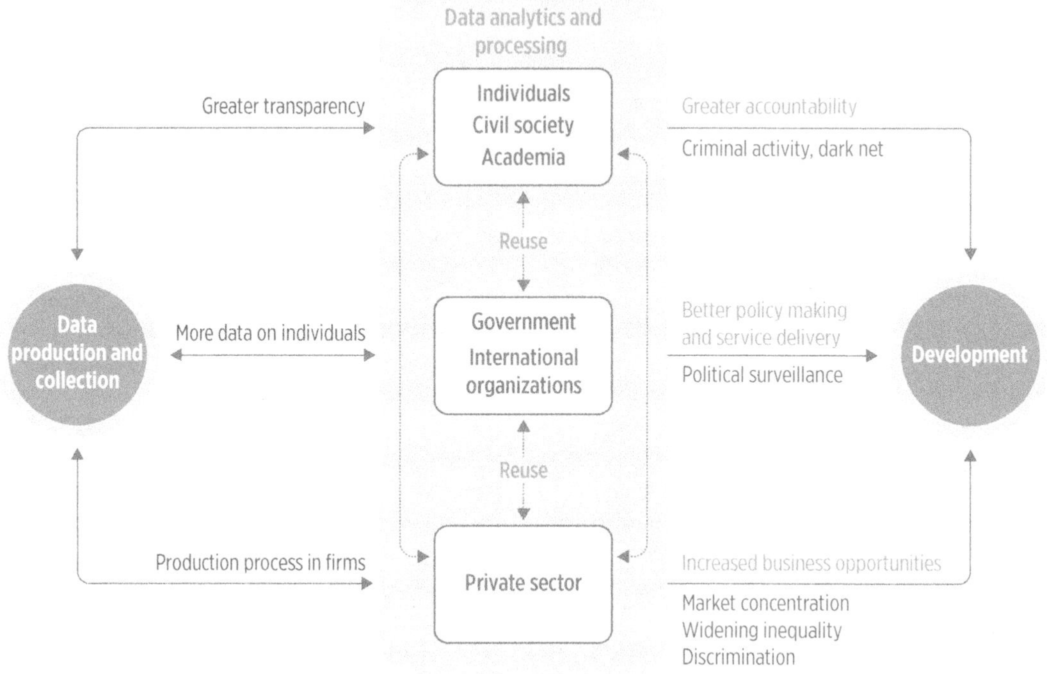

Source: WDR 2021 team.

Note: Positive impacts are shown in green; negative impacts are shown in red.

for specific purposes, often intended to improve policies and encourage development. However, without strong data systems in place to support data analysis in relevant applications, much of the potential for data to improve outcomes is unrealized.

Important factors in supporting successful national data systems include trained staff, budgetary autonomy for agencies that collect data, adequate data infrastructure, connected databases, and international partnerships (see chapter 9). However, these resources are often scarce in low-income countries, leaving these countries the least equipped to collect and effectively use the data necessary to assess and understand the scope and nature of the development problems they face and make inroads to solving them. Enhancing the capacity of client countries to collect, analyze, and utilize data therefore has been, and will continue to be, a priority of the World Bank Group, and it is a major focus of this Report. International organizations can help countries to address lack of funding, technical capacity, governance, and demand for public intent data and to overcome these barriers. Sovereign-supported multilateral and bilateral development institutions are also important collectors and disseminators of data in their own right, and they support country governments in their efforts to improve and deploy data better.

A better ability to exchange public intent data across many platforms (interoperability) could increase their impact on development. Despite their advantages in coverage, suitability for some types of analysis, and potential for informing and improving policy, public intent data are often stored in different government agencies and formatted in different ways. Fragmentation and incompatibilities thus limit a government's scope to use its data to the fullest extent to improve policies, service delivery, and targeting. Interoperability across public intent data sources is therefore an important goal.

The central role of government and international organizations in fostering development through data use and reuse is captured in figure 1.3 by the placement of this pathway in the center of the figure (see chapter 2).

Individuals, civil society, and academia. In the top pathway, making data widely available enables individuals and civil society to hold governments accountable for policy choices. Inputs from civil society provide a feedback mechanism through which policies can be adapted and improved, leading to more responsive governance. Civil society organizations themselves create data by collecting surveys and crowdsourcing information directly from citizens. Such data can foster discussion, government accountability, and transparency. Simply providing individuals with better access to their own data collected by government, international, or private sector actors is another way to enable citizens to advocate for themselves and improve their lives.

This pathway includes the use of administrative datasets by academic researchers to improve the quantity and quality of available evidence on social programs and policies.[41] For example, administrative linked employer-employee datasets have been used to document earnings inequality and to study the sources of its decline in Brazil[42] and to study underreporting of wages by formal firms[43] and the effects of business start-up programs in Mexico.[44] Often carried out in partnership with firms or governments, this type of research is being published increasingly in top academic journals.[45] However, broadening researchers' access to administrative datasets remains a challenge, even in countries with well-developed statistical systems.[46]

The private sector. Through the bottom pathway, data generated by the private sector also hold promise for improving the lives of the poor (see chapter 3). For one thing, data have become critically important in the production process of many firms. Indeed, the business models of some of the world's largest firms (such as Amazon, Google, and Facebook) are predicated on data. Some important platform business models emerging in middle-income countries (such as Grab in Indonesia and Mercado Libre in Latin America) could greatly expand market access opportunities for small and medium enterprises. Other data-based private solutions can directly improve the lives of poor people—such as digital credit, often applied for via cellphone, which facilitates financial inclusion. Private financial services providers are also using alternative credit scoring techniques that take advantage of users' digital footprints to train machine learning algorithms to identify, score, and underwrite credit for individuals who otherwise would lack documentation of their creditworthiness.

Data reuse, sharing, and repurposing for all pathways. Enabling data reuse and repurposing is central to realizing their value (see chapter 4). Such reuse can take place between actors within each of the three pathways, but also across pathways. The two-way arrow in figure 1.3 between private firms and government indicates the reuse and repurposing for public policy of data originally collected for commercial purposes and the reuse and repurposing of public intent data by firms. Similarly, the two-way arrow between individuals/civil society/academia and governments indicates the reuse, sharing, and repurposing of data between those parties. The final two-way arrows reflect the use of private sector data and data-driven applications by individuals/civil society/academia and the use of data and analysis generated by individuals/civil society/academia by firms.

The many examples of repurposing data to improve development outcomes include using geospatial location data from mobile phones, mobile call detail records, or social media (Facebook) and online search (Google) data to predict and trace the outbreak of disease, especially COVID-19 (box 1.4).[47] Online media and user-generated content can be used to map water/flood events in real time for water management and food security. Combining satellite imagery data from private and public sources can be used to monitor crop yields and forecast malnutrition.[48]

The COVID-19 experience has also shown how public statistics constructed from private sector data—on credit card spending, employment, and business revenues—can serve as a new tool for empirical research and policy analysis. In the United States, indicators disaggregated by ZIP code, industry, income group, and business size showed that small businesses and low-income workers providing in-person services within wealthier ZIP codes were hardest-hit by the reduction in consumer spending during the crisis.[49] The patterns suggest that widespread tax cuts or relief checks are not effective when people are afraid to go out and spend. Unemployment insurance benefits and grants or low-cost loans targeting struggling businesses are likely a better approach.[50]

Ways in which the same three pathways can harm development

Although use, reuse, and repurposing of data offer great prospects for fostering development, they simultaneously pose significant risks that must be managed to avoid negative development impacts. The mounting nature of such concerns has prompted calls for a new social contract around data. These risks can manifest themselves through public, private, and civil society pathways. Thus figure 1.3 also presents some concrete (though by no means exhaustive) illustrations (in red) of such negative impacts through each of the three pathways.

In the middle pathway, governments can abuse citizens' data for political ends. As public sector data systems improve and become increasingly interoperable, governments may accumulate a wide array of information about specific individuals. As long as public accountability is strong and state actors can be presumed to act in the broader public interest, this need not be a major concern. However, if those

Box 1.4 Using private intent data to tackle COVID-19

At the onset of the COVID-19 outbreak, governments began implementing policy measures to reduce social contact and curb the spread of the pandemic. Data collected through mobile phones, such as call detail records and global positioning system (GPS) location data, proved extremely valuable in quantifying the effectiveness of policies ranging from partial curfews to strict lockdowns.[a] These data enabled measurement of population density, travel patterns, and population mixing in real time and at high resolution, making it possible to better target policy interventions and inform epidemiological modeling. Analysis of GPS locations showed that by March 23, 2020, social distancing policies had helped reduce mobility in major US cities by half.[b] In Colombia, Indonesia, and Mexico, travel restrictions and lockdowns on mobility had different effects on mobility across socioeconomic groups. Those in the top decile of wealth reduced their mobility up to twice as much as those in the bottom decile.[c]

Despite the potential of deploying mobility data in the fight against COVID-19, their impact on policy has been limited in lower-income countries. Bottlenecks include a lack of technical expertise among government organizations; restrictions on data access, especially from mobile network operators; and a lack of investment and political will required to scale up onetime projects.[d]

A review of the academic literature produces a broader look at the impact of repurposed data on the study of COVID-19 (figure B1.4.1 and map B1.4.1). Between February and September 2020, more than 950 articles were published in scientific, medical, and technical journals that repurposed cellphone, social media, Google search, and other types of private intent data to track the disease and to offer policy and operational solutions (figure B1.4.1). Despite the relatively large number of articles in a short time frame, the coverage of lower-income countries was quite limited, especially in Africa (map B1.4.1). This pattern holds after adjusting

Figure B1.4.1 Use of repurposed data to study COVID-19: Published articles, by type of private intent data used

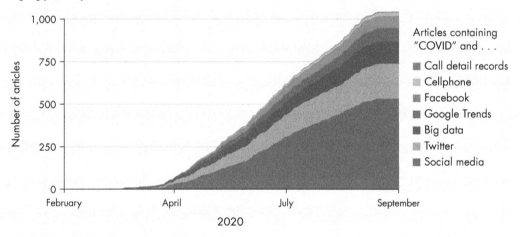

Articles containing "COVID" and . . .
- ■ Call detail records
- ▨ Cellphone
- ▦ Facebook
- ■ Google Trends
- ■ Big data
- ▨ Twitter
- ■ Social media

Source: WDR 2021 team, based on data from CORD-19 (COVID-19 Open Research Dataset) Semantic Scholar team, Ai2 (Allen Institute for AI), http://www.semanticscholar.org/cord19. Data at http://bit.do/WDR2021-Fig-B1_4_1.

Note: Figure shows the number of articles published in scientific, medical, and technical journals across time from February to September 2020. The cumulative sum across all categories is higher because some articles appear in more than one category.

(Box continues next page)

presumptions do not hold, significant perils arise. One clear risk is the potential to misuse such data for politically motivated surveillance or discrimination along the lines of ethnicity, religion, race, gender, disability status, or sexual orientation. Another concern is the possible use of data by political incumbents,

domestic political players, or even foreign actors to unduly influence electoral processes by privately targeting misinformation to marginal voters during campaigns. Civil society actors can also misuse data for surveillance (to recruit members for violent extremism, for example) or to unduly affect electoral

Box 1.4 **Using private intent data to tackle COVID-19** *(continued)*

Map B1.4.1 **Use of repurposed data to study COVID-19: Published articles, by country**

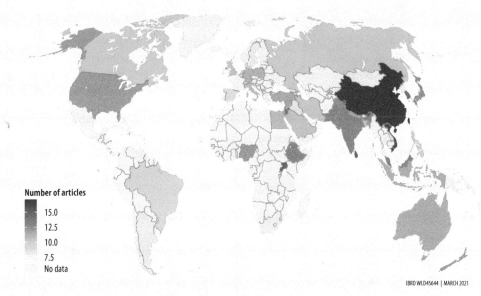

Number of articles

15.0
12.5
10.0
7.5
No data

IBRD WLD45644 | MARCH 2021

Source: WDR 2021 team, based on data from CORD-19 (COVID-19 Open Research Dataset) Semantic Scholar team, Ai2 (Allen Institute for AI), http://www.semanticscholar.org/cord19. Data at http://bit.do/WDR2021-Map-B1_4_1.

Note: Map shows the number of articles published in scientific, medical, and technical journals across countries from February to September 2020. Article counts are divided by the COVID-19 death incidence rate.

the number of articles for death rates associated with COVID-19 in each country, and it likely reflects the difficulties in accessing data and the limited research funding and capacity.

a. Oliver et al. (2020).
b. Klein et al. (2020).
c. Fraiberger et al. (2020).
d. Oliver et al. (2020).

processes, as can private firms, but governments are more likely to do so. Again, these examples of misuse of data are mentioned to be indicative rather than exhaustive of all possibilities.

In the top pathway, individuals and organized groups can inflict considerable harm through cyber-criminals who steal and manipulate sensitive information. The so-called dark net is a vast parallel network of hidden websites that can only be accessed using specific software tools and private authorizations. It acts as an underground digital platform for a wide array of criminal activities, facilitating illegal trade in drugs, counterfeit currency, stolen goods, credit card numbers, forged papers, firearms, and human organs. In addition to facilitating criminal activity in the real world, the internet can be the locus for cybercrime in the digital world, with burgeoning

security breaches leading to the theft of critical data and raising the risk of major disruptions to critical services. One recent study estimated the annual cost of such crime as between US$57 billion and US$110 billion in the United States alone.[51] Data service providers have a tendency to underinvest in cybersecurity because the economic consequences of any data security breach are largely borne by the clients whose data are compromised.

In the bottom pathway, private firms can potentially abuse consumers' data through anticompetitive practices. Data-driven platform businesses experience steeply increasing returns to scale as user communities expand, leading to positive network externalities that make them more and more attractive to additional users. This dynamic has led to strong market concentration in platform businesses—including e-commerce, search engines, and social media—raising concerns about abuse of market power. For services that are provided free of charge, abuse of dominance may manifest itself in declining quality of service, particularly in terms of the level of privacy offered to consumers. In other cases, use of algorithms can facilitate price collusion (tacit or otherwise). More broadly, data-driven businesses may exploit their vast information about consumer preferences and behavior to engage in aggressive or manipulative marketing techniques based on microtargeting of persuasive messages—a practice known as nudging—which may unduly influence consumers' choices or simply be a nuisance.[52]

Just as data can be reused for positive purposes, collecting and sharing sensitive data for ill-intentioned purposes can pose significant risks. For example, researchers at Cambridge Analytica developed a technique to map personality traits based on what people had "liked" on Facebook. The researchers paid users small sums to take a personality quiz and download an app that would scrape some private information from their profiles and those of their friends—an activity permitted at the time. Cambridge Analytica eventually obtained files for roughly 30 million users that contained enough information for the company to match users to other records and build psychographic profiles. However, only about 270,000 users—those who participated in the quiz—had consented to having their data harvested.[53] The outcome was that political campaigns were able to microtarget their political ads to individuals based on these profiles.

Although social media data can be reused to affect election outcomes, it is challenging to do so, and there is little solid evidence that the approach has had such effects thus far.[54] However, the Cambridge Analytica example demonstrates how private sector data can be leveraged by third parties (in this case, a political party) to attempt to influence voting behavior in ways the originators of the data (Facebook users and their friends) never intended.

The Cambridge Analytica example also highlights the importance of transparency as data are increasingly created, used, reused, and repurposed by a wider range of people, organizations, businesses, and other parties. At the most basic level, documentation of sources and collection and aggregation methods are crucial for data quality and for inspiring trust among users of data. But transparent documentation is not a priority in all countries, and some governments may consciously opt for data opacity, thereby significantly undermining public trust. In short, data policy options are fraught with complex political economic constraints.

A data governance framework to enforce the social contract for data

Data governance entails creating an environment of implementing norms, infrastructure policies and technical mechanisms, laws and regulations for data, related economic policies, and institutions that can effectively enable the safe, trustworthy use of public intent and private intent data to achieve development outcomes. By providing predictability and confidence that these rights are being protected and protections are enforceable, a robust and effectively implemented data governance framework can strengthen *trust* in the data system, thereby incentivizing the use of data-driven products and services, increasing their *value,* and ensuring a more *equitable* distribution of benefits. In effect, data governance enforces the social contract around data, by applying the principles of trust, value, and equity.

A data governance framework can be visualized as four distinct layers that build on and support one another (figure 1.4). The foundational layer is the policy framework for data infrastructure—both the policies that promote universal access to internet data services and the policies that ensure that countries have adequate infrastructure to exchange, store, and process data efficiently over the internet. The next layer consists of the legal and regulatory environment for data itself, which creates rules to enable the reuse and sharing of data while safeguarding against their potential abuse and misuse. This normative framework for data interacts in significant ways with wider economic policy issues represented in the third layer, which affect a country's ability to harness the economic value of data through competition, trade, and taxation. The fourth layer is the institutional ecosystem that ensures that data can deliver on their potential and that laws, regulations, and policies are effectively enforced.

Infrastructure policies. The digital character of modern data makes infrastructure indispensable for collecting, exchanging, storing, processing, and distributing data (see chapter 5). Individual access to data infrastructure is a prerequisite for both contributing one's own data and accessing the data of others. The powerful network benefits, which arise as more and more people are connected to data infrastructure, are the economic underpinning for universal service policies that have also been widely endorsed

Figure 1.4 Data governance layers at the national and international levels

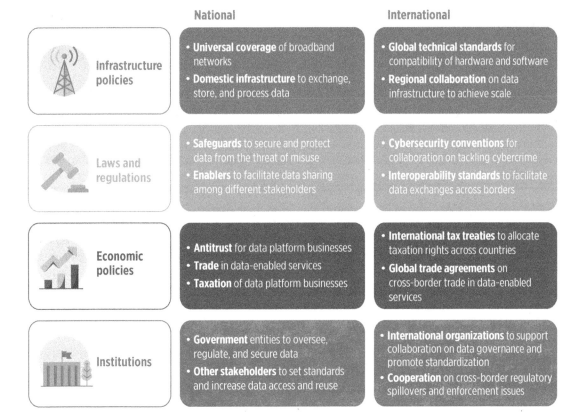

	National	International
Infrastructure policies	• **Universal coverage** of broadband networks • **Domestic infrastructure** to exchange, store, and process data	• **Global technical standards** for compatibility of hardware and software • **Regional collaboration** on data infrastructure to achieve scale
Laws and regulations	• **Safeguards** to secure and protect data from the threat of misuse • **Enablers** to facilitate data sharing among different stakeholders	• **Cybersecurity conventions** for collaboration on tackling cybercrime • **Interoperability standards** to facilitate data exchanges across borders
Economic policies	• **Antitrust** for data platform businesses • **Trade** in data-enabled services • **Taxation** of data platform businesses	• **International tax treaties** to allocate taxation rights across countries • **Global trade agreements** on cross-border trade in data-enabled services
Institutions	• **Government** entities to oversee, regulate, and secure data • **Other stakeholders** to set standards and increase data access and reuse	• **International organizations** to support collaboration on data governance and promote standardization • **Cooperation** on cross-border regulatory spillovers and enforcement issues

Source: WDR 2021 team.

politically. Significant policy efforts are needed to ensure adequate coverage of last-mile infrastructure that keeps pace with constantly evolving technological standards of performance. Policy makers also need to consider how to address demand-side factors, such as the affordability of handheld devices and data charges, as well as people's limited data literacy skills.

At the country level, affordable processing of data transactions and adequate speed call for increasingly sophisticated data infrastructure. A starting point is to facilitate the creation of internet exchange points that allow internet service providers to exchange domestic internet traffic across their respective networks without incurring expense and slowing speed by routing traffic overseas. A further step is to create a policy environment suitable for investment in colocation data centers. Such centers allow storage and retrieval of vast volumes of digital data, including local replicas of popular global internet content, and they can be used to provide dedicated access to overseas cloud computing capacity that facilitates increasingly sophisticated data processing and machine learning

techniques. Small-scale, regulatory deficiencies and inadequate competition all conspire to hold back the development of all forms of data infrastructure in many low- and middle-income countries, posing particular challenges for policy makers.

Laws and regulations. Legal and regulatory frameworks for data need to be adequately developed, with a balanced emphasis on both safeguards and enablers (see chapter 6). The legal and regulatory provisions to safeguard personal and nonpersonal data differ greatly because these two types of data are typically generated, used, and treated in very different ways.

Personally identifiable data convey information that is specific to a known individual, although identifiers (such as names, addresses, and social security numbers) that directly or indirectly point to a person (or entity) could be deleted.[55] Some types of personal data, such as health histories or banking transactions, may be more sensitive than others, such as shopping records. Nonpersonal data are generated about nonhuman subjects, including institutions or machines. They may include data on prices, traffic patterns, weather, and agricultural practices. In practice, the boundary between personal and nonpersonal data is becoming increasingly blurred as it becomes possible to infer personal characteristics from nonpersonal data, such as mobile phone records. Advances in artificial intelligence also are making the deidentification of personal data more challenging and making personal inferences from combining multiple sources of nonpersonal data possible, thereby blurring the boundaries between personal and nonpersonal data.

The nature of data safeguards for personal data versus nonpersonal data is quite different. For personal data, a rights-based approach to data protection is appropriate, emphasizing the rights of data subjects as well as the obligations of data users as the primary considerations. For nonpersonal data, intellectual property rights provide the relevant frame of reference, and there is greater scope to weigh the balance of economic interests between safeguards and enablers. Another important and underdeveloped aspect of data protection, affecting both personal and nonpersonal data, is cybersecurity.

Complementing such safeguards, greater access to data for reuse can be enabled by open data regulations and by provisions that ensure technical interoperability between different types of data, allowing them to be readily combined and repurposed. Data portability provisions, which allow individuals to move their own data from one service provider to another, also help enhance the agency of data subjects.

Economic policies. Because of the proliferation of data-driven platform business models, the design of legal frameworks for data governance carries significant implications for the real economy that are often overlooked (see chapter 7). Competition agencies grapple with the market power of globally dominant technology firms operating data-driven business models. Tax authorities struggle to collect revenues from platform businesses that often have scale in a market without any physical presence and can readily shift tax liabilities across international borders. Trade policy introduces tensions between the need to protect data domestically and the desire to benefit from a growing cross-border trade in data-based goods and services. In each case, decisions about the design of the domestic regulatory framework for data will materially affect economic performance.

Institutions. For effective enforcement of the normative framework, a suitable institutional ecosystem that encompasses both state and nonstate actors must be in place (see chapter 8). The proliferation of arrangements around the world suggests that there is no single institutional blueprint for the implementation of data governance frameworks. The important thing is to identify the critical functions needed to deliver on the safeguards and enablers embedded in legal statutes. Depending on the country context, it may make sense to assign some of these roles to existing institutions (such as the national statistical office or relevant sector regulators) or to create new institutions (such as data protection agencies or data intermediaries). Whatever the institutional architecture, common challenges facing the effective implementation of data governance policies include capacity and resource constraints, lack of institutional autonomy, difficulties adopting a data-driven culture, and problems of coordination across stakeholder groups.

International dimension. Although they are rooted in the domestic environment, data governance frameworks also have important international dimensions (as shown in figure 1.4 and further detailed in spotlights 7.2 and 8.1). In many instances, international treaties provide the overarching legal framework for the development of domestic legislation and regulations. International agreements are also critical in reaching resolution of long-standing data policy challenges such as how to treat cross-border data flows in international trade or how to allocate taxation rights for data transactions. At the institutional level, decisions made by policy makers and regulators, particularly in the larger global markets, will have important spillover effects in smaller countries, particularly those with which the markets have strong economic ties. These effects underscore the importance of cross-border cooperation in addressing common data governance challenges such as the regulation of market power in data-driven businesses. At the same time, data infrastructure is to a considerable extent cross-border in nature, with large volumes of data flowing to overseas storage and processing facilities and opportunities for regional collaboration around infrastructure development. Facilitation of such cross-border data movements also entails global harmonization of technical standards.

In addition, there is an important role for international cooperation in creating common standards and guidelines for statistical activities (spotlight 2.2). The creation of international measurement standards and protocols helps improve comparability of measures across countries in a way that allows national policy makers to understand their country's performance relative to that of their neighbors. Cross-country measurement of progress toward policy goals and, more generally, of statistical performance ensure that countries can benchmark and monitor their data achievements and identify and strengthen their weaknesses. Good data governance, both at the national and international levels, ensures that the various components work together to enable the effective and safe use of data in order to extract value in a trustworthy, equitable way.

Putting it all together: Establishing an integrated national data system

A well-functioning data governance framework ensures that infrastructure, laws and regulations, policies, and institutions work together to support the use of data in a way that aligns with the social contract for data. This framework defines the rules, and the associated compliance mechanisms, for how data can be safely used, reused, and shared by all stakeholders, including government entities, international organizations, civil society and individuals, academic institutions, and the private sector. To realize data's potential, this framework must be built around a data system that not only ensures that data transactions are safe, but also actively promotes access to data by all stakeholders (figure 1.5).

This Report concludes with an aspirational vision of an integrated national data system (INDS) that can deliver on the promise of producing high-quality data and then making data open in a way that it is both protected and accessible to be shared and reused by all stakeholders (chapter 9). Such an aspirational INDS works seamlessly with the governance structure. If the governance system is viewed as establishing the rules of the road (and the institutions governing those rules), the INDS can be envisioned as a network of highways that connects all users and ensures the safe passage of data to and from destinations.

A well-functioning INDS is powered by people: people to produce, process, and manage high-quality data; people to populate the institutions that

Figure 1.5 Data flow safely across all stakeholders in an integrated national data system

Source: WDR 2021 team.

safeguard and protect the data against misuse; and people to draft, oversee, and implement data strategies, policies, and regulations. The system also needs all people to have sufficient skills and knowledge to use data in ways that allow them to hold the public and private sectors accountable. All this requires robust data literacy within data institutions, government ministries, the private sector, and the general population.

There is no singular blueprint for how to build an INDS. It certainly must be funded sufficiently to implement the infrastructure and institutions necessary for the system to function well. Incentives need to be in place to produce, protect, and share data, and to create a data culture in which people demand transparency and accountability. But how countries move toward this vision of an INDS will depend on their current capacity and the parameters of the social contract for data. Although the path toward an INDS will differ for each country, this Report proposes a sequenced maturity model to help assess progress and identify areas for more attention to further the development of a well-functioning INDS.

The maturity model is based on a progression of three stages: first, establishing fundamentals; second, initiating data flows; and third, optimizing the system (chapter 8). Although progress within these stages will differ by country—and for a given country progress in dealing with certain types of data also may differ—these three stages nonetheless serve as a useful reference to help assess weak spots and gaps in the construction of an INDS.

Establishing fundamentals first requires taking stock to identify the existing data types and the data processing activities carried out by different actors. This analysis should focus on activities already taking place—both inside and outside of government—that present potential development opportunities for data use, reuse, and repurposing, along with risks. Uncovering gaps in the stock of data or bottlenecks in gaining access to these data can help prioritize efforts to address gaps and remove barriers. Governments should also engage with the private sector and civil society stakeholders to develop legislation, rules, and standards to safeguard data, while encouraging data collection, processing, and use. Other steps in establishing fundamentals include efforts to facilitate public-private data sharing and cross-border data transfers by establishing contracts with information management services (such as identification systems) or licenses for regulated entities (such as banks and telecom operators) that create provisions for secure, protected data transactions between public

and private actors. Ensuring that the fundamentals are in place also includes developing a data governance strategy with policies and laws that promote the objectives of the INDS and enforce compliance with rules.

The next phase is to ensure that *data begin to flow across all the stakeholders.* One path to this goal is to establish a government agency with sufficient power to leverage compliance across ministries and public sector agencies in how they manage and exchange data. In addition, the rules and standards that enable greater interoperability among datasets must be established. Creating interoperability allows for innovative new uses of multiple data files as these data become accessible to a more diverse set of users. It also allows for the development of measurement standards to ensure data quality.[56] Public-private and cross-border data flows can be encouraged through multistakeholder engagements with domestic and international actors to promote harmonization principles, standards, and practices. Such engagements are particularly important for data protection and cybersecurity, which require coordination to be effective.

To reach the *optimized stage,* the tools and methods that helped create data flows should be incorporated into a unified whole-of-government approach. Ongoing, recurrent investments in training increase the effective use of data for decision-making and accountability. Similarly, recurrent investments in infrastructure keep systems sufficiently modern and expand access. Data quality, data integration, and data synchronization should be integral parts of all processes at this stage. Meanwhile, the safe flow of data through the data system should be continually assessed and stress tested for weakness.

Organization of this Report

This Report is divided into three parts. Part I identifies the multiple channels through which data can support or impede the development process, making sense of the data landscape and pointing out the associated development opportunities and risks. This part provides a conceptual framework (figure 1.3), together with illustrations and examples from recent experience in low- and middle-income countries.

Part II, which describes the data governance layers presented in figure 1.4, focuses on data governance broadly defined to include data infrastructure policy (chapter 5), the legal and regulatory framework for data (chapter 6), the related economic policy implications (chapter 7), and institutions (chapter 8). These diverse elements are effectively the building blocks of a social contract that seeks to deliver the potential value of data equitably while safeguarding against harmful outcomes. Examples and case studies illustrate both the importance of establishing safeguards to prevent the misuse of data that could harm development objectives and how data can be better enabled to further development objectives.

Part III brings together the building blocks of the Report to present the vision of an integrated national data system (chapter 9).

Throughout the Report, spotlights at the end of chapters highlight relevant cases in low- and middle-income countries and internationally and explore various policy issues in more depth.

This Report was prepared against the backdrop of the COVID-19 pandemic. The pandemic itself is a vivid illustration of the usefulness of data in dealing with obstacles to development and the complexity of the associated governance challenges. Examples of how countries have used data as part of their response to COVID-19 are featured in chapters, using boxes and narratives to illustrate many of the issues addressed in the Report. Those issues include the deficiencies of public sector data systems and the complementarities between public intent and private intent data, as well as the legal and regulatory issues posed by accessing private intent data for public purposes. More broadly, through a discussion of the many ways in which data can help economic development, this Report aims to describe the challenges to realizing these gains, offer guidance on how to attain them, and propose safeguards for protecting citizens.

Notes

1. Rowntree (2000 [1901]).
2. World Bank (2016).
3. World Bank (2019).
4. The Report also builds on other themes featured in past World Bank reports, including the importance of building the data capacity of countries (see World Bank 2018). More generally, World Bank reports have long emphasized the importance of data, information, and knowledge for economic, social, and political development (see, for example, World Bank 2002). What has changed is the nature and amount of data available, the ways in which they are produced, and the ease with which they can be exchanged, reused, and shared to address development objectives. Thus the focus of this *World Development Report* is on data for better lives, particularly for the poor.
5. See, for example, OECD (2013, 2016, 2018a, 2018b, 2019).
6. Whitby (2020).
7. Grajalez et al. (2013).

8. Thorvaldsen (2017).
9. Bethlehem (2009).
10. Thorvaldsen (2017).
11. de Heer, de Leeuw, and van der Zouwen (1999).
12. Conseil constitutionnel, "Déclaration des Droits de l'Homme et du Citoyen de 1789" [Declaration of Human and Civic Rights of 26 August 1789], Paris, https://www.conseil-constitutionnel.fr/le-bloc-de-constitutionnalite/declaration-des-droits-de-l-homme-et-du-citoyen-de-1789.
13. Whitby (2020).
14. Bethlehem (2009).
15. Bethlehem (2009).
16. Musa et al. (2013).
17. Wallis and Robinson (1987).
18. Musa et al. (2013).
19. Dempsey (2012).
20. LGBTQI stands for lesbian, gay, bisexual, transgender, queer (or questioning), intersex.
21. OECD (2013).
22. Directive 95/46/EC on the protection of individuals with regard to the processing of personal data and on the free movement of such data (1995 Directive on Personal Data Protection, https://eur-lex.europa.eu/legal-content/EN/TXT/?uri=CELEX%3A31995L0046) was repealed and replaced in 2016 by Regulation (EU) 2016/679 on the protection of natural persons with regard to the processing of personal data and on the free movement of such data (EU GDPR, https://eur-lex.europa.eu/legal-content/en/TXT/?uri=CELEX%3A32016R0679).
23. Kilic et al. (2017).
24. Serajuddin et al. (2015).
25. Blank and Lutz (2017).
26. Abay et al. (2019); Carletto, Jolliffe, and Banerjee (2015); Desiere and Jolliffe (2018); Gourlay, Kilic, and Lobell (2019).
27. Lobell, Azzari, et al. (2020); Lobell, Di Tommaso, et al. (2020).
28. Jones and Tonetti (2020). Treating data as a nonrival input in a production function draws on the earlier literature that modeled information and ideas as nonrival inputs to production. See Romer (1990) and Radner and Stiglitz (1984).
29. For example, Statistics Canada (2019) estimated the value of data in Canada considering the direct labor cost of data production, associated indirect labor costs, and other related expenses such as human resources management and financial control. It quantified the total own-account investment in databases in 2018 as between Can$8 billion and Can$12 billion.
30. Two examples illustrate this approach. First, the US Department of Commerce (2014) found that government data helped US businesses generate at least US$24 billion a year. Second, Deloitte (2017) conducted a review of studies of the economic value of open data (public data available with no restrictions to users) to a wide range of users in the United Kingdom and found that satellite data from Landsat were worth US$2 billion a year in commercial applications, while public transport routing and scheduling data from Transport for London

generated economic benefits to passengers valued at £80 million a year.

31. Several illustrations of this approach suggest the magnitude of monetary benefits. PwC (2019) found that market capitalizations of data-intensive companies are twice as likely to be in the top industry quartile as those of companies operating in the same sector that are not data-intensive. Li, Nirei, and Yamana (2019) looked at the sums paid for acquisitions of data-intensive firms and their impact on the market capitalization of the acquiring firm. Frier (2018) examined the revenue streams that companies are able to generate from sales of data or associated advertising revenues, finding that Apple charges application developers a commission of 30 percent of their sales for accessing its consumer data, which has earned the company US$42.8 billion in sales over the past 10 years.

32. This is similar to suggesting that there is a nonconcavity in the value of data and information. It is also linked to the point that because ideas are nonrivalrous, they exhibit increasing marginal returns over a range. See Radner and Stiglitz (1984) and Romer (1990).

33. Juba and Le (2019).

34. Goldfarb and Tucker (2019).

35. Zingales (2017) notes that as the economic scale of firms becomes large in relation to governments, economic and political power may converge.

36. Cavallo (2013); Cavallo and Rigobon (2016).

37. Erkoyun (2020).

38. Nyeko (2019).

39. *Economist* (2019).

40. IMF (2019).

41. Cole et al. (2020).

42. Alvarez et al. (2018); Menezes-Filho et al. (2008).

43. Kumler, Verhoogen, and Frías (2020).

44. Kaplan, Piedra, and Seira (2011).

45. Chetty (2012); Cole et al. (2020).

46. Card et al. (2010).

47. Wesolowski et al. (2015).

48. Burke and Lobell (2017); Osgood-Zimmerman et al. (2018).

49. Chetty et al. (2020).

50. Rosalsky (2020).

51. CEA (2018).

52. Amnesty International (2019); Zuboff (2019).

53. Rosenberg, Confessore, and Cadwalladr (2018).

54. Hern (2018).

55. Kayaalp (2017).

56. Anyone wondering about the importance of establishing comparable definitions and developing precise instruments for these measures need only look at the US National Institute of Standards and Technology, established in 1901. It has been home to five Nobel laureates.

References

Abay, Kibrom A., Gashaw T. Abate, Christopher B. Barrett, and Tanguy Bernard. 2019. "Correlated Non-Classical Measurement Errors, 'Second Best' Policy Inference, and the Inverse Size–Productivity Relationship in Agriculture." *Journal of Development Economics* 139 (June): 171–84. https://doi.org/10.1016/j.jdeveco.2019.03.008.

Alvarez, Jorge, Felipe Benguria, Niklas Engbom, and Christian Moser. 2018. "Firms and the Decline in Earnings Inequality in Brazil." *American Economic Journal: Macroeconomics* 10 (1): 149–89. https://doi.org/10.1257/mac.20150355.

Amnesty International. 2019. "Surveillance Giants: How the Business Model of Google and Facebook Threatens Human Rights." Report POL 30/1404/2019, Amnesty International, London. https://www.amnesty.org/en/documents/document/?indexNumber=pol30%2f1404%2f2019&language=en.

Arrow, Kenneth J. 1962. "Economic Welfare and the Allocation of Resources for Invention." In *The Rate and Direction of Inventive Activity: Economic and Social Factors*, edited by National Bureau of Economic Research, 609–26. Princeton Legacy Library Series. Princeton, NJ: Princeton University Press.

Ball, Laura. 2009. "Cholera and the Pump on Broad Street: The Life and Legacy of John Snow." *History Teacher* 43 (1): 105–19.

Bethlehem, Jelke. 2009. "The Rise of Survey Sampling." Discussion Paper 09015, Statistics Netherlands, The Hague.

Blank, Grant, and Christoph Lutz. 2017. "Representativeness of Social Media in Great Britain: Investigating Facebook, LinkedIn, Twitter, Pinterest, Google+, and Instagram." *American Behavioral Scientist* 61 (7): 741–56. https://doi.org/10.1177/0002764217717559.

Burke, Marshall, and David B. Lobell. 2017. "Satellite-Based Assessment of Yield Variation and Its Determinants in Smallholder African Systems." *PNAS Proceedings of the National Academy of Sciences* 114 (9): 2189–94. https://doi.org/10.1073/pnas.1616919114.

Card, David E., Raj Chetty, Martin S. Feldstein, and Emmanuel Saez. 2010. "Expanding Access to Administrative Data for Research in the United States." White Paper, National Science Foundation, Alexandria, VA. http://www.rajchetty.com/chettyfiles/NSFdataaccess.pdf.

Carletto, Calogero, Dean Jolliffe, and Raka Banerjee. 2015. "From Tragedy to Renaissance: Improving Agricultural Data for Better Policies." *Journal of Development Studies* 51 (2): 133–48. https://doi.org/10.1080/00220388.2014.968140.

Carrière-Swallow, Yan, and Vikram Haksar. 2019. "The Economics and Implications of Data: An Integrated Perspective." Departmental Paper 19/16, Strategy, Policy, and Review Department, International Monetary Fund, Washington, DC.

Cavallo, Alberto. 2013. "Online and Official Price Indexes: Measuring Argentina's Inflation." *Journal of Monetary Economics* 60 (2): 152–65.

Cavallo, Alberto, and Roberto Rigobon. 2016. "The Billion Prices Project: Using Online Prices for Inflation Measurement and Research." *Journal of Economic Perspectives* 30 (2): 151–78.

CEA (Council of Economic Advisers). 2018. "The Cost of Malicious Cyber Activity to the U.S. Economy." CEA, White House, Washington, DC. https://www.whitehouse.gov/wp-content/uploads/2018/02/The-Cost-of-Malicious-Cyber-Activity-to-the-U.S.-Economy.pdf.

Chetty, Raj. 2012. "Time Trends in the Use of Administrative Data for Empirical Research." Paper presented at NBER Summer Institute 2012, National Bureau of Economic Research, Cambridge, MA, July 2–27. http://www.rajchetty.com/chettyfiles/admin_data_trends.pdf.

Chetty, Raj, John N. Friedman, Nathaniel Hendren, Michael Stepner, and Opportunity Insights Team. 2020. "How Did COVID-19 and Stabilization Policies Affect Spending and Employment? A New Real-Time Economic Tracker Based on Private Sector Data." NBER Working Paper 27431, National Bureau of Economic Research, Cambridge, MA. https://www.nber.org/system/files/working_papers/w27431/w27431.pdf.

Cole, Shawn, Iqbal Dhaliwal, Anja Sautmann, and Lars Vilhuber. 2020. *Handbook on Using Administrative Data for Research and Evidence-Based Policy*. Cambridge, MA: Abdul Latif Jameel Poverty Action Lab and Massachusetts Institute of Technology. https://admindatahandbook.mit.edu/book/v1.0-rc6/index.html.

DCMS (Department for Digital, Culture, Media, and Sport, United Kingdom). 2020. "UK National Data Strategy." Policy paper, DCMS, London. https://www.gov.uk/government/publications/uk-national-data-strategy/national-data-strategy.

de Heer, Wim, Edith Desirée de Leeuw, and Johannes van der Zouwen. 1999. "Methodological Issues in Survey Research: A Historical Review." *Bulletin of Sociological Methodology* 64 (1): 25–48.

Deloitte. 2017. "Assessing the Value of TfL's Open Data and Digital Partnerships." Deloitte LLP, London. http://content.tfl.gov.uk/deloitte-report-tfl-open-data.pdf.

Dempsey, Caitlin. 2012. "History of GIS." *GIS Lounge* (blog), May 14, 2012. https://www.gislounge.com/history-of-gis/.

Desiere, Sam, and Dean Jolliffe. 2018. "Land Productivity and Plot Size: Is Measurement Error Driving the Inverse Relationship?" *Journal of Development Economics* 130 (January): 84–98. https://doi.org/10.1016/j.jdeveco.2017.10.002.

Duch-Brown, Nestor, Bertin Martens, and Frank Mueller-Langer. 2017. "The Economics of Ownership, Access, and Trade in Digital Data." JRC Digital Economy Working Paper 2017-01, Joint Research Center, European Commission, Seville, Spain. https://ec.europa.eu/jrc/sites/jrcsh/files/jrc104756.pdf.

Economist. 2019. "The Net Tightens: A \$2bn Loan Scandal Sank Mozambique's Economy." August 22, 2019. https://www.economist.com/middle-east-and-africa/2019/08/22/a-2bn-loan-scandal-sank-mozambiques-economy.

Erkoyun, Ezgi. 2020. "Researchers Say New Model Shows Turkish Inflation Well Above Official Tally." Reuters, October 22, 2020. https://www.reuters.com/article/turkey-economy-inflation-int-idUSKBN2771EY.

Fraiberger, Samuel P., Pablo Astudillo, Lorenzo Candeago, Alex Chunet, Nicholas K. W. Jones, Maham Faisal Khan, Bruno Lepri, et al. 2020. "Uncovering Socioeconomic Gaps in Mobility Reduction during the COVID-19 Pandemic Using Location Data." ArXiv:2006.15195 [Physics.soc-ph], July 27, Cornell University, Ithaca, NY.

Frier, Sarah. 2018. "Is Apple Really Your Privacy Hero?" *Bloomberg Businessweek*, June 8, 2018. https://www.bloomberg.com/news/articles/2018-08-08/is-apple-really-your-privacy-hero.

Gillies, Robert J., Paul E. Kinahan, and Hedvig Hricak. 2015. "Radiomics: Images Are More Than Pictures, They Are Data." *Radiology* 278 (2): 563–77. https://doi.org/10.1148/radiol.2015151169.

Goldfarb, Avi, and Catherine Tucker. 2019. "Digital Economics." *Journal of Economic Literature* 57 (1): 3–43. https://doi.org/10.1257/jel.20171452.

Gourlay, Sydney, Talip Kilic, and David B. Lobell. 2019. "A New Spin on an Old Debate: Errors in Farmer-Reported Production and Their Implications for Inverse Scale–Productivity Relationship in Uganda." *Journal of Development Economics* 141 (November): 102376. https://www.sciencedirect.com/science/article/pii/S0304387818306588.

Grajalez, Carlos Gómez, Eileen Magnello, Robert Woods, and Julian Champkin. 2013. "Great Moments in Statistics." *Significance* 10 (6): 21–28.

Hallal, Pedro Curi, Fernando P. Hartwig, Bernardo L. Horta, Gabriel D. Victora, Mariângela F. Silveira, Cláudio José Struchiner, Luís Paulo Vidaleti, et al. 2020. "Remarkable Variability in SARS-CoV-2 Antibodies across Brazilian Regions: Nationwide Serological Household Survey in 27 States." *medRxiv* (May 30). https://www.medrxiv.org/content/10.1101/2020.05.30.20117531v1.

Hallal, Pedro Curi, Bernardo L. Horta, Aluísio J. D. Barros, Odir A. Dellagostin, Fernando P. Hartwig, Lúcia C. Pellanda, Cláudio José Struchiner, et al. 2020. "Trends in the Prevalence of COVID-19 Infection in Rio Grande do Sul, Brazil: Repeated Serological Surveys." *Ciência & Saúde Coletiva* 25 (supplement 1): 2395–401. https://doi.org/10.1590/1413-81232020256.1.09632020.

Hern, Alex. 2018. "Cambridge Analytica: How Did It Turn Clicks into Votes?" *Guardian*, May 6, 2018. https://www.theguardian.com/news/2018/may/06/cambridge-analytica-how-turn-clicks-into-votes-christopher-wylie.

IMF (International Monetary Fund). 2019. "Republic of Mozambique: Diagnostic Report on Transparency, Governance, and Corruption." IMF Country Report 19/276, IMF, Washington, DC. https://www.imf.org/en/Publications/CR/Issues/2019/08/23/Republic-of-Mozambique-Diagnostic-Report-on-Transparency-Governance-and-Corruption-48613.

Jones, Charles I., and Christopher Tonetti. 2020. "Nonrivalry and the Economics of Data." *American Economic Review* 110 (9): 2819–58. https://doi.org/10.1257/aer.20191330.

Juba, Brendan, and Hai S. Le. 2019. "Precision-Recall Versus Accuracy and the Role of Large Data Sets." *Proceedings of the AAAI Conference on Artificial Intelligence* 33 (01): 4039–48. https://doi.org/10.1609/aaai.v33i01.33014039.

Kaplan, David S., Eduardo Piedra, and Enrique Seira. 2011. "Entry Regulation and Business Start-Ups: Evidence from Mexico." *Journal of Public Economics* 95 (11–12): 1501–15. https://doi.org/10.1016/j.jpubeco.2011.03.007.

Kayaalp, Mehmet. 2017. "Modes of De-Identification." Paper presented at American Medical Informatics Association 2017 Annual Symposium, Washington, DC. November 6–8. https://www.ncbi.nlm.nih.gov/pmc/articles/PMC5977668.

Kilic, Talip, Umar Serajuddin, Hiroki Uematsu, and Nobuo Yoshida. 2017. "Costing Household Surveys for Monitoring Progress toward Ending Extreme Poverty and

Boosting Shared Prosperity." Policy Research Working Paper 7951, World Bank, Washington, DC.

Klein, Brennan, Timothy LaRock, Stefan McCabe, Leo Torres, Filippo Privitera, Lake Brennan, Moritz U. G. Kraemer, et al. 2020. "Assessing Changes in Commuting and Individual Mobility in Major Metropolitan Areas in the United States during the COVID-19 Outbreak." Network Science Institute, Northeastern University, Boston. https://www.networkscienceinstitute.org/publications/assessing-changes-in-commuting-and-individual-mobility-in-major-metropolitan-areas-in-the-united-states-during-the-covid-19-outbreak.

Koutroumpis, Pantelis, Aija Leiponen, and Llewellyn D. W. Thomas. 2020. "Markets for Data." *Industrial and Corporate Change* 29 (3): 645–60. https://doi.org/10.1093/icc/dtaa002.

Kumler, Todd, Eric Verhoogen, and Judith Frías. 2020. "Enlisting Employees in Improving Payroll Tax Compliance: Evidence from Mexico." *Review of Economics and Statistics* 102 (5): 881–96. https://doi.org/10.1162/rest_a_00907.

Leighton, Timothy G., and Andi Petculescu. 2016. "Guest Editorial: Acoustic and Related Waves in Extraterrestrial Environments." *Journal of the Acoustical Society of America* 140 (2): 1397–99. https://doi.org/10.1121/1.4961539.

Li, Wendy C. Y., Makoto Nirei, and Kazufumi Yamana. 2019. "Value of Data: There's No Such Thing as a Free Lunch in the Digital Economy." RIETI Discussion Paper 19-E-022, Research Institute of Economy, Trade, and Industry, Tokyo. https://www.rieti.go.jp/jp/publications/dp/19e022.pdf.

Lobell, David B., George Azzari, Marshall Burke, Sydney Gourlay, Zhenong Jin, Talip Kilic, and Siobhan Murray. 2020. "Eyes in the Sky, Boots on the Ground: Assessing Satellite- and Ground-Based Approaches to Crop Yield Measurement and Analysis." *American Journal of Agricultural Economics* 102 (1): 202–19. https://doi.org/10.1093/ajae/aaz051.

Lobell, David B., Stefania Di Tommaso, Calum You, Ismael Yacoubou Djima, Marshall Burke, and Talip Kilic. 2020. "Sight for Sorghums: Comparisons of Satellite- and Ground-Based Sorghum Yield Estimates in Mali." *Remote Sensing* 12 (1): 100. https://doi.org/10.3390/rs12010100.

Menezes-Filho, Naércio Aquino, Marc-Andreas Muendler, and Garey Ramey. 2008. "The Structure of Worker Compensation in Brazil, with a Comparison to France and the United States." *Review of Economics and Statistics* 90 (2): 324–46.

Musa, George J., Po-Huang Chiang, Tyler Sylk, Rachel Bavley, William Keating, Bereketab Lakew, Hui-Chen Tsou, and Christina W. Hoven. 2013. "Use of GIS Mapping as a Public Health Tool: From Cholera to Cancer." *Health Services Insights* 6 (November): 111–16. https://doi.org/10.4137/HSI.S10471.

Nyeko, Oryem. 2019. "Tanzania Drops Threat of Prison over Publishing Independent Statistics." Human Rights Watch, Dispatches, July 3. https://www.hrw.org/news/2019/07/03/tanzania-drops-threat-prison-over-publishing-independent-statistics.

OECD (Organisation for Economic Co-operation and Development). 2013. *The OECD Privacy Framework.* Paris: OECD. http://www.oecd.org/sti/ieconomy/oecd_privacy_framework.pdf.

OECD (Organisation for Economic Co-operation and Development). 2016. "Big Data: Bringing Competition Policy to the Digital Era." Report DAF/COMP(2016)14 (rev. November 29–30), Competition Committee, Directorate for Financial and Enterprise Affairs, OECD, Paris. https://one.oecd.org/document/DAF/COMP(2016)14/en/pdf.

OECD (Organisation for Economic Co-operation and Development). 2018a. *Rethinking Antitrust Tools for Multi-Sided Platforms 2018.* Paris: OECD. https://www.oecd.org/daf/competition/Rethinking-antitrust-tools-for-multi-sided-platforms-2018.pdf.

OECD (Organisation for Economic Co-operation and Development). 2018b. *Tax Challenges Arising from Digitalisation: Interim Report 2018.* Paris: OECD. http://dx.doi.org/10.1787/9789264293083-en.

OECD (Organisation for Economic Co-operation and Development). 2019. *Enhancing Access to and Sharing of Data: Reconciling Risks and Benefits for Data Re-use across Societies.* Paris: OECD. https://www.oecd-ilibrary.org/content/publication/276aaca8-en.

Oliver, Nuria, Bruno Lepri, Harald Sterly, Renaud Lambiotte, Sébastien Deletaille, Marco De Nadai, Emmanuel Letouzé, et al. 2020. "Mobile Phone Data for Informing Public Health Actions across the COVID-19 Pandemic Life Cycle." *Science Advances* 6 (23): eabc0764. https://doi.org/10.1126/sciadv.abc0764.

Osgood-Zimmerman, Aaron, Anoushka I. Millear, Rebecca W. Stubbs, Chloe Shields, Brandon V. Pickering, Lucas Earl, Nicholas Graetz, et al. 2018. "Mapping Child Growth Failure in Africa between 2000 and 2015." *Nature* 555 (7694): 41–47. https://doi.org/10.1038/nature25760.

PwC. 2019. "Putting a Value on Data." PwC, London. https://www.pwc.co.uk/issues/data-analytics/insights/putting-value-on-data.html.

Radner, Roy, and Joseph E. Stiglitz. 1984. "A Nonconcavity in the Value of Information." In *Bayesian Models in Economic Theory*, edited by Marcel Boyer and Richard E. Kihlstrom, 33–52. Studies in Bayesian Econometrics Series 5. Amsterdam: Elsevier.

Romer, Paul M. 1990. "Endogenous Technological Change." *Journal of Political Economy* 98 (5): S71–S102.

Rosalsky, Greg. 2020. "The Dark Side of the Recovery Revealed in Big Data." *Planet Money Newsletter*, October 27, 2020. https://www.npr.org/sections/money/2020/10/27/927842540/the-dark-side-of-the-recovery-revealed-in-big-data.

Rosenberg, Matthew, Nicholas Confessore, and Carole Cadwalladr. 2018. "How Trump Consultants Exploited the Facebook Data of Millions." *New York Times*, March 17, 2018. https://www.nytimes.com/2018/03/17/us/politics/cambridge-analytica-trump-campaign.html.

Rowntree, Benjamin Seebohm. 2000. *Poverty: A Study of Town Life*, 2d ed. Bristol, UK: Policy Press.

Serajuddin, Umar, Hiroki Uematsu, Christina Wieser, Nobuo Yoshida, and Andrew L. Dabalen. 2015. "Data Deprivation: Another Deprivation to End." Policy Research Working Paper 7252, World Bank, Washington, DC.

Statistics Canada. 2019. "The Value of Data in Canada: Experimental Estimates." *Daily*, July 10, 2019, Statistics Canada, Ottawa. https://www150.statcan.gc.ca/n1/pub/13-605-x/2019001/article/00009-eng.htm.

Stephens-Davidowitz, Seth. 2017. *Everybody Lies: Big Data, New Data, and What the Internet Can Tell Us about Who We Really Are*. Illus. ed. New York: Dey Street Books.

Thorvaldsen, Gunnar. 2017. *Censuses and Census Takers: A Global History*. Routledge Studies in Modern History Series. London: Routledge. https://doi.org/10.4324/97813 15148502.

UFPEL (Federal University of Pelotas). 2020. "FAPESP e Todos pela Saúde garantirão a continuidade do estudo EPICOVID-19 BR." Coordenação de Comunicação Social, Pró-Reitoria de Gestão da Informação e Comunicação, UFPEL, Pelotas, Rio Grande do Sul, Brazil. http://ccs2 .ufpel.edu.br/wp/2020/08/31/fapesp-e-todos-pela-saude -garantirao-a-continuidade-do-estudo-epicovid-19-br/.

US Department of Commerce. 2014. "Fostering Innovation, Creating Jobs, Driving Better Decisions: The Value of Government Data." Office of the Chief Economist, Economics and Statistics Administration, US Department of Commerce, Washington, DC. https://www.commerce .gov/files/fostering-innovation-creating-jobs-driving -better-decisions-value-government-data.

Wallis, Helen M., and Arthur Howard Robinson, eds. 1987. *Cartographical Innovations: An International Handbook of Mapping Terms to 1900*. Tring, UK: Map Collector Publications.

Wesolowski, Amy, Taimur Qureshi, Maciej F. Boni, Pål Roe Sundsøy, Michael A Johansson, Syed Basit Rasheed, Kenth Engø-Monsen, et al. 2015. "Impact of Human Mobility on the Emergence of Dengue Epidemics in Pakistan." *Proceedings of the National Academy of Sciences* 112 (38): 11887–92.

Whitby, Andrew. 2020. *The Sum of the People: How the Census Has Shaped Nations, from the Ancient World to the Modern Age*. New York: Basic Books.

World Bank. 2002. *World Development Report 2002: Building Institutions for Markets*. Washington, DC: World Bank; New York: Oxford University Press.

World Bank. 2016. *World Development Report 2016: Digital Dividends*. Washington, DC: World Bank.

World Bank. 2018. *Data for Development: An Evaluation of World Bank Support for Data and Statistical Capacity*. Washington, DC: Independent Evaluation Group, World Bank.

World Bank. 2019. *IC4D, Information and Communications for Development 2018: Data-Driven Development*. Washington, DC: World Bank. http://documents1.worldbank.org /curated/en/987471542742554246/pdf/128301-97814648 13252.pdf.

Yala, Adam, Peter G. Mikhael, Fredrik Strand, Gigin Lin, Kevin Smith, Yung-Liang Wan, Leslie Lamb, et al. 2021. "Toward Robust Mammography-Based Models for Breast Cancer Risk." *Science Translational Medicine* 13 (578): 1–11. https://doi.org/10.1126/scitranslmed.aba4373.

Zingales, Luigi. 2017. "Towards a Political Theory of the Firm." *Journal of Economic Perspectives* 31 (3): 113–30.

Zuboff, Shoshana. 2019. *The Age of Surveillance Capitalism: The Fight for a Human Future at the New Frontier of Power*. New York: Public Affairs. https://www.hbs.edu/faculty/Pages /item.aspx?num=56791.

Spotlight 1.1

Helping communities to gain the ability to collect and analyze their own data

A novel experiment in India empowered villagers—particularly women, many of them illiterate—to design their own process for collecting and deploying data to track changes in the quality of public services and in their living standards and to make better decisions in village meetings.

In 2014 the World Bank's Social Observatory, working closely with the Pudhu Vaazhvu Project of the South Asia Livelihoods team in the south Indian state of Tamil Nadu, developed a method called participatory tracking.[1] This effort built on the institutional context in India, whereby democratically elected village councils hold regular, open village meetings in which budget priorities are planned and monitored, and there is a network of women's self-help groups with a strong presence in every village in the state. Participatory tracking proceeded in three steps.

First, representatives of women's groups from 200 villages engaged in several weeks of deliberations to think about what constitutes the good life for them, turn those ideas into indicators measured using survey questions, and then test those questions in their villages through a simple questionnaire that took no more than 30 minutes to answer.

Second, the community-designed questionnaire was incorporated into tablet-based software. A member of each women's group was trained via video on how to administer the questionnaire in her own village. In the pilot, women were able to conduct a census of 40,000 households in about six weeks. Once the survey was conducted, the data were dispatched directly to a cloud server to prevent anyone from tampering with them.

About one-third of villagers could not read or write. Thus, the team developed ways of showing the data that would be understandable to people who were not literate.

Third, the Social Observatory team "coproduced" data visualizations with the community. Figure S1.1.1 provides an example, developed to demonstrate variations in decision-making within the household. If a member of the family has more authority over a decision, his or her face becomes bigger. If women have more authority, the colored background shades from dark gray toward dark green. The village median is displayed alongside that of another village for comparison. These data were presented at village planning meetings. They substantially improved the quality of deliberation by allowing citizens and officials to focus on the issues of concern rather than debate the facts about where decision-making power lay.

Versions of participatory tracking that focus more on the management of public goods and common property are being designed and will be scaled up in the Indian states of Tamil Nadu (where the pilot was developed) and Karnataka, which will cover more than 75 million people, and nationwide in Indonesia, which will cover another 145 million.

Figure S1.1.1 **A citizen-led method to ascertain who has authority in household decision-making in rural Indian villages**

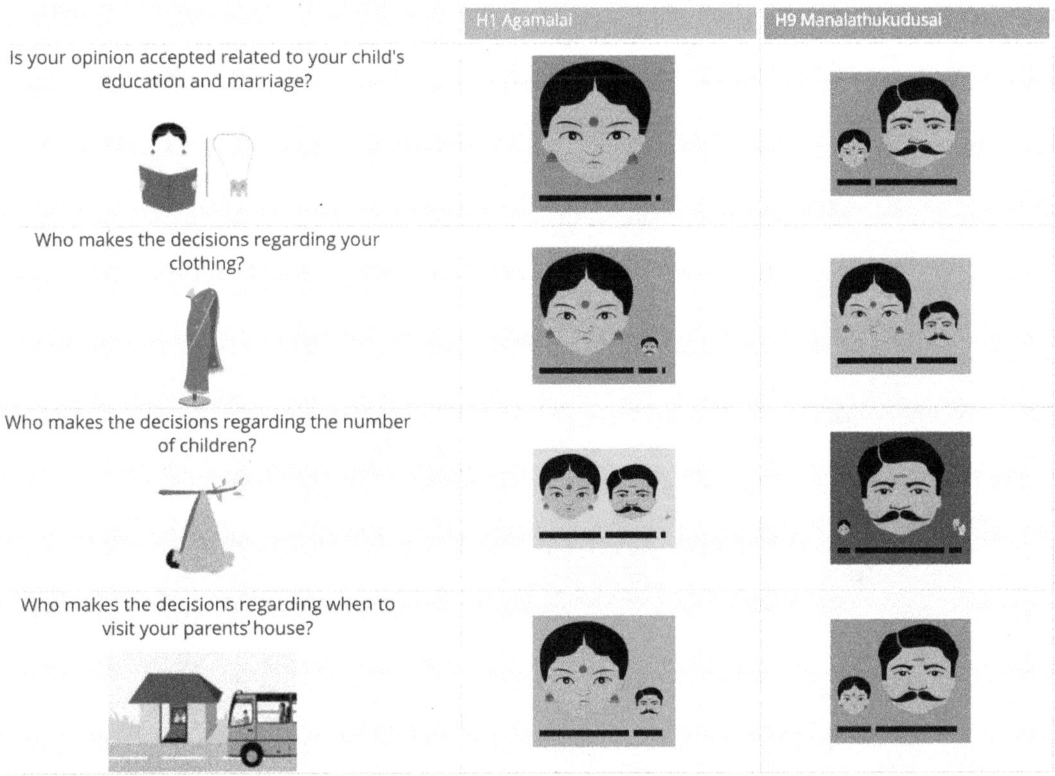

Source: Palaniswamy, Sakhamuri, and Xia 2017.

Note: The figure shows a screenshot of a data visualization developed to demonstrate variations in household decision-making. If a member of the family has more authority over a decision, his or her face becomes bigger. If women have more authority, the colored background shades from dark gray toward dark green.

Note

1. Palaniswamy, Sakhamuri, and Xia (2017).

Reference

Palaniswamy, Nethra, Smriti Sakhamuri, and Cassandra Xia. 2017. "Participatory Tracking: Customizing Visualizations." *Social Observatory* (blog), September 2017. http://socialobservatory.worldbank.org/articles/participatory-tracking-customizing-visualizations.

Spotlight 1.2

The importance of good data in helping low- and middle-income countries to manage debt during and after the COVID-19 pandemic

Improvements in the collection, reporting, and monitoring of data about debt will be critical to borrowers and creditors alike.

Data on public debt remain opaque in some countries, potentially enabling governments to overborrow and hide debts from their citizens and creditors, at least for some period (see the example of Mozambique from chapter 1). This vulnerability is compounded by the high (reported) debt levels of lower-income countries at the outset of the COVID-19 crisis and the changing composition of private creditors and debt instruments. In 2019 almost half of all low-income countries were either in debt distress or at high risk of it. As the pandemic pushes as many as 150 million people into extreme poverty,[1] countries may need to take on substantial additional debt, which could result in large debt overhangs that could take years to manage.

The proliferation of complex debt instruments may make it easier for governments to obscure their debt position. Moreover, the composition of creditors is changing: China, the largest creditor, increased its share of the combined debt owed by Debt Service Suspension Initiative (DSSI)-eligible countries to G-20 countries from 38 percent to 57 percent between 2013 and end-2019 (figure S1.2.1). These changes could create new exposures, especially regarding access to future debt. While most lower-income countries owe a relatively small share of their external public debt to private creditors, some countries, including Chad, Côte d'Ivoire, Ghana, Saint Lucia, and Zambia, owe as much as 50–60 percent to private creditors. Private sector participation in achieving a sustainable debt trajectory will become increasingly critical for many countries.

Recognizing the pressing need to manage the debt burden of low-income countries, the World Bank and

Figure S1.2.1 In six years, the composition of debt has shifted dramatically

DSSI-eligible countries' bilateral debt: Composition of creditors, 2013 and 2019

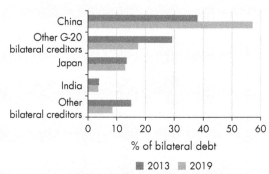

Source: World Bank, Debt Data (dashboard), https://datatopics.worldbank.org/debt/. Data at http://bit.do/WDR2021-Fig-S1_2_1.

Note: For more information, see "What Is the External Debt Reporting System (DRS)?" World Bank, Washington, DC, https://datahelpdesk.worldbank.org/knowledgebase/articles/381934-what-is-the-external-debt-reporting-system-drs. DSSI = Debt Service Suspension Initiative.

International Monetary Fund (IMF) have proposed the DSSI.[2] In managing current and future debt, governments and partners will need to improve the coverage, quality, timeliness, granularity, and transparency of debt data.[3] This effort requires investing in both the data themselves and in the systems for collecting, managing, analyzing, and reporting data, especially for countries where the risks are greatest. The World Bank and IMF have offered the following recommendations to the G-20:[4]

- *Establish clear and internationally harmonized concepts and definitions of debt.* Governments should adopt international reporting and statistical standards that clearly define debt concepts. New standards should be developed where gaps exist to improve the granularity of debt data.
- *Strengthen legal frameworks within countries.* Stronger legal frameworks have clearly defined organizational structures, roles, and responsibilities; sufficient monitoring, auditing, and compliance mechanisms in place to avoid conflicts of interest; internal controls to make sure that laws, procedures, and policies are followed; and well-coordinated debt management and other fiscal policies and financial frameworks.
- *Build a functional debt recording, management, and dissemination system.* A robust system is needed to facilitate the production and use of timely, accurate, high-quality, reliable, and complete data. The system should be interoperable with other key applications and be protected by appropriate security and data protection controls. Disseminating debt data openly in user-friendly formats and building the capability of systems to produce reports for borrowers and inform debt service transactions can facilitate the use of data.
- *Improve the organizational structure.* High-level government commitment and clear mandates are essential.[5] Effective coordination and accountability mechanisms can help to disentangle fragmented debt management functions across institutions and entities and ensure the timely sharing of data and analysis. Debt management offices should have the authority to collect data from state-owned enterprises or other indebted public entities.
- *Strengthen staff capacity.* Highly skilled staff with technical capacity to extract, analyze, and publish debt data are needed and should be retained and adequately compensated.

Multilateral institutions such as the World Bank and IMF play a critical role in improving debt transparency by improving coverage in the databases they manage, providing technical assistance, performing assessments on a country's current debt management framework, designing international standards on debt, and building awareness. Lenders, along with borrowers, also have a responsibility to report debt information fully, accurately, and transparently.

All of these steps will help creditors to assess accurately the debt sustainability of their potential borrowers, citizens to hold their governments accountable for the debt they assume, and borrowers to design strategies based on a clear understanding of the level, cost, and risk profile of their debt portfolio. Increased debt transparency will also help many low- and middle-income countries to assess and manage their external debt during and after the COVID-19 crisis and to work with policy makers toward achieving sustainable debt levels and terms.

Notes

1. World Bank (2020b).
2. World Bank (2020a).
3. IMF and World Bank (2018).
4. World Bank (2020a).
5. Teeling (2018).

References

IMF (International Monetary Fund) and World Bank. 2018. "G20 Notes on Strengthening Public Debt Transparency." IMF, Washington, DC, June 14, 2018. https://www.imf.org/external/np/g20/pdf/2018/072718.pdf.

Teeling, Gerry. 2018. "Debt Data Transparency." Background paper for Intergovernmental Group of Experts on Financing for Development, 2nd Session, United Nations Conference on Trade and Development, Geneva, November 7–9, 2018. https://unctad.org/system/files/non-official-document/tdb_efd2c03_Teeling_en.pdf.

World Bank. 2020a. "Debt Service Suspension and COVID-19." Factsheet, December 21, 2020, World Bank, Washington, DC. https://www.worldbank.org/en/news/factsheet/2020/05/11/debt-relief-and-covid-19-coronavirus.

World Bank. 2020b. *Poverty and Shared Prosperity 2020: Reversals of Fortune.* Washington, DC: World Bank. https://openknowledge.worldbank.org/bitstream/handle/10986/34496/9781464816024.pdf.

Data as a force for public good

Main messages

1. Public intent data, a foundation of public policies, can play a transformative role in the public sector. However, gaps in the availability, quality, and usability of these data are pervasive, particularly in low-income countries— the countries that stand to benefit most from improving public intent data.

2. Lack of resources, technical capacity, and data governance hamper the production of useful data for public policy. Lack of data literacy and demand for data limits their use for public policy.

3. These problems can be addressed through the high-level prioritization of data, including long-term financing, investments in human capital, and laws conducive to the safe production, exchange, and use of data. Some investments in better data have paid for themselves.

4. Ensuring a political commitment to and predictable government financing for the production of public intent data remains a central struggle in lower-income countries. The political will to prioritize funding for data systems can be stimulated by boosting the demand for data.

The central role of public intent data

Suppose a woman walks into a doctor's office and is given a diagnosis without examination by the doctor: no measurement of her heart rate, no recording of her symptoms, and no review of her medical history. The doctor just prescribes a medication. Such an approach, and such a world in which crucial data are not gathered, analyzed, and acted on, would not be welcome, to say the least.[1]

Yet all too often governments make decisions affecting people's well-being without understanding or even taking into account essential data. Designing policies without data is akin to a shot in the dark.[2] This problem is particularly acute in the poorest countries, where gaps in both the availability and the use of data are severest.[3]

Just as data gathered by a doctor can help improve a patient's diagnosis and ultimate well-being, data gathered by governments, international organizations, research institutions, and civil society can improve societal well-being by enhancing service delivery, prioritizing scarce resources, holding governments accountable, and empowering individuals. These data serve as the foundation for core functions of governments and their endeavors to reduce poverty. The data a doctor gathers often take the form of a conversation or some other means of communicating information between patient and doctor. In the same way, data gathered with the intent of informing public policy should enrich the policy dialogue and allow for systematic flows of information and communication among governments, their citizens, and commerce.

Such flows of information and communication require long-term investments in statistical capacity, infrastructure, data governance, data literacy, and data safeguards. These investments depend on one another. Failure in one area jeopardizes the value that data bring to development. Too often these investments are not made in the poorest parts of the world, contributing to data deprivations and poverty.

How should such deprivations be addressed? This chapter discusses the pathways through which data for public policy generate value for development, the obstacles to safe realization of value, and how those obstacles can be overcome.

Public intent data and development: Three pathways for adding value

Public intent data—data collected with the intent of serving the public good by informing the design,

execution, monitoring, and evaluation of public policy, or through other activities—are a prerequisite for many government functions. For that reason, government agencies are the primary producers of public intent data through censuses, surveys, and administrative data, among other things. Citizens, civil society organizations (CSOs), nongovernmental organizations (NGOs), academic institutions, and international organizations also contribute critically to the production of public intent data through surveys, crowdsourcing platforms, and other means. Data from firms can also be used for public policy—a topic that will be covered in chapter 4.[4] This chapter distinguishes between six types of public intent data that all serve the public good (box 2.1).

The discussion that follows uses country examples to describe three important pathways through which public intent data can bring value to development by (1) improving service delivery, (2) prioritizing scarce resources, and (3) holding governments accountable and empowering individuals. But these are not the only pathways. Others include regulating the economy and markets, fostering public safety and security, and improving dispute or conflict resolution.

The country examples reveal several conditions that should be in place to maximize the value of public intent data. The data need to be (1) produced with adequate spatial and temporal coverage (complete, timely, and frequent); (2) high in quality (granular, accurate, and comparable); (3) easy to use (accessible, understandable, and interoperable); and (4) safe to use (impartial, confidential, and appropriate)—see figure 2.1.[5] With these features, development-related data have the *potential* to transform development outcomes. For this potential to be realized, the data must be used explicitly to generate public good, including through the three pathways summarized in the following sections.

Pathway 1: Improving service delivery

Increasing access to government services. One of the fundamental ways in which public intent data can improve livelihoods is by increasing access to government services. More access often requires data representative of all residents. Use of administrative data, particularly foundational identification (ID) systems such as national IDs and civil registries as well as digital identification, ensures that all persons are covered and access is equitable. In Thailand at the turn of the century, only 71 percent of the population was covered by a public health insurance scheme that was intended to be universal. Yet the country had a near-universal foundational ID and population

Box 2.1 Six types of public intent data

 Administrative data—such as birth, marriage, and death records and data from identification systems; population, health, education, and tax records; and trade flow data—are generated by a process of registration or record keeping, usually by national authorities. Administrative data also include data used by governments to run projects, programs, and services. The digital revolution has created new types of administrative data—for example, when education and health inspectors' use of smartphone apps channels data to a central register.

 Censuses aim to systematically enumerate and record information about an entire population of interest, whether individuals, businesses, farms, or others. Most prominently, population and housing censuses record every person present or residing in a country and provide essential information on the entire population and their key socioeconomic conditions.

 Sample surveys draw on a smaller, representative sample of the entire population, typically from censuses, to collect detailed information more frequently. These surveys cover many domains such as household surveys, farm surveys, enterprise surveys, labor force surveys, and demographic and health surveys. Key official statistics, such as unemployment and national accounts, rely on survey data, often in combination with administrative data and census data.[a]

 Citizen-generated data are produced by individuals, often to fill gaps in public and private sector data or when the accuracy of existing data is in question. These data, which can have an important monitoring and accountability function, contribute to solving problems that

citizens face.[b] Examples include HarassMap, an Egyptian tool that maps cases of sexual harassment based on citizen reports, and ForestWatchers, a platform through which citizens monitor the deforestation of the Amazon.

 By contrast, *machine-generated data* are automatically generated by a sensor, application, or computer process without human interactions. An example is the sensors that monitor air pollution. These data emerge when devices are embedded with sensors and other technologies, allowing them to transfer data with each other, a system known as the Internet of Things.

 Geospatial data relate multiple layers of information based on their geographic locale. Public intent geospatial data include satellite imagery of the Earth such as that provided by the US National Aeronautics and Space Administration's Landsat program and the European Space Agency's Copernicus program; weather data; and cadastral (property and land record) data.[c]

These data types are neither exhaustive nor mutually exclusive. For example, all data sources can be geo-referenced and thus can be used in geospatial applications, and some administrative data and geospatial data can be machine-generated. Data sources are interoperable when they can be linked across and within these types though common numeric identifiers for persons, facilities, or firms; geospatial coordinates; time stamps; and common classification standards.

a. Sample surveys also include the surveys that are implemented by social media companies and target a sample of users who are active on their platforms. Examples include the Future of Business and Gender Equality at Home surveys conducted on the Facebook platform.
b. Meijer and Potjer (2018).
c. Such data sources are discussed in greater detail in chapter 4.

Figure 2.1 Certain data features can maximize the value of public intent data

Ensuring the data have adequate coverage	Ensuring the data are of high quality	Ensuring the data are easy to use	Ensuring the data are safe to use
• Completeness • Timeliness • Frequency	• Granularity • Accuracy • Comparability	• Accessibility • Understandability • Interoperability	• Impartiality • Confidentiality • Appropriateness

Source: WDR 2021 team, drawing on Jolliffe et al. (forthcoming).

registration system in which citizens and residents were issued a personal ID number when they were born or when their households were registered for the first time. Leveraging this register and the personal ID information from the existing public insurance scheme, the government was able to identify the population not covered and so was able to increase health insurance coverage from 71 percent to 95 percent.[6]

Machine-generated data also have the potential to markedly improve access to services such as water. In Kenya, sensors on water hand pumps, which are inoperable in one-third of rural Africa, provide real-time data on their functionality. This system helped reduce the average time to repair a broken pump from 27 days to three days and the median time from six days to one day (figure 2.2).[7]

Better preparing for and responding to emergencies. Public intent data can also lead to a better emergency response when disasters hit, whether environmental, financial, health, or conflict related. For example, weather data, especially weather forecasts, can help people anticipate and prepare for extreme events. The value of such data was revealed by two intense cyclones in the Bay of Bengal 14 years apart. The 1999 cyclone caught the Indian state of Odisha by surprise, causing massive devastation, killing more than 10,000 people, and destroying housing and public infrastructure. Since then, the Odisha State Disaster Management Authority and the government of Odisha have invested in weather forecast data and disaster response measures. When another cyclone hit in 2013, nearly 1 million people were evacuated to cyclone shelters, safe houses, and inland locations, and only 38 people died during and immediately after the storm.[8] These impressive results would not have been possible without the weather data that gave sufficient advance warning of the cyclone.

Mobile technologies have the potential to speed up emergency responses. In Uganda, a health reporting program that provides beneficiaries, health professionals, and the Ministry of Health with real-time health data by using text messaging was able to cut the response time to outbreaks of disease by half. The technology was used after the 2012 Ebola outbreak to help implement quarantines and other protective measures.[9] As these examples demonstrate, timely data can contribute to quick reactions to a crisis.

Generating useful knowledge. Data generated and used by academic institutions, think tanks, and international organizations play a vital role in ensuring that policies are evidence-based. Impact evaluations of reforms and development projects are frequently used to assess whether past policies have had the intended consequences and to improve program design. In the last few decades, numerous field experiments have tested policies in a real-life setting under strict statistical conditions that allow cause and effect to be ascertained. Findings from such experiments have been used to implement new policies and scale up existing programs. One estimate suggests that the new policies and programs built on the research findings have reached more than 400 million people worldwide.[10] In Brazil, evidence from 2,150 municipalities found that many mayors are willing to pay to learn the results of impact evaluations, and that informing mayors about research on a simple and effective policy increases the probability by 10 percentage points that their municipality implements the policy.[11]

Research also plays an important role in ensuring the accuracy of the data collected by governments, which is critical to preventing policy recommendations based on inaccurate or misleading data.[12] The World Bank's Living Standards Measurement Study (LSMS) program, while supporting the production of household survey data in 106 countries between 2011 and 2020,[13] has also drawn attention to the importance of research on survey methodologies and the role of better measurement in eliminating systematic measurement errors in self-reported survey data that otherwise bias empirical analyses and policy conclusions.[14] Much of the methodological research led by the LSMS is carried out in partnership with national statistical offices (NSOs), in turn facilitating the adoption of improved methods in downstream national surveys.

Pathway 2: Prioritizing scarce resources

Targeting resources and reaching marginalized populations and areas. When public intent data are granular—that is, they are tied to an individual or a specific location—they can help target resources and foster inclusion. In Croatia, data from the population census were

Figure 2.2 Improving access to water: Using real-time sensor data to reduce repair time for broken hand pumps in Kenya

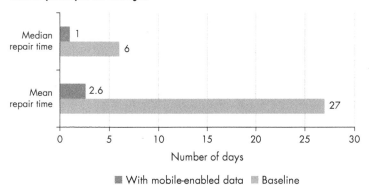

Source: SSEE 2014. Data at http://bit.do/WDR2021-Fig-2_2.

combined with household survey data and administrative data to create detailed maps of poverty and deprivations (map 2.1).[15] The maps revealed large differences in living standards across municipalities and within the territorial boundaries used for allocating funds from the European Union (EU).[16] More than one-third of the EU's annual budget—equivalent to more than €50 billion—is dedicated to investments in infrastructure, such as hospitals and schools, in less economically developed areas. Because the allocation of funds depends on an area's gross domestic product (GDP) per capita, poor municipalities situated in non-poor regions may not receive funding. Armed with the poverty map, Croatia responded with proposals for new geographical subdivisions that concentrate EU funds in the poorest areas.[17] This reordering, thanks to better data and analysis, has the potential to reduce inequality and pockets of poverty in Croatia.

A long-running and rich example of the value of granular data are the Demographic and Health Surveys, which cover topics such as HIV/AIDS and gender-based violence (see spotlight 2.1). Over the last few decades, data from 82 of these surveys, disaggregated by sex, have been used as inputs for developing laws banning domestic violence, developing HIV education programs, and more.[18] In Vietnam, a survey on gender-based violence revealed that more than half of women have experienced physical, sexual, or emotional abuse; that nearly half of these had physical injuries as a result; and that seven in eight did not seek any help. These data spurred a public discussion about the topic, informed the National Strategy on Gender Equality, and introduced counseling, health, legal, and shelter services for women subject to violence at home.[19]

Saving money and resources. Interoperability between geospatial data and government records can help governments save resources. Incomplete and out-of-date property and taxpayer records are an important reason that taxes remain uncollected in many low- and middle-income countries. In Tanzania, the government introduced a Geographic Information System for tax reporting and revenue collection. The system identified buildings via satellite imagery, collected and digitized data on their characteristics, and provided a comprehensive, up-to-date record of taxable properties. Using this new method, the city government of Arusha identified 102,904 buildings— nearly five times more than with earlier databases. One year after the system was introduced, the eight participating cities increased their revenue collection by 30 percent on average.[20]

Interoperable administrative data have also been used to increase efficiencies and save costs in public

Map 2.1 Reducing poverty: Mapping pockets of poverty in Croatia allowed better targeting of antipoverty funds

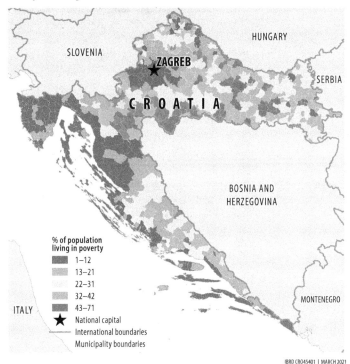

Source: World Bank 2016a. Data at http://bit.do/WDR2021-Map-2_1.

welfare systems. For example, in Argentina the government identified ineligible beneficiaries across various social programs using the country's system of unique taxpayer ID numbers. The exercise generated estimated savings of US$143 million over eight years.[21] More generally, investments in better data systems have been shown to pay for themselves.[22]

Monitoring progress and determining priorities. Public intent data can also help prioritize resources by monitoring progress on key indicators and deliverables over longer periods of time. Such monitoring is vital for creating and tracking national and international development goals. The Sustainable Development Goals (SDGs), for example, rely heavily on public intent data.[23] If the data needed to measure one of the targets were collected only every 10 years, tracking progress would become challenging.

Cross-country comparable composite indexes— often created by think tanks, research institutions, and international organizations—allow countries to benchmark their performance over time and against peers and to decide on priorities. These data can induce countries to respond with reforms in areas where they are lagging. Multidimensional poverty indexes, which measure poverty at the household and individual levels, track certain indicators in countries over time, helping countries decide on areas of focus. Costa Rica issued a presidential directive calling for use of such an index for budgetary planning and as an official measure for allocating resources and monitoring and evaluating social programs. The country has used the index to modify its budget allocation, which helped accelerate poverty reduction during a period of austerity without an increase in budget.[24]

Pathway 3: Holding government accountable and empowering individuals

Fostering transparency and increasing government accountability. CSOs and individuals are frequent producers and users of public intent data. Their demand for data can encourage transparency through data analysis and data feedback systems. In China, media and watchdog organizations in Beijing noted inconsistencies between official government data on air quality and data from independent air quality monitoring systems. Heightened concerns about air quality have fueled a dramatic expansion in publicly available, real-time data from thousands of air quality monitoring locations.[25] The central government launched a US$275 billion plan to improve air quality throughout the country, and the Beijing municipal government promised an additional US$160 billion toward that goal.[26]

Good data can also encourage transparency in and improve public procurement. Too often, public projects are not implemented adequately due to poor procurement such as inflated costs, corruption, or ghost contracts. Because 12 percent of global GDP is spent on public procurement, this finding matters tremendously for development outcomes.[27] In Uganda, in an attempt to improve procurement outcomes, local government entities made administrative procurement data from the bidding process down to the level of execution of contracts available to certain CSOs. These CSOs trained community members to understand the information in the contracts and conduct site checks to verify it. The findings revealed mismanagement of resources by contractors and government officials and a high dependence on noncompetitive contracts. Not only did Uganda undertake reforms to ensure that contracts were complying with national procurement standards, but the national public procurement agency also upgraded its procurement portal in line with international open contracting data standards, making Uganda the first African country to do so.[28]

Government accountability can also be enhanced through e-governance.[29] In Pakistan, a smartphone app that equips government health inspectors with real-time data on rural public health clinics led to a 74 percent increase in clinic inspections. In turn, doctor attendance rose by 18 percentage points, thereby improving health care services.[30]

Empowering individuals. Disadvantaged groups are sometimes left out of government efforts to collect data because governments fail to acknowledge inclusion of those groups as a policy objective. Citizens must then often collect the data needed to empower themselves. That data, such as on harassment and early warning systems, can help fill a gap that neither the public sector nor the private sector can fill. The map-based mobile app Safetipin allows users to report mobility and safety issues in cities related to lighting, walk paths, visibility, public transport, and security. Beyond informing citizens where it is safe to be in their city, these data can be used to conduct citywide audits. In Bogotá, Colombia, the city government wanted to use this tool to map safety around bike paths. The biking community helped collect images along 230 kilometers of bike paths in the city, which were then analyzed by Safetipin (map 2.2). This analysis supported the authorities in understanding where to improve lighting and add closed-circuit TV cameras.[31]

Public intent data can also empower individuals to make better choices through more information and knowledge. The digital revolution has greatly increased the accessibility of data, as well as how easily information can be spread. One example is providing smallholder farmers with agricultural information digitally, often through text messages, to increase their productivity. Such data transmission can improve on extension services, which rely on in-person agricultural advice and are more costly to sustain and whose quality is more difficult to ensure. A meta-analysis suggests that providing agricultural information increases yields by 4 percent and farmers' probability of increasing productivity-enhancing agrochemical inputs.[32] With more than 2 billion people living on smallholder farms, these numbers can have major effects on global poverty and shared prosperity.

Many of the features of public intent data that increase their value for development can also increase their potential for harm. Data may be misused for political surveillance and control or discrimination and exclusion, or they may inadvertently expose sensitive information about individuals.[33] For example, in República Bolivariana de Venezuela, a digital biometric fingerprint system was introduced initially for voter registration and identification, but it has since been integrated with other registers. Identification with the digital fingerprint has become mandatory to purchase basic goods such as food and medicine, which has led to numerous cases of stores refusing to sell young people, foreigners, and LGBTQI individuals such goods.[34] To avoid data being harmful in this and other ways, certain prerequisites must be put in place, notably robust data protection laws, independent oversight, and legal and technological solutions to safeguard the confidentiality of individuals and prevent misuse of data.

Gaps in the coverage, quality, and usability of public intent data

Despite the demonstrated value of public intent data, gaps in their availability, quality, and usability persist, particularly in poor countries. This section documents these gaps, drawing on the World Bank's Statistical Performance Indicators (SPI), described in box 2.2, as well as two other prominent indexes rating public intent data availability and quality.[35]

When the coverage of data is inadequate: Lack of timeliness, frequency, and completeness

Lack of timely and frequent data remains an issue in many thematic areas and across all types of public intent data. Timeliness is particularly an issue with survey and census data because long lags commonly occur between their collection and their release. For example, according to the Statistical Performance Indicators, half of low-income countries have not undertaken a population and housing census in the last 10 years, and 18 percent have not done so in the last 20 years.[36] The census has a foundational function in any statistical system and is critical for political representation and resource allocation. The costs of allowing the census to become outdated are demonstrable.[37] Monthly or quarterly industrial production indexes, which are important to track current economic activity, are available in only 9 percent of low-income countries, compared with 40 percent of lower-middle-income countries, 48 percent of upper-middle-income countries, and 64 percent of high-income countries.[38]

Ground-based sensors, deployed in Internet of Things systems, can measure some outcomes, such as air pollution, climatic conditions, and water quality, on a continual basis and at a low cost. However, adoption of these technologies is still too limited to provide timely data at scale, particularly in low-income countries.[39]

Lack of completeness is often less of a problem in census and survey data because they are designed to

Map 2.2 Improving public safety: The use of citizen-collected data in Bogotá led to greater safety around bike paths

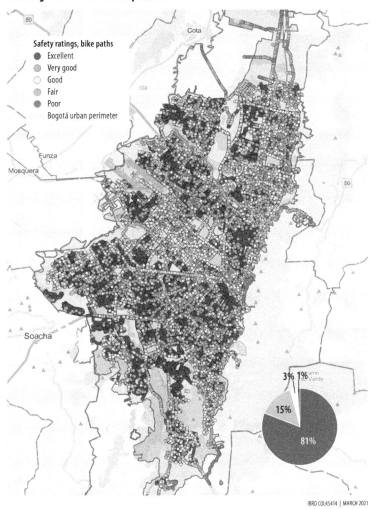

Safety ratings, bike paths
● Excellent
◔ Very good
○ Good
◑ Fair
● Poor
Bogotá urban perimeter

IBRD COL45414 | MARCH 2021

Source: Safetipin 2016.

Note: Safety ratings of poor to excellent for Bogotá bike paths are based on safety scores.

cover the entire population of interest. For administrative data, the story is different. Civil registration and vital statistics systems (births and deaths) are not complete in any low-income country, compared with completeness in 22 percent of lower-middle-income countries, 51 percent of upper-middle-income countries, and 95 percent of high-income countries.[40] These gaps leave about 1 billion people worldwide without official proof of identity.[41] More than one-quarter of children overall, and more than half of children in Sub-Saharan Africa, under the age of five are not registered at birth.[42]

Although population and housing censuses are designed to represent all individuals at the time of

The World Bank's Statistical Performance Indicators (SPI) measure statistical performance across 174 countries.[a] The indicators are grouped into five pillars: (1) data use, which captures the demand side of the statistical system; (2) data services, which looks at the interaction between data supply and demand such as the openness of data and quality of data releases; (3) data products, which reviews whether countries report on important indicators; (4) data sources, which assesses whether censuses, surveys, and other data sources are created; and (5) data infrastructure, which captures whether foundations such as financing, skills, and governance needed for a strong statistical system are in place. Within each pillar is a set of dimensions, and under each dimension is a set of indicators to measure performance. The indicators provide a time series extending at least from 2016 to 2019 in all cases, with some indicators going back to 2004. The data for the indicators are from a variety of sources, including databases produced by the World Bank, International Monetary Fund (IMF), United Nations (UN), Partnership in Statistics for Development in the 21st Century (PARIS21), and Open Data Watch—and in some cases, directly from national statistical office websites. The indicators are also summarized as an index, with scores ranging from a low of 0 to a high of 100.

a. World Bank, Statistical Performance Indicators (database), http://www.worldbank.org/spi; Dang et al. (2021a, 2021b).

the census, they can leave out some of the poorest and most vulnerable. Many vulnerable groups are hard to count in the first place, especially when census enumeration focuses on residence and the concept of the household. These groups include the displaced, the homeless, slum inhabitants, nomads, migrants, young children, and the disabled.[43] The extent of undercounting is difficult to measure systematically, but in 2013 it was estimated that globally between 170 million and 320 million people were missing from population census frames, with the poorest more likely to be missed.[44] As noted, in many countries the census determines the allocation of resources and political representation. Thus these omissions have real consequences and can disenfranchise vulnerable populations.[45] They also affect the representativeness of household surveys that use census-based sampling frames.[46]

Lower-income countries also are susceptible to coverage gaps in geospatial data, especially in some of the geospatial reference datasets such as administrative boundaries, postal codes, and maps. The Global Open Data Index of the Open Knowledge Foundation assesses the availability and openness of three such geospatial datasets in 94 countries: administrative boundaries, addresses and locations, and national maps. The assessment reveals that all three datasets are often incomplete in lower-income countries (figure 2.3).

Similarly, the road network coverage of the open mapping platform OpenStreetMap is complete in many high-income countries, but less so in lower-income countries. OpenStreetMap is a citizen-generated geospatial application that relies on its users to digitize the location of roads and other infrastructure. Its coverage disparities reflect the barriers to making this type of data work for the poorest countries. In India, by 2015 only 21 percent of the road network had been digitized.[47]

Figure 2.3 Gaps in geospatial datasets are especially large in lower-income countries

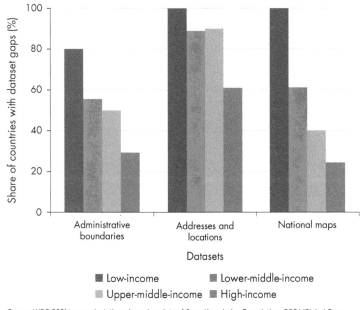

Source: WDR 2021 team calculations, based on data of Open Knowledge Foundation, GODI (Global Open Data Index) (database), https://index.okfn.org/. Data at http://bit.do/WDR2021-Fig-2_3.

When data quality is poor: Lack of granularity, accuracy, and comparability

Lack of granularity can occur when data are not available at the desired level of disaggregation. The gaps in data on women and girls are particularly severe. Only 10 of the 54 gender-specific indicators (19 percent) in the SDGs are widely available, based on international standards for measurement, and only 24 percent of the available gender-specific indicators are from 2010 or later.[48] Gaps in sex-disaggregated data related to the COVID-19 pandemic are also pervasive, causing knowledge of the gender impacts of the pandemic to be incomplete (box 2.3).

Box 2.3 Gender data and the COVID-19 pandemic

The COVID-19 pandemic was not gender-blind; it affected men and women differently and may have exacerbated gender inequalities.[a] Yet knowledge of the gender impacts of COVID-19 is incomplete because of data gaps across all dimensions of well-being. At the most basic level, data are lacking on COVID-19 infections and deaths among men and women. In March 2020, only 61 percent of reported COVID-19 cases were disaggregated by sex, and these data were provided by 26 countries. By November 2020, reporting had grown to 80 countries, but the proportion still stood at 60 percent. The reporting was irregular throughout 2020, as shown in figure B2.3.1.

Understanding the gender dimensions of the COVID-19 impacts extends well beyond case and mortality data. The data systems in place prior to the pandemic had notable gender data gaps that hampered the ability to track impacts and inform policy. For example, monitoring impacts on jobs requires regular and timely data on informal employment where women predominate. However, only 41 percent of low-income countries (LICs) and lower-middle-income countries (LMICs) report data on informal jobs disaggregated by sex. And in seven of the 10 countries where the recent economic contraction is severest, less than 38 percent of Sustainable Development Goal economic opportunity indicators are available by sex.[b] Furthermore, preexisting biases in face-to-face household survey design and implementation bled into phone surveys implemented during the pandemic, limiting measurement of the gender-related impacts of the crisis. These biases include designing phone surveys aimed at household heads and lack of survey content on time use.

There are also notable gaps in the gender data needed to inform policy design and effectiveness. Although the expansion of social protection programs is arguably the largest policy response to offset the economic impacts of the crisis, comparable sex-disaggregated measures of social protection coverage are largely unavailable. Data on personal identification cards and mobile phone ownership should inform program design decisions, especially as countries scale up digital platforms. Yet data

Figure B2.3.1 Proportion of COVID-19 cases reported with sex-disaggregated data for 190 countries

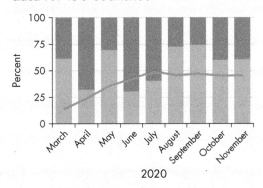

Sources: Global Health 50/50, University College London, COVID-19 Sex-Disaggregated Data Tracker (database), November 30, 2020, data release, https://globalhealth5050.org/the-sex-gender-and-covid-19-project/; Global Change Data Lab, University of Oxford, Our World in Data, Coronavirus Pandemic (COVID-19) (database), https://ourworld indata.org/coronavirus; calculations of Open Data Watch, Washington, DC. Data at http://bit.do/WDR2021-Fig-B2_3_1.

on gender differences in ownership of personal identity cards are missing for more than a third of countries. Less than a quarter of LICs and LMICs report data on mobile phone ownership by women.[c]

Even though the pandemic created new demands for statistics, it also interrupted the supply. More than half of LICs and LMICs reported that the COVID-19 pandemic affected national statistical offices' ability to produce socioeconomic statistics.[d] This problem requires immediate attention, but building effective, gender-aware data systems will require sustained financial and human capital investments.

Sources: Mayra Buvinic (Center for Global Development), Lorenz Noe (Data2x), and Eric Swanson (Open Data Watch), with inputs from the WDR 2021 team.

a. UN Women (2020).
b. Buvinic, Noe, and Swanson (2020).
c. Buvinic, Noe, and Swanson (2020).
d. UNSTATS and World Bank (2020).

Although data disaggregated at the individual level are central to understanding and addressing conditions that uniquely affect the lives of women, men, children, adults, the elderly, and persons with disabilities, the required data are not being sufficiently produced. For example, survey data on ownership of physical and financial assets have traditionally been collected at the household rather than the individual level, limiting their usefulness in understanding women's relative wealth, rights, and decision-making power in their families.[49] Monetary poverty estimates are also based on household-level measures of resources, and "poor individuals" are identified based on the poverty status of their entire households, regardless of differences within households among women, men, and children in access to and use of resources.[50] Meanwhile, gaps remain in the adoption and proper implementation of the survey questions developed by the Washington Group on Disability Statistics—questions that are critical for obtaining internationally comparable estimates on disabilities and for disaggregating relevant SDG indicators by disability status.[51]

Finally, despite the enormous potential of geographically granular data for targeting policies effectively, such disaggregated data are rarely available comprehensively. According to the 2020 Open Data Inventory, about 90 percent of official statistics, even when they are available, are not consistently reported at the regional level (first administrative division), and almost none are consistently reported at the district level (second administrative division).

Poor accuracy of data can limit their usefulness. For those collecting individual-level data through household surveys, a concern is the choice of survey respondents. Relying on proxy respondents to elicit individual-level information—a common cost-saving mechanism in large-scale household surveys—has been shown to produce wrong estimates of gender differences in asset ownership, labor market outcomes, decision-making, and control of income.[52] Reported levels of income, wages, and firm profits vary, depending on the length of the period over which they are recalled by survey respondents.[53] The length of recall also matters for the accuracy of survey data on agricultural production, health, and labor.[54]

Accuracy is also a concern for administrative data. One reason for the proliferation of survey data is the perception that administrative records are unreliable and incomplete.[55] A study of multiple African countries found overreporting of vaccination rates in health information systems by 5 percent of countries and of primary enrollment rates in education management systems by a third. This data inflation appears

to be connected to making aid flows conditional on results, creating an incentive to misreport.[56]

Data quality concerns and methodological challenges also characterize data produced by the Internet of Things. For example, the quality of data generated by low-cost commercial sensors used for air pollution monitoring has been found to vary widely when benchmarked against reference measurements.[57] Sensors must be calibrated to the specific conditions in which they are used to yield accurate results, but the calibration process remains expensive and time-consuming.[58]

Lack of comparability is particularly a concern among low-income countries. Only 40 percent of low-income countries, 20 percent of countries in fragile and conflict-affected situations (FCS), and 40 percent of countries in Sub-Saharan Africa (figure 2.4) have at least three comparable estimates of extreme poverty.[59] It is therefore difficult to understand changes in living standards over time and design policies to eradicate poverty. Recent innovations in data collection in these countries suggest a slightly more optimistic picture for the future.[60] It is also important to note that some lack of comparability over time is necessary, particularly when adopting new global standards.

When data are not easy to use: Lack of accessibility, understandability, and interoperability

Lack of data accessibility prohibits actors from using data. According to an assessment of the Open Data Inventory, lower-income countries lag far behind in overall data openness (table 2.1), although even high-income countries have mediocre openness scores. Only 11 percent of low-income countries consistently make data available with a license classifiable as open, compared with 19 percent of lower-middle-income countries, 22 percent of upper-middle-income countries, and 44 percent of high-income countries.

The Open Data Inventory assessment also reveals some limitations to machine readability. To the extent that governments publish official statistics, only 37 percent of low-income countries make at least some of these available in machine readable formats, compared with 51 percent of lower-middle-income countries, 61 percent of upper-middle-income countries, and 81 percent of high-income countries.

One reason for lack of data accessibility is that data systems in the public sector can be very fragmented. The health sector, for example, often has many different health information systems because of its tendency to have many different service providers. These include many private providers whose data are often

Figure 2.4 Lower-income countries, especially those affected by fragility and conflict, have less comparable poverty data than other country groups

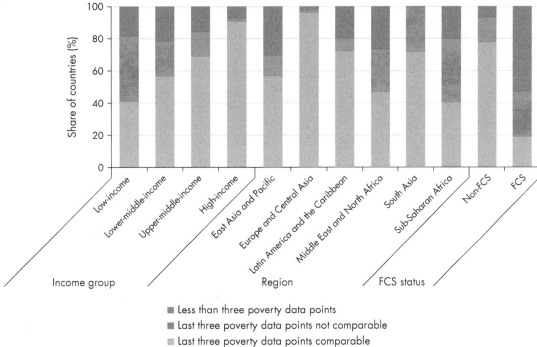

■ Less than three poverty data points
■ Last three poverty data points not comparable
■ Last three poverty data points comparable

Source: WDR 2021 team calculations, based on World Bank, PovcalNet: Data (database), http://iresearch.worldbank.org/PovcalNet/data.aspx. Data at http://bit.do/WDR2021-Fig-2_4.

Note: Only those economies with at least one international poverty estimate are included. FCS status refers to the World Bank's "Classification of Fragile and Conflict-Affected Situations" (World Bank 2020a).

Table 2.1 Assessment of the openness of data, by country income group

Indicator	Low-income	Lower-middle-income	Upper-middle-income	High-income
Openness score (0–100)	38	47	50	66
Available in machine readable format (%)	37	51	61	81
Available in nonproprietary format (%)	75	85	81	84
Download options available (%)	56	68	68	78
Open terms of use/license (%)	11	19	22	44

Source: WDR 2021 team calculations, based on 2020/21 Open Data Inventory indicators (Open Data Watch, ODIN [Open Data Inventory] [database], https://odin.opendatawatch.com/), also used as part of the World Bank's Statistical Performance Indicators database, http://www.worldbank.org/spi.

Note: The openness score is the average by country income group on a scale of 0–100. All other indicators are the percentage of published data averaged by country income group.

unavailable to the Ministry of Health. In Ethiopia, a study of the health sector found 228 different digital health information applications, of which only 39 percent sent data to the Ministry of Health.[61] Administrative data, in particular, are too often siloed in different systems, prohibiting their effective use for monitoring and policy design. Although data coordination within agencies is often limited, the challenge of siloed systems is even greater across government agencies.[62]

Lack of understandability prevents even those data that are accessible from generating value. To be

understandable, data must be well disseminated, backed up with sufficient metadata, responsive to user needs, and, for certain purposes, summarized and visualized for the user. A majority of countries have data portals and provide metadata for their published data—practices that facilitate wider data use.[63] Low-income countries perform comparatively well in the data portal and metadata categories, but even here they lag. A larger gap remains in terms of advance release calendars, which commit government units to release data on a predetermined timetable. Only

Table 2.2 Data dissemination practices and openness, by country income group

Indicator	Low-income	Lower-middle-income	Upper-middle-income	High-income
NSO uses advance release calendar	30	75	92	98
NSO has data portal	84	91	95	92
NSO has conducted user satisfaction survey	10	20	19	33
NSO makes metadata available	63	91	97	100

Source: Cameron et al. 2019.

Note: Data are for 2019. The percentages reflect the proportion of the population in each income group whose national statistical office (NSO) has the listed attribute.

30 percent of NSOs in low-income countries publish such calendars, compared with almost all high-income countries. Across the board, only a few NSOs utilize user satisfaction surveys, which could play an important role in gauging and understanding data demand (table 2.2).

Limitations to interoperability. The use of common standards, methodologies, and classifications across public intent data sources ensures interoperability and enables data integration. Common and unified identification is needed across producers of public intent data for geographic divisions below the national level, such as regions, states, and districts. There is significant scope for expanding the use of georeferencing in censuses, surveys, and collection of administrative data, particularly in low-income settings. The use of common and unified personal identifiers to match data across multiple data sources is more contentious because of privacy and equity concerns, and robust data protection legislation is a prerequisite for their use.[64] Personal identification also requires trust and comprehensive civil registration and vital statistics systems, which have so far been elusive in the poorest countries. The use of tokenized identifiers in line with privacy by design principles is a potential solution.[65]

Adhering to set methodologies and standards in line with international best practices greatly increases the interoperability and usability of public intent data. The World Bank's Statistical Performance Indicators capture this aspect of public intent data systematically. Under the indicator on data infrastructure, standards related to systems of national accounts, employment status, consumption, consumer price indexes, and government finance statistics, among others, are assessed. The indicator shows a strong income gradient in the adherence to international best-practice standards and methodologies.[66] For example, the International Classification of Status in Employment is being used in two-thirds

Figure 2.5 Lower-income countries are less likely than other countries to adhere to international best-practice statistical standards and methodologies

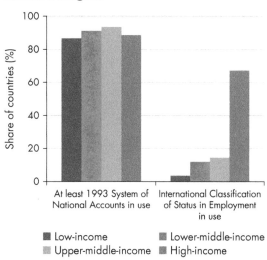

Source: WDR 2021 team calculations, based on World Bank, Statistical Performance Indicators (database), http://www.worldbank.org/spi. Data at http://bit.do/WDR2021-Fig-2_5.

of high-income countries but in only 7 percent of low-income countries (figure 2.5). By contrast, a large share of all countries globally is using at least the 1993 international standards for the System of National Accounts (SNA 1993).

When data are not safe to use: Lack of impartiality, confidentiality, and appropriateness for development

Gaps also remain in the safety of data. These can occur when data are not immune to influence from stakeholders, when they are not stored securely, or when they are not properly deidentified. For example, Greece's debt statistics appear to have deliberately misrepresented the country's financial situation in the lead-up to the 2009 euro crisis, and data breaches are all too common in government and private sector databases.[67]

Similarly, deidentifying individuals has not always proved to be enough to maintain confidentiality. In the 1990s, the governor of Massachusetts in the United States approved making deidentified medical records of state employees available for researchers. Although key identifiers such as name and address were removed from the data, by triangulating the information available with other public information a researcher was able to identify the medical records of the governor and other individuals (see chapter 6 for more details).[68] One way to minimize these concerns is to ensure that only appropriate data are produced—data that measure concepts of interest, have a clear policy purpose, and are not produced from attempts to collect excessive information or surveil individuals. Such data, of course, can still be misused and mishandled.

Why data gaps persist: The political economy of public intent data

The previous two sections describe how public intent data can yield great value for development, yet gaps in public intent data are severe, particularly in low-income countries—the countries that stand to benefit most from the data. Why do these data gaps persist? This section answers that question, complementing existing data sources with structured interviews with NSOs across all income groups and geographical regions.[69] This approach requires digging one level deeper and understanding the main roadblocks on the pathways to data for public policy, or conversely, the enablers of public intent data. The main roadblocks identified are lack of financing, technical capacity, data governance, and demand for data (figure 2.6).

A common reason for these roadblocks is lack of understanding of and commitment to the use of data for policy making. In a positive feedback loop, realizing the value of public intent data increases understanding of the potential of the data, leading to a commitment to the further production and use of public intent data. To spearhead such commitments, SDG Target 17.18 calls for increasing the availability of high-quality, timely, and disaggregated reliable data, and SDG Target 17.19 calls for developing measurements of progress related to statistical capacity building.

Deficiencies in financing

Underinvestment and misaligned investment priorities are perpetuating data gaps.

Figure 2.6 A positive feedback loop can connect enablers and features of public intent data with greater development value

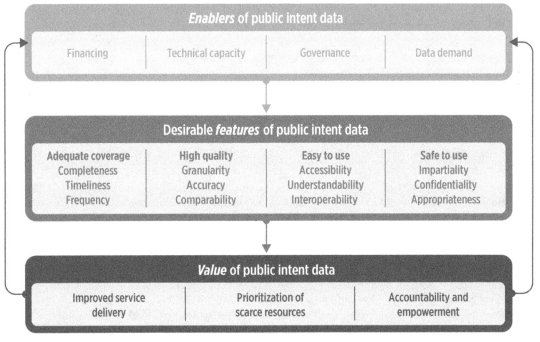

Source: WDR 2021 team.

Figure 2.7 Most countries do not fully fund their national statistical plans

Bar chart. Y-axis: Share of countries with fully funded plan (%), from 0 to 100.

Income group:
- Low-income: 0
- Lower-middle-income: 41
- Upper-middle-income: 61
- High-income: 93

Region:
- Sub-Saharan Africa: 22
- South Asia: 43
- Latin America and the Caribbean: 50
- Middle East and North Africa: 69
- East Asia and Pacific: 74
- Europe and Central Asia: 94

FCS status:
- FCS: 3
- Non-FCS: 48

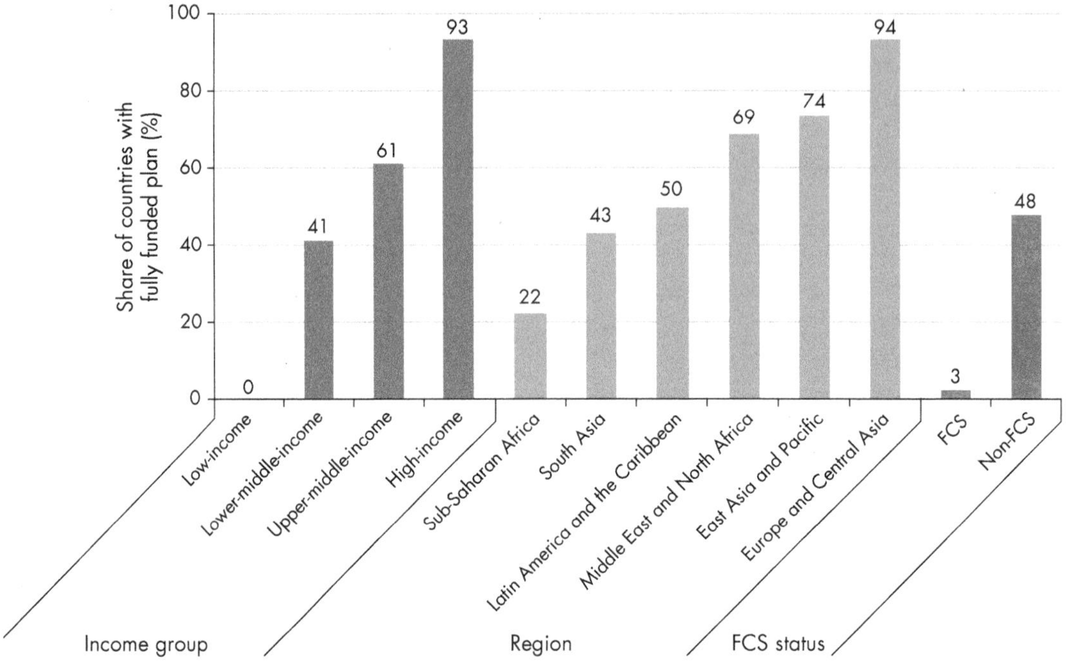

Source: WDR 2021 team calculations, based on indicators collected by the Partnership in Statistics for Development in the 21st Century (PARIS21) that are also used as Statistical Performance Indicators (World Bank, http://www.worldbank.org/spi). Data at http://bit.do/WDR2021-Fig-2_7.

Note: Having a fully funded national statistical plan under implementation is Sustainable Development Goal Indicator 17.18.3. FCS = fragile and conflict-affected situations.

Underinvestment by governments. Underinvestment in public intent data systems is widespread. Only half of countries had a national statistical plan that was fully funded in 2019 (figure 2.7).[70] Lack of national funding for statistics is especially a struggle for fragile and conflict-affected countries, countries in Sub-Saharan Africa, and low-income countries. Whereas 93 percent of high-income countries have a fully funded national statistical plan, not a single low-income country has one. A recent review of public financing of statistics found that seven of 10 low- and middle-income countries analyzed funded less than half of their respective national statistical plans, with country contributions ranging from 9 percent to 77 percent.[71]

This problem is more pressing in low-income countries with less government revenue to spend on multiple priorities. However, the cost of public data systems is modest relative to that of other government functions. Decision-makers in budget offices may not fully understand how much funding is needed to produce high-quality data or lack the incentives to prioritize data. How well public data systems are funded is thus also a matter of high-level government officials recognizing the value of public intent data and offering leadership to encourage collection of them.[72] A key factor in such an effort is the perceived relevance and credibility of public intent data and its producers.[73]

Another reason for lack of funding for data is the absence of a benchmark guiding how much governments should spend, unlike for other areas of government spending. For example, the Education 2030 Framework for Action urges countries to allocate at least 4–6 percent of GDP or at least 15–20 percent of their total public expenditure to education. The Abuja Declaration urges countries to spend at least 15 percent of their annual budget to improve the health sector.[74] No similar guidelines are found on data.

Underinvestment by donors. Donors also invest relatively little in public intent data. The share of total official development assistance devoted to statistics has ranged between 0.35 percent and 0.4 percent in recent years, or US$693 million in 2018.[75] The combination of national and donor contributions leaves a funding gap of between US$100 million and US$700 million a year globally to upgrade public intent data systems, depending on the scope of improvements.[76]

Misalignment of investment priorities. Beyond the size of investments in public intent data, how donors invest matters as well. With insufficient government funding of data and with donors stepping in to fill needs, the risk is that donor priorities will be funded at the expense of national priorities and that donors, instead of national stakeholders, will become the main clients of NSOs.[77]

Because investments in data tend to be small, donors have limited incentives to make longer-term commitments that strengthen data systems such as technical capacity, research and development, infrastructure, or recording of administrative data. Instead, many investments prioritize the production of new data or specific survey efforts such as a one-off survey on a specific topic.[78] In particular, donor priorities skew toward monitoring and international reporting.[79] Although most national governments subscribe to international reporting, there is arguably a more immediate need for frequent and highly geographically disaggregated data and strong administrative data systems for the effective day-to-day functioning of government.[80]

Within the development community, lack of donor coordination can undermine public intent data systems, leading to duplication of and parallel systems for data collection. Each project uses its own set of indicators to report results instead of relying on and strengthening country data systems.[81] Such situations can arise if donors need to fulfill their internal reporting requirements or are suspicious of the accuracy of government-reported data.

Lack of funding is also an issue for citizen-generated data. Interviews with representatives from NGOs in Argentina, Kenya, and Nepal revealed that lack of funding can constrain the collection of citizen-generated data.[82] Similarly, although the cost of sensors has steadily fallen over the last few years, the costs of equipment, deployment, and transmission, as well as the lack of off-the-shelf tools for environments facing resource constraints, are still major barriers to the generation and use of machine-generated data, especially in smallholder agriculture.[83]

Deficiencies in technical capacity

Data gaps are also persisting because of underqualified, understaffed, and underpaid data producers and lack of technology and infrastructure.

Lack of qualified staff, proper staff renumeration, and career incentives. The gaps in public intent data also stem from limited technical capacity, especially in lower-income countries—a result in part of the limited and misaligned resources previously discussed. A shortage of skilled data scientists, statisticians, and economists across public data systems is a critical constraint on the performance of the data producers and the production of data, especially at a time when data from digital sources are becoming more important.

The absence of key personnel in strategic positions who have a commitment to data is especially costly because of the importance of relationships between ministries and NSOs and with civil society as a catalyst for the flow of data and information.[84]

According to a global survey of NSOs conducted by PARIS21, after a shortage of funds the biggest obstacle to countries' successful development of capacity is lack of skilled staff to implement programs.[85] In a list of 15 goals for capacity development, 86 percent of African NSOs selected strengthening human resources as one of their five most important goals, higher than any other category. It is particularly difficult for NSOs to recruit new staff with the skills needed to achieve their objectives. When reporting the most frequent methods of human resource development, only 7 percent of NSOs reported recruitment of staff with new skill sets, and most of these NSOs were in high-income countries.[86]

Recruitment and retention of skilled staff are difficult without competitive pay scales and career tracks.[87] Consultations with NSOs revealed that differences in pay scales across government entities especially make it difficult for NSOs to recruit skilled staff. In Ethiopia, the Central Statistical Agency follows civil service rules and regulations for remuneration of staff, whereas research institutes and universities have their own rules and regulations.

A common challenge for other government agencies that produce data is that they lack designated data scientists or statisticians. This is particularly problematic when other agency staff may lack the time and capacity to make better use of the data collected within their institution.[88]

Lack of technology, software, and infrastructure. Even when producers of public intent data have staff with the skills needed to collect, process, and disseminate those data, they often lack the technological infrastructure to be effective in their work. Constraints in technology and information technology (IT) infrastructure compound constraints in technical capacity. For example, as part of the Global COVID-19 Survey of NSOs, many NSOs in low- and middle-income countries noted their need for software to collect data remotely to meet new data demands.[89] In the PARIS21 survey, the option most selected to achieve priorities for a national statistical system in the medium term is acquiring up-to-date technology and infrastructure.[90] Technological shortcomings also constrain the ability of individuals to produce data themselves because many types of citizen-generated data rely on phone or web technologies.[91]

Deficiencies in governance

In addition to shortages of skills and funding, various failures and problems with data governance impede the potential of public intent data from being realized. At the national level, clear institutional mandates and good coordination among the data-producing agencies are critical for the exchange, interoperability, and timely publication of data.[92] In practice, exchanges of data across ministries and between ministries and NSOs and beyond are rare, even in well-resourced and high-capacity environments.[93] The absence of clear mandates, responsibilities, and incentives to effectively coordinate data production and data exchanges can obstruct collaboration and lead to duplication of data-gathering efforts.[94]

Deficiencies in the legal framework. The legal framework governing data production and data exchanges is a common barrier. Outdated statistical laws can make it difficult for NSOs and data-producing agencies to operate and collaborate effectively in light of recent changes in the data landscape, such as the proliferation of new data types, sources, and producers. In Chile, the National Institute of Statistics (INE) has had difficulties accessing key data from other public institutions in a timely fashion, primarily because the national statistical law is not sufficiently clear in authorizing INE's access to statistical information. When the law was passed in 1970, data exchanges were not a concern. Although a process to modernize the law has been at the forefront of political discussions for a decade, a revised version has yet to be formally implemented. This issue is a concern more generally because the older the national statistical law, the lower is statistical performance in general and data openness in particular at any country income level (figure 2.8).

Other important elements of the legal framework are regulations governing data protection and the right to information. When these safeguards are lacking or weak, data exchanges can entail serious risks to data protection.[95] Lack of comprehensive data protection regulations is a problem in many parts of the world.[96] A review of African countries found that only 28 percent had procedures in place to ensure deidentification of data before publication.[97] Without a requirement to share data and guidance on how to treat confidential information, any risk-averse government employee would face few incentives to share data, especially confidential data, considering the possibly high costs should confidentiality be breached. The absence of comprehensive data protection legislation can also facilitate misuse of data such as for political control or discrimination.[98]

Independence of the NSO. The legal, financial, and institutional independence of the NSO is an important element of a successful public intent data system, especially its data quality and openness.[99] The

Figure 2.8 The older a country's statistical laws, the lower is its statistical performance and the less open are its data

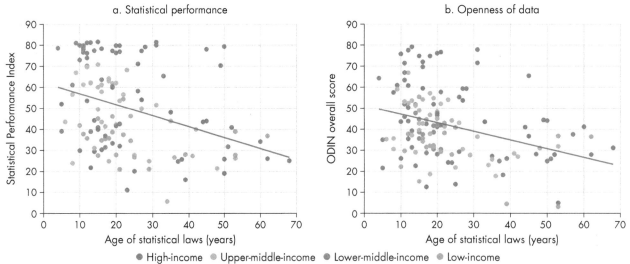

Sources: WDR 2021 team, based on UNSTATS (Statistics Division, Department of Economic and Social Affairs, United Nations), UNSTATS (database), https://unstats.un.org/unsd/dnss/cp/searchcp.aspx; Partnership in Statistics for Development in the 21st Century (PARIS21), https://paris21.org/knowledge-database?keyword=&type%5B%5D=Statistical-Legislation-Country-Documents&date-from=&date-to=&page=; World Bank, World Development Indicators (database), https://databank.worldbank.org/source/world-development-indicators. Data at http://bit.do/WDR2021-Fig-2_8.

Note: In panel a, the regression coefficient on age, controlling for GDP per capita, is −0.48, p < .01; in panel b, −0.39, p < .01. For the Statistical Performance Indicators, see World Bank, Statistical Performance Indicators (database), http://www.worldbank.org/spi. For the Open Data Inventory (ODIN), see Open Data Watch, https://odin.opendatawatch.com/.

Figure 2.9 Greater NSO independence and freedom of the press are positively correlated with better statistical performance

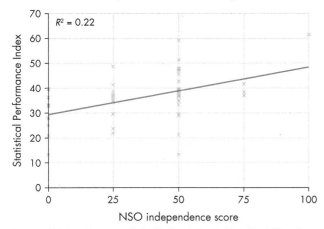

a. NSO independence and statistical performance

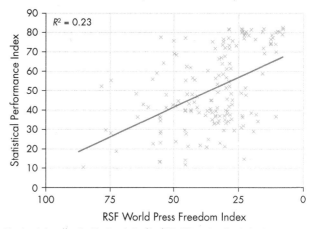

b. Freedom of the press and statistical performance

Sources: NSO independence score: Mo Ibrahim Foundation, Ibrahim Index of African Governance (database), http://mo.ibrahim.foundation/iiag/; World Press Freedom Index: Reporters Without Borders, 2020 World Press Freedom Index (database), https://rsf.org/en/ranking_table. Data at http://bit.do/WDR2021-Fig-2_9.

Note: The x's represent countries. Panel a shows only African countries, and panel b shows all countries with data available. The NSO independence score ranges from 0 to 100. The World Press Freedom Index ranges from 100 to 0—lower values imply greater press freedom. For the Statistical Performance Index, see World Bank, Statistical Performance Indicators (database), http://www.worldbank.org/spi. NSO = national statistical office; RSF = Reporters Without Borders.

independence of producers of public intent data also reinforces the credibility of and trust in the data and its producers, which encourages data use in both government and civil society.[100]

An indicator capturing the independence of NSOs in all African nations is included in the Ibrahim Index of African Governance.[101] The indicator measures the institutional autonomy and financial independence of an NSO. A perfect score indicates that an NSO is able to publish data without clearance from another government branch and has sufficient funding to do so. A higher score on the NSO independence indicator is highly correlated with statistical performance as captured by the World Bank's SPI (figure 2.9, panel a). In 2019 the average score on NSO independence was 34 out of 100, with low-income African countries scoring below average. These findings illustrate that NSO independence is precarious, particularly in lower-income countries. Anecdotes of attacks on NSO independence around the world suggest that fragile NSO independence is not limited to the African context.[102] For example, in 2007 the Argentine government began interfering with the independence of Argentina's NSO, the National Institute of Statistics and Censuses (INDEC). The effort initially focused on the consumer price index and later expanded to other official statistics, casting doubt especially on reported inflation statistics. Recognizing the harmful effects of these measures, by 2015 a new government had undertaken efforts to rebuild the institute, and INDEC resumed the delivery of trustworthy statistics

with transparency and complete adherence to international principles.[103]

A government's interest in having an independent national statistical system can be affected by several competing factors. On the one hand, a government may have a vested interest in curtailing statistical independence and the production and dissemination of reliable data, fearing these could expose poor policy decisions and performance, dilute power, and increase public scrutiny and pressure.[104] In this case, lack of independence and the availability of reliable data would make it harder to hold governments accountable.[105] On the other hand, an independent statistical system producing reliable data in a transparent fashion best informs government decision-making and increases citizens' trust in government data and public institutions in general.[106] Such transparency can also facilitate favorable capital market and investment conditions and foster GDP growth.[107] Finally, international cooperation can boost statistical independence and data transparency when adherence to standards of data quality and the independence of their producers is required for accession to international organizations or agreements. An example is Colombia's successful bid to join the Organisation for Economic Co-operation and Development (OECD).[108]

Civil society performs a vital function in demanding transparency and holding government accountable. Citizen-generated data can be used to challenge official statistics when their accuracy or impartiality are in question. A free and empowered press is a critical check on government power in general and on government interference with statistical independence and data transparency in particular. Greater press freedom, as measured in the World Press Freedom Index compiled by Reporters Without Borders,[109] is highly correlated with statistical performance as well as with statistical independence, regardless of a country's size or income level (figure 2.9, panel b).

Deficiencies in data demand

Even when high-quality data are available and accessible, they must be put to an appropriate use to have an impact on development. As such, lack of data use is blocking the path to development.

Low levels of data literacy. Several barriers to data use remain. Low levels of data literacy among both policy makers and civil society are one barrier.[110] Potential data users need to have both a conceptual understanding of how data can inform policy questions and the technical skills to extract the relevant information from data. An analysis of the use of statistics in news articles in 32 countries in four languages revealed considerable scope for journalists to improve their critical engagement with statistics—and that finding is likely to apply to civil society at large.[111] For policy makers as well, data literacy is frequently identified as a barrier

to data use.[112] Among the general population, comparably low literacy and numeracy rates in lower-income countries fundamentally diminish the pool of potential data users.[113]

Lack of incentives for and interest in data use. Even when policy makers have the skills to use data, they may not be interested in exercising those skills because they do not attach value to data. Accordingly, another major factor affecting demand for public intent data is lack of incentives to use the data.[114] When political leaders exhibit a commitment to data use, they can generate expectations for civil servants to rely on data more frequently and create incentives for accountability. "Political champions," as well as changes in administration or individual government officials, often create opportunities for data-driven policy making.[115] A data-literate society plays a major role in creating these political commitments to data use by demanding—and rewarding—the justification of policy decisions with data.

Low trust in the quality of public intent data. Another reason for lack of data use is the often low trust in the quality of public intent data. Although data users can check for signs of internal coherence, the accuracy of data cannot be inferred from the data alone, and incorrect statistics can take years to be detected, if they are detected at all.[116] A survey of data producers and users in 140 countries found that NSO officials have much greater confidence in the quality of national statistics than ministry officials have.[117]

Lack of infrastructure to access and use the data. A final reason for lack of data use is related to the infrastructure needed to access and use data. For example, internet access is key to obtaining data, but penetration rates are lower in poorer countries. The exclusive sharing of data via online channels may exclude large shares of potential data users who are hampered by limited internet connectivity.[118] And certain users may be unaware that data are available for use.[119] Lack of internet connectivity, reliable power, and data centers are also major challenges in the use of Internet of Things systems and sensor data.[120]

Use of public intent data by a diverse group of actors often translates into greater demand for high-quality data. The rise in demand can drive investment in data and capacity, setting off a virtuous cycle of increasing data demand and supply (figure 2.10). For example, government ministries' reliance on and demand for high-quality data have been associated with NSOs in Latin America exhibiting higher capacity.[121] In the same region, demand for and interest in accurate and high-quality statistics in civil

Figure 2.10 Data supply and demand can generate either virtuous or vicious cycles of data production and use

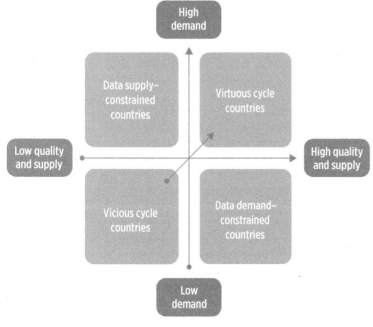

Source: Adapted from Sanga (2013).

society, academia, the media, and the private sector have led to better funding, autonomy, and capacity in national statistical systems.[122] Conversely, countries with a low supply of data are likely to use data less, creating a vicious cycle of data production and use. In general, countries can benefit from assessing whether their constraints are primarily on the supply side or the demand side for data. They can then use such an assessment to prioritize data-related policies and maximize their return on development.[123]

Realizing the potential of public intent data

To maximize the impact of public intent data on development, governments need to address the financing, technical capacity, governance, and data demand roadblocks. This section describes policies to overcome these foundational challenges. Figure 2.11 summarizes some of the main policies governments can enact, categorized by the actors and barriers they primarily address. International organizations also have a role to play, and spotlight 2.2 discusses how they can contribute to addressing the key roadblocks.

Chapter 9 builds on the analysis in this section, specifically in the domain of data governance, laying out a bold vision for an integrated national data system. Such a system can transform the role the public sector plays in the data modernization agenda by incorporating public intent data alongside private intent data, integrating the users and producers of both, and enabling safe data exchanges.

Figure 2.11 Policies to realize the potential of public intent data

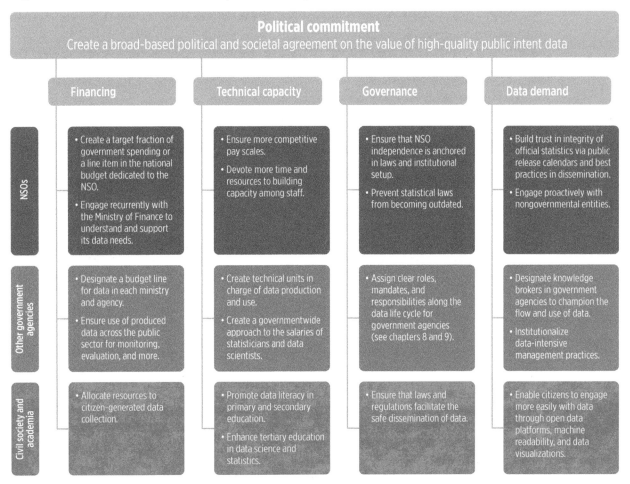

Source: WDR 2021 team.

Note: The figure summarizes policies governments can enact, categorized by the actors and barriers the policies are primarily addressing. Many policies span several actors and barriers but are placed into one box here for simplification. The role of the private sector in realizing the potential of public intent data is discussed in chapter 4. The role of international organizations is examined in spotlight 2.2. NSO = national statistical office.

A common reason for the four roadblocks on the pathways to data for public policy just described is the lack of a political understanding and appreciation of the value of data for policy making. Achieving high-quality production and use of public intent data requires an unequivocal high-level political commitment to data for development, even when data do not yield politically convenient insights. A broad-based political and societal agreement on the value of public intent data is the most effective way to ensure a robust political commitment to data. Such a social contract for data can build the trust of all participants that they will not be harmed in the production, exchange, and use of data. Actors from across the public sector, private sector, civil society, and academia can play an important role in demanding and encouraging agreement. One mechanism for formulating such broad agreement and formalizing a commitment to data is confirming the importance of data in countries' national development plans. Another mechanism is formulating a national data strategy—a topic discussed in greater detail in chapters 8 and 9.

Financing needs: Strengthening and sustaining financial resources for data producers

Most low-income and lower-middle-income countries severely underspend on data. Securing sustainable financing is an enduring struggle for data producers and users. To reap the full value of data for development, governments must raise current spending levels drastically. At the same time, it is painfully hard to obtain and benchmark how much governments are spending on data. Thus one priority is to improve the statistics on government spending on data.

One way to increase the priority given to financing of data is to establish a target (percentage) for the government expenditure on the national statistical system. Such a target can be derived with a view toward the resources needed to fully fund the national statistical plan or be based on the spending of peer countries that have achieved sufficient funding. If a government commits to such a target through a national development plan or through other means, it arms data producers during later budget negotiations.

Another way to implement stable and transparent government financing is to insert a line item in the national budget dedicated to the NSO. The absence of such a budget line has been a problem for even high-income countries. For example, the European Union's statistical agency, Eurostat, recently saw its budget line merged into an overarching digitization and modernization budget, raising fears that funding for

statistical needs could be at risk. Conversely, one of the biggest steps in ensuring the independence of the United Kingdom's Office for National Statistics in 2007 was giving the office authority over how it uses its budget. Similarly, data-producing ministries and other government agencies could each receive a designated budget line for the production, processing, management, and safe sharing of the administrative data they produce. Other investment priorities should be closing existing coverage gaps in vital statistics and other registers and including populations that are hard to reach.

The Ministry of Finance has a special role to play as the most influential actor in budget negotiations for government-financed producers of public intent data. Recurrent engagement with, and consequently systematic use of, public intent data and official statistics by the Ministry of Finance is also likely to improve the funding for data producers and the NSO in particular.[124] As documented in the examples earlier in this chapter, it is important that the Ministry of Finance understand that investing in data may improve budgets through increased revenue collection and elimination of duplication in beneficiaries, among other things.

Stable government financing can also be secured by ensuring that data play a role in government programs and projects. When government projects have numerical targets, data management and data analysis are a must. Where relevant, the legislature could require that government program budgets be supported or justified by evidence, necessitating the use of data and therefore funding for data. Although linking funding for data to monitoring government targets may also create disincentives in producing accurate data, resisting such disincentives must be at the core of an NSO's mission to ensure credibility of and trust in official statistics.

Sometimes the financing for data is sufficient, but the resources need to be better spent. Government funding of citizen-generated data, for example, can complement that of other public intent data and be a less costly alternative. But doing so requires that civil society data platforms have sufficient capabilities and resources for community outreach, coordination, monitoring of data collection, and quality assessments of the data.[125]

Technical capacity needs: Investing in human capital for production of public intent data

Once more and better funding is provided, investment in technical capacity is a top priority. Such an effort should start with human capital: investing in statisticians, data scientists, and applied economists across the public sector and in data literacy in the population at large. These investments would promote demand for public intent data and bolster the credibility of and trust in public intent data producers. These goals could be achieved through a combination of education and training initiatives.

Meanwhile, the public sector at large and the NSO in particular should seek qualified statisticians, applied economists, and data scientists. One way of doing so is to create a governmentwide approach to the formulation of salary scales and renumeration of the positions across the public sector, including in the NSO, the central bank, and line ministries. Such an approach could minimize differentials in salary scales within and across government agencies and subsequently create an opportunity to adopt more competitive salary scales to attract and retain talent.

A strategic area in which NSO capabilities in low- and middle-income countries could be strengthened is research on the development of improved methods and standards for data production. The capacity to conduct such methodological research is critical to improving the availability, quality, and usability of public intent data. NSOs could establish a business line on experimental statistics, which may serve as an avenue for participating in cutting-edge, multidisciplinary research efforts centered on integrating public intent and private intent data. Low-capacity NSOs, however, will have to strengthen, and in certain cases create, capabilities in data science and geographic information systems. Twinning arrangements between NSOs with established programs on experimental statistics and those beginning to build these capabilities may be one way to accelerate progress. These activities are also aligned with the call for international organizations to sustain investments in the search for improved methods of data collection, curation, and analysis (see spotlight 2.2).

Beyond NSOs, data-related capabilities in ministries and other government agencies are often insufficient. They could remedy the situation by first creating technical units in charge of data production, processing, management, and dissemination to improve data quality. These units could also develop ministry-specific action plans for capacity building, and should be empowered by receiving the financial, technological, and human resources they need to fulfill their mandated roles in the national data system. Their goal would be delivery of high-quality knowledge disseminated in accordance with a ministry-specific public release calendar.

Capacity building should also be pursued in a country's education system.[126] In line with the aspirations of SDG Target 4.6, primary and secondary educational institutions should elevate foundational numeracy and statistical literacy skills so that, like general literacy, they are part of the fundamental curricula. These skills would empower an informed public of data users and create a pool of potential candidates for specialized data professions. In tertiary education and data-driven academic fields, advanced education on statistics should be enhanced in ways that equip future technocrats with data skills that meet policy makers' demands.

An example at the country level is Politeknik Statistika, a highly selective university established by Statistics Indonesia in 1958. Politeknik Statistika awards bachelor's degrees, with an emphasis on applied training in official statistics, in preparation for statistical careers at Statistics Indonesia and the public sector at large. Examples at the regional level include the Ecole Nationale Supérieure de Statistique et d'Economie Appliquée (ENSEA) in Côte d'Ivoire and the Eastern Africa Statistical Training Center (EASTC) in Tanzania.

Degree and certificate programs with a data science theme, including those offered online, can facilitate development of statistical capacity in techniques that cut across statistics and computer science, such as artificial intelligence and machine learning. A noteworthy example is the Think Data Science Program that was launched in 2019 by the Palestinian Central Bureau of Statistics (PCBS), in partnership with the Arab American University in West Bank and Gaza. As part of this program, students have to complete a graduation project at the PCBS, which gets accredited by the Ministry of Higher Education.

Finally, investments in human capital should be accompanied by investments in physical infrastructure, IT platforms, and software capabilities (see chapter 5).

Governance needs: Making laws and regulations conducive to production and use of quality data

Effective use of public intent data depends on having in place a governmentwide national data strategy or another high-level document that outlines the roles, responsibilities, and mandates of various government agencies. Such arrangements are discussed in detail in chapters 8 and 9.

The NSO must be truly independent, impartial, and nonpolitical. Its independence should be anchored in laws and an institutional setup that curtails political interference in official statistics and other public data products.[127] Debatable is whether placement of the NSO under the executive branch of government leaves it open to attacks on its independence. On the one hand, it is important that the NSO be positioned to inform public debate and policy. But this may be difficult to achieve if the NSO is administratively separated from other parts of the government and does not maintain a close relationship with influential ministries such as the Ministry of Finance or Treasury and the Ministry of Commerce or Industry. On the other hand, reporting to a specific ministry or an individual as part of the executive branch leaves the NSO vulnerable to being questioned, pressured, or otherwise influenced in its involvement with politically sensitive statistical activities.

Another way to safeguard against the politicization of data is by making deidentified public intent datasets publicly available and accessible. Ensuring the creation and dissemination of deidentified public intent datasets is partly a political task and partly a technical one.

On the political front, the NSO and other government agencies must promote open data for development. These agencies should ensure that statistical laws and regulations permit the public dissemination of deidentified public intent data—both aggregated data and microdata. They should also actively engage with data users to cultivate a shared understanding of the value of reusing open data for research and for design and evaluation of public policy. Administrative data in particular are often not accessible beyond the ministry collecting the data.

On the technical front, safeguarding the confidentiality of subjects of public intent data production is an unconditional requirement. Confidential data include both personally identifiable information and the geographic coordinates of data subjects, including communities, households, facilities, and establishments. Although best practices, standards, and tools for microdata deidentification are available,[128] the risk of disclosure is increasing with enhancements in the interoperability of public intent data. These trends call for continued improvement of deidentification techniques. Building capabilities within technical units of ministries and NSOs in the use of analytical tools to remove sensitive information, spatially deidentify microdata, and deal responsibly with the risk of disclosure will also foster a better culture of open data.

Data demand needs: Expanding the use of public intent data

The precondition for the widespread use and reuse of data is greater data literacy among the citizenry at large and government decision-makers. The integrity of and public trust in official statistics are also critical to the demand for data. The integrity of official statistics is closely tied to the perceived independence and trustworthiness of the NSO. Existing best practices can ensure integrity of and trust in the computation of official statistics and the timing of their release, even in the face of political pressures. A first set of practices centers on effective outreach and communication about NSO products. These practices include publishing a release calendar and providing a public explanation of potential deviations from release dates, as well as publicly disseminating meticulous documentation and metadata allowing findings to be replicated. Other best practices include refraining from participating in national politics and carrying out periodic outreach efforts to cultivate public understanding and acceptance of the importance of an independent statistical agency.

NSOs could also increase use of and demand for their data by engaging proactively with and listening to stakeholders in government, academia, the private sector, CSOs, and the media.[129] These engagements may have multiple objectives such as disseminating statistical outputs, understanding and responding to user needs, exploring links between NSO data products and other data, and strengthening statistical literacy. Statistics Canada, Statistics Indonesia, and Mexico's National Institute of Statistics and Geography (INEGI) have engaged in recurrent training of journalists in print, radio, television, and digital media outlets on official statistics. INEGI has expanded its work program on data and statistics related to crime and victimization in Mexico in response to the growing demands from policy makers and data users. Elsewhere, the Palestinian Central Bureau of Statistics regularly disseminates official statistics on important international observances, such as International Workers' Day and International Women's Day.

Closely involving civil society in the use and production of data is critical. This involvement can be achieved by establishing advisory boards composed of independent technical experts who can help prepare national statistical strategies in view of the needs of all users—not only the needs of various government agencies.

Data visualization is another way in which NSOs could increase the reach of official statistics and the public's understanding of them. It does little good to achieve greater mastery of advanced analytics without also ensuring that the policy makers designing and enacting interventions that improve lives understand and appreciate the value added by data.[130] Distilling complex phenomena into compelling visuals and narratives for broad audiences is a timeless idea that can effectively influence public debate and policy making (for a pioneering example, see box 1.2 in chapter 1).

From the perspective of government ministries and agencies, one way to jump-start data use in planning and policy making is through the institutionalized adoption of data-intensive management practices. In Rwanda, as part of the nationwide Imihigo performance contracts launched in 2006, mayors commit to setting development targets. Each target is subsequently evaluated and ranked by the national government with respect to its achievement and whether it was monitored appropriately.[131] Management of these contracts not only requires large amounts of data to evaluate performance, but, more important, puts data on development outcomes at the center of the policy discourse.[132]

When low data literacy or appreciation of data are barriers to their use, knowledge brokers can facilitate data use in the public sector. A knowledge broker points policy makers to the relevant data and creates value through collaboration.[133] The important role of knowledge brokers is highlighted by evidence from a survey conducted by AidData: policy makers reported that they learn about sources of data primarily through personal interactions.[134]

The role of knowledge broker can be fulfilled by government officials and by outsiders. Central analytical units and technical staff in line ministries can serve as intermediaries for NSOs seeking to reach senior officials and increase data use, presenting data in both technical and nontechnical ways tailored to the needs of decision-makers.[135] Another useful technique is joint analytical exercises by the government and researchers. Collaboration between external researchers and policy makers is a major facilitator of the use of evidence and data.[136]

If governments address these financing, human capital, governance, and data demand roadblocks, the value of public intent data can be maximized. Chapter 9 discusses sequencing of the required government interventions, placing such activities within an integrated national data system. Another way in which data can lead to better lives is via the private sector. That is the topic of the next chapter.

Notes

1. Unfortunately, in some contexts this scenario is not too far from reality. For example, Das and Hammer (2007) found that doctors in New Delhi often perform only a fraction of the recommended examinations and tests when patients present with common yet dangerous health conditions.
2. As just one example, in Ethiopia a 2016 study by Rogger and Somani (2018) surveying 1,831 officials of 382 organizations spanning three tiers of government revealed officials' significant lack of knowledge about their area of work. Half thought that their district's population was at least 50 percent larger or smaller than it was. Government staff in the educational sector were on average 38 percent off when estimating primary enrollment figures.
3. Cameron et al. (2019).
4. See chapter 1 for more information on the distinction between public intent data and private intent data, chapter 3 for a discussion of private intent data, and chapter 4 for a discussion of how both kinds of data can be repurposed.
5. See Jolliffe et al. (forthcoming) for a lengthier discussion of these 12 features of public intent data and examples of how they can generate value for development.
6. World Bank (2018d).
7. SDSN TReNDS (2018b); SSEE (2014).
8. Hallegatte et al. (2017).
9. SDSN TReNDS (2018a).
10. J-PAL (2018).
11. Hjort et al. (2019).
12. Arezki et al. (2020), for example, show that imprecise definitions of employment in the Middle East and North Africa blur the lines between unemployment and informality and distort the role of women and rural areas in national labor markets.
13. The World Bank LSMS team provided the number of countries in which LSMS-supported survey data production took place from 2011 to 2020.
14. Abay et al. (2019); Arthi et al. (2018); Carletto, Gourlay, and Winters (2015); Carletto, Savastano, and Zezza (2013); Carletto et al. (2017); De Weerdt, Gibson, and Beegle (2019); Desiere and Jolliffe (2018); Dillon et al. (2019); Gaddis et al. (2019); Gourlay, Kilic, and Lobell (2019); Kilic et al. (2017, 2018).
15. World Bank (2016a, 2017a).
16. The EU uses a Nomenclature of Territorial Units for Statistics, known as NUTS, for the purpose of allocating funds. Many EU countries have a hierarchy of three NUTS levels. The second level, NUTS 2, is used for allocation of funds. In the accompanying text, NUTS 2 is referred to as areas.
17. Government of Croatia (2019).
18. Open Data Watch (2015b).
19. Data2x (2019).

20. McCluskey and Huang (2019) and unpublished notes shared with the WDR 2021 team. The 30 percent refers to own-source revenue collection—that is, the part of the revenue collection that the cities themselves oversee in contrast to revenue they receive from national authorities and more.

21. World Bank (2018c). See also World Bank (2020b).

22. Roseth, Reyes, and Amézaga (2019) and references cited therein provide evidence of an up-to-date census generating savings to the government many times its cost. The value of public intent data to the private sector is discussed in spotlight 3.1 and elsewhere.

23. The SDG on clean water and sanitation relies on a mix of household surveys, population and housing censuses, and administrative data (SDSN 2015). Earth observation data are used for the SDGs on sustainable cities and communities, life below water, life on land, and more (Anderson et al. 2017). Citizen-generated data are often used when government data are missing and to verify government data (Lämmerhirt et al. 2018). In the Philippines, for example, the NSO identified more than 80 relevant SDG indicators where data are missing and CSOs could provide inputs through community-based monitoring systems (PARIS21 and PSA 2020).

24. MPPN (2017).

25. Yin et al. (2020). See World Air Quality Index Project, World's Air Pollution: Real-Time Air Quality Index (database), https://waqi.info/, and OpenAQ, OpenAQ (database), https://openaq.org/, for publicly available, real-time data from air quality monitoring stations around the globe, including those in China.

26. Open Data Watch (2015a).

27. Bosio and Djankov (2020).

28. AFIC (2018); GPSA (2020).

29. World Bank (2017c).

30. Callen et al. (2019). Petrov, Gurin, and Manley (2016) and Verhulst and Young (2017) contain many other examples and channels through which open data may lead to better development outcomes.

31. Safetipin (2016).

32. Fabregas, Kremer, and Schilbach (2019).

33. For example, in several high-profile cases researchers have been able to reidentify individuals from publicly available microdata, even though the data had been published in a deidentified fashion (Heffetz and Ligett 2014).

34. Díaz (2018); Fundación Reflejos de Venezuela (2016); Privacy International (2019). LGBTQI stands for lesbian, gay, bisexual, transgender, queer (or questioning), intersex.

35. Open Data Watch, ODIN (Open Data Inventory) (database), https://odin.opendatawatch.com/; Open Knowledge Foundation, GODI (Global Open Data Index) (database), https://index.okfn.org/.

36. WDR 2021 team calculations based on 2019 Statistical Performance Indicators (World Bank, Statistical Performance Indicators [database], http://www.worldbank.org /spi). As of December 2014, 21 countries had not completed a census during the 2010 round of the population and housing census (Statistics Division, Department of Economic and Social Affairs, United Nations, World Population and Housing Census Programme [database], http://mdgs.un.org/unsd/demographic-social /census/index.cshtml).

37. See estimates in, for example, Roseth, Reyes, and Amézaga (2019) and references cited therein.

38. WDR 2021 team calculations based on 2019 Statistical Capacity Indicators (World Bank, Statistical Capacity Indicators [database], https://datatopics.worldbank .org/statisticalcapacity/SCIdashboard.aspx).

39. López-Vargas, Fuentes, and Vivar (2020).

40. WDR 2021 team calculations based on 2019 Statistical Performance Indicators (World Bank, Statistical Performance Indicators [database], http://www.worldbank .org/spi).

41. Desai, Diofasi, and Lu (2018); World Bank, Global ID4D Dataset (Identification for Development Global Dataset) (database), https://datacatalog.worldbank.org /dataset/identification-development-global-dataset.

42. United Nations (2019b).

43. Carr-Hill (2013); Randall (2015); Seltzer and Walker (2020); Toulemon (2017).

44. Carr-Hill (2013).

45. Jerven (2019).

46. Where vital registration systems function well, administrative records can be used to update census population counts. But these systems are weak in lower-income countries. Gaps in registration will likely leave out more vulnerable people than the census, especially seasonal migrants and the displaced (Dunning, Gelb, and Raghavan 2014). The use of administrative records from nongovernment actors can supplement official records.

47. Maron (2015).

48. UN Women (2018). Gender-specific SDG indicators are those that explicitly call for disaggregation by sex or that refer to gender equality as the underlying objective.

49. Doss, Kieran, and Kilic (2020). Administrative recording of land titles can serve the function of documenting asset ownership at the individual level. However, land and property ownership registries are among the less developed administrative recording systems globally. According to the Global Open Data Index, these data are available in less than one-quarter of countries, even in high-income nations, and are rarely openly available.

50. World Bank (2017b). Advances have been made in intrahousehold poverty estimation based on structural models and existing household survey data—that is, clothing expenditures for women, men, and children (Lechene, Pendakur, and Wolf 2019). The predictions provided by these models, however, have yet to be validated in the context of randomized survey experiments that collect detailed, individual-disaggregated consumption data that can, in turn, be used to compute observed estimates of intrahousehold poverty among women, men, and children. These observed estimates can, in turn, be compared with predictions stemming from structural models, based on the data elicited through prevailing approaches to household survey data collection.

51. Tiberti and Costa (2020); UN Women (2018). Similarly, individual-disaggregated data on time use are required to monitor SDG Target 5.4. Yet of the 84 countries known to have conducted time use surveys in the past, only 24 percent of them have collected data since 2010.

52. Ambler et al. (2020); Bardasi et al. (2011); Chen and Collins (2014); Deere, Alvarado, and Twyman (2012); Fisher, Reimer, and Carr (2010); Jacobs and Kes (2015); Kilic and Moylan (2016); Kilic, Moylan, and Koolwal (2020); Kilic et al. (2020).

53. See de Mel, McKenzie, and Woodruff (2009); de Nicola and Giné (2014); Gibson and Kim (2010).

54. Arthi et al. (2018); Das, Hammer, and Sánchez-Paramo (2012); Deininger et al. (2012); Gaddis et al. (2019); Kilic et al. (2018); Wollburg, Tiberti, and Zezza (2020).

55. Sandefur and Glassman (2015).

56. Sandefur and Glassman (2015).

57. Karagulian et al. (2019).

58. Antony et al. (2020); Morawska et al. (2018).

59. Similar findings were reported in Beegle et al. (2016).

60. See Hoogeveen and Pape (2020) for more information on such innovations. The last two poverty data points are comparable in 60 percent of countries in FCS and in 75 percent of low-income and Sub-Saharan African countries.

61. FMOH (2018).

62. CTO (2018).

63. Custer and Sethi (2017); Kiregyera (2017).

64. However, under secure circumstances authorized third-party researchers can be allowed to match individual-level records across multiple data sources to generate insights that rely on individual-level matching.

65. Privacy by design refers to proactively embedding privacy considerations in the design of information technology and data systems. See examples from Austria, Estonia, and India covered in *ID4D Practitioner's Guide: Version 1.0* (World Bank 2019b).

66. WDR 2021 team calculations based on the 2019 Statistical Performance Indicators (World Bank, Statistical Performance Indicators [database], http://www.worldbank.org/spi).

67. Katsimi and Moutos (2010).

68. Heffetz and Ligett (2014).

69. In particular, the team had discussions with the NSOs of Canada, Chile, Ethiopia, India, Indonesia, Mexico, the United Kingdom, and West Bank and Gaza.

70. See United Nations (2019b) for similar findings.

71. Calleja and Rogerson (2019). McQueston (2013) found similar results.

72. Dargent et al. (2020); OECD (2017).

73. United Nations (2019b).

74. UNESCO (2016); WHO (2011).

75. PARIS21 (2020).

76. Calleja and Rogerson (2019).

77. Sethi and Prakash (2018).

78. Calleja and Rogerson (2019). National governments also tend to prioritize covering ongoing expenses for collecting data over onetime investments in systems.

79. Lange (2020).

80. Calleja and Rogerson (2019); Sandefur and Glassman (2015); World Bank (2018a).

81. Sanna and McDonnell (2017).

82. Piovesan (2015).

83. Antony et al. (2020); Hosman (2014); López-Vargas, Fuentes, and Vivar (2020); Pham, Rahim, and Cousin (2016).

84. Allard et al. (2018).

85. PARIS21 (2018).

86. PARIS21 (2018).

87. Dargent et al. (2020).

88. Allard et al. (2018); Johnson, Massey, and O'Hara (2015).

89. Fu and Schweinfest (2020); UNSTATS and World Bank (2020).

90. PARIS21 (2018).

91. Lämmerhirt et al. (2018).

92. OECD (2019).

93. Allard et al. (2018).

94. Calleja and Rogerson (2019); Khan, Wales, and Stuart (2015).

95. OECD (2019).

96. Amnesty International (2019); Privacy International (2013); United Nations (2019a).

97. Van Belle et al. (2018).

98. Amnesty International (2019); Privacy International (2013); United Nations (2019a).

99. Independence of the national statistical system underpins the UN Statistical Commission's 1994 Fundamental Principles of Official Statistics. The commission highlighted its concern for independence in its 2015 *United Nations Fundamental Principles of Official Statistics: Implementation Guidelines* (UNSTATS 2015).

100. Childs et al. (2019); Taylor (2016).

101. Mo Ibrahim Foundation, Ibrahim Index of African Governance (IIAG) (database), http://mo.ibrahim.foundation/iiag/.

102. Bodin (2011); Todesca (2017); Trewin (2018); von Oppeln-Bronikowski et al. (2015).

103. Todesca (2017).

104. Hoogeveen and Nguyen (2019); Taylor (2016); World Bank (2016b, 2017c).

105. Desiere, Staelens, D'Haese (2016); Jerven (2014).

106. Brackfield (2012); World Bank (2018a).

107. Arezki et al. (2020); Cady (2005); Cady and Pellechio (2006); Kubota and Zeufack (2020).

108. Dargent et al. (2020).

109. See Reporters Wthout Borders, 2020 World Press Freedom Index (database), https://rsf.org/en/ranking_table.

110. World Bank (2016b, 2018a).

111. Klein, Galdin, and Mohamedou (2016).

112. Custer and Sethi (2017); Kiregyera (2017).

113. WDR 2021 team based on information in World Bank, "Literacy Rate, Adult Total (% of People Ages 15 and Above)," https://data.worldbank.org/indicator/se.adt.litr.zs.

114. World Bank (2017c).

115. Manning, Goldman, and Hernández Licona (2020).

116. Hoogeveen and Nguyen (2019).

117. Sethi and Prakash (2018).

118. Custer and Sethi (2017); World Bank (2018a).
119. Custer and Sethi (2017); Kiregyera (2017).
120. ITU (2016); López-Vargas, Fuentes, and Vivar (2020); Pham, Rahim, and Cousin (2016).
121. Dargent et al. (2020).
122. Dargent et al. (2020).
123. Scott (2005).
124. World Bank (2019a).
125. Lämmerhirt et al. (2018).
126. OECD (2017).
127. Bodin (2011); Todesca (2017); Trewin (2018); von Oppeln-Bronikowski et al. (2015).
128. For more information on resources and tools related to the anonymization of microdata, see World Bank and PARIS21 Consortium, Microdata Anonymization (database), International Household Survey Network, PARIS21 Consortium, https://ihsn.org/anonymization.
129. Snorrason (2018).
130. Ashby (2019).
131. World Bank (2018b).
132. Krätke and Byiers (2014).
133. Head (2016); Manning, Goldman, and Hernández Licona (2020).
134. Masaki et al. (2017).
135. Sethi and Prakash (2018).
136. Oliver et al. (2014).

References

Abay, Kibrom A., Gashaw T. Abate, Christopher B. Barrett, and Tanguy Bernard. 2019. "Correlated Non-Classical Measurement Errors, 'Second Best' Policy Inference, and the Inverse Size-Productivity Relationship in Agriculture." *Journal of Development Economics* 139 (June): 171–84. https://doi.org/10.1016/j.jdeveco.2019.03.008.

AFIC (Africa Freedom of Information Center). 2018. "Eyes on the Contract: Citizens' Voice in Improving the Performance of Public Contracts in Uganda." 2nd Monitoring Report, AFIC, Kampala, Uganda. https://africafoicentre .org/download/eyes-on-the-contract-citizens-voice -in-improving-the-performance-of-public-contracts-in -uganda/.

Allard, Scott W., Emily R. Wiegand, Collen Schlecht, A. Rupa Datta, Robert M. Goerge, and Elizabeth Weigensberg. 2018. "State Agencies' Use of Administrative Data for Improved Practice: Needs, Challenges, and Opportunities." *Public Administration Review* 78 (2): 240–50.

Ambler, Kate, Cheryl Doss, Caitlin Kieran, and Simone Passarelli. 2020. "He Says, She Says: Exploring Patterns of Spousal Agreement in Bangladesh." *Economic Development and Cultural Change*. Published ahead of print, November 16. https://doi.org/10.1086/703082.

Amnesty International. 2019. "New Technologies and Their Impact on the Promotion and Protection of Human Rights in the Context of Assemblies: Submission to the Office of the United Nations High Commissioner for Human Rights," Amnesty International, London. https://www.amnesty.org/download/Documents /IOR4012842019ENGLISH.pdf.

Anderson, Katherine, Barbara Ryan, William Sonntag, Argyro Kavvada, and Lawrence Friedl. 2017. "Earth Observation in Service of the 2030 Agenda for Sustainable Development." *Geo-Spatial Information Science* 20 (2): 77–96.

Antony, Anish Paul, Kendra Leith, Craig Jolley, Jennifer Lu, and Daniel J. Sweeney. 2020. "A Review of Practice and Implementation of the Internet of Things (IoT) for Smallholder Agriculture." *Sustainability* 12 (9): 3750.

Arezki, Rabah, Daniel Lederman, Amani Abou Harb, Nelly Youssef, Louis William El-Mallakh, Rachel Yuting Fan, Asif Mohammed Islam, et al. 2020. "Middle East and North Africa Economic Update, April 2020: How Transparency Can Help the Middle East and North Africa." World Bank Other Operational Studies 33475, World Bank, Washington, DC.

Arthi, Vellore, Kathleen Beegle, Joachim De Weerdt, and Amparo Palacios-López. 2018. "Not Your Average Job: Measuring Farm Labor in Tanzania." *Journal of Development Economics* 130 (January): 160–72.

Ashby, Deborah. 2019. "Pigeonholes and Mustard Seeds: Growing Capacity to Use Data for Society." *Journal of the Royal Statistical Society: Series A (Statistics in Society)* 182 (4): 1121–37.

Bardasi, Elana, Kathleen Beegle, Andrew Dillon, and Pieter Serneels. 2011. "Do Labor Statistics Depend on How and to Whom the Questions Are Asked? Results from a Survey Experiment in Tanzania." *World Bank Economic Review* 25 (3): 418–47.

Beegle, Kathleen, Luc Christiaensen, Andrew L. Dabalen, and Isis Gaddis. 2016. *Poverty in a Rising Africa.* Africa Poverty Report. Washington, DC: World Bank.

Bodin, Jean-Louis. 2011. "How to React When the Independence of Statisticians and the Integrity of Statistics Are Endangered?" *Statistical Journal of the IAOS* 27 (1–2): 59–69.

Bosio, Erica, and Simeon Djankov. 2020. "How Large Is Public Procurement?" *Let's Talk Development* (blog), February 5, 2020. https://blogs.worldbank.org/developmenttalk /how-large-public-procurement.

Brackfield, David. 2012. "OECD Work on Measuring Trust in Official Statistics." *Bulletin of the ISI 58th World Statistics Congress of the International Statistical Institute, 2011* (December 2012): 3721–26. The Hague, Netherlands: International Statistical Institute.

Buvinic, Mayra, Lorenz Noe, and Eric Swanson. 2020. "Understanding Women's and Girls' Vulnerabilities to the COVID-19 Pandemic: A Gender Analysis and Data Dashboard of Low- and Lower-Middle Income Countries." Data2x, United Nations Foundation, Washington, DC.

Cady, John. 2005. "Does SDDS Subscription Reduce Borrowing Costs for Emerging Market Economies?" *IMF Staff Papers* 52 (3): 503–17.

Cady, John, and Anthony J. Pellechio. 2006. "Sovereign Borrowing Cost and the IMF's Data Standards Initiatives." IMF Working Paper WP/06/78, International Monetary Fund, Washington, DC.

Calleja, Rachel, and Andrew Rogerson. 2019. "Financing Challenges for Developing Statistical Systems: A

Review of Financing Options." PARIS21 Discussion Paper 14, Partnership in Statistics for Development in the 21st Century, Paris.

Callen, Michael, Saad Gulzar, Ali Hasanain, Muhammad Yasir Khan, and Arman Rezaee. 2019. "Data and Policy Decisions: Experimental Evidence from Pakistan." King Center on Global Development Working Paper 1055, Stanford University, Stanford, CA.

Cameron, Grant James, Hai-Anh H. Dang, Mustafa Dinc, James Stephen Foster, and Michael M. Lokshin. 2019. "Measuring the Statistical Capacity of Nations." Policy Research Working Paper 8693, World Bank, Washington, DC.

Carletto, Calogero, Sydney Gourlay, Siobhan Murray, and Alberto Zezza. 2017. "Cheaper, Faster, and More Than Good Enough: Is GPS the New Gold Standard in Land Area Measurement?" *Survey Research Methods* 11 (3): 235–65.

Carletto, Calogero, Sydney Gourlay, and Paul Winters. 2015. "From Guesstimates to GPStimates: Land Area Measurement and Implications for Agricultural Analysis." *Journal of African Economies* 24 (5): 593–628.

Carletto, Calogero, Sydney Savastano, and Alberto Zezza. 2013. "Fact or Artifact: The Impact of Measurement Errors on the Farm Size–Productivity Relationship." *Journal of Development Economics* 103 (July): 254–61.

Carr-Hill, Roy. 2013. "Missing Millions and Measuring Development Progress." *World Development* 46 (June): 30–44.

Chen, J. Joyce, and LaPorchia A. Collins. 2014. "Let's Talk about the Money: Spousal Communication, Expenditures, and Farm Production." *American Journal of Agricultural Economics* 96 (5): 1272–90.

Childs, Jennifer Hunter, Aleia Clark Fobia, Ryan King, and Gerson Morales. 2019. "Trust and Credibility in the US Federal Statistical System." *Survey Methods: Insights from the Field*, February 22. https://surveyinsights.org/?p=10663.

CTO (Office of the Chief Technology Officer, US Department of Health and Human Services). 2018. "The State of Data Sharing at the US Department of Health and Human Services." US Department of Health and Human Services, Washington, DC. https://www.hhs.gov/sites/default/files/HHS_StateofDataSharing_0915.pdf.

Custer, Samantha, and Tanya Sethi, eds. 2017. "Avoiding Data Graveyards: Insights from Data Producers and Users in Three Countries." AidData, Global Research Institute, College of William and Mary, Williamsburg, VA.

Dang, Hai-Anh, Mustafa Dinc, Juderica Diaz, Hiroko Maeda, John Pullinger, Umar Serajuddin, Brian Stacy, et al. 2021a. "Measuring the Statistical Performance of Countries: An Overview of Updates to the World Bank Statistical Capacity Index." World Bank, Washington, DC.

Dang, Hai-Anh, John Pullinger, Umar Serajuddin, and Brian Stacy. 2021b. "Statistical Performance Index: A New Tool to Measure Country Statistical Capacity." Policy Research Working Paper, World Bank, Washington, DC.

Dargent, Eduardo, Gabriela Lotta, José Antonio Mejía-Guerra, and Gilberto Moncada. 2020. "Who Wants to Know? The Political Economy of Statistical Capacity

in Latin America." Inter-American Development Bank, Washington, DC.

Das, Jishnu, and Jeffrey Hammer. 2007. "Money for Nothing: The Dire Straits of Medical Practice in Delhi, India." *Journal of Development Economics* 83 (1): 1–36.

Das, Jishnu, Jeffery Hammer, and Carolina Sánchez-Paramo. 2012. "The Impact of Recall Periods on Reported Morbidity and Health Seeking Behavior." *Journal of Development Economics* 98 (May): 76–88.

Data2x. 2019. "Data Breaks the Silence on Violence against Women: A Case Study of Vietnam." Gender Data Impact Case Study, United Nations Foundation, Washington, DC. https://data2x.org/wp-content/uploads/2020/02/Impact-Case-Studies-Vietnam-4P.pdf.

Deere, Carmen Diana, Gina E. Alvarado, and Jennifer Twyman. 2012. "Gender Inequality in Asset Ownership in Latin America: Female Owners vs Household Heads." *Development and Change* 43 (2): 505–30.

Deininger, Klaus, Calogero Carletto, Sara Savastano, and James Muwonge. 2012. "Can Diaries Help in Improving Agricultural Production Statistics? Evidence from Uganda." *Journal of Development Economics* 98 (May): 42–50.

de Mel, Suresh, David J. McKenzie, and Christopher M. Woodruff. 2009. "Measuring Microenterprise Profits: Must We Ask How the Sausage Is Made?" *Journal of Development Economics* 88 (1): 19–31.

de Nicola, Francesca, and Xavier Giné. 2014. "How Accurate Are Recall Data? Evidence from Coastal India." *Journal of Development Economics* 106 (January): 52–65.

Desai, Vyjayanti T., Anna Diofasi, and Jing Lu. 2018. "The Global Identification Challenge: Who Are the 1 Billion People without Proof of Identity?" *Voices* (blog), April 25, 2018. https://blogs.worldbank.org/voices/global-identification-challenge-who-are-1-billion-people-without-proof-identity.

Desiere, Sam, and Dean Mitchell Jolliffe. 2018. "Land Productivity and Plot Size: Is Measurement Error Driving the Inverse Relationship?" *Journal of Development Economics* 130 (January): 84–98. https://doi.org/10.1016/j.jdeveco.2017.10.002.

Desiere, Sam, Lotte Staelens, and Marijke D'Haese. 2016. "When the Data Source Writes the Conclusion: Evaluating Agricultural Policies." *Journal of Development Studies* 52 (9): 1372–87.

De Weerdt, Joachim, John Gibson, and Kathleen Beegle. 2019. "What Can We Learn from Experimenting with Survey Methods?" LICOS Discussion Paper 418, LICOS Center for Institutions and Economic Performance, Faculty of Economics and Business, Katholieke Universiteit Leuven, Leuven, Belgium.

Díaz, Marianne. 2018. "El Cuerpo Como Dato." @Derechos-Digitales América Latina, Santiago, Chile. https://www.derechosdigitales.org/wp-content/uploads/cuerpo_DATO.pdf.

Dillon, Andrew, Sydney Gourlay, Kevin McGee, and Gbemisola Oseni. 2019. "Land Measurement Bias and Its Empirical Implications: Evidence from a Validation Exercise." *Economic Development and Cultural Change* 67 (3): 595–624.

Doss, Cheryl Renee, Caitlin Kieran, and Talip Kilic. 2020. "Measuring Ownership, Control, and Use of Assets." *Feminist Economics* 26 (3): 144–68.

Dunning, Casey, Alan Gelb, and Sneha Raghavan. 2014. "Birth Registration, Legal Identity, and the Post-2015 Agenda." CGD Policy Paper 046, Center for Global Development, Washington, DC.

Fabregas, Raissa, Michael M. Kremer, and Frank Schilbach. 2019. "Realizing the Potential of Digital Development: The Case of Agricultural Advice." *Science* 366 (6471): eaay3038.

Fisher, Monica, Jeffrey J. Reimer, and Edward R. Carr. 2010. "Who Should Be Interviewed in Surveys of Household Income?" *World Development* 38 (7): 966–73.

FMOH (Federal Ministry of Health, Ethiopia). 2018. *eHealth Apps Inventory*. Addis Ababa: FMOH.

Fu, Haishan, and Stefan Schweinfest. 2020. "COVID-19 Widens Gulf of Global Data Inequality, While National Statistical Offices Step Up to Meet New Data Demands." *Data Blog*, June 5, 2020. https://blogs.worldbank.org/opendata/covid-19-widens-gulf-global-data-inequality-while-national-statistical-offices-step-up.

Fundación Reflejos de Venezuela. 2016. "El drama de ser transgénero e intentar comprar en un supermercado." Fundación Reflejos de Venezuela, Caracas.

Gaddis, Isis, Gbemisola Oseni, Amparo Palacios-López, and Janneke Pieters. 2019. "Measuring Farm Labor: Survey Experimental Evidence from Ghana." Policy Research Working Paper 8717, World Bank, Washington, DC.

Gibson, John, and Bonggeun Kim. 2010. "Non-Classical Measurement Error in Long-Term Retrospective Recall Surveys." *Oxford Bulletin of Economics and Statistics* 72 (5): 687–95.

Gourlay, Sydney, Talip Kilic, and David B. Lobell. 2019. "A New Spin on an Old Debate: Errors in Farmer-Reported Production and Their Implications for the Inverse Scale–Productivity Relationship in Uganda." *Journal of Development Economics* 141 (November): 1–35. https://www.sciencedirect.com/science/article/pii/S0304387818306588.

Government of Croatia. 2019. "Gov't Launches Changes to Country's Statistical Subdivision." News release, January 23. https://vlada.gov.hr/news/gov-t-launches-changes-to-country-s-statistical-subdivision/25178.

GPSA (Global Partnership for Social Accountability). 2020. "Making Public Contracts Work for People: Experiences from Uganda." GPSA, World Bank, Washington, DC. https://www.thegpsa.org/stories/making-public-contracts-work-people-experiences-uganda.

Hallegatte, Stéphane, Adrien Vogt-Schilb, Mook Bangalore, and Julie Rozenberg. 2017. *Unbreakable: Building the Resilience of the Poor in the Face of Natural Disasters*. Climate Change and Development Series. Washington, DC: World Bank.

Head, Brian W. 2016. "Toward More 'Evidence-Informed' Policy Making?" *Public Administration Review* 76 (3): 472–84.

Heffetz, Ori, and Katrina Ligett. 2014. "Privacy and Data-Based Research." *Journal of Economic Perspectives* 28 (2): 75–98.

Hjort, Jonas, Diana Moreira, Gautam Rao, and Juan Francisco Santini. 2019. "How Research Affects Policy: Experimental Evidence from 2,150 Brazilian Municipalities." NBER Working Paper 25941, National Bureau of Economic Research, Cambridge, MA.

Hoogeveen, Johannes, and Nga Thi Viet Nguyen. 2019. "Statistics Reform in Africa: Aligning Incentives with Results." *Journal of Development Studies* 55 (4): 702–19.

Hoogeveen, Johannes, and Utz Pape, eds. 2020. *Data Collection in Fragile States: Innovations from Africa and Beyond*. Cham, Switzerland: Palgrave Macmillan.

Hosman, Laura. 2014. "Emerging Markets: Top ICT Hardware Challenges." Inveneo, San Francisco.

ITU (International Telecommunication Union). 2016. "Harnessing the Internet of Things for Global Development." ITU, Geneva. https://www.itu-ilibrary.org/science-and-technology/harnessing-the-internet-of-things-for-global-development_pub/80d1ac90-en.

Jacobs, Krista, and Aslihan Kes. 2015. "The Ambiguity of Joint Asset Ownership: Cautionary Tales from Uganda and South Africa." *Feminist Economics* 21 (3): 23–55.

Jerven, Morten. 2014. "The Political Economy of Agricultural Statistics and Input Subsidies: Evidence from India, Nigeria, and Malawi." *Journal of Agrarian Change* 14 (1): 129–45.

Jerven, Morten. 2019. "The Problems of Economic Data in Africa." In *Oxford Research Encyclopedia of Politics*. Oxford, UK: Oxford University Press. https://doi.org/10.1093/acrefore/9780190228637.013.748.

Johnson, David S., Catherine Massey, and Amy O'Hara. 2015. "The Opportunities and Challenges of Using Administrative Data Linkages to Evaluate Mobility." *Annals of the American Academy of Political and Social Science* 657 (1): 247–64.

Jolliffe, Dean, Talip Kilic, Daniel Gerszon Mahler, and Philip Randolph Wollburg. Forthcoming. "Under What Conditions Are Data Valuable for Development?" WDR 2021 background paper, World Bank, Washington, DC.

J-PAL (Abdul Latif Jameel Poverty Action Lab). 2018. "Annual Report 2018 and a Look Ahead to 2019." J-PAL, Massachusetts Institute of Technology, Cambridge, MA. https://www.povertyactionlab.org/sites/default/files/2018-annual-report-web-ready.pdf.

Karagulian, Federico, Maurizio Barbiere, Alexander Kotsev, Laurent Spinelle, Michel Gerboles, Friedrich Lagler, Nathalie Redon, et al. 2019. "Review of the Performance of Low-Cost Sensors for Air Quality Monitoring." *Atmosphere* 10 (9): 506.

Katsimi, Margarita, and Thomas Moutos. 2010. "EMU and the Greek Crisis: The Political-Economy Perspective." *European Journal of Political Economy* 26 (4): 568–76. https://doi.org/10.1016/j.ejpoleco.2010.08.002.

Khan, Amina, Joseph Wales, and Elizabeth Stuart. 2015. "Country Priorities for Data Development: What Does History Tell Us?" Report, Overseas Development Institute, London. https://www.odi.org/sites/odi.org.uk/files/odi-assets/publications-opinion-files/9695.pdf.

Kilic, Talip, and Heather G. Moylan. 2016. "Methodological Experiment on Measuring Asset Ownership from a

Gender Perspective (MEXA)." Technical Report, World Bank, Washington, DC.

Kilic, Talip, Heather G. Moylan, John Ilukor, Clement Mtengula, and Innocent Pangapanga-Phiri. 2018. "Root for the Tubers: Extended-Harvest Crop Production and Productivity Measurement in Surveys." Policy Research Working Paper 8618, World Bank, Washington, DC.

Kilic, Talip, Heather G. Moylan, and Gayatri B. Koolwal. 2020. "Getting the (Gender-Disaggregated) Lay of the Land: Impact of Survey Respondent Selection on Measuring Land Ownership." Policy Research Working Paper 9151, World Bank, Washington, DC.

Kilic, Talip, Goedele Van den Broeck, Gayatri B. Koolwal, and Heather G. Moylan. 2020. "Are You Being Asked? Impacts of Respondent Selection on Measuring Employment." Policy Research Working Paper 9152, World Bank, Washington, DC.

Kilic, Talip, Alberto Zezza, Calogero Carletto, and Sara Savastano. 2017. "Missing(ness) in Action: Selectivity Bias in GPS-Based Land Area Measurements." *World Development* 92 (April): 143–57.

Kiregyera, Ben. 2017. "Supporting Implementation of Fundamental Principles of Official Statistics in the African Region." *Statistical Journal of the IAOS* 33 (4): 863–67.

Klein, Thilo, Anaïs Galdin, and El Iza Mohamedou. 2016. "An Indicator for Statistical Literacy Based on National Newspaper Archives." Paper presented at International Association of Statistics Education's 2016 Roundtable Conference, "Promoting Understanding of Statistics about Society," Berlin, July 19–22, 2016. http://iase-web .org/Conference_Proceedings.php?p=Promoting _Understanding_of_Statistics_about_Society_2016.

Krätke, Florian, and Bruce Byiers. 2014. "The Political Economy of Official Statistics: Implications for the Data Revolution in Sub-Saharan Africa." PARIS21 Discussion Paper 5, Partnership in Statistics for Development in the 21st Century, Paris. http://ecdpm.org/wp-content/uploads /DP-170-Political-Economy-Official-Statistics-Africa -December-2014.pdf.

Kubota, Megumi, and Albert Zeufack. 2020. "Assessing the Returns on Investment in Data Openness and Transparency." Policy Research Working Paper 9139, World Bank, Washington, DC.

Lämmerhirt, Danny, Jonathan Gray, Tommaso Venturini, and Axel Meunier. 2018. "Advancing Sustainability Together? Citizen-Generated Data and the Sustainable Development Goals." Global Partnership for Sustainable Development Data, United Nations, New York. http://www .data4sdgs.org/resources/advancing-sustainability -together-citizen-generated-data-and-sustainable -development.

Lange, Simon. 2020. "Key Trends in Development Cooperation for National Data and Statistical Systems." OECD Development Policy Paper 31, Organisation for Economic Co-operation and Development, Paris.

Lechene, Valérie, Krishna Pendakur, and Alex Wolf. 2019. "OLS Estimation of the Intra-Household Distribution of Consumption." IFS Working Paper W19/19, Institute for Fiscal Studies, London.

López-Vargas, Ascensión, Manuel Fuentes, and Marta Vivar. 2020. "Challenges and Opportunities of the Internet of Things for Global Development to Achieve the United Nations Sustainable Development Goals." *IEEE Access* 8: 37202–13.

Manning, Richard, Ian Goldman, and Gonzalo Hernández Licona. 2020. "The Impact of Impact Evaluation." UNU-WIDER Working Paper 2020/20, United Nations University–World Institute for Development Economics Research, Helsinki.

Maron, Mikel. 2015. "How Complete Is OpenStreetMap?" *Mapbox* (blog), November 19, 2015. https://blog.mapbox .com/how-complete-is-openstreetmap-7c369787af6e.

Masaki, Takaaki, Samantha Custer, Agustina Eskenazi, Alena Stern, and Rebecca Latourell. 2017. "Decoding Data Use: How Do Leaders Source Data and Use It to Accelerate Development?" AidData, Global Research Institute, College of William and Mary, Williamsburg, VA.

McCluskey, William, and Chyi-Yun Huang. 2019. "The Role of ICT in Property Tax Administration: Lessons from Tanzania." CMI Brief 6, Chr. Michelsen Institute, Bergen, Norway.

McQueston, Kate. 2013. "Autonomy, Independence, and Capacity of National Statistics Offices." Background paper, Center for Global Development, Washington, DC; African Population and Health Research Council, Nairobi.

Meijer, Albert, and Suzanne Potjer. 2018. "Citizen-Generated Open Data: An Explorative Analysis of 25 Cases." *Government Information Quarterly* 35 (4): 613–21.

Morawska, Lidia, Phong K. Thai, Xiaoting Liu, Akwasi Asumadu-Sakyi, Godwin Ayoko, Alena Bartonova, Andrea Bedini, et al. 2018. "Applications of Low-Cost Sensing Technologies for Air Quality Monitoring and Exposure Assessment: How Far Have They Gone?" *Environment International* 116 (July): 286–99.

MPPN (Multidimensional Poverty Peer Network). 2017. "Using the MPI to Determine National Budgets in Costa Rica." *Dimensions* 4 (August): 14–18, Oxford Poverty and Human Development Initiative, Oxford Department of International Development, University of Oxford, Oxford, UK. https://www.mppn.org/wp -content/uploads/2017/08/Dim_4_ENGLISH_online .pdf.

OECD (Organisation for Economic Co-operation and Development). 2017. *Development Co-operation Report 2017: Data for Development.* Paris: OECD.

OECD (Organisation for Economic Co-operation and Development). 2019. *The Path to Becoming a Data-Driven Public Sector.* OECD Digital Government Studies Series. Paris: OECD. https://doi.org/10.1787/059814a7-en.

Oliver, Kathryn, Simon Innvar, Theo Lorenc, Jenny Woodman, and James Thomas. 2014. "A Systematic Review of Barriers to and Facilitators of the Use of Evidence by Policymakers." *BMC Health Services Research* 14 (January 3), article 2. https://doi.org/10.1186/1472-6963-14-2.

Open Data Watch. 2015a. "Breathe Deep: Air Quality Reform in China." Data Impacts Case Studies, Open Data Watch, Washington, DC. https://dataimpacts.org/project/data -help-china-breath-better/.

Open Data Watch. 2015b. "Disaggregated Data: Impacts of Demographic and Health Surveys." Data Impacts Case Studies, Open Data Watch, Washington, DC. https://dataimpacts.org/project/health-surveys/.

PARIS21 (Partnership in Statistics for Development in the 21st Century). 2018. "Survey Results: New Approaches to Capacity Development and Future Priorities, CD4.0 Survey." PARIS21, Paris. https://paris21.org/capacity-development-40/cd40-survey.

PARIS21 (Partnership in Statistics for Development in the 21st Century). 2020. "Partner Report on Support to Statistics: PRESS 2019." PARIS21, Paris. https://paris21.org/sites/default/files/inline-files/PARIS21_Press%202019_WEB.pdf.

PARIS21 (Partnership in Statistics for Development in the 21st Century) and PSA (Philippine Statistics Authority). 2020. *Use of Citizen-Generated Data for SDG Reporting in the Philippines: A Case Study.* Paris: PARIS21. https://paris21.org/sites/default/files/inline-files/PSA-report-FINAL.pdf.

Petrov, Oleg, Joel Gurin, and Laura Manley. 2016. "Open Data for Sustainable Development." Connections: Transport and ICT, Note 2016-5, World Bank, Washington, DC.

Pham, Congduc, Abdur Rahim, and Philippe Cousin. 2016. "Low-Cost, Long-Range Open IoT for Smarter Rural African Villages." In *2016 IEEE International Smart Cities Conference (ISC2)*, edited by Institute of Electrical and Electronics Engineers, 512–17. Red Hook, NY: Curran Associates.

Piovesan, Federico. 2015. "Statistical Perspectives on Citizen-Generated Data." DataShift, Civicus, Johannesburg. http://civicus.org/thedatashift/wp-content/uploads/2015/07/statistical-perspectives-on-cgd_web_single-page.pdf.

Privacy International. 2013. "Biometrics: Friend or Foe of Privacy?" Privacy International, London. https://privacyinternational.org/news-analysis/1409/biometrics-friend-or-foe-privacy.

Privacy International. 2019. "Submission to the Special Rapporteurship on Economic, Social, Cultural, and Environmental Rights of the Inter-American Commission on Human Rights Regarding the Situation of Economic, Social, Cultural, and Environmental Rights in the Region." TEDIC, InternetLab, Derechos Digitales, Fundación Karisma, Dejusticia, Asociación por los Derechos Civiles, and Privacy International, Privacy International, London.

Randall, Sara. 2015. "Where Have All the Nomads Gone? Fifty Years of Statistical and Demographic Invisibilities of African Mobile Pastoralists." *Pastoralism* 5, article 22.

Rogger, Daniel Oliver, and Ravi Somani. 2018. "Hierarchy and Information." Policy Research Working Paper 8644, World Bank, Washington, DC.

Roseth, Benjamin, Angela Reyes, and Karla Yee Amézaga. 2019. "The Value of Official Statistics: Lessons from Intergovernmental Transfers." IDB Technical Note 1682, Inter-American Development Bank, Washington, DC. https://publications.iadb.org/publications/english/document/The_Value_of_Official_Statistics_Lessons_from_Intergovernmental_Transfers_en.pdf.

Safetipin. 2016. "Bogota: A Safety Analysis Report." Safetipin, Gurgaon, India. https://safetipin.com/report/bogota-report-2016/.

Sandefur, Justin, and Amanda Glassman. 2015. "The Political Economy of Bad Data: Evidence from African Survey and Administrative Statistics." *Journal of Development Studies* 51 (2): 116–32.

Sanga, Dimitri. 2013. "The Challenges of the Narrative of African Countries' Development: Data Demand and Supply Mismatches." Paper presented at conference "African Economic Development: Measuring Success and Failure," School for International Studies, Simon Fraser University, Vancouver, Canada, April 18–20, 2013.

Sanna, Valentina, and Ida McDonnell. 2017. "Data for Development: DAC Member Priorities and Challenges." OECD Development Co-Operation Working Paper 35, OECD, Paris.

Scott, Christopher. 2005. "Measuring Up to the Measurement Problem: The Role of Statistics in Evidence-Based Policy-Making." Partnership in Statistics for Development in the 21st Century, Paris. https://paris21.org/sites/default/files/MUMPS-full.pdf.

SDSN (United Nations Sustainable Development Solutions Network). 2015. "Data for Development: A Needs Assessment for SDG Monitoring and Statistical Capacity Development." SDSN, New York. https://sustainabledevelopment.un.org/content/documents/2017Data-for-Development-Full-Report.pdf.

SDSN TReNDS (United Nations Sustainable Development Solutions Network–Thematic Research Network on Data and Statistics). 2018a. "Data Sharing via SMS Strengthens Uganda's Health System: A Case Study of mTRAC, Uganda." SDSN TReNDS, New York. http://www.data4sdgs.org/sites/default/files/2018-09/mTRAC%20CaseStudy_FINAL.pdf.

SDSN TReNDS (United Nations Sustainable Development Solutions Network–Thematic Research Network on Data and Statistics). 2018b. "Handpump Data Improves Water Access." SDSN TReNDS, New York. http://www.data4sdgs.org/sites/default/files/2018-12/Smart%20Handpump%20Case%20Study.pdf.

Seltzer, Judith, and Deborah Klein Walker. 2020. "Counting Children in the US 2020 Census: Assure Our Future Is Represented." *NAM Perspectives* Commentary, National Academy of Medicine, Washington, DC. https://doi.org/10.31478/202003d.

Sethi, Tanya, and Mihir Prakash. 2018. "Counting on Statistics: How Can National Statistical Offices and Donors Increase Use?" AidData, Global Research Institute, College of William and Mary, Williamsburg, VA. https://www.aiddata.org/publications/counting-on-statistics.

Snorrason, Hallgrímur. 2018. "Securing the Independence of Official Statistics: Introductory Remarks." *Statistical Journal of the IAOS* 34 (2): 145–47.

SSEE (Smith School of Enterprise and the Environment). 2014. "From Rights to Results in Rural Water Services: Evidence from Kyuso, Kenya." Water Programme Working Paper 1, SSEE, University of Oxford, Oxford, UK. https://www.smithschool.ox.ac.uk/publications/reports/SSEE-rights-to-results_final_March2014.pdf.

Taylor, Matthew. 2016. "The Political Economy of Statistical Capacity: A Theoretical Approach." IDB Discussion Paper IDP-DP-471, Inter-American Development Bank, Washington, DC.

Tiberti, Marco, and Valentina Costa. 2020. "Disability Measurement in Household Surveys: A Guidebook for Designing Household Survey Questionnaires." LSMS Guidebook, Living Standards Measurement Study, World Bank, Washington, DC. http://documents.world bank.org/curated/en/456131578985058020/Disability -Measurement-in-Household-Surveys-A-Guidebook-for -Designing-Household-Survey-Questionnaires.

Todesca, Jorge A. 2017. "Political Power and the Argentine Statistical System: The Case of INDEC1." *Statistical Journal of the IAOS* 33 (4): 875–83.

Toulemon, Laurent. 2017. "Undercount of Young Children and Young Adults in the New French Census." *Statistical Journal of the IAOS* 33 (2): 311–16.

Trewin, Dennis. 2018. "What Does an Independent Official Statistical Agency Mean in Practice?" *Statistical Journal of the IAOS* 34 (2): 165–69.

UNESCO (United Nations Educational, Scientific, and Cultural Organization). 2016. "Education 2030: Incheon Declaration and Framework for Action." Document ED-2016/WS/28, Institute for Information Technologies in Education, UNESCO, Paris. http://uis.unesco.org/sites/default /files/documents/education-2030-incheon-framework -for-action-implementation-of-sdg4-2016-en_2.pdf.

United Nations. 2019a. "Extreme Poverty and Human Rights: Note by the Secretary-General." Document A/74/493, United Nations, New York. https://undocs.org/A/74/493.

United Nations. 2019b. *The Sustainable Development Goals Report 2019*. New York: United Nations.

UNSTATS (Statistics Division, Department of Economic and Social Affairs, United Nations). 2015. *United Nations Fundamental Principles of Official Statistics: Implementation Guidelines*. New York: United Nations. https:// .unstats.org/unsd/dnss/gp/Implementation_Guidelines _FINAL_without_edit.pdf.

UNSTATS (Statistics Division, Department of Economic and Social Affairs, United Nations) and World Bank. 2020. "Monitoring the State of Statistical Operations under the COVID-19 Pandemic: Highlights from the Second Round of a Global COVID-19 Survey of National Statistical Offices." World Bank, Washington, DC.

UN Women. 2018. *Turning Promises into Action: Gender Equality in the 2030 Agenda for Sustainable Development*. New York: UN Women.

UN Women. 2020. "COVID-19 and Its Economic Toll on Women: The Story behind the Numbers." *News and Events*, September 16, 2020. https://www.unwomen.org /en/news/stories/2020/9/feature-covid-19-economic -impacts-on-women.

Van Belle, Jean-Paul. 2018. *Africa Data Revolution Report 2018: Status and Emerging Impact to Open Data in Africa*. With contributions by Danny Lämmerhirt, Carlos Iglesias, Paul Mungai, Hubeidatu Nuhu, Mbongeni Hlabano, Tarik Nesh-Nash, and Sarang Chaudhary. Washington, DC: World Wide Web Foundation. https:// webfoundation.org/docs/2019/03/Africa-data-revolution -report.pdf.

Verhulst, Stefaan G., and Andrew Young. 2017. "Open Data in Developing Economies: Toward Building an Evidence Base on What Works and How." Governance Lab, New York University, New York. https://odimpact.org/files /odimpact-developing-economies.pdf.

von Oppeln-Bronikowski, Sibylle, Christine Kronz, Irina Meinke, and Hannah Wirtzfeld. 2015. "How Can Professional and Ethical Frameworks Strengthen Statisticians in Their Practical Work?" *Statistical Journal of the IAOS* 31 (4): 513–22.

WHO (World Health Organization). 2011. "The Abuja Declaration: Ten Years On." WHO, Geneva. https://www.who .int/healthsystems/publications/abuja_report_aug_2011 .pdf?ua=1.

Wollburg, Philip, Marco Tiberti, and Alberto Zezza. 2020. "Recall Length and Measurement Error in Agricultural Surveys." *Food Policy*. Published ahead of print, December 1, 2020. https://doi.org/10.1016/j.foodpol.2020.102003.

World Bank. 2016a. *Croatia: Small-Area Estimation of Consumption-Based Poverty (Poverty Maps)*. Washington, DC: World Bank. https://razvoj.gov.hr/UserDocs Images//Istaknute%20teme/Kartom%20siroma%C5% A1tva//Croatia%20Small-Area%20Estimation%20of%20 Consumption-Based%20Poverty%20(Poverty%20Maps) .pdf.

World Bank. 2016b. *World Development Report 2016: Digital Dividends*. Washington, DC: World Bank.

World Bank. 2017a. "Index of Multiple Deprivation: Conceptual Framework for Identifying Lagging Municipalities and Towns in Croatia." World Bank, Washington, DC. https://razvoj.gov.hr/UserDocsImages//Istaknute%20 teme/Kartom%20siroma%C5%A1tva//Index%20of%20 Multiple%20Deprivation%20-%20Conceptual%20 framework_18.06.2019.pdf.

World Bank. 2017b. "Monitoring Global Poverty: Report of the Commission on Global Poverty." World Bank, Washington, DC. https://openknowledge.worldbank.org /bitstream/handle/10986/25141/9781464809613.pdf.

World Bank. 2017c. *World Development Report 2017: Governance and the Law*. Washington, DC: World Bank.

World Bank. 2018a. *Data for Development: An Evaluation of World Bank Support for Data and Statistical Capacity*. Washington, DC: Independent Evaluation Group, World Bank.

World Bank. 2018b. *Improving Public Sector Performance: Through Innovation and Inter-Agency Coordination*. Global Report: Public Sector Performance. Washington, DC: World Bank.

World Bank. 2018c. "Public Sector Savings and Revenue from Identification Systems: Opportunities and Constraints." World Bank, Washington, DC.

World Bank. 2018d. "The Role of Digital Identification for Healthcare: The Emerging Use Cases." Identification for Development (ID4D), World Bank, Washington, DC.

World Bank. 2019a. *IC4D, Information and Communication for Development 2018: Data-Driven Development*. Washington, DC: World Bank. http://documents1.worldbank.org/curated

/en/987471542742554246/pdf/128301-9781464813
252.pdf.

World Bank. 2019b. *ID4D Practitioner's Guide: Version 1.0.*
Washington, DC: World Bank. http://documents1
.worldbank.org/curated/en/248371559325561562/pdf
/ID4D-Practitioner-s-Guide.pdf.

World Bank. 2020a. "Classification of Fragile and Conflict-
Affected Situations." *Brief*, July 9, World Bank, Washington, DC. https://www.worldbank.org/en/topic
/fragilityconflictviolence/brief/harmonized-list-of
-fragile-situations.

World Bank. 2020b. "West Africa Unique Identification for
Regional Integration and Inclusion Program, Phase 2."
Project Appraisal Document, Report PAD3556, World
Bank, Washington, DC.

Yin, Peng, Michael Brauer, Aaron J. Cohen, Haidong Wang,
Jie Li, Richard T. Burnett, Jeffrey D. Stanaway, et al. 2020.
"The Effect of Air Pollution on Deaths, Disease Burden,
and Life Expectancy across China and Its Provinces,
1990–2017: An Analysis for the Global Burden of Disease
Study 2017." *Lancet Planetary Health* 4 (9): 386–98.

Spotlight 2.1
Deploying data to curtail violence against women and girls

For too long, violence against women and girls has been a deep, dark secret. Now, data collection efforts around the world are shedding light on this tragic problem and leading to solutions.

Violence against women and girls (VAWG) is a global pandemic. One out of three women and girls (35 percent) worldwide between the ages of 15 and 49 has experienced physical violence, sexual violence, or both. At least 200 million girls and women have undergone female genital mutilation (FGM), and in at least 11 countries, more than half of women ages 15–49 have undergone FGM (figure S2.1.1).[1] We know

Figure S2.1.1 Prevalence of female genital mutilation in women ages 15–49, by country income level, 2010–19

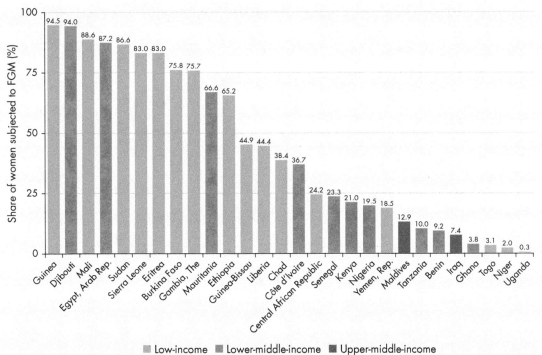

Source: Adapted from Kashiwase and Pirlea 2019. Data are drawn from the World Bank World Development Indicators, https://databank.worldbank.org/FGM-Prevalence/id/a4f22755 (SH.STA.FGMS.ZS), using data from Demographic and Health Surveys, Multiple Indicator Cluster Surveys, and UNICEF. Data at http://bit.do/WDR2021-Fig-S2_1_1.

Note: FGM = female genital mutilation; UNICEF = United Nations Children's Fund.

these facts because representative population-based studies have been undertaken to understand the prevalence of VAWG. These studies have used a standardized methodology in more than 90 countries across all regions and all income groups. For example, data for 55 low- and middle-income countries are available through a standardized module measuring VAWG, and this module has been incorporated in the Demographic and Health Surveys (DHSs).[2]

The availability and accessibility of reliable, comparable, and nationally representative VAWG data are leading to solutions, including laws banning domestic violence.[3] Moreover, the data are informing diagnostic work, prevention and response efforts, and policies in low- and middle-income settings in key areas such as health, education, social protection, and governance. For instance, kNOwVAWdata,[4] an initiative led by the United Nations Population Fund (UNFPA), collects VAWG data on 27 countries in Asia and the Pacific, shedding light on why survivors are not accessing services. The World Bank has used these data as a basis for its analytical and operational work. In the Great Lakes region of Africa, an in-depth analysis of DHS data helped to identify and target emergency and women's health activities and to prevent and respond to VAWG in Uganda. In 2019 Peru's president welcomed an in-depth analysis of VAWG data and expenditures, setting the stage for a national results-oriented budgetary plan to reduce VAWG that was supported by the Ministry of Economy and Finance and the Ministry of Women and Vulnerable Populations.

Investing in data to understand the barriers preventing survivors of violence from using essential support services

In addition to amassing data on the prevalence of VAWG, many countries and agencies that provide essential services to survivors of violence keep track of service-based data. Data on reported cases of VAWG allow countries to understand who is seeking help, when, for what types of violence, and how often. Various barriers, including fear and lack of knowledge, may prevent women from seeking services; data help countries to understand and address these barriers. For instance, service-based data can be

used to monitor important life-saving measures, like providing victims with post-exposure prophylactics (PEP) within 72 hours of a sexual assault. Tracking how many survivors receive PEP can unveil barriers related to the supply chain of essential medicines or gaps in the training of health service staff.

Integrating service-based data with data representative of a given population can yield important insights. The Gender-Based Violence Information Management System (GBVIMS) provides a global example.[5] This multiagency initiative facilitates the safe, ethical, effective, and efficient standardization and coordination of service-based data. While such efforts are critical, it is also important to ensure that investments in gender-based violence data systems do not divert limited funds and staffing away from the provision of services to the survivors of violence. Separate streams of investment—and greater investment—in service provision and data systems are necessary.

The first and foremost purpose of the GBVIMS and service-based data is to improve the quality and accessibility of services for survivors of VAWG. But for these systems to be effective, several foundational issues must be addressed. First, efforts to integrate data should be driven by the needs of women and girls seeking services, not by the ease of access to centrally located data. Second, to overcome silos and promote national monitoring, coordination is needed across multiple institutions with different mandates and data systems.

Addressing the surge in VAWG during the COVID-19 pandemic

VAWG has surged during the COVID-19 pandemic.[6] Lockdown measures designed to contain the spread of the virus as well as the economic and health stresses associated with this crisis have contributed to an increase in violence—especially intimate partner violence.[7] In the early days of the pandemic, the UNFPA warned that 31 million additional cases of gender-based violence could occur as a result of six months of lockdowns.[8] Complicating matters, providing services has become more difficult because some resources have been diverted to the COVID-19 response and some services have been suspended altogether.[9]

Reliable data are crucial to understanding and addressing this situation. However, collecting reliable data on VAWG has been especially challenging during the COVID-19 pandemic. Face-to-face data collection, the predominant mode in low- and middle-income countries, has been widely suspended. The alternatives—remote data collection through telephone, text messaging, or the Web—increase the risk of violence: confidentiality is nearly impossible to ensure, and even electronic communications leave traces.[10] Instead, sources of indirect information should be used: for instance, service-based data or key informant interviews with frontline workers.

Collecting VAWG data ethically

Special care must be taken when handling data on VAWG. Soberingly, collecting VAWG data can and has caused women to experience more violence. Ethical and safety guidelines must be followed when considering both the collection and sharing of such data. These guidelines identify minimum standards for the collection of VAWG data, such as the ability to offer referrals for support to all who say they have experienced violence; the ability to guarantee confidentiality and privacy for survivors when collecting and reporting on data; and the commitment to use the data collected for increased and improved action. The World Health Organization (WHO) has issued the following guidelines:

- "Putting Women First: Ethical and Safety Recommendations for Research on Domestic Violence against Women" (2001)[11]
- "Ethical and Safety Recommendations for Interviewing Trafficked Women" (2003)[12]
- "Sample Design, Ethical and Safety Considerations, and Response Rates" (2005)[13]
- "Ethical and Safety Recommendations for Researching, Documenting, and Monitoring Sexual Violence in Emergencies" (2007)[14]
- "Ethical and Safety Recommendations for Intervention Research on Violence against Women" (2016),[15] building on lessons from the publication "Putting Women First: Ethical and Safety Recommendations for Research on Domestic Violence against Women" (2001)

The Sexual Violence Research Initiative of the Medical Research Council in Pretoria, South Africa, has also issued important guidelines:

- Ethical and Safety Recommendations for Research on Perpetration of Sexual Violence (2012)[16]

Notes

1. Female genital mutilation "does not provide any health benefits, but rather causes serious risks for women's health, including chronic infections and pain, menstrual problems, and complications in childbirth" (Kashiwase and Pirlea 2019). See also United Nations Children's Fund, Female Genital Mutilation (dashboard), updated February 2020, https://data.unicef.org/topic/child-protection/female-genital-mutilation/.
2. The country count is as of August 2020. For DHS data on violence against women and girls, see ICF International, STATcompiler (DHS Program STATcompiler) (database), http://www.statcompiler.com/. Select "Choose Indicator" and, from the dropdown menu, "Physical or sexual violence committed by husband/partner." Then click "Next," "Filter by World Region," "Select All," and "Next." The data will appear and can be augmented and refined by choosing more categories from the "Indicators" and "Countries" menus on the right.
3. For case studies of the impact of VAWG data on policy, see "Disaggregated Data: Impacts of Demographic and Health Surveys," Data Impacts Case Studies, Open Data Watch, https://dataimpacts.org/project/health-surveys/.
4. See Measuring Prevalence of Violence against Women in Asia-Pacific (dashboard), Regional Office for Asia and the Pacific, United Nations Population Fund, https://asiapacific.unfpa.org/knowvawdata.
5. See GBVIMS (Gender-Based Violence Information Management System) (dashboard), Inter-Agency GBVIMS Steering Committee, https://www.gbvims.com/.
6. Bettinger-Lopez and Bro (2020); Johnson et al. (2020).
7. United Nations (2020); UNDP (2020).
8. UNFPA (2020).
9. Johnson et al. (2020).
10. UN Women (2020).
11. WHO (2001).
12. WHO (2003).
13. García-Moreno et al. (2005).
14. WHO (2007).
15. WHO (2016).
16. Jewkes, Dartnall, and Sikweyiya (2012).

References

Bettinger-Lopez, Caroline, and Alexandra Bro. 2020. "A Double Pandemic: Domestic Violence in the Age of COVID-19." *In Brief* (blog), May 13, 2020. https://www.cfr.org/in-brief/double-pandemic-domestic-violence-age-covid-19.

García-Moreno, Claudia, Henrica A. F. M. Jansen, Mary Ellsberg, Lori Heise, and Charlotte Watts. 2005. "Sample Design, Ethical and Safety Considerations, and Response Rates." In *WHO Multi-Country Study on Women's Health and Domestic Violence against Women: Initial Results on Prevalence, Health Outcomes, and Women's Responses*, ch. 3, 19–24. Geneva: World Health Organization. https://www.who.int/reproductivehealth/publications/violence/24159358X/en/.

Jewkes, Rachel, Elizabeth Dartnall, and Yandisa Sikweyiya. 2012. "Ethical and Safety Recommendations for Research on Perpetration of Sexual Violence." Sexual Violence Research Initiative, Gender and Health Research Unit, Medical Research Council, Pretoria, South Africa.

Johnson, Katy, Lindsey Green, Muriel Volpellier, Suzanne Kidenda, Thomas McHale, Karen Naimer, and Ranit Mishori. 2020. "The Impact of COVID-19 on Services for People Affected by Sexual and Gender-Based Violence." *International Journal of Gynecology and Obstetrics* 150 (3): 285–87. https://doi.org/10.1002/ijgo.13285.

Kashiwase, Haruna, and Florina Pirlea. 2019. "200 Million Women and Girls in the World Today Have Undergone Female Genital Mutilation." *Data Blog* (blog), September 27, 2019. https://blogs.worldbank.org/opendata/200-million-women-and-girls-world-today-have-undergone-female-genital-mutilation.

United Nations. 2020. "Policy Brief: The Impact of COVID-19 on Women." United Nations, New York.

UNDP (United Nations Development Programme). 2020. "Gender-Based Violence and COVID-19." UNDP Brief, UNDP, New York. https://www.undp.org/content/undp/en/home/librarypage/womens-empowerment/gender-based-violence-and-covid-19.html.

UNFPA (United Nations Population Fund). 2020. "Millions More Cases of Violence, Child Marriage, Female Genital Mutilation, Unintended Pregnancy Expected due to the COVID-19 Pandemic." *News* (blog), April 28, 2020. https://www.unfpa.org/news/millions-more-cases-violence-child-marriage-female-genital-mutilation-unintended-pregnancies.

UN Women (United Nations Entity for Gender Equality and the Empowerment of Women). 2020. "Violence against Women and Girls: Data Collection during COVID-19." UN Women, New York. https://www.unwomen.org/en/digital-library/publications/2020/04/issue-brief-violence-against-women-and-girls-data-collection-during-covid-19.

WHO (World Health Organization). 2001. "Putting Women First: Ethical and Safety Recommendations for Research on Domestic Violence against Women." Document WHO/FCH/GWH/01.1, Department of Gender and Women's Health, Family and Community Health, WHO, Geneva. https://www.who.int/gender/violence/womenfirtseng.pdf.

WHO (World Health Organization). 2003. "WHO Ethical and Safety Recommendations for Interviewing Trafficked Women." Health Policy Unit, London School of Hygiene and Tropical Medicine, London; WHO, Geneva.

WHO (World Health Organization). 2007. "WHO Ethical and Safety Recommendations for Researching, Documenting, and Monitoring Sexual Violence in Emergencies." WHO, Geneva. https://www.who.int/gender/documents/OMS_Ethics&Safety10Aug07.pdf.

WHO (World Health Organization). 2016. *Ethical and Safety Recommendations for Intervention Research on Violence against Women: Building on Lessons from the WHO Publication* Putting Women First: Ethical and Safety Recommendations for Research on Domestic Violence against Women. Geneva: WHO.

Spotlight 2.2
The role of international organizations in improving public intent data

International organizations can aid countries bilaterally to address challenges regarding funding, technical capacity, governance, and data demand and create global public goods to overcome these barriers.

More and better financing for data production

Coalitions of international organizations and development partners can provide coordinated global solutions for activities that fulfill specific data needs. Governments can finance such activities either under national budgets or through loans or grants from multilateral development banks. For example, the World Bank's Data for Policy Package identifies a core set of social, economic, and sustainability statistics crucial for monitoring and evaluating development outcomes and provides governments with loans or grants to address these data needs. For relatively lower income, data-deprived countries, this aid can help governments to prioritize which gaps to fill and supplement scarce national funding. Another example is the 50x2030 Initiative to Close the Agricultural Data Gap, a multipartner initiative that seeks to transform agricultural data systems across 50 low- and middle-income countries by 2030. It uses innovative funding mechanisms, leveraging donor funding to mobilize national funding and create national ownership.

Advancing research and development in methods and tools

In addition to investing in improvements in the technical capacity of data producers and users, international organizations can also foster technical capacity more broadly by providing global public goods through research and development in methods of data collection, curation, and analysis. For example, they can support innovations in data capture, including through portable sensors and mobile applications. These innovations must be validated rigorously through methodological research activities that compare the relative accuracy, cost-effectiveness, and feasibility of new and traditional methods of data collection. Based on such research, guidelines can be formulated for integrating validated innovations into surveys, censuses, and administrative records. International organizations can play an important role in carrying out such research and promoting these innovations and associated guidelines. Partnerships between international organizations and national statistical offices (NSOs) in methodological research and development increase the likelihood that innovations in data capture will be adopted and implemented.

Developing, disseminating, and implementing global standards for statistical activities

International organizations can also support efforts to develop, disseminate, and implement international standards and guidelines for statistical activities. International statistical standards and guidelines need to be disseminated and adopted at the country level for data to be comparable across countries and hence for policy makers to be able to compare their performance with that of their peers. Among many examples are the Systems of National Accounts developed by the United Nations in collaboration with several other partners; the International Labour Organization's International Standard Classification of Occupations; and the monitoring and harmonization of data related to drinking water, sanitation, and hygiene by the World Health Organization and United Nations Children's Fund (UNICEF). Technical collaboration—including joint research among like-minded international organizations, NSOs, technical partners, and academia—is critical to the successful production of international standards and guidelines, as are international forums for peer review, discussion, endorsement, and promotion of these public goods.

Coordinating actions to ensure the effective diffusion of public goods and funding activities

In the absence of coordination, organizations might finance overlapping activities or fragment investments, overwhelm national data systems, or produce conflicting standards and guidelines. The Inter-Agency and Expert Working Groups as well as the Intersecretariat Working Groups, under the aegis of the United Nations Statistical Commission, provide a platform for catalyzing collaborative work on the

development of standards and should continue to be supported with periodic reviews of their terms of reference and desired outputs. Awareness of these working groups needs to be expanded, particularly within international organizations, to assure coordinated actions within an organization.

Making data accessible and compatible with national priorities and spurring local demand

To satisfy increasing demand for data, international organizations should make their own data, syntax files, and metadata widely available and easily accessible beyond their own institutions. The data that international organizations require, such as data on the Sustainable Development Goals, affect the data produced by countries and can even crowd out the domestic production of data. It is thus imperative for such standards and goals to be made compatible with the interests, priorities, and goals of countries. When this is the case, the data maintained by international organizations can spur local demand for cross-country data, foster their continued production, and create a virtuous cycle of data production and use.

Data as a resource for the private sector

Main messages

1. Businesses are reaping tremendous value from both data created through businesses' economic activities and data shared by governments. Used as an input in data-driven decision-making, those data can spur innovation in products and services and reduce transaction costs, ultimately boosting productivity, export competitiveness, and growth.

2. Use of data in the production process of firms may help tilt the playing field toward poor people and underserved populations (who can trade across platforms and access free services) by reducing fragmentation in markets. However, it can also exacerbate domestic inequalities where foundational skills, infrastructure, and finance are not widely available in countries.

3. Use of data by businesses can also tilt the playing field away from poor countries, whose local enterprises may struggle to compete with large global players in part because of economies of scale and scope from data.

4. Although the use of data in the production process presents many opportunities to solve development challenges, policy makers should heed the risks this use presents for the concentration of economic power, patterns of inequality, and protection of the rights of individuals.

Creating value and solving development challenges through data-driven business models

For millennia, farming and food supply have depended on access to accurate information. When will the rains come? How large will the yields be? What crops will earn the most money at market? Where are the most likely buyers located? Today, that information is being collected and leveraged at an unprecedented rate through data-driven agricultural business models. In India, farmers can access a data-driven platform that uses satellite imagery, artificial intelligence (AI), and machine learning (ML) to detect crop health remotely and estimate yield ahead of the harvest. Farmers can then share such information with financial institutions to demonstrate their potential profitability, thereby increasing their chance of obtaining a loan. Other data-driven platforms provide real-time crop prices and match sellers with buyers.

For remote populations around the world, receiving specialized medical care has been nearly impossible without having to travel miles to urban areas. Today, telehealth clinics and their specialists can monitor and diagnose patients remotely using sensors that collect patient health data and AI that helps analyze such data.

Innovations like these herald the promise of business models that apply data to create new and better goods and services, helping to address development challenges in the process. Both private intent and public intent data are increasingly being used by firms to create value in the production process. At the same time, data are continually being produced as a by-product of economic activity, creating digital footprints that drive the data economy. With their growing capacity to collect, store, and process that data, businesses find that their ability to extract value from this data has been rising exponentially in recent years.

The COVID-19 crisis has created urgent demands for the private sector to adopt data-driven solutions to deal with the pandemic and increase resilience and productivity for recovery. Big Tech companies have been one of the few winners during the crisis as consumers purchase more goods and services online. As businesses shift toward recovery, the new reality will likely accelerate trends toward data-driven technologies that allow for automation and traceability in value chains.

For all their promise, however, the accelerating pace of these trends also comes with risks related to the concentration of economic power, greater inequality, and protection of the rights of individuals.

The degree to which individuals can benefit from the data-driven economy—including consumers, entrepreneurs, and job seekers—will differ according to their access to finance, education levels, skills, and technology. In charting a way forward, policy makers—across all stages of development of their country's data-driven economy—should remain alert to these risks so that the use of data by firms contributes to broadly shared benefits.

The role of data in the production process of firms

The role of data in the production process can be conceptualized in different ways, depending on the specificities of the firms, industries, technologies, and types of data being considered. There is as yet no overarching theory or consensus on the role of data in the production process. The categories that follow summarize various ways of understanding the role of data in the creation of value by firms—as a factor of production, as a productivity enhancer, as a by-product, or as an output.

Data as a factor of production. For some firms, data are considered an input central to their business, essential to fulfillment of their core objectives. In this context, data have been referred to as a factor of production—on a par with labor, capital, and land—that is a primary determinant of output and productivity.[1] For example, many social media platforms are built around monetizing their users' data for advertising.

Data as a productivity enhancer. Data may also be conceptualized as a driver of total factor productivity (TFP). Increases in TFP reflect a more efficient use of factors of production often thought to be driven by technological change. Businesses use data along with various technologies to become more productive by improving their business processes, learning more about their clients and customers, developing new products, or making better data-driven decisions.[2] In this context, the addition of data to the production process makes the main factors of production more efficient, leading to better performance. According to one study, in the US health care sector the use of big data has been associated with a 0.7 percent increase in productivity growth per year.[3] Other studies have found that among 179 large publicly traded US firms the adoption of data-driven decision-making has led to an increase in productivity of 5–6 percent.[4]

Data as a by-product of the production process. Data are often passively created as a by-product of economic activities. For example, call detail records (CDRs) are a by-product of telephone usage. Observed data on consumers' browsing and buying patterns are a by-product of online e-commerce. Data created in this way can be used in the production of new products or services, either by the firm that produced the original data or by other firms with which the data are shared, such as under commercial arrangements. For example, e-commerce platforms use data created as a by-product of transactions on their platform to improve their product offerings; credit card companies sometimes sell their transaction data for a specific location to firms involved in tourism in that location; and new firms use CDRs for commercial purposes, including analytics and advertising.[5]

Data as an output. For some firms, data are the primary output of the production process. Examples are data intermediaries, including rating services such as Nielsen; pollsters such as Gallup; and data aggregators such as dataPublica.[6] These data are then used either by other firms in their production processes or by government in policy making.

In all cases, data have a role in creating value for the economy, but the way in which data play into the production process differs by context.

Pathways to development

Whether the use of data in the production process is conceptualized as a factor of production or a driver of productivity, its transformative effects on development can be summarized by four channels:

1. *Quality improvements in existing products and services.* This channel includes the use of data-driven decision-making to provide consumers with better health diagnostics, better credit scoring, better search results, and more personalized product recommendations.
2. *Cost reduction in delivering products and services.* Data and analytics can reduce the costs of delivery, which can then lower prices (subject to markets being sufficiently competitive). For example, better credit scoring can reduce the cost of delivering loans and lead to lower interest rates on loans. Sensor-based agricultural devices and platforms that take and analyze soil readings can inform farmers how much fertilizer they should apply, which should reduce wastage and costs.
3. *Greater innovation in development of new products and services.* Examples include the development of new financial products, smart contracts and supply chain tracking services, new products that rely on applications such as online maps or translation, and new consumer goods based on analysis of purchasing trends.

4. *More effective intermediation and lower transaction costs.* Platform firms can help solve market failures and lower the entry and transaction costs for firms that connect to those platforms. This happens in part by reducing information asymmetries, thereby increasing trust in those firms. Distributed ledger technologies (DLTs) not only can reduce transaction costs but also enhance trust through secure transactions. Better intermediation can disrupt traditional market structure and reduce the market power of intermediaries, particularly in sectors such as agriculture where they have traditionally played a central role in the value chain.

These four channels to increasing the impact of data on development are driven by two key effects. First, analytics applied to data can reveal patterns that *allow better data-driven decision-making.* Second, data can help to *facilitate transactions, including by matching the suppliers of goods and services with those who demand them.* In this way, the use of data can help overcome market failures, with positive effects on productivity, growth, jobs, and welfare (figure 3.1).

Data-driven businesses and the technologies that help them create value

Data-intensive analytics can be used to discover new insights, enhance decision-making, and optimize processes. When data are characterized by the "3 V's"— volume, velocity, and variety—they can serve as inputs to big data analytics. Such analytics typically require new methodologies and technologies to enable enhanced decision-making (box 3.1). This chapter focuses on the development impact of business models that use data-intensive technology or analytics as their key value drivers, whether they are technology firms (the providers of data-intensive technological solutions) or traditional firms and entrepreneurs (the adopters of data-intensive technologies).

Firms may use various data-driven technologies by themselves or in combination. A key business model that has emerged using data-intensive technologies are *data-driven platform businesses,* which use data, along with AI/ML and other analytics, to intermediate between distinct user groups to match supply with demand. By overcoming informational asymmetries and reducing search costs, these businesses facilitate market exchanges and generate more data on users and their behavior. Some may also use a combination of other technologies. For example, the platform GrainChain uses DLT to broker secure transactions

Figure 3.1 The role of data in the production process: Pathways to development

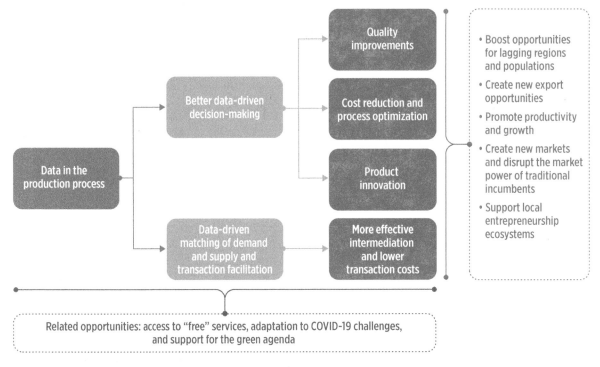

Source: WDR 2021 team.

Box 3.1 Technologies and methods that support data-driven decision-making and intermediation

Technology that supports data-intensive analytics: artificial intelligence, including machine learning

Artificial intelligence (AI) and machine learning (ML) can help firms analyze their data with less manual effort. AI is the development and use of any device that perceives its environment and takes actions that maximize its chance of success of reaching a defined goal (including learning and adapting to its environment). It is not a single technology but a family of technologies. Machine learning is one application of AI. The algorithms that underlay AI rely on inputs of large amounts of data to learn and produce accurate and valuable insights. Based on adoption patterns, studies predict that firms responsible for about 70 percent of economic output will have adopted at least one type of AI technology by 2030.[a]

Data-intensive analytic applications and big data analytics sometimes require that data be processed in different formats and distributed across different locations. These may include cloud computing, bio-inspired computing, or quantum computing. They also require the

capacity to store big datasets and to clean them to correct inaccuracies.

Technology that collects data and actions insights from analytics: smart devices and devices connected through the Internet of Things (IoT)

Devices include sensors and monitors that generate data. Smart devices rely on these "machine-generated" data to improve their operations, often using AI. Devices are increasingly being connected to the IoT, which allows them to receive and send data from and to other IoT devices on ground moisture, climate and air quality, individuals' health metrics, firm asset performance, and the movement of goods through supply chains. IoT and machine-generated data from devices are poised to multiply exponentially the data generated by businesses, with potential for development in agriculture, health, manufacturing, and transportation (such as driverless vehicles). IoT devices already exceed the number of internet users and are forecast to reach 25 billion by

(Box continues next page)

2025, with the introduction of fifth-generation (5G) wireless technology.

Technology that creates transparency and trust in data records: distributed ledger technology, including blockchain

Distributed ledger technology (DLT) is a distributed database in which data are recorded, shared, and synchronized across the nodes (or devices) of a network. Blockchain is a type of DLT whereby information is consolidated into "blocks" that are linked in a way in which they can add information layers to the ledger, which

cannot be changed (in an "append-only" fashion). Blockchain records transactions, tracks assets, or transfers value between two parties in a verifiable and permanent way without the need for a central coordinating entity. Because everyone participating in the blockchain can see all transactions, the technology engenders peer-to-peer trust and has several applications, including enabling payments, smart contracts, supply chain tracking, and resolving data protection and security issues in the IoT.

a. MGI (2018).

---

between buyers and sellers of agricultural commodities, while employing Internet of Things (IoT) devices to accurately measure variables such as commodity weight. In those platform businesses that earn a significant proportion of their revenue from advertising, data collected through the platform are used to inform that advertising. Platform models are a key focus of this chapter and of many of the economic policy issues raised in chapter 7 because of their importance to low- and middle-income countries.

The extent to which data-intensive technologies can be deployed relies on the presence of key infrastructure, most fundamentally network coverage. There is also the challenge of bringing more people online, especially in countries with a gap between the number of people who have access to networks and those who are online. This gap is a function of affordability, the existence of local content, and digital skills (see chapter 5). As more people and devices come online and data usage matures, the network capacity needed will grow, requiring sufficient spectrum to be made available for mobile use—especially in lower-income countries where mobile is the predominant technology. Although 4G technology is sufficient for many IoT uses, 5G will be needed for those uses that require ultra-reliability and low latency such as smart energy grids and autonomous vehicles. Reliability of connection is important for DLT applications that must keep a reliable and consistent record of data. Storage and analysis of the data generated through IoT devices and platform business models depend on cloud computing (remote storage and processing infrastructure) and the ability to transmit data over the internet to data centers either locally or abroad. Beyond data infrastructure, most technology

applications require a suite of other foundational systems to create value, including reliable payment systems and logistics networks, transport infrastructure, and address systems. Data infrastructure policy is discussed further in chapter 5.

Figure 3.2 summarizes how data are used as an input to and produced as a by-product of economic activity. It illustrates how data created through economic activity can be used as an input to either the same economic activity or new activities.

Focus on platform firms in low- and middle-income countries

Platform businesses, one of the most ubiquitous and transformative data-driven models today, reduce transaction costs and alleviate market failures.[7] Ranging from start-ups to businesses operating at scale, they are a mix of both locally grown and foreign firms, and they are expanding across low- and middle-income countries. More than 300 digital platforms headquartered in Africa were active across major Sub-Saharan African economies as of 2020.[8] In Asia, a study looking at local platforms that had reached scale identified 62 major local platforms with an individual market capitalization of at least US$800 million as of 2016, half of which were located in China.[9]

The diversity of new platforms is evident in recent research examining both start-ups and scaled platforms. At least 959 platform firms have established a physical presence in a sample of 17 low- and middle-income countries[10] from all regions across four sectors that are important for jobs or economic productivity: e-commerce, transport and logistics (including both freight and passenger transport), agriculture, and

Figure 3.2 The role of data in economic activity

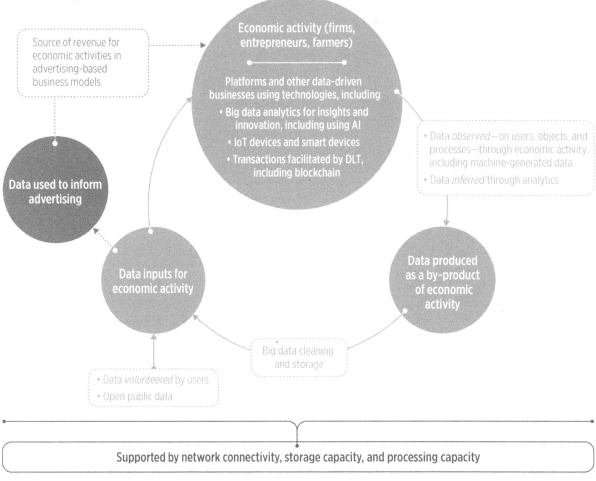

Platforms and other data-driven businesses using technologies, including

- Big data analytics for insights and innovation, including using AI
- IoT devices and smart devices
- Transactions facilitated by DLT, including blockchain

Economic activity (firms, entrepreneurs, farmers)

Source of revenue for economic activities in advertising-based business models

Data used to inform advertising

Data *observed*—on users, objects, and processes—through economic activity, including machine-generated data

Data *inferred* through analytics

Data inputs for economic activity

Data produced as a by-product of economic activity

Big data cleaning and storage

- Data *volunteered* by users
- Open public data

Supported by network connectivity, storage capacity, and processing capacity

Source: WDR 2021 team.

Note: AI = artificial intelligence; DLT = distributed ledger technology; IoT = Internet of Things.

tourism.[11] In the sample, Bangladesh, Brazil, Indonesia, Kenya, and Nigeria have relatively high numbers of platform firms when controlling for gross domestic product (GDP) per capita (figure 3.3, panel a).

Across the countries in the sample, most platform firms are recent entrants—55 percent were established in the past five years.[12] Only 11 percent of firms were established more than 10 years ago. Firms also tend to be small—over 80 percent have 50 or fewer employees, and almost half (47 percent) have 10 or fewer (figure 3.3, panel b). Most firms have remained active (defined as having an active and up-to-date online presence) since they were established; the average share of firms currently active across regions is more than 80 percent. Sub-Saharan Africa is an outlier: nearly half of its firms appear to be inactive.[13]

E-commerce has the highest share of platform firms in 82 percent of countries in the sample, with the highest shares in South Asia and the Middle East

and North Africa and the lowest in Europe and Central Asia. The agriculture sector tends to have the smallest share of firms across regions, with the exception of Sub-Saharan Africa. The importance of e-commerce in the data economy is also reflected in web traffic.

Although local data-driven firms are on the rise in low- and middle-income countries, foreign-headquartered firms have a significant presence, underscoring the global nature of the data-driven economy. Their presence is also a reminder that the platform economy is still nascent in lower-income countries relative to high-income economies (partly due to issues around trust, lack of digital skills, and lack of access to finance). Of the top 25 websites in terms of traffic in the 17 low- and middle-income countries sampled, 59 percent belong to firms with foreign headquarters on average[14]—however, the figure varies across countries (figure 3.4). Although the presence of firms from high-income countries in lower-income countries is

Figure 3.3 Platform firms are numerous in some lower-income countries but tend to be small

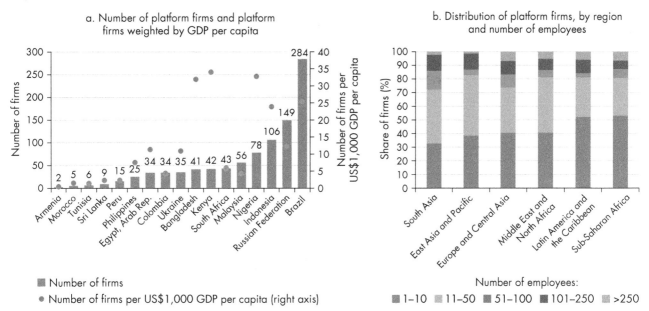

a. Number of platform firms and platform firms weighted by GDP per capita

b. Distribution of platform firms, by region and number of employees

■ Number of firms
● Number of firms per US$1,000 GDP per capita (right axis)

Number of employees:
■ 1–10 ■ 11–50 ■ 51–100 ■ 101–250 ■ >250

Sources: Nyman and Stinshoff (forthcoming), based on information from Crunchbase, Crunchbase (database), https://www.crunchbase.com/; World Bank, Digital Development (database), https://www.worldbank.org/en/topic/digitaldevelopment; Dow Jones and Company, Factiva (database), https://professional.dowjones.com/factiva/; Thomson Reuters Foundation, "Inclusive Economies," http://www.trust.org/inclusive-economies/; Alexa Internet, "The Top 500 Sites on the Web, by Country" (accessed April 2020), https://www.alexa.com/topsites/countries; World Bank, World Development Indicators (database), https://datatopics.worldbank.org/world-development-indicators/.

Note: Panel a shows the number of platform firms and platform firms weighted by gross domestic product (GDP) per capita in selected low- and middle-income countries The total sample of platform firms is 959. Per capita GDP is in constant 2010 US dollars for 2019. Panel b shows the share of firm sizes in terms of number of employees by region in a sample of 595 active platform firms.

Figure 3.4 The importance of domestic versus foreign-headquartered firms differs across countries as indicated by firm share of top websites

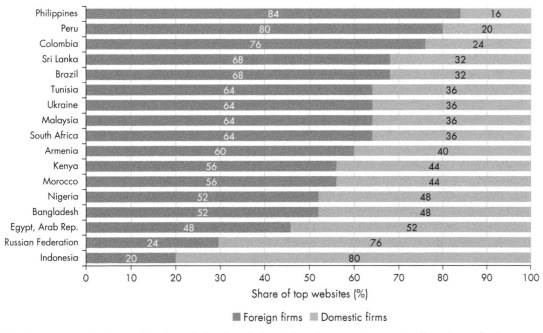

■ Foreign firms ▫ Domestic firms

Source: WDR 2021 team, based on Alexa Internet, "The Top 500 Sites on the Web, by Country" (accessed April 2020), https://www.alexa.com/topsites/countries.

Note: The figure shows the percentage of websites for firms with foreign headquarters versus domestic headquarters among the top 25 websites per country based on traffic. Headquarters is understood to be the global headquarters, not the domestic or regional office. Total sample size is 425 websites.

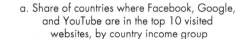

Figure 3.5 Users visit and spend more time on Facebook, Google, and YouTube than other websites

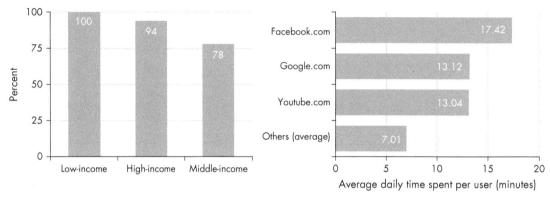

a. Share of countries where Facebook, Google, and YouTube are in the top 10 visited websites, by country income group

b. Daily time spent on website (global average): Facebook, Google, and YouTube versus other top 10 visited websites

Source: WDR 2021 team, based on data from Alexa Internet, "The Top 500 Sites on the Web, by Country" (accessed April 2020), https://www.alexa.com/topsites/countries.

Note: Sample of 1,270 websites (top 10 websites in 127 countries).

widespread, the opposite is not true. Only 15 percent of digital firms headquartered in Sub-Saharan Africa operate outside the region, and the majority of those have expanded to the Middle East and North Africa.[15]

The leading global platforms are highly relevant to the digital ecosystems of lower-income countries and their citizens, particularly for online search and social media. Google, YouTube (which is owned by Google), and Facebook are among the top 10 most visited websites in 62 of 77 low- and middle-income countries (figure 3.5, panel a). These platforms also have the highest average daily time spent on the site per user globally (figure 3.5, panel b). In online markets where firms compete for the attention of viewers, such popularity can significantly intensify these platforms' market power in advertising (which is, in turn, important for suppliers of other products) and increase the amount of data being collected about users. Google's Next Billion Users initiative is specifically aimed at developing products and services for lower-income countries. Facebook has launched an app aimed at providing free data in lower-income countries. WhatsApp (owned by Facebook) is by far the most used mobile application globally in terms of time.[16] Because of the global nature of these firms, dynamics in overseas markets that affect the strategies and policies of these large platforms will have repercussions for those in low- and middle-income countries.

Data traffic over the internet is also highly concentrated in a few companies. Six US companies generate more than 40 percent of the world's internet

data flows (figure 3.6, panel a). Across the top 25 websites (by traffic) in the 17 sampled countries featured in figure 3.4, some 60 percent is owned by five firms headquartered in the United States (Google, Microsoft, Facebook, Verizon, and Amazon). Significant non-US parent companies include Naspers (headquartered in South Africa), Alibaba (China), and Jumia (which has its operations largely in Nigeria)—see figure 3.6, panel b.

Data inputs for economic activity

The "digital footprint" and data collection by firms

Everything a digital user does leaves a trail, whether it is making a phone call, sending a text, conducting an online search, posting on social media, or making a digital transaction. The digital footprint of an individual or business is their collection of traceable digital activities and communications on the internet or other digital media. Data collected through devices—particularly IoT devices—can also capture insights on individuals and firms. For firms, such insights are gained from data on throughput and efficiency, spare capacity, and asset quality, among other things. For individuals, they typically involve health and biometric data.

Digital footprints can be actively created when a user makes a choice to share information, such as by posting on social media or volunteering information to register for services. Or they can be passively

Figure 3.6 Internet traffic in low- and middle-income countries is concentrated in several US-based firms

a. Share of global internet traffic by firm, 2018 (% of total)

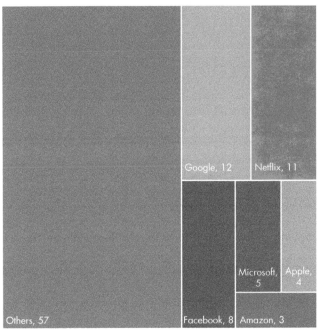

b. Ten most visited parent firms among the top 25 websites

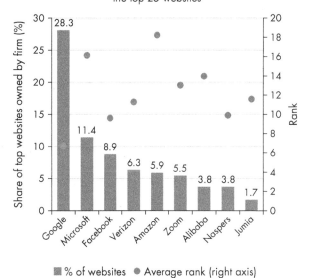

■ % of websites ● Average rank (right axis)

Source: Sandvine 2019. Data at http://bit.do/WDR2021-Fig-3_6_a.

Note: "Others" refers to file sharing, marketplace, security, and virtual private network (VPN) messaging, as well as cloud and audio streaming.

Source: Nyman and Stinshoff (forthcoming), based on information in Alexa Internet, "The Top 500 Sites on the Web, by Country" (accessed April 2020), https://www.alexa.com/topsites/countries.

Note: The panel shows the percentage of the top 25 websites owned by the listed parent organizations in the sample. Traffic rank is from a low of 1 (more traffic) to a high of 20 (least traffic). Total sample includes 425 websites from 17 low- and middle-income countries. Ownership is defined as majority shareholding.

created, when data are left behind as a by-product of other activities such as an Internet Protocol (IP) address, search history, or internet clicks. Firms typically collect both active and passive data. Often, this information is collected at exceedingly high frequency and microgranularity.

Big data and ML algorithms enable firms to draw inferences about the characteristics of individuals (such as attitudes and socioeconomic status) and other businesses (such as performance, capacity, and reputation). In low- and middle-income countries, digital footprints are best known for their ability to predict repayment behavior. However, applications also extend to the development of new products and improvements in service delivery across the economy, to the development of analytical tools for businesses, and, importantly, to the creation of consumer profiles that can be used to sell advertising services—a practice that ultimately subsidizes many of the "free" products that consumers use today. A number of risks have been identified and concerns raised about these methods and applications. These are discussed later in the chapter.

Data collected through mobile phone use has been one of the fastest-growing sources of user information and behavior. CDRs held by mobile network operators (MNOs) contain certain data on every call and text made, including the telephone number of the caller and receiver, the date and time of the interaction, and the associated cellphone tower. This information is primarily collected for billing purposes but can be used as well to identify the behavior, mobility patterns, and social networks of users. MNOs can also track data on use of value-added services, internet services, and mobile money transactions.[17]

Data-driven firms—including e-commerce, online search, and social media firms—produce, in addition, data on behavioral patterns that can be detected by noting the time, frequency, and extent of transactions or communications made. Several variables that can help predict economic status are available to platform firms, including the device type of their users (desktop, tablet, mobile), the operating system (Windows, iOS, Android), and the channel through which a user arrived at the firm's home page. For example, having an iOS device consistently correlates with being in the top quartile of the income distribution in the United States.[18] A study in Germany found that the time of day that purchases were made on an e-commerce site was predictive of a consumer's self-control and repayment behavior. People who made purchases between noon and 6 p.m. were half as likely to default on their payment for the products bought as those who made purchases between midnight and 6 a.m. Consumers coming from a price comparison website were roughly half as likely to default as customers directed to the site via search engine ads, consistent with research on impulse shopping.[19]

Finally, firms collect data that are generated as a result of phenomena that are not attributable to a specific individual or business. These data are often generated by machines or devices and can include data on traffic, weather and climatic conditions, and network usage in the case of computing or network industries. This Report highlights many examples of using this type of data for development purposes.

The use of open public intent data by businesses

Public intent data are also used by businesses for commercial purposes, particularly where those data are nonpersonal and where there are positive spill-overs from the private use of such data. The use of open public intent data by private firms is prevalent in advanced economies with advanced national data systems, although there are also examples from low-income and emerging economies. Spotlight 3.1 discusses these uses in greater detail.

The positive development impacts of data used in the production process

This section presents examples of potential positive development impacts that data used in firms' production processes can facilitate (following the third development pathway of data generated by private firms described in chapter 1). It then turns to the risks stemming from the use of data by firms that policy makers need to consider. These examples are included to help set out what the current production possibility frontier might look like going forward. Although many of the examples may be outliers, they can indicate what may be possible and what countries may want to aspire to.

Boosting opportunities for lagging regions and populations by reducing market fragmentation. Data-driven business models can lower entry costs to markets and provide new opportunities for small firms and

low-income households.[20] Firms in less populated areas can expand their access to markets through data-driven platforms, which match sellers and buyers, and through the logistics services of e-commerce platforms, which provide support in bringing products to market from more remote areas. Costs associated with distance are as much as 65 percent lower for online vendors active on global e-commerce platforms, compared with those for offline vendors.[21] Lower-income countries could reap substantial benefits from such e-commerce platforms: the cost-reduction effects of platforms tend to be greater for exporting countries that are unknown or less trustworthy to consumers (as measured by corruption indexes).[22]

In China's rural (and traditionally lower-income) Taobao Villages, where annual e-commerce transaction volumes exceed 10 million yuan and at least 10 percent of households engage in e-commerce, rural households trading goods on the Taobao platform have significantly higher incomes and higher income growth than those that do not.[23] These data are suggestive of the large benefits of data-driven business models in lagging regions, but the evidence base is just beginning to develop, and not all signs are encouraging. For example, a recent randomized trial in China that connected rural villages to e-commerce found little evidence of income gains for rural producers and workers. Understanding what factors led to Taobao success and meager gains for other Chinese villages is a crucial part of the future research agenda.

Creating new export opportunities. Not only can entrepreneurs market their goods remotely, but intangible data-enabled services now flow across borders. The boom in data-enabled services creates opportunities for new entrants in global trade and may foster economic growth for countries traditionally lagging in access to global markets. For example, the rise in Indian services exports has been associated with gains in per capita income and a decline in urban and rural poverty head count ratios.[24] The Indian digital services industry has also created employment, especially for women and in smaller cities with populations of about 1 million or less, which can help bridge economic and social inequalities.[25]

The Philippines is another important beneficiary, exporting an estimated US$23 billion in services enabled by information technology (IT)—equivalent to almost half of the country's merchandise trade exports and more than double its total agricultural exports.[26] In Africa, Senegal, a low-income country, boasts a dynamic digital services sector focused on business services as well as apps and software solutions geared toward regional markets. Mauritius has developed a fast-growing export-oriented digital business services industry, diversifying its services-centered economy away from the country's tourism sector.[27] Such expansion into digital services has proven important in light of the tourism collapse provoked by the COVID-19 pandemic. Studies show that trade in services, in particular IT-enabled business services, is not as prone to sudden collapses as other forms of global trade.[28]

Promoting productivity and growth. Although evidence from lower-income countries is scant, across four industries (hotels, restaurants, taxis, and retail trade) in 10 member countries of the Organisation for Economic Co-operation and Development (OECD)[29] the average service provider enjoyed bigger increases in the overall productivity of labor and capital in countries with relatively high online platform development between 2011 and 2017.[30] Increased e-sales activities accounted for 18 percent of the labor productivity growth in 14 European countries from 2003 to 2010.[31] There is also some evidence from Europe of a smaller productivity gap between large and small firms in the sectors that use online sales most.[32]

Machine learning could fundamentally revolutionize innovation, bringing data to the core of the growth process.[33] Empirical evidence on 18,000 US manufacturing plants between 2005 and 2010 finds that firms with more intensive data usage are significantly more productive due to not only technology adoption but also data-driven decision-making.[34] Globally, AI could deliver additional economic output of about US\$13 trillion between 2018 and 2030 (netting out competition effects and transition costs), boosting global GDP by about 1.2 percent a year, according to a 2018 modeling exercise.[35]

Of course, not all countries will be affected similarly, and the evidence base for low- and middle-income countries needs to be developed. The focus in this chapter on data-driven business models and productivity enhancement through data reveals an imbalance toward case studies from higher-income countries. That imbalance is itself a sign of the lopsided distribution of benefits deriving from data.

Creating new markets and disrupting the market position of traditional incumbents. E-money platforms, among others, have challenged traditional banks and other service providers in transferring funds to and from accounts. For example, M-Pesa reached 9.5 million customers within its first three years in operation in Kenya, a country with only 8.4 million bank accounts.[36] Electronic freight exchanges such as uShip and Mober that match carriers with cargo holders have triggered global logistics providers such as Schenker and DHL to develop their own digital exchanges. Incumbent taxi providers who were protected by fixed license caps are now exposed to competition from ride-hailing apps, which can improve inclusion of some parts of the population. For example, in Mexico City the proportion of female drivers with Uber (5 percent) is higher than in Mexico's taxi industry (0.5–2.5 percent).[37] A 2017 study of 2,000 firms in 60 countries found that digital entrants boost the size of an industry by both realizing latent demand and taking market share from incumbents.[38] Indeed, the study showed that the profits of incumbents fall significantly in response to competition from digital entrants, and the slowest-growing incumbents are the most affected. These effects should translate into welfare benefits for users through more affordable products and greater innovation, although the benefits are less likely felt by the lowest income groups because they do not participate in these markets as consumers or suppliers.

Supporting local entrepreneurship ecosystems. An ecosystem is an interconnected set of services accessed through a single integrated experience. Facebook, for example, enables users to shop, make hotel bookings, message contacts, read the news, and chat with a doctor—all with different firms but through a single interface. Successful data-driven firms often spark new business models through complementary products and aftermarkets. Such local ecosystems, consisting of symbiotic and interdependent firms, frequently rise up around leading multinational platforms. The leading global platforms are therefore highly relevant for the digital ecosystems of countries and their citizens.

Ecosystems built around larger firms can enable lower-income economies to build digital capabilities, especially because they integrate data across a series of services to increase the scale and scope of datasets. For example, Apple's Healthkit platform offers Apple device users the option to share their health and activity data across applications on their smartphones. This integration allows researchers, hospitals, and developers of health care and fitness apps to access valuable data to inform patient care, marketing, and product development. The development of a healthy ecosystem relies on provision of access to data and systems.

Related opportunities arising from data-driven business models

Three related opportunities can arise from data-driven business models that are not linked directly to the four channels discussed earlier. Evidence is just emerging, but it indicates that these models could be important for lower-income countries.

Providing nominally "free" services to consumers. Nominally "free" or "zero price" services have become an integral part of our lives. Free messaging services, video communication, social connection tools, search engines, map services, storage, and translation and payment apps are now commonplace and increasingly being developed with low-income consumers in mind. Google is rolling out scaled-down search and e-mail apps for low-end smartphones, as well as voice search in various dialects to overcome literacy challenges. Free services also offer important inputs for other data-driven businesses. Digital start-ups often rely on integration with digital payment systems, cloud storage, and online analytical tools. For transformative business models that match and connect users in different geographic locations, online map services are a crucial input.

The welfare gains of nominally "free" digital goods are substantial. However, they are likely to be underestimated because they are not captured in GDP—they have a nominal price of zero. A recent study found that including the welfare gains from Facebook would add between 0.05 and 0.11 percentage points to GDP growth per year in the United States.[39]

"Free" services reflect the very low marginal cost of replicating and distributing data and certain digital services. But they are ultimately made possible on a large scale because firms can monetize data through advertising and data sales, thereby giving rise to the idea that users in fact "pay with their data." This approach is reflected in the revenue structure of some of the tech giants. Mobile advertising made up 84 percent of Google's total revenue in 2019,[40] while Alibaba earns more than half its global revenues from advertising.[41]

Both Google and Facebook have offered free internet access in lower-income countries. Facebook's schemes have been criticized for mining the data of low-income users while initially defying net neutrality rules and offering access to only a limited set of sites.[42] Meanwhile, Google attempted to monetize its free Wi-Fi service (rolled out in nine middle-income countries) by showing ads to users, but it recently discontinued these services because they have proven unprofitable.[43]

More limited opportunities in low- and middle-income countries for monetizing data may therefore limit the ability of firms operating locally to offer free services. Facebook's average revenue per user in the United States and Canada was US$41.41 in 2019, whereas it was US$2.48 in all countries except the United States, Canada, and European and Asia-Pacific countries. Firms focused on lower-income countries may find it difficult to replicate the free services offered by firms that operate globally and can cross-subsidize their operations with global advertising.

Adapting to new ways of doing business because of the COVID-19 pandemic. Urgent demands have surfaced for the private sector to adopt data-driven solutions to deal with the pandemic and increase resilience and productivity for recovery. Firms will also need to increasingly invest in the transparency and traceability of value chains, increase their reliance on automation in the production process, and make more precise predictions about their demand and input supply that anticipate disruptions. Data-driven technologies will play a critical role in helping firms adapt. Smart connected devices and robots that automate previously manual processes while collecting and analyzing data will serve as a key input in this reengineering of business processes during the recovery. AI that can predict consumption and production trends, combined with platforms that provide matching through data analysis, may also create on-demand labor forces.

Although the intensifying adoption of data-driven business models can be an opportunity, these trends also hold risks for the international competitiveness of those countries not at the technological frontier, with implications for jobs and inequality.

Impacts on the green and sustainability agenda. The increased use of data-intensive technologies contributes to global carbon emissions. And yet these technologies can also help firms better manage their environmental footprint and become sustainable, while allowing sectors such as agriculture to adapt to climate change. By improving the efficiency and traceability of supply chains and production processes, these technologies can reduce waste, enable circular solutions, promote sustainable sourcing of inputs, and empower consumers to make more environmentally responsible decisions. By making energy systems more efficient (including through automated tracking of energy use), they can facilitate the adoption of renewable energy through better management of performance. Data-driven farming can help farmers adapt to climate change while rationalizing use of harmful inputs. However, the net impact of such technologies on the environment will depend on several factors, including responsible actions by consumers and the decarbonization of the energy sector.

How use of data in the production process is transforming sectors

New business models that use data to drive value are springing up in low- and middle-income economies. The data and technology that can be most transformative depend on the types of market failures that need to be solved and the development channels that are possible. This differs across sectors.

Finance

Some 1.7 billion adults worldwide did not have a bank account as of 2017.[44] At least 200 million small firms in low- and middle-income countries have unmet credit needs estimated at US$2.2 trillion.[45] Several market failures are to blame. First, the high cost of traditional banking relative to the low-value transactions and balances of low-income individuals makes it less viable or attractive for traditional banking to serve this market segment. Second, information asymmetries between financial institutions and low-income borrowers make it difficult to assess credit risk, thereby limiting the supply and raising the price of credit. Finally, formal financial services lack relevant products and services for low-income users. Digitization and data analytics can help overcome these challenges to make services more accessible, affordable, and secure.

Alternative credit scoring algorithms. Financial service providers are increasingly adopting alternative credit scoring techniques that take advantage of users' digital footprints to train ML algorithms to identify, score, and underwrite credit for individuals who otherwise lack documentation of their creditworthiness.

Two early movers that have achieved scale—Lenddo (Philippines) and Cignifi (operating in Africa, Asia, and Latin America)—use data that consumers volunteer about their cellphone use patterns, digital transactions, and social media and web browsing activity to build algorithms that map behavioral patterns and score the creditworthiness of borrowers.

Payment and transaction histories have also enabled e-commerce firms to move into lending. Ant Financial's MYbank app links directly to users' Alibaba transaction data to score and extend credit.[46] Amazon's small business loan operation (which operates in China, India, and other countries) relies on a seller's sales performance on Amazon to decide whether to extend credit. Destácame, a Chile-based alternative credit scoring start-up and the first of its kind in Latin America, uses data on utilities payments for its credit scoring.

Psychometric tests, which assess the abilities, attitudes, and personality traits of individuals, are also being used to screen borrowers. LenddoEFL provides financial institutions with psychometric tools that analyze applicants' answers on an online quiz, including factors such as how long it takes applicants to answer and how they interact with the web interface. LenddoEFL claims to have made more than 12 million credit assessments through more than 50 client financial institutions around the world.[47]

Notwithstanding the opportunities these approaches offer, observers have raised concerns that using algorithms in this way can discriminate against individuals and reinforce existing racial, gender, and economic inequalities. Lenddo, for example, has been known to rate consumers as less creditworthy if they are friends on Facebook with someone who was late paying back a loan.[48] Algorithmic bias is discussed later in this chapter and in chapters 4 and 6.

Payment systems. Digital payments are by definition flows of electronic data. They are central to powering e-commerce and other online transactions, while simultaneously generating data on purchasing patterns that can provide insights into a plethora of consumer characteristics.

Mobile payments in particular have reduced the transaction costs of transferring resources, enabling new ways for households and firms to make payments, save, and send remittances. The well-documented benefits of mobile money in lower-income countries include lowering transaction and transport costs; encouraging saving through the relatively safe storage of value in a digital format; empowering female users through greater privacy, thereby increasing their bargaining power within families; and allowing more effective risk sharing between households.[49] In India, mobile money has improved the ability of households to share risk, providing welfare benefits of 3–4 percent of income on average.[50] Research also has found a significant link between the use of the mobile financial service M-Pesa and a reduction in poverty among Kenyans, with greater impacts on female-headed households through changes in financial behavior and movement of labor from subsistence farming to secondary jobs and entrepreneurship.[51]

Use of transaction data for product development. Digital payments generate large amounts of data on how people make purchases and transfers, which can be especially important in economies that run largely on cash and among demographic groups that have a small digital footprint. These data can enable firms to see which regions and market segments are expanding, understand user preferences and behavior to target services such as microcredit, and predict fraud and increase security within and between platforms. For example, Mastercard's Tourism Insights service allows the tourism industry to make better investments by leveraging big data to provide information on travelers' preferences.[52] In South Africa, TymeBank offers customers incentives to link their debit cards to their retail loyalty programs, providing access to data on customer spending that are used for product design.

Distributed ledger technology, including blockchain. Blockchain eliminates the need for financial intermediaries, drastically reducing settlement time and making transfers almost instantaneous. The use of digital technology can embed rules into smart contracts, including automated execution of contract. The explicit terms and payments of DLT can simplify complex negotiation and verification processes.[53] DLTs' use of smart contracts in the provision of loans and credit can also improve trust. This is especially important for new and smaller firms that lack the requisite credit histories and collateral.

Despite the promise of blockchain, there are serious challenges to its widespread adoption, including unclear or unfavorable regulatory approaches and lack of user understanding. Adopting blockchain where the technology does not address the underlying issue or consumer needs is also problematic.

Agriculture

Managing production and marketing risks is a key challenge for smallholder farmers and agribusinesses. Remote sensing and geographic information systems, together with data analytics, provide insights into farming operations and propel the development of smart farming, which can help manage production and financial risks. For example, NubeSol, an Indian agtech firm, provides sugarcane growers with a monthly yield map of their plots, with forecasts of yields and recommendations on inputs such as fertilizer based on remote sensing and data analytics.

JD Digits (JDD), a technology firm in China, is adopting AI techniques and big data to provide credit to farmers who raise pigs. Farms install AI-enabled cameras that can recognize pigs' faces, as well as IoT technology to transmit data about the farms' physical conditions. If a pig with feeding abnormalities has been identified, the algorithm can quickly extract information about its growth history and immune status to provide customized feeding care. The IoT system adjusts farm conditions such as humidity, temperature, and lighting based on real-time data on the farm. Using information about farm operations, JDD also carries out credit assessments to provide farmers with loans, which has reduced their nonperforming loan ratio to nearly zero.

Platforms are using data as well to provide a range of services and products along the value chain, including by reducing idle capacity in machinery. Hello Tractor, which emerged in Nigeria, operates a platform connecting tractor owners and farmers who lack their own equipment. Data about tractor locations and availability are monitored using an installed device and then transmitted to Hello Tractor's mobile app platform, which farmers can use to submit a booking request. In this way, farmers are able to find the most cost-effective available tractor, and tractor owners are able to monitor the use of equipment. Another agriculture platform, DigiCow, pioneered in Kenya, keeps digital health records on cows and matches farmers with qualified veterinary services.

Integrated, data-focused solutions are emerging along the whole agriculture value chain. Digifarm, a mobile platform offered by Safaricom in Kenya, provides farmers with one-stop access to a suite of products, including financial and credit services, quality farm products, and customized information on best farming practices. Mobile money data from M-Pesa and data on the way people behave on the app are taken into consideration to provide farmers with tailored products and services.

As agriculture supply chains become more complex, margins imposed by different intermediaries mount, which raises the prices paid by consumers and depresses the income earned by farmers. Food traceability concerns also increase.[54] Data-based solutions can improve food traceability, while disrupting traditional market structures by reducing the need for intermediaries. In Haiti, blockchain solutions have allowed mango farmers to maintain ownership of their produce until the final sale to US retailers by facilitating traceability and direct payments. Employed in conjunction with other value chain components such as third-party logistics services, intermediaries that previously held substantial market power are circumvented. Customers can scan a QR code on the final product to access information about where the mango comes from, how it was packaged and transported, and the costs involved at each step.[55] Similarly, Walmart has collaborated with IBM to trace mangoes from South and Central America to the United States. Participants in this process cannot edit information because of the decentralization feature of blockchain technology, which ensures trust and transparency.[56]

Personal data protection has specific complexities for farmers. Data on their farms are identifiable and could be used to reveal personal details such as their wealth and income. However, farmers could also benefit from using and pooling their data to develop commercial insights. The governance regime for agriculture thus requires special considerations (see the further discussion of governance issues in chapter 8).

Health

To deliver individual health care in lower-income countries, data-driven applications require complementary improvements in infrastructure and basic health services before they can become truly transformational. Some business models show promise in helping overcome such challenges, which include high logistical costs, counterfeiting of pharmaceuticals, difficulties in coordinating health care resources, and low supplies of specialist expertise, especially in rural areas. With strong mobile phone penetration, rising investment in digitizing health information, and developments in cloud computing, more health-focused businesses in low- and middle-income countries are likely to adopt data-intensive advances in coming years. Although such advances hold promise, the sensitive nature of health data implies an acute need for policy makers to be aware of the risks posed by the improper collection and use of these data.

Telehealth (mHealth and eHealth). Telehealth makes use of data and connected devices to deliver care remotely. In rural areas where the ratio of doctors to patients is low, telehealth is a useful way to access consultations and disease diagnosis. The model has also played an important role during the COVID-19 pandemic, where remote diagnosis has been necessary.

Mobile apps combined with AI technology and wearable devices can provide in-the-field diagnoses and recommendations. For example, Colorimetrix, an app that allows a smartphone camera to read results from color-based tests for diabetes, kidney disease, and urinary tract infections, was designed specifically with lower-income economies in mind. Algorithms are used to compare the result with stored calibration values. Results are delivered to the smartphone, allowing for further analysis of results for trends. The hope is that such apps will eventually also be able to detect HIV, malaria, and tuberculosis.[57]

Accuhealth Chile monitors patients in remote areas by using a range of connected medical sensors. Both quantitative data on patients' progress and qualitative data collected through custom-created questionnaires are sent to a virtual clinical service that conducts patient triage based on algorithmic analysis. Accuhealth is also using predictive algorithms to make service delivery more cost-efficient.

In Cameroon, CardioPad was locally designed to improve the access of patients living in rural areas to cardiovascular health care. The CardioPad tablet is paired with sensors that collect data on the patient's health statistics and transmit them over a mobile network to hospitals where cardiologists can make a diagnosis.

Drug verification. Substandard or falsified medical products will be an urgent health care challenge in the next decade, according to the World Health Organization (WHO).[58] An estimated one-tenth of medical products in low- and middle-income countries, particularly antimalarials and antibiotics, are substandard or falsified.[59]

Mobile authentication services such as mPedigree offer people in countries such as Ghana, India, Kenya, and Nigeria an easy way to check the authenticity of medicine. Launched in Ghana in 2007, mPedigree allows pharmaceutical manufacturers to add a code to their packaging that consumers can then verify using their mobile phones. mPedigree has also begun using its consumer authentication data to monitor for anomalies in real time so that it can then generate warnings to brand owners, regulators, and consumers.[60]

Supplies management. Digital platforms can also help manage supplies in countries where centralized provision is deficient or lacking. LifeBank is a Nigerian platform firm that matches hospitals requesting blood with potential donors based on current demand and location maps of all institutions involved in blood distribution. Information about the donation, collection, screening, storage, and delivery procedures are recorded on a blockchain, thereby increasing confidence in blood quality. LifeBank claims to have reduced the average delivery time from about 24 hours to 45 minutes.[61] During the COVID-19 crisis, the platform has also extended its services to matching medical equipment.

Education

Despite significant improvements in school enrollment over the last decades, an average student in low-income countries performs worse than 95 percent of the students in high-income countries.[62] Lack of teaching resources and learning tools and the traditional one-size-fits-all approach in education have made it difficult to tailor instruction to students' individual abilities and needs, particularly where classrooms are overcrowded.[63] Recent advances in big data and AI offer opportunities to provide individualized learning experiences for students. Machine learning and data analytics techniques can help identify students' behavioral patterns (such as mistakes made frequently in tests) usually in a more efficient way than teachers. For example, by memorizing and understanding students' learning paths, Byju, a digital supplemental learning platform in India, suggests tailored learning materials such as videos, quizzes, and flashcards that match the needs of individual students. Besides analyzing individual learning behaviors, the platform also analyzes aggregate data on how all students learn on its platform. If many students are having trouble with similar types of problem sets, the system flags the need to add more explanatory videos or materials to the entire platform.

In China, Squirrel Ai Learning is another firm specializing in intelligent adaptive education. Students start with a short diagnostic test to leave a digital footprint reflecting their knowledge level so that the teaching system can provide a tailored curriculum, which is updated as the student proceeds through learning modules. Based on its comparison trials among middle school students, Squirrel Ai Learning claims that its system does a better job of improving math test scores than traditional classroom teaching.[64]

During the COVID-19 pandemic, digital platforms that support live video communication have been playing an indispensable role in transitioning to online learning. As of May 2020, more than 140 countries had closed schools, affecting more than 60 percent of enrolled students.[65] Lark, for example, is providing educational institutions in India with free cloud storage and video conference services. Dingtalk, a communication platform that supports video conferencing and attendance tracking, has connected more than 50 million students with teachers in China.

Transport and logistics

Data-driven firms in transport and logistics provide matching services to facilitate the use of assets by other market participants. By automating decision-making and navigation, these models increase the efficiency of service delivery and the management of supply chains. Prominent applications are for digital freight matching, digital courier logistics, and IoT-enabled cold storage.

Digital freight matching. These platforms (often dubbed "Uber for trucks") match cargo and shippers with trucks for last-mile transport. In lower-income countries, where the supply of truck drivers is highly fragmented and often informal, sourcing cargo is a challenge, and returning with an empty load contributes to high shipping costs. In China, the empty load rate is 27 percent versus 13 percent in Germany and 10 percent in the United States.[66]

Digital freight matching overcomes these challenges by matching cargo to drivers and trucks that are underutilized. The model also uses data insights to optimize routing and provide truckers with integrated services and working capital. Because a significant share of logistics services in lower-income countries leverage informal suppliers, these technologies also represent an opportunity to formalize services. Examples include Blackbuck (India), Cargo X (Brazil), Full Truck Alliance (China), Kobo360 (Ghana, Kenya, Nigeria, Togo, Uganda), and Lori (Kenya, Nigeria, Rwanda, South Sudan, Tanzania, Uganda). In addition to using data for matching, Blackbuck uses various data to set reliable arrival times, drawing on global positioning system (GPS) data and predictions on the length of driver stops. Lori tracks data on costs and revenues per lane, along with data on asset utilization, to help optimize services. Cargo X charts routes to avoid traffic and reduce the risk of cargo robbery. Kobo360 chooses routes to avoid armed bandits based on real-time information shared by drivers. Many of the firms also allow shippers to track their cargo in real time. Data on driver characteristics and behavior have allowed platforms to offer auxiliary services to address the challenges that truck drivers face. For example, some platforms offer financial products to help drivers pay upfront costs, such as tolls, fuel, and tires, as well as targeted insurance products.

Kobo360 claims that its drivers increase their monthly earnings by 40 percent and that users save an average of about 7 percent in logistics costs.[67] Lori claims that more than 40 percent of grain moving through Kenya to Uganda now moves through its platform, and that the direct costs of moving bulk grain have been reduced by 17 percent in Uganda.[68]

Digital courier logistics. The growth of on-demand couriers enables small merchants and the growing e-commerce industry to reach customers rapidly and reliably in expanding urban areas. Data-driven matching and route optimization overcome high search costs and traffic congestion and provide verification of safety standards through customer reviews.

The prime example of this business model is Gojek, which is reportedly utilized by more than 1 million motorcycle drivers serving 500,000 micro, small, and medium enterprises (MSMEs)—including more than 120,00 MSMEs since the onset of the COVID-19 pandemic.[69] Established in Indonesia in 2010 as a call center to connect consumers to courier delivery services, the company leveraged its data on consumer behavior to expand into digital courier services in 2015. Its app now offers various logistics services, including delivery of food and groceries and medicines and pharmaceuticals. Gojek uses AI and ML for matching, forecasting (to inform drivers where to go ahead of a surge in demand), and dynamic pricing. Through its 8 billion pings with drivers per day, Gojek claims it generates 4–5 terabytes of data every day.

IoT-enabled cold storage. According to WHO, 19.4 million people across the globe lacked access to routine life-saving vaccines in 2018, partly because of lack of efficient cold chain systems.[70] IoT-enabled cold storage solutions allow the transport and storage of temperature-sensitive food and medication, with greater control and tracking by the freight owner. For vaccines, the ability to track temperature can help ensure confidence in integrity before dispensation, even before further testing.

Gricd, a Nigerian start-up founded in 2018, utilizes solar-powered, IoT-enabled mobile refrigeration boxes whose internal probes collect temperature data and transmit it to a server. Real-time information on location and temperature can be accessed by freight owners online or via a mobile app, ensuring that the cold chain is effectively monitored and maintained.

Social media as a tool for connecting to markets

High marketing and advertising costs hinder smaller businesses trying to reach new markets and customers. Meanwhile, high search costs and frictions related to contract enforcement raise prices for buyers and inhibit trade.[71] Social media provide a low-cost sales platform for firms domestically and abroad and reduce search costs for consumers. They enable products to be better targeted to consumers and can reduce marketing costs by as much as 90 percent, compared with traditional television marketing.[72] Social media platforms also allow sellers to incorporate market intelligence into their product development through real-time feedback and gathering of online data.[73] Given these advantages, it is not surprising that nearly half of all enterprises in the European Union had used social media for advertising purposes as of 2017.[74]

Reaching markets through social media could disproportionately advantage smaller firms over larger ones, as suggested by the high proportion of small entrepreneurs who use Facebook. In 2018, nearly four in 10 Facebook business users were single-person firms connecting across 42 countries

(including low- and middle-income), although single-person firms are only one-tenth of the general population of firms.[75] Businesses run by women are more likely to leverage online tools to facilitate business success than businesses run by men.[76]

On the buyer side, social connections can increase trade by building trust, including by reducing information asymmetries and providing a substitute for the formal mechanisms of contract enforcement.[77] According to a study of 180 countries and 332 European regions, social connectedness tends to increase exports—particularly to those countries with a weak rule of law—and to lower prices, especially for goods whose prices are not transparent and that are not traded on exchanges.[78]

Some potential risks and adverse outcomes of data-driven businesses to be addressed by policy

Despite the potential transformative effects of data-driven firms, policy makers need to take into account several (often interrelated) risks and adverse outcomes to ensure that the use of data in the productive processes of firms safely fulfills their potential. The relevance and immediacy of these concerns depend on the data intensity of a country's economy. However, because of the global nature of many large data-driven firms market dynamics in one country can often have spillover effects internationally. This concern should not discourage policy makers from fostering a data-driven economic ecosystem in their country, but they should put the appropriate safeguards and enablers in place to ensure that data-driven markets remain competitive and vibrant—and that gains are shared broadly across society—as the data intensity of the economy increases. These topics are covered in part II of this Report.

Potential to increase the propensity for dominant firms to emerge

Proprietary data can provide a firm with a competitive advantage over rivals. Because data are often created as a by-product of a firm's economic activities, once a firm has invested in the fixed cost of building capacity to collect data, the marginal cost of creating additional data is low. Moreover, better targeting of a firm's offering can attract more users, thereby leveraging network effects between platform users that can lead to a "winner-takes-most" dynamic or, at the least, a scale advantage that new entrants find difficult to overcome.[79] For example, an e-commerce platform that incorporates more consumer data creates a more customized shopping experience, with more accurate product recommendations, more preordered shopping baskets, and more consumer reviews. A platform with a greater number of consumers will also attract more suppliers through indirect network effects, raising users' costs of switching to competing platforms. The distribution of web traffic, a proxy for concentration in the e-commerce sector, is skewed toward a few larger platforms. Among 631 business-to-consumer online marketplaces in Africa, 56 percent of web visitors went to 1 percent of sites in 2019.[80] Jumia alone had 24 percent of users.

Data can also ease a platform's entry into adjacent markets. Well-known examples are M-Pesa's move from money transfers into savings and loan products; Uber's entry into food and freight delivery; and Google's evolution from search to shopping, maps, and other markets. By combining multiple types of data, platforms can benefit from the broader scope of their data, which has spurred a growing number of mergers aimed at accumulating data (a prime example is Facebook's acquisition of WhatsApp).[81]

The potential of a platform business to acquire market power depends on its business model, including the types of users that interact on the platform and its revenue model, which affect the type of data that gives firms a competitive advantage (figure 3.7). For example, firms that rely on advertising revenue require frequently updated consumer data to create holistic consumer profiles. Platforms that earn a fee

based on their transactions conducted may rely more on historical data on product demand and consumer profiles for a smaller range of products. The type of data required affects, in turn, the ease with which firms can access or replicate the data they need. Where platforms rely on volunteered or observed consumer data, firms with greater market power may be able to collect data more easily because consumers have fewer options—meaning those firms can further entrench their market positions.

The greater propensity for dominance in data-driven markets raises the risk that smaller or more traditional firms will be excluded, hindering local entrepreneurship and posing risks for consumer welfare. These effects can be exacerbated in developing markets, where entrants find it harder to raise start-up capital and hire from the limited supply of skilled programmers and data scientists. For example, of the total private market funding received by the 10 highest-funded disruptive tech firms in Africa, 77 percent went to firms owned by the three largest African internet companies (two by Naspers, two by Jumia, and one by Ringier One Africa Media).[82] Where few large data-driven players currently operate or where a few large firms provide much-needed goods and services, the risks may be less immediately apparent. However, because of the dynamism of such markets and their tendency to tip toward concentrated structures, it is important that policy makers safeguard against dominance that forestalls entry and innovation.

Figure 3.7 Risks to market structure and market power stemming from platform firms

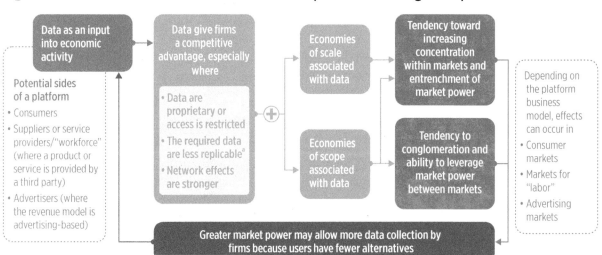

Source: WDR 2021 team.

a. Such data include observed and inferred data and data requiring frequent updating.

On DLT platforms, data access is not controlled by one institution, thus reducing the extent to which the benefits of network effects can entrench market power. However, private blockchains still require a central authority or institution that decides who can participate in the system, thereby placing power in the hands of the institution that acts as the gatekeeper. By contrast, public blockchains such as Bitcoin do not require a central authority but rather "proof-of-work" (a system to deter frivolous or malicious uses of computing power) to participate. This system, in turn, generates very high energy costs because it requires computing power and resource usage.[83]

Phenomena linked to the issue of dominance and market structure are described in the sections that follow.

Tension between cooperation and competition in data-driven ecosystems. Complementary products are built around larger platforms. These innovations can become central to the business models of the larger platforms. For example, Amazon, Uber, and Airbnb would not be able to operate without the payment systems embedded in their services. However, this network structure also means that firms are dependent on accessing the systems and data of other firms that could become rivals in the future.

Typically, firms access the systems and data of other firms through application programming interfaces (APIs) provided by the core platform in the ecosystem. APIs link platforms to other platforms and to developers of digital services. Through APIs, a platform or digital service provider will typically either draw data from or provide data to other firms to support its own functioning or support the functioning of other players. In markets where data are a key input, the owners of valuable data are gatekeepers in the development of smaller entrepreneurs.

The emergence of potential competition from complementors may provoke the lead platform to restrict its API. For example, when Twitter perceived a competitive threat from LinkedIn, Twitter restricted the use of its API in 2012 to prevent users' Tweets from appearing on LinkedIn's platform. In Kenya, developers have complained about M-Pesa's refusal to share its API.[84] In the United States, developers testifying before Congress in 2020 accused Apple of mimicking their products and of citing privacy concerns to restrict how third-party developers collect location data.[85] Chapter 7 covers competition issues.

Data-driven mergers and acquisitions. In recent years, waves of acquisitions by large local players have occurred in e-commerce in China and India and in transportation in Southeast Asia, where Uber exited eight Southeast Asian markets after selling its businesses to Grab, the region's leading platform.[86] Of the mergers involving digital platforms that have undergone review by antitrust authorities around the world, 82 percent involved an acquisition by a very large firm.[87] Mergers of two very large firms were the most common type of transaction. Chapter 7 covers issues related to mergers in more detail.

Suboptimal exchange of data. Although the broad use, reuse, and repurposing of data by firms can generate larger gains, market mechanisms may generate specific patterns of data exchange and reuse below the level that yields the greatest social welfare.[88] Regulators must take several steps to balance the costs and benefits of mandating data sharing to address these concerns. First, they should protect individuals' rights related to personal data. Second, they should recognize that mandated data sharing would dampen firms' incentives to invest in data collection if firms must share data with competitors or potential competitors. And, third, they should take into account that data sharing could jeopardize the provision of free or subsidized services if a firm relies on monetization of its data to cross-subsidize these services. Optimal data sharing between firms could be lower in countries where data are less important to the economy.[89] The right balance may differ in high-income and lower-income economies, although policy makers in some lower-income countries may wish to adopt a forward-looking viewpoint in this area to set the stage for future advances in their data economies. These issues are further discussed in chapters 6 and 7.

Linked to data sharing is the debate over property rights or access rights to data generated as a by-product of economic activity—for example, in terms of individuals versus firms in the case of personal data or in terms of owners of devices or applications versus the party using the device or application. This issue is taken up in chapter 6.

Potential for exploitation of individuals

Excessive data collection. Data collected by firms tracking users across third-party websites, applications, and devices can raise concerns. This practice is dominated by a small number of large firms—for example, a major part of Google's data collection occurs when a user is not directly engaged with any of its products.[90] Recent literature suggests that the vast amounts of data collected in this manner may be deemed excessive under existing European competition laws, where the focus is on the anticompetitive harm that may occur whether or not data protection rules are infringed.[91] More generally, both data protection authorities and competition authorities have noted that firms often understate and obscure their actual data practices, preventing consumers from making informed choices.[92] Excessive collection of data on children and other vulnerable groups is of particular concern (such as in the education, health, and financial sectors), especially in countries and locales where individuals lack adequate knowledge to protect against these risks. These issues are further discussed in chapters 6 and 7.

Insufficient governance of data held by private firms. Firms choose how much to invest in cybersecurity and data protection, but that investment may fall short of the level that yields the greatest social welfare because firms do not fully internalize the value of privacy and security to the individual user or the need to engender trust in the data economy. Infrastructure service providers may tend to underinvest in cybersecurity because the economic consequences of any breach in data security are largely borne by the clients whose data are compromised. A 2018 report by the US Council of Economic Advisers estimated that malicious cyberactivity cost the US economy between US\$57 billion and US\$109 billion in 2016, representing between 0.31 and 0.58 percent of that year's GDP.[93] Governments may need to provide incentives or regulations to offset the tendency of firms to underinvest in cybersecurity, including imposing adequate penalties for data breaches.[94]

Pricing, discrimination, and algorithmic risks. Because firms have so much information on customers' personal characteristics and purchase histories, they can adjust their offerings to charge higher or lower prices based on an individual's price sensitivity. This practice can allow low-income sectors of society to be served that otherwise would not be. It can also help firms clear their stock, thereby reducing wastage. However, such price and quality discrimination can also harm some consumers. This kind of price discrimination is not inherently bad—it is a transfer of surplus from consumers to producers, and governments can use taxes and transfers to distribute it back again—but data and data-driven business models do make it easier to discriminate by price.

Algorithms can facilitate anticompetitive behavior by firms, ultimately harming individuals through higher prices. Algorithms can be trained to collude independently by surreptitiously following the behavior of a price leader, or they may be unintentionally biased because of inherent bias in their training data. This bias can magnify marginalization because the most vulnerable populations are often those that are least represented in digital data. Although algorithms

hold the promise of impartiality, this promise is not always realized because ultimately they reflect the same biases in human judgment and behavior (due to logic bias and flawed assumptions) reflected in their training datasets. But because algorithmic decision-making is opaque, the potential biases and anticompetitive effects may be difficult to detect.

In algorithmic decision-making, including credit scoring, these risks could lead to discrimination along socioeconomic lines that entrenches existing inequalities.[95] Groups with more limited access to mobile phones, the internet, and bank accounts, such as women, may become less visible in data and decision-making if algorithmic bias is perpetuated through use of biased datasets. If decisions are based on data about those with whom a person interacts, such as friends and neighbors, this, too, may amplify discriminatory effects. For example, a poor credit score for an individual may contribute to lower scores for those in their neighborhood or social network. Furthermore, alternative scoring tools may be used to identify vulnerable individuals susceptible to predatory loans and other product offerings.[96]

These concerns suggest the need to establish a system of oversight, inspection, and auditing of firms' algorithms. However, adequate standardized legal and regulatory frameworks to deal with risks from AI and regulatory capacity to determine harm and the appropriate safeguards are lacking.

Indirect management of the workforce through algorithms. Remotely collecting data on workers and service providers to drive automated or semiautomated decision-making on parameters such as task allocations, performance evaluations, and incentives for certain types of behavior has become particularly prevalent in the gig economy.[97] In addition to the risks algorithmic management raises for bias and discrimination, the practice makes it easier for firms to avoid classifying individuals as employees and thus avoid providing workers with benefits. Better understanding of the organizational and welfare impacts of algorithmic management and data collection on workers would help identify appropriate protections.

Potential to increase inequality within and among countries

Adoption of data-driven business models could widen gaps within countries, between countries, and between different types of firms, different types of workers, and individuals in different income groups.

Within a country, the impact of the data-driven economy on individuals—as consumers, entrepreneurs, or job seekers—will depend on their access to finance, education levels, skills, and technology. Although selling through platforms can close the productivity gaps between large and small firms for those small firms that go down this sales channel, overall smaller firms and entrepreneurs around the world lag their larger counterparts in adopting basic technologies such as fast broadband, having an internet presence, selling online, and utilizing cloud computing. Although the gig economy provides opportunities for job creation, only those who have the assets and skills to participate (such as cars, mobile devices, and literacy) will be able to benefit. And even though automated decision-making may mean more efficient and cost-effective service delivery for some individuals, it may lead to greater bias and discrimination against others.

Likewise, the degree to which a country can benefit from the data-driven economy depends on its underlying infrastructure, capabilities, and scale. The amount of data that can be derived locally depends on a country's level of digital economic activity. Firms from larger, more connected economies—or firms that already operate across countries—with access to larger datasets will have an advantage that only grows with time. Firms from low- and middle-income countries are more likely to lack both access to finance to cover the initial costs of collecting and managing their data and the analytical capabilities to derive value from them. When combined with fewer (or more uncertain) opportunities for monetizing data, either now or in the future (such as through advertising or development of new products), firms from lower-income economies also have less incentive to invest in collecting and analyzing data, which can worsen inequality between countries on a macro level.

Discouraging international data-driven firms from operating or locating in lower-income countries (such as through restrictive data policies) is not a viable solution because it deprives the local economy of the pro-growth and development benefits that data-driven firms can provide. Moreover, it prevents the development of a local ecosystem of data-driven entrepreneurs built around these larger firms—a scenario that could slow the advancement of infrastructure and capabilities needed for lower-income countries to bridge the gap in the longer term. Instead, governments can seek to harness the positive welfare effects of the data-driven economy while mitigating the risks to inequality through a combination of digital inclusion policies, public investments, and robust legal and regulatory tools. These are the topics of part II of this Report.

Notes

1. EIU (2012); Manyika et al. (2011).
2. Fernando (2021).
3. Manyika et al. (2011).
4. Brynjolfsson, Hitt, and Kim (2012); Brynjolfsson and McElheran (2016b).
5. von Mörner (2017).
6. Magalhaes and Roseira (2017); Stott (2014).
7. Evans and Schmalensee (2016); Gawer (2014).
8. This figure is according to the database constructed by the i2i Facility. The database covers eight Sub-Saharan African countries: Ghana, Kenya, Nigeria, Rwanda, South Africa, Tanzania, Uganda, and Zambia. See Africa's Digital Platforms Database, Insight2Impact (i2i), http://access.i2ifacility.org/Digital_platforms/.
9. Evans (2016); Evans and Gawer (2016).
10. The countries in the sample are Armenia, Bangladesh, Brazil, Colombia, the Arab Republic of Egypt, Indonesia, Kenya, Malaysia, Morocco, Nigeria, Peru, the Philippines, the Russian Federation, South Africa, Sri Lanka, Tunisia, and Ukraine. These countries were selected based on data availability and to provide a combination of countries of different sizes and levels of economic development across regions.
11. See Nyman and Stinshoff (forthcoming), who base their data on information provided by Crunchbase, Crunchbase (database), https://www.crunchbase.com/; Dow Jones and Company, Factiva (database), https://professional.dowjones.com/factiva/; Thomson Reuters Foundation, "Inclusive Economies," http://www.trust.org/inclusive-economies/. E-commerce includes both business-to-business (B2B) and business-to-consumer (B2C) business models (excluding agriculture wholesale). Transport includes passenger transport and freight transport/logistics, with the latter accounting for about 67 percent of firms in this category on average. Agriculture includes platforms where the main business focus is agriculture, including both marketplace and financial services. Tourism includes booking platforms and accommodation sharing.
12. Data on the founding year were available for 75 percent of firms in the database.
13. A firm is considered closed if the website cannot be found or accessed via internet research, or if the domain is for sale. A firm is confirmed closed if an article noting the firm's exit was found.
14. Sites are ordered by their Alexa traffic rank, calculated using a combination of average daily visitors and pageviews over the past month. The site with the highest combination of visitors and pageviews is ranked 1. See Alexa Internet, "The Top 500 Sites on the Web, by Country" (accessed April 2020), https://www.alexa.com/topsites/countries.
15. Analysis of data from World Bank, Digital Business Indicators (database), https://www.worldbank.org/en/research/brief/digital-business-indicators.
16. Total session time of over 85 billion hours was recorded from May to June 2018, according to data from 2020 on data software development kits, mobile app downloads,

and revenue and usage data from Apptopia, Data (database), https://apptopia.com/.

17. Kumar and Muhota (2012). See UN Global Working Group on Big Data for Official Statistics for an overview of mobile phone data types and their potential use (UNGWG 2019).

18. Bertrand and Kamenica (2018).

19. Berg et al. (2018).

20. Platforms, IoT devices, and blockchain reduce asymmetric information about the quality and trustworthiness of smaller suppliers. For platforms, user reviews partly serve this purpose. For example, better-rated sellers on eBay have higher prices and higher revenues—see Houser and Wooders (2005); Livingston (2002); Lucking-Reiley et al. (2007); Melnik and Alm (2002)—and sellers with low ratings exit from eBay's platform (Cabral and Hortaçsu 2010).

21. Lendle et al. (2012).

22. Lendle et al. (2012).

23. Luo and Niu (2019).

24. De and Raychaudhuri (2008).

25. Balchin et al. (2016).

26. Data are as of 2018 and come from World Trade Organization, Trade Profiles (database), https://www.wto.org/english/res_e/statis_e/trade_profiles_list_e.htm.

27. Balchin et al. (2016).

28. Borchert and Mattoo (2019).

29. The 10 countries are Belgium, France, Germany, Hungary, Italy, Poland, Spain, Sweden, the United Kingdom, and the United States.

30. Bailin et al. (2019).

31. Falk and Hagsten (2015).

32. Calculations of the European Investment Bank (EIB) and World Bank based on EIB (2019).

33. Aghion, Jones, and Jones (2017); Cockburn, Henderson, and Stern (2019).

34. Brynjolfsson and McElheran (2016a).

35. MGI (2018).

36. IFC (2009).

37. Eisenmeier (2018).

38. Bughin and van Zeebroeck (2017). The authors estimate that tapping latent demand could increase industry size by 0.5 percent a year.

39. Brynjolfsson et al. (2019).

40. Alphabet Inc. (2019); Clement (2020).

41. Alibaba Group (2019); McNair (2018).

42. West and Biddle (2017).

43. Singh (2020).

44. Demirgüç-Kunt et al. (2018).

45. Manyika et al. (2016).

46. Ant Financial is an affiliate company of the Alibaba Group.

47. LenddoEFL (2020).

48. Lobosco (2013).

49. Aron and Muellbauer (2019).

50. Patnam and Yao (2020).

51. Suri and Jack (2016).

52. Mastercard (2017). In May 2020, Mastercard and the Caribbean Hotel and Tourism Association (CHTA) launched a Tourism Insights platform that looks at travel trends from search patterns to in-market spending for the Dominican Republic, Jamaica, and Puerto Rico (*Jamaica Observer* 2020).

53. Baruri (2016).

54. Creydt and Fischer (2019).

55. Open Access Government (2019).

56. Kamath (2018).

57. Levy (2014).

58. The World Health Organization (WHO 2018) defines as substandard "authorized medical products that fail to meet either their quality standards or specifications, or both" and falsified "medical products that deliberately/fraudulently misrepresent their identity, composition or source."

59. WHO (2018).

60. Taylor (2016).

61. Google (2021).

62. World Bank (2017).

63. Rouhiainen (2019).

64. Hao (2019).

65. UNESCO (2020).

66. Future Hub (2020).

67. Gerretsen (2020).

68. Okello (2018).

69. Estimates are provided by Gojek. See Universitas Indonesia (2020).

70. WHO (2019).

71. See, for example, Aker (2010); Allen (2014); Eaton and Kortum (2002); Jensen (2007); Simonovska and Waugh (2014); Startz (2017).

72. See LYFE Marketing "Traditional Media vs. Social Media Advertising: Cost Comparison," https://www.lyfemarketing.com/traditional-media-versus-social-media/.

73. Rumo Arongo Ndiege (2019).

74. EU Open Data Portal, Eurostat, "Social Media Use by Type, Internet Advertising" (dataset), https://data.europa.eu/euodp/en/data/dataset/MTxwCIIEx8RhOhZMmgWvg.

75. Facebook, OECD, and World Bank (2017).

76. Facebook, OECD, and World Bank (2017).

77. Bailey et al. (2020).

78. Bailey et al. (2018).

79. A model developed by Farboodi et al. (2019) shows that data accumulation increases the skewness of firm size distribution as large firms generate more data and invest more in active experimentation. Although there has been less research on DLT applications, Benos, Garratt, and Gurrola-Perez (2019) suggested that similar dynamics would also push these markets to concentration.

80. See ecomConnect, International Trade Centre, African Marketplace Explorer (dashboard), https://ecomconnect.org/page/african-marketplace-explorer.

81. Argentesi et al. (2019).

82. CB Insights (2020). Private market funding refers to the total amount of money a firm has received, including from financial institutions and venture funding. Money raised in public markets is excluded.

83. IRGC (2017).

84. Riley and Kulathunga (2017).

85. Romm (2020).

86. Evans (2016).
87. Very large firms have more than 10,000 employees and more than US$1 billion in revenues. See Nyman and Barajas (forthcoming).
88. In the presence of privacy concerns and negative externalities in data sharing, the market may instead generate too much data sharing. See Acemoglu et al. (2019).
89. Jones and Tonetti (2019).
90. Schmidt (2018).
91. Robertson (2020).
92. Kemp (2019).
93. CEA (2018).
94. Gordon et al. (2015); Kashyap and Wetherilt (2019).
95. McGregor, Murray, and Ng (2019).
96. Hurley and Adebayo (2017).
97. Mateescu and Nguyen (2019).

References

Acemoglu, Daron, Ali Makhdoumi, Azarakhsh Malekian, and Asuman Ozdaglar. 2019. "Too Much Data: Prices and Inefficiencies in Data Markets." NBER Working Paper 26296, National Bureau of Economic Research, Cambridge, MA. https://doi.org/10.3386/w26296.

Aghion, Philippe, Benjamin F. Jones, and Charles I. Jones. 2017. "Artificial Intelligence and Economic Growth." NBER Working Paper 23928, National Bureau of Economic Research, Cambridge, MA.

Aker, Jenny C. 2010. "Information from Markets Near and Far: Mobile Phones and Agricultural Markets in Niger." *American Economic Journal: Applied Economics* 2 (3): 46–59. https://doi.org/10.1257/app.2.3.46.

Alibaba Group. 2019. "Alibaba Group Announces March Quarter and Full Fiscal Year 2019 Results." Press release, May 15, 2019, Hangzhou, China. https://www.alibaba group.com/en/news/press_pdf/p190515.pdf.

Allen, Treb. 2014. "Information Frictions in Trade." *Econometrica* 82 (6): 2041–83.

Alphabet Inc. 2019. "Form 10-K: Annual Report Pursuant to Section 13 or 15(D) of the Securities Exchange Act of 1934." US Securities and Exchange Commission, Washington, DC. https://abc.xyz/investor/static/pdf/20200204_alphabet_10K.pdf?cache=cdd6dbf.

Argentesi, Elena, Paolo Buccirossi, Emilio Calvano, Tomaso Duso, Alessia Marrazzo, and Salvatore Nava. 2019. "Ex-post Assessment of Merger Control Decisions in Digital Markets." With contributions by Elena Salomone and Anna Violini, Lear, Rome. https://www.learlab.com/wp-content/uploads/2019/06/CMA_past_digital_mergers_GOV.UK_version-1.pdf.

Aron, Janine, and John Muellbauer. 2019. "The Economics of Mobile Money: Harnessing the Transformative Power of Technology to Benefit the Global Poor." *VoxEU.Org*, May 7, 2019. https://voxeu.org/article/economics-mobile-money.

Bailey, Michael, Rachel Cao, Theresa Kuchler, Johannes Stroebel, and Arlene Wong. 2018. "Social Connectedness: Measurement, Determinants, and Effects." *Journal of Economic Perspectives* 32 (3): 259–80.

Bailey, Michael, Abhinav Gupta, Sebastian Hillenbrand, Theresa Kuchler, Robert J. Richmond, and Johannes Stroebel. 2020. "International Trade and Social Connectedness." NBER Working Paper 26960, National Bureau of Economic Research, Cambridge, MA. https://doi.org/10.3386/w26960.

Bailin, Alberto, Peter Gal, Valentine Millot, and Stéphane Sorbe. 2019. "Like It or Not? The Impact of Online Platforms on the Productivity of Incumbent Service Providers." OECD Economics Department Working Paper 1548, Organisation for Economic Co-operation and Development, Paris. https://doi.org/10.1787/080a17ce-en.

Balchin, Neil, Bernard Hoekman, Hope Martin, Maximiliano Mendez-Parra, Phyllis Papadavid, David Primack, and Dirk Willem te Velde. 2016. "Trade in Services and Economic Transformation." SET Report, Supporting Economic Transformation, Overseas Development Institute, London. https://set.odi.org/wp-content/uploads/2016/11/SET-Trade-in-Services-and-Economic-Transformation_Final-Nov2016.pdf.

Baruri, Pani. 2016. "Blockchain Powered Financial Inclusion." PowerPoint presentation, Cognizant, Teaneck, NJ. http://pubdocs.worldbank.org/en/710961476811913780/Session-5C-Pani-Baruri-Blockchain-Financial-Inclusion-Pani.pdf.

Benos, Evangelos, Rodney Garratt, and Pedro Gurrola-Perez. 2019. "The Economics of Distributed Ledger Technology for Securities Settlement." *Ledger* 4 (November): 121–56. https://doi.org/10.5195/ledger.2019.144.

Berg, Tobias, Valentin Burg, Ana Gombović, and Manju Puri. 2018. "On the Rise of the FinTechs: Credit Scoring Using Digital Footprints." FDIC CFR Working Paper 2018-04, Center for Financial Research, Federal Deposit Insurance Corporation, Arlington, VA. https://www.fdic.gov/analysis/cfr/2018/wp2018/cfr-wp2018-04.pdf.

Bertrand, Marianne, and Emir Kamenica. 2018. "Coming Apart? Cultural Distances in the United States over Time." NBER Working Paper 24771, National Bureau of Economic Research, Cambridge, MA. https://doi.org/10.3386/w24771.

Borchert, Ingo, and Aaditya Mattoo. 2009. "The Crisis-Resilience of Services Trade." *Service Industries Journal* 30 (13): 2115–36.

Brynjolfsson, Erik, Avinash Collis, Walter Erwin Diewert, Kevin J. Fox, and Felix Eggers. 2019. "GDP-B: Accounting for the Value of New and Free Goods in the Digital Economy." NBER Working Paper 25695, National Bureau of Economic Research, Cambridge, MA.

Brynjolfsson, Erik, Lorin M. Hitt, and Heekyung Hellen Kim. 2012. "Strength in Numbers: How Does Data-Driven Decision-Making Affect Firm Performance?" In *International Conference on Information Systems 2011 (ICIS 2011)*, vol. 1, edited by Association for Information Systems, 541–58. Red Hook, NY: Curran Associates.

Brynjolfsson, Erik, and Kristina McElheran. 2016a. "Data in Action: Data-Driven Decision Making in U.S. Manufacturing." CES Working Paper 16-06, Center for Economic Studies, US Census Bureau, Washington, DC. https://www2.census.gov/ces/wp/2016/CES-WP-16-06.pdf.

Brynjolfsson, Erik, and Kristina McElheran. 2016b. "The Rapid Adoption of Data-Driven Decision-Making."

American Economic Review 106 (5): 133–39. https://doi.org/10.1257/aer.p20161016.

Bughin, Jacques, and Nicolas van Zeebroeck. 2017. "The Best Response to Digital Disruption." *MIT Sloan Management Review* 58 (4): 80–86. https://sloanreview.mit.edu/article/the-right-response-to-digital-disruption/.

Cabral, Luís, and Ali Hortaçsu. 2010. "The Dynamics of Seller Reputation: Evidence from eBay." *Journal of Industrial Economics* 58 (1): 54–78.

CB Insights. 2020. "The Fintech 250: The Top Fintech Companies of 2020." Research Report, CB Insights, New York. https://www.cbinsights.com/research/report/fintech-250-startups-most-promising/.

CEA (Council of Economic Advisers). 2018. "The Cost of Malicious Cyber Activity to the U.S. Economy." CEA, White House, Washington, DC. https://www.whitehouse.gov/wp-content/uploads/2018/02/The-Cost-of-Malicious-Cyber-Activity-to-the-U.S.-Economy.pdf.

Clement, Jessica. 2020. "Google: Annual Advertising Revenue 2001–2019." Statista, New York. https://www.statista.com/statistics/266249/advertising-revenue-of-google/.

Cockburn, Iain M., Rebecca Henderson, and Scott Stern. 2019. "The Impact of Artificial Intelligence on Innovation: An Exploratory Analysis." In *The Economics of Artificial Intelligence: An Agenda*, edited by Ajay Agrawal, Joshua Gans, and Avi Goldfarb, 115–46. Cambridge, MA: National Bureau of Economic Research; Chicago: University of Chicago Press. https://www.nber.org/books-and-chapters/economics-artificial-intelligence-agenda/impact-artificial-intelligence-innovation-exploratory-analysis.

Creydt, Marina, and Markus Fischer. 2019. "Blockchain and More: Algorithm Driven Food Traceability." *Food Control* 105 (November): 45–51. https://doi.org/10.1016/j.foodcont.2019.05.019.

De, Prabir, and Ajitava Raychaudhuri. 2008. "Is India's Services Trade Pro-Poor? A Simultaneous Approach." Markhub Working Paper 16, Macao Regional Knowledge Hub, United Nations Economic and Social Commission for Asia and the Pacific, Macao SAR, China.

Demirgüç-Kunt, Asli, Leora Klapper, Dorothe Singer, Saniya Ansar, and Jake Hess. 2018. *The Global Findex Database 2017: Measuring Financial Inclusion and the Fintech Revolution*. Washington, DC: World Bank. https://doi.org/10.1596/978-1-4648-1259-0.

Eaton, Jonathan, and Samuel Kortum. 2002. "Technology, Geography, and Trade." *Econometrica* 70 (5): 1741–79. https://doi.org/10.1111/1468-0262.00352.

EIB (European Investment Bank). 2019. "EIB Group Survey on Investment and Investment Finance 2019: EU Overview." Economics Department, European Investment Bank, Luxembourg. https://www.eib.org/en/publications/econ-eibis-2019-eu.

Eisenmeier, Siegfried R. J. 2018. "Case Study: Ride-Sharing Platforms in Developing Countries: Effects and Implications in Mexico City." P4P Commission Background Paper 3, Pathways for Prosperity Commission on Technology and Inclusive Development, Blavatnik School of Government, University of Oxford, Oxford, UK. https://pathwayscommission.bsg.ox.ac.uk/sites/default/files/2019-09/ride-sharing_platforms_in_developing_countries.pdf.

EIU (Economist Intelligence Unit). 2012. "The Deciding Factor: Big Data and Decision-Making." Business Analytics, Capgemini, Paris.

Evans, David S., and Richard Schmalensee. 2016. *Matchmakers: The New Economics of Multisided Platforms*. Boston: Harvard Business Review Press.

Evans, Peter C. 2016. "The Rise of Asian Platforms." Emerging Platform Economy Series 3, Center for Global Enterprise, New York. https://www.thecge.net/web/viewer.html?file=/app/uploads/2016/11/FINALAsianPlatformPaper.pdf.

Evans, Peter C., and Annabell Gawer. 2016. "The Rise of the Platform Enterprise: A Global Survey." Emerging Platform Economy Series 1, Center for Global Enterprise, New York. https://www.thecge.net/app/uploads/2016/01/PDF-WEB-Platform-Survey_01_12.pdf.

Facebook, OECD (Organisation for Economic Co-operation and Development), and World Bank. 2017. "Future of Business Survey: Gender Management in Business." Factworks, San Mateo, CA. https://fbnewsroomes.files.wordpress.com/2017/02/future-of-business-survey-gender-management-in-business-january-20171.pdf.

Falk, Martin, and Eva Hagsten. 2015. "E-Commerce Trends and Impacts across Europe." *International Journal of Production Economics* 170 (December): 357–69. https://doi.org/10.1016/j.ijpe.2015.10.003.

Farboodi, Maryam, Roxana Mihet, Thomas Philippon, and Laura Veldkamp. 2019. "Big Data and Firm Dynamics." NBER Working Paper 25515, National Bureau of Economic Research, Cambridge, MA. https://doi.org/10.3386/w25515.

Fernando, Jason. 2021. "Factors of Production." *Investopedia*, January 3, 2021. https://www.investopedia.com/terms/f/factors-production.asp.

Future Hub. 2020. "E-Logistics Transforming Mid-Mile Freight Logistics in Emerging Markets: Stories Told and Untold." *Future Insight* (blog), June 30, 2020. http://www.fhub.io/blog/e-logistics-transforming-mid-mile-freight-logistics-in-emerging-markets.

Gawer, Annabell. 2014. "Bridging Differing Perspectives on Technological Platforms: Toward an Integrative Framework." *Research Policy* 43 (7): 1239–49.

Gerretsen, Isabelle. 2020. "Trucking App Kobo360 Wants to Speed Up Deliveries across Africa." *CNN Business: Innovate Africa*, April 16, 2020. https://www.cnn.com/2020/04/16/tech/kobo-360-trucks-spc-intl/index.html.

Google. 2021. "How Doctors, Dispatch Drivers, and Blood Donors Are Coming Together to Save Lives across Africa." *Search On*, Lifebank, Google, Mountain View, CA. https://about.google/stories/lifebank/#:~:text=By%20designing%20a%20system%20to,take%20your%20time%20to%20solve.

Gordon, Lawrence A., Martin P. Loeb, William Lucyshyn, and Lei Zhou. 2015. "Increasing Cybersecurity Investments in Private Sector Firms." *Journal of Cybersecurity* 1 (1): 3–17. https://doi.org/10.1093/cybsec/tyv011.

Hao, Karen. 2019. "China Has Started a Grand Experiment in AI Education: It Could Reshape How the World Learns." *MIT Technology Review*. https://www.technologyreview.com/2019/08/02/131198/china-squirrel-has-started-a-grand-experiment-in-ai-education-it-could-reshape-how-the/.

Houser, Daniel, and John Wooders. 2005. "Hard and Soft Closes: A Field Experiment on Auction Closing Rules." In *Experimental Business Research: Economic and Managerial Perspectives*, vol. 2, edited by Amnon Rapoport and Rami Zwick, 123–31. Dordrecht, the Netherlands: Springer.

Hurley, Mikella, and Julius Adebayo. 2017. "Credit Scoring in the Era of Big Data." *Yale Journal of Law and Technology* 18 (1): 148–216.

IFC (International Finance Corporation). 2009. "M-Money Channel Distribution Case, Kenya: Safaricom M-PESA." IFC, Washington, DC. https://www.ifc.org/wps/wcm/connect/e0d2a9bd-16b9-4a36-8498-0b2650b9af8b/Tool%2B6.7.%2BCase%2BStudy%2B-%2BM-PESA%2BKenya%2B.pdf?MOD=AJPERES&CVID=jkCVy-n.

IRGC (International Risk Governance Center). 2017. "Governing Risks and Benefits of Distributed Ledger Technologies." IRGC, Geneva. https://irgc.org/wp-content/uploads/2018/09/IRGC.-2017.-Governing-risks-and-benefits-of-DLTs.-Highlights.pdf.

Jamaica Observer. 2020. "Mastercard, CHTA Launch Tourism Insights Platform." May 8, 2020. http://www.jamaicaobserver.com/business-report/mastercard-chta-launch-tourism-insights-platform_193696?profile=1442.

Jensen, Robert. 2007. "The Digital Provide: Information (Technology), Market Performance, and Welfare in the South Indian Fisheries Sector." *Quarterly Journal of Economics* 122 (3): 879–924. http://www.jstor.org/stable/25098864.

Jones, Charles I., and Christopher Tonetti. 2019. "Nonrivalry and the Economics of Data." NBER Working Paper 26260, National Bureau of Economic Research, Cambridge, MA. https://ideas.repec.org/p/nbr/nberwo/26260.html.

Kamath, Reshma. 2018. "Food Traceability on Blockchain: Walmart's Pork and Mango Pilots with IBM." *JBBA, Journal of the British Blockchain Association* 1 (1): 3712. https://doi.org/10.31585/jbba-1-1-(10)2018.

Kashyap, Anil K., and Anne Wetherilt. 2019. "Some Principles for Regulating Cyber Risk." *AEA Papers and Proceedings* 109 (May): 482–87. https://doi.org/10.1257/pandp.20191058.

Kemp, Katharine. 2019. "Concealed Data Practices and Competition Law: Why Privacy Matters." Report UNSWLRS 53, University of New South Wales Law Research Series, UNSW Law, University of New South Wales, Sydney.

Kumar, Kabir, and Kim Muhota. 2012. "Can Digital Footprints Lead to Greater Financial Inclusion?" CGAP Brief, Consultative Group to Assist the Poor, Washington, DC. https://www.cgap.org/sites/default/files/researches/documents/CGAP-Brief-Can-Digital-Footprints-Lead-to-Greater-Financial-Inclusion-Jul-2012.pdf.

LenddoEFL. 2020. "Product Briefs." LenddoEFL, Singapore. https://lenddoefl.com/resources.

Lendle, Andreas, Marcelo Olarreaga, Simon Schropp, and Pierre-Louis Vezina. 2012. "There Goes Gravity: How eBay Reduces Trade Costs." Policy Research Working Paper 6253, World Bank, Washington, DC.

Levy, Stephen. 2014. "Colorimetrix App Turns Smartphones into Lab Test Readers." *MD+DI*, March 19, 2014. https://www.mddionline.com/digital-health/colorimetrix-app-turns-smartphones-lab-test-readers.

Livingston, Jeffrey A. 2002. "How Valuable Is a Good Reputation? A Sample Selection Model of Internet Auctions." *Review of Economics and Statistics* 87 (3): 453–65.

Lobosco, Katie. 2013. "Facebook Friends Could Change Your Credit Score." *CNN Business*, August 27, 2013. https://money.cnn.com/2013/08/26/technology/social/facebook-credit-score/index.html.

Lucking-Reiley, David, Doug Bryan, Naghi Prasad, and Daniel Reeves. 2007. "Pennies from eBay: The Determinants of Price in Online Auctions." *Journal of Industrial Economics* 55 (2): 223–33.

Luo, Xubei, and Chiyu Niu. 2019. "E-Commerce Participation and Household Income Growth in Taobao Villages." Poverty and Equity Global Practice Working Paper 198, World Bank, Washington, DC.

Magalhaes, Gustavo, and Catarina Roseira. 2017. "Open Government Data and the Private Sector: An Empirical View on Business Models and Value Creation." *Government Information Quarterly* 37 (3): 101248. https://doi.org/10.1016/j.giq.2017.08.004.

Manyika, James, Michael Chui, Brad Brown, Jacques Bughin, Richard Dobbs, Charles Roxburgh, and Angela Hung Byers. 2011. "Big Data: The Next Frontier for Innovation, Competition, and Productivity." McKinsey Global Institute, New York.

Manyika, James, Susan Lund, Marc Singer, Olivia White, and Chris Berry. 2016. "Digital Finance for All: Powering Inclusive Growth in Emerging Economies." McKinsey Global Institute, New York. https://www.mckinsey.com/~/media/McKinsey/Featured%20Insights/Employment%20and%20Growth/How%20digital%20finance%20could%20boost%20growth%20in%20emerging%20economies/MG-Digital-Finance-For-All-Full-report-September-2016.ashx.

Mastercard. 2017. "Leveraging Big Data to Drive Tourism Revenue." Mastercard Tourism Insights, Mastercard, Purchase, NY. https://www.mastercard.us/content/dam/public/mastercardcom/na/us/en/documents/tourism-insights-summary.pdf.

Mateescu, Alexandra, and Aiha Nguyen. 2019. "Explainer: Algorithmic Management in the Workplace." February, Data & Society Research Institute, New York. https://datasociety.net/wp-content/uploads/2019/02/DS_Algorithmic_Management_Explainer.pdf.

McGregor, Lorna, Daragh Murray, and Vivian Ng. 2019. "International Human Rights Law as a Framework for Algorithmic Accountability." *International and Comparative Law Quarterly* 68 (2): 309–43.

McNair, Corey. 2018. "Global Ad Spending Update: Alibaba, Facebook, and Google to Capture Over 60% of Digital Ad Dollars in 2019." *eMarketer*, November 20, 2018, Insider Intelligence, New York. https://www.emarketer.com/content/global-ad-spending-update.

Melnik, Mikhail I., and James Alm. 2002. "Does a Seller's Ecommerce Reputation Matter? Evidence from eBay Auctions." *Journal of Industrial Economics* 50 (3): 337–49.

MGI (McKinsey Global Institute). 2018. "Notes from the AI Frontier: Modeling the Impact of AI on the World Economy." Discussion Paper, MGI, New York. https://www.mckinsey.com/~/media/McKinsey/Featured%20Insights/Artificial%20Intelligence/Notes%20from%20the%20frontier%20Modeling%20the%20impact%20of%20AI%20on%20the%20world%20economy/MGI

-Notes-from-the-AI-frontier-Modeling-the-impact-of-AI-on-the-world-economy-September-2018.ashx.

Nyman, Sara, and Rodrigo Barajas. Forthcoming. "Antitrust in the Digital Economy: A Global Perspective." World Bank, Washington, DC.

Nyman, Sara, and Clara Stinshoff. Forthcoming. "A Mapping of Digital Platform Firms in Developing Economies." WDR 2021 background paper, World Bank, Washington, DC.

Okello, Ron. 2018. "TechCrunch Battlefield Africa Winner Lori Systems Expands into Three New Countries; Wins Multiple Bids Associated with $4B Railroad Project." *Business Wire*, August 18, 2018. https://www.businesswire.com/news/home/20180918005205/en/TechCrunch-Battlefield-Africa-Winner-Lori-Systems-Expands.

Open Access Government. 2019. "World Bank Blockchain Pilot Shows Fresh Narrative for Haiti's Farmers." *Blockchain News*, March 25, 2019. https://www.openaccessgovernment.org/world-bank-blockchain-haitis-farmers/61205/.

Patnam, Manasa, and Weijia Yao. 2020. "The Real Effects of Mobile Money: Evidence from a Large-Scale Fintech Expansion." IMF Working Paper WP/20/138, International Monetary Fund, Washington, DC. https://www.imf.org/en/Publications/WP/Issues/2020/07/24/The-Real-Effects-of-Mobile-Money-Evidence-from-a-Large-Scale-Fintech-Expansion-49549.

Riley, Thyra A., and Anoma Kulathunga. 2017. *Bringing E-money to the Poor: Successes and Failures.*" Directions in Development: Finance Series. Washington, DC: World Bank.

Robertson, Viktoria H. S. E. 2020. "Excessive Data Collection: Privacy Considerations and Abuse of Dominance in the Era of Big Data." *Common Market Law Review* 57 (1): 161–90.

Romm, Tony. 2020. "Companies Burned by Big Tech Plead for Congress to Regulate Apple, Amazon, Facebook, and Google." *Washington Post*, January 18, 2020.

Rouhiainen, Lasse. 2019. "How AI and Data Could Personalize Higher Education." *Harvard Business Review*, October 14. https://hbr.org/2019/10/how-ai-and-data-could-personalize-higher-education.

Rumo Arongo Ndiege, Joshua. 2019. "Social Media Technology for the Strategic Positioning of Small and Medium-Sized Enterprises: Empirical Evidence from Kenya." *EJISDC, Electronic Journal of Information Systems in Developing Countries* 85 (2): e12069. https://doi.org/10.1002/isd2.12069.

Sandvine. 2019. "The Mobile Internet Phenomena Report, February 2019." Sandvine, Fremont, CA. https://www.sandvine.com/hubfs/downloads/phenomena/2019-mobile-phenomena-report.pdf.

Schmidt, Douglas C. 2018. "Google Data Collection." Digital Content Next, New York. https://digitalcontentnext.org/wp-content/uploads/2018/08/DCN-Google-Data-Collection-Paper.pdf.

Simonovska, Ina, and Michael Waugh. 2014. "The Elasticity of Trade: Estimates and Evidence." *Journal of International Economics* 92 (1): 34–50.

Singh, Manish. 2020. "Google Ends Its Free Wi-Fi Program Station." *TechCrunch*, February 17, 2020. https://social.techcrunch.com/2020/02/17/google-ends-its-free-wi-fi-program-station/.

Startz, Meredith. 2017. "The Value of Face-to-Face: Search and Contracting Problems in Nigerian Trade." *VoxDev*, July 31, 2017. https://voxdev.org/topic/firms-trade/value-face-face-search-and-contracting-problems-nigerian-trade#:~:text=My%20estimates%20suggest%20that%20search,one%20sixth%20of%20consumer%20spending.

Stott, Andrew. 2014. "Open Data for Economic Growth." Working Paper 89606, World Bank, Washington, DC. http://documents.worldbank.org/curated/en/131621468154792082/Open-data-for-economic-growth.

Suri, Tavneet, and William Jack. 2016. "The Long-Run Poverty and Gender Impacts of Mobile Money." *Science* 354 (6317): 1288–92. https://science.sciencemag.org/content/354/6317/1288.

Taylor, Phil. 2016. "Marie Stopes Turns to MPedigree for Tracking Technology." Securing Industry, Bromsgrove, UK. https://www.securingindustry.com/pharmaceuticals/marie-stopes-turns-to-mpedigree-for-tracking-technology/s40/a2723/.

UNESCO (United Nations Educational, Scientific, and Cultural Organization). 2020. "Education: From Disruption to Recovery." UNESCO, Paris. https://en.unesco.org/covid19/educationresponse.

UNGWG (United Nations Global Working Group on Big Data for Official Statistics). 2019. "Handbook on the Use of Mobile Phone Data for Official Statistics." Draft, Statistics Division, Department of Economic and Social Affairs, United Nations, New York. https://unstats.un.org/bigdata/task-teams/mobile-phone/MPD%20Handbook%2020191004.pdf.

Universitas Indonesia. 2020. "Dampak Ekonomi Gojek 2019: dan Peran Ekosistem Gojek di Indonesia Saat Pandemi COVID-19." Demographics Institute, Faculty of Economics and Business, University of Indonesia, Depok, Indonesia. https://drive.google.com/file/d/1RgVRNJaszs36-3z_smhsqBegrufhNWw/view.

von Mörner, Moritz. 2017. "Application of Call Detail Records: Chances and Obstacles." *Transportation Research Procedia* (25): 2233–41. https://doi.org/10.1016/j.trpro.2017.05.429.

West, Sarah, and Ellery Roberts Biddle. 2017. "Facebook's Free Basics Doesn't Connect You to the Global Internet, But It Does Collect Your Data." *Global Voices Advox*, July 27, 2017. https://advox.globalvoices.org/2017/07/27/facebooks-free-basics-doesnt-connect-you-to-the-global-internet-but-it-does-collect-your-data/.

WHO (World Health Organization). 2018. "Substandard and Falsified Medical Products." Fact Sheet, WHO, Geneva. https://www.who.int/news-room/fact-sheets/detail/substandard-and-falsified-medical-products.

WHO (World Health Organization). 2019. "The Global Vaccine Action Plan (2011–2020): Review and Lessons Learned." Report WHO/IVB/19.07, Strategic Advisory Group of Experts on Immunization, WHO, Geneva. http://www.who.int/immunization/global_vaccine_action_plan/en/.

World Bank. 2017. *World Development Report 2017: Governance and the Law.* Washington, DC: World Bank.

Spotlight 3.1
The huge potential of open data for business applications

Public intent data play a foundational role as a system of reference for the entire economy.

Public intent data add tremendous value to the economy as a whole and to various sectors. The gross value added from public data is estimated to range from 0.4 percent to 1.4 percent of GDP, according to a 2016 meta-study that focused mainly on high-income countries.[1] Specific public intent data products also yield great value for particular sectors. For example, Denmark's open access dataset of addresses generated direct economic benefits of €62 million (over DKr 450 million) between 2005 and 2009, returning the €2 million (roughly DKr 15 million) cost of investments in data many times over.[2] This example is relevant for low- and middle-income countries, where the lack of addresses and address datasets have been a barrier to the development of data-driven transport and logistics services.

Creating value using public intent data

Entrepreneurs create value using public intent data in ways similar to how they use other data. First, companies use public intent data to *improve their operations*. US retailers, for example, combine data from the American Community Survey with their own sales data to customize inventory regionally.[3] On the operations side, businesses rely on price-level data to set wages and allowances, among many other uses.[4] Second, firms use public intent data to *develop new products or services, including research and analytics services*.[5] For example, the global energy analytics sector depends on data from the Energy Information Administration to monitor worldwide patterns of energy use.[6] Other businesses use data to provide new forms of advice to their customers. Farmerline, a company in Ghana, combines government meteorological and administrative

data with proprietary data to provide advice to farmers via text message. Firms also rely on demographic statistics and business registers to inform their decisions about whether and how to enter new markets. Finally, firms may act as *data intermediaries* (see chapter 8), aggregating and repackaging government data in more accessible, user-friendly formats.

The changing landscape of business sectors driven by public data

While businesses driven by public data have been studied in high-income economies in some detail,[7] there is little systematic information on private sector use of public intent data and their value to the economy in lower-income countries. Nevertheless, a handful of sources shed light on the business use of public intent data, including in emerging economies.[8]

These sources indicate that companies using public intent data span a wide range of sectors in both high-income and low- and middle-income economies. Around the world, the technology sector clearly dominates. In low- and middle-income economies, the research and consulting sector is the second most frequent user of public intent data. Companies using such data tend to be young and small in terms of the number of employees, with a large majority of global companies that use GovLab's OpenData500 Global Network database having 200 or fewer employees. In terms of the data used, half of the US-based OpenData500 companies use data from multiple government agencies. The US Census Bureau is one of the most used sources (16 percent). Similarly, in Mexico, the national statistics office, the National

Institute of Statistics and Geography (INEGI), is the most important source of public intent data for businesses, with 88 percent of companies reporting that they use INEGI data. Among the 200 firms in low- and middle-income countries included in the Open Data Impact Map compiled by the Open Data for Development Network, geospatial data are the most commonly used type of public intent data (41 percent), followed by demographic data (36 percent), economic data (30 percent), and health data (27 percent).

These assessments indicate that the business sector that uses public data is much smaller in most low- and middle-income countries than in high-income economies. This pattern is related closely to challenges with public intent data in general.[9] In many cases, national data systems are limited with respect to the amount of data being produced as well as their quality and usability, timeliness, openness, and accessibility (see chapter 2).[10] Indeed, companies driven by open data surveyed by the World Bank

Figure S3.1.1 Private company use of public data is extremely valuable in the United States, suggesting the value of open government data

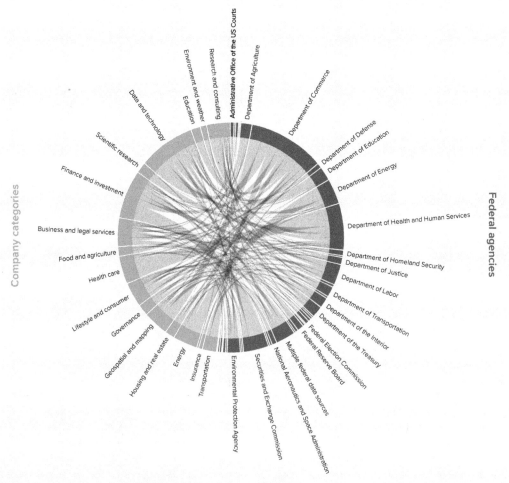

Source: Verhulst and Caplan 2015. Data at http://bit.do/WDR2021-Fig-S3_1_1. © The GovLab. Used with permission of The GovLab; further permission required for reuse.

Note: The figure centers on 500 US firms. Starting with the right-hand, purple-shaded half of the circle, the gray lines emanating from the federal agencies show which type of private sector firms have used data from which government departments. The portion of the semicircle for each department reflects the number of firms using its data. Moving to the left-hand, green-shaded half of the circle, the gray lines emanating from the private sector reveal which categories of company have used data from which government agency. For example, firms in the finance and investment sector have used open data from 19 US departments and agencies.

reported poor quality and lack of openness of and accessibility to public intent data as major concerns.[11] The more active public data–driven business sectors in Mexico and other Latin American countries illustrate the potential for low- and middle-income countries. Realizing this potential requires better financing mechanisms and high-capacity, integrated, and open national data systems (see chapter 9).

Figure S3.1.1 visualizes the huge potential of open data. The figure centers on 500 firms based in the United States. It reveals widespread private sector use of publicly available federal government data, though data from some agencies are used more than from others. For example, fewer firms use open data from the Department of Agriculture than from the Department of Commerce (home of the US Census and many other important data), as evidenced by a smaller portion of the circle allocated to the Department of Agriculture. But, even in the case of agriculture, firms from seven distinct sectors have used the Department of Agriculture's open data. Figure S3.1.1 also reveals that companies from some sectors rely on many types of government data. For example, firms in the finance and investment sector have used open data from 19 US departments and agencies. The intricacies of the connections reveal the great potential for data use, reuse, and repurposing. Such uses have only begun to be exploited in both higher-income and lower-income countries.

Notes

1. Lateral Economics (2014).
2. McMurren, Verhulst, and Young (2016).
3. Hughes-Cromwick and Coronado (2019).
4. Hughes-Cromwick and Coronado (2019).
5. Gurin, Bonina, and Verhulst (2019); Magalhaes and Roseira (2017).
6. Hughes-Cromwick and Coronado (2019).
7. See, for example, Hughes-Cromwick and Coronado (2019); Lateral Economics (2014); Manyika et al. (2013); and Stott (2014).
8. See Morrison and Lal Das (2014); Center for Open Data Enterprise, Open Data Impact Map (database), https://opendataimpactmap.org/.
9. Gurin, Bonina, and Verhulst (2019).
10. Gurin, Bonina, and Verhulst (2019).
11. Morrison and Lal Das (2014).

References

Gurin, Joel, Carla Bonina, and Stefaan Verhulst. 2019. "Open Data Stakeholders: Private Sector." In *The State of Open Data: Histories and Horizons*, edited by Tim Davies, Stephen B. Walker, Mor Rubinstein, and Fernando Perini, 418–29. Cape Town, South Africa: African Minds; Ottawa: International Development Research Centre. https://www.idrc.ca/en/book/state-open-data-histories-and-horizons.

Hughes-Cromwick, Ellen, and Julia Coronado. 2019. "The Value of US Government Data to US Business Decisions." *Journal of Economic Perspectives* 33 (1): 131–46. https://doi.org/10.1257/jep.33.1.131.

Lateral Economics. 2014. "Open for Business: How Open Data Can Help Achieve the G20 Growth Target." Omidyar Network, Redwood City, CA. https://lateraleconomics.com.au/wp-content/uploads/omidyar_open_business.pdf.

Magalhaes, Gustavo, and Catarina Roseira. 2017. "Open Government Data and the Private Sector: An Empirical View on Business Models and Value Creation." *Government Information Quarterly* 37 (3): 101248. https://doi.org/10.1016/j.giq.2017.08.004.

Manyika, James, Michael Chui, Peter Groves, Diana Farrell, Steve Van Kuiken, and Elizabeth Almasi Doshi. 2013. *Open Data: Unlocking Innovation and Performance with Liquid Information*. New York: McKinsey Global Institute. https://www.mckinsey.com/business-functions/mckinsey-digital/our-insights/open-data-unlocking-innovation-and-performance-with-liquid-information.

McMurren, Juliet, Stefaan Verhulst, and Andrew Young. 2016. "Denmark's Open Address Data Set: Consolidating and Freeing-Up Address Data." The GovLab, New York University, New York; Omidyar Network, Redwood City, CA. https://odimpact.org/case-denmarks-open-address-data-set.html.

Morrison, Alla, and Prasanna Lal Das. 2014. "New Surveys Reveal Dynamism, Challenges of Open Data-Driven Businesses in Developing Countries." *Data Blog* (blog), December 15, 2014. https://blogs.worldbank.org/opendata/new-surveys-reveal-dynamism-challenges-open-data-driven-businesses-developing-countries.

Stott, Andrew. 2014. "Open Data for Economic Growth." Working Paper 89606, World Bank, Washington, DC. http://documents.worldbank.org/curated/en/131621468154792082/Open-data-for-economic-growth.

Verhulst, Stefaan, and Robyn Caplan. 2015. "Open Data: A Twenty-First-Century Asset for Small and Medium-Sized Enterprises." The GovLab, New York University, New York. https://www.thegovlab.org/static/files/publications/OpenData-and-SME-Final-Aug2015.pdf.

Creative reuses of data for greater value

Main messages

1. Innovations in repurposing and combining public intent and private intent data are opening doors to development impacts previously unimaginable. These innovations can inform and advance policy goals, help governments improve and target service delivery, and empower individuals and civil society.

2. When private intent data are repurposed for public purposes, they can help fill data gaps and provide real-time and finer-scale insights. When public intent and private intent data are combined, some or many of the limitations of each data type can be overcome.

3. Private intent data can be difficult to understand, monitor, and regulate. They may also miss the poorest or other marginalized populations and perpetuate discrimination and biases. Data protection is a key issue. Responsive regulation and consumer protection measures are needed, along with recognition of which populations are omitted from an analysis.

4. Using private intent data for effective policy making requires short- and long-term coordinated investments in training, data partnerships, and research. Best practices and guidelines need to be developed.

The power of repurposing and combining different types and sources of data

Lack of data and information is no more apparent than during a crisis such as the COVID-19 pandemic or an earthquake. Urgent questions— What is happening? How can we help?—should receive good answers, and right away.

Consider the earthquake that devastated Haiti in 2010. Large donations of supplies and money poured into the country within days of the disaster, but delivering relief was difficult because vast numbers of people scattered. Censuses were no longer useful in helping responders direct relief to the people who needed it most. Using data from mobile phones, researchers were later able to demonstrate that they could have pinpointed population movements in

almost real time. They found that one-third of the estimated 630,000 residents of the capital, Port-au-Prince, had fled the city.[1] Even though this study was retrospective, it demonstrated how real-time, spatially pinpointed information like this could have expedited relief efforts and saved countless lives had it been accessed contemporaneously. This example highlights an emerging question in development research: When a pressing crisis such as the Haiti earthquake or the COVID-19 pandemic emerges, what data can complement traditional public intent data to solve complex development challenges?

Recent technological shifts in lower-income countries—such as the adoption of mobile phones, social media, digital transactions, and mobile money—have generated a wealth of granular private intent data (see chapter 3 and box 4.1) suited to a wide range of secondary uses.[2] These data are being leveraged to

Box 4.1 Using cellphones to combat COVID-19

After the onset of the COVID-19 outbreak, governments began implementing policy measures to reduce social contact and curb the spread of the pandemic. Data collected through mobile phones, such as call detail records and global positioning system (GPS) location data, have been extremely valuable in quantifying the effectiveness of policies, ranging from partial curfews to strict lockdowns. These data enable measurement of population density, travel patterns, and population mixing in real time and at high resolution, making it possible to better

target policy interventions and improve epidemiological modeling.[a] Analysis of GPS locations showed that by March 23, 2020, social distancing policies had helped reduce mobility in major US cities by half.[b] In Colombia, Indonesia, and Mexico, the impact of nonpharmaceutical interventions (such as travel restrictions and lockdowns) on mobility differed by socioeconomic group. Smartphone users living in the top 20 percent wealthiest neighborhoods in Jakarta, Indonesia, reduced their mobility up to twice as much as those living in the bottom 40 percent

Map B4.1.1 Mapping the home location of smartphone users in Jakarta, 2020

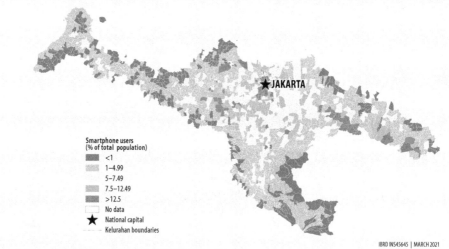

Smartphone users
(% of total population)
- <1
- 1–4.99
- 5–7.49
- 7.5–12.49
- >12.5
- No data
- ★ National capital
- Kelurahan boundaries

IBRD INS45645 | MARCH 2021

Source: Fraiberger et al. 2020. Data at http://bit.do/WDR2021-Map-B4_1_1.

Note: This map of Jakarta's metropolitan area shows the spatial distribution of smartphone users' home location as a percentage of Jakarta's total population.

(Box continues next page)

Box 4.1 **Using cellphones to combat COVID-19** *(continued)*

Figure B4.1.1 **Smartphone location data reveal the changes in the time users spend at home in Jakarta**

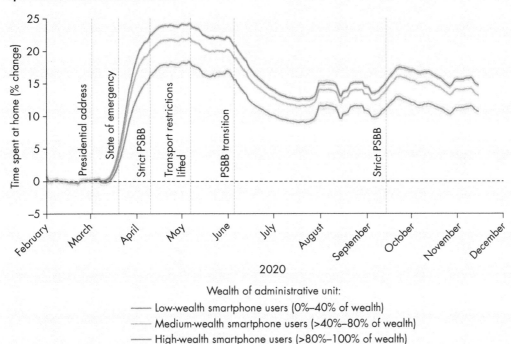

Wealth of administrative unit:
—— Low-wealth smartphone users (0%–40% of wealth)
—— Medium-wealth smartphone users (>40%–80% of wealth)
—— High-wealth smartphone users (>80%–100% of wealth)

Source: Adapted from Fraiberger et al. 2020. Data at http://bit.do/WDR2021-Fig-B4_1_1.

Note: Figure shows the changes in the time users spent at home from February 1 to November 15, 2020, relative to the baseline period. PSBB = *Pembatasan Sosial Berskala Besar* (large-scale social restrictions).

(map B4.1.1 and figure B4.1.1).[c] Using an epidemiological model and estimates of population movements derived from mobile phone data, research in China found that nonpharmaceutical interventions implemented in late January 2020 led to a 98.5 percent reduction in the number of COVID-19 cases one month later.

Meanwhile, mobile phones have proved to be a valuable tool for contact tracers seeking to alert individuals who may have been in contact with an infected person.[d]

Although both private companies and government actors have produced mobile phone applications for contact tracing (such as the Corona app 100m in the Republic of Korea, TraceTogether in Singapore, and COVIDSafe in Australia), their efficacy relative to more traditional forms of contact tracing has not yet been established. Digital contact tracing also raises important concerns about data protection,[e] prompting researchers worldwide to develop contact tracing technologies that preserve privacy. Examples are the Private Kit: Safe Paths developed by the Massachusetts Institute of Technology (MIT) and the Decentralized Privacy-Preserving Proximity Tracing

(DP3T) protocol developed by a consortium of European research institutions.

Despite the potential of deploying mobility data in the fight against COVID-19, their impact on policy thus far has been limited, especially in lower-income countries. Bottlenecks include a lack of technical expertise among government organizations; restrictions on data access, especially by mobile network operators; and lack of the investments and political will required to scale up one-time projects.[f] To ensure that mobility data can be made accessible and useful for policy purposes, it is important for all stakeholders—governments, mobile phone operators, technology companies, and researchers—to collaborate and form interdisciplinary teams to facilitate readiness and responsiveness to future crises.

a. Buckee et al. (2020).
b. Klein et al. (2020).
c. Fraiberger et al. (2020).
d. Servick (2020b).
e. Servick (2020a).
f. Oliver et al. (2020).

monitor the effectiveness of policy measures and predict outcomes of long-standing concern to development practitioners and policy makers.

Technological advances in the private sector have turned data into an integral component of the production process, leading to gains in productivity and generating even more data that can be repurposed for development. Specifically, the same approaches that are transforming efficiency and innovation in the private realm are being repurposed to tackle development bottlenecks in poor countries, making the development process more efficient, innovative, agile, and flexible. Because of the nonrivalrous nature of data, private companies also are able to reuse and repurpose publicly collected data, which can generate welfare-enhancing economies of scope.[3]

That said, the reuse of private intent data is not a panacea and may pose unique challenges for policy making. For example, data created by businesses to track mobile phone users may miss the poorest populations who do not have these technologies. Similarly, the data required to target customer experiences and to achieve business gains are different from the sociodemographic information on which policy makers rely to design inclusive policy. Furthermore, many of the algorithms used to process private intent data are considered trade secrets and thus lack the transparency required for effective policy making. Transparency and oversight are also important considerations when giving private companies access to sensitive data such as those related to facial recognition and surveillance (see chapter 6).

Despite these challenges, combining public intent and private intent data can offer real-time insights that not only are inclusive of the entire population (or nearly so) but also are more precisely estimated for specific population segments and localities. This is especially important for the poorest people in the poorest countries, which have the largest data gaps. Too often, individuals on the lowest end of the income distribution remain on the margins when government, civil society, and the private sector lack the data to effectively allocate and target resources based on need. Leveraging all available data may reveal insights for the poor and marginalized that were previously unattainable.

This chapter begins by showcasing innovative uses of public intent and private intent data for aiding development policy. Examples include data repurposing and synergies to improve predictions of disease spread, streamline service delivery, and allocate aid in disaster recovery. The chapter then turns to an exploration of the challenges that arise when private intent data are repurposed or when public intent and private intent data are combined. It concludes with a framework within which policy makers and funders could invest in the human capital, data partnerships, and research needed to gain useful insights from these new types and combinations of data.

Features of private intent data that can overcome gaps in public intent data

Private intent data are an alluring candidate to overcome public intent data gaps and offer new perspectives on development problems. These types of data are increasingly large in scale, "always on," zoomed in, and, at times, less biased.

Big data. Private intent data are typically labeled "big data,"[4] recognizing their wide reach and scope. The growing rates of mobile phone and social media usage enable information to be gathered from all users on these platforms. Although this process may underrepresent certain parts of the population in countries with lower usage rates, ever-larger portions of a population are being brought into the fold as the rates of mobile phone ownership and internet connectivity continue to increase, even in lower-income countries. When private intent data are repurposed toward a public goal, their volume and reach can not only inform first-order policy goals of poverty reduction and service delivery, but also facilitate efforts to detect and study rare events, such as fraud, corruption, or criminal activity, through techniques such as anomaly detection.

"Always on" data. Private intent data are always on[5] because the daily use of new technologies entails constant data collection. Call detail records (CDRs) and apps that log locations pinpointed by satellite-based global positioning systems (GPS) offer traces of where cellphone users travel throughout the day. When a sudden and unexpected shock hits, such as a natural disaster or a disease outbreak, such data can provide precious real-time information on human mobility and call density. The timeliness of private intent data therefore contrasts with public intent data, which are generally collected at intervals of 1, 5, or 10 years and thus are not always very timely. In Africa, for example, 14 of 59 countries did not conduct any surveys from 2000 to 2010, impeding the construction of nationally representative poverty measures.[6] This critical situation sparked the call for a "data revolution" by the United Nations in 2014, pushing for an increase in data collection efforts in Africa and elsewhere.[7] Although the situation is improving, with the average number of surveys per country per year increasing from 0.5 in 1990 to 1.5 in 2010,[8] the

lack of timeliness of public intent data has resulted in huge knowledge gaps, which are particularly glaring following major economic shocks such as COVID-19. Meanwhile, private intent data are increasingly being used to help fill these gaps.

"Zoomed in" data. Private intent data can zoom in on individuals and locations. Private companies want to know who is using their products or services and in what ways they can optimize their offerings and operations. Private intent data zoom into individuals to collect key metrics such as transaction histories to predict consumer behavior and bolster successful products. Internet Protocol (IP) addresses, browsing histories, and smartphone app logs add to a rich dataset that companies collect on a single person over time. Tracking whether app users enter a store or whether IP addresses in a neighborhood are searching for products on their site enable companies to better plan their store locations and stock their supplies. These data are now being applied to the public sphere, ranging from improving population maps[9] to helping decision-makers target and optimize critical development resources. A key challenge to using individual data patterns to allocate resources or establish eligibility for products and services is data manipulation: individuals may strategically change browsing or other data usage behavior to appear more favorable in ranking criteria used by data algorithms to make allocation decisions. More research and policy deliberations are needed to design algorithms and decision rules that account for such user manipulation.

Potentially less biased data. Private intent data potentially reveal less "biased" information about people than surveys or polls because researchers observe actual behavior instead of relying on responses. Although it is possible that respondents misreport answers during surveys, they have little incentive to do so when searching the internet. For that reason, the Google internet search engine has been dubbed a "digital truth serum."[10] This finding may apply especially to opinions on sensitive topics such as racism. Few will admit their opinions in surveys, but they are revealed through internet searches and can influence political outcomes, among others.[11] However, the algorithms used by search engines are considered private trade secrets and are usually optimized for private benefit—not public benefit. Without knowledge of the workings of these algorithms, users of search engine outcomes as an exclusive source of data may find they lead to biased and discriminatory policy predictions.

Overall, combining public intent and private intent data is a powerful way to gain aggregate population insights in real time, if enough attention is given to addressing representativeness, discrimination, and transparency. Calibrating private intent data with census and survey data is one way to estimate population-level needs.

The next section offers a broad range of innovative examples of applications of private intent data to public policy and instances in which public intent and private intent data have been combined to promote inclusive and timely development solutions.

New insights from repurposing and combining data

The last decade has seen a surge in innovative research that repurposes private intent data and combines it with public intent data to tackle development issues. In the spring and summer of 2020 when the COVID-19 outbreak reached global dimensions, more than 950 scientific and medical articles were published that used private intent data to tackle the pandemic (box 4.2). Researchers' ability to respond quickly to the pandemic builds on a growing trend of research that combines diverse data to tackle emerging issues.

Monitoring public health

Monitoring public health is a key area that could benefit from repurposing and combining public intent and private intent data. In many lower-income countries, infectious diseases routinely pose large health threats. Five of the top 10 causes of death in low-income countries are communicable diseases, including lower respiratory infections, diarrheal diseases, HIV/AIDS, malaria, and tuberculosis.[12] Viruses have been responsible for more deaths than all armed conflicts around the world over the last century.[13] Especially in countries where data are limited, new big private intent data sources can help inform public policy interventions to reduce the mortality and morbidity rates from infectious diseases. Identification of hotspots can help disease control programs target activities more effectively to those areas, reducing infection rates both directly and indirectly in destination areas that are receiving infected travelers.[14]

As early as 2008, researchers began exploring how mobile phone data could be used to measure population mobility and then be applied to the study of epidemics.[15] A seminal study applied this research at scale for all of Kenya using mobile phone data on nearly 15 million individuals to identify sources of imported malaria infections stemming from human mobility.[16] During the 2014 Ebola outbreak in West Africa, researchers highlighted the potential benefits

Box 4.2 Leveraging private intent data to tackle COVID-19

Between February and September 2020, more than 950 articles were published in scientific, medical, and technical journals that repurposed cellphone, social media, Google search, and other types of big private intent data to better understand the spread of COVID-19 and to offer policy and operational solutions (figure B4.2.1). Despite the relatively large number of articles in a short time span, coverage of lower-income countries was low, especially those in Africa (map B4.2.1). Lack of expertise, poor training, difficult access to data, and limited research support are key areas that funders could address to ensure innovative uses of data in and about lower-income countries.

Figure B4.2.1 Use of repurposed data to study COVID-19: Published articles, by type of private intent data used

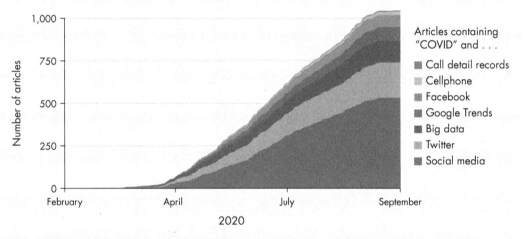

Source: WDR 2021 team, based on data from CORD-19 (COVID-19 Open Research Dataset) Semantic Scholar team, Ai2 (Allen Institute for AI), http://www.semanticscholar.org/cord19. Data at http://bit.do/WDR2021-Fig-B4_2_1.

Note: Figure shows the number of articles published in scientific, medical, and technical journals across time from February to September 2020. The cumulative sum across all categories is higher because some articles appear in more than one category.

(Box continues next page)

of using mobile phone data in the design of public policy.[17] However, use of these analytics at the time of the crisis remained limited.[18]

After onset of the COVID-19 pandemic, countries began to deploy this type of research and to pair mobile phone data with public intent data. Belgium formed a Data Against COVID-19 task force to analyze deidentified mobile phone data. These data are being used to monitor changes in human mobility trends due to lockdown measures and to inform decisions related to appropriate lockdown measures. In the Republic of Korea, mobile phone data are being used to aid contact tracing efforts to contain disease spread. By combining mobile phone data with medical facility records, credit card transaction logs, and closed-circuit television recordings, the government is identifying people at risk of exposure.[19] Lower-income countries such as Ghana and Mozambique are beginning to use deidentified mobile phone data to combat the pandemic, typically with the support of international organizations that provide analytical skills for processing the data.[20]

Other types of big data are also being enlisted to create measures of mobility that can improve the effectiveness of the pandemic response. Facebook disease prevention maps are being used to study COVID-19 and have been expanded to include colocation maps that measure comingling among people living in different areas and trends in whether individuals are staying near their homes or continuing to go to other locations.[21] Google has produced a new set of measures to track the response to policies aimed at flattening the curve of the COVID-19 pandemic.[22] Other sources of data for GPS locations have been

Box 4.2 **Leveraging private intent data to tackle COVID-19** *(continued)*

Map B4.2.1 **Uses of repurposed data to study COVID-19: Published articles, by country**

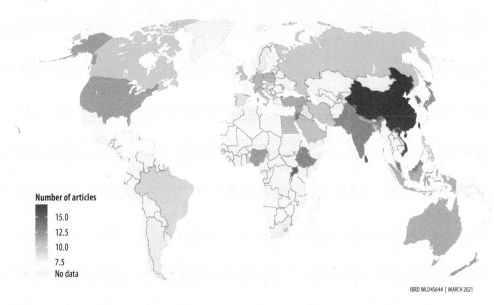

Number of articles

15.0
12.5
10.0
7.5
No data

IBRD WLD45644 | MARCH 2021

Source: WDR 2021 team, based on data from CORD-19 (COVID-19 Open Research Dataset) Semantic Scholar team, Ai2 (Allen Institute for AI), http://www.semanticscholar.org/cord19. Data at http://bit.do/WDR2021-Map-B4_2_1.

Note: Map shows the number of articles published in scientific, medical, and technical journals across countries from February to September 2020. Article counts are divided by the COVID-19 death incidence rate.

used by data analytics firms such as Baidu, Cuebiq, and Unacast to assess the impacts of social distancing measures for COVID-19.[23] GPS data provide better approximation of locations and mobility at a finer spatial resolution, but their availability is limited by smartphone penetration and usage. In many lower-income countries, smartphone penetration is still low, and even those individuals with smartphones may only selectively turn on data or GPS because of high costs and drain on battery life.

The potential of new data sources for supporting public health and epidemiology efforts goes far beyond measures of mobility.[24] Efforts are under way to use data tools as early warning systems for outbreaks and for understanding disease dynamics and routes of transmission. For example, the company BlueDot provides infectious disease surveillance services using advanced data analytics. It was able to warn of the outbreak of COVID-19 before the official announcement in early January 2020 by analyzing news reports, disease networks, and official

proclamations.[25] A similar prediction was made for the 2015–16 Zika outbreak that affected an estimated 1 million people, mainly in Latin America.[26] By combining online news sources, Google search queries, Twitter posts, and government disease reports, local outbreaks could have been detected two to three weeks earlier, a retrospective study estimates.[27] Combining public intent and private intent data sources has also improved forecasts for Ebola in West Africa[28] and dengue in Southeast Asia.[29] Improved forecasting of disease outbreaks and associated population movements is essential for efficient response measures to curb incidence rates.[30]

Another open and fertile source of synergy is data collected by wearables and other biotech devices. For example, the Kinsa HealthWeather app tracks fevers around the United States via smart thermometers and uses the aggregate data to create prediction models for the spread of disease. This type of application is particularly relevant in crises such as COVID-19, where timely reporting of case growth can help accurately map disease spread and enable timely and appropriate public policy responses.

Targeting resource allocations and responses during crises

Approximately 20–30 million people worldwide are displaced every year because of natural disasters such as storms, floods, droughts, and geological events.[31] Over the last decade, about 600,000 people lost their lives to natural disasters, most of them in low- and middle-income countries.[32] Effective disaster prevention, mitigation, response, and recovery require timely, cost-effective data at fine spatial scales. However, many countries lack the adequate early warning systems and advanced geological tools to aid in this process—at times with devastating consequences. During the 2018 earthquake and tsunami in Central Sulawesi, Indonesia, the government could have minimized the human cost had the country's warning system of buoys and seismographic sensors not been defective.[33] As climate change continues to increase the frequency and damage of natural disasters, lower-income countries will likely bear the brunt of the economic and human impacts. Spotlight 4.1 highlights the importance of improved meteorological data for lower-income countries to confront enhanced climate risks.

Recent data innovations have revealed that nontraditional sources of private intent data such as mobile phone usage, social media activity, online queries, crowdsourcing platforms, and remote sensing technologies can facilitate disaster management.[34] These devices and activities are not a replacement for advanced geological and meteorological equipment, which can predict disasters and offer early warnings. They can, however, help in government efforts to prevent loss and provide relief when such events occur. Various studies in both lower- and higher-income countries have found that scraping social media platforms for posts related to seismic activity produces an in situ impact profile of seismic damage similar to the ones produced by advanced geological instruments, the traditional source of such data.[35] Similarly, Tweets have been analyzed for disaster-related keywords to detect earthquakes in Australia and New Zealand.[36] Deidentified CDR data are a good predictor of population movement for weather-related disasters such as floods. For example, the textual content of Tweets was used to understand how people were reacting to the 2011 floods in Thailand. Messages were classified by their content to help highlight precise needs in affected communities.[37]

The geospatial nature of social media posts can further help prioritize resource allocation in times of dire need. Moreover, combining geographic and social media analytics can enhance aid recovery efforts after a disaster. In the aftermath of the 2014 earthquake in Napa, California, researchers trained a machine learning algorithm to extract disaster-related semantics from Tweets and paired this information with geolocations to identify spatial hotspots.[38] From these data, they were able to infer a disaster footprint and assess damage. They also learned that this method was transferrable to other social media platforms and locations, with tweaks for cultural differences in social media use. Similarly, researchers studying Hurricane Irma, which hit Florida in 2017, found that sentiment analysis[39] on geolocated Tweets could be used to guide resource allocation.[40] Social media and mobile records have also proven useful in tracking recovery efforts. After Hurricane Sandy slammed into the New York City area in 2012, researchers analyzed Tweet topics and sentiment to see how those who experienced the disaster were coping, compared with those who did not experience it.

Finally, governments have long used satellite imagery to assess damage in the aftermath of natural disasters. However, this imagery usually lacks the spatial resolution needed for a granular assessment. It is typically considered public intent data, but a growing number of private companies are launching their own remote sensing technologies and data collection. The start-up Cloud to Street uses private satellite data to provide near real-time flood assessments to assist disaster recovery and adaptive planning. In three days in 2018, it was able to build a flood monitoring system to help the Democratic Republic of Congo deploy resources to 16,000 asylum seekers who had sought refuge along the flood-prone banks of the Congo River. Cloud to Street leveraged high-resolution private intent satellite data with data about cropland, population, and public assets (such as roads and infrastructure) to generate real-time impact estimates served on an interactive web platform and with automated alerts. As decision-makers transitioned from disaster response to recovery, Cloud to Street transitioned to using freely available satellite images—an effort that enabled longer-term support with fewer resources.[41]

Mapping poverty and targeting service delivery more precisely

Timely, reliable data on population characteristics are vital for responsive social and economic policy making. Mobile CDR and remote sensing data have recently been used to predict poverty patterns on a granular level and in a timely fashion, thereby helping to better target government services. Use of these data sources costs a fraction of that for fielding censuses or household surveys. Similar data from social media, online engagement, and satellite imagery are reducing the constraints to collecting data on the most vulnerable and hard-to-reach populations. Moreover, the same algorithms that Google and Facebook use for online consumer marketing can be tweaked to direct resources to people living in poverty. In the same way that these tech firms predict the advertising that may interest consumers based on their digital behavior, development actors can use digital behavior to predict whether people are economically vulnerable.[42]

Research relying on data from Rwanda reveals that past histories of mobile phone use extracted from CDRs are a reliable predictor of socioeconomic status as validated against survey data.[43] Moreover, the researchers find that the predicted characteristics of millions of mobile phone users can be aggregated to the same distribution of wealth across the entire country or at the cluster level—approximately equivalent to a village in rural areas or a ward in urban areas—as that indicated by traditional data sources. Such highly localized poverty maps can be used to effectively target policies, programs, and resources to the poorest. These methods can also improve demographic targeting of services by gender, age, and income level. For example, CDR data have been used to identify the gender of phone users,[44] as well as to identify the ultrapoor.[45]

Beyond the realm of CDRs, research in higher-income countries has shown that online browsing history and social media activity can also reliably predict household income. Social media footprints were used in Spain to infer city-level behavioral measures and predict socioeconomic output, specifically unemployment.[46] Similarly, data from Yelp reviews of retail shops were used to measure changes in gentrification and predict local housing prices.[47] Equipped with real-time and localized insights and trends, policy makers can better inform policies to target areas that have been affected by short-term economic shocks or long-term economic shifts.

Remote sensing technology is yet another novel way to collect population characteristics, predict poverty patterns, and improve public service delivery.[48] Researchers have relied on publicly available data from Africa to both calibrate and validate machine learning models. The Demographic and Health Survey (DHS) sponsored by the United States Agency for International Development (USAID) and the World Bank's Living Standards Measurement Study (LSMS) surveys provide high-resolution data on household wealth and consumption expenditures. When calibrated with these surveys, satellite imagery can predict poverty. At the survey cluster level, when used with survey data from Malawi, Nigeria, Rwanda, Tanzania, and Uganda satellite imagery can explain 55–75 percent of the variation in wealth and consumption per capita. Estimates of economic well-being using this approach outperformed both similar estimates using satellite readings of nighttime light in the same countries and estimates using mobile phone data in Rwanda. Critically, this approach has been shown to work reasonably well for predicting wealth and poverty in countries when they are excluded from the sample used to train the model, suggesting the approach is scalable across other countries, at least in Africa.

Ensuring road safety in transport and transit

Road transport is an important element of economic development. Access to transport and mobility are highly correlated with income and quality of life. Even though lower-income countries have only half of the world's vehicles, they account for 90 percent of road traffic fatalities. In 2011 the World Health Organization (WHO) and the World Bank launched a Decade of Action for Road Safety, and they have provided funding and technical assistance to build systems aimed at reducing injuries and deaths on the road. Despite these efforts, little progress has been reported in low- and middle-income countries, and the number of fatalities remains high.[49]

A new and growing body of literature studies how alternative sources of data can be used to make progress toward achieving national road safety outcomes. In the public sector, for example, a study in Nigeria provided road safety agents with a monitoring system to investigate and record road safety events via mobile phone.[50] Access to this mobile phone–based database helped disseminate information better and enabled agents to respond faster to road accidents. Such transit monitoring practices are becoming more widespread, especially in the private sector. Commercial banks in Kenya now require a tracking device in minibuses before approving loans to bus service owners. As a result, today most long-range buses in the country are equipped with GPS.[51] This technology advancement serves the dual purpose of tracking assets under lien for the bank's private benefit and promoting safer driving for public benefit.

Social media analytics have also been applied in the private sector to understand the traffic safety culture. A recent study in Washington State in the United States mined Twitter data to understand the patterns, behaviors, and attitudes related to road safety.[52] The study conducted sentiment analysis based on traffic-related keywords to extract latent views on topics such as safe driving measures, accidents, law enforcement and patrolling, and accident-causing behavior. It found that sentiment analysis using social media posts can be used in developing policies to improve traffic safety relevant to specific contexts. This type of sentiment analysis could be applied in lower-income countries as well, with substantial benefits. Techniques are also being developed to fill in gaps in data on the number and location of accidents in lower-income countries. Recently, researchers developed an algorithm to identify and geolocate crashes from Twitter feeds to substantially increase the digital data available to prioritize road safety policies. Spotlight 4.2 describes how car crash danger zones were pinpointed in Nairobi, Kenya, by combining police reports and crowdsourced data.[53]

More broadly, research in this area has focused on the transit industry to answer broader development questions in the realm of private sector development. For example, a study in Kenya found that providing bus owners with data on their employees' driving behavior can improve firm operations.[54] Specifically, they placed GPS devices in Kenya's inner-city public transport vehicles and tracked a variety of data that captured driving behavior, including acceleration, jerk, location, and timestamp to measure the number of daily safety violations. The main contribution of this data innovation was to correct informational asymmetry: once minibus owners could track driving performance, drivers could receive more generous contracts for better performance. In turn, drivers operated in a manner less damaging to the vehicle, more frequently met targets, and reduced underreporting of revenues. Thus incentives between the company (principal) and the drivers (agents) were better aligned. These types of data can also provide governments with feedback to use in redesigning their road infrastructure and guide interventions to reduce accidents.

Monitoring illegal fishing and deforestation

Recent advances in combining public intent and private intent data are also improving the monitoring of natural resource extraction. Box 4.3 features one example: identifying illegal fishing in protected ocean waters.

Efforts to monitor deforestation have also begun to leverage public and private datasets. Combining data in this way has enabled indigenous groups to patrol their forest reserves and defend against encroachment. With the aid of open-access or cheaper private satellite imagery, cloud computing, community observations, and publicly available property maps, community-based forest monitoring has become increasingly effective in identifying encroachment.[55] In addition, through social media and platforms such as Global Forest Watch the international community can better help local groups hold governments accountable in achieving national sustainable development commitments.[56] Similar data are being used by companies to ensure that their suppliers are meeting sustainability standards for forest products. A recent initiative, Radar Alerts for Detecting Deforestation (RADD), was launched by the world's 10 largest palm oil producers and buyers to monitor illegal deforestation in palm oil plantations.[57] By funding development of a system to detect illegal deforestation using public radar imagery, property maps, and private procurement data, this initiative may signal a shift from civil society monitoring the private sector to the private sector monitoring itself to ensure that company commitments are met.

Keeping governments accountable

Emerging data types are enabling civil society to better monitor corruption. Utilizing crowdsourced data and web scraping, social media discussion boards are emerging as ways in which local leaders can act against corrupt officials and receive real-time feedback on the impact of anticorruption policies.[58] Data reported in newspapers have been used to target corruption, thereby allowing civil society organizations to press for stricter governance measures. A systematic, real-time view of corruption trends can be gained from the news flow indices of corruption (NIC) constructed by the International Monetary Fund (IMF), drawing on country-specific searches of more than 665 million news articles.[59] Regressing the NIC onto the real per capita gross domestic product (GDP) revealed that changes in corruption levels as measured by the NIC indicators were associated with 3 percent lower economic growth over the next two years. Combined with election data, NIC data have helped identify countries that had peaks in corruption before or after elections. These findings can prove helpful to international responses to corruption.

Private sector data are making it possible for international organizations and civil society actors to monitor policy and report on important events

Box 4.3 Preventing illegal fishing in protected maritime areas

Monitoring illegal fishing in Marine Protected Areas (MPAs) is difficult because of their size and distance from land. The boundaries of MPAs are curated and made open access by the United Nations Environment Programme (UNEP) and the International Union for Conservation of Nature (IUCN). Yet identifying boats in vast expanses of the ocean requires innovative uses of data that are not publicly available. Global Fishing Watch has data partnerships with the firm ORBCOMM to access raw data from commercial trawlers' automatic identification systems (AIS), which provides the real-time geographic coordinates of each trawler to help avoid collisions and provide other traffic services. AIS data can be combined with optical and radar imagery from satellites to detect illegal fishing activity (figure B4.3.1). By overlaying MPA boundaries on AIS data used to identify boats and determining fishing behaviors from the time spent in specific areas, researchers found that 59 percent of MPAs in the European Union were commercially trawled. In areas that were heavily fished, the presence of sensitive species (such as sharks, rays, and skates) was 69 percent lower.[a]

Figure B4.3.1 Public intent and private intent data can be combined to detect illegal fishing activity

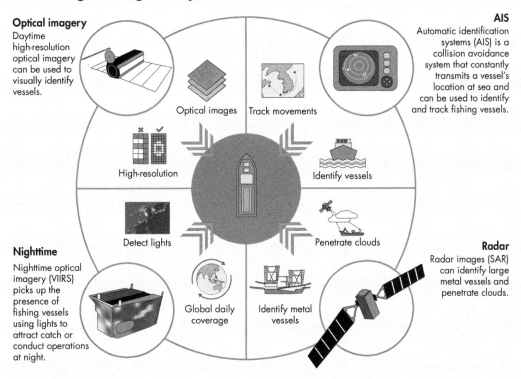

Optical imagery
Daytime high-resolution optical imagery can be used to visually identify vessels.

AIS
Automatic identification systems (AIS) is a collision avoidance system that constantly transmits a vessel's location at sea and can be used to identify and track fishing vessels.

Optical images   Track movements

High-resolution   Identify vessels

Detect lights   Penetrate clouds

Nighttime
Nighttime optical imagery (VIIRS) picks up the presence of fishing vessels using lights to attract catch or conduct operations at night.

Radar
Radar images (SAR) can identify large metal vessels and penetrate clouds.

Global daily coverage   Identify metal vessels

Source: Infographic taken on July 8, 2020, globalfishingwatch.org. © Global Fishing Watch. Used with permission of Global Fishing Watch; further permission required for reuse.

Note: Public intent data include satellite data. Private intent data include data from trawlers' collision avoidance systems.

a. Dureuil et al. (2018).

such as elections in real time. The Inter-American Development Bank, in partnership with governments in Latin America, has launched a website that uses crowdsourced civic feedback to monitor public works projects.[60] Similarly, Civic Cops, a start-up in India, provides a suite of digital platforms to connect governments with civil society, notably offering a service that allows civic complaints and citizen service requests to be filed by mobile phone and directed to the corresponding public authorities. Civic engagement data have also been used to monitor elections in lower-income countries. For example, in Sierra Leone's 2012 elections a collection of citizen journalists traveled throughout the country and reported election activity through SMS text messages, which were then posted on a Tumblr website, pegged to a Google map, and disseminated on Twitter.[61]

Benchmarking policy priorities

Private intent data repurposed by international organizations, civil society actors, and private companies are being used to track policy goals and benchmark policy priorities. These initiatives are invaluable because they provide unique and comparable data across countries that are not collected by national governments.

The data being harvested and disseminated to promote financial inclusion have been widely recognized by policy makers as critical to reducing poverty and achieving inclusive economic growth. Partnering with the polling firm Gallup Inc., the World Bank launched the Global Findex database in 2011, the world's most comprehensive database on how adults save, borrow, make payments, and manage risks (map 4.1). This dataset was created by adding a module to the Gallup World Poll, which offers a standing global survey that produces comparable data across countries and across time. Researchers, private companies, and international organizations use these data to understand the lives of people everywhere.[62] The Global Findex database has become a mainstay of global efforts to promote financial inclusion. In addition to being widely cited by scholars and development practitioners, Global Findex data have been used to track progress toward the World Bank's goal of universal financial access by 2020 and the United Nations' Sustainable Development Goals (SDG Target 8.10).

Data synergies can also help in critical policy areas such as food security in both times of normality and crises such as the COVID-19 pandemic. The potential

Map 4.1 Private intent data can provide unique and comparable information not collected by national governments, such as the number of adults who lack a formal financial account

Globally, 1.7 billion adults lacked a formal financial account in 2017

Number of adults without an account
— 200 million
— 100 million
— 10 million
— 1 million

IBRD WLD45646 | MARCH 2021

Source: World Bank, Global Findex (Global Financial Inclusion Database), https://globalfindex.worldbank.org/. Data at http://bit.do/WDR2021-Map-4_1.

Note: Data are not displayed for economies in which the share of adults without an account is 5 percent or less.

to combine geospatial data with farmer output and market pricing can improve the logistics and management of critical food systems. Meanwhile, international organizations have partnered with companies to create public intent surveys to track progress toward the SDGs and inclusive development. For example, in 2014 the United Nations Food and Agriculture Organization (FAO) began to add questions to the Gallup World Poll to collect data for its Food Insecurity Experience Scale (addressing SDG 2). In 2015 the International Labour Organization (ILO) and Walk Free Foundation added questions that measure the incidence of modern slavery (addressing SDG Target 8.7). Through a partnership with Facebook, in 2018 the World Bank and the Organisation for Economic Co-Operation and Development (OECD) launched the Future of Business biannual survey.[63] The survey targets active micro, small, and medium enterprises (MSMEs) that host a Facebook business page. Using these data, researchers have been able to study the gender pay gap across 97 countries.[64]

Apart from surveys, companies are beginning to repurpose their own data for the public good. During the COVID-19 pandemic, Google began releasing updated community mobility reports for 135 countries.[65] These reports rely on users' location data to show daily changes in mobility patterns at the country or state/provincial level, such as fewer trips to transit stations, retail stores, parks, grocery stores, pharmacies, workplaces, or residential addresses. These data give public health officials and the general public a way to benchmark a region's response to COVID-19 relative to other regions and over time. Because the data are collected systematically across countries, they can also be used to compare behavioral responses across the world. Another example of a private company repurposing its own data for public benefit is the internet speed test company Ookla, which provides a global index for internet speeds that ranks countries for their mobile and fixed broadband.[66] These data can be used by governments and funders to prioritize investments in broadband coverage.

Researchers are also combining global public intent and private intent datasets to prioritize funding streams for donors. One example is in the digital agricultural space, where farmers can access extension services on their cellphones. Digital agricultural interventions offer a solution to the dearth of agricultural extension agents in many lower-income countries, where the ratio of farmers to extension agents often exceeds 1,000 to 1.[67] Digital services can provide farmers with expert scientific advice based on their local field, market, and climatic conditions. Yet most small-scale farmers live in areas with lower 3G and 4G coverage than in areas with relatively high shares of large-scale farms (map 4.2 and figure 4.1).[68] This

Map 4.2 Agricultural extension services can be tailored to the slower, older broadband internet accessible to many small-scale farmers

Mobile network coverage on farms
- 4G
- 3G
- 2G
- None

IBRD WLD45647 | MARCH 2021

Source: Mehrabi et al. 2020. Data at http://bit.do/WDR2021-Map-4_2.

Figure 4.1 Gaps in network coverage differ across farm sizes, affecting agricultural extension services

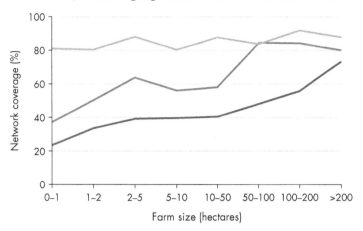

Internet service: ⎯⎯ 2G ⎯⎯ 3G ⎯⎯ 4G

Source: Mehrabi et al. 2020. Data at http://bit.do/WDR2021-Fig-4_1.

finding suggests that the wave of digital agricultural services should focus on 2G solutions (such as voice and text messaging) to ensure that small-scale farmers are reached. Combining private intent broadband coverage data from the data aggregation company Mosaik (now part of Ookla) with public intent farm size data yields localized estimates of broadband usage at 10 square kilometer resolution. This type of analysis can be used in making decisions about the deployment of infrastructure to support the faster broadband required for digital services that depend on smartphones.

Limitations in using private intent data for development

Despite the enormous potential offered by private intent data through repurposing and synergies, several important limitations and challenges affect their use for development projects. These issues should be taken into account in the design of future research and public policy.

Data coverage and representativeness

A key limitation of most private intent data is their lack of representativeness. Private intent data are often a by-product of the use of digital technologies such as mobile phones or the internet. Having access to these technologies typically requires infrastructure resources such as electricity or broadband that are distributed unequally in lower-income countries. In addition, because smartphone ownership is skewed toward those who can afford the phones, the

data collected through these technologies primarily highlight the characteristics of a relatively wealthier share of the population. A 2012 study combining CDRs and surveys found that mobile phone owners in Rwanda were wealthier, better educated, and predominantly male.[69] Similar conclusions emerged from an analysis of the population of mobile phone owners in Kenya.[70] The lack of representativeness is even more pronounced in social media data, which typically require that users be literate in addition to having internet access. Moreover, because of the access charges associated with internet use, only the wealthy can afford to use the internet on their mobile devices. Estimates from Ghana, Kenya, Nigeria, and Senegal suggest that less than one-third of the population uses internet on a mobile phone, and less than 15 percent in Mozambique, Rwanda, Tanzania, and Uganda.[71] To overcome the lack of representativeness of private intent data, development practitioners often rely on statistical methods to combine them with public intent data.

One important source of alternative data is satellite imagery, which can be either public intent or private intent, depending on the application. Images collected by satellites have the advantage of being fully representative of the population, and they are well suited to picking up measures of building density that are highly correlated with population density and, by extension, economic well-being. Satellite data, however, come with an important limitation—they are typically available only for aggregated geographic units such as grids or villages. So-called "bottom-up" statistical techniques combine survey data with remote sensing indicators to permit greater geospatial precision (box 4.4).

Data profiling and discrimination

Because of the complexity and unstructured nature of private intent data, data scientists are increasingly relying on modern machine learning methods and algorithms to analyze them.[72] These algorithms can contain millions of parameters, which can be extremely costly and time-consuming to calibrate.[73] Machine learning experts thus typically rely on algorithms that are "pre-trained" using very large quantities of private intent data to make them easy to use for a variety of tasks. Although these algorithms are extremely useful for extracting insights from complex datasets, researchers in recent years realized that biases in the data used to calibrate these algorithms could contribute to discrimination,[74] with adverse consequences for people's welfare. Other research found that a machine learning tool created

Combined data sources, by improving the representativeness and precision of survey data, enable indicators to be reported at finer spatial scales. One statistical approach to improving representativeness typically used when combining survey data with mobile phone data or satellite imagery is to average the data from different sources using a common geographic unit of analysis. For example, a welfare measure such as an asset index could be averaged across all households in a village (enumeration area). The results are then related to satellite imagery or mobile phone data. This procedure works well when extrapolating from imagery to predict average consumption for countries or large areas not covered by a survey. This method can also be used to generate local estimates of welfare within a country, provided that an appropriate statistical method is used to directly incorporate information from the sample into the estimation procedure to obtain more precise estimates.

Facebook engineers have used deep-learning algorithms to detect buildings in satellite imagery, allowing them to downscale population estimates from the census to a much finer spatial resolution. However, these methods have significant drawbacks. Predictions based on models specified at aggregate levels will generally not deliver precise estimates unless they are combined in an appropriate way with survey-based estimates. Precision is an important consideration because most national statistical offices will not publish imprecise estimates due to quality concerns. Furthermore, geographic downscaling relies on a few key assumptions. Facebook assumes the population is distributed in proportion to the "built-up area," which leads to inconsistencies between the estimates and the census. For example, because a smaller portion of buildings in urban areas are residential, relying on built-up area to distribute population could exaggerate population counts in urban areas compared with rural ones.

An alternative method for estimating the population of small areas is to use "bottom-up" methods that draw on data from survey listing exercises rather than "top-down" disaggregation of census data. "Bottom-up" techniques offer the important advantage of being able to produce updated population estimates without a census at a fraction of the cost. They use survey data to calibrate a model that relates population in the areas sampled by the survey to remote sensing indicators. Geospatial indicators that predict population density include the geographic size of the village, the number of buildings, the extent of built-up area, and the presence of nighttime lights. The model can then be used to generate population estimates nationwide. Similar methods can be used to generate more precise estimates of nonmonetary poverty.[a] They likely could be applied to a variety of socioeconomic indicators, including monetary poverty, labor market outcomes, health outcomes, and educational attainment.

a. Masaki et al. (2020).

---

to predict the future criminal behavior of defendants in the United States embedded racial discrimination: black defendants were twice as likely as their white counterparts to be falsely classified as future criminals.[75] Similarly, image search engines such as Flickr, which have been the source of training data for various computer vision algorithms, have been shown to overrepresent light-skinned men between the ages of 18 and 40, leading to poorer performance by these algorithms when making predictions of underrepresented categories such as women or minorities.[76]

Similar issues arise when machine learning algorithms are pre-trained using text containing racist and sexist stereotypes. Text generation algorithms trained on massive online text databases that were scraped from the web, such as the GPT-2 database created by Open AI, have been found to generate racist and anti-Semitic text in response to specific inputs.[77] When trained on Google News, word-embedding algorithms aimed at measuring the similarity between words tend to propagate the sexist biases reflected in the text, highlighting similarities between "man" and "computer programmer," whereas "woman" appears to be associated with "homemaker."[78] Arguably, such discrimination can have larger consequences in lower-income countries, which typically lack safety nets and social protection mechanisms.

Data transparency and manipulation
Both the data-generating process and the algorithms used to process private intent data suffer from a lack of transparency. The algorithms used by search engines

are not public, and they are constantly optimized to improve users' experience. This process can lead to inaccurate predictions of policy outcomes, such as the notorious Google Flu Trends index. In 2009 a team of scientists at Google published a paper describing an innovative method to predict the number of flu cases in the United States using the volume of search terms related to the flu on Google.[79] Their Google Flu Trends index was initially able to predict official numbers ahead of the US Centers for Disease Control and Prevention (CDC), until it made headlines in 2013 for incorrectly predicting twice the number of actual flu cases. Scientists investigating what went wrong realized that many search terms used as predictors were associated with the onset of winter instead of the onset of colds.[80] This "overfitting" is a major concern when private intent datasets containing high-dimensional data (that is, data with a high number of features or independent variables) are used to nowcast policy outcomes that are infrequently observed. New generations of forecasting models based on private intent data should aim to rely on information coming from multiple private data sources to avoid being too dependent on the idiosyncrasies of a single source.

Even when accurate, predictive models are often so opaque that their predictions cannot be easily communicated to policy makers. Because machine learning is increasingly used to shape development policies, more research is needed to make complex algorithms transparent and interpretable, thereby increasing their legitimacy and ensuring they do not contribute to unequal outcomes. More research is also needed to understand trade-offs between interpretability and predictive performance. For example, researchers have estimated models using data to predict poverty from satellite imagery in both Sri Lanka and Uganda by focusing on objects in images that correlate with standards of living such as roads, buildings, and cars.[81] In each country, the interpretable model performed as well as commonly used black-box computer vision algorithms, indicating that model interpretability does not necessarily come at the cost of performance. The performance of image recognition algorithms may be constrained, however, because they are initially trained to detect a wide variety of objects using millions of images, which may not isolate the most important portions of the images for the specific purpose of predicting poverty.

An additional challenge of relying on algorithms to design policy is that they can be manipulated. People can change their behavior in response to algorithmic decision-making to trick the system and maximize their interests. For example, the nonprofit

GiveDirectly facilitates direct cash transfers to poor households. As a proxy for poor living conditions, satellite imagery was initially used to target households with thatched roofs. When GiveDirectly's methods became common knowledge, some families pretended to live in a thatched structure near their home to qualify for the aid.[82] This concern about manipulation increasingly motivates the design of machine learning algorithms that assign more weight to personal characteristics less likely to be subject to manipulation.[83]

Investments in data innovations: Building a culture of data

Effectively leveraging new types of data requires investing in human capital, data sharing, and research in lower-income countries. This section describes areas in which governments, donors, and advocates of corporate social responsibility can help promote innovative uses of data for public benefit in lower-income countries, thereby helping to build a culture for the use of data and evidence.

Investing in people

Building the skills of analysts and decision-makers. Leveraging the comparative advantages of public intent and private intent data requires a long-term approach to enhancing domestic human capital in lower-income countries. Investments in human capital should focus on decision-makers and analysts. Strengthening the data and statistical literacy of decision-makers can help them understand the potential utility and limitations of these new data sources. This understanding is key for them to champion a data innovation agenda and advocate for the required human, technological, and financial resources. Analysts, on the other hand, need unique skill sets to leverage private intent data that bridge many disciplines, including statistics, economics, computer science, geographic information systems (GIS), and the multidisciplinary field of data science. Although many of these skills are akin to those needed to bolster the capacities of national statistical offices (NSOs), teams with exposure to private sector data and data systems will be able to work more efficiently across data types and foster collaboration.

At the country level, it is critical to build analysts' skills to integrate public intent and private intent data for public policy design and evaluation. These skills include *data engineering* to manage, process, and link public intent and private intent data; *analyzing* integrated datasets using traditional statistical and econometric methods and the latest advances in machine learning; and *visualizing* the emerging insights. These skills must be augmented with acute awareness of the *ethics* and *data protection* dimensions of public intent and private intent data sources. Several competency frameworks developed for big data analytics are useful for a more granular understanding of the skill sets required for data acquisition, processing, analysis, visualization, and reporting.[84] These broad directions for capacity building focus on catalyzing the use of new data sources, in contrast to the recommendations presented in chapter 2, which focus on strengthening data production within the public sector.

Enhancing tertiary education. The long-term process of acquiring these skills begins by enhancing tertiary education. Because of the wide array of competencies that data scientists are expected to possess, university and graduate degree programs may have to be altered, particularly in lower-income countries. Students need the foundational statistical skills central to understanding and using public intent data, as well as the frontier skills in artificial intelligence (AI) and machine learning at the heart of leveraging the value from the integration of public intent and private intent data. The curricula of degree programs—in the fields of statistics, economics, computer science, and GIS—could be revised to align formal education with the practical demands of jobs in data analytics. In addition, new degree, graduate, and certificate programs with a data science theme could be established.

Promoting partnerships with universities and private companies in higher-income countries. Such partnerships

can be instrumental in achieving these education goals and enhancing training in contemporary data topics such as machine learning and AI. These types of initiatives can help tailor research in lower-income countries that leverages private intent data to local contexts and hires more local researchers. This would be a welcome trend because this research field has been predominantly led by principal investigators who are not nationals of these countries.

Proficiency with AI is one of the most coveted data skill sets. It involves feeding computers large amounts of data to train them to identify patterns and make predictions. For example, seismic activity data are crunched by computers to learn how to predict earthquakes,[85] and satellite images of agricultural areas are processed to estimate crop yields.[86] According to an analysis of self-reported job skills on the professional network platform LinkedIn, the United States leads in AI, followed by China (see figure 4.2).[87] Low- and middle-income countries need to catch up to these emerging trends in skills. In South Africa, the minister of communications and digital technologies argues there is no shortage of talent in the Africa region, but rather a lack of visionary policy makers to drive digitization and enable key infrastructure such as data centers and cloud computing.[88]

Technical training can sometimes be obtained cheaply or at no cost. Some digital companies provide free online training, and their certifications often attract job seekers.[89] Cisco's Networking Academy has trained more than 10 million people in low- and

Figure 4.2 Artificial intelligence specialists gravitate to the US market, no matter where they are educated

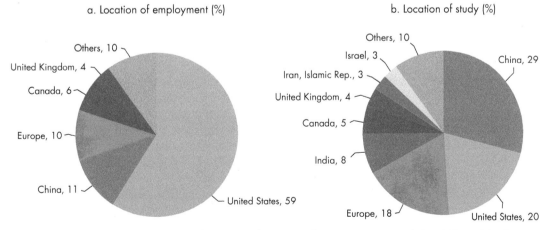

Source: MacroPolo, "The Global AI Talent Tracker," https://macropolo.org/digital-projects/the-global-ai-talent-tracker/. Adapted with permission of MacroPolo/Paulson Institute; further permission required for reuse. Data at http://bit.do/WDR2021-Fig-4_2.

Note: Country affiliations are based in panel a on the headquarters of institutions in which researchers currently work and in panel b on the country in which researchers received their undergraduate degree.

middle-income countries, often in partnership with local academic institutions with no or low-cost tuition. It also offers free online courses.[90] Although basic tech knowledge is needed to participate in these options, these offerings suggest that relevant training can be obtained in many developing countries at low cost provided good broadband internet connectivity is available. Popular cloud data management and analytical applications also feature graphical user interfaces, making it easier for those without advanced coding skills to use them.

Increasing training, mentorship, and on-the-job training. Improvements along the formal education supply chain can be augmented by on-the-job training efforts that target a broad coalition of data producers and users across the public sector, academia, and civil society. Increasing access to online training platforms (such as DataCamp and Coursera) and online degree and certificate programs, as well as free courses offered by prestigious universities in higher-income countries, can help build capacity across an impressive array of topics related to both foundational and frontier data analytics. These activities could be supplemented by continued support of emerging data science initiatives that provide scope for collaboration, mentorship, and learning, including the Deep Learning Indaba Institute,[91] Data Science Africa conferences,[92] and the competition platform Zindi.[93]

Skills training companies and platforms have recently surfaced supporting the development of digital data skills in developing countries and linking trainees to employers. Upskilling platforms such as Andela and Gebeya in Africa and Revelo in Brazil train students in data analytics and software development. Andela, founded in 2014, is training young people to meet the demand for information technology (IT) talent globally and within Africa. Gebeya, founded in 2016, matches trainees with companies in Africa.[94] And data labeling companies such as CloudFactory in Kenya and Nepal and Samasource in Kenya are creating jobs for cleaning, categorizing, and labeling data used for AI applications.[95]

As for its continued support of short-term training and mentorship programs in lower-income countries, the international community should evaluate the conditions for achieving sustained improvements in local capacity to identify short-term capacity-building models that hold promise.

Strengthening data literacy among senior leadership and creating institutional environments that encourage the use of sophisticated data and evidence. The big push to build an army of data scientists for jobs in the public sector, private sector, and civil society must be complemented with efforts to create enabling institutional and leadership environments (see chapter 8) that place a high premium on the use of data and evidence—both internally for management of these institutions and externally for understanding and producing policies that enhance welfare.

To help strengthen data literacy, especially in low-capacity settings, regional and international development partners can leverage their expertise or technical partnerships to provide governments with technical assistance. They can also organize objective peer reviews for gauging the relevance and accuracy of complex research that hinges on the integration of public intent and private intent data sources, including efforts sponsored by international agencies themselves (see spotlight 2.2).

On the whole, strengthening the data literacy of the senior leadership of public sector institutions will not guarantee that they will seek data and evidence when designing policies, especially if their insights do not appear to contribute to the political objectives of their government (see chapter 8). As discussed in chapter 2, mutually reinforcing constraints in financing, human capital, data governance, and data demand must be overcome as part of a long-term, holistic plan backed by domestic support from politicians of the major political parties, academia, and civil society.

In the short term, strengthening human capital in NSOs and line ministries in lower-income countries in the production and use of public intent data will indirectly contribute to the pool of skill sets required for public intent and private intent data to be integrated into official statistics and knowledge products generated within the public sector (see chapters 2 and 9 for further discussion). International organizations can provide these institutions with technical assistance to cultivate open data practices and to build skills in the creation and dissemination of public use census, survey, and administrative datasets that are subject to international best practices in deidentification. This effort can catalyze downstream research that brings together public intent and private intent data sources.

Statistical capacity-building projects financed by international organizations and traditionally focused on the production and use of public intent data should be expanded systematically to allow for investments in skills critical to the integration of public intent and private intent data sources. NSOs could establish a business line on *experimental statistics* (that is, statistics that leverage new data sources and methods to better respond to users' needs and can be viewed as official statistics "in the making"). This business line would provide a more direct route to investing in staff who can conduct cutting-edge research grounded in synergies among public intent and private intent data sources.[96]

Revamping NSOs to perform nontraditional roles with private intent data. In general, for NSOs to maintain relevance in a landscape in which they no longer generate the majority of the data, they should be empowered data stewards endowed with qualified staff who can perform nontraditional roles. NSOs must be able to field requests for accessing confidential data that can be used to calibrate and validate models that fuse public intent and private intent data sources. By pursuing a work program on experimental statistics, NSOs should aspire to be proactive contributors to research that would assess the public intent data requirements of synergistic applications. The Data Science Campus in the United Kingdom's Office for National Statistics (ONS) is an example of a unit in an NSO that is tasked with leveraging the latest advances in data science and the synergies between public intent and private intent data sources to serve the public good. The Campus works on data science projects not only for the ONS, but also for the UK government as well as international organizations in collaboration with partners from academia and the private sector.[97] Twinning arrangements between the NSOs in high-income countries with similar initiatives and NSOs in low- and middle-income countries can be one way to strengthen NSO capabilities in low-capacity environments to create units akin to the ONS Data Science Campus.

NSOs will also need to grapple with data protection issues. They must, for example, determine whether spatially deidentified data are sufficient for calibration purposes and what minimum volume and scope of confidential data will have to be accessed for specific applications. NSOs also can carefully identify applications in which access to confidential data are not required. However, accommodating requests for applications with well-defined and well-articulated confidential data needs or responding to time-sensitive requests tied to immediate policy needs (such as a humanitarian or disaster response) ultimately require that NSOs have personnel who are trained in data protection and law and who can enter into and enforce data sharing agreements to mitigate data protection risks. To fulfill these roles, NSOs must receive a significant infusion of financial and human capital and should consider actively engaging—at least in the short term—international organizations or academic institutions and research organizations, at both the local and international levels, to bridge the gaps in internal institutional and technical capacity.

Investing in data accessibility. Accessing private intent data remains challenging, especially in lower-income countries. Large barriers, such as protecting customers and maintaining competitive advantages, prevent companies from sharing their data. In addition, pulling data from a company's database requires computing and human resources that are typically outside of a business's key performance indicators. If a public organization has poorly formulated requests for a company's data, compiling and exporting data can become a time-intensive burden on companies. Even if a company is willing and able to share its data, because of the diversity of private intent data types it is difficult to create standards to share data. Shared data must have clear documentation, be in a usable format that is interoperable with other private and public datasets for integration, and have been deidentified. Creating these types of standards may require third parties to coordinate efforts and will place more resource burdens on companies.

Utilizing data collaboratives and research partnerships. These cooperative arrangements are essential ways for different sectors, research institutions, and governments to share data. The Open Data Lab describes data collaboratives as moving beyond public-private partnerships to pool data resources that researchers use for public benefit.[98] A successful example can be found in Nairobi, Kenya, where researchers have partnered with local government agencies to develop spatially integrated road safety datasets with inputs from administrative, social media, private, and traditional sources (see spotlight 4.2 for details).

Data collaboratives can be coordinated by civil society or universities, or through corporate social responsibility programs. Facebook's Data for Good initiative is an example of how technology companies can be incentivized to share their data through corporate social responsibility programs. By leveraging customer data and engaging with civil society and university partners, Facebook is offering a suite of innovative datasets intended to aid public policy decisions. Offerings range from mobility data and downscaled population maps to data on electric grid coverage.

Data collaboratives and research partnerships could provide companies' application programming interfaces (APIs) and cloud services through tiers made available to the public sector. Social media platforms such as Twitter provide APIs so that users can download their text data using free tiers.

Private companies could be encouraged to share their data at reduced cost for public initiatives, with special grants for researchers or tax breaks for the data provider. Cloud computing services, such as Google Cloud and Amazon Web Services, are offering small education grants to researchers to access the computing infrastructure needed to leverage these datasets, which are often large. Flowminder, a Swedish nongovernmental organization, provides code, instructions, and support for mobile network operators to aggregate, deidentify, and share their CDR data. Their open-source tool, FlowKit, provides APIs, code, and databases to aid companies sharing these sensitive records with researchers.[99]

Trusted intermediaries are building platforms that provide researchers with private intent data or facilitate sending programming code to private companies, which can, in turn, run the code with their private intent data on behalf of the researcher and share aggregated research insights. Opportunity Insights, a nonpartisan, nonprofit research organization based at Harvard University, offers a Track the Recovery platform that gives researchers access to near real-time economic data to understand the COVID-19 policy response in the United States. As the broker of the data sharing agreements, Opportunity Insights deidentifies data to facilitate sharing by protecting customers' and companies' data. For example, they protect companies' data through aggregation and by creating relative indicators that mask actual revenue and profit. OPAL ("Open Algorithms") takes a different approach. OPAL is a nonprofit partnership created by groups at MIT Media Lab, Imperial College London, the financial company Orange, the World Economic Forum, and the Data-Pop Alliance. Its platform allows researchers to send companies certified open-source algorithms that are then run behind the companies' firewalls.

Despite the promise of these innovative data-sharing pathways, many are not available in lower-income countries. For example, these countries rarely participate in data collaboratives, according to data compiled by the Open Data Lab.[100] A similar trend can be seen in the limited number of studies on lower-income countries that leveraged private intent data in the early stages of the COVID-19 pandemic (box 4.2). More investments are needed in accessing private intent data for public benefit in lower-income countries.

Investing in research

Investments in research are needed to develop methods and enable lower-income countries to grow research programs that leverage private intent data for public policy. The research community can achieve quick wins by focusing on foundational areas such as testing whether validated methods in one region translate to contexts where data are sparse. Over the longer term, research strategies would benefit from building validation and training datasets in lower-income countries to avoid issues similar to data profiling and discrimination when using pre-trained models from higher-income countries. The selections that follow describe some of the high-priority research needed to advance the use of private intent data for public benefit in the short and long term.

Shorter-term research needs. Because much of the current innovation in using private intent data is led by researchers and technology companies in higher-income countries, many of the available methods are not tailored to the development context.[101] Even when a solution is developed for and validated in a particular lower-income country, understanding whether and when the solution can be extended to other lower-income countries can enable research in data-sparse contexts. For example, even though international phone call usage correlates with wealth more strongly in Rwanda than in Balkh province in Afghanistan, such a finding can still be useful in contexts such as Balkh province.[102] Similarly, granular poverty maps that use digital trace data from mobile phones hold great potential for better targeting social services, but the patterns that algorithms use to make poverty predictions may differ from context to context.[103] Research is needed to determine when granular poverty estimates created for one country can be transferred to another country and when they will lead to misleading maps.

In the short term, researchers also need to produce methods that preserve privacy while combining public intent and private intent data. As more datasets are made available to researchers and decision-makers, more opportunities arise to reverse-engineer traditional deidentification methods. If these risks are not eliminated, individuals and companies may be reluctant to share their data. One example of how public intent data are being designed to prevent de-anonymization is the GPS data collected from household surveys for the Demographic and Health Survey and the Living Standards Measurement Study. Even if surveys collect GPS-based locations for communities and households, the resulting data are not included in public use datasets to ensure the confidentiality of respondents. Any third-party user that obtains DHS- or LSMS-type survey data has access only to spatially offset locations of survey enumeration areas. For example, a household's location is represented using the 10 square kilometer area within which the house is located. These surveys are also good examples of providing documentation that makes the precision and accuracy of the deidentified data explicit.

Concerns about data protection have limited the eagerness to share data, even in critical times such as during the Ebola crisis. Historically, data deidentification techniques have maintained equilibrium between the producers and consumers of data, preserving individuals' privacy while limiting information loss. However, deidentification techniques have proven to be increasingly imperfect with high-dimensional private intent data. Despite the use of standard deidentification techniques, one study found that four data points were enough to reidentify 95 percent of individuals in a mobile phone dataset of 1.5 million people.[104] In this context, new data sharing frameworks have been proposed to mitigate privacy risks while maximizing the informative potential of private intent data. Researchers have proposed four models for use of mobile phone data, depending on the level of risk tolerance and the number of potential third-party users.[105] The Social Science One initiative, which allows researchers from academic institutions to access Facebook data at scale,[106] is an example of how new data sharing frameworks could be applied to access private intent data, paving the way for future public-private collaborations. As noted, more research will be needed to design methods that allow the privacy of private intent data to be protected, while minimizing the loss of precision associated with using these data in applications aimed to inform public policy.[107]

In a context of low data and coding literacy, off-the-shelf programming tools can lead to more effective and responsible use of private intent data. Flowminder's FlowKit is an example of an open-source solution that helps companies to deidentify, clean, and export their data effectively for policy applications.[108] Using FlowKit, Flowminder and its partners have been able to rapidly integrate CDRs into the COVID-19 response. Aequitas is another open-source toolkit that provides an intuitive way to audit machine learning models for discrimination and bias.[109] These types of tools enable researchers to access data and companies to share data without the need for specialized skills to collate and deidentify the datasets. Ideally, these research tools should be designed to promote access to data and to share technical knowledge between lower-income countries, from higher-income countries to lower-income countries, or from lower-income countries to higher-income countries. Research funding would not only operate on short-term project cycles

but also support the institutional setup of research labs and institutes in lower-income countries.

Longer-term research needs. These needs include devising best practices and quality standards. Most decision-makers will not be well versed in the latest data methods. Best practices and quality standards can facilitate trust in leveraging new data types for policy. These types of standards and governing institutions are available for public intent data. Conceivably, then, they could be translated for private intent data. For example, traditional data collection using sample surveys has many imperfections, but by studying them extensively, the research community has come up with ways to address them or quantify the errors they introduce.[110] In the same way, researchers need to study the limitations of private intent data and develop the appropriate quality standards for their use in public policy. For example, there is currently no consensus on the criteria needed to determine whether a poverty map is fit for use in resource allocations.

International organizations can play a major role in this process by providing platforms for discussing, formulating, and promoting these practices and standards (see spotlight 8.1). The working groups established under the auspices of the United Nations Statistical Commission on household surveys, open data, and big data may provide insight into the types of commissions that could be established.[111]

Coordinating investment

In the longer term, coordinated investment in high-quality training data from lower-income countries will also be needed. Currently, private intent data are mostly repurposed for machine learning applications, which require high-quality data collected on location via remote sensing to train algorithms. For example, over the last five years pioneering research on small-scale farming systems has successfully combined high-quality georeferenced survey data with high-resolution, multispectral satellite imagery from public sources (Sentinel-2) and private sources (Planet and Maxar, formerly Digital Globe) to obtain crop yield estimates on individual plots.[112] These efforts have shown the importance of using high-quality ground data—including georeferenced plot outlines and objective measures of crop yields—to calibrate and validate remote sensing models that can, in turn, churn out high-resolution grids for crop types and crop yields for entire regions and countries.

One of the challenges preventing the rapid scale up of these efforts is the lack of knowledge on the required volume and content of georeferenced microdata that should be collected through surveys to inform downstream remote sensing applications capable of meeting needs for spatially disaggregated estimation and reporting. These challenges could be addressed by research. Similarly, to analyze natural language data to, for example, measure attitudes on certain topics in the population, researchers typically rely on pre-trained language models (that is, models already trained on a large corpus of text). The lack of these pre-trained language models in languages other than the major ones has been a barrier to the analysis of text data in low- and middle-income countries.[113] If the people in these countries are themselves the designers, curators, and owners of location-specific, high-quality training data to test private intent data, the center of research gravity would naturally shift toward lower-income countries.

Table 4.1 summarizes selected short- and long-term research needs. Answers to the questions listed in the table will vary in accordance with the development

Table 4.1 Selected research gaps to be addressed to advance the use of private intent data for development

Research area	Examples of research gaps
Societal impacts	• How do we ensure that algorithmic-based policy making can lead to fair outcomes? • How can we increase the transparency and interpretability of policy predictions using private intent data? • How can we design algorithms that can be safeguarded against manipulation? • What are the trade-offs between granularity and precision, and what is the optimal mix for targeting of development programs?
Quality standards	• How can standards be created, agreed on, updated, and communicated to the general development community? Who needs to be part of these conversations? • To ensure that policy makers can trust and use results, what should the standards be for accuracy and precision for frontier applications that use private intent data or that combine public intent and private intent data?
External validity[a]	• How promising is the approach of building models in countries that have data and applying them to countries with limited data? • How can issues akin to data profiling and discrimination be avoided when using pre-trained models from higher-income countries in cases of novel development use? • To what extent can applications that combine public intent survey data with private intent data predict values calculated from census data within a country?
Machine learning	• How does the approach to machine learning and spatial feature selection need to change from common machine learning tasks to more specialized tasks that will aid development policy? • Which features best predict spatial variation in development outcomes in different contexts? What are the trade-offs between predictive accuracy and cost?
Training and validation data	• What should be the required volume of and approach to public intent data collection for calibrating and validating machine learning algorithms that combine public intent and private intent data?
Deidentification[b]	• How do deidentification methods need to change to protect individuals and companies when private intent data are used for public benefit? • How does (spatial) deidentification of public intent data affect the accuracy and precision of applications that use public intent data to calibrate and validate machine learning algorithms that combine public intent and private intent data?
Capturing longitudinal change	• How do accuracy and precision differ in applications that aim to estimate longitudinal change versus obtaining cross-sectional predictions for the same development outcome? • What features best predict longitudinal change in different contexts? • How can we ensure the stability over time of algorithms aimed at predicting changes in policy outcomes? • When public intent survey data are combined with imagery—specifically, spatial features (predictors) extracted via deep-learning techniques—in order to derive high-resolution estimates of a development outcome, how do the spatial, spectral,[c] and temporal resolution of satellite imagery affect the accuracy and precision of the predictions for the outcome of interest? • Do these effects vary based on the decisions on the size of satellite imagery grids that are processed for extracting spatial features?

a. External validity relates to the research findings of one location holding true in another location.
b. The term deidentification is used instead of anonymization because, although data are processed to deidentify any individual, these data may become identifiable in the future as computing and machine learning advance. Thus data may never be truly anonymized.
c. "Spectral" refers to different wavelengths on the visual spectrum. Satellite images typically have multiple "bands" that capture different spectral ranges.

outcome/process that researchers are aiming to better measure and understand through the use and augmentation of private intent data. For example, the requirements for high-resolution estimation of population density will differ from requirements for estimating crop yields.

The growing availability and use of private intent data for development purposes have potentially large benefits, especially when paired with public intent data. However, the way forward requires a conducive and enabling environment that trains both analysts and higher-level decision-makers to consider critically issues of data protection, discrimination, manipulation, representativeness, and transparency. Repurposing and combining public intent and private intent data are central to getting more value from data, but the benefits must be shared equitably while safeguarding against harmful outcomes. Part II of this Report describes the building blocks of a social contract that enables such data flows, including infrastructure policies, legal and regulatory frameworks for data, related economic policies, and the institutions of data governance.

Notes

1. Bengtsson et al. (2011).
2. Chetty et al. (2020); Oliver et al. (2020).
3. Beraja, Yang, and Yuchtman (2020).
4. Salganik (2017).
5. Salganik (2017).
6. Serajuddin et al. (2015).
7. IEAG (2014).
8. Demombynes and Sandefur (2015).
9. Tiecke and Gros (2016).
10. Stephens-Davidowitz (2017).
11. For the 2008 and 2012 US presidential elections, Stephens-Davidowitz (2017) found that an area's search rate for terms with racial overtones was a robust negative predictor of presidential candidate Barack Obama's vote share.
12. WHO (2008).
13. Adda (2016).
14. Ihantamalala et al. (2018); Milusheva (2020); Wesolowski et al. (2012).
15. González, Hidalgo, and Barabási (2008); Le Menach et al. (2011); Tatem et al. (2009).
16. Wesolowski et al. (2012).
17. Wesolowski et al. (2012).
18. Peak et al. (2018). After the outbreak, they studied how mobile phone data for Sierra Leone could have been used to evaluate the impacts of interventions meant to decrease travel during the epidemic.
19. COVID-19 National Emergency Response Center (2020).
20. Burns (2020).
21. Chang et al. (2020); Maas et al. (2019).
22. Aktay et al. (2020).

23. Lai et al. (2020); Pepe et al. (2020).
24. Salathé et al. (2012).
25. McCall (2020).
26. PAHO and WHO (2016).
27. McGough et al. (2017).
28. Kraemer et al. (2019).
29. Yang et al. (2017).
30. Milinovich et al. (2014).
31. Internal Displacement Monitoring Center (IDMC), Data of GIDD (Global Internal Displacement Database), https://www.internal-displacement.org/database/displacement-data.
32. Ritchie and Roser (2019).
33. BBC News (2018); CNN Indonesia (2018).
34. Bengtsson et al. (2011); Lu, Bengtsson, and Holme (2012); Wilson et al. (2016).
35. Robinson, Power, and Cameron (2013).
36. Robinson, Power, and Cameron (2013).
37. Kongthon et al. (2012).
38. Resch, Usländer, and Havas (2018).
39. Sentiment analysis is the process of computationally identifying and categorizing opinions expressed in a piece of text, especially to determine whether the writer's attitude toward a topic or product is positive, negative, or neutral. See "sentiment analysis," Lexico, Oxford University Press, https://www.lexico.com/en/definition/sentiment_analysis.
40. Reynard and Shirgaokar (2019).
41. See "Case Study 5: Delivering Remote Flood Analytics as a Scalable Service," pages 61–68 in Sylvester (2019).
42. Blumenstock, Cadamuro, and On (2015); Jean et al. (2016); Yeh et al. (2020).
43. Blumenstock, Cadamuro, and On (2015).
44. Frias-Martinez, Frias-Martinez, and Oliver (2010).
45. Aiken et al. (2020).
46. Llorente et al. (2015).
47. Glaeser, Kim, and Luca (2018).
48. Blumenstock (2016).
49. Bonnet, Lechat, and Ridde (2018).
50. Williams, Idowu, and Olonade (2015).
51. Kelley, Lane, and Schönholzer (2020).
52. Dai and Sujon (2019).
53. Milusheva et al. (2020).
54. Kelley, Lane, and Schönholzer (2020).
55. Pratihast et al. (2014).
56. See World Resources Institute, Global Forest Watch (dashboard), https://www.globalforestwatch.org/.
57. WRI (2019).
58. See, for example, Janaagraha Centre for Citizenship and Democracy, I Paid a Bribe (dashboard), https://www.ipaidabribe.com/about-us#gsc.tab=0.I.
59. Hlatshwayo et al. (2018).
60. Inter-American Development Bank, "Countries That Have Already Implemented the Investment Map Initiative," https://www.iadb.org/en/reform-modernization-state/countries.
61. Marshall (2012).
62. Deaton (2008); Falk et al. (2018). For a list of projects that have used Gallup World Poll data, see Gallup, "Working Together to Change the World," https://www.gallup

.com/analytics/318176/public-sector-success-stories
.aspx.
63. Goldstein, Gonzalez Martinez, and Papineni (2019).
64. Goldstein, Gonzalez Martinez, and Papineni (2019).
65. See Google, Community Mobility Reports (database), https://www.google.com/covid19/mobility/?hl=en.
66. See Ookla, Speedtest Global Index (database), https://www.speedtest.net/global-index.
67. Davis et al. (2010).
68. Mehrabi et al. (2020).
69. Blumenstock and Eagle (2012).
70. Wesolowski et al. (2012).
71. Frankfurter et al. (2020).
72. Jean et al. (2016).
73. Strubell, Ganesh, and McCallum (2019).
74. Zou and Schiebinger (2018).
75. Angwin et al. (2016).
76. Buolamwini and Gebru (2018).
77. Wallace et al. (2019).
78. Bolukbasi et al. (2016).
79. Ginsberg et al. (2009).
80. Lazer et al. (2014).
81. Ayush et al. (2020); Engstrom, Hersh, and Newhouse (2017).
82. Blumenstock (2018).
83. Björkegren, Blumenstock, and Knight (2020).
84. Carretero, Vuorikari, and Punie (2017); GSS (2016); Vale and Gjaltema (2020).
85. Perol, Gharbi, and Denolle (2018).
86. RTI International, "Impact: Using Satellite Images and Artificial Intelligence to Improve Agricultural Resilience," https://www.rti.org/impact/using-satellite-images-and-artificial-intelligence-improve-agricultural-resilience.
87. Perisic (2018).
88. ITU (2020).
89. Flowers (2019).
90. Cisco Systems, "Cisco Networking Academy," https://www.cisco.com/c/en/us/about/csr/impact/education/networking-academy.html.
91. Deep Learning Indaba Institute, https://deeplearningindaba.com/2020/.
92. Data Science Africa, http://www.datascienceafrica.org/.
93. Zindi (2020).
94. Buckholtz (2019).
95. Kaye (2019).
96. See, for example, the related efforts under the European Statistical System by Eurostat, Statistics Denmark, Destatis (Germany), National Statistics Institute (Spain), ISTAT (Italy), Central Statistical Bureau of Latvia, Statistics Netherlands, Statistics Poland, Statistics Portugal, National Institute of Statistics (Romania), Statistics Finland, Statistics Iceland, and the Federal Statistical Office (Switzerland)—see European Statistical System, Eurostat, "Experimental Statistics," Luxembourg, https://ec.europa.eu/eurostat/web/ess/experimental-statistics.
97. For more information on the ONS Data Science Campus and its projects, see Data Science Campus,

Office for National Statistics, "Data Science for Public Good: Projects," https://datasciencecampus.ons.gov.uk/projects/.
98. GovLab, Tandon School of Engineering, New York University, "Data Collaboratives," https://datacollaboratives.org/.
99. Flowminder Foundation, "FlowKit CDR Analytics Toolkit," https://flowkit.xyz/.
100. GovLab, Tandon School of Engineering, New York University, "Data Collaboratives," https://datacollaboratives.org/.
101. Blumenstock (2018).
102. Aiken et al. (2020).
103. Blumenstock (2018).
104. de Montjoye et al. (2013).
105. de Montjoye et al. (2013).
106. Social Science One, Institute for Quantitative Social Science, Harvard University, "Building Industry-Academic Partnerships," https://socialscience.one/home.
107. Dwork and Roth (2014).
108. Flowminder Foundation, "FlowKit CDR Analytics Toolkit," https://flowkit.xyz/.
109. Saleiro et al. (2019).
110. Bethelehem (2009).
111. United Nations Statistical Commission, Statistics Division, Department of Economic and Social Affairs, United Nations, "Active Groups under the Statistical Commission by Pillar and Type of Group," https://unstats.un.org/unsd/statcom/groups/.
112. Burke and Lobell (2017); Gourlay, Kilic, and Lobell (2019); Jain et al. (2016); Lambert et al. (2018); Lobell et al. (2020).
113. Zindi (2020).

References

Adda, Jérôme. 2016. "Economic Activity and the Spread of Viral Diseases: Evidence from High Frequency Data." *Quarterly Journal of Economics* 131 (2): 891–941.

Aiken, Emily L., Guadalupe Bedoya, Aidan Coville, and Joshua Evan Blumenstock. 2020. "Targeting Development Aid with Machine Learning and Mobile Phone Data: Evidence from an Anti-Poverty Intervention in Afghanistan." In *COMPASS '20: Proceedings of the 3rd ACM SIGCAS Conference on Computing and Sustainable Societies*, 310–11. New York: Association for Computing Machinery.

Aktay, Ahmet, Shailesh Bavadekar, Gwen Cossoul, John Davis, Damien Desfontaines, Alex Fabrikant, Evgeniy Gabrilovich, et al. 2020. "Google COVID-19 Community Mobility Reports: Anonymization Process Description (Version 1.0)." April 8, 2020. https://arxiv.org/abs/2004.04145v1.

Angwin, Julia, Jeff Larson, Surya Mattu, and Lauren Kirchner. 2016. "Machine Bias: There's Software Used across the Country to Predict Future Criminals, and It's Biased against Blacks." *ProPublica*, May 23, 2016. https://www.propublica.org/article/machine-bias-risk-assessments-in-criminal-sentencing.

Ayush, Kumar, Burak Uzkent, Marshall Burke, David B. Lobell, and Stefano Ermon. 2020. "Generating

Interpretable Poverty Maps Using Object Detection in Satellite Images." Cornell University, Ithaca, NY. http://arxiv.org/abs/2002.01612.

BBC News. 2018. "Indonesia Earthquake and Tsunami: How Warning System Failed the Victims." *BBC News*, October 1, 2018. https://www.bbc.com/news/world-asia-45663054.

Bengtsson, Linus, Xin Lu, Anna Thorson, Richard Garfield, and Johan von Schreeb. 2011. "Improved Response to Disasters and Outbreaks by Tracking Population Movements with Mobile Phone Network Data: A Post-Earthquake Geospatial Study in Haiti." *PLoS Medicine* 8 (8): e1001083. https://doi.org/10.1371/journal.pmed.1001083.

Beraja, Martin, David Y. Yang, and Noam Yuchtman. 2020. "Data-Intensive Innovation and the State: Evidence from AI Firms in China." NBER Working Paper 27723, National Bureau of Economic Research, Cambridge, MA. https://www.nber.org/papers/w27723.

Bethlehem, Jelke. 2009. "The Rise of Survey Sampling." Discussion Paper 09015, Statistics Netherlands, The Hague.

Björkegren, Daniel, Joshua Evan Blumenstock, and Samsun Knight. 2020. "Manipulation-Proof Machine Learning." Cornell University, Ithaca, NY. http://arxiv.org/abs/2004.03865.

Blumenstock, Joshua Evan. 2016. "Fighting Poverty with Data." *Science* 353 (6301): 753–54. https://doi.org/10.1126/science.aah5217.

Blumenstock, Joshua Evan. 2018. "Don't Forget People in the Use of Big Data for Development." *Nature* 561 (7722): 170–72. https://doi.org/10.1038/d41586-018-06215-5.

Blumenstock, Joshua Evan, Gabriel Cadamuro, and Robert On. 2015. "Predicting Poverty and Wealth from Mobile Phone Metadata." *Science* 350 (6264): 1073–76. https://doi.org/10.1126/science.aac4420.

Blumenstock, Joshua Evan, and Nathan Eagle. 2012. "Divided We Call: Disparities in Access and Use of Mobile Phones in Rwanda." *Information Technologies and International Development* 8 (2): 1–16.

Bolukbasi, Tolga, Kai-Wei Chang, James Zou, Venkatesh Saligrama, and Adam Kalai. 2016. "Man Is to Computer Programmer as Woman Is to Homemaker? Debiasing Word Embeddings." July 21, Cornell University, Ithaca, NY. https://arxiv.org/abs/1607.06520.

Bonnet, Emmanuel, Lucie Lechat, and Valéry Ridde. 2018. "What Interventions Are Required to Reduce Road Traffic Injuries in Africa? A Scoping Review of the Literature." *PLoS ONE* 13 (11): e0208195. https://doi.org/10.1371/journal.pone.0208195.

Buckee, Caroline O., Satchit Balsari, Jennifer Chan, Mercè Crosas, Francesca Dominici, Urs Gasser, Yonatan H. Grad, et al. 2020. "Aggregated Mobility Data Could Help Fight COVID-19." *Science* 368 (6487): 145–46. https://doi.org/10.1126/science.abb8021.

Buckholtz, Alison. 2019. "Africa's IT Talent Pool." *IFC Insights* (blog), December 2019. https://www.ifc.org/wps/wcm/connect/news_ext_content/ifc_external_corporate_site/news+and+events/news/insights/africa-it-talent.

Buolamwini, Joy, and Timnit Gebru. 2018. "Gender Shades: Intersectional Accuracy Disparities in Commercial Gender Classification." In *PMLR, Proceedings of Machine Learning Research*, vol. 81, *FAT 2018, Conference on Fairness,* *Accountability, and Transparency, 23–24 February 2018, New York, NY, USA,* edited by Sorelle A. Friedler and Christo Wilson, 77–91. Cambridge, MA: MIT Press. https://dam-prod.media.mit.edu/x/2018/02/06/Gender%20Shades%20Intersectional%20Accuracy%20Disparities.pdf.

Burke, Marshall, and David B. Lobell. 2017. "Satellite-Based Assessment of Yield Variation and Its Determinants in Smallholder African Systems." *PNAS, Proceedings of the National Academy of Sciences* 114 (9): 2189–94. https://doi.org/10.1073/pnas.1616919114.

Burns, Sarah. 2020. "How Anonymized Mobile Data Are Helping Ghana Fight COVID-19." Global Partnership for Sustainable Development Data, United Nations, New York. https://www.data4sdgs.org/news/how-anonymized-mobile-data-are-helping-ghana-fight-covid-19.

Carretero, Stephanie, Riina Vuorikari, and Yves Punie. 2017. "DigComp 2.1: The Digital Competence Framework for Citizens, with Eight Proficiency Levels and Examples of Use." JRC Working Paper JRC106281, Joint Research Center, EU Science Hub, Seville, Spain.

Chang, Meng-Chun, Rebecca Kahn, Yu-An Li, Cheng-Sheng Lee, Caroline O. Buckee, and Hsiao-Han Chang. 2020. "Modeling the Impact of Human Mobility and Travel Restrictions on the Potential Spread of SARS-CoV-2 in Taiwan." *medRxiv*, April 11, 2020. https://doi.org/10.1101/2020.04.07.20053439.

Chetty, Raj, John N. Friedman, Nathaniel Hendren, Michael Stepner, and the Opportunity Insights Team. 2020. "How Did COVID-19 and Stabilization Policies Affect Spending and Employment? A New Real-Time Economic Tracker Based on Private Sector Data." NBER Working Paper 27431, National Bureau of Economic Research, Cambridge, MA. https://doi.org/10.3386/w27431.

CNN Indonesia. 2018. "BNPB: Seluruh Buoy Deteksi Tsunami di Indonesia Rusak." *CNN Indonesia*, September 30, 2018. https://www.cnnindonesia.com/nasional/20180930160115-20-334439/bnpb-seluruh-buoy-deteksi-tsunami-di-indonesia-rusak.

COVID-19 National Emergency Response Center. 2020. "Contact Transmission of COVID-19 in South Korea: Novel Investigation Techniques for Tracing Contacts." *Osong Public Health and Research Perspectives* 11 (1): 60–63. COVID-19 National Emergency Response Center, Epidemiology and Case Management Team, Korea Centers for Disease Control and Prevention, Cheongju, Republic of Korea. https://doi.org/10.24171/j.phrp.2020.11.1.09.

Dai, Fei, and Mohhammad Sujon. 2019. "Measuring Current Traffic Safety Culture via Social Media Mining." WTSC Report 2019-AG-2856, Washington Traffic Safety Commission, Olympia, WA. http://wtsc.wa.gov/wp-content/uploads/dlm_uploads/2019/10/Measuring-Traffic-Safety-Culture-via-Social-Media-Mining_Oct2019-1.pdf.

Davis, Kristin E., Burton Swanson, David Amudavi, Daniel Ayalew Mekonnen, Aaron Flohrs, Jens Riese, Chloe Lamb, and Elias Zerfu. 2010. "In-Depth Assessment of the Public Agricultural Extension System of Ethiopia and Recommendations for Improvement." IFPRI Discussion Paper 01041, International Food Policy Research Institute,

Washington, DC. https://www.ifpri.org/publication/depth-assessment-public-agricultural-extension-system-ethiopia-and-recommendations.

Deaton, Angus S. 2008. "Income, Health, and Well-Being around the World: Evidence from the Gallup World Poll." *Journal of Economic Perspectives* 22 (2): 53–72. https://doi.org/10.1257/jep.22.2.53.

Demombynes, Gabriel, and Justin Sandefur. 2015. "Costing a Data Revolution." *World Economics* 16 (3): 99–112.

de Montjoye, Yves-Alexandre, César A. Hidalgo, Michel Verleysen, and Vincent D. Blondel. 2013. "Unique in the Crowd: The Privacy Bounds of Human Mobility." *Scientific Reports* 3 (1): 1376. https://doi.org/10.1038/srep01376.

Dureuil, Manuel, Kristina Boerder, Kirsti A. Burnett, Rainer Froese, and Boris Worm. 2018. "Elevated Trawling inside Protected Areas Undermines Conservation Outcomes in a Global Fishing Hot Spot." *Science* 362 (6421): 1403–07. https://doi.org/10.1126/science.aau0561.

Dwork, Cynthia, and Aaron Roth. 2014. "The Algorithmic Foundations of Differential Privacy." *Foundations and Trends in Theoretical Computer Science* 9 (3–4): 211–407. http://dx.doi.org/10.1561/0400000042.

Engstrom, Ryan, Jonathan Samuel Hersh, and David Locke Newhouse. 2017. "Poverty from Space: Using High-Resolution Satellite Imagery for Estimating Economic Well-Being." Policy Research Working Paper 8284, World Bank, Washington, DC.

Falk, Armin, Anke Becker, Thomas Dohmen, Benjamin Enke, David Huffman, and Uwe Sunde. 2018. "Global Evidence on Economic Preferences." *Quarterly Journal of Economics* 133 (4): 1645–92. https://doi.org/10.1093/qje/qjy013.

Flowers, Andrew. 2019. "Indeed Tech Skills Explorer: Fastest-Rising Tech Skills." *Occupation Spotlight* (blog), November 26, 2019. https://www.hiringlab.org/2019/11/26/fastest-rising-tech-skills/.

Fraiberger, Samuel P., Pablo Astudillo, Lorenzo Candeago, Alex Chunet, Nicholas K. W. Jones, Maham Faisal Khan, Bruno Lepri, et al. 2020. "Uncovering Socioeconomic Gaps in Mobility Reduction during the COVID-19 Pandemic Using Location Data." Cornell University, Ithaca, NY. http://arxiv.org/abs/2006.15195.

Frankfurter, Zoe, Klaudia Kokoszka, David Locke Newhouse, Ani Rudra Silwal, and Siwei Tian. 2020. "Measuring Internet Access in Sub-Saharan Africa (SSA)." *Poverty and Equity Notes* 31 (August), World Bank, Washington, DC. https://openknowledge.worldbank.org/bitstream/handle/10986/34302/Measuring-Internet-in-Access-in-Sub-Saharan-Africa-SSA.pdf?sequence=1.

Frias-Martinez, Vanessa, Enrique Frias-Martinez, and Nuria Oliver. 2010. "A Gender-Centric Analysis of Calling Behavior in a Developing Economy Using Call Detail Records." In *Artificial Intelligence for Development: Papers from the AAAI Spring Symposium*, edited by Association for the Advancement of Artificial Intelligence, 37–42. Technical Report SS-10-01. Menlo Park, CA: AAAI Press.

Ginsberg, Jeremy, Matthew H. Mohebbi, Rajan S. Patel, Lynnette Brammer, Mark S. Smolinski, and Larry Brilliant. 2009. "Detecting Influenza Epidemics Using Search Engine Query Data." *Nature* 457 (February): 1012–14. https://www.nature.com/articles/nature07634.

Glaeser, Edward L., Hyunjin Kim, and Michael Luca. 2018. "Nowcasting Gentrification: Using Yelp Data to Quantify Neighborhood Change." *AEA Papers and Proceedings* 108 (May): 77–82.

Goldstein, Markus P., Paula Gonzalez Martinez, and Sreelakshmi Papineni. 2019. "Tackling the Global Profitarchy: Gender and the Choice of Business Sector." Policy Research Working Paper 8865, World Bank, Washington, DC. https://openknowledge.worldbank.org/handle/10986/31747.

González, Marta C., César A. Hidalgo, and Albert-László Barabási. 2008. "Understanding Individual Human Mobility Patterns." *Nature* 453 (7196): 779–82.

Gourlay, Sydney, Talip Kilic, and David B. Lobell. 2019. "A New Spin on an Old Debate: Errors in Farmer-Reported Production and Their Implications for Inverse Scale–Productivity Relationship in Uganda." *Journal of Development Economics* 141 (November): 102376. https://doi.org/10.1016/j.jdeveco.2019.102376.

GSS (Government Statistical Service, UK). 2016. "Competency Framework for the Government Statistician Group (GSG)." GSS, Office of National Statistics, London.

Hlatshwayo, Sandile, Anne Oeking, Manuk Ghazanchyan, David Corvino, Ananya Shukla, and Lamin Leigh. 2018. "The Measurement and Macro-Relevance of Corruption: A Big Data Approach." IMF Working Paper WP/18/195, International Monetary Fund, Washington, DC. http://dx.doi.org/10.5089/9781484373095.001.

IEAG (Independent Expert Advisory Group on a Data Revolution for Sustainable Development). 2014. "A World That Counts: Mobilising the Data Revolution for Sustainable Development." Data Revolution Group, United Nations, New York.

Ihantamalala, Felana Angella, Vincent Herbreteau, Feno M. J. Rakotoarimanana, Jean Marius Rakotondramanga, Simon Cauchemez, Bienvenue Rahoilijaona, Gwenaëlle Pennober, et al. 2018. "Estimating Sources and Sinks of Malaria Parasites in Madagascar." *Nature Communications* 9 (1): 3897.

ITU (International Telecommunication Union). 2020. "Africa Is at the AI Innovation Table and 'Ready for the Next Wave.'" *ITU News*, June 23, 2020. https://www.itu.int/en/myitu/News/2020/06/23/07/55/AI-for-Good-2020-Africa-innovation.

Jain, Meha, Amit Srivastava, Balwinder Singh, Rajiv Joon, Andrew Mcdonald, Keitasha Royal, Madeline Lisaius, et al. 2016. "Mapping Smallholder Wheat Yields and Sowing Dates Using Micro-Satellite Data." *Remote Sensing* 8 (November): 860. https://doi.org/10.3390/rs8100860.

Jean, Neal, Marshall Burke, Michael Xie, W. Matthew Davis, David B. Lobell, and Stefano Ermon. 2016. "Combining Satellite Imagery and Machine Learning to Predict Poverty." *Science* 353 (6301): 790–94. https://doi.org/10.1126/science.aaf7894.

Kaye, Kate. 2019. "These Companies Claim to Provide 'Fair-Trade' Data Work: Do They?" *MIT Technology Review*, August 7. https://www.technologyreview.com/2019/08/07/133845/cloudfactory-ddd-samasource-imerit-impact-sourcing-companies-for-data-annotation//.

Kelley, Erin, Gregory Lane, and David Schönholzer. 2020. "Monitoring in Target Contracts: Theory and Experiment in Kenyan Public Transit." Paper presented at Virtual BREAD/CEPR/STICERD/TCD Conference on Development Economics, October 1–3, 2020. https://youtu.be/TU-_xDR3x7I.

Klein, Brennan, Timothy LaRock, Stefan McCabe, Leo Torres, Filippo Privitera, Lake Brennan, Moritz U. G. Kraemer, et al. 2020. "Assessing Changes in Commuting and Individual Mobility in Major Metropolitan Areas in the United States during the COVID-19 Outbreak." Network Science Institute, Northeastern University, Boston. https://www.networkscienceinstitute.org/publications/assessing-changes-in-commuting-and-individual-mobility-in-major-metropolitan-areas-in-the-united-states-during-the-covid-19-outbreak.

Kongthon, Alisa, Choochart Haruechaiyasak, Jaruwat Pailai, and Sarawoot Kongyoung. 2012. "The Role of Twitter during a Natural Disaster: Case Study of 2011 Thai Flood." In 2012 Proceedings of PICMET '12: Technology Management for Emerging Technologies, edited by Institute of Electrical and Electronics Engineers, 2227–32. Red Hook, NY: Curran Associates.

Kraemer, Moritz U. G., Nick Golding, Dionisio Bisanzio, Samir Bhatt, David M. Pigott, S. E. Ray, O. J. Brady, et al. 2019. "Utilizing General Human Movement Models to Predict the Spread of Emerging Infectious Diseases in Resource Poor Settings." Scientific Reports 9 (March): 5151. https://doi.org/10.1038/s41598-019-41192-3.

Lai, Shengjie, Nick W. Ruktanonchai, Liangcai Zhou, Olivia Prosper, Wei Luo, Jessica R. Floyd, Amy Wesolowski, et al. 2020. "Effect of Non-Pharmaceutical Interventions to Contain COVID-19 in China." Nature 585 (7825): 410–13. https://doi.org/10.1038/s41586-020-2293-x.

Lambert, Marie-Julie, Pierre C. Sibiry Traoré, Xavier Blaes, Philippe Baret, and Pierre Defourny. 2018. "Estimating Smallholder Crops Production at Village Level from Sentinel-2 Time Series in Mali's Cotton Belt." Remote Sensing of Environment 216 (October): 647–57. https://doi.org/10.1016/j.rse.2018.06.036.

Lazer, David, Ryan Kennedy, Gary King, and Alessandro Vespignani. 2014. "The Parable of Google Flu: Traps in Big Data Analysis." Science 343 (6176): 1203–05. https://doi.org/10.1126/science.1248506.

Le Menach, Arnaud, Andrew J. Tatem, Justin M. Cohen, Simon I. Hay, Heather Randell, Anand P. Patil, and David L. Smith. 2011. "Travel Risk, Malaria Importation, and Malaria Transmission in Zanzibar." Scientific Reports 1: 93. https://www.nature.com/articles/srep00093.

Llorente, Alejandro, Manuel Garcia-Herranz, Manuel Cebrian, and Esteban Moro. 2015. "Social Media Fingerprints of Unemployment." PLoS ONE 10 (5): e0128692. https://doi.org/10.1371/journal.pone.0128692.

Lobell, David B., George Azzari, Marshall Burke, Sydney Gourlay, Zhenong Jin, Talip Kilic, and Siobhan Murray. 2020. "Eyes in the Sky, Boots on the Ground: Assessing Satellite- and Ground-Based Approaches to Crop Yield Measurement and Analysis." American Journal of Agricultural Economics 102 (1): 202–19. https://doi.org/10.1093/ajae/aaz051.

Lu, Xin, Linus Bengtsson, and Petter Holme. 2012. "Predictability of Population Displacement after the 2010 Haiti Earthquake." PNAS, Proceedings of the National Academy of Sciences of the United States of America 109 (29): 11576–81. https://doi.org/10.1073/pnas.1203882109.

Maas, Paige, Shankar Iyer, Andreas Gros, Wonhee Park, Laura McGorman, Chaya Nayak, and P. Alex Dow. 2019. "Facebook Disaster Maps: Aggregate Insights for Crisis Response and Recovery." In Conference Proceedings: 16th International Conference on Information Systems for Crisis Response and Management, edited by Zeno Franco, José J. González, and José H. Canós, 836–47. Valencia, Spain: Polytechnic University of Valencia.

Marshall, Sarah. 2012. "Citizen Journalists Report Sierra Leone Elections by SMS." Journalism, November 20, 2012. https://www.journalism.co.uk/news/citizen-journalists-report-sierra-leone-elections-by-sms-/s2/a551240/.

Masaki, Takaaki, David Locke Newhouse, Ani Rudra Silwal, Adane Bedada, and Ryan Engstrom. 2020. "Small Area Estimation of Non-Monetary Poverty with Geospatial Data." Policy Research Working Paper 9383, World Bank, Washington, DC.

McCall, Becky. 2020. "COVID-19 and Artificial Intelligence: Protecting Health-Care Workers and Curbing the Spread." Lancet Digital Health 2 (4): e166–e167. https://doi.org/10.1016/S2589-7500(20)30054-6.

McGough, Sarah F., John S. Brownstein, Jared B. Hawkins, and Mauricio Santillana. 2017. "Forecasting Zika Incidence in the 2016 Latin America Outbreak Combining Traditional Disease Surveillance with Search, Social Media, and News Report Data." PLoS Neglected Tropical Diseases 11 (1): e0005295.

Mehrabi, Zia, Mollie J. McDowell, Vincent Ricciardi, Christian Levers, Juan Diego Martinez, Natascha Mehrabi, Hannah Wittman, et al. 2020. "The Global Divide in Data-Driven Farming." Nature Sustainability 4 (February 2021): 154–60. https://doi.org/10.1038/s41893-020-00631-0.

Milinovich, Gabriel J., Gail M. Williams, Archie C. A. Clements, and Wenbiao Hu. 2014. "Internet-Based Surveillance Systems for Monitoring Emerging Infectious Diseases." Lancet Infectious Diseases 14 (2): 160–68. https://doi.org/10.1016/S1473-3099(13)70244-5.

Milusheva, Sveta. 2020. "Managing the Spread of Disease with Mobile Phone Data." Journal of Development Economics 147 (November): 102559. https://doi.org/10.1016/j.jdeveco.2020.102559.

Milusheva, Sveta, Robert Marty, Guadalupe Bedoya, Elizabeth Resor, Sarah Williams, and Arianna Legovini. 2020. "Can Crowdsourcing Create the Missing Crash Data?" In COMPASS '20: Proceedings of the 3rd ACM SIGCAS Conference on Computing and Sustainable Societies, 305–06. New York: Association for Computing Machinery. https://doi.org/10.1145/3378393.3402264.

Oliver, Nuria, Bruno Lepri, Harald Sterly, Renaud Lambiotte, Sébastien Deletaille, Marco De Nadai, Emmanuel Letouzé, et al. 2020. "Mobile Phone Data for Informing Public Health Actions across the COVID-19 Pandemic Life Cycle." Science Advances 6 (23): eabc0764. https://doi.org/10.1126/sciadv.abc0764.

PAHO (Pan American Health Organization) and WHO (World Health Organization). 2016. "Zika Cases and Congenital Syndrome Associated with Zika Virus Reported by Countries and Territories in the Americas: Cumulative Cases, 2015–2016." PAHO, Washington, DC. https://www.paho.org/hq/dmdocuments/2016/2016 -dec-29-phe-ZIKV-cases.pdf.

Peak, Corey M., Amy Wesolowski, Elisabeth zu Erbach-Schoenberg, Andrew J. Tatem, Erik Wetter, Xin Lu, Daniel Power, et al. 2018. "Population Mobility Reductions Associated with Travel Restrictions during the Ebola Epidemic in Sierra Leone: Use of Mobile Phone Data." International Journal of Epidemiology 47 (5): 1562–70.

Pepe, Emanuele, Paolo Bajardi, Laetitia Gauvin, Filippo Privitera, Brennan Lake, Ciro Cattuto, and Michele Tizzoni. 2020. "COVID-19 Outbreak Response: A Dataset to Assess Mobility Changes in Italy Following National Lockdown." Scientific Data 7: 230. https://doi.org/10.1038 /s41597-020-00575-2.

Perisic, Igor. 2018. "How Artificial Intelligence Is Already Impacting Today's Jobs." Economic Graph (blog), September 17, 2018. https://economicgraph.linkedin.com/blog /how-artificial-intelligence-is-already-impacting-todays -jobs.

Perol, Thibaut, Michaël Gharbi, and Marine Denolle. 2018. "Convolutional Neural Network for Earthquake Detection and Location." Science Advances 4 (2): e1700578. https://doi.org/10.1126/sciadv.1700578.

Pratihast, Arun Kumar, Ben DeVries, Valerio Avitabile, Sytze De Bruin, Lammert Kooistra, Mesfin Tekle, and Martin Herold. 2014. "Combining Satellite Data and Community-Based Observations for Forest Monitoring." Forests 5 (10): 2464–89. https://doi.org/10.3390/f5102464.

Resch, Bernd, Florian Usländer, and Clemens Havas. 2018. "Combining Machine-Learning Topic Models and Spatiotemporal Analysis of Social Media Data for Disaster Footprint and Damage Assessment." Cartography and Geographic Information Science 45 (4): 362–76.

Reynard, Darcy, and Manish Shirgaokar. 2019. "Harnessing the Power of Machine Learning: Can Twitter Data Be Useful in Guiding Resource Allocation Decisions during a Natural Disaster?" Transportation Research Part D: Transport and Environment 77 (December): 449–63.

Ritchie, Hannah, and Max Roser. 2019. "Natural Disasters." Our World in Data. Global Change Data Lab and Oxford Martin Program on Global Development, University of Oxford, Oxford, UK. https://ourworldindata.org/natural -disasters.

Robinson, Bella Fay, Robert Power, and Mark Cameron. 2013. "A Sensitive Twitter Earthquake Detector." In WWW '13: Proceedings of the 22nd International Conference on World Wide Web, 999–1002. New York: Association for Computing Machinery. https://dl.acm.org/doi/10.1145 /2487788.2488101.

Salathé, Marcel, Linus Bengtsson, Todd J. Bodnar, Devon D. Brewer, John S. Brownstein, Caroline Buckee, Ellsworth M. Campbell, et al. 2012. "Digital Epidemiology." PLoS Computational Biology 8 (7): e1002616.

Saleiro, Pedro, Benedict Kuester, Loren Hinkson, Jesse London, Abby Stevens, Ari Anisfeld, Kit T. Rodolfa, et al. 2019. "Aequitas: A Bias and Fairness Audit Toolkit." Cornell University, Ithaca, NY. https://arxiv.org/abs /1811.05577.

Salganik, Matthew J. 2017. Bit by Bit: Social Research in the Digital Age. Princeton, NJ: Princeton University Press.

Serajuddin, Umar, Hiroki Uematsu, Christina Wieser, Nobuo Yoshida, and Andrew L. Dabalen. 2015. "Data Deprivation: Another Deprivation to End." Policy Research Working Paper 7252, World Bank, Washington, DC.

Servick, Kelly. 2020a. "Cellphone Tracking Could Help Stem the Spread of Coronavirus: Is Privacy the Price?" Science, March 22. https://www.sciencemag.org/news/2020/03 /cellphone-tracking-could-help-stem-spread-coronavirus -privacy-price.

Servick, Kelly. 2020b. "COVID-19 Contact Tracing Apps Are Coming to a Phone Near You: How Will We Know Whether They Work?" Science, May 21. https://www .sciencemag.org/news/2020/05/countries-around-world -are-rolling-out-contact-tracing-apps-contain-corona virus-how.

Stephens-Davidowitz, Seth. 2017. Everybody Lies: Big Data, New Data, and What the Internet Can Tell Us about Who We Really Are. New York: HarperCollins.

Strubell, Emma, Ananya Ganesh, and Andrew McCallum. 2019. "Energy and Policy Considerations for Deep Learning in NLP." Proceedings of 57th Annual Meeting of the Association for Computational Linguistics, Florence, Italy, July 2019.

Sylvester, Gerard, ed. 2019. "E-Agriculture in Action: Big Data for Agriculture." Food and Agriculture Organization of the United Nations and International Telecommunication Union, Bangkok. http://www.fao.org/3/ca5427en /ca5427en.pdf.

Tatem, Andrew J., Youliang Qiu, David L. Smith, Oliver Sabot, Abdullah S. Ali, and Bruno Moonen. 2009. "The Use of Mobile Phone Data for the Estimation of the Travel Patterns and Imported Plasmodium Falciparum Rates among Zanzibar Residents." Malaria Journal 8 (December): 287. https://doi.org/10.1186/1475-2875-8-287.

Tiecke, Tobias G., and Andreas Gros. 2016. "Connecting the World with Better Maps." Facebook Engineering (blog), February 22, 2016. https://engineering.fb.com/core-data /connecting-the-world-with-better-maps/.

Vale, Steven, and Taeke Gjaltema. 2020. "High-Level Group for the Modernisation of Official Statistics." United Nations Economic Commission for Europe, Geneva. https://statswiki.unece.org/display/hlgbas/High-Level+ Group+for+the+Modernisation+of+Official+Statistics.

Wallace, Eric, Shi Feng, Nikhil Kandpal, Matt Gardner, and Sameer Singh. 2019. "Universal Adversarial Triggers for Attacking and Analyzing NLP." Cornell University, Ithaca, NY. http://arxiv.org/abs/1908.07125.

Wesolowski, Amy, Nathan Eagle, Abdisalan M. Noor, Robert W. Snow, and Caroline O. Buckee. 2012. "Heterogeneous Mobile Phone Ownership and Usage Patterns in Kenya." PLoS ONE 7 (4): e35319. https://doi.org/10.1371/journal.pone .0035319.

WHO (World Health Organization). 2008. "The Top 10 Causes of Death." *Fact Sheets* (blog), May 24, 2008. https://www.who.int/news-room/fact-sheets/detail/the-top-10-causes-of-death.

Williams, Kehinde, Adebayo Peter Idowu, and Emmanuel Olonade. 2015. "Online Road Traffic Accident Monitoring System for Nigeria." *Transactions on Networks and Communications* 3 (1): 10–30. https://doi.org/10.14738/tnc.31.589.

Wilson, Robin, Elisabeth zu Erbach-Schoenberg, Maximilian Albert, Daniel Power, Simon Tudge, Miguel Gonzalez, Sam Guthrie, et al. 2016. "Rapid and Near Real-Time Assessments of Population Displacement Using Mobile Phone Data Following Disasters: The 2015 Nepal Earthquake." *PLoS Currents* 8 (February 24). https://doi.org/10.1371/currents.dis.d073fbece328e4c39087bc086d694b5c.

WRI (World Resources Institute). 2019. "Palm Oil Industry to Jointly Develop Radar Monitoring Technology to Detect Deforestation." Press release, October 31, 2019. https://www.wri.org/news/2019/10/release-palm-oil-industry-jointly-develop-radar-monitoring-technology-detect.

Yang, Shihao, Samuel C. Kou, Fred Lu, John S. Brownstein, Nicholas Brooke, and Mauricio Santillana. 2017. "Advances in Using Internet Searches to Track Dengue." *PLoS Computational Biology* 13 (7): e1005607.

Yeh, Christopher, Anthony Perez, Anne Driscoll, George Azzari, Zhongyi Tang, David B. Lobell, Stefano Ermon, et al. 2020. "Using Publicly Available Satellite Imagery and Deep Learning to Understand Economic Well-Being in Africa." *Nature Communications* 11 (1): 2583. https://doi.org/10.1038/s41467-020-16185-w.

Zindi. 2020. "GIZ AI4D Africa Language Challenge, Round 2: $6,000 USD." *Competitions*, June 1, 2020. https://zindi.africa/competitions/ai4d-african-language-dataset-challenge.

Zou, James, and Londa Schiebinger. 2018. "AI Can Be Sexist and Racist: It's Time to Make It Fair." *Nature* 559 (7714): 324–26. https://doi.org/10.1038/d41586-018-05707-8.

Spotlight 4.1

Gathering, sharing, and using better data on weather, water, and climate from low- and middle-income countries

Two-way flows of data between local, regional, and international meteorological centers have high value for social and economic development.

The need for weather and climate information is growing rapidly as people are becoming more vulnerable to natural hazards, including those exacerbated by climate change. To support economic and social development, all countries need to have access to sufficiently accurate, reliable, and understandable weather, water, and climate data (as stated in the Sustainable Development Goals).[1] This is the case everywhere, but particularly in low- and middle-income countries, which are bearing the brunt of losses from natural hazards.[2]

Scientific and technological advances have brought weather prediction systems to a level where they can provide weather intelligence to inform the decisions of individuals and groups of individuals.[3] But such data are useful for decision-making only if more high-quality observational data are shared, assimilated, or used to adjust model outputs. While satellites provide most of the data for models, local data play several critical roles. Scientists from national meteorological services work with regional and global centers to calibrate global models at national and local scales.

The more local data are shared internationally, the better the weather predictions produced by global centers can be applied locally. Exchanging more and better data internationally and doing so more frequently have many direct benefits, yielding better-performing models, more accurate local forecasts, and improved verification of forecasts, helping to monitor, improve, and compare the quality of forecasts and forecasting systems.

Recognizing the benefit of sharing national data with regional and global forecasting centers, Ukraine recently increased the number of weather stations reporting data to the European Centre for Medium-Range Weather Forecasts (ECMWF) from 30 to 130.[4] The extra data produced by these stations will help to improve global forecasts and thus regional and national forecasts. In particular, local observations of near-surface temperature and humidity will improve estimates of soil moisture, which influence regional and global forecasts of near-surface temperature and rainfall. Additional data on snow depth from Denmark, Hungary, the Netherlands, Romania, Sweden, and Switzerland have improved forecasts of air temperature in the northern hemisphere.

More data are now being shared in real time between ECMWF and all 37 countries participating in the Regional Integrated Multi-Hazard Early Warning System for Africa and Asia (RIMES).[5] The Bangladesh Meteorological Department, for example, has increased from 10 to 32 the number of stations sharing observational data taken every three hours and provided nearly 40 years of historical data. The total number of stations added by all RIMES members is now 500 and is expected to increase to 1,500 soon, leading to a significant improvement in the accuracy and lead time of weather forecasts.

However, these data are not categorized as essential data, as defined by the World Meteorological Organization,[6] and are not considered open data from the perspective of their use and reuse. For this reason, RIMES needs to ensure that these data are protected by nondisclosure agreements. In return, ECMWF shares high-resolution digital forecast products with each participating country, with the aim of improving national forecasts and deepening the technical collaboration between RIMES countries and ECMWF. With access to these high-resolution forecast products from ECMWF, countries can focus more efforts on

Map S4.1.1 Large gaps remain in global reporting on basic weather data

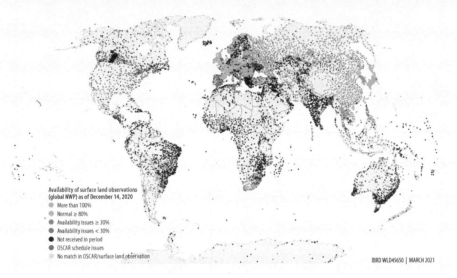

Availability of surface land observations
(global NWP) as of December 14, 2020
- More than 100%
- Normal ≥ 80%
- Availability issues ≥ 30%
- Availability issues < 30%
- Not received in period
- OSCAR schedule issues
- No match in OSCAR/surface land observation

IBRD WLD45650 | MARCH 2021

Source: World Bank map, based on data from WDQMS (WIGOS Data Quality Monitoring System) (webtool), World Meteorological Organization, Geneva, https://wdqms.wmo.int. Data at http://bit.do/WDR2021-Map-S4_1_1.

Note: Snapshot of World Meteorological Organization Integrated Global Observing System interactive map showing observations of surface temperature measured on a typical day (December 14) in 2020. NWP = numerical weather prediction; OSCAR = Observing Systems Capability Analysis and Review Tool.

applying forecast information to the needs of their population and on building skills in data analytics.[7]

As map S4.1.1 shows, significant gaps in reporting basic weather data still exist. Important steps to take are getting countries to recognize the value of sharing their data and to participate in improving the models. In time, it is anticipated that open data policies similar to the European Union Directive will apply to meteorological data everywhere, characterizing these data as having high value for social and economic development. The German Meteorological Service, for example, has started openly sharing all of the data it uses for its public tasks.[8] Now more than 500 petabytes of data are downloaded monthly and used by a wide range of industries in Germany to improve their economic performance.

Notes

1. See United Nations, Sustainable Development Goals: Decade of Action (dashboard), https://www.un.org/sustainabledevelopment/decade-of-action/.
2. Hallegatte, Bangalore, and Vogt-Schilb (2016).
3. Charts Catalogue (weather map repository), European Centre for Medium-Range Weather Forecasts, https://apps.ecmwf.int/webapps/opencharts/?.
4. ECMWF (2018).
5. Rimes (2020).
6. Zillman (2019).
7. ECMWF (2020).
8. See Deutscher Wetterdienst, Open Data Server (dashboard), https://www.dwd.de/EN/ourservices/opendata/opendata.html.

References

ECMWF (European Centre for Medium-Range Weather Forecasts). 2018. "Extra Weather Station Data Improve ECMWF's Forecasts." *News*, June 18, 2018. https://www.ecmwf.int/en/about/media-centre/news/2018/extra-weather-station-data-improve-ecmwfs-forecasts.

ECMWF (European Centre for Medium-Range Weather Forecasts). 2020. "ECMWF Moves towards a Policy of Open Data." *News*, October 7, 2020. https://www.ecmwf.int/en/about/media-centre/news/2020/ecmwf-moves-towards-policy-open-data.

Hallegatte, Stéphane, Mook Bangalore, and Adrien Vogt-Schilb. 2016. "Socioeconomic Resilience: Multi-Hazard Estimates in 117 Countries." Policy Research Working Paper 7886, World Bank, Washington, DC.

RIMES (Regional Integrated Multi-Hazard Early Warning System for Africa and Asia). 2020. "37 RIMES Countries Agree to Share Data and Focus on Impact Forecasting and Forecast-Based Action for 2021–2025." RIMES, Asian Institute of Technology, Pathumthani, Thailand, November 26, 2020. https://www.rimes.int/?q=node/630.

Zillman, John W. 2019. "Origin, Impact, and Aftermath of WMO Resolution 40." *WMO Bulletin* 68 (2): 69–71. https://library.wmo.int/doc_num.php?explnum_id=10077.

Spotlight 4.2
Making roads safer by repurposing private intent traffic data

Developing spatially integrated datasets that leverage administrative, social media, private, and more traditional sources can help to pave the way for smart and socially beneficial investments and policies.

Reducing road mortality by half (Sustainable Development Goal 3.6) could save 675,000 lives a year. Yet the countrywide investments in regulation, enforcement, education, and infrastructure needed to attain this ambitious target are often out of reach. Resource constraints require countries to make smart choices on where and how to invest. Knowing where and when road traffic crashes happen can help to prioritize investments where they matter most. Unfortunately, many countries facing these difficult choices have little or no data on road traffic crashes and inadequate capacity to analyze the data they do have. Official data on road traffic crashes capture only 56 percent of fatalities in low- and middle-income countries, on average.[1]

Crash reports exist, yet they are buried in piles of paper or collected by private operators instead of being converted into useful data or disseminated to the people who need the information to make policy decisions. In Kenya, where official figures underreport the number of fatalities by a factor of 4.5,[2] the rapid expansion of mobile phones and social media provides an opportunity to leverage commuter reports on traffic conditions as a potential source of data on road traffic crashes.

Big data mining, combined with digitization of official paper records, has demonstrated how disparate data can be leveraged to inform urban spatial analysis, planning, and management.[3] Researchers worked in close collaboration with the National Police Service to digitize more than 10,000 situation reports spanning from 2013 to 2020 from the 14 police stations in Nairobi to create the first digital

and geolocated administrative dataset of individual crashes in the city. They combined administrative data with data crowdsourced using a software application for mobile devices and short message service (SMS) traffic platform, Ma3Route, which has more than 1.1 million subscribers in Kenya. They analyzed 870,000 transport-related tweets submitted between 2012 and 2020 to identify and geolocate 36,428 crash reports by developing and improving natural language processing and geoparsing algorithms.[4]

To verify the accuracy of crowdsourced reports and the efficiency of the algorithms, the team dispatched a motorcycle delivery company to the site of the reported crash minutes after each new crash report was received for a subset of reports. In 92 percent of cases, a crash was verified to have occurred in the stated location or nearby. By combining these sources of data, researchers were able to identify the 5 percent of roads (crash black spots) where 50 percent of the road traffic deaths occur in the city (map S4.2.1).

This exercise demonstrates that *addressing data scarcity can transform an intractable problem into a more manageable one.* In this case, investing in the safety of a 6,200-kilometer road network is intractable. Digitizing and analyzing administrative data and variables on injuries and deaths can help to narrow down the locations and times of the day and week that are associated with the most severe crashes. The analysis offers an invaluable road map for future regulation, infrastructure, and enforcement efforts.

More insights can be gained by integrating existing data and collecting further information, such as

Map S4.2.1 By combining police reports and crowdsourced data, researchers were able to identify the 5 percent of roads where half of the crashes occur in Nairobi

● Crashes geolocated from police situation reports
● Crashes identified by crowdsourced reports that were geolocated and clustered into individual crashes

IBRD KEN45648 | MARCH 2021

Source: Milusheva et al. 2020.

Note: Data shown are for July 2017–July 2018.

Uber and Waze data on average speeds on road segments and on road obstacles; Google Maps data on land use; and weather data on driving conditions. The researchers also invested in a massive data collection effort that is surveying the infrastructure and videotaping and coding the behavior of road users in 200 crash black spots in the city. The analysis of these new data will generate hypotheses to optimize the policy response to the road safety problem.

Overall, developing spatially integrated datasets that leverage administrative, social media, private, and more traditional sources can help to fill data gaps and pave the way for smart and socially beneficial investments and policies.

Notes

1. WDR 2021 and World Health Organization (WHO) team calculations based on a comparison of reported deaths from the WHO *Global Status Report on Road Safety* (WHO 2018).
2. WHO (2018).
3. Milusheva et al. (2020).
4. The new algorithms build on work by Finkel, Grenager, and Manning (2005); Gelernter and Balaji (2013); and Ritter et al. (2011).

References

Finkel, Jenny Rose, Trond Grenager, and Christopher Manning. 2005. "Incorporating Non-local Information into Information Extraction Systems by Gibbs Sampling." In *43rd Annual Meeting of the Association for Computational Linguistics: Proceedings of the Conference*, edited by Kevin Knight, Hwee Tou Ng, and Kemal Oflazer, 363–70. New Brunswick, NJ: Association for Computational Linguistics. https://www.aclweb.org/anthology/P05-1045.

Gelernter, Judith, and Shilpa Balaji. 2013. "An Algorithm for Local Geoparsing of Microtext." *GeoInformatica* 17 (4): 635–67. https://doi.org/10.1007/s10707-012-0173-8.

Milusheva, Sveta, Robert Marty, Guadalupe Bedoya, Elizabeth Resor, Sarah Williams, and Arianna Legovini. 2020. "Can Crowdsourcing Create the Missing Crash Data?" In *COMPASS '20: Proceedings of the 3rd ACM SIGCAS Conference on Computing and Sustainable Societies*, 305–06. New York: Association for Computing Machinery. https://doi.org/10.1145/3378393.3402264.

Ritter, Alan, Sam Clark, Mausam, and Oren Willi Etzioni. 2011. "Named Entity Recognition in Tweets: An Experimental Study." In *Conference on Empirical Methods in Natural Language Processing: Proceedings of the Conference*, 1524–34. Stroudsburg, PA: Association for Computational Linguistics.

WHO (World Health Organization). 2018. *Global Status Report on Road Safety 2018*. Geneva: WHO. https://www.who.int/publications/i/item/9789241565684.

PART II

Aligning data governance with the social contract

5. Data infrastructure policy: Ensuring equitable access for poor people and poor countries

6. Data policies, laws, and regulations: Creating a trust environment

7. Creating value in the data economy: The role of competition, trade, and tax policy

8. Institutions for data governance: Building trust through collective action

CHAPTER

5

Data infrastructure policy: Ensuring equitable access for poor people and poor countries

Main messages

① As new mobile technologies emerge, policy makers should proactively facilitate their rollout by promoting service competition, where possible, and infrastructure sharing, where necessary.

② Universal service policies should incorporate measures designed to ease the demand-side barriers often faced by those who do not seek data services even when they are locally available. These measures include programs to improve the affordability of handsets and data services, while enhancing the digital literacy of excluded groups.

③ To ensure high-speed, cost-effective data services, policy makers should facilitate development of domestic data infrastructure that allows local storage, processing, and exchange of data so that data need not travel through distant overseas facilities.

④ A competitive market and open governance arrangements are two policies that support the creation of internet exchange points. Establishment of colocation data centers will depend on a stable investment climate for private sector investors, combined with the availability of low-cost reliable sources of clean energy.

Data infrastructure as a source of inequity

Infrastructure is a prerequisite for collecting, exchanging, storing, processing, and distributing modern data because of its digital character. Harnessing the full economic and social value of modern data services calls for digital infrastructure that is universally accessible, while also offering adequate internet speed at affordable cost. Yet the developing world is lagging behind, with major gaps between rich and poor people on broadband connectivity, and a substantial divide emerging between rich and poor countries in the availability of data infrastructure. Well-designed infrastructure policies are needed to redress these adverse trends.

Concerns about inequities in access to data infrastructure stem from growing evidence of a link with economic activity. Numerous studies have found that broadband infrastructure boosts economic growth,[1] increasing productivity[2] and employment[3] while enabling digital enterprises. For example, the arrival of fiber-optic submarine cables in Africa has had positive effects on employment from the entry of new firms, greater productivity, and higher exports.[4] More broadly, a 10 percent increase in data centers results in an expansion of exports in data-related services of about 1.6 percent.[5] As a growing share of economic activity becomes data-enabled, it is important to ensure that poor people and poor countries are not excluded from such opportunities by the absence of suitable data infrastructure.

Data infrastructure forms a supply chain that originates in global data storage centers and data processing facilities known as cloud computing platforms (figure 5.1). From there, data pass through

Figure 5.1 The data infrastructure supply chain

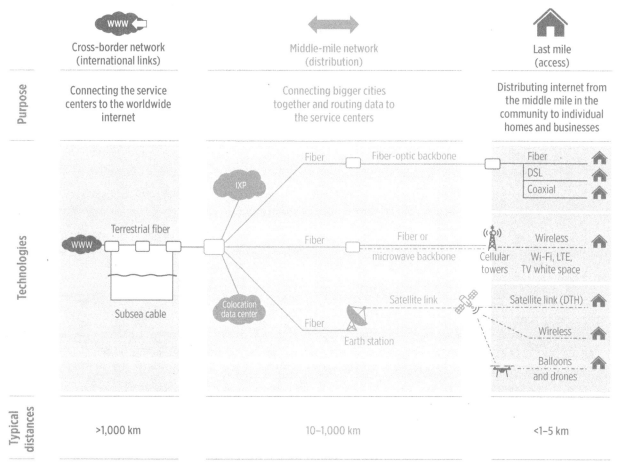

Source: Adapted from World Bank (2019c).

Note: DSL = digital subscriber line; DTH = direct-to-home; IXP = internet exchange point; km = kilometers; LTE = Long-Term Evolution; WWW = World Wide Web (internet).

internet exchange points (IXPs) for transfer to users. Data then flow in and out of countries through an intercontinental network of submarine cables. Once on domestic soil, data are distributed through national fiber-optic and microwave backbone networks until they reach a proximate location for distribution to local communities, whether through wired connections, or wireless signals provided by mobile (or cellular) networks. Finally, data are exchanged with individuals, businesses, and public institutions through *fixed* lines or *wireless* signals from cellular towers, and increasingly with inanimate machines, cameras, and sensors connected to what is known as the Internet of Things (IoT). Data travel thousands of kilometers along this seamless infrastructure supply chain at breathtaking speeds of 200,000 kilometers per second—meaning that digital data can, in principle, circle the globe five times within a second.[6]

Data traffic is growing rapidly around the world. Internet data usage rose from 4.6 to 13 gigabytes per person per month between 2012 and 2017.[7] Four trends are driving the explosion in data traffic. First, the number of internet users is growing. More than half of the world's population is now online, up from less than one-third in 2010, and that share is forecast to reach two-thirds by 2023. Second, the number of connected devices on the IoT already exceeds the number of human users and is forecast to reach 25 billion by 2025 with the diffusion of 5G technology.[8] Third, internet speeds are continually increasing, which supports growing data volumes. By 2023 the speed of broadband service provided over fixed networks is expected to double from 2018 levels,[9] even as the speed of broadband service provided over fixed networks triples. Fourth, video accounts for three-fifths of internet traffic, and associated quality improvements are increasing video data traffic.[10] A two-hour movie in standard definition uses 1.4 gigabytes of data, whereas ultra-high definition uses 18 gigabytes.[11]

Although most data traffic is still carried over fixed networks, data traffic carried over wireless networks is forecast to rise to more than 20 percent of the global total by 2022, up from only 3 percent in 2012. This shift is driven by the greater prevalence of mobile traffic in emerging nations, with China and India alone accounting for more than 40 percent of the world's mobile data traffic as of 2018.

Both poor *people* and poor *countries* face fundamental inequities in their ability to access data infrastructure. To participate in the data-driven economy, *people* require internet connectivity. It entails both access to last-mile internet infrastructure—increasingly provided through a wireless signal—and ownership of a data-enabled mobile handset (also known as a smartphone)—or alternatively a full-blown fixed line connection. Such connectivity makes it possible for people to both have access to data about other people (and increasingly other things) and provide their own data to others. Large swathes of the population remain excluded from the internet, particularly the poor, the uneducated, the elderly, those living in rural areas, and—in some parts of the world—women. This complex situation reflects both the supply-side challenges entailed in rolling out coverage of the latest mobile technologies and the demand-side barriers preventing potential users from taking up the service even when it becomes available. Moreover, because of the growing volumes of data underpinning economic and social activity, connectivity is meaningful only if it can be provided at affordable cost and adequate speed.

Unless *countries* have access to modern data infrastructure, connectivity (even when available) will remain prohibitively expensive and slow. Such infrastructure begins with adequate international bandwidth to permit fluid and unconstrained access to the global internet commons. As traffic grows, local IXPs are needed to prevent domestic data transfers from being diverted across vast distances overseas. The addition of domestic colocation data centers—wholesale storage facilities that host other companies' data—allows substantial volumes of popular overseas content to be stored locally, further improving internet performance. It may also permit direct access to cloud computing platforms, greatly enhancing data processing capabilities. Although almost all countries now enjoy access to global internet submarine cables through either direct coastal access points or cross-border land connections, domestic data infrastructure—such as IXPs, colocation data centers, and cloud computing platforms—remain nascent across low- and middle-income nations, leaving them to contend with low internet speeds and high data charges.

This chapter unpacks the underlying issues that explain the data inequities faced by poor people and poor countries, with an emphasis on identifying appropriate policy responses. The chapter updates, complements, and extends the earlier treatment of related issues in *World Development Report 2016: Digital Dividends*. For this reason, coverage of supply-side issues is on a relatively high level, whereas the demand-side barriers, as well as the emerging challenges posed by development of domestic data infrastructure, receive more attention.

Connecting poor people

Many individuals in low- and middle-income nations use basic cellphones for applications such as text messaging and mobile money. These applications have had tremendous development impacts, even without using much data or requiring broadband internet access.[12] Beyond such basic telephony applications, access to broadband internet, in combination with ownership of a feature phone or smartphone, greatly enriches an individual's ability to use data for a better life. Social media connect family and friends; online government services and shopping websites save individuals time and money; online learning and telemedicine provide new, accessible, and inexpensive ways of delivering education and health. The COVID-19 pandemic is reinforcing the importance of access to broadband internet for remote learning and home working, as well as improving the overall resilience of economies to shocks of various kinds (see spotlight 5.1).

In the context of low- and middle-income countries, wireless broadband networks have emerged as the most relevant technology for accessing data services. The impacts of wireless broadband are greater than those of wired broadband in these nations,[13] particularly because the expansion of fixed broadband is relatively limited and has yet to reach the minimum threshold to have a statistically significant effect on economic growth.[14] Even in upper-middle-and high-income nations, where fixed broadband is more prevalent users spend most of their time online on mobile phones. Among the poorest in these countries, many only use wireless networks to access the internet (figure 5.2).[15]

The world's political commitment to universal access for internet was most recently articulated in a 2019 report of the United Nations Broadband Commission for Sustainable Development, which calls for 75 percent access to broadband worldwide by 2025—65 percent in developing economies and 35 percent in least developed countries.[16] The United Nations also encourages all countries to adopt by 2025 a national plan for universal access to broadband. These targets reflect a reappraisal by the international community following the failure to reach Sustainable Development Goal (SDG) 9, Target 9.c, which called for "universal and affordable access to the internet in least developed countries by 2020."[17]

From an economic standpoint, public policy support for universal coverage of telecommunications and data services has hinged on positive network externalities. In other words, the economic value

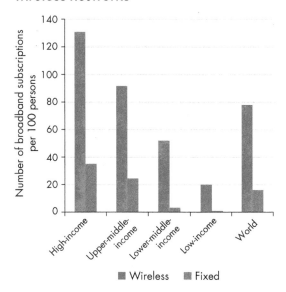

Figure 5.2 The developing world overwhelmingly accesses data using wireless networks

Source: WDR 2021 team, based on data from International Telecommunication Union, Statistics (database), https://www.itu.int/en/ITU-D/Statistics/Pages/stat/default.aspx. Data at http://bit.do/WDR2021-Fig-5_2.

Note: Data are for 2019.

of communications infrastructure rises as more members of a society are connected because such growth exponentially increases the number of pairs of people who can communicate with each other.[18] Such positive externalities have underpinned the case for providing public subsidies to ensure that universal access can be achieved. Furthermore, as the internet becomes the central platform for much of social and economic life, providing all citizens with an opportunity to access this platform is increasingly a matter of social inclusion.

The shortfall of digital connectivity in the developing world can be understood in terms of three different types of gaps. The *coverage gap* refers to the fact that last-mile digital infrastructure has yet to reach all inhabited locales. The *usage gap* refers to the fact that, even when coverage becomes available, uptake of the service by the affected population will typically not be universal. The *consumption gap* refers to the fact that, even when people do take up the service, data consumption is typically too low to support basic economic and social functions. The discussion that follows focuses primarily on people, but small firms face many of the same barriers.

Although all but 8 percent of the world's population is covered by a wireless broadband network (figure 5.3, panel a), this overall figure hides significant

Figure 5.3 Gaps in 3G wireless broadband internet coverage have been shrinking, but usage gaps remain stubbornly high

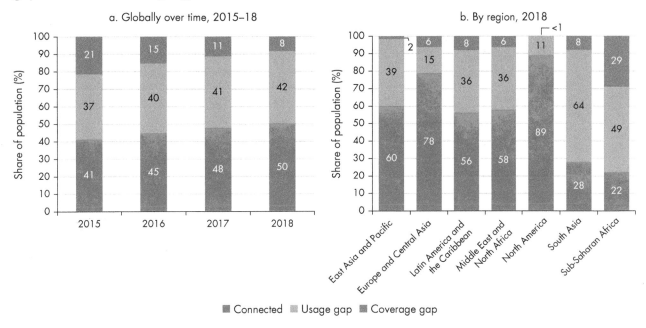

a. Globally over time, 2015–18

b. By region, 2018

■ Connected ■ Usage gap ■ Coverage gap

Sources: WDR 2021 team, based on 2015 and 2018 data in ITU (2018a). Data at http://bit.do/WDR2021-Fig-5_3.

regional differences (figure 5.3, panel b). The *coverage gap* is less than 1 percent in North America, but as high as 29 percent in Sub-Saharan Africa. The *usage gap* encompassed 42 percent of the world's population in 2018, but as much as 64 percent of the population of South Asia, where more than 1 billion people are covered by a broadband signal without making use of the internet. Although the 3G coverage gap has shrunk by more than half over the last five years thanks to successful rollout of last-mile infrastructure on the supply side, the usage gap has remained remarkably stable, indicating the persistence of barriers on the demand side. Indeed, as of 2018 more than four in five of the unserved persons worldwide lived in areas where 3G signal coverage was already available.

Ultimately, the three gaps are interrelated because improving service uptake and data consumption also contribute to commercial viability, increasing the revenues generated by any particular investment in network coverage. Thus progress on closing the usage gap and narrowing the consumption gap will further help eliminate the coverage gap.

Closing the coverage gap

In 2018 more than 600 million people lived without access to the internet, a far cry from the United Nations' SDG target of universal and affordable access to the internet by 2020.[19] Most of those who are unconnected live in lower-income nations. Estimates suggest that achieving universal broadband internet access by 2030 will require an investment of approximately US$100 billion in Africa alone.[20]

The coverage gap is typically reported relative to 3G technology, which delivers speeds of 42 megabytes per second, making it the first generation able to support data-rich smartphone applications. However, rapid innovation in the mobile communications sector leads to a new generation of technology just about every decade, ushering in substantial improvements in speed and bandwidth and making universal coverage something of a moving target. In fact, 4G technology, offering speeds of 400 megabytes per second, is already widely available in the developing world (figure 5.4). If 4G were used as the relevant technological benchmark, the coverage gap would rise from 8 percent to 20 percent in 2018, and the problem of access would no longer be confined solely to Sub-Saharan Africa.

In 2019 5G technology became commercially available in 23 high-income economies and China, with a global coverage gap of 95 percent by the end of the first year. The new 5G technology is revolutionary because of both its exceptionally high speed of 1,000 megabytes per second, as well as its greatly enhanced

Figure 5.4 Globally, the coverage of wireless technologies reflects their constant upgrading

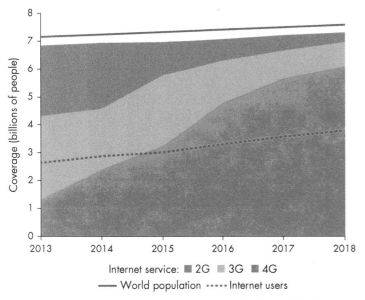

Internet service: ■ 2G ■ 3G ■ 4G
—— World population ····· Internet users

Source: WDR 2021 team, based on data in ITU (2018a). Data at http://bit.do/WDR2021-Fig-5_4.

capacity to transmit a large amount of sensor-based data from the IoT in near real time, offering numerous applications across different economic sectors. Forecasts suggest that one-third of mobile subscriptions could be 5G by 2025.[21]

This Report finds that under current conditions, 5G stand-alone technology (that is, technology not dependent on 4G for signaling) does not seem to be broadly viable across low- and middle-income countries, outside of major urban areas. However, developing 5G non–stand-alone technology as an incremental evolution of 4G greatly improves its viability. It could then become a cost-effective technology for meeting population coverage in densely populated middle-income countries once data traffic grows to the point that large numbers of users are demanding many gigabytes of data per month.[22] Viability could also be greatly improved by adopting regulations that promote sharing of infrastructure and policies that limit the burden of taxes and spectrum license fees on investors.[23]

Past investments in fiber-optic backbone networks and cellular towers (under 3G) have had a significant impact on the viability of the newer wireless technologies (such as 4G and 5G). Countries at an earlier stage of infrastructure development will find it challenging to leapfrog ahead, but for others investments in the fiber-optic backbone will continue to provide payoffs as countries upgrade to more advanced technologies.

The coverage gap reflects the lack of commercial viability associated with serving remote populations in the absence of any government intervention. Closing this gap calls for concerted efforts to drive down the cost of service provision, as well as better design of government policies on universal service access. Among the main policy measures to cut costs are those aimed at strengthening competition in the sector, enabling the sharing of infrastructure, improving the availability and affordability of the wireless spectrum, and exploiting new technologies.

Reducing retail costs. Individuals' access to reliable high-speed data services depends on both extensive last-mile coverage and proximity to the national fiber-optic backbone infrastructure. Limited retail competition can lead to high profit margins inflating charges to customers for last-mile access.[24] In addition, costs may be relatively high due to limited electricity coverage in outlying areas, forcing operators to rely on their own higher-cost diesel power generation for base stations instead of being able to draw energy from the public grid.[25] Meanwhile, recent innovations in wireless cellular technologies may reduce the cost of last-mile rollout. For example, in Japan Rakuten recently achieved 40 percent reductions in the cost of traditional cellular networks through migration to a cloud-based, software-driven environment.[26]

Introducing fiber-optic backbone competition. The greater the proximity of users to backbone infrastructure, the stronger are the mobile signals and the faster the data download speeds. In Africa, 45 percent of the population lives more than 10 kilometers away from fiber-optic network infrastructure—more than in any other region.[27] Relative to microwave links, fiber-optic backbones offer greater carrying capacity at higher speeds. Yet many countries in Africa still need to upgrade from microwave to fiber-optic technology— an estimated 250,000 kilometers of fiber-optic cable are needed across the continent.[28] Deployment of fiber-optic cable can cost as much as US$70,000 per kilometer[29]—a high entry barrier for building national fiber-optic backbones.

As a result, competition is often limited, and, in the absence of regulation, high wholesale prices and limited network development may result. Lack of competition is further exacerbated when backbone infrastructure operators are vertically integrated, providing both wholesale and retail services.[30] In the absence of robust competition, some countries have opted for state-owned backbone development, based on vendor financing, but this approach crowds out private investment and unnecessarily adds to the public debt. A competitive backbone market may be a preferable alternative policy, with government taking on a coordinating role, inviting multiple operators to participate, enforcing open access and cost-based pricing, and offering incentives to existing or new operators to invest in less lucrative areas to complete the infrastructure backbone.

Enabling sharing of infrastructure. Another way to increase coverage by keeping costs down is to create a regulatory environment that facilitates the sharing of infrastructure both across sectors and within digital infrastructure markets.[31] The cost of broadband transmission and core network deployment can be reduced by using existing railway lines, power transmission grids, and pipelines, or by coordinating with road construction to lay ducts along highways. In emerging markets, and particularly in the poorest countries where demand may be thin and infrastructure costs and the associated risks relatively high, operators could be allowed to share backhaul infrastructure (such as fiber-optic cable) or local facilities (such as communication towers). Sharing of infrastructure has great potential to accelerate digital connectivity. Recent estimates suggest that the cost of deploying 5G mobile network technology could be reduced by more than 40 percent by sharing antenna sites.[32] However, the tensions between promoting competition and enabling cooperation in the market for digital infrastructure must be carefully balanced, with cooperation encouraged only in market segments that cannot efficiently support more than one operator.

Improving the availability and affordability of the spectrum. Making adequate spectrum available at relatively low cost is important for reducing coverage gaps. A low-frequency spectrum is attractive for rural areas because it provides wider coverage, requiring a lower density of cellular towers to cover a given area and reducing investment costs. Governments have often delayed the migration from analog to digital television, which releases coveted low-frequency spectrum for wireless broadband use. Some governments auction frequencies with elevated reserve prices that raise investment costs and are then passed on to users through higher prices. For example, in Senegal operators boycotted the 4G spectrum auction because of the high reserve price—CFAF 30 billion (US$49.86 million).[33] Other governments charge recurring fees for the use of spectrum, raising the cost of deploying infrastructure in rural areas.

Exploiting new technologies. Emerging niche technologies—such as TV white space (TVWS), hot air balloons, and low-orbit satellites—promise to significantly reduce last-mile deployment costs in remote areas, although many have yet to scale up commercially.

TVWS uses the buffer frequencies between TV channels to provide broadband internet access. It is already being used successfully in Colombia to connect rural schools and coffee plantations in geographically challenging locations such as mountainous rainforests.[34] Two innovative solutions that have been proposed to reach remote rural areas are high-altitude platform station (HAPS) systems, which use a network of hot air balloons to provide unserved locations with connectivity,[35] and low-Earth orbiting (LEO) satellites. Iridium—which in 1998 became the first LEO to launch—today has slightly more than 1 million subscribers, mainly in niche markets such as the maritime aviation sectors and emergency services, as well as oil and gas.[36] Yet neither HAPS nor LEO satellites have proved they can provide direct consumer broadband access in rural areas on a sustainable basis at an affordable price.

Reforming universal service funds. Adopting these approaches to driving down costs can substantially expand the coverage attainable on a commercially viable basis. Nonetheless, some remote pockets will not reach universal access without some form of state support. Many countries have created universal service funds to harness public resources to subsidize infrastructure rollout in unserved areas. These funds are typically financed by obligatory levies charged on operators. However, for a variety of reasons many of these funds have proven to be unsuccessful (Kenya is one of the few exceptions in Africa).[37] Funds often suffer from poor design, lack of spatial planning to guide fund allocations, a mismatch between funds collected and disbursed, political interference, and failure to incorporate sustainability factors such as training and education, maintenance, and energy supply.[38] For example, in Africa more than US$400 million worth of universal service funds have not been disbursed.[39] A study of countries with universal service funds in the Asia-Pacific region found that they did not experience higher internet growth than countries without funds—except Malaysia and Pakistan, where the funds were transparent, efficient, and targeted extension of the national fiber-optic backbones.[40]

Tackling the usage gap

Of the 3.8 billion people not using the internet in 2018, 3.1 billion lived within range of a wireless broadband signal.[41] Government efforts to provide universal service access have traditionally focused on eliminating the coverage gap through rolling out the supply of infrastructure, but such policies should increasingly be oriented toward addressing the demand-side barriers that limit service uptake, thereby creating such a sizable usage gap.

Targeting the most critical underserved segments. Although traditional universal service policies have largely focused on directing public support to underserved rural *communities*, there is considerable scope to target demand-side policy measures to particular categories of under-served *individuals* irrespective of their location. A suite of large sample household surveys conducted in 22 developing countries in 2017/18 reveal that people who do not connect to broadband service even when it is available are significantly more likely to be poor (in the bottom 40 percent of the national income distribution), less educated (having only a primary education), elderly (over 50 years old), and female.[42] Of these, the largest effect is associated with education: completion of primary education adds 35 percentage points to the likelihood of internet uptake.

Also noteworthy is the significant gender digital divide. Globally, some 250 million fewer women than men use the internet. In low-income countries, only one in seven women is online, compared with one in five men.[43] Women are somewhat more likely than men to be challenged by digital literacy issues and to face additional obstacles to being online. For example, in many countries lack of family approval for women owning a cellphone is a major barrier.[44]

Broadly, three reasons have been put forward to explain the usage gap in low- and middle-income countries. First, people find it difficult to afford a mobile device or data services. Second, they lack the digital literacy needed to use the internet.[45] Or, third, they do not see internet services offering any content or application of relevance to their lives. The household surveys conducted in 22 developing countries in 2017/18 found that the reasons most frequently cited by people for not taking up data services are related to digital literacy (69 percent), followed by affordability concerns (15 percent) and relevance issues (12 percent)—see figure 5.5.[46] Digital literacy limitations appear to dominate in South Asia, whereas affordability concerns are more prominent in some African countries. These different constraints are not, however, mutually exclusive. A person who becomes digitally literate and therefore more motivated to access the internet may then face affordability challenges not relevant before.

Individuals are also attracted to using the internet when family members or friends do so, particularly when it comes to social media. Analysis conducted for this Report found that social network effects have a significant positive impact on the usage of wireless internet in low- and middle-income countries. Individuals whose five closest friends are using an online social network are 63 percent more likely to use the internet than those whose closest friends are not already active on social media.[47]

Addressing the widespread problem of digital literacy. In the 2017/18 household surveys, digital literacy was the most fundamental reason given for not using the internet. More than 84 percent of those surveyed who

Figure 5.5 In low- and middle-income countries, nearly 70 percent of those who do not use the internet are held back by deficiencies in digital literacy

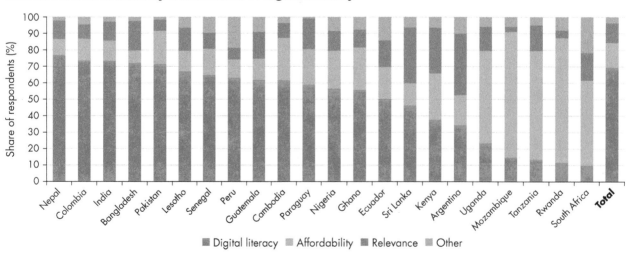

Source: Chen 2021. Data at http://bit.do/WDR2021-Fig-5_5.

Note: Respondents to the survey conducted for this Report had access to internet service. Responses to the digital literacy category included "Do not know what internet is" and "Do not know how to use internet." Responses to the affordability category included "No access device" and "Too expensive." Responses to the relevance category included "No interest/not useful" and "No relevant content in local language."

were either uneducated or had completed only a primary school education stated they "do not know what internet is" or "do not know how to use internet."[48]

Various initiatives are under way to teach basic digital skills. Mobile industry association GSMA has developed a Mobile Internet Skills Training Toolkit based on a "train the trainers" approach.[49] Results from a pilot project in Bangladesh found that mobile internet usage among the beneficiary group more than tripled, with 19 percent of group members becoming regular mobile data users.[50] In early 2017, the Rwandan government launched the Digital Ambassadors Program, which trained 5,000 youth posted to all 30 districts in the country to provide digital skills training to 5 million Rwandans over a four-year period.[51] Field studies conducted in Burkina Faso, Mali, Senegal, and Tanzania found that audio and icon-based interfaces and a stripped-down version of the internet ("internet lite") helped students overcome their digital literacy limitations.[52] Despite these examples, there is little evidence that digital literacy programs are operating at the scale needed to significantly improve the uptake of data services, or that they are being suitably integrated with efforts to address the more fundamental underlying problem of basic literacy.

Once people become digitally literate, a key determinant of using the internet is availability of local language content.[53] Social media usage grows rapidly as the relevant apps become available in local languages much sooner than internet content.[54]

Making digital devices more affordable. Poor people wishing to avail themselves of internet access must first be able to afford a mobile device. However, according to one study, the cost of even an entry-level device exceeds 20 percent of the monthly income in more than half of low- and middle-income nations.[55] Another study found that the cost of a low-end US$42 smartphone is more than 80 percent of the monthly income in low-income countries.[56]

Efforts are under way to make entry-level internet devices more affordable. Mobile operators are creating partnerships to obtain inexpensive handsets or are bundling mobile phones with subscriptions. Pan-African operator MTN collaborated with China Mobile to launch a US$20 smartphone targeted at 10 million first-time users.[57] In India, Jio offers an internet-enabled phone for Rs 699 (US$9.21), provided the customer spends at least Rs 1,500 (US$19.77) a year on service charges.[58] Although most branded phones are manufactured in East Asia, several countries have created reassembly plants to manufacture inexpensive mobile phones locally. In Ethiopia, a Chinese company is assembling about 1 million phones a year

for export throughout the region.[59] In Costa Rica and Malaysia, universal service funds have been used to subsidize internet devices for low-income users.[60]

Taxes, import duties, and other fees also affect device affordability. Despite the low purchasing power of their populations, low-income countries on average impose the highest customs duties on mobile phones, adding 7 percent to prices on average. One study found that several mainly low- and middle-income countries applied handset excise taxes (beyond the regular sales tax) and activation fees.[61] Ownership is also affected by substantial gender gaps in low- and middle-income countries; the share of men owning mobile devices is 20 percentage points higher than the share of women.[62]

Narrowing the consumption gap

Even among people who connect to the internet and subscribe to data services, a wide consumption gap remains in *wireless* data usage across country income levels and regions, with the data usage per capita in high-income countries more than 30 times higher than that in low-income countries (figure 5.6). The consumption gap is even wider if *fixed* broadband is considered. The number of fixed broadband subscriptions is much higher in high-income economies, and because of more favorable data plans, these subscriptions support much higher levels of consumption than mobile subscriptions—potentially as much as 100 times more.[63]

The consumption gap raises questions about how much data are "enough" to meet basic social and economic needs. In 2019 the Alliance for Affordable Internet (A4AI) stated that 1 gigabyte of data per month was sufficient to benefit from the internet in a meaningful way,[64] but later it revised its estimate of "meaningful connectivity" to unlimited access as a result of the burgeoning use of data during the COVID-19 pandemic.[65] Based on a detailed empirical examination of data consumption patterns, this Report estimates that 660 megabytes per month is adequate to meet basic needs for e-government services, online shopping, browsing news, medical and educational information, and the like, rising steeply toward 6 gigabytes per month if a certain amount of social media and video-related usage is also included.[66]

Two fundamental drivers of low data consumption are the struggle to afford data usage charges and the technical constraints on network performance. These two drivers can be related. Problems with affordability translate into lower usage, which, in turn, means lower revenue streams and weaker incentives to invest in better network performance.

Figure 5.6 Inequities in mobile data consumption across country income groups and regions are huge

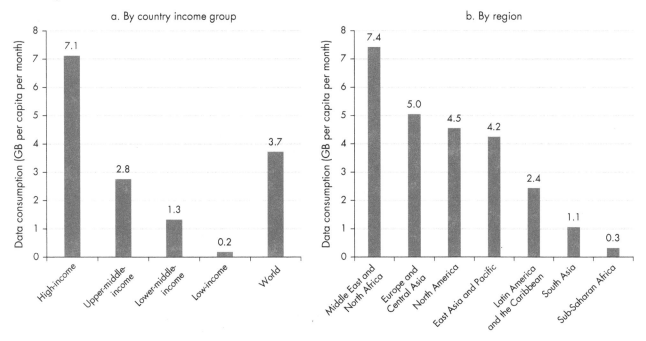

a. By country income group

b. By region

Source: WDR 2021 team. Data at http://bit.do/WDR2021-Fig-5_6.

Note: Data are for 2018. Figures include averages of 119 economies with data. GB = gigabytes.

Tackling affordability constraints. Many internet users in low- and middle-income nations limit their mobile data usage because of affordability constraints (figure 5.7). A survey carried out in 11 emerging countries found that a median of 48 percent of respondents had difficulty paying for their mobile data usage, and 42 percent frequently or occasionally restrict the amount of data they use.[67] Instead of purchasing large amounts of data on a monthly basis, users buy it in small amounts when they have the money. Many mobile operators offer a variety of data bundles to cater to this pattern. MTN Zambia, for example, has 17 prepaid data plans, ranging from one-hour plans, including 5 megabytes of data, to weekly bundles offering unlimited access to popular social media applications.[68]

What is an affordable level of expenditure on data services has been the subject of some debate. The Alliance for Affordable Internet established a normative affordability threshold of 2 percent of monthly income linked to a normative consumption threshold of 1 gigabyte per month.[69] This threshold was subsequently adopted by the UN Broadband Commission.[70] According to these norms, data services could be considered generally affordable to the average consumer, except in low-income countries. The reality is that the actual expenditure on data services (known as average

revenue per user or ARPU) and the associated data consumption levels both fall well below these norms. In fact, it is only when the cost per gigabyte of data drops below 0.5 percent of gross national income (GNI) per capita that data consumption reaches and eventually exceeds the 1 gigabyte threshold (figure 5.8).

The amount of data that people can afford to consume is itself a function of the prices that operators offer across different markets, as well as over time. In India, rapid entry of mobile operators offering 4G service in 2016 boosted coverage from 4 percent in 2015 to 94 percent in 2018.[71] Intensifying competition led to a dramatic price drop from US$4.41 to US$0.17 per gigabyte per month from 2014 to 2018 and a surge in consumption per subscriber from 0.3 to 7.7 gigabytes per month over the same period.[72] Similarly, in Cambodia intense competition has brought down the cost per gigabyte of data from US$4.56 in 2013 to one of the world's lowest at US$0.13 in 2019, driving up data consumption to 6.9 gigabytes per capita per month—the highest mobile data usage per capita of any low- or lower-middle-income nation. This increase was achieved through a combination of measures such as migrating spectrum and users to 4G to achieve lower operating costs, outsourcing construction work, and moving software to the cloud.[73] As a result of the low data charges, Cambodian consumers devote

Figure 5.7 The monthly price for 1 gigabyte of data is unaffordable in low-income countries

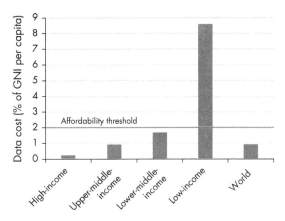

Source: Cable.co.uk, Worldwide Mobile Data Pricing 2020: The Cost of 1GB of Mobile Data in 228 Countries (dashboard), https://www.cable.co.uk /mobiles/worldwide-data-pricing/. Data at http://bit.do/WDR2021 -Fig-5_7.

Note: Data are as of 2018. The affordability threshold is 2 percent of monthly income. Prices are the median prices of the economies in the group. GNI = gross national income.

Figure 5.8 Data consumption is very sensitive to market prices and service affordability

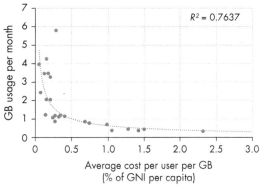

Source: WDR 2021 team. Data at http://bit.do/WDR2021-Fig-5_8.

Note: Each circle represents a country. GB = gigabyte; GNI = gross national income.

96 percent of their information and communication technology (ICT) spending to data services, having largely moved away from voice and text.

Interestingly, users in low-income countries typically spend much more on voice and text services—between 2 and 4 percent of monthly income—than they do on data services. Because traditional voice and text can alternatively be provided on over-the-top (OTT) data-based services, which bypass traditional distribution and use only a small amount of data, users could substantially reduce their overall ICT expenditure by substituting data for voice and text services.

Addressing technical constraints. Slow speeds also discourage consumers from using more data. Downloading 250 megabytes takes 17 seconds at a speed of 100 megabytes per second, but as long as three minutes at a speed of 10 megabytes per second.[74] The speed dividends arising from migration to the next generation of mobile technology clearly drive higher levels of data consumption. For example, in India during 2018 a 2G subscriber consumed just 0.5 gigabytes per month, rising to 5.3 gigabytes per month for a 3G subscriber and 9.7 gigabytes per month for a 4G subscriber.[75]

Regulatory policies and retail competition drive migration to higher-generation mobile technologies. Transitions to next generations can be encouraged by early release of competitively priced spectrum. The auction of 3G spectrum in Thailand in 2012 was designed to support rapid upgrade from 2G by incorporating license conditions for coverage, pricing, and quality. Within two years, all license conditions were exceeded, with nearly universal 3G coverage, upgrading of three-quarters of subscriptions, lower prices, and service speeds exceeding license requirements by tenfold.[76]

Allowing operators to "refarm" their spectrum holdings can also accelerate migration to next-generation mobile. In contrast to regulatory policies that tie new mobile technologies to specific frequencies that are then auctioned, refarming allows operators to launch new mobile technology using their own spectrum. This encourages them not only to be more efficient in their use of spectrum, but also to rapidly upgrade their existing subscribers to reclaim the spectrum used for the older technology. About three-quarters of the spectrum used for 4G around the world has been refarmed: 25 percent from switching from analog to digital television broadcasting and 50 percent from operators using their own spectrum.[77]

Nonetheless, many operators try to recapture their original capital expenditure before upgrading to a new generation of wireless technology.[78] To overcome this issue, Rwanda created a public-private partnership to roll out a 4G/LTE (Long-Term Evolution) network that covered almost 99 percent of the population by the end of 2019—the highest level in the world. However, because of the high cost of obtaining a 4G/LTE–compatible device, as well as technical challenges with the migration of voice services, service uptake has been modest, with most Rwandans continuing to use slow 2G technology for mobile data.[79]

Connecting poor countries

The high cost and low speed of internet services have emerged as key drivers of data consumption in the developing world. One reason is that many low-income countries lack their own domestic data infrastructure, relying instead on overseas facilities to exchange data (via internet exchange points), store data (at colocation data centers), and process data (on cloud platforms). This reliance requires them to transfer large volumes of data in and out of the country (see "tromboning" in figure 5.9), for which they pay a substantial penalty: prices that are several times higher than those in countries with their own infrastructure. They also experience slower speeds that can be an order of magnitude lower. This situation can be avoided by creating IXP infrastructure at the national level, eventually complemented by colocation data centers.

Consider a user who wants to view an educational video online. The request is uploaded as a small packet of data with address information and goes from the user's device to the national backbone and onward to the internet service provider (ISP). Often in lower-income countries, the video is not available domestically, obliging the ISP to route the request overseas, where it finds its destination—say, in California. The video is then downloaded back to the user. Such a circuitous process for accessing content incurs significant charges from international carriers while prejudicing service quality. This same operation would be much faster and cheaper if a replica of this content were stored at a local colocation data center that could be accessed via a local IXP.

This example illustrates how international bandwidth is a critical part of the data infrastructure, enabling data to be sent to and retrieved from anywhere in the world. The global internet bandwidth stood at 463 terabytes per second in 2019, almost tripling from 2015. Sub-Saharan Africa had the fastest growth in bandwidth of any region over the 2015–19 period. It grew by 53 percent a year, reflecting a large increase in capacity because of the deployment of new submarine cables. However, Sub-Saharan Africa continues to lag other regions in total capacity.

Most international internet traffic is carried over the world's dense web of some 400 undersea fiber-optic cables, spanning more than 1 million kilometers.[80] Almost all coastal economies are now connected to undersea cables (map 5.1). Submarine cable ownership has diversified from consortiums of telecommunication operators to include wholesale operators and increasingly big content providers such as Amazon, Google, and Microsoft.[81] Notably, Facebook recently announced plans to lay the 2Africa submarine cable around Africa. It will have nearly three times the capacity of all the undersea cables currently serving the continent.[82] The growing convergence of content provision and carriage of content will require greater regulatory oversight to ensure that carriage is provided in an open, nondiscriminatory manner.

Before establishing a submarine cable connection, countries used costly, low-capacity satellite links. Connection to submarine cables has dramatically lowered wholesale international bandwidth prices. Results in Africa over the last decade have been dramatic, with the price of 1 megabit per second dropping from US$3,500 to US$29 in Mauritania and from US$1,174 to US$73 in Togo.[83] In Tonga, the submarine cable increased capacity by more than 100 times, while prices dropped from US$495 to US$155 per megabit per second.[84] Nonetheless, restrictive policies for access to submarine cable landing stations may

Figure 5.9 The presence of domestic data infrastructure facilitates national data exchanges

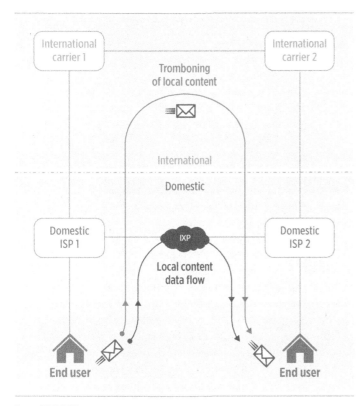

Source: WDR 2021 team.

Note: ISP = internet service provider; IXP = internet exchange point.

Map 5.1 The global fiber-optic cable submarine network reaches all corners of the world, but data infrastructure is unevenly developed

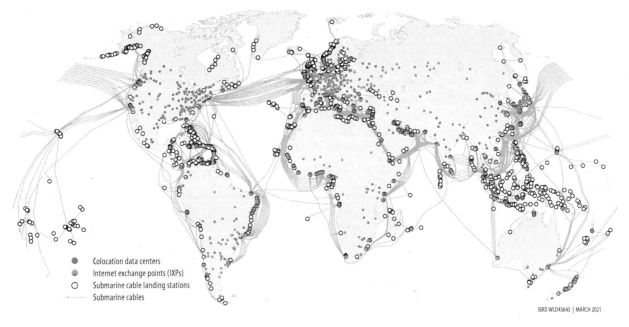

Colocation data centers
Internet exchange points (IXPs)
Submarine cable landing stations
Submarine cables

IBRD WLD45643 | MARCH 2021

Sources: PeeringDB, Interconnection Database, https://www.peeringdb.com/; PCH Packet Clearing House, Packet Clearing House Report on Internet Exchange Point Locations (database), accessed December 14, 2020, https://www.pch.net/ixp/summary; TeleGeography, Submarine Cables (database), https://www.submarinecablemap.com/. Data at http://bit.do/WDR2021-Map-5_1.

prevent the full benefits of this reduction in wholesale prices to feed through into retail tariffs.

Despite such progress, huge price differences persist for the exchange of data traffic. For example, the cost of exchanging data is around US$0.45 per megabyte per second in North America and US$0.62 per megabyte per second in London, compared with US$2.38 in São Paulo and US$5.00 in Johannesburg.[85] These stark differences in costs may in part reflect the limited development of domestic data infrastructure in low- and middle-income countries.

Strengthening data infrastructure

Without a domestic capability to exchange data, countries are totally reliant on international bandwidth. As noted, such bandwidth is expensive and slower than exchanging traffic locally. Such reliance also affects service resilience, since a country is completely shut off from the internet if there is any disruption to international bandwidth. For example, after a trawler snapped a submarine cable in 2018, Mauritania was offline for two days, and nine other West African countries experienced internet outages.[86] Although there will always be a need for international bandwidth, an appropriate balance is needed between relying on overseas infrastructure and developing domestic facilities.[87]

The economic case for domestic data infrastructure hinges on whether the present value of the resulting cost savings and speed improvements for data transactions over the life of such infrastructure exceeds the associated immediate up-front investment in facilities. The cost of developing IXPs is relatively modest and likely can be supported even in nascent markets so long as the sector is not monopolistic. As for colocation data centers, the investments are more sizable. There are also significant scale economies associated with the development of the associated power infrastructure that may account for as much as 40 percent of investment costs. The operating expenses are also largely fixed; about half of them are related to energy for cooling the facilities. Because exceptionally high levels of reliability and security are needed for colocation data centers, market dynamics favor hyperscale service providers with established reputations. This requirement further reinforces the case for larger-scale facilities in countries that have a relatively stable investment climate, including low levels of disaster risk, and the availability of clean, reliable, and cost-effective sources of energy or natural sources of cooling such as water bodies.

Creating internet exchange points. By keeping data traffic in the country, IXPs can reduce reliance on international bandwidth, lowering costs and improving performance. One study covering Latin America noted that "local bits" are cheaper than "exported bits," finding that the region spent around US$2 billion a year for international bandwidth—a sum that could be reduced by one-third through greater use of IXPs.[88] IXPs reduce the time it takes to retrieve data, enhancing user engagement. In Rwanda, it is 40 times faster to access a locally hosted website (<5 milliseconds) than one hosted in the United States or Europe (>200 milliseconds).[89]

As of June 2020, there were 556 IXPs across the globe.[90] Europe, with the largest number, accounts for 37 percent of the world total, while Africa has just 9 percent and accounts for less than 2 percent of global IXP traffic, although that traffic is growing rapidly.[91] Stark differences in the availability of IXPs are evident across country income groups, particularly when population differences are taken into account.

IXPs are often established initially by universities or as nonprofit associations of ISPs, located in small server rooms with technical tasks carried out by volunteers. As greater volumes of traffic are exchanged and new participants join, a more sustainable technical and operational environment is needed. Governance arrangements are then formalized, staff hired, and equipment upgraded. Eventually, the IXP grows to the point where many participants want to join without having to deploy a physical connection to the exchange. This leads to the creation of multiple IXPs in different locations, with the central IXP relocated to a colocation data center. For example, DE-CIX, an IXP in Frankfurt, Germany, began operations 25 years ago in an old post office when three ISPs interconnected their networks.[92] Today, it is the world's leading IXP, spread over more than three dozen data centers and linking almost 1,000 participants, with average traffic of more than 6 terabytes per second.

Developing colocation data centers. Data centers have emerged as a vital component of the digital infrastructure ecosystem. In a data center, networked computers provide remote storage, processing, and distribution of data. The centers are mainly operated by global information technology (IT) companies, governments, and enterprises that host other companies' data (colocation data centers). Data centers range from small rooms in organizations where data are kept on storage devices connected to computer servers to giant warehouse-like facilities where thousands of servers are arranged on racks. Colocation data centers offer companies multiple advantages, including the physical space to store a growing amount of data, the security associated with high industry reliability standards (as they almost never shut down), and easy internet access due to their growing association with IXPs.[93]

Globally, some 3,700 data centers are connected to the internet.[94] The disparities in data center penetration among country income levels are wide, particularly when taking population differences into account (figure 5.10). Although there are more than three data centers per million inhabitants in North America, the ratio is only 0.8 per million in South Asia and Sub-Saharan Africa. In fact, there are more data centers in the state of California than in all of Sub-Saharan Africa. These disparities may be related to lower income and thus demand, but they also reflect shortcomings in the investment climate.

Major colocation data center companies have largely shunned investing in low- and middle-income economies. This lack of investment is often attributed to a lack of demand, as well as an aversion to a country's perceived high risk of natural disasters, unpredictable political environment, barriers to doing business, and unreliable energy and internet infrastructure.[95] However, certain large businesses in low-income countries, such as those in the financial

Figure 5.10 Data infrastructure is relatively scarce in low- and middle-income countries

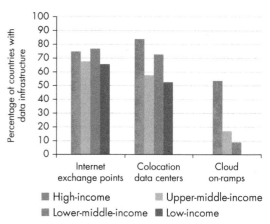

Source: WDR 2021 team, adapted from PeeringDB, https://www.peeringdb.com/. Data at http://bit.do/WDR2021-Fig-5_10.

Note: The figure depicts data centers connected to the internet. Data were extracted in June 2020.

sector and other service industries, already have in-house data storage systems that, if aggregated, could create the scale necessary for colocation data centers.

Regional players are filling the void left by the large global data center providers. For example, Africa Data Centres (part of the Liquid Telecom Group) has colocation facilities in Kenya, Rwanda, South Africa, and Zimbabwe. Although some of the scale issues associated with developing colocation data centers could potentially be overcome through regional collaboration around shared facilities, the case for such an approach hinges on the existence of strong regional fiber-optic network connectivity to ensure that data can be transferred rapidly and reliably to any shared regional data facility; competitive pricing of such data transfers; and regional harmonization of the regulatory framework to support agile cross-border data transfers (as discussed in chapter 7).

Despite mounting concerns about the environmental impact of data centers, there is evidence that the industry is taking aggressive action to curtail emissions and that availability of renewable energy is a factor in attracting investment (see spotlight 5.2).

Climbing the data infrastructure ladder. A country's development of data infrastructure can be envisioned as a series of stages that over time lower costs and improve performance (figure 5.11).[96] The stages progress from having no domestic IXP (stage 0), to establishing an IXP (stage 1), to attracting content providers and deploying data centers that host a diverse group of participants (stage 2), to locating

the IXP alongside a colocation data center (stage 3). As countries move up the ladder, more data are exchanged nationally, and reliance on costly international bandwidth is consequently reduced, lowering retail prices, raising speed, and allowing higher data consumption.

Drawing on industry registries capturing the availability of data infrastructure globally in 2020, it is possible to build a comprehensive picture of domestic data infrastructure in the developing world. At stage 0 are 28 of the countries surveyed for this Report, none of which has an IXP, and these include almost half of the low-income country group. Underlying barriers are often responsible for the lack of an IXP: 10 of these countries are small island states where the scale of traffic is insufficient; four are in fragile and conflict-affected situations that impede the development of the data ecosystem; and five are monopolies where the sole national telecom operator is also in effect the IXP.

At stage 1 are 29 countries in which IXPs connect local ISPs. These include more than a third of low- and lower-middle-income countries. These IXPs are often located on the premises of government agencies or at academic institutions, typically in a small server room and in some cases using equipment provided through development assistance. For example, the African Internet Exchange System (AXIS) project, financed by the European Union, established IXPs in 14 African nations.[97] The IXPs in this group of nations often generate limited amounts of traffic, sometimes because not all ISPs participate in the IXP. In some

Figure 5.11 Countries develop domestic data infrastructure in stages

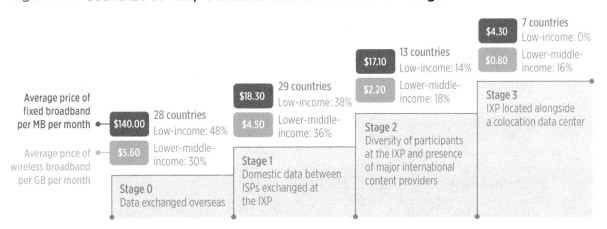

Source: Comini, Srinivasan, and Minges, forthcoming.

Note: Data provide close to global coverage for the year 2020 and are compiled from a variety of industry sources, including Packet Clearing House, CAIDA, PeeringDB, EURO-IX, and AF-IX. Amounts are in US dollars. GB = gigabyte; ISP = internet service provider; IXP = internet exchange point; MB = megabit.

countries, regulatory restrictions forbid participants that are not ISPs from joining the IXP.

The 13 countries at stage 2 have IXPs with non-ISP participants. Less than one-fifth of low- and lower-middle-income countries fall into this group. This group generally has numerous and diverse participants in the IXP, including all ISPs, as well as government agencies, local cloud providers, and national content companies, among others. Often, they have a Google Global Cache, a subset of Google's most popular content,[98] as well as content delivery networks (CDNs). However, large international content and cloud providers do not always use the IXP either because it is not located in a neutral data center or because its governance is not organized according to an open multistakeholder model.

At stage 3 are seven countries with IXPs colocated in data centers with international content participants. There are no low-income countries in this category, and only a minority of lower-middle-income countries. These arrangements often include multiple IXPs located in several data centers to facilitate participation. The Kenya Internet Exchange Point (KIXP) illustrates how this results in a dense network, enabling many participants to exchange data. KIXP is operated by a nonprofit organization representing technology companies, and its board follows international IXP best practices. KIXP has no restrictions on the types of organization that can connect to the exchange. It is located in colocation data centers in Kenya's two largest cities, Nairobi and Mombasa. Participants include national, regional, and international ISPs; government agencies; financial companies; and international content and cloud providers such as Amazon, Facebook, Google, and Microsoft.

Empirical evidence suggests that the benefits to countries of moving up the data infrastructure ladder are substantial. The average cost per gigabyte of wireless data per month drops from US$5.60 in countries at stage 0 to US$0.80 in countries at stage 3, while the corresponding cost per megabit for fixed data drops from US$140.00 to US$4.30 per month.

Nonetheless, the full benefits of developing domestic data infrastructure become apparent only when the local market is sufficiently competitive. For example, because of its strategic geographic location on the Horn of Africa, Djibouti's DjIX is a regional hub handling the exchange of considerable volumes of internet traffic. However, even though Djibouti's data infrastructure provides valuable services to neighboring countries, the monopolistic market structure of the national telecommunications sector does not allow these advantages to be passed on to domestic consumers, who face some of the most unaffordable internet charges in the world.[99]

Policy makers have an important role to play in shepherding IXPs through these various stages of development. In the early stages, demand remains incipient, and it is not possible to benefit from scale economies in infrastructure development. Governments and academic institutions can help initially with nascent IXPs by providing facilities and resources for training. Encouraging ISPs to exchange traffic locally helps boost demand for data services by reducing the cost of exchange. If needed, governments may have to mandate participation, particularly where dominant operators have been resistant. As their IXPs grow, governments can reduce their role, encouraging IXPs to become self-sustaining. Open IXP policies and multistakeholder governance are important for attracting non-ISPs to the membership, including large content providers. Government insistence on control over IXP practices discourages private sector investment in the data ecosystem.[100] A supportive regulatory environment for IXPs, as well as attention to sound governance practices, should ensure that multiple ISPs as well as universities, large enterprises, and other significant users make full use of the available IXP infrastructure. For example, in 2011 Bolivia legally mandated the creation of a national IXP requiring the participation of local ISPs. However, traffic growth was limited until 2018, when improved governance arrangements incentivized greater reliance on the IXP by local market players.[101]

Accessing cloud platforms

Just as there is growing reliance on colocation data centers to store data, the processing of data is being handled increasingly by cloud platforms. Cloud platforms essentially enable users to access scalable data storage and computing resources across the internet or other digital networks as and when required. Continual enhancements in cutting-edge computing capabilities, combined with significant improvements in the capacity and speed of processing, transmitting, and storing data, are making cloud computing increasingly important in the delivery of public and private services.[102]

Cloud platforms offer significant benefits in terms of security, resilience, scale, and flexibility. Security is arguably better on large cloud computing platforms than what many businesses or governments could achieve in-house.[103] Strong security features include ongoing data backups, redundant sites, and industry certifications, as well as adherence to national data protection regulations. However, moving data to the cloud environment also presents new vulnerabilities such as reduced visibility of assets and operations, or the possibility that applications used to access cloud services could be compromised. IT infrastructure becomes more resilient as digital data and computing power become geographically distributed. This resiliency is enhanced by classifying services by region and availability zones and connecting data centers in the same geographic area. Cloud computing is attractive because it is often cheaper to share resources on a common platform than to replicate hardware, software, and storage requirements on individual company sites. Small enterprises can then outsource IT activities that they otherwise would not be able to provide internally, while benefiting from the flexibility of immediate upgrades to the most recent analytics and storage technology.

As broadband connectivity has become more widely available around the world, cloud computing has been growing rapidly, with industry revenues exceeding US$180 billion in 2018, up 27 percent over the previous year.[104] A few large companies dominate the cloud space, with almost all software and IT services firms based in the United States. These hyperscale providers operate cloud data centers mainly in high-income countries, with just a handful in large middle-income nations such as Brazil and South Africa, though not elsewhere in the developing world.

Free cloud services funded by advertising, such as webmail and online social networks, are already widely used in low- and middle-income nations. Google Docs provides word processing, spreadsheet, and presentation software used by millions around the world.[105] IBM offers several free services on its cloud.[106] However, sophisticated cloud services such as storage and analysis of vast amounts of data can be costly for developing economies because of the cost of moving data internationally and the resulting sacrifice in terms of speed.

One potential solution is to develop cloud platforms at the regional level by aggregating demand to achieve economies of scale. Regional harmonization of regulations for data security, data protection,[107] and data sovereignty could further reduce compliance costs and help induce major cloud providers to locate closer to low- and middle-income countries. For example, in March 2019 Microsoft launched the first data centers from a large cloud provider in Africa, with locations in Cape Town and Johannesburg, South Africa, and potential wider relevance to southern Africa.[108]

Another approach is for countries with colocation data centers to encourage the creation of "on-ramps" to cloud computing services. These are prevalent in some 80 percent of high-income countries but only in about 10 percent of middle-income countries such as India and Indonesia, and not at all in low-income countries.

Cloud on-ramps are private connections between data centers and cloud providers. They allow clients to interact directly with overseas cloud providers through domestic IXPs located in colocation data centers without needing to use the internet to access cloud services.[109] This process provides greater security and reliability because data are not transmitted to the cloud over public infrastructure but rather directly via the on-ramp. Performance in terms of speed is also greatly improved and costs are significantly lowered because the cloud provider is responsible for managing and routing the data traffic from the domestic colocation data center to its cloud data center overseas using the on-ramp. At the same time, cloud services create demand for data centers because some applications require very high speed, which can only be achieved when computational power is located close to the user at the network's "edge."[110] This description underscores the complementarities between different types of data infrastructure, such as IXPs, colocation data centers, and cloud computing.

Big data analysis is increasingly taking place over distributed cloud networks because the considerable processing power needed is available only on the cloud. Data are stored in one or more places and processed in others. The cloud has also enabled a new collaborative environment for software development in which developers from around the world participate in modifying code. The world's largest open-source platform, GitHub, hosts more than 100 million repositories used by 50 million developers worldwide.[111] The growth in new software projects is mainly coming from low- and middle-income nations, with Africa expanding more rapidly than any other region. Open-source repositories in Africa created by software developers grew 40 percent in 2019.[112]

Without skilled human resources, countries will be limited in their ability to apply modern data infrastructure to achieving economic and social impacts. Workers are needed to create and maintain data infrastructure, as well as to collect, store, manage, and analyze large amounts of data. Although the skills needed to collect, store, and manage data are available in many parts of the world, those for analyzing big datasets are limited. Data scientists—specialists in math, computer, and analytical skills—who derive value from large datasets are in short supply, and low- and middle-income countries are at a disadvantage in the global market for technical skills (see box 5.1).

Box 5.1 The brain drain—ICT professionals

Available data on the supply of and demand for information and communication technology (ICT) skills paint two distinct pictures.[a] Among country income groups, there does not seem to be wide divergence in the proportion of students graduating with ICT degrees, which typically falls in the 7–8 percent range overall, yet with marked discrepancies between men and women (figure B5.1.1, panel a). However, employment of ICT professionals is strongly correlated with country income groups, since these workers account for 2.1 percent of total employment in high-income nations, dropping to 0.1 percent in low-income countries (figure B5.1.1, panel b).

The mismatch between supply and demand in low- and middle-income economies prompts outward migration toward better employment opportunities in countries where the digital sector is more developed. Evidence of this brain drain already exists: all countries except high-income are experiencing large outflows of skilled tech workers (figure B5.1.2, panel a). Even where skilled data workers have opportunities in low- and middle-income countries, wage differentials could be a driver of migration. The average wages for ICT employees are significantly higher in high-income nations (figure B5.1.2, panel b), and significant wage differentials exist across regions.

Figure B5.1.1 Low- and middle-income countries are educating ICT professionals but not retaining them

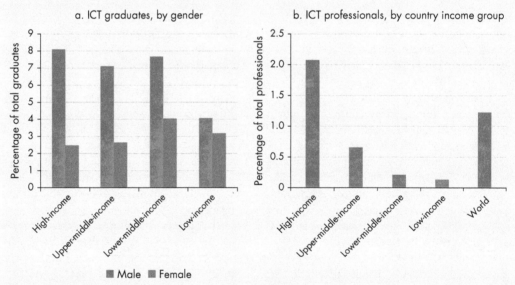

a. ICT graduates, by gender

b. ICT professionals, by country income group

■ Male ■ Female

Sources: Institute for Statistics, United Nations Educational, Scientific, and Cultural Organization, Data of UIS.Stat (database), http://data.uis .unesco.org/; International Labour Organization, ILOSTAT Database, http://www.ilo.org/ilostat/. Data at http://bit.do/WDR2021-Fig-B5_1_1.

Note: For ICT graduates, panel a presents the latest available data between 2015 and 2018 for 120 economies. For ICT professionals, panel b plots the latest available data between 2016 and 2019 for 73 economies. Country income group percentages are collective country averages. ICT = information and communication technology.

(Box continues next page)

Conclusions and recommendations

Low- and lower-middle-income countries continue to face major challenges in connecting themselves to the vital infrastructure that underpins the data-driven economy. Many have yet to develop their own IXPs and remain reliant on slow, expensive international data transfers to access the World Wide Web. Colocation data centers that allow further local storage and processing of data, as well as caching of internet content, are still not prevalent in low- and lower-middle-income countries, while global cloud computing resources are almost entirely concentrated in high-income countries, with a limited availability of on-ramps to facilitate access by the developing world.

Box 5.1 The brain drain—ICT professionals (continued)

Figure B5.1.2 Major wage differentials for ICT professionals create a brain drain, especially in low- and middle-income countries

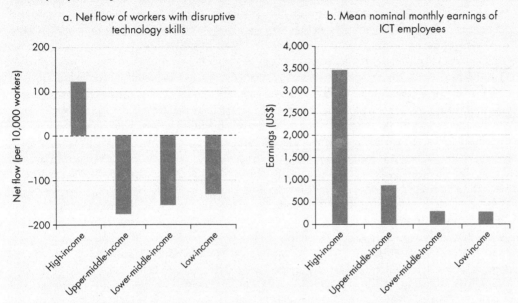

a. Net flow of workers with disruptive technology skills

b. Mean nominal monthly earnings of ICT employees

Sources: International Labour Organization, ILOSTAT Database, http://www.ilo.org/ilostat/; LinkedIn data (2015–19). Data at http://bit.do/WDR2021-Fig-B5_1_2.

Note: According to LinkedIn dataset classification, "disruptive technology skills" include knowledge and skills in areas of materials science, aerospace engineering, development tools, data science, robotics, artificial intelligence, human computer interaction, genetic engineering, nanotechnology, and fintech. ICT = information and communication technology.

The relative penetration rate of data science skills—relevant to artificial intelligence—across comparable occupations is four times higher in high-income countries than in low-income countries.[b] Given salary differentials of 5–10 times between data scientists in low- and high-income countries, it is estimated that workers with these skills in low-income countries are 33 percent more likely to migrate than workers from high-income countries. There was a net outflow of at least 70,000 workers from low- and middle-income countries every year from 2015 to 2019.[c]

a. Data from the national statistical office on data skills are lacking in both availability and specificity, particularly for low- and middle-income countries. New sources of data, such as the professional networking platform LinkedIn, are emerging as sources of timely and granular information on the labor market, albeit with limited representativeness. The LinkedIn data used in this Report have been validated against international metrics where available to assess coverage and representativeness (Zhu, Fritzler, and Orlowski 2018).
b. Estimation based on the Skills Genome Benchmarking Methodology, using LinkedIn's Skills Genome Country-Occupation data. This method allows a fair comparison of the penetration of data science skills of all countries in the dataset with that of a chosen benchmark (low-income countries, in this case) by controlling for common occupations among each country and the benchmark.
c. WDR 2021 team calculations, based on Zhu, Fritzler, and Orlowski (2018).

At the same time, in poor countries large swathes of the poorest and most disadvantaged segments of society continue to be excluded from access to broadband data services. For low-income countries, particularly in Africa, the coverage gap for broadband signal remains significant, affecting 30 percent of the population. A major concern is the usage gap—the vast majority of those who do not have data access today live within range of a mobile signal, but they face either affordability or literacy challenges that prevent them from making use of the service. The COVID-19 pandemic has drawn growing attention to the consumption gap, which highlights the limited volumes of data usage in the developing world and the implications for the population's ability to access data-based services such as tele-education.

Connecting poor people

When it comes to connecting people to data infrastructure, the following steps are recommended.

Keep costs down through competition. Governments should prioritize all measures to drive down the cost of service provision. Lower costs improve the commercial viability of services, thereby reducing coverage gaps and accelerating technology upgrades. They also help to improve service affordability, thereby reducing usage and consumption gaps. Governments have two possible levers for reducing costs. The most fundamental is creating competitive pressures along the supply chain, including both its wholesale and retail tiers, while addressing structural impediments such as vertical integration. In addition, governments could create a regulatory environment that supports sharing bottleneck infrastructures in areas with low data traffic that could not otherwise support competitive provision of data infrastructure.

Harness private sector investment. To develop digital infrastructure governments should rely on the private sector wherever possible. This calls for privatization of state-owned incumbents and a policy of avoiding state investment (such as through vendor-financed models) in segments such as the national fiber-optic backbone where the private sector is willing to invest. The entry of new market players is an important market trend, including the growing role of content providers in building backbone infrastructure, which will require careful consideration of competition and regulatory issues such as net neutrality.[113] With the advent of 5G, industrial players are also expected to become more active in the development of ICT infrastructure.

Rethink universal service policies. The underperformance of traditional universal service funds points to the need to rethink and modernize government policy measures to support universal service. Measures such as license coverage obligations should be considered. The role of innovative technologies (such as TV white space) and new entrants (such as content providers) in reaching remote populations are also relevant. Supply-side subsidies should be competitively awarded and carefully targeted to those pockets that cannot be reached effectively after considering all other available measures. Furthermore, universal service funds could be redirected to addressing the usage gap by funding digital literacy programs or supporting access to lower-cost mobile devices. This would entail targeting such resources more toward

disadvantaged population segments than to underserved geographic areas.

Calibrate fiscal regimes carefully. The governments of poor countries have typically regarded digital infrastructure and associated data services as a potential fiscal cash cow (through taxes, fees, and other charges) in the context of low mobilization of public sector revenues. This view has led to relatively high indirect taxes on mobile devices and data services, significant import duties on equipment, and in some cases high reservation fees for spectrum access. However, there are important trade-offs between the fiscal revenues generated by the sector in the short term and the pace of digital infrastructure rollout and service uptake in the longer term, which also has implications for economic growth and associated tax revenues over time. The design of the fiscal regime for digital infrastructure and data services must therefore be carefully thought through to balance these competing policy objectives. There may be a case for giving lighter tax treatment to low-end mobile devices to support uptake by disadvantaged groups.

Support upgrades to new technologies. Governments need to create an environment that enables accelerated upgrades to higher-generation technologies. The fiber-optic backbone is a critical prerequisite for further upgrade of networks to 4G and 5G technologies. Thus measures to expand this network at any stage, in partnership with the private sector, would be a no-regrets strategy. In addition, allowing reform of the spectrum so that operators can repurpose existing spectrum allocations would be a helpful strategy. License conditions could also be used to package such regulatory allowances with obligations for data service providers to provide wide-ranging service coverage. Finally, the complexity of these new technologies will require adequate investments in cybersecurity protection.[114]

Connecting poor countries

When connecting countries to data infrastructure, the following steps are recommended.

Progressively develop domestic data infrastructure. Governments need to pay much more attention to the specific infrastructure required to support the sharing, storage, and processing of large volumes of data. To participate in the data-driven economy on a competitive basis, countries must be able to perform high-volume data operations at the greatest possible speed and lowest possible cost. The infrastructures that can meet these performance goals are internet exchange points, colocation data centers, and cloud computing.

Promote creation of internet exchange points. IXPs remain scarce across the developing world, and even where they do exist they often fail to achieve their potential. Governments have a role in creating the enabling conditions for such institutions to emerge and be widely utilized. Better governance models are needed so that IXPs can develop and become sustainable. Collaboration between IXPs and key stakeholders such as ISPs, government entities, research networks, and content providers can help to raise awareness, expand skills, and create the trust essential for IXPs to be successful.

Create a favorable environment for colocation data centers. Neutral, privately owned colocation data centers are an essential part of data infrastructure and critical for promoting the digital economy. They are a secure venue in which local and international companies can store their data and help support the local hosting industry. The willingness of private investors to install such facilities in low- and middle-income countries is affected by concerns about the enabling environment—in particular, the availability of clean and secure energy sources, as well as relative political stability and ease of doing business. Governments can catalyze the market by moving their online services to data centers and by encouraging businesses to host locally to create economies of scale, while establishing a solid data protection framework to build trust.

Secure on-ramps to the cloud. Cloud computing creates tremendous opportunities for low- and middle-income nations to gain remote access to advanced computing facilities for data management and analytics. The cloud also enables collaborative creation of software, thereby giving software developers around the world opportunities to participate. However, cloud data centers and on-ramps are mainly located in upper-middle- and high-income nations. Low-income countries could induce the major cloud providers to locate closer through a regional approach that aggregates demand and harmonizes compliance requirements for security, data protection, and sovereignty. Governments also need to foster an enabling environment that encourages cloud providers to locate in local data centers in order to provide an on-ramp to their services.

Invest in and retain human resources. Realization of the potential for data infrastructure to contribute to economic development depends on adequate human resources, particularly in frontier areas such as data science and artificial intelligence. Although there is an acute global scarcity of these skills, evidence suggests that low- and middle-income nations are producing some graduates in these fields. However, wage differentials in a highly competitive global market are leading to a powerful brain drain effect, preventing those countries from harnessing these skills. The brain drain is often exacerbated by the lack of opportunities arising from undeveloped local data infrastructure. Governments need to stimulate their digital economies by encouraging private investment in fiber-optic backbones and data centers that generate direct and indirect employment.

The recommendations presented here are organized within the maturity model framework in table 5.1, recognizing that different countries may be at different stages of developing data infrastructure.

Table 5.1 Recommendations for data infrastructure improvements sequenced according to a maturity model

Stage of country	Connecting people	Connecting countries
Establishing fundamentals	Eliminate coverage gaps by reducing costs through wholesale and retail competition, as well as infrastructure sharing arrangements, and, where still required, providing well-crafted state support.	Ensure adequate international bandwidth. Create a competitive market environment for international gateways and internet service providers.
Initiating data flows	Narrow usage gaps through digital literacy campaigns, investment in basic education, lower taxation and import duties on low-end handsets, and support of local ventures for manufacturing handsets.	Encourage creation of the first domestic IXP and facilitate participation by all relevant domestic players. Allow additional IXPs to emerge and players to formalize and mature. Encourage arrangements to cache popular international internet content on local servers.
Optimizing the system	Upgrade digital networks to the latest generation to improve speed and efficiency and facilitate higher consumption.	Create a supportive environment in which colocation data centers can emerge, integrate with IXPs, and provide on-ramp access to cloud services.

Source: WDR 2021 team.

Note: IXPs = internet exchange points.

Notes

1. Briglauer and Gugler (2019); Czernich et al. (2011); Katz and Callorda (2018); Koutroumpis (2018); Minges (2015).
2. Bertschek and Niebel (2016).
3. Shapiro and Hassett (2012).
4. Hjort and Poulsen (2019).
5. van der Marel (2020).
6. See "How Does Data Travel on the Internet?" *Networking Guides*, https://networkingguides.com/how-does-data-travel-over-the-internet/.
7. Cisco (2018).
8. Ericsson (2020).
9. Cisco (2020).
10. Monash University (2020).
11. Sandvine (2019).
12. Text messages allow traders to check on agricultural prices, remind the sick when to take their medicine, and help nurses register births. Mobile money has unleashed add-on services in microinsurance, agriculture, and transportation, and it is facilitating the deployment of off-grid energy by allowing users to repay the cost of solar panels with micropayments. Development agencies can make conditional cash transfers to mobile money accounts, reducing costs and increasing security.
13. Katz and Callorda (2018).
14. Czernich et al. (2009).
15. Anderson and Kumar (2019).
16. Broadband Commission (2019).
17. For further details on Sustainable Development Goal 9, Target 9.c, see Department of Economic and Social Affairs, United Nations, "Goals: 9, Build Resilient Infrastructure, Promote Inclusive and Sustainable Industrialization and Foster Innovation," https://sdgs.un.org/goals/goal9.
18. See, for example, Michie (1997) or Madden (2010).
19. SDG Target 9.c states: "Significantly increase access to information and communications technology and strive to provide universal and affordable access to the Internet in least developed countries by 2020" (Department of Economic and Social Affairs, United Nations, "Goals: 9, Build Resilient Infrastructure, Promote Inclusive and Sustainable Industrialization and Foster Innovation," https://sdgs.un.org/goals/goal9).
20. Broadband Commission (2019).
21. Ericsson (2020).
22. Oughton et al. (2018).
23. Oughton et al. (2018).
24. World Bank (2016).
25. GSMA (2019c).
26. Kapko (2020).
27. Broadband Commission (2019).
28. Broadband Commission (2019).
29. GSMA (2019b).
30. See World Bank (2019c). One example is Liquid Telecom, which has rolled out 70,000 kilometers of fiber-optic cable through several African nations. See Liquid Telecom, "Our Network," https://www.liquid telecom.com/about-us/our_network.
31. For example, landlocked Mongolia's north-south fiber-optic backbone connecting it to China and the Russian Federation runs along the railway (Tsolmondelger 2019).
32. Strusani and Houngbonon (2020).
33. UN-OHRLLS (2017).
34. See the information on the Adopting TV White Spaces Project in Colombia (ITU 2018c, 33).
35. Loon (2020).
36. Iridium Communications (2020).
37. Intelecom Research and Consultancy (2016).
38. GSMA (2013).
39. World Wide Web Foundation and A4AI (2018).
40. ESCAP (2017).
41. ITU (2018a).
42. Chen (2021).
43. ITU (2018b).
44. GSMA (2020).
45. The United Nations Educational, Scientific, and Cultural Organization (UNESCO) defines digital literacy as "the ability to access, manage, understand, integrate, communicate, evaluate and create information safely and appropriately through digital technologies for employment, decent jobs and entrepreneurship. It includes competences that are variously referred to as computer literacy, ICT literacy, information literacy and media literacy" (Law et al. 2018).
46. Chen (2021).
47. Chen (2021).
48. Chen (2021).
49. GSMA (2017).
50. GSMA (2019a).
51. See Ministry of ICT and Innovation, "Digital Ambassadors Programme," Kigali, Rwanda, https://www.minict.gov.rw/projects/digital-ambassadors-programme.
52. Radovanović et al. (2020).
53. Internet Society (2015).
54. Silver and Smith (2019).
55. GSMA (2019a).
56. A4AI (2020).
57. MTN (2020).
58. JioPhone, "Jio Digital Life," Reliance Jio Infocomm Ltd, Mumbai, India, https://www.jio.com/en-in/jiophone.
59. *New China* (2018).
60. A4AI (2020).
61. GSMA (2019d).
62. GSMA (2020).
63. Telefónica S.A., "Quarterly Results: 2020 January–September," https://www.telefonica.com/en/web/shareholders-investors/financial_reports/quarterly-reports/.
64. A4A1 (2019).
65. Sonia (2020).
66. Chen and Minges (2021).
67. Silver et al. (2019).
68. ITU (2018c).
69. See Alliance for Affordable Internet, "Affordable Internet Is '1 for 2'," https://a4ai.org/affordable-internet-is-1-for-2.

70. See "Advocacy Target 2" (Broadband Commission 2020).

71. BBC News (2019a).

72. BBC News (2019b).

73. Based on information provided by one of Cambodia's seven mobile operators, Smart (Smart Axiata 2019).

74. See the speed graph provided by West Central Telephone Association, Sebeka, MN, https://www.wcta.net/speed-demo/.

75. TRAI (2019).

76. Malisuwan, Tiamnara, and Suriyakrai (2015).

77. Sanni (2016).

78. Capitel (2016).

79. RURA (2019).

80. TeleGeography, Submarine Cables (database), https://www.submarinecablemap.com/.

81. Miller (2019).

82. Ahmad and Salvadori (2020).

83. See World Bank, "West Africa Regional Communications Infrastructure Project, APL 2," https://projects.worldbank.org/en/projects-operations/project-detail/P123093.

84. World Bank (2019a).

85. See TeleGeography, Submarine Cable Frequently Asked Questions, https://www2.telegeography.com/submarine-cable-faqs-frequently-asked-questions.

86. Baynes (2018).

87. The development of domestic data infrastructure should not be confounded with the question of data localization. Data localization, a regulatory issue discussed at some length under the trade section of chapter 7, concerns the adoption of government restrictions requiring that a country's data be stored and sometimes processed on national territory, often with associated government controls on cross-border data transfers. Although domestic data infrastructure is a prerequisite for data localization, the development of domestic data infrastructure serves many other critical functions. In particular, it supports the cost-effective exchange of data among domestic parties and facilitates the access of country nationals to data from other jurisdictions by allowing copies of such data to be stored locally.

88. Agudelo et al. (2014).

89. Internet Society (2017).

90. The count of the number of IXPs in the world differs depending on the source. For example, PeeringDB (https://www.peeringdb.com/) reported 786 in June 2020. The variations are often due to differences in definitions (such as whether private peering facilities are included).

91. See Packet Clearing House, "Packet Clearing House Report on Internet Exchange Point Locations," https://www.pch.net/ixp/summary.

92. DE-CIX (2015).

93. Dobran (2018). Colocation data centers are vulnerable to physical and cybersecurity threats. They may be an attractive target for cybercriminals because they host large amounts of data and private information, all in the same location. However, because they have more resources, colocation sites can invest in better security protections than what could be achieved in-house for a typical small or medium-size business.

94. PeeringDB, https://www.peeringdb.com/.

95. C&W (2016).

96. Comini, Srinivasan, and Minges (forthcoming).

97. EU-AITF (2018).

98. See Interconnect Help, Google, "Introduction to GGC," https://support.google.com/interconnect/answer/9058809?hl=en.

99. Comini, Srinivasan, and Minges (forthcoming).

100. Balancing Act (2019).

101. Comini, Srinivasan, and Minges (forthcoming).

102. UNCTAD (2013).

103. All large cloud providers have International Organization for Standardization/International Electrotechnical Commission (ISO/IEC) 27000 certification compliant with regulatory and legal requirements that relate to the security of information (ISO/IEC, "Popular Standards: ISO/IEC 27001, Information Security Management," https://www.iso.org/isoiec-27001-information-security.html).

104. IDC (2019).

105. See Google, "Google Docs," https://www.google.com/docs/about/.

106. International Business Machines, "IBM Cloud: Free Tier," https://www.ibm.com/cloud/free.

107. See chapter 7 for a discussion about data localization regulations.

108. Keane (2019).

109. See DP Facilities, "The Critical Role Data Centers Play in Today's Enterprise Networks: Part 3, Why Cloud On-Ramps Are Key for an Enterprise Migrating to the Cloud," https://www.dpfacilities.com/blog/cloud-onramps-are-key-to-migration/.

110. World Bank (2019b).

111. GitHub, "Where the World Builds Software," https://github.com/.

112. GitHub, "The 2020 State of the OCTO–VERSE," https://octoverse.github.com/.

113. Because of the complexity of the topic, this chapter does not address the issue of net neutrality and its impact on market regulation and competition.

114. With their distributed routing approach and software-driven design, 5G networks present an array of new cybersecurity challenges that must be addressed before these networks are widely deployed. Moreover, IoT devices are often manufactured without adequate cybersecurity protections, and they have security vulnerabilities. These vulnerabilities can be exploited by bad actors who can gain access to the network or harness the computational power of an IoT device for other malicious purposes, such as distributed denial of service attacks. A forthcoming World Bank 5G flagship report will address in detail the cybersecurity issues raised by the uptake of the 5G technology.

References

A4AI (Alliance for Affordable Internet). 2019. "The 2019 Afford-ability Report." October, World Wide Web Foundation, Washington, DC. https://a4ai.org/affordability-report.

A4AI (Alliance for Affordable Internet). 2020. "From Luxury to Lifeline: Reducing the Cost of Mobile Devices to Reach Universal Internet Access." August 6, World Wide Web Foundation, Washington, DC. https://docs.google.com/document/d/1YFXbUr-WoLTOAXs9QEtlf8oEBsrakQ_lLeHUyb-6oEY/edit.

Agudelo, Mauricio, Raúl Katz, Ernesto Flores-Roux, María Cristina Duarte Botero, Fernando Callorda, and Taylor Berry. 2014. *Expansión de infraestructura regional para la interconexión de tráfico de internet en América Latina.* Caracas, República Bolivariana de Venezuela: Devel-opment Bank of Latin America. http://scioteca.caf.com/handle/123456789/522.

Ahmad, Najam, and Kevin Salvadori. 2020. "Building 2Africa, a Transformative Subsea Cable to Better Con-nect Africa." *Connectivity, Networking, & Traffic* (blog), May 13, 2020. https://engineering.fb.com/2020/05/13/connectivity/2africa/.

Anderson, Monica, and Madhumitha Kumar. 2019. "Digital Divide Persists Even as Lower-Income Americans Make Gains in Tech Adoption." *Fact Tank, News in the Numbers* (blog), May 7, 2019. https://www.pewresearch.org/fact-tank/2019/05/07/digital-divide-persists-even-as-lower-income-americans-make-gains-in-tech-adoption/.

Balancing Act. 2019. "Ugandan Government and Regulator Want to Take Control of Local IXP: The Latest in a Dis-turbing Pattern of Regulatory Interventions." *Balancing Act News*, July 12. https://www.balancingact-africa.com/news/telecoms-en/45586/ugandan-government-and-regulator-want-to-take-control-of-local-ixp-the-latest-in-a-disturbing-pattern-of-regulatory-interventions.

Baynes, Chris. 2018. "Entire Country Taken Offline for Two Days after Undersea Internet Cable Cut." *Independent*, April 11. https://www.independent.co.uk/news/world/africa/mauritiana-internet-cut-underwater-cable-offline-days-west-africa-a8298551.html.

BBC News. 2019a. "Mobile Data: Why India Has the World's Cheapest." *BBC News*, March 18. https://www.bbc.com/news/world-asia-india-47537201.

BBC News. 2019b. "Reliance Jio: India's Cheapest Data Pro-vider to Raise Prices." *BBC News*, November 20. https://www.bbc.com/news/world-asia-india-50484594.

Bertschek, Irene, and Thomas Niebel. 2016. "Mobile and More Productive? Firm-Level Evidence on the Pro-ductivity Effects of Mobile Internet Use." *Telecommu-nications Policy* 40 (9): 888–98. https://doi.org/10.1016/j.telpol.2016.05.007.

Briglauer, Wolfgang, and Klaus Gugler. 2019. "Go for Giga-bit? First Evidence on Economic Benefits of High-Speed Broadband Technologies in Europe." *JCMS, Journal of Common Market Studies* 57 (5): 1071–90. https://doi.org/10.1111/jcms.12872.

Broadband Commission (United Nations Broadband Commission for Sustainable Development). 2019. *Con-necting Africa through Broadband: A Strategy for Doubling Connectivity by 2021 and Reaching Universal Access by 2030.* October. Geneva: Broadband Commission Working Group on Broadband for All, International Telecommu-nication Union. https://www.broadbandcommission.org/Documents/working-groups/DigitalMoonshotfor Africa_Report.pdf.

Broadband Commission (United Nations Broadband Com-mission for Sustainable Development). 2020. *The State of Broadband 2020: Tackling Digital Inequalities; A Decade for Action.* September. Geneva: International Telecommuni-cation Union. https://broadbandcommission.org/Pages/targets/Target-3.aspx.

Buckholtz, Alison. 2019. "Africa's IT Talent Pool." *IFC Insights* (blog), December 2019. https://www.ifc.org/wps/wcm/connect/news_ext_content/ifc_external_corporate_site/news+and+events/news/insights/africa-it-talent.

C&W (Cushman and Wakefield). 2016. "Data Centre Risk Index." C&W, London. https://verne-global-lackey.s3.amazonaws.com/uploads%2F2017%2F1%2Fb5e0a0da-5ad2-01b3-1eb8-8f782f22a534%2FC%26W_Data_Centre+Risk_Index_Report_2016.pdf.

Capitel. 2016. "Economics of Mobile Data in Frontier and Emerging Markets." Techno-Commercial Planning and Transaction Advisory in Telecoms, Media, and Technology, Capitel, Gurgaon, India; Singapore. https://capitelpartners.com/wp-content/uploads/2018/04/Capitel-Economics-of-mobile-data.pdf.

Chen, Rong. 2021. "A Demand-Side View of Mobile Internet Adoption in the Global South." Policy Research Work-ing Paper 9590, World Bank, Washington, DC. http://documents.worldbank.org/curated/en/492871616350929155/A-Demand-Side-View-of-Mobile-Internet-Adoption-in-the-Global-South.

Chen, Rong, and Michael Minges. 2021. "Minimum Data Consumption: How Much Is Needed to Support On-Line Activities, and Is It Affordable?" Digital Development: Analytical Insights, Note 3, World Bank, Washington, DC. http://pubdocs.worldbank.org/en/742001611762098567/Analytical-Insights-Series-Jan-2021.pdf.

Cisco. 2018. "Cisco Visual Networking Index: Forecast and Trends, 2017–2022." White Paper, November, Cisco Systems, San Jose, CA. https://cloud.report/Resources/Whitepapers/eea79d9b-9fe3-4018-86c6-3d1df813d3b8_white-paper-c11-741490.pdf.

Cisco. 2020. "Cisco Annual Internet Report (2018–2023)." White Paper, March, Cisco Systems, San Jose, CA. https://www.cisco.com/c/en/us/solutions/collateral/executive-perspectives/annual-internet-report/white-paper-c11-741490.html.

Comini, Niccolo, Sharada Srinivasan, and Michael Minges. Forthcoming. "The Role of a National Data Infrastruc-ture: Internet Exchange Points, Content Delivery Net-works, and Data Centers." WDR 2021 background paper, World Bank, Washington, DC.

Czernich, Nina, Oliver Falck, Tobias Kretschmer, and Ludger Woessmann. 2009. "Broadband Infrastructure and Eco-nomic Growth." CESifo Working Paper 2861 (December), Munich Society for the Promotion of Economic Research, Center for Economic Studies, Ludwig Maximilian Uni-versity and Ifo Institute for Economic Research, Munich. https://www.cesifo.org/DocDL/cesifo1_wp2861.pdf.

Czernich, Nina, Oliver Falck, Tobias Kretschmer, and Ludger Woessmann. 2011. "Broadband Infrastructure and Economic Growth." *Economic Journal* 121 (552): 505–32. doi:10.1111/j.1468-0297.2011.02420.x.

DE-CIX (Deutscher Commercial Internet Exchange). 2015. "DE-CIX: From the Interconnection of Three Internet Service Providers back in 1995 to the World's Leading Internet Exchange." DE-CIX Exchange, Frankfurt. https://www.de-cix.net/Files/d4167da7aafe0da34f384181606db6b8572cf2c1/DE-CIX_From-the-interconnection-of-three-ISP-to-the-worlds-leading-IX.pdf.

Dobran, Bojana. 2018. "Data Center Tier Classification Levels Explained (Tier 1, 2, 3, 4)." *PhoenixNAP* (blog), May 2, 2018. https://phoenixnap.com/blog/data-center-tiers-classification.

Ericsson. 2020. "Mobility Report." Ericsson, Stockholm. https://www.ericsson.com/4adc87/assets/local/mobility-report/documents/2020/november-2020-ericsson-mobility-report.pdf.

ESCAP (United Nations Economic and Social Commission for Asia and the Pacific). 2017. "The Impact of Universal Service Funds on Fixed-Broadband Deployment and Internet Adoption in Asia and the Pacific." Asia-Pacific Information Superhighway (AP-IS) Working Paper, ICT and Development Section, Information and Communications Technology and Disaster Risk Reduction Division, ESCAP, Bangkok, Thailand. https://www.unescap.org/sites/default/files/Universal%20Access%20and%20Service%20Funds.pdf.

EU-AITF (European Union–Africa Infrastructure Trust Fund). 2018. "EU–Africa Infrastructure Trust Fund: Annual Report 2017." European Investment Bank, Luxembourg. https://www.eib.org/attachments/country/eu_africa_infrastructure_trust_fund_annual_report_2017_en.pdf.

GSMA (GSM Association). 2013. *Universal Service Fund Study*. London: GSMA. https://www.gsma.com/publicpolicy/wp-content/uploads/2016/09/GSMA2013_Report_SurveyOfUniversalServiceFunds.pdf.

GSMA (GSM Association). 2017. *Connected Society: Mobile Internet Skills Training Toolkit; A Guide for Training People in Basic Mobile Internet Skills*. London: GSMA. https://www.gsma.com/mobilefordevelopment/connected-society/mistt/.

GSMA (GSM Association). 2019a. "Connected Society: Mobile Internet Skills Training Toolkit; Banglalink Pilot Evaluation." GSMA, London. https://www.gsma.com/mobilefordevelopment/resources/mobile-internet-skills-training-toolkit-banglalink-pilot-evaluation/.

GSMA (GSM Association). 2019b. "Connected Society: The State of Mobile Internet Connectivity 2019." GSMA, London. https://www.gsma.com/mobilefordevelopment/resources/the-state-of-mobile-internet-connectivity-report-2019/.

GSMA (GSM Association). 2019c. "GSMA Connected Society: Closing the Coverage Gap; How Innovation Can Drive Rural Connectivity." GSMA, London. https://www.gsma.com/mobilefordevelopment/wp-content/uploads/2019/07/GSMA-Closing-The-Coverage-Gap-How-Innovation-Can-Drive-Rural-Connectivity-Report-2019.pdf.

GSMA (GSM Association). 2019d. "Rethinking Mobile Taxation to Improve Connectivity." GSMA, London. https://www.gsma.com/publicpolicy/wp-content/uploads/2019/02/Rethinking-mobile-taxation-to-improve-connectivity_Feb19.pdf.

GSMA (GSM Association). 2020. "Connected Women: The Mobile Gender Gap Report 2020." GSMA, London. https://www.gsma.com/mobilefordevelopment/wp-content/uploads/2020/05/GSMA-The-Mobile-Gender-Gap-Report-2020.pdf.

Hjort, Jonas, and Jonas Poulsen. 2019. "The Arrival of Fast Internet and Employment in Africa." *American Economic Review* 109 (3): 1032–79.

IDC (International Data Corporation). 2019. "Worldwide Public Cloud Services Revenue Grows to Nearly $183 Billion in 2018, Led by the Top 5 Service Providers and Accelerating Public Cloud Services Spending in China." IDC, Framingham, MA. https://www.idc.com/getdoc.jsp?containerId=prUS45411519.

Intelecom Research and Consultancy. 2016. "ICT Access Gaps Study: Final Report." Communications Authority of Kenya, Nairobi. https://ca.go.ke/wp-content/uploads/2018/02/ICT-Access-Gaps-Report-April-2016-.pdf.

Internet Society. 2015. "Local Content: An Internet Society Public Policy Briefing." *Public Policy*, Internet Society, Reston, VA. https://www.internetsociety.org/policybriefs/localcontent/.

Internet Society. 2017. "The Benefits of Local Content Hosting: A Case Study." Internet Society, Reston, VA. https://www.internetsociety.org/wp-content/uploads/2017/08/ISOC_LocalContentRwanda_report_20170505.pdf.

Iridium Communications. 2020. *2019 Annual Report: Reliability Above All*. McLean, VA: Iridium Communications. https://investor.iridium.com/annual-reports.

ITU (International Telecommunication Union). 2018a. *ICTs, LDCs, and the SDGs: Achieving Universal and Affordable Internet in the Least Developed Countries*. Thematic Report: ITU Development, LDCs and Small Island Developing States Series. Geneva: ITU. https://www.itu.int/en/ITU-D/LDCs/Pages/Publications/LDCs/D-LDC-ICTLDC-2018-PDF-E.pdf.

ITU (International Telecommunication Union). 2018b. "ITU's Approach to Bridging the Digital Gender Divide." *ITU News*, October 22, 2018. https://www.itu.int/es/myitu/News/2020/05/22/11/16/ITU-s-approach-to-bridging-the-digital-gender-divide.

ITU (International Telecommunication Union). 2018c. *Report on the WSIS Stocktaking 2018*. Geneva: ITU.

Kapko, Matt. 2020. "Rakuten Mobile Delivers Its Virtualized Reality." *SDxCentral News*, April 8, 2020. https://www.sdxcentral.com/articles/news/rakuten-mobile-delivers-its-virtualized-reality/2020/04/.

Katz, Raul, and Fernando Callorda. 2018. "The Economic Contribution of Broadband, Digitization, and ICT Regulation." Thematic Report: Regulatory and Market Environment Series, International Telecommunication Union, Geneva. https://www.itu.int/pub/D-PREF-EF.BDR-2018.

Keane, Tom. 2019. "Microsoft Opens First Datacenters in Africa with General Availability of Microsoft Azure." *Microsoft Azure Announcements* (blog), March 6, 2019. https://azure.microsoft.com/en-us/blog/microsoft-opens

-first-datacenters-in-africa-with-general-availability-of
-microsoft-azure/.

Koutroumpis, Pantelis. 2018. "The Economic Impact of Broadband: Evidence from OECD Countries." Ofcom, London. https://www.ofcom.org.uk/__data/assets/pdf _file/0025/113299/economic-broadband-oecd-countries .pdf.

Law, Nancy, David Woo, Jimmy de la Torre, and Gary Wong. 2018. *A Global Framework of Reference on Digital Literacy Skills for Indicator 4.4.2.* Information Paper 51, UIS/2018/ICT/IP/51. Montreal: Institute for Statistics, United Nations Educational, Scientific, and Cultural Organization. http://uis.unesco.org/sites/default/files /documents/ip51-global-framework-reference-digital -literacy-skills-2018-en.pdf.

Loon. 2020. "The Stratosphere." Loon, Mountain View, CA. https://loon.com/static/pdfs/Stratosphere_Whitepaper _May1.pdf.

Madden, Gary. 2010. "Economic Welfare and Universal Service." *Telecommunications Policy* 34 (1–2): 110–16. https://www.sciencedirect.com/science/article/abs/pii /S0308596109001141.

Malisuwan, Settapong, Noppadol Tiamnara, and Nattakit Suriyakrai. 2015. "A Post-Auction Review of 2.1 GHz Spectrum Licensing Obligations in Thailand." *International Journal of Innovation, Management, and Technology* 6 (4): 285–89. https://doi.org/10.7763/IJIMT.2015.V6.616.

Manulis, Mark, Chris P. Bridges, Richard Harrison, Venkkatesh Sekar, and Andy Davis. 2020. "Cyber Security in New Space: Analysis of Threats, Key Enabling Technologies, and Challenges." *International Journal of Information Security.* Published ahead of print, May 12, 2020. https:// link.springer.com/article/10.1007/s10207-020-00503-w.

Michie, Jonathan. 1997. "Network Externalities: The Economics of Universal Access." *Utilities Policy* 6 (4): 317–24. http://www.sciencedirect.com/science/article/pii/S095 717879700026X.

Miller, Jayne. 2019. "This Is What Our 2019 Submarine Cable Map Shows Us about Content Provider Cables." *TeleGeography* (blog), March 19, 2019. https://blog.tele geography.com/this-is-what-our-2019-submarine-cable -map-shows-us-about-content-provider-cables.

Minges, Michael. 2015. "Exploring the Relationship between Broadband and Economic Growth." Background paper, *World Development Report 2016: Digital Dividends,* World Bank, Washington, DC. http://documents.worldbank.org /curated/en/178701467988875888/Exploring-the-relation ship-between-broadband-and-economic-growth.

Monash University. 2020. "World's Fastest Internet Speed from a Single Optical Chip." *ScienceDaily,* May 22, 2020. https://www.sciencedaily.com/releases/2020/05/2005 22095504.htm.

MTN. 2020. "#Good Together: Sustainability Report for the Year Ended 31 December 2019." March 31, 2020, MTN Group, Johannesburg, South Africa. https://www.mtn .com/wp-content/uploads/2020/03/MTN-Sustainability -report.pdf.

New China. 2018. "Chinese Phone Maker Celebrates 100-Mln-USD Export Milestone in Ethiopia." *New China,* November 21, 2018. http://www.xinhuanet.com/english/2018-11 /21/c_137622555.htm.

Oughton, Edward, Zoraida Frias, Tom Russell, Douglas Sicker, and David D. Cleevely. 2018. Towards 5G: Scenario-Based Assessment of the Future Supply and Demand for Mobile Telecommunications Infrastructure." *Technological Forecasting and Social Change* 133 (August): 141–55. https://doi.org/10.1016/j.techfore.2018 .03.016.

Radovanović, Danica, Christine Holst, Sarbani Banerjee Belur, Ritu Srivastava, Georges Vivien Houngbonon, Erwan Le Quentrec, Josephine Miliza, Andrea S. Winkler, and Josef Noll. 2020. "Digital Literacy Key Performance Indicators for Sustainable Development." *Social Inclusion* 8 (2): 151–67. https://doi.org/10.17645/si.v8i2.2587.

RURA (Rwanda Utilities Regulatory Authority). 2019. "Statistics Report for Telecom, Media, and Broadcasting Sector as of the Fourth Quarter of the Year 2019." ICT Quarterly Statistics Report, RURA, Kigali, Rwanda. https://rura.rw /fileadmin/Documents/ICT/statistics/ICT_Quarterly _Statistics_report_as_of_December_2019.pdf.

Sandvine. 2019. "The Global Internet Phenomena Report." Sandvine, Fremont, CA. https://www.sandvine.com/hubfs /Sandvine_Redesign_2019/Downloads/Internet%20 Phenomena/Internet%20Phenomena%20Report%20 Q32019%2020190910.pdf.

Sanni, Shola. 2016. "How to Implement Spectrum Re-Farming." GSM Association, London. https://www.gsma .com/spectrum/wp-content/uploads/2017/11/10-Day-2 -Session-3-How-to-Implement-Spectrum-Refarming -Shola-Sanni.pdf.

Shapiro, Robert J., and Kevin A. Hassett. 2012. "The Employment Effects of Advances in Internet and Wireless Technology: Evaluating the Transitions from 2G to 3G and from 3G to 4G." NDN and New Policy Institute, Washington, DC. http://www.sonecon.com/docs/studies /Wireless_Technology_and_Jobs-Shapiro_Hassett -January_2012.pdf.

Silver, Laura, and Aaron Smith. 2019. "In Some Countries, Many Use the Internet without Realizing It." *Fact Tank, News in the Numbers* (blog), May 2, 2019. https://www .pewresearch.org/fact-tank/2019/05/02/in-some -countries-many-use-the-internet-without-realizing-it/.

Silver, Laura, Emily A. Vogels, Mara Mordecai, Jeremiah Cha, Raea Rasmussen, and Lee Rainie. 2019. "Mobile Divides in Emerging Countries." *Internet & Technology* (blog), November 20, 2019. https://www.pewresearch .org/internet/2019/11/20/mobile-divides-in-emerging -economies/.

Smart Axiata. 2019. "Sweating Assets to Drive Down Cost/ GB." Slide presentation at "Axiata Analyst & Investor Day," Smart Axiata, Phnom Penh, Cambodia. https:// axiata.listedcompany.com/misc/6c_Operational _Excellence_in_Action-Smart.pdf.

Sonia, Jorge. 2020. "Covid-19 Shows We Need More Than Basic Internet Access: We Need Meaningful Connectivity." Alliance for Affordable Internet, Washington, DC. https://a4ai.org/covid-19-shows-we-need-more-than -basic-internet-access-we-need-meaningful-connectivity/.

Strusani, Davide, and Georges Vivien Houngbonon. 2020. "Accelerating Digital Connectivity through Infrastructure Sharing." EMCompass Note 79, International Finance Corporation, Washington, DC. https://www.ifc

.org/wps/wcm/connect/Publications_EXT_Content/IFC
_External_Publication_Site/Publications_Listing_Page
/EMCompass-Note-79-Digital-Infrastructure-Sharing.

TRAI (Telecom Regulatory Authority of India). 2019. "Wire-
less Data Services in India: An Analytical Report." TRAI,
New Delhi. https://trai.gov.in/sites/default/files/Wireless
_Data_Service_Report_21082019.pdf.

Tsolmondelger, Odkhuu. 2019. "ICT Infrastructure along
Transport Network." Presentation, November 20, 2019,
Information Communications Network LLC, Ulaan-
baatar, Mongolia. https://www.unescap.org/sites/default
/files/ICT%20Infrastructure%20Along%20Transport%20
Network%2C%20Mongolia%20NetCom.pdf.

UNCTAD (United Nations Conference on Trade and
Development). 2013. *Information Economy Report 2013:
The Cloud Economy and Developing Countries.* Geneva:
United Nations. https://unctad.org/system/files/official
-document/ier2013_en.pdf.

UN-OHRLLS (Office of the High Representative for the Least
Developed Countries, Landlocked Developing Countries,
and Small Island Developing States). 2017. "Leveraging
Investments in Broadband for National Development:
The Case of Rwanda and Senegal." UN-OHRLLS, United
Nations, New York. https://unohrlls.org/custom-content
/uploads/2017/07/Leveraging-Investments-in-Broadband
-for-National-Development-2017.pdf.

van der Marel, Erik. 2020. "Sources of Comparative Advan-
tage in Data-Related Services." Working Paper EUI
RSCAS 2020/30, Robert Schuman Center for Advanced
Studies, Global Governance Programme-393, European
University Institute, San Domenico di Fiesole (FI), Italy.
http://hdl.handle.net/1814/66987.

World Bank. 2016. *World Development Report 2016: Digital
Dividends.* Washington, DC: World Bank. https://www
.worldbank.org/en/publication/wdr2016.

World Bank. 2019a. "Implementation Completion and
Results Report, Tonga: Pacific Regional Connectivity
Program." Report No. ICR00004623, World Bank, Wash-
ington, DC. http://documents.worldbank.org/curated
/en/844361556573010769/Tonga-Pacific-Regional
-Connectivity-Program-Project.

World Bank. 2019b. *Information and Communications for
Development 2018: Data-Driven Development.* Washington,
DC: World Bank. https://openknowledge.worldbank.org
/handle/10986/30437.

World Bank. 2019c. *Innovative Business Models for Expanding
Fiber-Optic Networks and Closing the Access Gaps.* Washington, DC: Digital Development Partnership, World
Bank. https://documents.worldbank.org/en/publication
/documents-reports/documentdetail/674601544534500
678/main-report.

World Wide Web Foundation and A4AI (Alliance for Affordable Internet). 2018. "Universal Service and Access
Funds: An Untapped Resource to Close the Gender
Digital Divide." World Wide Web Foundation, Washington, DC. https://webfoundation.org/research/closing
-gender-digital-divide-in-africa.

Zhu, Tingting Juni, Alan Fritzler, and Jan Alexander Kaz-
imierz Orlowski. 2018. "World Bank Group–LinkedIn
Data Insights: Jobs, Skills, and Migration Trends; Methodology and Validation Results." World Bank, Washington, DC. https://datacatalog.worldbank.org/dataset
/world-bank-group-linkedin-digital-data-development
/resource/b16c3403-2d59-45ca-bc31.

Spotlight 5.1

How the COVID-19 pandemic has recalibrated expectations of reasonable data consumption and highlighted the digital divide

Massive increases in data traffic herald greater use of online platforms and underscore the importance of including currently excluded users.

Around the world, the COVID-19 pandemic has resulted in millions of people using videoconferencing for working and learning from home and other activities. The three main platforms reported around 700 million daily users in March–April 2020. Adding in other platforms, the number of users was equal to roughly one-tenth of the world's population. Zoom's average number of users jumped from 10 million in December 2019 to 300 million in April 2020.[1] Cisco's Webex recorded 324 million users in March 2020, doubling from January 2020.[2] Microsoft Teams had 75 million daily users in April 2020.[3] Being homebound also resulted in more use of social media, video streaming, and online gaming.[4]

These online activities have driven massive increases in data traffic. In Spain, internet traffic increased 40 percent in the week following the shutdown, while mobile data traffic rose 25 percent.[5] The German internet exchange DE-CIX, one of the world's largest, recorded a 10 percent increase in traffic during the first two weeks in March, when shelter-at-home was implemented in the country, breaking the world record for data throughput. Videoconferencing traffic on DE-CIX rose 50 percent, and gaming and social media traffic grew 25 percent.[6]

For the most part, telecommunications networks have stood up well to this massive increase in traffic. Networks are engineered to handle peak traffic, resulting in large parts of the day where capacity is more than sufficient. Similar to flattening the curve

for COVID-19, telecommunications operators worked to smooth fluctuations in traffic flows during the height of the pandemic in spring 2020. Widespread deployment of high-capacity fiber-optic backbone and access networks has proved vital for dealing with the surge in traffic. During COVID-19, regulators have increased mobile data capacity by releasing spectrum,[7] and streaming video services have reduced traffic 25 percent by using compression technology.[8] Some telecommunications operators have increased their data allowances, and some have provided free data and smartphones to health workers.

Telecommunication networks have thus far proved up to the task in the new social distancing world for those who already have access, but limitations have prevented the transition of vital public services, such as education, to the online space, with major repercussions for schooling. Many predict that videoconferencing will continue to be used more after the pandemic, though not at the same high level.

The ability to use Web conferencing tools has shone a spotlight on the digital divide. Many students around the world have been excluded from online learning because they lack broadband access and computers. Concerns about security surround video conferencing[9] and data privacy for big data analytics used during the pandemic.[10] Telecommunication companies have also been criticized for waiting for a crisis to offer pro-consumer data allowances.

Notes

1. Zoom (2020).
2. Mukherjee (2020).
3. Spencer, Nadella, and Hood (2020).
4. Sandvine (2020).
5. See Telefónica (2020).
6. DE-CIX (2020).
7. GSMA (2020).
8. Florance (2020).
9. Paul (2020).
10. OECD (2020).

References

DE-CIX (Deutscher Commercial Internet Exchange). 2020. "Internet Exchange Operator DE-CIX Sees a Strong Change in Internet User Behavior." Press Release, March 18, 2020. https://www.de-cix.net/en/about-de-cix/media-center/press-releases/internet-exchange-operator-de-cix-sees-a-strong-change-in-internet-user-behavior.

Florance, Ken. 2020. "Reducing Netflix Traffic Where It's Needed While Maintaining the Member Experience." *Innovation* (blog), March 21, 2020. https://about.netflix.com/en/news/reducing-netflix-traffic-where-its-needed.

GSMA (GSM Association). 2020. "Keeping Everyone and Everything Connected: How Temporary Access to Spectrum Can Ease Congestion during the COVID-19 Crisis." *Newsroom* (blog), March 31, 2020. https://www.gsma.com/newsroom/blog/keeping-everyone-and-everything-connected-how-temporary-access-to-spectrum-can-ease-congestion-during-the-covid-19-crisis/.

Mukherjee, Supantha. 2020. "Cisco's Webex Draws Record 324 Million Users in March." *Technology News* (blog), April 3, 2020. https://www.reuters.com/article/us-cisco-systems-webex-idUSKBN21L2SY.

OECD (Organisation for Economic Co-operation and Development). 2020. "Tracking and Tracing COVID: Protecting Privacy and Data while Using Apps and Biometrics." OECD Policy Responses to Coronavirus (COVID-19), OECD, Paris. https://read.oecd-ilibrary.org/view/?ref=129_129655-7db0lu7dto&title=Tracking-and-Tracing-COVID-Protecting-privacy-and-data-while-using.

Paul, Kari. 2020. "Zoom Releases Security Updates in Response to 'Zoom-Bombings.'" *Guardian*, April 23, 2020. http://www.theguardian.com/technology/2020/apr/23/zoom-update-security-encryption-bombing.

Sandvine. 2020. "The Global Internet Phenomena Report: COVID-19 Spotlight." Sandvine, Fremont, CA. https://www.sandvine.com/phenomena.

Spencer, Michael, Satya Nadella, and Amy Hood. 2020. "Microsoft Fiscal Year 2020 Third Quarter Earnings Conference Call." Microsoft, Redmond, WA, April 29, 2020. https://www.microsoft.com/en-us/Investor/events/FY-2020/earnings-fy-2020-q3.aspx.

Telefónica. 2020. "Operators Advise a Rational and Responsible Use of Telecommunication Networks to Cope with Traffic Increases." News Release, March 15, 2020. https://www.telefonica.com/documents/737979/145808680/pr-usoresponsable-redes.pdf/874e69ed-a201-92b3-4d54-60de558d0084?version=1.0.

Zoom. 2020. "Zoom: Annual Report, Fiscal 2020." Zoom Video Communications, San Jose, CA. https://investors.zoom.us/static-files/28614884-1d63-477a-9148-a7039796f19c.

Spotlight 5.2
Data's carbon footprint

Data infrastructure is becoming increasingly energy efficient and turning to renewable sources of energy. Increased use of information and communication technology solutions such as videoconferencing could help to reduce global carbon dioxide emissions by one-fifth by 2030.

Data infrastructure consumes significant amounts of energy, with environmental consequences, including global warming. Electricity consumption for data infrastructure amounted to 1 percent of the global total in 2018 (231 terawatt-hours) (figure S5.2.1, panel a). Although data traffic grew 100 percent from 2015 to 2018, associated electricity consumption rose just 16 percent, and its share of total global consumption remains constant. Huge gains in energy

efficiency have made this possible. One reason is a shift from smaller data centers to more efficient larger ones, particularly among some of the bigger players in China, Japan, and the United States. Modernization of telecommunication networks is also contributing. Fiber-optic cable is 85 percent more energy efficient than vintage copper wires, while each successive generation of wireless technology conserves more energy than the previous one. For

Figure S5.2.1 Worldwide greenhouse gas emissions from data consumption have been flat, even though electricity consumption has been growing

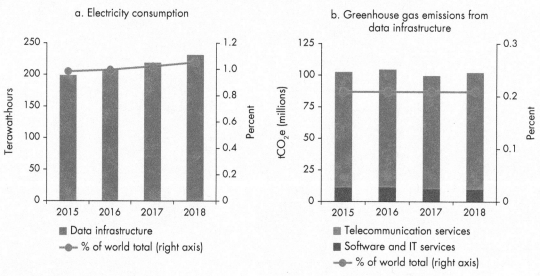

Source: World Bank, original research based on annual reports from 49 companies in 26 countries. Data at http://bit.do/WDR2021-Fig-S5_2_1.

Note: Data were derived from environmental reports of companies accounting for 90 percent of data traffic. IT = information technology; tCO_2e= tonnes of carbon dioxide equivalent.

example, 4G can be more than 50 times more energy efficient than 2G.[1]

Despite rising electricity consumption, greenhouse gas (GHG) emissions from data infrastructure have been flat since 2015, equivalent to 0.2 percent of the global total (see figure S5.2.1, panel b). This is due to the rising share of renewables in the electricity mix used by data centers.[2] For example, Equinix, one of the world's leading data center operators, increased its share of renewable energy from less than one-third in 2014 to 92 percent in 2018, leading to a two-thirds reduction in GHG emissions.[3] Moreover, the tech giants—Apple, Google, and Microsoft—have switched to 100 percent renewable energy, while completely offsetting their GHG emissions. Apple generates more than 600 megawatt-hours of its own energy through one of the largest investments in renewables outside of utility companies,[4] while Google is the world's largest nonutility buyer of renewable energy. Digital companies already account for one-quarter of the world's renewable energy purchases,[5] and they are encouraging their downstream suppliers to follow suit.[6]

Access to renewable energy is becoming an important factor in deciding where to expand data infrastructure for dozens of major investors. For example, Equinix seeks markets with favorable renewable energy policies when deciding on the location of new data centers.[7] Foreign operators are developing renewable energy projects in low- and middle-income nations. For example, Vodafone Group is constructing a utility-scale solar park in the Arab Republic of Egypt.[8]

Data infrastructure is also playing a significant role in reducing emissions, as demonstrated by the COVID-19 outbreak. The massive use of video conferencing, fueled by the pandemic, has greatly reduced fuel consumption associated with travel—potentially on a permanent basis.[9] Increased use of information and communication technology (ICT) solutions could lead to a 20 percent reduction in global carbon dioxide (CO_2) emissions by 2030.[10] This reduction is almost 10 times greater than the ICT sector's own footprint during the same period and translates into as much potential emissions reduction as the mobility, manufacturing, agriculture, building, and energy sectors combined.

Notes

1. IEA (2020).
2. There are, nonetheless, some subtleties of environmental accounting. Direct emissions from electricity are reported on either a market basis or a location basis (Equinix 2019). Market basis reflects the emissions from the electricity that a company is purchasing, which may differ from the electricity that the company is using at its location. Location-based emissions are higher, yet most companies report market-based emissions.
3. Equinix (2019).
4. Apple (2019).
5. Ambrose (2020).
6. In 2018 Apple announced that 23 of its suppliers had committed to 100 percent clean energy (Apple 2018).
7. Nareit (2019).
8. Vodafone (2019).
9. Darrow (2020).
10. GeSI (2015).

References

Ambrose, Jillian. 2020. "Tech Giants Power Record Surge in Renewable Energy Sales." *Guardian*, January 28, 2020. https://www.theguardian.com/environment/2020/jan/28/google-tech-giants-spark-record-rise-in-sales-of-renewable-energy.

Apple. 2018. "Apple Now Globally Powered by 100 Percent Renewable Energy." Press Release, April 9, 2018. https://www.apple.com/newsroom/2018/04/apple-now-globally-powered-by-100-percent-renewable-energy/.

Apple. 2019. "2019 Environmental Responsibility Report." Apple Inc., Cupertino, CA, April 2019. https://www.apple.com/environment/pdf/Apple_Environmental_Responsibility_Report_2019.pdf.

Darrow, Barb. 2020. "Zoom Taps Oracle to Keep Schools Teaching, Businesses Running, Friends and Family Connected." *Oracle News Connect* (blog), April 28, 2020. https://www.oracle.com/corporate/blog/zoom-selects-oracle-042820.html.

Equinix. 2019. "2018 Corporate Sustainability Report: Connecting with Purpose." Equinix, Redwood City, CA. https://sustainability.equinix.com/wp-content/uploads/2019/12/Sustainability-Report-2018.pdf.

GeSI (Global e-Sustainability Initiative). 2015. #SMARTer2030: *ICT Solutions for 21st Century Challenges*. Brussels: Global e-Sustainability Initiative. http://smarter2030.gesi.org/downloads/Full_report.pdf.

IEA (International Energy Agency). 2020. "Data Centres and Data Transmission Networks." Tracking Report, IEA, Paris, June 2020. https://www.iea.org/reports/data-centres-and-data-transmission-networks.

Nareit. 2019. "REIT Industry ESG Report." Nareit, Washington, DC, June 2019. https://www.reit.com/sites/default/files/media/PDFs/Research/Nareit2019_Sustainability Report_webv3.pdf.

Vodafone. 2019. "Sustainable Business Report 2019." Vodafone Group Plc, Newbury, UK. https://www.vodafone.com/content/dam/vodcom/sustainability/pdfs/sustainable business2019.pdf.

Data policies, laws, and regulations: Creating a trust environment

Main messages

1. Trust in data transactions is sustained by a robust legal and regulatory framework encompassing both *safeguards*, which prevent the misuse of data, and *enablers*, which facilitate access to and reuse of data.

2. Safeguards must differentiate between *personal data*, requiring a rights-based approach with individual protection, and *nonpersonal data*, allowing a balancing of interests in data reuse.

3. Enablers for data sharing are typically more developed for *public intent data*, where public policy and law mandating data access and sharing are more readily established, than for *private intent data*, where governments have more limited influence.

4. Creation of a trust environment remains a work in progress worldwide, especially in low-income countries. There is no one-size-fits-all legal and regulatory framework. In countries with weak regulatory environments, the design of suitable safeguards and enablers may have to be carefully adapted to local priorities and capacities.

A trust framework of data safeguards and enablers

With the growing recognition of the use, misuse, and underuse of data, responsible governance of data has gained importance, resulting in new global legal and regulatory standards. This movement was propelled by the revelations in 2013 by US whistleblower Edward Snowden of global surveillance by Western democracies,[1] followed by the Cambridge Analytica scandal in 2018.[2] In response, countries enacted major policies to protect data. A series of epochal rulings by India's Supreme Court identified a constitutional right to privacy, and the country is now considering new data protection legislation. In the European Union (EU), its General Data Protection Regulation (GDPR) came into force in 2018 with its application beyond the EU's borders,[3] and it inspired similar legislation in other jurisdictions, such as the US state of California.[4] China implemented its Personal Information Standard in 2018, promulgated its Civil Code in 2020, and introduced a new draft Personal Data Protection Law for public consultation in 2020.[5] Despite these important advances regarding personal data, legal frameworks for data governance across much of the developing world remain a patchwork, raising concerns about the ability of lower-income countries to benefit from the development opportunities emerging from the burgeoning global data economy.

This greater attention to the use and reuse of personal data is part of an evolving social contract around data, which remains under negotiation across the globe (see spotlight 6.1 for an example of how COVID-19 is creating new challenges for using data while protecting rights). With a view toward informing this process, this chapter lays out the legal mechanisms that enable trusted and trustworthy domestic and cross-border data transactions for the use and reuse of both personal and nonpersonal data. Whether the focus is on the collection, use, transfer, or processing of data between businesses, or among citizens, businesses, and governments, each of these interactions is a data transaction with the potential to create value—as long as both parties trust the overall process sufficiently. However, a variety of factors can undermine trust. These may include the absence, weakness, or uneven application of the legal framework; weak institutions and law enforcement or lack of effective ways for parties to enforce their rights; practices that unfairly benefit certain actors; skewed or lopsided incentives (see chapter 8); and poor or insecure infrastructure (see chapter 5).

From a normative perspective, trust is a function of both "hard law" and "soft law." *Hard law* includes domestic, regional, and international law, as well as case law and statutory law that originate from tort, contract, and competition law. Some of the issues embedded in domestic law have their origins in well-hewn and commonly agreed standards derived from international law, conventions, and treaties. Emerging applications of trust law and competition law may also play a valuable role in strengthening the normative framework for data.

Whereas *hard law* is shaped by state actors, *soft law* includes standards, terms and conditions of use, norms, and codes of conduct and other voluntary frameworks used by nonstate actors, including industry participants and civil society (see chapter 8). These soft law elements can play an equally valuable role in governing data use according to needs and cultural specificity.[6]

A central claim of this Report is that use of data for development purposes requires a legal framework for data governance that includes both safeguards and enablers. *Safeguards* generally refers to those norms and legal frameworks that ensure and promote trust in the data governance and data management ecosystem by avoiding and limiting harm arising from the misuse of data or breaches affecting their security and integrity. *Enablers* generally refers to those policies, laws, regulations, and standards that facilitate the use, reuse, and sharing of data within and between stakeholder groups through openness, interoperability, and portability. Whereas the approach to safeguards differs markedly for personal and nonpersonal data, a common set of enablers is relevant to both categories.

For the collection and processing of *personal data*, this Report proposes a rights-based approach, whereby access to personal data must first be adequately safeguarded before enabling use and reuse. This two-step process helps to rebalance power asymmetries between data holders/subjects and data controllers/users that can undermine trust. For the purposes of this chapter, personal data include not only data directly provided by an individual, but also personally identifiable information and machine-generated information that can readily be linked to an individual (such as mobile phone data).[7]

For *nonpersonal data*, this Report advocates a balance of interests approach to safeguards and enablers, recognizing that trade-offs typically arise between increasing data access and safeguarding intellectual property rights (IPRs) over nonpersonal data. The focus is thus on a legal framework that enables the (re)use and sharing of data through regulatory predictability, data openness, and portability (the ability to readily transfer data from one service to another based on clear legal and technical standards). Of growing importance are data that blend both personal and nonpersonal sources—so-called mixed data.

The creation, collection, and use or processing of personal and nonpersonal data by public or private sector entities in both domestic and cross-border contexts interact in a dynamic way in a three-dimensional legal/regulatory space in which different elements of the legal framework apply (see figure 6.1). The underlying type of data does not necessarily determine how the data might be treated legally across the data value chain; that depends on how such data are used or processed. For example, data that may start off as public sector and personal data (such as household survey, health, or geolocation data) may end up as private sector and nonpersonal data (when integrated as part of a proprietary algorithm and perfectly deidentified). Similarly, data that start out as private data may end up in the public domain if published as open data or shared with government under a data sharing agreement. These dynamic shifts in data uses may change the legal treatment of that data accordingly.

The trust framework encompassing safeguards and enablers is underpinned by rule of law and good governance principles. These include certainty, transparency, accountability, nondiscrimination, fairness, inclusiveness, and openness. They are subject to due process limitations such as necessity and proportionality. Transparency, accountability, and certainty in rulemaking can be reinforced by ensuring that laws and regulations are developed according to good regulatory practices. These include supporting consultative rulemaking[8] and ensuring that regulations are based on evidence, with stakeholder impacts and spillover effects fully considered through regulatory impact analysis.[9] In addition, recent developments in regulatory design have included efforts to adapt regulations to the digital age. Mechanisms such as regulatory sandboxes and laboratories help make regulations more agile and readily adaptable to evolving circumstances. By drafting principle-based and technologically neutral laws and regulations, policy makers help them remain relevant as technologies evolve and reduce compliance burdens.

To capture the current robustness and completeness of normative frameworks for data governance around the world, the chapter draws on a new Global Data Regulation Survey conducted exclusively for

Figure 6.1 Envisioning the multidimensional nature of the legal framework for trust

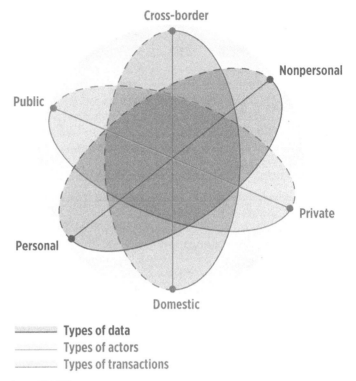

	Types of data
	Types of actors
	Types of transactions

Source: WDR 2021 team.

this Report.[10] It collected information on attributes of the regulatory framework in 80 countries (covering 80 percent of the world's population) selected from global regions and country income groups across the development spectrum. The survey entails a detailed assessment of domestic laws, regulations, and administrative requirements, reflecting the regulatory status of each country as of June 1, 2020. Survey results are summarized in a variety of subindexes that capture different aspects of the regulatory environment for safeguards and enablers.

This chapter focuses squarely on the legal dimension of data governance. Chapter 7 then examines the resulting economic trade-offs, and chapters 8 and 9 discuss the design of institutional ecosystems to support implementation and enforcement.

Building safeguards for trusted data use

The term *safeguards* refers to the trust environment around the collection and use of data. It includes supporting individuals' agency—that is, their ability to exercise control—over how their personal data are used, through mechanisms such as consent, rights of use of data, and regimes that allow reuse of data for "legitimate purposes" without express consent. Safeguards also encompass how data are secured and accessed, covering the obligations of those who collect, process, or use data to take precautions to ensure the integrity of the data and protect data rights, including intellectual property rights and other limitations on the use of nonpersonal data (see figure 6.1).

Safeguards are analyzed primarily according to whether they are related to personal data, nonpersonal data, or mixed data. The degree of sensitivity of these types of data differs markedly, leading to various legal approaches.

Safeguards for personal data, nonpersonal data, and mixed data

Safeguards for personal data are grounded in a rights-based framework that has evolved over time (see figure 6.2). These safeguards have their origin in the establishment of the "rule of law" in conjunction with the expression of individual rights in the Enlightenment and were codified in international law after

World War II. They were further refined in the context of analog data in the 1970s and 1980s with the Fair Information Practices, the Council of Europe's Convention 108 for the Protection of Individuals with regard to Automatic Processing of Personal Data,[11] and the first guidelines issued by the Organisation for Economic Co-operation and Development (OECD). Safeguards must necessarily adapt to technological change and will continue to evolve accordingly. For example, the OECD guidelines were updated after the launch in 1995 of the World Wide Web, and Convention 108 was updated to Convention 108+ in response to the entry into force of the GDPR.

Safeguards for nonpersonal data entail a more straightforward balancing of economic incentives and interests, grounded in IPRs as typically enshrined in domestic law.

For datasets containing mixed data, it is the responsibility of the data processing entity to ensure that personal data are protected. This compliance challenge has become more acute in recent years because source data and collection methods have evolved and

Figure 6.2 The evolution of data protection

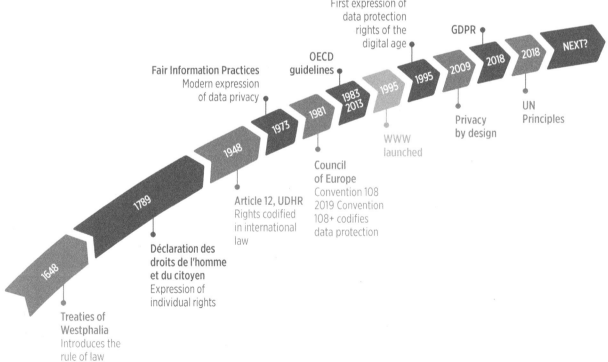

Source: WDR 2021 team.

Note: This figure shows a clear arc from historical concepts of rights governing interactions between the state and the individual (and between states) to principles guiding data protection. EU = European Union; GDPR = General Data Protection Regulation; OECD = Organisation for Economic Co-operation and Development; UDHR = Universal Declaration of Human Rights; UN = United Nations; WWW = World Wide Web.

blurred the distinction between the traditional legal definitions of personal and nonpersonal data.

The Global Data Regulation Survey conducted for this Report provides an overview of the extent to which good-practice data safeguards have been adopted. Across the 80 countries surveyed, about 40 percent of the elements of good-practice regulatory safeguards are in place. Although scores range considerably, from less than 35 percent in low-income countries to more than 50 percent in high-income countries, the results highlight that even among the latter the regulatory framework is far from complete. Of the high-income countries included in the survey, Australia, the United Kingdom, and Uruguay stand out as those with the most advanced safeguards. Among the strongest middle-income countries are Colombia, Moldova, and Nigeria. Other low- and middle-income nations that have endeavored to develop safeguard regulatory frameworks are Benin, Mexico, and Turkey. Mauritius, a standout among its middle-income peers, performs well on most safeguard measures. It has deliberately designed and implemented policies based on best practices and has distinguished itself as one of the first Sub-Saharan African countries to ratify Convention 108+. In Latin America, Uruguay is one of two countries to have received an adequacy determination from the European Commission.

Overarching safeguards for cybersecurity and cybercrime

A key element in establishing trust in the data ecosystem for both personal and nonpersonal data is ensuring the security of the network infrastructure and elements over which data flow.

Cybercrime laws effectively give teeth to cybersecurity policies. Although there is no universally accepted definition of cybercrime, the concept encompasses both a narrow view—criminal activities targeting information and communication technologies (ICT) and software—and a broader view—traditional crimes committed in cyberspace.[12] In practice, the scope of cybercrime is typically understood to include unauthorized access to a computer system (sometimes called hacking), unauthorized monitoring, data alteration or deletion, system interference, theft of computer content, misuse of devices, and offenses related to computer content and function.[13]

Cybercrime knows no borders. The crime can be committed from any computer, no matter where, connected to the internet or from a public or private entity that relies on ICT systems. Similarly, the impact of the crime can be felt anywhere, even outside the jurisdiction where the cybercriminal is physically located. Thus to be truly effective, a cybercrime law needs to extend beyond dealing with criminal activity within a subnational or national jurisdiction and become a tool to maximize cross-border cooperation.[14] This requirement entails the legal notion of dual criminality, which establishes that a criminal activity in one jurisdiction is also a criminal activity in another.[15] It also demands practical collaboration, usually achieved through mutual legal assistance treaties (MLATs).

Countries enter into MLATs either through bilateral treaties with other countries or by adhering to an instrument that features a built-in MLAT process, such as the Council of Europe's Budapest Convention of 2001. The main legal instrument for cybersecurity in Europe and beyond, this convention provides for balancing security interests with respect for human rights.[16] Sixty-five countries have acceded to the convention, with an additional 12 states participating as observers.[17] Of the members and observers, 26 countries are lower-middle-income. Recently, some governments have been sidestepping the MLAT process by making requests for evidence directly to foreign law enforcement agencies and allowing them to do likewise. In this vein, the United States adopted the Clarifying Lawful Overseas Use of Data (CLOUD) Act of 2018, which authorizes the US government to enter into bilateral agreements with foreign governments, allowing the parties to remove any legal barriers that would prevent the other party from seeking and obtaining data directly from the service providers in the other country under certain circumstances.[18] This has attracted comment for potentially sidestepping legal protections for personal data.[19] The European Union is considering a draft regulation with similar provisions.[20]

Cybersecurity encompasses the data protection requirements for the technical systems used by data processors and controllers, as well as the establishment of a national Computer Security Incident Response Team (CSIRT), an expert group that handles computer security incidents (see chapter 8). In addition to dealing with the criminal behaviors discussed, cybersecurity also builds trust by addressing unintentional data breaches and disclosures (such as those resulting from badly configured servers) and holding firms accountable.

Overall, the Global Data Regulation Survey reveals a low level of uptake of cybersecurity measures (figure 6.3). None of the low-income countries included in the survey has legally imposed a full range of security measures on data processors and controllers. Even among high-income countries, barely 40 percent

Figure 6.3 Gaps in the regulatory framework for cybersecurity are glaring across country income groups

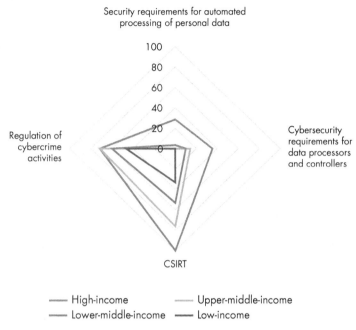

Security requirements for automated processing of personal data

Regulation of cybercrime activities

Cybersecurity requirements for data processors and controllers

CSIRT

—— High-income   —— Upper-middle-income
—— Lower-middle-income   —— Low-income

Source: WDR 2021 team, based on World Bank, Global Data Regulation Survey, https://microdata .worldbank.org/index.php/catalog/3866. Data at http://bit.do/WDR2021-Fig-6_3.

Note: The figure shows the percentage of countries in each country income group that had adopted good-practice legal and regulatory frameworks for cybersecurity and cybercrime as of 2020. CSIRT = Computer Security Incident Response Team.

of those surveyed require data processors and controllers to comply with these security requirements, such as by adopting an internal policy establishing procedures for preventing and detecting violations; establishing the confidentiality of data and systems that use or generate personal data; appointing a personal data processing or information security officer or manager; performing internal controls; assessing the harm that might arise from a data breach; or introducing an awareness program among employees. CSIRTs are far more prevalent. They can be found in all high-income countries and in about one-third of low-income countries.

Among the lower-middle-income group, a good reflection of best practice is the comprehensive cybersecurity requirements in Kenya's new Data Protection Act. It requires data controllers to consider measures such as pseudonymization and encryption of data; an ability to restore the availability of and access to personal data in the event of a physical or technical incident; and mechanisms to identify internal and external risks to personal data that are reasonably foreseeable. It also requires steps to ensure that safeguards are established, effectively implemented,

and continually updated in response to new risks or deficiencies.

Safeguarding personal data

To better address underlying concerns about the power asymmetries between (individual) data subjects and data processors and collectors, this Report advocates an approach based on control over personal data rather than one grounded in data ownership (see spotlight 6.2). Under the rights-based approach to protection of personal data, individuals have fundamental rights regarding their personal data. These rights are both substantive and procedural.

Substantive rights include measures preventing the unauthorized disclosure of personal data and the use of personal data for unwarranted surveillance, unfair targeting, exclusion, discrimination, unjust treatment, or persecution. Such substantive rights also require purpose specification, data minimization, and storage limitations.

Procedural rights are built around the concepts of necessity, transparency,[21] accountability, proportionality, and due process. They include rights to receive notice about and to object to how data are used and rights of access to correct and erase data (including the right to be forgotten),[22] as well as rights to redress and remedy. These rights are grounded mainly in domestic law. The absence of a harmonized global legal framework for protection of personal data affects cross-border data transactions involving personal data, which are especially limited in lower-middle-income countries (see chapter 7).

Adoption of data protection laws is comparatively widespread.[23] Nearly 60 percent of countries surveyed for this Report have adopted such laws, ranging from 40 percent of low-income countries to almost 80 percent of high-income countries (figure 6.4). Yet the quality of such legislation is uneven, with important good-practice elements often lacking. Legal frameworks for the protection of personal data should typically include individual rights to challenge the accuracy and object to the use of personal data and parallel requirements for data processors to limit the purpose of data use, minimize the volume of data collected, and limit the time frame for data storage. These legal provisions are much less prevalent in low- and middle-income countries than in high-income countries. Although many lower-middle-income countries have laws on the books, their enforcement is uneven: only some 40 percent of low-income and lower-middle-income countries have created a data protection authority, compared with some 60 percent of high-income countries.

Figure 6.4 Progress on personal data protection legislation differs markedly across country income groups

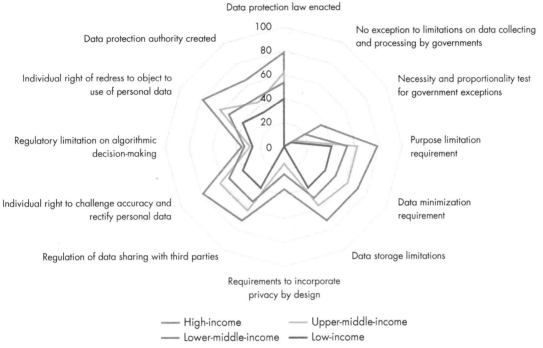

Source: WDR 2021 team, based on World Bank, Global Data Regulation Survey, https://microdata.worldbank.org/index.php/catalog/3866. Data at http://bit.do/WDR2021-Fig-6_4.

Note: The figure shows the percentage of countries in each country income group that had adopted good-practice legal and regulatory frameworks to safeguard personal data as of 2020.

The uneven quality of data protection legislation affects in practice the effectiveness of safeguards for personal data.

After many years in the making, both Kenya and Nigeria recently updated their legal regimes for data protection. In 2019 Kenya's new Data Protection Act entered into force, while Nigeria's National Information Technology Development Agency issued a new Data Protection Regulation. Both instruments reflect many of the elements contained in the GDPR. India is also debating landmark data protection legislation.

Requiring consent or other lawful bases for data collection and processing. Most data protection laws rely on individual consent as one lawful means of limiting how data about individuals can be collected and used.[24] The appropriate lawful basis for data processing depends on factors that include how the data will be used and the relationship between the parties. For example, consent may not be the appropriate basis for data processing by public authorities.[25]

The consent model has normative and practical limitations. Current commercial practices often adopt a "tick the box" approach to obtaining consent, and they are more often based on incentives to limit corporate liability than on a desire to ensure that consent is "informed" (that is, that individuals fully understand what will happen to the information they have authorized for collection and are effectively in control of how their data will be further used and shared). Privacy notices are often long, complex documents written by companies' legal teams. It is, then, difficult for people to read all the disclosure documents on the websites they visit or for all the apps on their smartphones.

This difficulty is particularly acute in the developing world, where literacy rates remain low and individuals face language and technical barriers to understanding privacy notices. In such cases, data processors should take extra care to obtain informed consent through adapted means. Firms can use consent to justify collecting and processing excessive amounts of data, especially in countries where data protection authorities may not have enough resources to monitor and enforce compliance with other obligations, such as data minimization. Addressing these concerns would require taking a more user-centric approach to obtaining informed consent for the collection of volunteered data, including using simplified terms of service and embedding responsible data collection practices in operations to avoid collecting excessive amounts of data.

Although consent may still be an appropriate lawful basis in some instances (such as when data are volunteered by individuals), newer technologies involving passive data collection (such as by the Internet of Things) and merging or linking datasets to make inferences pose further challenges to the consent model.

Alternatives to consent include relying on other lawful bases for processing personal data, including resorting to a "legitimate purpose" test or fiduciary duty requirement. A legitimate purpose test would limit the use of personal data to what is compatible, consistent, and beneficial to data subjects based on the original purpose for which the data were collected. Under this approach, data could still be used for more wide-ranging purposes if they are anonymized or aggregated to, for example, develop new products and services, or to make risk assessments without impinging on the data subject's rights. Relying on a fiduciary duty approach would require data collection and processing firms to always act in the best interests of data subjects and in ways that are not detrimental to them. Legally obligating providers to act in the best interests of their customers can help establish trust and confidence among customers that their data are being used responsibly. Examples of fiduciary duty breaches include using customer data to unfairly manipulate purchasing decisions. Another alternative to these approaches that might require less oversight is to ban use of certain types of data outright based on identified possible misuses of personal data.[26]

In principle, the limitations on the use of personal data enshrined in data protection legislation apply to all parties that process or control personal data. Nevertheless, governments may choose to create exceptions to these compliance and liability limitations for data processing by public sector entities. The Global Data Regulation Survey indicates that these exceptions are widespread in all surveyed countries that have data protection legislation (figure 6.4). Most of these exceptions are limited and pertain to specific data uses, such as in relation to national security as in Brazil and India[27] or in transactions involving health data as in Gabon. Other countries have passed laws that provide for more wide-ranging exceptions, including exemption from the requirement to obtain consent from data holders when performing lawful government functions such as service delivery.[28]

Where such government exceptions exist, good practice calls for them to be transparent and objective. They should also be limited in scope and duration (such as through sunset provisions) to respect due process limitations. These exceptions must be "necessary and proportionate" to the intended objectives—limitations designed to ensure that any established exceptions are lawful and balanced against the objective being sought.[29] Furthermore, exceptions should be consistent with international human rights law. More than one-third of high-income countries require justification for the exceptions, while less than 10 percent of surveyed low-income countries place such process limitations on government action. This lack of limitations creates additional opportunities for unchecked state surveillance or mission creep, thereby undermining trust in data use.[30]

Meeting technological challenges. Rapid technological progress in data processing, machine learning, and artificial intelligence (AI) pose challenges to current data protection frameworks. In particular, traditional data protection is based on the notion that information is volunteered by the data subject, whereas data analysis is increasingly based on observed data (obtained from passive scraping of information from devices and social media accounts) or inferred data[31] (generated from a vast array of correlates using statistical techniques). In addition, AI and machine learning rely on large-scale datasets to function, creating tensions with established data protection principles such as data minimization. Although linking these data sources provides a fuller picture of the individual, the linked data could also have a negative impact on the subject if used in decisions such as on credit or employment, with limited enforceability of the protections applicable to volunteered data, including accessing and seeking correction of erroneous information.

The increasingly widespread practice of linking datasets to feed algorithms also stretches the limits of technical mechanisms to protect personal data, such as anonymization. Unlike pseudonymized data, once data are thoroughly deidentified legally they are no longer considered to be personal data. Thus they can be published or used outside the scope of data protection law, even if the original source contains personal data.[32] Although anonymization techniques can protect individual datasets, research has shown that linking datasets enables the reidentification of individuals in deidentified data and risks blurring the boundary between personal and nonpersonal data.[33] At the same time, anonymization techniques can reduce the size and accuracy of datasets, affecting their value to third parties once published.[34]

Even when anonymization techniques can deidentify individuals, concerns are growing about the use of such data to identify groups of people who could be targeted for surveillance or discrimination (including groups defined by ethnicity, race, religion, or sexual orientation).[35] Data protection laws need to keep pace with technological efforts aimed at deanonymization.[36] Laws could require data users to adopt a holistic approach[37] to data protection that can be adapted to different risks from data uses,[38] including protecting data by design and default.

Adopting "data protection by design." Data protection by design embeds data protection practices into the initial design phase of data-driven products and services[39] through a combination of hardware and software features, legal and administrative provisions, and privacy-enhancing technologies (PETs) using encryption[40] and statistical techniques.[41] Such measures complement and enhance existing legal data protection in ways that reduce the risk of identifiability of data.[42]

Data protection by design has evolved from "privacy by design," which was first adopted as an international standard in 2010. It was later recognized by its inclusion in the Mauritius Declaration on the Internet of Things in 2014,[43] with a new International Organization for Standardization (ISO) standard under development.[44] The concept—originally developed in Canada[45]—has been integrated into data protection regulation and practice in the European Union,[46] as well as Australia (State of Victoria);[47] Hong Kong SAR, China;[48] and the United Kingdom.[49] Nevertheless, the Global Data Regulation Survey indicates limited uptake of data protection or privacy by design approaches. Less than 20 percent of the countries surveyed have adopted such requirements, ranging from 36 percent uptake in the high-income countries surveyed to negligible adoption in middle-income countries (figure 6.4). An interesting exception is Benin, which mandates "data protection by design" in its Digital Code Act.

PETs are often used to deidentify data at the source (for example, by relying on anonymization and aggregation) to reduce their identifiability. The result may be a trade-off between the level of data protection afforded and the resulting usefulness of the data (for data uses requiring granular or identifiable characteristics such as gender or age). Research showing the ease of reidentifying previously deidentified data (using only four data points[50] or when linking datasets) has highlighted the limitations of current anonymization methods and has prompted the development of new techniques.[51] Separately, the value of encryption-based PETs may be limited if law enforcement authorities argue that back doors should be included in these systems.

These limitations have also prompted the emergence of other mechanisms to protect personal data, including personal information management systems (PIMS) such as Safe Sharing sites[52] and personal data stores.[53] These tools can help users store, use, and manage how their personal information is shared with third parties. To address certain cyber-vulnerabilities and technical features of data protection by design and act as effective safeguards, PETs should be accompanied by supporting organizational and behavioral measures.[54]

Dealing with automated processing. The growing use of algorithms for automated processing of personal data can add significant value through the application of predictive analytics, but it poses additional regulatory and societal challenges. These include algorithmic bias, risks to personal data protection, and lack of transparency, accountability, and other procedural safeguards (such as redress) to ensure that decisions made on the basis of automated processing are conducted in compliance with due process.[55] Only about 30 percent of countries included in the Global Data Regulation Survey have put in place measures to restrict decision-making based on automatically processed personal data (figure 6.4). Among the relatively small number of countries whose laws address this, Côte d'Ivoire has included provisions in its data protection act that prohibit the use of automated processing of personal data in judicial decision-making to prevent bias.[56]

Automated processing of personal data in the criminal justice sector is an example of controversial public sector use of these technologies—especially those using facial recognition—that can perpetuate biases.[57] A 2016 study conducted in Oakland, California, found that, despite survey data showing an even distribution of drug use across racial groups, algorithmic predictions of police arrests were concentrated in predominantly African-American communities, creating feedback loops that reinforced patterns of structural or systemic bias in the history of police arrests.[58] Algorithms can also introduce racial biases when facial recognition algorithms are trained predominantly on data from Caucasian faces, significantly reducing their accuracy in recognizing other ethnicities.[59] Evidence suggests that racial[60] and gender[61] bias in private sector uses of AI for decision-making is also prevalent.

Additional challenges within the public sector include a lack of transparency and accountability in the use of automated decision-making systems. Many of the technologies procured by public sector entities are developed by private sector corporations. Thus, the underlying algorithms may be subject to copyright or other IPRs that restrict the ability to undertake independent third-party audits. The use of such technologies by the public sector, without implementation of the appropriate audits and grievance redress mechanisms, may impair public trust in data processing by institutions and lead to discrimination or otherwise unfair decisions.

Because of these challenges, as the uptake in AI technologies and automated decision-making systems increases in both the public and private sectors, some principles for algorithmic regulation are emerging at both the national and international levels. Internationally, the focus has frequently been on developing guiding principles based on data ethics. For example, OECD and the Group of Twenty (G-20) published two closely related sets of principles on ethical AI in 2019 that highlight the need to ensure transparency, explainability, and inclusion of unrepresented or vulnerable groups in the design and implementation of AI systems.[62] Fulfilling this need will require significant capacity-building efforts to promote responsible use of AI in lower-income countries.

Principles grounded in data ethics can be applied to other types of data uses that may have important societal impacts. Human rights-based frameworks, for example, can provide useful guiding principles for responsible data use.[63] Some countries have made efforts to support transparency and accountability in the use of AI and automated decision-making systems in the public sector by publishing the source code of algorithms in public registers,[64] revising procurement rules, and developing charters,[65] regulations, or certifications.[66] In February 2020, a Dutch court ruled that an automated surveillance system developed to detect welfare fraud in the Netherlands (SyRI) violated human rights by not meeting a "fair balance" between its objectives and its risk to privacy. It then halted the system.[67]

Relying on competition and consumer protection laws. In countries where data protection legislation is not yet in place, other statutory instruments—notably, consumer protection and competition legislation—have been leveraged to protect the data rights of individuals, notwithstanding the rights' distinct legal focus. Under a rights-based approach, data protection law is generally aimed at achieving individual agency, whereas consumer protection law aims to promote economic fairness for consumers, and competition law strives for fairness among businesses. These approaches are complementary, but they are not an adequate substitute for the scope and protection of a rights-based data protection legal framework. Nonetheless, consumer protection agencies may have wider-ranging powers than data protection authorities,[68] equipping them to address some of the issues underlying misuse of personal data, such as unfair consumer practices or competition· concerns (see chapter 7 for further discussion of data and competition issues).[69]

Safeguarding nonpersonal data

Safeguards for the domestic use and reuse of nonpersonal data revolve around the protection of intellectual property rights fit for the digital age, as well as cybersecurity measures. Various contractual elements affecting how entities use and reuse nonpersonal data (and even mixed data) are also relevant, including contracts themselves (terms and conditions, assignment of liability and remedies), as well as industry standards, codes of conduct, and audit requirements. Soft law tools include the use of standards to broker trust among entities exchanging data.

Nonpersonal data produced by the private sector can be protected under copyright, although copyright is limited to protecting creative expression, such as compilations, as opposed to raw data. Some governments have introduced innovations to overcome these limitations.[70] Observing that while the rights to data utilization may be controlled by contract but are not always specified in terms, Japan's Ministry of Economy, Trade and Industry updated application of the Unfair Competition Prevention Act to provide protection for industrial data by publishing guidelines along with model contract clauses for data transactions.[71] India's Ministry of Electronics and Information Technology published a draft governance framework for nonpersonal data, recommending clarifications on the scope, classification, rights of use of nonpersonal data, and creation of a nonpersonal data authority.[72]

Governments may also wish to establish rules to support the reuse of public sector data by preventing the private sector from setting excessively high prices for the use of licensed data-driven products and services developed using public sector, or otherwise "high value," data. One mechanism is to mandate firms to license such products on fair, reasonable, and non-discriminatory (FRAND) terms by considering them "essential data infrastructure." Governments may, however, find that IPR protection of nonpersonal data conflicts with other policies that encourage the interoperability of data systems and the free reuse of datasets.

Protection of nonpersonal data under an IPR regime is currently more prevalent in upper-middle-income countries than in most of the low-income countries surveyed. Fifty percent of upper-middle-income countries protect nonpersonal data under their respective IPR frameworks. For example, Brazil's copyright law covers the use of databases containing "economic rights."[73] Similarly, in Bangladesh programming codes, data, and charts are deemed to be the property of the owner, as indicated in the 2000 Copyright Act.

Creating enablers for data sharing

This section examines a variety of enablers, including those related to electronic transactions (e-transactions), data sharing policies (including open data, access to information regimes, open licensing), and exceptions to the liability of data intermediaries.

Enablers are primarily analyzed according to the domain of the data—that is, whether data are generated or controlled, or both, by the public or private sector. This approach highlights the varying margin of control that governments have over these two types of data. For public sector data, governments can employ several policy and legal tools to directly mandate access to and sharing of data—indeed, some already do so for certain health, patent, and even airline passenger data. By contrast, most data transactions involving the private sector are based on voluntary contractual agreements. The government's role is largely limited to creating incentives to promote private sector data sharing. Although the discussion here deals mainly with domestic data transactions, many of the enablers can be adapted to cross-border data transactions (see chapter 7).

Across the 80 countries surveyed for this Report, just under half (47 percent) of the elements of a good-practice regulatory framework for enabling data use and reuse are in place. The scores range considerably, from 30 percent among low-income countries to 62 percent among high-income countries. Although Estonia and the United Kingdom stand out among the high-income countries surveyed for the most advanced enablers, their performance is matched in the middle-income group by Mexico. Several other low- and middle-income nations are

also making progress establishing regulatory frameworks to enable data reuse, such as China, Colombia, Indonesia, and Nigeria.

Overarching enablers for electronic transactions

Many data uses or transfers are executed via electronic transactions. Individuals using their data to transact online need assurance that their data are being used in a safe and secure manner. Laws governing e-commerce and e-transactions provide an overarching legal framework that helps create trust in both public and private sector online data transactions, which, in turn, encourages use of data online.

Introducing e-commerce laws. A good-practice regulatory environment for electronic transactions begins with foundational e-commerce legislation, which is a prerequisite to the widespread use of more sophisticated online credentials. Such laws are relatively widespread; more than 70 of the countries surveyed, including about 70 percent of low-income countries surveyed, have such laws. And there is little variation across country income groups (figure 6.5). Legal recognition of electronic signatures is one of the few areas in which high-income countries remain far ahead of low- and middle-income countries.

Establishing legal equivalence of paper-based and electronic communications. In a legal framework, the central issue is to establish that a data transfer will not be denied legal value merely because it is done electronically—that is, the online transaction, contract, or communication has legal equivalence to physical transactions, and electronic evidence has probative value.[74] For example, electronic contracts and signatures are given the same legal value as a wet ink signature on a paper contract, and digital evidence has the same value as physical evidence.[75] The majority of surveyed countries' e-commerce legislation includes such provisions (figure 6.5), an unsurprising finding given that model laws on e-commerce were promulgated in the late 1990s.[76] For example, provisions enabling e-transactions are found in Morocco's Law No. 53-05 (2007), and good-practice provisions are embedded in Thailand's Electronic Transactions Act (2019 amendments).

Authenticating parties to an online transaction. Special legal treatment surrounds the manner in which parties to an online transaction are authenticated. Most laws governing e-transactions take a layered approach to the digital authentication of parties to a transaction, with built-in recognition that certain types of online transactions require greater degrees of reliability about the identity of parties, while others

Figure 6.5 Adoption of e-commerce and related legislation is widespread across country income groups

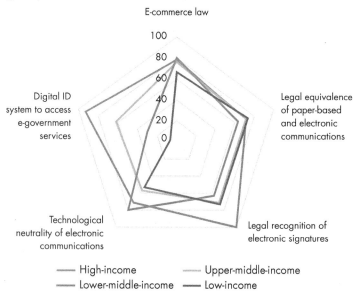

Source: WDR 2021 team, based on World Bank, Global Data Regulation Survey, https://microdata .worldbank.org/index.php/catalog/3866. Data at http://bit.do/WDR2021-Fig-6_5.

Note: The figure shows the percentage of countries in each country income group that had adopted good-practice legal and regulatory frameworks for e-commerce as of 2020.

require lower levels of assurance. Some—such as land transactions and certain family law matters, including marriage and divorce—are generally outside the scope of these laws because of the sensitive nature of the transaction. For transactions requiring a high level of assurance, public or private key infrastructure is often recognized in e-transaction laws as providing robust authentication, and it is backed up by a digital certification process.[77] Other trust services may also be specified as a basis for verifying and validating electronic signatures, seals, or time stamps; verifying and validating certificates to be used for website authentication; and a range of activities related to data transfers.[78]

Introducing digital identification. An important tool for authentication of parties to a digital transaction is a trusted digital identification system with widespread coverage, allowing individuals to securely prove their identity in online settings. Currently, an estimated 1 billion people worldwide do not have government-recognized proof of their identity (and many more do not have the means to securely and reliably prove who they are in the digital world).[79] Although the use of digital identity verification and authentication tools is on the rise, driven in part by advances in connectivity as well as growth in digital

payments and services,[80] fewer than half of surveyed countries have government-recognized digital identification systems that would enable people to remotely authenticate themselves to access e-government services. Those that do are mainly higher-income nations (figure 6.5).

Ensuring technical neutrality of online systems. E-transaction laws should be principle-based and technology-neutral so that they accommodate a wide range of technical solutions and avoid requiring specific authentication technologies to the exclusion of others. Such requirements avoid capture of the e-transaction or authentication market and help laws adapt as technologies evolve.[81] Technology neutrality is also a feature of digital identity programs and of some digital identity laws.[82]

Enabling reuse of public intent data

The challenges with sharing and reusing public sector data abound. They include barriers to the real-time provision of data; data not being shared or published in reusable formats (standardized and machine readable with metadata); and data not being provided at reasonable cost. Usage is also affected by the quality or relevance of the data being shared. Political economy factors, including the absence of a data sharing culture in public administration and lack of coordination among government entities, can further impede the exchange of public sector data (see chapter 8).

Overcoming these challenges can yield considerable returns. An impact assessment of the 2003 Directive on the Reuse of Public Sector Information found that in the European Union the direct economic value of public sector information was €52 billion in 2017, potentially rising to €194 billion by 2030.[83] In recognition of such potential value, national governments have ramped up efforts to use policy, legal, and regulatory tools to mandate data sharing within and beyond the public sector.

A good-practice regulatory environment for enabling reuse of public sector data would include foundational legislation on open data and access to information, as well as digital identity verification and authentication; a data classification policy; adoption of syntactic and semantic interoperability; and user-friendly licensing arrangements. The surveyed countries have adopted about half of such good practices, ranging, on average, from less than 30 percent by low-income countries to two-thirds by high-income countries (figure 6.6).

Legislation to promote and regulate the publication and use of public sector data (open government data) can be passed as stand-alone open data acts, such as in the Republic of Korea and Mexico; embedded in other related legislation, such as the laws mandating data sharing in Australia,[84] India, and the United Kingdom;[85] or through broader e-government omnibus legislation, such as France's Law for a Digital Republic.[86] The matter can also be tackled at the supranational level, such as through the European Union's Open Data Directive of 2019 (replacing the Public Sector Reuse Directive of 2003), which includes a list of "high value datasets"[87] to be published at no charge as key inputs to the development of AI.

Open data policies or laws and access to information (ATI) legislation (also known as right to information or freedom of information) play complementary roles as enablers for the use and sharing of public sector data. Open data policies or laws require public disclosure of data as the general rule (ex ante disclosure) rather than waiting for an individual request for access to information (ex post disclosure).[88] In countries that have passed open data policies without any legal foundation, the publication of open government data relies on the cooperation of holders of public sector data to publish their data. By contrast, ATI legislation provides citizens and firms with a legally enforceable right to compel disclosure.[89]

Open Barometer, an organization that compiles a global measure of how governments are publishing and using open data for accountability, innovation, and social impact, recommends aligning access to information and open data. This alignment would entail amending ATI laws to provide for proactive disclosure of data and mandating that nonpersonal data will be open by default, available in machine readable formats, and published under an open license to enable reuse outside government.

About one-third of surveyed countries have open data legislation, and more than 70 percent have ATI legislation (figure 6.6). Whereas ATI legislation is widespread in countries across all stages of development, adoption of open licensing regimes is more common in high-income countries.

Establishing open data policies. A country's public sector data being prepared for publication can be classified on a spectrum from closed to open. According to the Open Knowledge Foundation, for data to be considered open it must be "freely used, re-used and redistributed by anyone—subject only, at most, to the requirement to attribute and sharealike."[90] Open data are thought to be the most decisive approach governments can use to enhance access to public sector data and enable their reuse by third parties to

Figure 6.6 Regulations enabling access to and reuse of public intent data are unevenly developed across country income groups

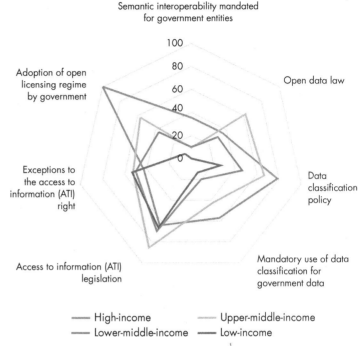

Source: WDR 2021 team, based on World Bank, Global Data Regulation Survey, https://microdata.worldbank.org/index.php/catalog/3866. Data at http://bit.do/WDR2021-Fig-6_6.

Note: The figure shows the percentage of countries in each country income group that had adopted good-practice legal and regulatory frameworks to enable access, use, and reuse of public intent data as of 2020.

create value.[91] According to the Open Data Institute, key elements of a robust data policy include a clear definition of open data and a general declaration of principles that should guide the publication and reuse of open data.[92]

Geospatial and transportation data are often prioritized for publication by governments under open data initiatives.[93] However, certain categories of data may not be suitable for publication as open data, including personal data and data with national security implications. Care must be taken to ensure that personal data are not published on open data portals without adequate protective measures and a conscious assessment of the associated risks. A data protection impact assessment can be used to evaluate the risks of data processing and ensure that data are adequately safeguarded before being shared.[94]

As open data systems mature, governments should move from merely promoting access to data to facilitating use of data. A key enabling reform is ensuring that data and metadata are "open by default," available in a machine readable format and by bulk download or via application programming interfaces (APIs)— computing interfaces and code that allow data to be readily transmitted between one software product or application and another. A survey conducted by the Open Data Barometer found that less than 10 percent of governments that have established open data portals include a provision for data to be open by default. Moreover, only half of the datasets published are in a machine readable format, and only one-quarter of datasets have an open license.[95]

Ensuring unified data classification standards. A key enabler of data reuse is a data classification policy that categorizes types of data according to objective and easily implementable criteria across the different stages of the data life cycle.[96] Data classification policies typically entail categorizing data according to their sensitivity (such as classified, confidential, or business use only). Although data classification policies are found in more than half of the countries surveyed (figure 6.6), their practical effects are limited because in less than one-third of countries is the application of data classification policies mandatory for government database applications or document management systems.

Restricted data (data that cannot be published as open data) could possibly be shared bilaterally by agreement (such as with memoranda of understanding). Alternatively, innovative mechanisms, including data pools and data sandboxes, allow data to be accessed and processed in a controlled environment, subject to specific restrictions on data use. For example, data could be analyzed at a secure data repository (whether virtual or physical) but not taken off-site.[97]

Allowing access to information. ATI legislation is a key complementary enabler for increasing access to public sector data that have not been published on an open data platform. Such legislation provides the legal means for enforcement of public sector disclosure.[98] As with open data legislation, ATI legislation can be more or less effectively implemented, depending on how broadly the exemption categories for disclosure are drafted or interpreted and how restrictively data classification policies are applied at the working level. If government entities claim that much of their data are "sensitive" and therefore fall under one of the exceptions for disclosure under ATI statutes, then the usefulness of such legislation for enabling public data access may be limited. This concern is warranted because nearly half the countries included in the Global Data Regulation Survey—across the income spectrum—have placed significant exceptions on an individual's rights to access public information under such laws (figure 6.6).

Another limit to the impact of ATI legislation is its scope of application, which is necessarily limited to public sector data. Open data policies, although originating in the public sector, can be voluntarily adopted by the private sector. However, there is no general legal equivalent to ATI requests to compel the disclosure of private sector data. Currently, the majority of private sector data sharing is undertaken on a contractual basis. Certain experts have argued that expanding the scope of laws mandating access to private sector data, consistent with competition law, could be the "next frontier in data governance."[99]

Promoting interoperability of data and systems. For the value of data—including open data—to be fully harnessed, legislation must go beyond promoting access to data and ensure that data can be used more effectively by combining or linking datasets. Doing so requires provisions governing the interoperability of data (and metadata) and their quality, as well as the modalities under which data should be published. These good-practice characteristics include publishing data in a machine readable format (under FAIR principles that govern the findability, accessibility, interoperability, and reuse of data)[100] and ideally via APIs.[101] Interoperability of data and systems can be supported by adopting harmonized standards— ideally, open standards. Open standards are often determined by sectoral or international standard setting organizations (SSOs) in order to support the interoperability of data and systems within a particular market or sector. They are therefore designed collaboratively based on user needs.[102]

Public intent data should also be published under an open license and at no charge or at a marginal price to cover the costs of dissemination or reproduction.[103] Nearly 48 percent of the surveyed countries have adopted some form of open licensing regime for public intent data. All the high-income countries covered in the survey have done so, compared with about 40 percent of middle-income countries. Other countries, such as Jordan and Mauritius,[104] have adopted Creative Commons Attribution 4.0 International Licenses for government datasets released as open data. In Jordan, datasets published by the government are open to all and licensed under a Jordanian Open Government Data License, which allows the use, reuse, and sharing of data, in compatibility with the Creative Commons (CC-BY) license.[105] To ensure that data prioritized for publication meet the needs of nongovernmental actors in the private sector and civil society, these decisions should be guided by consultations with multiple stakeholders (see chapter 8).

Enabling access to and the seamless transfer of public sector data between different entities within the public sector and with end users (including individuals and businesses) requires ensuring the interoperability of information technology (IT) systems (including platforms) and data (syntactic and semantic interoperability). As defined by ISO, syntactic interoperability enables "the *formats* of the exchanged information [to] be understood by the participating systems," while semantic interoperability enables the "meaning of the data model within the context of a subject area to be understood by the participating systems."[106] Effective data and systems interoperability requires the implementation of several technical protocols and a government interoperability platform.

In addition to technical enablers for interoperability across the whole of government, an enabling legal and regulatory framework is often required. This framework mandates the use of the government's interoperability platform and data exchange protocols, ensuring that all government entities connect to and use the platform as a vehicle for exchanging data. Very few countries surveyed have adopted a full range of common technical standards (such as the FAIR principles) that enable the interoperability of systems, registries, and databases (figure 6.6). Estonia is among the few countries surveyed that has established standards for open APIs for government to government (G2G), government to business (G2B), and government to consumer (G2C) services; standardized communications protocols for accessing metadata; and developed semantic catalogues for data and metadata.

A distinct advantage of implementing interoperability is the possibility of applying the once-only principle to access to data, which reduces the administrative burden. Citizens and businesses are asked to provide their data only once, thereby requiring public sector entities to internally share and reuse data—with the appropriate safeguards—in the provision of administrative services. Because the risk of data breaches and misuse increases when data are stored in centralized or decentralized but linked repositories, the once-only principle should be complemented with robust legal and technical data protection as well as cybersecurity and cybercrime safeguards, implemented in a citizen-centered and trustworthy manner, with sufficient capacity for implementation

(see chapter 8).[107] This once-only principle was integrated into the European eGovernment Action Plan (2016–20) for implementation across the European Union,[108] with the intention of enabling both domestic and cross-border interoperability. It is also one of the pillars of the 2015 Digital Single Market strategy[109] and The Once-Only Principle Project (TOOP),[110] which has been piloted under the European Union's Horizon 2020 framework.[111] At the national level, Austria, Belgium, Denmark, Estonia, the Netherlands, Portugal, and Spain have integrated the once-only principle into domestic law for application across government or on a sector basis.[112]

Enabling reuse of private intent data

The majority of business-to-business (B2B) and business-to-government (B2G) data transactions are governed by bilateral data sharing agreements sourced in contract law.[113] Consequently, policy and legal interventions to encourage access to private sector data focus on mitigating the legal and technical challenges that discourage the use and sharing of data by private sector entities. Governments also maintain a greater margin of control over private sector data transactions involving personal data, which are subject to personal data protection and privacy legislation (or competition and consumer protection laws).

As appreciation has grown of the strategic value of private sector data for enabling evidence-based policy making and promoting innovation and competition in key sectors (see chapter 4), some governments have enacted legislation mandating the sharing of private sector data deemed to be in the public interest and whose voluntary sharing by the private sector would, otherwise, have been too costly to incentivize.[114] Many of the sectors prioritized by such legislation (including utilities and transportation) are considered to be particularly relevant for the development of AI.

At the European level, the 2019 EU Open Data Directive[115] requires the European Commission to adopt a list of high-value datasets to be provided free of charge, in machine readable formats, via APIs, and where relevant, via bulk download. These datasets, considered to have "high commercial or societal potential," include geospatial data, Earth observation data, meteorological data, data about corporate ownership, mobility data, and data from publicly funded research projects.[116] At the national level, France's Law for a Digital Republic (2016) includes provisions mandating making private sector data available according to open standards for the creation of "public interest datasets."[117] Another relevant example is the UK

Digital Economy Act (2017), which enables researchers to gain access to deidentified data for research purposes.[118] At the subnational level, cities such as New York, San Francisco, and São Paulo have also made legal attempts to promote public-private data sharing by requiring certain private sector platforms to share their commercial data for regulatory purposes and to spur the development of smart cities.[119]

A good-practice regulatory environment for enabling reuse of private sector data encompasses data portability and voluntary licensing of access to essential data (figure 6.7). On average, surveyed countries have adopted less than 20 percent of such good practices for enabling private sector reuse of data, which is less than half the level of uptake found for enablers related to public sector data.

Promoting open licensing. Licensing regimes, which provide permission to use an otherwise proprietary dataset, can be effective enablers of innovation and competition. They can encourage holders of data-related intellectual property rights to invest in products and markets, knowing that they can control access to licensed products and receive returns on their investments.[120] Licensing of intellectual property rights is often voluntary, but in some cases it is implemented on a compulsory basis by regulators or industry participants to avoid market distortions.[121] Voluntary licensing on FRAND terms can be a useful mechanism in enabling the development of open standards because the terms allow companies to share technology and data.[122] The adoption of such licensing regimes, however, remains rare, especially in low- and middle-income nations (figure 6.7). Korea and the United Kingdom are among the few surveyed countries that have done so.

A range of open licenses are available for use with data. Open data licenses (Open Database Licenses, or ODbLs) provide users with the legal rights to freely share, modify, and use a database without regard to copyright or other intellectual property rights or limitations around data ownership. These license agreements are published by the Open Data Commons, which makes available a set of legal tools and licenses to help users publish, provide, and use open data.[123] The ODbL license sets out user rights, establishes the correct procedure for attributing credit, and specifies how to modify data to facilitate their sharing and comparability. Another form of open license for data is issued by Creative Commons, an international network devoted to educational access and expanding the range of creative works available for others to build on legally and to share.[124] Under the license, any person can use, copy, publish, distribute, transmit, or process the data and make them available to third parties. They can also develop new derivatives of the data by combining them with other data or using them in a product or service, as long as they are attributed to the publisher(s) using a specified statement.[125]

Requiring data portability. Voluntary data transactions between parties are greatly facilitated by data portability. The right to personal data portability is designed to facilitate data transfers with the aim of increasing an individual's choice and control over data about them. More fundamentally, the right to personal data portability is aimed at "rebalancing the relationship" between data generators/providers and data controllers (including data users and platforms) by mitigating the risk of locking in consumer data. On a more systemic level, this right is intended to foster competition between companies.[126]

Portability can be broken down into three distinct rights: first, to receive a copy of the data provided by the data generator to the data collector or user (including data consumers and platforms); second, to transmit data to another data collector/user;

Figure 6.7 Adoption of enablers for sharing private intent data lags those for public intent data across country income groups

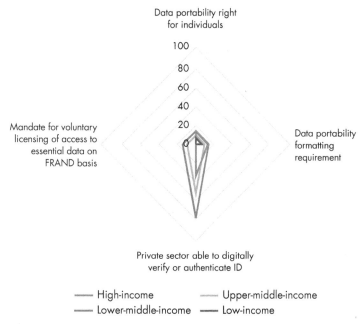

Source: WDR 2021 team, based on World Bank, Global Data Regulation Survey, https://microdata .worldbank.org/index.php/catalog/3866. Data at http://bit.do/WDR2021-Fig-6_7.

Note: The figure shows the percentage of countries in each country income group that had adopted good-practice legal and regulatory frameworks to enable access to, sharing, and reuse of private intent data as of 2020. FRAND = fair, reasonable, and non-discriminatory; ID = identification.

and third, to request a direct transfer from one data collector/user to another.[127]

Although data portability rights extend to the raw data provided by the data subject (interpreted to include observed data), they do not appear to extend to inferred data (based on drawing inferences from the raw data provided), which are increasingly being used to develop AI.[128] Enabling the direct transfer of (personal or nonpersonal) data to another provider requires that the source and host data formats and systems are fully interoperable through the implementation of APIs.[129] At present, interoperability is encouraged, not mandated, by the GDPR[130] and EU regulations on the free flow of nonpersonal data.[131] Alternatives to direct portability include storing personal data in personal information management systems,[132] although their uptake is limited.[133]

In the European Union, the right to personal data portability is mandated by Article 20 of the GDPR and considered one of its most significant innovations.[134] Little more than 10 percent of countries surveyed have enacted data portability rights for individuals. By contrast, the portability of nonpersonal data is not mandated, but only encouraged as a means of promoting competition and enabling the development of competitive sectors using AI and big data.[135]

Individuals' ability to enforce their right to data portability can in practice be supported by requiring data to be transferred in a standard machine readable format. The surveyed countries that grant individuals data portability rights all include formatting requirements to support data portability (figure 6.7). For example, in the Philippines the 2012 Data Protection Act grants data portability rights to data subjects and empowers the National Privacy Commission to specify the format and technical requirements to enable data portability.[136] Using a somewhat different approach, Australia created a specific "consumer data right" in August 2019[137] to enable data portability through its Competition and Consumer Act 2010.[138] The act follows a phased sectoral approach to implementation,[139] which enables common standards to be adapted to sector-specific needs while being made publicly available on the open-source platform GitHub.[140]

Despite these advances, technical limitations and legal uncertainties challenge effective enforcement of data portability rights. At the same time, cybersecurity risks, such as improper access or identity theft, could increase if portability is not accompanied by robust security measures.

In the absence of specific laws or regulations mandating interoperability and portability standards, some private sector actors have developed their own mechanisms. One example is the collaborative Data Transfer Project.[141] Data format standardization is a key component of enabling data portability in practice: the right to data portability cannot be exercised if data are not downloaded in a format common to other service providers. In practice, despite the source code and APIs being open source, the leadership of this project raises broader questions about the first mover advantage that Big Tech companies have in setting de facto standards and markets for B2B data sharing between platforms.

Using APIs to enable effective interoperability and portability. APIs can be used to either enable data sharing (such as through open APIs) and portability or limit access to data, depending on how they are designed.[142] Although APIs are technical in nature, technolegal frameworks can be developed to determine access and control rules for third parties. These rules can include setting controls to ensure the syntactic and synthetic portability of data; the identity of the API users; the type and amount of data transacted; and the controls on the identifiability of data.[143] APIs designed with access and control mechanisms that enable the selection of a limited amount of data can provide users with more flexibility than if they downloaded bulk data.[144] That said, because APIs can expose data to unauthorized access during data transfers, they may prove challenging to use effectively in lower-middle-income countries that do not have sufficient technical capacity to respond to cybersecurity risks.

Fully leveraging APIs to enable effective interoperability and portability requires ensuring that they are developed according to common standards. These standards can be developed through regulation or by industry, based on a multistakeholder approach. Examples of successful initiatives include the Berlin Group, which has developed common API standards for the European banking industry.[145] Cases from the financial services sector (such as the UK Open Banking Initiative and implementation of the European Union's Second Payment Service Directive) may provide helpful lessons for the effective implementation of these mechanisms as enablers for data reuse and sharing.

Forging data partnerships. An alternative modality for private sector data sharing is through data public-private partnerships (PPPs) entered into on mutually agreed contractual terms between private sector entities or between government and businesses. For example, the traffic application Waze has partnered with more than 1,000 cities and other local public sector entities through its Connected Citizens Program[146] to exchange traffic data and derive insights to inform mobility projects, manage traffic and congestion, support emergency response, and share data with citizens through a cloud-based platform.[147]

Data partnerships pose several challenges. Partnerships between large companies and small and medium enterprises may raise concerns about fairness because of asymmetries in information or market power. Partnerships between public and private entities may lead to conflicts of interest because of the government's dual role as data user and data regulator.[148] In either case, partnerships may create uncertainties around the allocation of the legal liability associated with the use of the data, as well as potential compliance costs due to lack of harmonization of legal frameworks applicable to both parties.[149] Some of these risks can be mitigated by developing contract guidelines or standard contractual terms to harmonize provisions and rectify information asymmetries. Some public sector initiatives have attempted to develop such standard terms to promote data sharing.[150]

Not all data sharing partnerships are designed for profit. Some businesses provide their data and digital tools at no charge to governments, academia, and nongovernmental organizations for "social good." Data philanthropy,[151] particularly in the area of big data, has enabled the World Bank,[152] together with UN agencies—the World Health Organization (WHO), United Nations Development Programme (UNDP), World Food Programme (WFP), and United Nations Children's Fund (UNICEF)—and others, to leverage companies' data stock and digital capabilities to fully exploit the value of data for development, while benefiting the private sector through positive externalities.

Limiting intermediary liability. One of the great enablers of the flow of data across the internet are rules limiting the liability of intermediaries for content that flows over their platforms. The intermediary liability concept has roots in US telecommunications law dating back to the 1930s,[153] and it has been informed by subsequent US case law.[154] Crucially, this exemption from liability was extended to "interactive computer services" (internet service providers) in Section 230 of the 1996 amendments to the Communications Act of 1934[155] and in the Digital Millennium Copyright Act.[156] The advent of data platform business models has led to growing requests from users for the "take-down" of their personal information and has triggered an ongoing debate between privacy advocates and Big Tech about responsibility for fundamental issues of

freedom of expression and transparency of knowledge. Liability exemptions have been criticized as harboring defamatory conduct, encouraging harassment online, and undermining attempts by law enforcement to attribute conduct to specific individuals.[157] Nevertheless, freedom of expression advocates continue to support shielding intermediaries from liability.[158] The rapidly changing landscape is creating significant regulatory uncertainty for Big Tech firms (see the overview and chapter 1 for a discussion on the broader policy considerations relating to content moderation and mis/disinformation).

Recommendations for crafting a holistic legal framework

Any new social contract on data must rest on the foundation of a comprehensive legal and regulatory framework that helps build trust between stakeholders, integrating both safeguards and enablers. As the results of the Global Data Regulation Survey suggest, the development and robustness of different aspects of the legal and regulatory framework are quite uneven, with relatively consistent patterns across country income groups (table 6.1). These divergences may be exacerbated by differences in implementation. E-commerce legislation is the only area in which all country income groups are doing comparatively well. Development is at an intermediate level in areas such as enabling reuse of public intent data, safeguarding both personal and nonpersonal data, protecting cybersecurity, and combating cybercrime. By far the weakest area of performance of the surveyed countries is enablers for private intent data. Overall, the average scores of high-income countries are not very high in absolute terms, warranting an advanced (green) classification in table 6.1 in only one case. And the score differential between high- and low-income countries is relatively small (rarely more than 30 points). Both findings indicate the novel challenges of developing a sound data governance legal framework and the significant progress all countries need to make.

To fill the many remaining gaps in the legal framework and further strengthen existing provisions, this Report offers several recommendations. Overall, the underlying legal framework needs to be approached holistically. Although different elements of the legal framework can be viewed in a modular fashion, the elaboration of particular laws needs to touch on all critical aspects. The crafting of such a coherent legal framework should take into account both evolving best practices and local conditions based on robust

Table 6.1 Certain elements of the regulatory framework are much better developed than others, but performance is generally low

Average score, by country group	Safeguards			Enablers		
	Cybersecurity and cybercrime	Personal data	Nonpersonal data	E-commerce and e-transactions	Public intent data	Private intent data
High-income	73	59	43	86	69	30
Upper-middle-income	57	46	29	74	62	20
Lower-middle-income	55	43	38	72	44	15
Low-income	39	31	47	59	28	3
Global	56	44	38	73	50	17

Source: WDR 2021 team, based on World Bank, Global Data Regulation Survey, https://microdata.worldbank.org/index.php/catalog/3866.

Note: The table shows the average score for good-practice data governance by theme across country income groups as of 2020. Colors refer to the level of the regulatory framework: ▨ = advanced level (scores of 75–100); ▨ = moderate level (scores of 50–75); ▧ = evolving level (scores of 25–50); and ■ = basic level (scores below 25).

stakeholder consultation. There is no one-size-fits-all solution.

Recommendations for strengthening safeguards

Adopt and implement personal data protection legislation. One of the biggest contributors to the trust framework is the adoption of personal data protection legislation following a rights-based approach. For countries that lack data protection legislation or enforcement agencies, the existing consumer protection legislation and competition law can be leveraged to remedy certain manifestations of the misuse of personal data. Although such legislation and laws may be helpful, their scope of application is limited, making them complements to, not substitutes for, personal data protection legislation.

Introduce more meaningful models of consent. Traditional approaches to consent, developed in an analog age, are an increasingly uncomfortable fit in the modern digital age. Furthermore, in lower-income countries, where literacy challenges continue to affect a significant share of the population, reliance on "consent," as traditionally applied, will continue to be problematic as more people access the internet and permit their data to be used and reused. To ensure that consent remains a meaningful legal basis for using data, new models should be seriously considered, including those that shift responsibility for data protection from individuals to the collectors and users of the data.

Expand protection to mixed data and group privacy. New data uses, fueled by innovative analytical techniques and the growth of algorithm-based technologies such

as big data and the Internet of Things, are blurring the distinction between personal and nonpersonal data. At present, only personal data fall within the scope of most current data protection laws, while anonymized personal data are considered nonpersonal data. In view of the ease of reidentifying and linking datasets, which opens the door to deriving sensitive or discriminatory insights from the processing of nonpersonal data, policy makers should consider expanding the scope of data protection legislation to protect such mixed data. A related issue is that current provisions for personal data protection, which focus on the individual, do not preclude the identification and potential misuse of data attributes pertaining to homogeneous groups (including those defined by ethnicity, race, religion, or sexual orientation). These protections are particularly important in complex or fragile sociopolitical environments or emergency contexts because of the increased risk of misuse of such data for targeting or surveillance.

Adopt data protection by design and default. Privacy-enhancing technologies are important complements of data protection legislation, allowing privacy to be embedded in data-driven products and services right from the design phase. These standards can play a valuable role in safeguarding fundamental data rights in contexts in which weak institutional capacity diminishes the legal enforceability of those rights. However, for technical mechanisms to have teeth, they must be underpinned by a robust legal framework that creates the rights and limits on use that privacy-enhancing technologies reinforce. Because of the utility of data protection and privacy by design, policy makers should consider building more of these requirements into their regulatory frameworks, while maintaining technological neutrality.

Prioritize cybersecurity measures. Protecting individuals' and groups' rights in data is one thing; protecting the infrastructure and systems over which those data flow—cybersecurity—is another. From a legal perspective, these protections are gained by adopting cybercrime legislation that balances security concerns with other fundamental rights. Too few countries have adopted serious legal provisions to ensure cybersecurity, leading to mounting social and economic risks. This gap should be addressed as a matter of urgency.

Recommendations for strengthening enablers

Build a robust yet flexible foundation for electronic transactions. Digital transactions should be granted legal equivalence to the analog variety, with limited exceptions. Robust authentication should be technology neutral to ensure a level playing field for a wide variety of approaches to authenticating transactions and related trust services.

Make data open by default and easy to access. Countries should strengthen open data policies by calling for open-by-default approaches to public sector data through legislation across the whole of government. Datasets to be published should be prioritized using input from end users. End users should not be charged (or should pay a limited price) for public intent data.

Consistently apply reasonable norms for data classification. Implementation of open data policies or laws requires the consistent application of clear, reasonable data classification policies.

Adopt open standards and sharing-friendly licenses. Policy makers should strengthen open access to public intent data, including adoption of open standards and sharing-friendly licenses.

Strengthen access to information provisions. Access to information legislation should be expanded to cover the proactive and transparent disclosure of nonsensitive data. Exceptions to disclosure will be necessary and should be proportionate. ATI laws should provide for regular public disclosure of ATI requests received and rejected, and justification for any rejection, ideally on an open platform.

Promote the interoperability of data and systems. Improving the use and sharing of data will rely on developing and applying unified technical standards to support the interoperability of data and systems. Interoperability of systems entails adoption of common technical protocols and a government interoperability platform. Data can be made interoperable by ensuring that they are classified and processed according to common standards and published in a machine readable format.

Support data portability. The right to data portability should be strengthened by requiring data to be in a structured, commonly used, and machine readable format. Interoperable data and systems can help achieve continuous data portability, where proportionate and technically feasible. As an alternative or complement to direct portability, personal information management systems can help users receive and manage their data, but their uptake is currently limited. The enforcement of data portability rights depends on adequate market competition, enabling users to switch providers. For data portability to be meaningful, there is also a need to address the lack of clear understanding of these rights by data subjects, as well as the implementation challenges faced by micro, small, and medium enterprises.

Promote sharing of private intent data. Governments can incentivize the sharing of private sector data by promoting data sharing agreements and enhancing intellectual property rights. Together, these measures can help reduce incentives for data hoarding and leverage the reusability of data. In the case of public interest data, and particularly under emergency situations, governments should increasingly consider mandating private sector data sharing, subject to suitable conditions and safeguards.

A maturity model for strengthening the legal and regulatory framework

The urgency of applying these measures will depend on how far a country's legal and regulatory framework for data has evolved. Countries should develop sound, comprehensive policies based on best practices adapted to their circumstances. Building on this foundation, countries should then enact robust legislation buttressed by multistakeholder consultation, followed by clear time-bound implementation procedures to ensure accountability. The identified measures can tentatively be mapped onto the maturity model framework summarized in table 6.2. Although certain safeguarding and enabling elements are considered foundational, the ability to build an effective legal regime for trusted data use is dependent on ensuring that the overall framework is both internally coherent and aligned with the country's policy orientation, data culture, and social contract on data.

Table 6.2 Recommendations organized according to a maturity model based on data safeguards and enablers

Stage of country's data system	Safeguards	Enablers
Establishing fundamentals	Conduct a baseline needs assessment. Develop a comprehensive policy framework based on best practices that does the following: • Safeguards personal, nonpersonal, and evolving categories of data and promotes greater equity around data • Enhances the security of systems and infrastructure that protect against misuse of data • Expands individuals' agency and control over their personal data • Promotes certainty and predictability, integrating the fundamental safeguards discussed in this chapter such as data protection and cybersecurity.	Conduct a baseline needs assessment. Develop a comprehensive policy framework based on best practices that enables the use and sharing of data for development purposes, ensuring access, openness, interoperability, portability, predictability, and transparency, while integrating the fundamental enablers discussed in this chapter, such as electronic transactions.
Initiating data flows	Elaborate a legal framework that embodies policy prerogatives that include: • Personal data protection • Promotion of cybersecurity and combating of cybercrime • Regulation of competition • Provisions in the legal framework to provide for establishment of the relevant enforcement institutions.	Elaborate a legal framework that embodies policy prerogatives that include: • Legal recognition of e-transactions • Access to information • Intellectual property rights for nonpersonal data • Openness of public intent data, including the use of licenses that encourage data sharing • Data classification principles.
Optimizing the system	Promote awareness of safeguards: • Domestically, through adoption of data protection by design and default, together with associated cybersecurity measures • Internationally, through cross-border interoperability of data protection standards • Address more complex issues such as mixed data and group rights • Ensure that the capacity of the institutions responsible for overseeing these activities is sufficient • Establish metrics to monitor and evaluate the implementation and enforcement of these policies and laws.	Consider issues such as data portability and increasing incentives around sharing of private intent data. Ensure that the capacity of the institutions responsible for overseeing these activities is sufficient. Establish metrics to monitor and evaluate the implementation of these policies, laws, and institutions.

Source: WDR 2021 team.

Notes

1. Gellman (2013).
2. Confessore (2018).
3. A framework for data protection existed in the EU prior to the GDPR—the 1995 Data Protection Directive. Because a directive requires incorporation into domestic law, several European countries adopted their own data protection regimes, in some cases with even more stringent protections (such as Germany). However, adoption of the GDPR is a significant evolution in three key dimensions. First, as a regulation that applies directly to all EU members, it has harmonized data protection law across the EU. Second, it has supported enforcement through the introduction of significant fines. And,

third, it has applied extraterritorially to cross-border data transactions involving data subjects in the EU.

4. Attorney General's Office, California Department of Justice, California Consumer Privacy Act (CCPA), https://oag.ca.gov/privacy/ccpa.
5. China's revision of its civil code will enter into force in 2021. Articles 1032–1039 grant certain rights to individuals. These provisions may be superseded by the expected introduction of a new law on protection of personal information. See, for example, Dong (2020) and Fang, Bigg, and Zhang (2020). China also published for consultation a draft law on personal data protection that in many respects mirrors provisions of the GDPR (Zhang and Yin 2020).

6. See Fisher and Streinz (2021) and Lessig (1999).

7. Personally identifiable information refers to information that can be used to distinguish or trace the identity of a data subject. Examples of such information are the subject's name, national identity number, or biometric records, alone or when combined with other personal or identifying information that is linked or linkable to a specific data subject, such as date and place of birth or mother's maiden name.

8. PMC (2019).

9. A regulatory impact analysis (RIA), also known as a regulatory impact assessment, is defined by the Organisation for Economic Co-operation and Development (OECD) as "a systemic approach to critically assessing the positive and negative effects of proposed and existing regulations and nonregulatory alternatives. As employed in OECD countries it encompasses a range of methods. It is an important element of an evidence-based approach to policy making" (OECD, "Regulatory Impact Analysis," https://www.oecd.org /regreform/regulatory-policy/ria.htm). According to data from the World Bank's Global Indicators of Regulatory Governance (GIRG), 86 out of 186 countries surveyed carry out RIAs on either a regular or a semi-regular basis (World Bank, Global Indicators of Regulatory Governance [dashboard], https://rulemaking .worldbank.org/). However, although most high-income countries carry out RIAs (45 out of 59, or 76 percent), only 12 percent of low- and middle-income countries do so. Moreover, even though all OECD high-income countries except for Italy and Chile have developed specific RIA guidelines, only three countries in Sub-Saharan Africa (Kenya, South Africa, and Uganda) have set requirements. For more details, see Deighton-Smith, Erbacci, and Kauffmann (2016); ITU (2014); World Bank (2018); World Bank, "Key Findings," https:// rulemaking.worldbank.org/en/key-findings.

10. Chen (2021). To access the World Bank's Global Data Regulation Survey and its results, see https:// microdata.worldbank.org/index.php/catalog/3866.

11. COE (2018).

12. See, generally, page 70 of World Bank and United Nations (2017).

13. World Bank and United Nations (2017).

14. World Bank and United Nations (2017).

15. In the absence of dual criminality, if an activity is criminal in jurisdiction X but is not in jurisdiction Y, then the authorities in X could not extradite a criminal in Y.

16. Treaty Office, Directorate of Legal Advice and Public International Law, Council of Europe, "Details of Treaty No. 185: Convention on Cybercrime," https://www.coe.int /en/web/conventions/full-list/-/conventions/treaty/185.

17. Cybercrime, Council of Europe, "Parties/Observers to the Budapest Convention and Observer Organisations to the T-CY," https://www.coe.int/en/web/cybercrime /parties-observers.

18. U.S. Clarifying Lawful Overseas Use of Data Act ("CLOUD" Act), 18 U.S. Code §2523, https://www.justice .gov/dag/page/file/1152896/download.

19. LOC (2018).

20. Council of the European Union (2019).

21. EC (2018a).

22. EC (2014).

23. Sources differ on the number of data protection laws enacted around the world: 128 countries, according to the United Nations Conference on Trade and Development, Data Protection and Privacy Legislation Worldwide (dashboard), https://unctad.org/page/data -protection-and-privacy-legislation-worldwide; 116 countries, according to DLA Piper (2020); and 142 countries (as of 2019), according to Greenleaf and Cottier (2020), as referenced by Anderson and Renieris (2020).

24. Consent is not the only basis for data processing, but it remains a centerpiece because of its historical legacy. Even in the GDPR, consent is one among many grounds for legitimate data processing. See, for example, GDPR Article 6.1 (EU 2018a).

25. See Recital 43 of the GDPR (EU 2018c).

26. For example, the US Fair Credit Reporting Act bans certain types of data from being used to determine an individual's creditworthiness (FTC 2018).

27. Section 35 of the Personal Data Protection Bill currently under discussion in India states that, in the event of an imminent threat to the sovereignty or integrity of the country or security of the state, the government has the power to exempt public sector entities from application of the bill entirely (Parliament of India 2019).

28. Sections 13(1) and (2) of India's Personal Data Protection Bill (2018) state that, until and unless such a threat occurs, personal data may be processed without procuring consent from the user in the following cases: "(1) Personal data may be processed if such processing is necessary for any function of Parliament or any State Legislature. (2) Personal data may be processed if such processing is necessary for the exercise of any function of the State authorised by law for: (a) the provision of any service or benefit to the data principal from the State; or (b) the issuance of any certification, license or permit for any action or activity of the data principal by the State" (Personal Data Protection Bill, 2018, https://www.meity.gov.in/writereaddata/files/Personal _Data_Protection_Bill,2018.pdf).

29. See Article 8 of the European Convention on Human Rights on the right to respect for private and family life (ECHR 2010). The European Court of Human Rights (ECHR) has interpreted limitations to the right as subject to a "legitimate aim" necessary to fulfill a "pressing social need" and "proportionate to the legitimate aim pursued" (ECHR 2020, 12). These due process restrictions apply even in emergency situations—see Article 15 (ECHR 2010). Such situations could include war or pandemic. The European Data Protection Board (EDPB 2018), civil society organizations such as the Electronic Frontier Foundation (see, for example, Gelman 1998), and Article 19 of the European Convention have enshrined these principles into data protection rules and guidelines. See Electronic Frontier Foundation, "13 International Principles on the Application of Human

Rights to Communication Surveillance," https://www.eff.org/files/2014/01/05/13p-onepagerfinal.pdf.

30. Ben-Avie and Tiwari (2019).

31. According to the World Economic Forum, "volunteered data" are data that are "created and explicitly shared by individuals, e.g., social network profiles"; "observed data" are "captured by recording the actions of individuals, e.g., location data when using cell phones"; and "inferred data" are "data about individuals based on an analysis of volunteered or observed information, e.g., credit scores" (WEF 2011).

32. Austin and Lie (2019). See also Recital 26 of the GDPR: "The principles of data protection should therefore not apply to anonymous information, namely information which does not relate to an identified or identifiable natural person or to personal data rendered anonymous in such a manner that the data subject is not or no longer identifiable" (EU 2018b). Pseudonymized data, however, still count as personally identifiable information.

33. Austin and Lie (2019); de Montjoye et al. (2013). Additional research argues that only three data points are needed for reidentification in most cases (Sweeney 2000). There is also much recent research on the limits and durability of these deidentifying technologies (Lubarsky 2017).

34. Austin and Lie (2019). For example, scientific research may require certain personally identifiable information characteristics (such as age and gender) for accuracy.

35. Current international guidelines for data collection and processing, such as the 2013 OECD guidelines and the United Nations Data Privacy, Ethics and Protection Principles (UNSDG 2017), and leading legal frameworks such as the European Union's General Data Protection Regulation (EU 2018f), focus on protecting personal data and professionally identifiable information. For a broader discussion, see Taylor, Floridi, and van der Sloot (2017).

36. Krämer, Senellart, and de Streel (2020).

37. A purpose-driven approach to data protection should involve determining as threshold questions what data should be collected and what data should be shared. Anonos, "Schrems II Webinar Summary: Lawful Data Transfers," https://www.schremsii.com/faqs-and-summary-edps-noyb-webinar.

38. In other words, focus on the ways in which the data will and may be used and what its potential impacts may be. For this reason, tools such as data protection impact assessments (and, when appropriate, human rights impact assessments, such as when high-risk, data-driven technologies are being used) can help identify risks that must be mitigated through the appropriate legal, technical, and organizational means.

39. Cavoukian (2011).

40. For example, homomorphic encryption allows analysis of encrypted data. Similar in purpose, federated learning techniques allow data to be processed and analyzed without having to send raw data to a central server (Homomorphic Encryption Standardization, "Homomorphic Encryption," https://homomorphicencryption.org/; Potey, Dhote, and Sharma 2016). That said, encryption is not a silver bullet for compliance. Encryption may be an effective safeguard while data are in storage or in transit, but it may not provide sufficient protection for processing if data must be de-encrypted before computation.

41. Newer techniques that have emerged in response to challenges around deidentification include K-anonymity (works by aggregating data attributes) and differential privacy (works by introducing random noise into datasets)—see Austin and Lie (2019); Dwork (2006); Sweeney (2000).

42. The European Commission's guidance on privacy by design is clear that these techniques should not be a substitute for robust legal protections: "The term 'Privacy by Design' means nothing more than 'data protection through technology design.' Behind this is the thought that data protection in data processing procedures is best adhered to when it is already integrated in the technology when created. . . . The text of the law leads one to conclude that often several protective measures must be used with one another to satisfy statutory requirements. In practice, this consideration is already performed in an early development phase when setting technology decisions. Recognized certification can serve as an indicator to authorities that the persons responsible have complied with the statutory requirements of 'Privacy by Design'" (Intersoft Consulting, "GDPR: Privacy by Design," https://gdpr-info.eu/issues/privacy-by-design/). Also see DSGVO-Portal, "Recital 78 GDPR | General Data Protection Regulation," https://www.dsgvo-portal.de/gdpr_recital_78.php.

43. The Mauritius Declaration on the Internet of Things states: "Data processing starts from the moment the data are collected. All protective measures should be in place from the outset. We encourage the development of technologies that facilitate new ways to incorporate data protection and consumer privacy from the outset. Privacy by design and default should no longer be regarded as something peculiar. They should become a key selling point of innovative technologies" (EDPS 2014, 2).

44. The International Organization for Standardization has created a technical committee for a new ISO standard on Consumer Protection: Privacy by Design for Consumer Goods and Services (ISO 2018).

45. Cavoukian (2010).

46. According to the European Commission: "Companies/organisations are encouraged to implement technical and organisational measures, at the earliest stages of the design of the processing operations, in such a way that safeguards privacy and data protection principles right from the start ('data protection by design'). By default, companies/organisations should ensure that personal data is processed with the highest privacy protection (for example only the data necessary should be processed, short storage period, limited accessibility) so that by default personal data isn't made accessible to an indefinite number of persons ('data protection

by default')." European Commission, "What Does Data Protection 'by Design' and 'by Default' Mean?" https://ec.europa.eu/info/law/law-topic/data-protection/reform/rules-business-and-organisations/obligations/what-does-data-protection-design-and-default-mean_en.

47. OVIC (2020).

48. See PCPD (2012) for materials on the data protection framework in China.

49. ICO (2018).

50. de Montjoye at al. (2013). Additional research argues that only three data points are needed for reidentification in most cases (Sweeney 2000).

51. These new techniques include statistical approaches such as K-anonymity, which aggregates data attributes (Sweeney 2002); differential privacy, which introduces random noise (Dwork 2006); and encryption techniques such as homomorphic encryption, which conduct analysis on encrypted data (Potey, Dhote, and Sharma 2016).

52. Austin and Lie (2019).

53. See Hasselbalch and Tranberg (2016). An explanation of a personal data store is offered in Mydex, "What Is a Personal Data Store?" https://pds.mydex.org/what-personal-data-store-0.

54. ENISA (2014). Also see the recommendation by the European Union Agency for Cybersecurity (ENISA) that it may be necessary to overlay several privacy by design or pseudonymization techniques in order to meet the GDPR's threshold (ENISA 2019).

55. The OECD Recommendation on Artificial Intelligence "identifies five complementary values-based principles for the responsible stewardship of trustworthy AI" (OECD 2019c). In particular, according to principle 2 on human-centered values and fairness, "AI actors should respect the rule of law, human rights, and democratic values throughout the AI system life cycle. These include freedom, dignity and autonomy, privacy and data protection, nondiscrimination and equality, diversity, fairness, social justice, and internationally recognized labor rights." These actors should also "implement mechanisms and safeguards, such as capacity for human determination, that are appropriate to the context." According to principle 3 on transparency and explainability, "AI actors should commit to transparency and responsible disclosure regarding AI systems." One of the aims should be "to enable those adversely affected by an AI system to challenge [the] outcome based on plain and easy-to-understand information." As of May 2019, 44 countries had adhered to the OECD Recommendation and the five principles (OECD 2019c).

56. See Loi N° 2013-450 relative à la protection des données à caractère personnel [Law 2013-450 on the protection of personal data], *Journal Officiel de la Republique de Côte d'Ivoire*, August 8, 2013, 474–82.

57. Controversies around the use of facial recognition and other AI-based technologies for law enforcement have been in the public eye in the United Kingdom since 2019, when the UK Information Commissioner Office launched an investigation into the use of facial recognition technology in King's Cross in London, on the grounds that it might raise data protection concerns. Subsequently, the UK High Court's decision in favor of the use of facial recognition by the South Wales Police, after the claimant argued that its use would be a violation of privacy, was the first legal challenge to the use of facial recognition by police in the world. See ICO (2019); Nilsson (2019); Smith (2016).

58. The 2016 study conducted by the Human Rights Data Analysis Group using 2010 and 2011 data from the Oakland police department and other sources compared a mapping of drug use based on survey data from the victims of crime with another based on algorithmic analysis of police arrests. The study showed that biased source data could reinforce and potentially amplify racial bias in law enforcement practices (Lum 2016). Data on arrests showed that African-American neighborhoods have on average 200 times more drug arrests than other areas in Oakland (NIST 2020; Smith 2016).

59. Hill (2020).

60. Noble (2018).

61. Dastin (2018).

62. Organisation for Economic Co-operation and Development, http://www.oecd.org/going-digital/ai/principles/; G-20 (Japan-led), https://www.meti.go.jp/press/2019/06/20190610010/20190610010-1.pdf.

63. HLCM (2018).

64. Cision (2020); City of Amsterdam (2020); City of Helsinki (2020).

65. DCMS (2019); Stats NZ (2019). For a subnational example, see Nantes City's Metropolitan Charter on Data (Ville de Nantes 2019). At a national level, France's Etalab has developed a map of algorithmic systems in use across public sector entities in France and is providing ministries, departments, and agencies with guidance on their reporting and other accountability requirements (Etalab 2020a, 2020b).

66. See Canada's responsible use of AI in government programs, including Guiding Principles, lists of certified providers of AI services, and its Algorithmic Impact Assessment (TBS 2020).

67. Henley and Booth (2020).

68. The mandate of the US Federal Trade Commission (FTC) includes hearing and adjudicating cases involving unfair competition or unfair or deceptive acts under Section 5 of the FTC Act (see Federal Trade Commission, Federal Trade Commission Act, https://www.ftc.gov/enforcement/statutes/federal-trade-commission-act). According to the FTC, "when companies tell consumers they will safeguard their personal information, the FTC can and does take law enforcement action to make sure that companies live up [to] these promises. The FTC has brought legal actions against organizations that have violated consumers' privacy rights, or misled them by failing to maintain security for sensitive consumer information, or caused substantial consumer injury. In many of these cases, the FTC has charged the defendants with violating Section 5 of the FTC Act, which bars unfair

and deceptive acts and practices in or affecting commerce. In addition to the FTC Act, the agency also enforces other federal laws relating to consumers' privacy and security" (see Federal Trade Commission, "Privacy and Security Enforcement," https://www.ftc.gov/news-events/media-resources/protecting-consumer-privacy/privacy-security-enforcement).

69. Hoofnagle, Hartzog, and Solove (2019).

70. In the context of its 2020 European Data Strategy, the EU may adopt a new Data Act in 2021, which would update the IPR framework currently in force (including a possible revision of the 1996 Database Directive) to support the use and reuse of nonpersonal data (EC 2020b).

71. See, for example, Contract Guidelines on Data Utilization Rights, updating the Unfair Competitive Prevention Act of 2018 (METI 2020).

72. MeitY (2020).

73. See World Intellectual Property Organization, "Brazil: Law No. 9.610 of February 19, 1998 (Law on Copyright and Neighboring Rights, as amended by Law No. 12.853 of August 14, 2013)," WIPO Lex (database), https://wipolex.wipo.int/en/legislation/details/17474.

74. See, generally, the two model laws promulgated by the United Nations Commission on International Trade Law (UNCITRAL 1998, 2001).

75. For purposes of this discussion, no distinction is drawn between "electronic" signatures and "digital" signatures, although commonly "digital" signatures are associated with the use of public key infrastructure (PKI). For a more detailed explanation of PKI and the differences between e-signatures and digital signatures, see UNCITRAL (2001, 26–27; https://www.uncitral.org/pdf/english/texts/electcom/ml-elecsig-e.pdf).

76. UNCITRAL (1998).

77. Public key infrastructure (PKI) has been defined as follows: "The framework and services that provide for the generation, production, distribution, control, accounting, and destruction of public key certificates. Components include the personnel, policies, processes, server platforms, software, and workstations used for the purpose of administering certificates and public-private key pairs, including the ability to issue, maintain, recover, and revoke public key certificates" (https://nvlpubs.nist.gov/nistpubs/SpecialPublications/NIST.SP.800-53r4.pdf).

78. EU (2014, article 3[15]).

79. See, generally, World Bank, ID4D Data: Global Identification Challenge by the Numbers (dashboard), https://id4d.worldbank.org/global-dataset; Sustainable Development, Department of Economic and Social Affairs, United Nations, "The 17 Goals," https://sdgs.un.org/goals. Sustainable Development Goal (SDG) 16.9 states: "By 2030, provide legal identity for all, including birth registration."

80. World Bank (2019).

81. UNCITRAL (1998).

82. National Assembly, Togo (2020).

83. EC (2018c).

84. The Australian government's Data Sharing and Release Act of 2018 was drafted based on the results of a report of the Productivity Commission (PC 2017). The purpose of the act is to (1) promote better sharing of public sector data, (2) build trust in use of public data, (3) dial up or down appropriate safeguards, (4) maintain the integrity of the data system, and (5) establish institutional arrangements (see Department of the Prime Minister and Cabinet, "Data Sharing and Release Reforms," https://www.pmc.gov.au/public-data/data-sharing-and-release-reforms). This is expected to lead to (1) more efficient and effective government services for citizens; (2) more well-informed government programs and policies; (3) greater transparency around government activities and spending; (4) economic growth from innovative data use; and (5) research solutions to current and emerging social, environmental, and economic issues. The purpose of the act is thus to move the paradigm from one that restricts access to identifiable data to one that authorizes release if appropriate data safeguards are in place. To complement the Data Sharing and Release Act, the government published a best-practice guide outlining good-practice principles based on the Five Safes Framework to manage the risks of disclosure and designed to assess whether and how to share data (PMC 2019). By enabling a privacy by design approach to data sharing by focusing on controls and benefits instead of merely reducing the level of detail in the data to be shared, the principles help maximize the usefulness of the data.

85. National Archives (2019).

86. Section 1 of France's Law for a Digital Republic lays out provisions on open government data (Légifrance 2016). Also see Dodds (2016).

87. They include geospatial, meteorological, and mobility data, as well as statistics and data on corporate ownership and Earth observation and the environment.

88. Noveck (2017).

89. Noveck (2017).

90. See Open Knowledge Foundation (2020).

91. OECD (2013, 2019a); Ubaldi (2013); Vickery (2012).

92. Dodds (2016).

93. OECD (2019a).

94. Austin and Lie (2019); Dodds (2016).

95. World Wide Web Foundation (2017).

96. For general principles, see ISO and IEC (2016, sec. 8.2). For a practical example, see Data.NSW (2020).

97. OECD (2019a).

98. OECD (2019a).

99. Austin and Lie (2019).

100. Wilkinson et al. (2016).

101. See Article 3: "Art. L. 300-4.- Any provision made electronically under this book is done in an open standard, easily reusable and exploitable by an automated processing system" of the French Republic (Légifrance 2016).

102. Because the development of open standards is often undertaken with input from leading industry participants, who frequently integrate their firms'

proprietary technical standards into the design, SSOs may require the application of patent rights on FRAND terms. The adoption of FRAND licensing terms can therefore become a condition for participation in SSOs. The obligation to offer FRAND licenses to new market entrants usually extends to third-party technology providers whether or not they are SSO members. For further details, see Ragavan, Murphy, and Davé (2016).

103. The Open Knowledge Foundation's definition of open data ("Open Definition") sets out conditions for the availability and access of data, its reuse and redistribution, and universal participation. On the latter, "everyone must be able to use, re-use and redistribute—there should be no discrimination against fields of endeavor or against persons or groups. For example, 'noncommercial' restrictions that would prevent 'commercial' use, or restrictions of use for certain purposes (e.g. only in education), are not allowed." See Open Knowledge Foundation (2020; https://okfn.org/opendata/).

104. MITCI (2017).

105. Council of Ministers, Jordan (2019).

106. ISO and IEC (2017).

107. EDRi (2015). Ensuring sufficient resources and technical capacity to effectively discharge these functions is critical. For example, Estonia's X-Tee data exchange and interoperability platform is continuously monitored to mitigate cyberthreats (RIA 2020). See chapter 8 for further details on implementation.

108. EC (2016).

109. As the European Commission notes: "Online public services are crucial to increasing the cost-efficiency and quality of the services provided to citizens and companies. One example of increased efficiency is the 'Once Only' principle—only in 48% of cases do public administrations reuse information about the citizen or companies that is already in their possession without asking again. The extension of this principle, in compliance with data protection legislation, would generate an annual net saving at the EU level of around EUR 5 billion per year by 2017. The Commission will launch a pilot project for the 'Once-Only' principle for businesses and citizens and explore the possibility of an EU wide e-safe solution (a secure online repository for documents). Extending 'Once-Only' across borders would further contribute to the efficiency of the Digital Single Market" (EC 2015, 16).

110. TOOP (2021).

111. See European Commission, "Horizon 2020," https://ec.europa.eu/programmes/horizon2020/en.

112. SCOOP4C, "Stakeholder Community: Once-Only Principle for Citizens," https://www.scoop4c.eu/.

113. OECD (2019a).

114. OECD (2019a).

115. EU (2019b).

116. EC (2020a).

117. Légifrance (2016). This covers, for example, data from delegated public services or data that are relevant for targeting welfare payments or constructing national statistics (OECD 2019a).

118. The UK Digital Economy Act enables accredited researchers to gain access to deidentified data for research purposes (National Archives, United Kingdom 2017, c. 30, Chap. 5). The act regulates data sharing practices for the purposes of research using public data, but it does not govern data sharing in other contexts (Austin and Lie 2019).

119. Finch and Tene (2018).

120. OECD (2019b).

121. Ragavan, Murphy, and Davé (2016).

122. FRAND licensing regimes have been designed to be an effective competition law remedy (see the *Apple vs. Samsung* cases), but infringements of FRAND terms involve contractual remedies between the patent holder and the SSO (or third party). However, experts have argued that the pro-innovation and competitive effects of licensing regimes depend on how they are implemented. Indeed, some have argued that an "excessive reliance" on FRAND terms may be counterproductive.

123. Open Knowledge Foundation, "Open Data Commons Open Database License (ODbL) v1.0," https://opendatacommons.org/licenses/odbl/1-0/.

124. Creative Commons, "Open Data," https://creativecommons.org/about/program-areas/open-data/.

125. MoICT (2017).

126. See the European Union's Free Flow of Nonpersonal Data Regulation (EU 2018e), the Payment Services Directive (EU 2015), the Digital Content Directive (EU 2019a), and certain sectoral regulations, in addition to the right to data portability for personal data enshrined in Article 20 of the GDPR. See also Borgogno and Colangelo (2019).

127. Article 20 of the GDPR (EU 2016).

128. The European Commission notes: "In general, given the policy objectives of the right to data portability, the term 'provided by the data subject' must be interpreted broadly, and should exclude 'inferred data' and 'derived data,' which include personal data that are created by a service provider (for example, algorithmic results). A data controller can exclude those inferred data but should include all other personal data provided by the data subject through technical means provided by the controller" (EC 2017). This approach contrasts with that of other legal frameworks, such as the California Consumer Protection Act (CCPA), that are broader in scope covering inferred data (see OneTrust DataGuidance and FPF 2019).

129. Krämer, Senellart, and de Streel (2020).

130. See Recital 68 of the GDPR: "Data controllers should be encouraged to develop interoperable formats that enable data portability. . . . The data subject's right to transmit or receive personal data concerning him or her should not create an obligation for the controllers to adopt or maintain processing systems which are technically compatible. . . . Where technically feasible, the data subject should have the right to have the personal data transmitted directly from one controller to another" (EU 2018d).

131. See Article 6, "Porting of Data," of the EU Regulation on the Free Flow of Non-personal Data: "The Commission shall *encourage and facilitate* [emphasis added] the development of self-regulatory codes of conduct at Union level ('codes of conduct'), in order to contribute to a competitive data economy" (EU 2018e, 67).

132. PIMS can help individuals control their ported data through mechanisms that simplify the process. They can include mechanisms that support individual control over ported data such as schema mappings (which convert data from the sender's format to the receiver's) or functionalities that centralize and help visualize consent and rights management for portability or broader data protection. However, these mechanisms have not been standardized across the industry to date, which affects the broader sustainability of the business model and their adoption as an alternative to other enforcement mechanisms.

133. Measures such as shifting to authentication mechanisms (like privacy seals) and open-source solutions that are more user friendly may support the adoption of PIMS as alternatives for consumers, especially if the reliability of these solutions are certified to promote trust (Krämer, Senellart, and de Streel 2020).

134. The first right to portability mandated by EU law was the portability of phone numbers, following the Universal Services Directive, based on a legislative effort to create competition in the telecommunications sector (Zanfir-Fortuna and Hondagneu-Messner 2019).

135. Borgogno and Colangelo (2019).

136. Congress of the Philippines (2012).

137. The "consumer data right" aims to "give Australians greater control over their data, empowering their consumers to choose to share their data with trusted recipients only for the purposes they have authorized" (Treasury, Australia 2020).

138. See Part IVD in Federal Register of Legislation, Australia (2019).

139. The act begins with the telecommunications, banking, and energy sectors before rolling out across the economy.

140. The data standards body has released version 1.6.0 of the consumer data standards, which represent high-level standards and are in accordance with the rules and phasing timetable of the Australian Competition and Consumer Commission. See Data61, Commonwealth Scientific and Industrial Research Organisation, "Consumer Data Standards," https://consumer datastandards.gov.au/consumer-data-standards/.

141. At present, the Data Transfer Project is at the pilot stage, making it difficult to measure the impact of the project on enabling continuous portability of data. It remains an interesting model of private sector–led cooperation to develop standard and interoperable data formats that could be scaled up. See Google, "Data Transfer Project," https://datatransferproject.dev/. The founding members of the Data Transfer Project were Google and Facebook. They were later joined by Apple, Microsoft, and Twitter.

142. Borgogno and Colangelo (2019).

143. OECD (2019a).

144. This was a point of discussion at the international policy workshop "Data for Better Lives: Enablers and Safeguards" hosted by the World Bank and the German Federal Ministry of Economic Cooperation and Development in Washington, DC, June 9–10, 2020.

145. See Berlin Group, "PSD2 Access to Bank Accounts," https://www.berlin-group.org/psd2-access-to-bank -accounts.

146. Waze (2018).

147. Google, "Waze for Cities: Working Together for a Smarter, More Sustainable Future," *Waze*, https://www .waze.com/ccp. Waze and other companies have been sharing data with local governments in Brazil since the 2016 Rio Olympics under their Connected Citizens Program. Their platform is designed to support public entities with urban planning, traffic optimization, law enforcement, and emergency service provision (Huyer and Cecconi 2020).

148. OECD (2019a).

149. Huyer and Cecconi (2020).

150. These include Japan's "Contract Guidance on Utilization of AI and Data" (METI 2018); the Netherlands' Dare-2-Share Cooperation Agreement (Dare 2 Share Ministries, "Terms and Conditions," https://www .dare2share.org/about/terms-and-conditions/); and the European Union's proposed "Guidance on Private Sector Data Sharing" (EC 2018b). Japan's Ministry of Economy, Trade and Industry (METI) developed the "Contract Guidance on Utilization of AI and Data" as a resource for businesses entering a data sharing agreement. It highlights factors and terms to be considered for inclusion when drafting a contract using data or AI, including sample clauses.

151. Kirkpatrick (2014).

152. See "Development Data Partnership," https://data partnership.org/.

153. GPO (2018).

154. Kosseff (2019, 27).

155. GPO (2018, at sec. 230).

156. LOC (1998).

157. Kosseff (2019, 5).

158. See Electronic Frontier Foundation, "Manila Principles on Intermediary Liability," https://www.manila principles.org/.

References

Anderson, Thea, and Elizabeth M. Renieris. 2020. "Data Protection and Digital Infrastructure before, during, and after a Pandemic." Omidyar Network, Redwood City, CA. https://omidyar.com/data-protection-and-digital -infrastructure-before-during-and-after-a-pandemic/.

Austin, Lisa M., and David Lie. 2019. "Safe Sharing Sites." *NYU Law Review* 94 (4): 591–623. https://www.nyulawreview .org/issues/volume-94-number-4/safe-sharing-sites/.

Ben-Avie, Jochai, and Udbhav Tiwari. 2019. "India's New Data Protection Bill: Strong on Companies, Step Backward on Government Surveillance." *Open Policy and Advocacy* (blog), December 10, 2019. https://blog.mozilla.org/net policy/2019/12/10/indias-new-data-protection-bill-strong -on-companies-weak-on-gov.

Borgogno, Oscar, and Giuseppe Colangelo. 2019. "Data Sharing and Interoperability: Fostering Innovation and Competition through APIs." *Computer Law and Security Review* 35 (5): 105314. https://doi.org/10.1016/j.clsr.2019.03.008.

Cavoukian, Ann. 2010. "Privacy by Design: The Definitive Workshop; A Foreword by Ann Cavoukian, Ph.D." *Identity in the Information Society* 3 (2): 247–51. https://doi.org /10.1007/s12394-010-0062-y.

Cavoukian, Ann. 2011. "PbD, Privacy by Design, the 7 Foundational Principles: Implementation and Mapping of Fair Information Practices." Information and Privacy Commissioner of Ontario, Toronto.

Chen, Rong. 2021. "Mapping Data Governance Legal Frameworks around the World: Findings from the Global Data Regulation Diagnostic." Policy Research Working Paper 9615, World Bank, Washington, DC. http:// documents.worldbank.org/curated/en/58133161781768 0243/Mapping-Data-Governance-Legal-Frameworks -Around-the-World-Findings-from-the-Global-Data -Regulation-Diagnostic.

Cision. 2020. "Helsinki and Amsterdam First Cities in the World to Launch Open AI Register." *Cision News*, September 28, 2020. Cision, Chicago. https://news.cision.com /fi/city-of-helsinki/r/helsinki-and-amsterdam-first -cities-in-the-world-to-launch-open-ai-register,c3204076.

City of Amsterdam. 2020. "What Is the Algorithm Register?" *City of Amsterdam Algorithm Register Beta.* https:// algoritmeregister.amsterdam.nl/en/ai-register/.

City of Helsinki. 2020. "What Is an Artificial Intelligence Register?" *City of Helsinki Artificial Intelligence Register.* https://ai.hel.fi/.

COE (Council of Europe). 2018. "Convention 108+: Convention for the Protection of Individuals with Regard to the Processing of Personal Data." COE, Strasbourg. https://rm.coe .int/convention-108-convention-for-the-protection-of -individuals-with-regar/16808b36f1.

Confessore, Nicholas. 2018. "Cambridge Analytica and Facebook: The Scandal and the Fallout So Far." *New York Times*, April 4, 2018. https://www.nytimes.com/2018/04/04/us /politics/cambridge-analytica-scandal-fallout.html.

Congress of the Philippines. 2012. "Republic Act No. 10173: An Act Protecting Individual Personal Information in Information and Communications Systems in the Government and the Private Sector, Creating for This Purpose a National Privacy Commission, and for Other Purposes." August 12, 2012, Lawphil Project, Arellano Law Foundation, Manila. https://lawphil.net/statutes/repacts/ra2012 /ra_10173_2012.html.

Council of Ministers, Jordan. 2019. "Jordan Open Government Data License." Issue version 1.0, Open Government Data Platform. https://portal.jordan.gov.jo/OGD -License_en.pdf.

Council of the European Union. 2019. "Regulation of the European Parliament and of the Council on European Production and Preservation Orders for Electronic Evidence in Criminal Matters." Interinstitutional File 2018/0108(COD), Council of the European Union, Brussels.

https://data.consilium.europa.eu/doc/document/ST -10206-2019-INIT/en/pdf.

Dastin, Jeffrey. 2018. "Amazon Scraps Secret AI Recruiting Tool That Showed Bias against Women." *Reuters*, October 10, 2018. https://www.reuters.com/article/us -amazon-com-jobs-automation-insight/amazon-scraps -secret-ai-recruiting-tool-that-showed-bias-against -women-idUSKCN1MK08G.

Data.NSW. 2020. "NSW Government Information Classification, Labelling, and Handling Guidelines." Data.NSW, Data Analytics Center, Customer, Delivery, and Transformation, Department of Customer Service, Government of New South Wales, Sydney. https://www .digital.nsw.gov.au/sites/default/files/NSW%20Info%20 Classification%20Labelling%20and%20Handling%20 Guidelines%202020%20V2.1_1.pdf.

DCMS (Department for Digital, Culture, Media, and Sport, United Kingdom). 2019. "Digital Charter." Policy Paper, DCMS, London. https://www.gov.uk/government /publications/digital-charter/digital-charter.

Deighton-Smith, Rex, Angelo Erbacci, and Céline Kauffmann. 2016. "Promoting Inclusive Growth through Better Regulation: The Role of Regulatory Impact Assessment." OECD Regulatory Policy Working Paper 3, Organisation for Economic Co-operation and Development, Paris. https://doi.org/10.1787/5jm3tqwqp1vj-en.

de Montjoye, Yves-Alexandre, César A. Hidalgo, Michel Verleysen, and Vincent D. Blondel. 2013. "Unique in the Crowd: The Privacy Bounds of Human Mobility." *Scientific Reports* 3 (1): article 1376. https://doi.org/10.1038 /srep01376.

DLA Piper. 2020. *Data Protection Laws of the World.* London: DLA Piper. https://www.dlapiperdataprotection.com /index.html?t=about&c=AO.

Dodds, Leigh. 2016. "How to Write a Good Open Data Policy." *Guides.* Open Data Institute, London.

Dong, Marissa Xiao. 2020. "China: The Civil Code Strengthens Civil Law Protection around Privacy and Personal Information." *Conventus Law*, June 12, 2020. http:// www.conventuslaw.com/report/china-the-civil-code -strengthens-civil-law/.

Dwork, Cynthia. 2006. "Differential Privacy." In *Automata, Languages and Programming: 33rd International Colloquium, ICALP 2006, Venice, Italy, July 10–14, 2006, Proceedings, Part II*, edited by Michele Bugliesi, Bart Preneel, Vladimiro Sassone, and Ingo Wegener, 1–12. Lecture Notes in Computer Science Series, Vol. 4052. Berlin: Springer. https:// link.springer.com/chapter/10.1007%2F11787006_1.

EC (European Commission). 2014. "Guidelines on the Implementation of the Court of Justice of the European Union Judgment on 'Google Spain and INC v. Agencia Española de Protección de Datos (AEPD) and Mario Costeja González' C-131/12." Document WP225, Directorate C (Fundamental Rights and Union Citizenship), Directorate General Justice, EC, Brussels. https://ec.europa.eu /newsroom/article29/item-detail.cfm?item_id=667236.

EC (European Commission). 2015. "A Digital Single Market Strategy for Europe." Document COM(2015) 192 final, EC, Brussels. https://eur-lex.europa.eu/legal-content/EN /TXT/PDF/?uri=CELEX:52015DC0192&from=EN.

EC (European Commission). 2016. "EU eGovernment Action Plan 2016–2020: Accelerating the Digital Transformation of Government." Document COM(2016) 179 final, EC, Brussels. https://eur-lex.europa.eu/legal-content/EN/TXT/?uri=CELEX:52016DC0179.

EC (European Commission). 2017. "Article 29 Data Protection Working Party: Guidelines on the Right to Data Portability." Document WP242 rev.01, Directorate C (Fundamental Rights and Rule of Law), Directorate General Justice and Consumers, EC, Brussels. https://ec.europa.eu/newsroom/article29/item-detail.cfm?item_id=611233.

EC (European Commission). 2018a. "Article 29 Working Party: Guidelines on Consent under Regulation 2016/679." Document WP259 rev.01, Directorate C (Fundamental Rights and Union Citizenship), Directorate General Justice, EC, Brussels. https://ec.europa.eu/newsroom/article29/document.cfm?action=display&doc_id=51030.

EC (European Commission). 2018b. "Guidance on Private Sector Data Sharing." Text. Shaping Europe's Digital Future—European Commission. https://ec.europa.eu/digital-single-market/en/guidance-private-sector-data-sharing.

EC (European Commission). 2018c. Study to Support the Review of Directive 2003/98/EC on the Re-Use of Public Sector Information: Final Report. Luxembourg: Publications Office of the European Union. https://data.europa.eu/doi/10.2759/373622.

EC (European Commission). 2020a. "European Legislation on Open Data and the Re-Use of Public Sector Information." Shaping Europe's Digital Future: Policy. Data Policy and Innovation (Unit G.1), EC, Brussels. https://ec.europa.eu/digital-single-market/en/european-legislation-reuse-public-sector-information.

EC (European Commission). 2020b. "A European Strategy for Data." Communication COM(2020) 66 final, Brussels, EC. https://ec.europa.eu/info/sites/info/files/communication-european-strategy-data-19feb2020_en.pdf.

ECHR (European Court of Human Rights). 2010. "European Convention on Human Rights." ECHR and Council of Europe, Strasbourg. https://www.echr.coe.int/documents/convention_eng.pdf.

ECHR (European Court of Human Rights). 2020. Guide on Article 8 of the European Convention on Human Rights: Right to Respect for Private and Family Life, Home and Correspondence, rev. ed. Strasbourg: ECHR. https://www.echr.coe.int/documents/guide_art_8_eng.pdf.

EDPB (European Data Protection Board). 2018. "Guidelines 2/2018 on Derogations of Article 49 under Regulation 2016/679." Guidelines. EDPB, Brussels. https://edpb.europa.eu/sites/edpb/files/files/file1/edpb_guidelines_2_2018_derogations_en.pdf.

EDPS (European Data Protection Supervisor). 2014. "Mauritius Declaration on the Internet of Things." 36th International Conference of Data Protection and Privacy Commissioners, Balaclava, Mauritius, October 14, 2014. https://edps.europa.eu/sites/edp/files/publication/14-10-14_mauritius_declaration_en.pdf.

EDRi (European Digital Rights). 2015. "A Truly Digital Single Market?" June, EDRi, Brussels. https://edri.org/files/DSM_Analysis_EDRi_20150617.pdf.

ENISA (European Union Agency for Cybersecurity). 2014. "Privacy and Data Protection by Design: From Policy to Engineering." ENISA, Heraklion, Greece. https://data.europa.eu/doi/10.2824/38623.

ENISA (European Union Agency for Cybersecurity). 2019. "Pseudonymisation Techniques and Best Practices: Recommendations on Shaping Technology According to Data Protection and Privacy Provisions." ENISA, Heraklion, Greece. https://www.enisa.europa.eu/publications/pseudonymisation-techniques-and-best-practices.

Etalab. 2020a. "Algorithmes de Nantes Métropole." data.gouv.fr, October 7, 2020, Etalab, Paris. https://www.data.gouv.fr/en/datasets/algorithmes-de-nantes-metropole/.

Etalab. 2020b. "Les algorithmes publics: enjeux et obligations" [Public sector algorithms: challenges and obligations]. guides.etalab.gouv.fr, Etalab, Paris. https://guides.etalab.gouv.fr/algorithmes/guide/#_1-a-quoi-servent-les-algorithmes-publics.

EU (European Union). 2014. "Regulation (EU) No 910/2014 of the European Parliament and of the Council of 23 July 2014 on Electronic Identification and Trust Services for Electronic Transactions in the Internal Market and Repealing Directive 1999/93/EC." Official Journal of the European Union L 257/73 (August 8). https://ec.europa.eu/futurium/en/system/files/ged/eidas_regulation.pdf.

EU (European Union). 2015. "Directive (EU) 2015/2366 of the European Parliament and of the Council of 25 November 2015 on Payment Services in the Internal Market, Amending Directives 2002/65/EC, 2009/110/EC and 2013/36/EU and Regulation (EU) No 1093/2010, and Repealing Directive 2007/64/EC." Official Journal of the European Union L 337/35 (December 23). https://eur-lex.europa.eu/legal-content/EN/TXT/PDF/?uri=CELEX:32015L2366&from=EN.

EU (European Union). 2016. "Regulation (EU) 2016/679 of the European Parliament and of the Council of 27 April 2016 on the Protection of Natural Persons with Regard to the Processing of Personal Data and on the Free Movement of Such Data, and Repealing Directive 95/46/EC (General Data Protection Regulation)." Official Journal of the European Union L 119/1 (May 4). https://eur-lex.europa.eu/eli/reg/2016/679/oj.

EU (European Union). 2018a. "Art. 6 GDPR: Lawfulness of Processing." GDPR.Eu, November 14, 2018. Proton Technologies, Calgary, Canada. https://gdpr.eu/article-6-how-to-process-personal-data-legally/.

EU (European Union). 2018b. "Recital 26: Not Applicable to Anonymous Data." GDPR.Eu, November 14, 2018. Proton Technologies, Calgary, Canada. https://gdpr.eu/recital-26-not-applicable-to-anonymous-data/.

EU (European Union). 2018c. "Recital 43: Freely Given Consent." GDPR.Eu, November 14, 2018. Proton Technologies, Calgary, Canada. https://gdpr.eu/recital-43-freely-given-consent/.

EU (European Union). 2018d. "Recital 68: Right of Data Portability." GDPR.Eu, November 14, 2018. Proton Technologies, Calgary, Canada. https://gdpr.eu/recital-68-right-of-data-portability/.

EU (European Union). 2018e. "Regulation (EU) 2018/1807 of the European Parliament and of the Council of 14 November 2018 on a Framework for the Free Flow of Non-personal Data in the European Union." Official Journal of the European Union L 303, 61 (November 10): 78–68. https://eur-lex.europa.eu/legal-content/EN/TXT/PDF/?uri=OJ:L:2018:303:FULL&from=EN.

EU (European Union). 2018f. "What Is GDPR, the EU's New Data Protection Law?" *GDPR.Eu*, May 25, 2018. Proton Technologies, Calgary, Canada. https://gdpr.eu/what-is-gdpr/.

EU (European Union). 2019a. "Directive (EU) 2019/770 of the European Parliament and of the Council of 20 May 2019 on Certain Aspects Concerning Contracts for the Supply of Digital Content and Digital Services." *Official Journal of the European Union* L 136/1 (May 22). https://eur-lex.europa.eu/legal-content/EN/TXT/PDF/?uri=CELEX:32019L0770&from=EN.

EU (European Union). 2019b. "Directive (EU) 2019/1024 of the European Parliament and of the Council of 20 June 2019 on Open Data and the Re-Use of Public Sector Information." *Official Journal of the European Union* L 172/56 (June 26). https://eur-lex.europa.eu/legal-content/EN/TXT/PDF/?uri=CELEX:32019L1024&from=EN.

Fang, Sammy, Carolyn Bigg, and John Zhang. 2020. "New Chinese Civil Code Introduces Greater Protection of Privacy Rights and Personal Information." *Insights*, June 9, 2020, DLA Piper, London. https://www.dlapiper.com/en/uk/insights/publications/2020/06/new-chinese-civil-code-introduces-greater-protection-of-privacy-rights-and-personal-information/.

Federal Register of Legislation, Australia. 2019. "Competition and Consumer Act 2010, No. 51, 1974." *Compilation* 121. Sydney: Office of Parliamentary Counsel. http://www.legislation.gov.au/Details/C2019C00317/Html/Volume_1.

Finch, Kelsey, and Omer Tene. 2018. "Smart Cities: Privacy, Transparency, and Community." In *The Cambridge Handbook of Consumer Privacy*, edited by Evan Selinger, Jules Polonetsky, and Omer Tene, 125–48. Cambridge Law Handbooks Series. Cambridge, UK: Cambridge University Press. https://doi.org/10.1017/9781316831960.007.

Fisher, Angelina, and Thomas Streinz. 2021. "Confronting Data Inequality." WDR 2021 background paper, World Bank, Washington, DC. https://papers.ssrn.com/sol3/papers.cfm?abstract_id=3825724.

FTC (Federal Trade Commission, United States). 2018. *Fair Credit Reporting Act, 15 U.S.C § 1681*, rev. ed. Washington, DC: FTC. https://www.ftc.gov/system/files/documents/statutes/fair-credit-reporting-act/545a_fair-credit-reporting-act-0918.pdf.

Gellman, Barton. 2013. "Edward Snowden, after Months of NSA Revelations, Says His Mission's Accomplished." *Washington Post*, December 23, 2013. https://www.washingtonpost.com/world/national-security/edward-snowden-after-months-of-nsa-revelations-says-his-missions-accomplished/2013/12/23/49fc36de-6c1c-11e3-a523-fe73f0ff6b8d_story.html.

Gelman, Robert B. 1998. *Protecting Yourself Online: The Definitive Resource on Safety, Freedom, and Privacy in Cyberspace*. With Stanton McCandlish and Members of the Electronic Frontier Foundation. New York: HarperCollins.

GPO (Government Publishing Office, United States). 2018. *Communications Act of 1934, as Amended*. United States Code, 2018 ed. Title 47: *Telecommunications*. Washington, DC: GPO. https://www.govinfo.gov/app/details/USCODE-2018-title47/USCODE-2018-title47-chap5-subchapI-sec151.

Greenleaf, Graham, and Bertil Cottier. 2020. "2020 Ends a Decade of 62 New Data Privacy Laws." *Privacy Laws and Business International Report* 163: 24–26. https://papers.ssrn.com/sol3/papers.cfm?abstract_id=3572611.

Hasselbalch, Gry, and Pernille Tranberg. 2016. "Personal Data Stores Want to Give Individuals Power over Their Data." *Dataethics* (blog), September 27, 2016. https://dataethics.eu/personal-data-stores-will-give-individual-power-their-data/.

Henley, Jon, and Robert Booth. 2020. "Welfare Surveillance System Violates Human Rights, Dutch Court Rules." *Guardian*, February 5, 2020. https://www.theguardian.com/technology/2020/feb/05/welfare-surveillance-system-violates-human-rights-dutch-court-rules.

Hill, Kashmir. 2020. "Wrongfully Accused by an Algorithm." *New York Times*, August 3, 2020. https://www.nytimes.com/2020/06/24/technology/facial-recognition-arrest.html.

HLCM (High-Level Committee on Management, United Nations). 2018. "Personal Data Protection and Privacy Principles." HLCM, Chief Executives Board for Coordination, United Nations, Geneva. https://unsceb.org/personal-data-protection-and-privacy-principles.

Hoofnagle, Chris Jay, Woodrow Hartzog, and Daniel J. Solove. 2019. "The FTC Can Rise to the Privacy Challenge, but Not without Help from Congress." *Brookings TechTank* (blog), August 8, 2019. https://www.brookings.edu/blog/techtank/2019/08/08/the-ftc-can-rise-to-the-privacy-challenge-but-not-without-help-from-congress/.

Huyer, Esther, and Gianfranco Cecconi. 2020. "Business-to-Government Data Sharing." Analytical Report 12, European Data Portal, European Commission, Luxembourg. https://www.europeandataportal.eu/sites/default/files/analytical_report_12_business_government_data_sharing.pdf.

ICO (Information Commissioner's Office). 2018. *Guide to the General Data Protection Regulation (GDPR)*. Wilmslow, UK: ICO. https://ico.org.uk/media/for-organisations/guide-to-data-protection/guide-to-the-general-data-protection-regulation-gdpr-1-1.pdf.

ICO (Information Commissioner's Office). 2019. "The Use of Live Facial Recognition Technology by Law Enforcement in Public Places." *Information Commissioner's Opinion*, 2019/01, October 31, 2019. https://ico.org.uk/media/about-the-ico/documents/2616184/live-frt-law-enforcement-opinion-20191031.pdf.

ISO (International Organization for Standardization). 2018. "ISO/PC 317: Consumer Protection: Privacy by Design for Consumer Goods and Services." *Taking Part: Technical Committee*, ISO, Geneva. https://www.iso.org/committee/6935430.html.

ISO (International Organization for Standardization) and IEC (International Electrotechnical Commission). 2016. "ISO/IEC 27011:2016(en): Information Technology, Security Techniques, Code of Practice for Information Security Controls Based on ISO/IEC 27002 for Telecommunications Organizations." Online Browsing Platform, ISO, Geneva, https://www.iso.org/obp/ui/#iso:std:iso-iec:27011:ed-2:v1:en.

ISO (International Organization for Standardization) and IEC (International Electrotechnical Commission). 2017. "ISO/IEC 19941:2017, Information Technology, Cloud Computing, Interoperability, and Portability." Online

Browsing Platform, ISO, Geneva. https://www.iso.org/obp/ui/#iso:std:iso-iec:19941:ed-1:v1:en.

ITU (International Telecommunication Union). 2014. "Using Regulatory Impact Analysis to Improve Decision Making in the ICT Sector." ITU, Geneva.

Kirkpatrick, Robert. 2014. "A Big Data Revolution for Sustainable Development." In *The Global Compact International Yearbook 2014*, edited by United Nations Global Compact Office, 33–35. New York: United Nations; Münster, Germany: macondo publishing.

Kosseff, Jeff. 2019. *The Twenty-Six Words That Created the Internet*. Ithaca, NY: Cornell University Press.

Krämer, Jan, Pierre Senellart, and Alexandre de Streel. 2020. "Making Data Portability More Effective for the Digital Economy: Economic Implications and Regulatory Challenges." Center on Regulation in Europe, Brussels. https://cerre.eu/publications/report-making-data-portability-more-effective-digital-economy/.

Légifrance. 2016. "Loi no 2016-1321 du 7 octobre 2016 pour une République numérique." *Journal officiel de la République française*, October 8, 2016, Légifrance, Direction de l'information légale et administrative, Paris. https://www.legifrance.gouv.fr/download/file/SJ9w29KN2wvvWjcmiPwHr3BoLa5rYk6ys5dm_FwTPZs=/JOE_TEXTE.

Lessig, Lawrence. 1999. *Code and Other Laws of Cyberspace*. New York: Basic Books.

LOC (Library of Congress, United States). 1998. "H. R. 2281 Digital Millennium Copyright Act: 105th Congress (1997–1998)." *Congress.gov*, October 28, 1998, LOC, Washington, DC. https://www.congress.gov/bill/105th-congress/house-bill/2281.

LOC (Library of Congress, United States). 2018. "H. R. 4943, CLOUD Act: 115th Congress (2017–2018)." *Congress.gov*, February 6, 2018, LOC, Washington, DC. https://www.congress.gov/bill/115th-congress/house-bill/4943.

Lubarsky, Boris. 2017. "Re-Identification of 'Anonymized' Data." *Georgetown Law Technology Review* (April): 202–13. https://georgetownlawtechreview.org/re-identification-of-anonymized-data/GLTR-04-2017/.

Lum, Kristian. 2016. "Predictive Policing Reinforces Police Bias." *HRDAG: Human Rights Data Analysis Group*, October 10. http://hrdag.org/2016/10/10/predictive-policing-reinforces-police-bias/.

MeitY (Ministry of Electronics and Information Technology). 2020. "Report by the Committee of Experts on Non-Personal Data Governance Framework." 111972/2020/CL & ES. MeitY, New Delhi. https://www.huntonprivacyblog.com/wp-content/uploads/sites/28/2020/08/mygov_15945338195506367l.pdf.

METI (Ministry of Economy, Trade, and Industry, Japan). 2018. "METI Formulates 'Contract Guidance on Utilization of AI and Data.'" News release, June 15, 2018. https://www.meti.go.jp/english/press/2018/0615_002.html.

METI (Ministry of Economy, Trade, and Industry, Japan). 2020. "Unfair Competition Prevention Act." *Policy Index*. Intellectual Property Policy Office, METI, Tokyo. https://www.meti.go.jp/english/policy/economy/chizai/chiteki/index.html.

MITCI (Ministry of Technology, Communication, and Innovation, Mauritius). 2017. "National Open Data Policy." MITCI, Quatre Bornes, Mauritius. https://mitci.govmu.org/Documents/Strategies/Mauritius%20Open%20Data%20Policy%20May%202017.pdf.

MoICT (Ministry of Information and Communication Technology, Jordan). 2017. "Open Government Data Policy." MoICT, Amman, Jordan. https://modee.gov.jo/ebv4.0/root_storage/en/eb_list_page/open_government_data_policy_2017.pdf.

National Archives, United Kingdom. 2017. "Digital Economy Act 2017." *legislation.gov.uk*, National Archives, London. https://www.legislation.gov.uk/ukpga/2017/30/contents/enacted.

National Archives, United Kingdom. 2019. "Guidance on the Implementation of the Re-use of Public Sector Information Regulations 2015: For Public Sector Bodies." Version 1.1, National Archives, London. https://www.nationalarchives.gov.uk/documents/information-management/psi-implementation-guidance-public-sector-bodies.pdf.

National Assembly, Togo. 2020. "Loi Relative a l'Identification Biometrique des Personnes Physiques au Togo" [Law on the biometric measurement of natural persons in Togo]. National Assembly, Open Session, September 3. http://www.assemblee-nationale.tg/images/biometrie%20loi%20AN.pdf.

Nilsson, Patricia. 2019. "Police Fear Bias in Use of Artificial Intelligence to Fight Crime." *Financial Times*, September 15, 2019. https://www.ft.com/content/5753689c-d63e-11e9-a0bd-ab8ec6435630.

NIST (National Institute of Standards and Technology). 2020. "NIST Study Evaluates Effects of Race, Age, Sex on Face Recognition Software." *News*, December 19, 2019, updated May 18, 2020, NIST, US Department of Commerce, Gaithersburg, MD. https://www.nist.gov/news-events/news/2019/12/nist-study-evaluates-effects-race-age-sex-face-recognition-software.

Noble, Safiya Umoja. 2018. *Algorithms of Oppression: How Search Engines Reinforce Racism*. New York: NYU Press. https://nyupress.org/9781479837243/algorithms-of-oppression.

Noveck, Beth Simone. 2017. "Rights-Based and Tech-Driven: Open Data, Freedom of Information, and the Future of Government Transparency." *Yale Human Rights and Development Law Journal* 19 (1): article 1. https://digitalcommons.law.yale.edu/yhrdlj/vol19/iss1/1.

OECD (Organisation for Economic Co-operation and Development). 2013. *The OECD Privacy Framework*. Paris: OECD. http://www.oecd.org/sti/ieconomy/oecd_privacy_framework.pdf.

OECD (Organisation for Economic Co-operation and Development). 2019a. *Enhancing Access to and Sharing of Data: Reconciling Risks and Benefits for Data Re-Use across Societies*. Paris: OECD. https://doi.org/10.1787/276aaca8-en.

OECD (Organisation for Economic Co-operation and Development). 2019b. "Licensing of IP Rights and Competition Law." Background Note DAF/COMP(2019)3, Competition Committee, Directorate for Financial and Enterprise Affairs, OECD, Paris. https://one.oecd.org/document/DAF/COMP(2019)3/en/pdf.

OECD (Organisation for Economic Co-operation and Development). 2019c. "Recommendation of the Council on Artificial Intelligence." *OECD Legal Instruments*, OECD/LEGAL/0449, adopted on May 22, 2019. https://

legalinstruments.oecd.org/en/instruments/OECD
-LEGAL-0449.

OneTrust DataGuidance and FPF (Future of Privacy Forum). 2019. "Comparing Privacy Laws: GDPR v. CCPA." OneTrust, London; FPF, Washington, DC. https://fpf .org/wp-content/uploads/2019/12/ComparingPrivacy Laws_GDPR_CCPA.pdf.

Open Knowledge Foundation. 2020. "What Is Open Data?" *Open Data Handbook: Guide.* London: Open Knowledge Foundation. https://opendatahandbook.org/guide/en /what-is-open-data/.

OVIC (Office of the Victorian Information Commissioner). 2020. "Victorian Protective Data Security Framework, Version 2.0." OVIC, Melbourne. https://ovic.vic.gov.au /wp-content/uploads/2020/02/Victorian-Protective-Data -Security-Framework-V2.0.pdf.

Parliament of India. 2019. "The Personal Data Protection Bill, 2019." Bill No. 373 of 2019, Parliament of India, New Delhi. https://dataprotectionindia.in/act/.

PC (Productivity Commission, Australia). 2017. *Data Availability and Use.* Productivity Commission Inquiry Report 82. Canberra: PC. https://www.pc.gov.au/inquiries /completed/data-access/report/data-access.pdf.

PCPD (Office of the Privacy Commissioner for Personal Data, Hong Kong SAR, China). 2012. "Privacy by Design Conference." PCPD, Hong Kong SAR, China. https:// www.pcpd.org.hk/pbdconference/index.html.

PMC (Department of the Prime Minister and Cabinet, Australia). 2019. "Best Practice Guide to Applying Data Sharing Principles." PMC, Canberra. https://www.pmc .gov.au/resource-centre/public-data/data-sharing -principles.

Potey, Manish M., C. A. Dhote, and Deepak H. Sharma. 2016. "Homomorphic Encryption for Security of Cloud Data." *Procedia Computer Science* 79 (January): 175–81. https://doi .org/10.1016/j.procs.2016.03.023.

Ragavan, Srividhya, Brendan Murphy, and Raj Davé. 2016. "FRAND v. Compulsory Licensing: The Lesser of the Two Evils." *Duke Law and Technology Review* 14 (1): 83–120.

RIA (Information System Authority, Estonia). 2020. "Data Exchange Layer X-Tee." RIA, Tallinn, Estonia. https:// www.ria.ee/en/state-information-system/x-tee.html#: ~:text=X%2Dtee%2C%20the%20data%20exchange,data %20based%20on%20an%20agreement.

Smith, Jack, IV. 2016. "Crime-Prediction Tool May Be Reinforcing Discriminatory Policing—Business Insider." *Business Insider,* October 10, 2016. https://www.businessinsider .com/predictive-policing-discriminatory-police-crime -2016-10?r=UK.

Stats NZ (Statistics New Zealand). 2019. "Algorithm Charter." Stats NZ, Wellington, New Zealand. https://data .govt.nz/assets/Uploads/Draft-Algorithm-Charter-for -consultation.pdf.

Sweeney, Latanya. 2000. "Simple Demographics Often Identify People Uniquely." Data Privacy Working Paper 3, Carnegie Mellon University, Pittsburgh.

Sweeney, Latanya. 2002. "k-Anonymity: A Model for Protecting Privacy." *International Journal of Uncertainty, Fuzziness and Knowledge-Based Systems* 10 (05): 557–70. https://doi .org/10.1142/S0218488502001648.

Taylor, Linnet, Luciano Floridi, and Bart van der Sloot, eds. 2017. *Group Privacy: New Challenges of Data Technologies.* Philosophical Studies Series, vol. 126. Cham, Switzerland: Springer.

TBS (Treasury Board of Canada Secretariat). 2020. "Responsible Use of Artificial Intelligence (AI)." *Canada.ca,* July 28, 2020, TBS, Ottawa. https://www.canada.ca/en /government/system/digital-government/digital -government-innovations/responsible-use-ai.html.

TOOP (The Once-Only Principle Project). 2021. "The Once-Only Principle Project." Tallinn University of Technology, Tallinn, Estonia. https://www.toop.eu/about.

Treasury, Australia. 2020. *Inquiry into Future Directions for the Consumer Data Right.* Canberra: Treasury. https://treasury .gov.au/sites/default/files/2020-12/cdrinquiry-accessible final.pdf.

Ubaldi, Barbara. 2013. "Open Government Data: Towards Empirical Analysis of Open Government Data Initiatives." OECD Working Paper on Public Governance 22, Organisation for Economic Co-operation and Development, Paris. https://doi.org/10.1787/5k46bj4f03s7-en.

UNCITRAL (United Nations Commission on International Trade Law). 1998. "UNCITRAL Model Law on Electronic Commerce (1996) with Additional Article 5 bis as Adopted in 1998." UNCITRAL, Vienna. https://uncitral.un.org/en /texts/ecommerce/modellaw/electronic_commerce.

UNCITRAL (United Nations Commission on International Trade Law). 2001. "UNCITRAL Model Law on Electronic Signatures (2001)." UNCITRAL, Vienna. https://uncitral .un.org/en/texts/ecommerce/modellaw/electronic _signatures.

UNCITRAL (United Nations Commission on International Trade Law). 2009. *Promoting Confidence in Electronic Commerce: Legal Issues on International Use of Electronic Authentication and Signature Methods.* Vienna: United Nations. https://www.uncitral.org/pdf/english/texts/electcom/08 -55698_Ebook.pdf.

UNSDG (United Nations Sustainable Development Group). 2017. "Data Privacy, Ethics, and Protection: Guidance Note on Big Data for Achievement of the 2030 Agenda." UNSDG, New York. https://unsdg.un.org/sites/default /files/UNDG_BigData_final_web.pdf.

Vickery, Graham. 2012. "Review of Recent Studies on PSI Re-use and Related Market Developments." Information Economics, Paris.

Ville de Nantes (City of Nantes, France). 2019. "Charte métropolitaine de la donnée" [Metropolitan data charter]. *Nantes Métropole,* May 2019, Ville de Nantes, France. https://metropole.nantes.fr/charte-donnee.

Waze. 2018. "Waze Celebrates 600 Connected Citizens Program Partners." *Waze,* Google, Mountain View, CA. https://medium.com/waze/waze-celebrates-600 -connected-citizens-program-partners-36945fbceb66.

WEF (World Economic Forum). 2011. "Personal Data: The Emergence of a New Asset Class." In collaboration with Bain & Company, Inc., WEF, Geneva. http://www3.we forum.org/docs/WEF_ITTC_PersonalDataNewAsset _Report_2011.pdf.

Wilkinson, Mark D., Michel Dumontier, IJsbrand Jan Aalbersberg, Gabrielle Appleton, Myles Axton, Arie Baak,

Niklas Blomberg, et al. 2016. "The FAIR Guiding Principles for Scientific Data Management and Stewardship." *Scientific Data* 3 (March 15): 160018. https://doi.org/10.1038/sdata.2016.18.

World Bank. 2018. "Global Indicators of Regulatory Governance: Worldwide Practices of Regulatory Impact Assessments." World Bank, Washington, DC. http://documents1.worldbank.org/curated/en/905611520284525814/Global-Indicators-of-Regulatory-Governance-Worldwide-Practices-of-Regulatory-Impact-Assessments.pdf.

World Bank. 2019. *ID4D Practitioner's Guide: Version 1.0.* October 2019. Washington, DC: World Bank. https://documents.worldbank.org/en/publication/documents-reports/documentdetail/248371559325561562/id4d-practitioner-s-guide.

World Bank and United Nations. 2017. *Combatting Cybercrime: Tools and Capacity Building for Emerging Economies.* Washington, DC: World Bank. http://documents.worldbank.org/curated/en/355401535144740611/Combatting-Cybercrime-Tools-and-Capacity-Building-for-Emerging-Economies.

World Wide Web Foundation. 2017. *Open Data Barometer: Global Report*, 4th ed. Washington, DC: World Wide Web Foundation. https://opendatabarometer.org/doc/4thEdition/ODB-4thEdition-GlobalReport.pdf.

Zanfir-Fortuna, Gabriela, and Sasha Hondagneu-Messner. 2019. "CPDP 2019 Panel: Understanding the Limits and Benefits of Data Portability." Future of Privacy Forum, 2019 Computers, Privacy, and Data Protection Conference, Brussels, February 26, 2019. https://fpf.org/2019/02/26/cpdp-2019-panel-understanding-the-limits-and-benefits-of-data-portability/.

Zhang, Gil, and Kate Yin. 2020. "A Look at China's Draft of Personal Data Protection Law." *Privacy Tracker*, International Association of Privacy Professionals, Portsmouth, NH. https://iapp.org/news/a/a-look-at-chinas-draft-of-personal-data-protection-law/.

Spotlight 6.1

The evolving social contract on data: Balancing data sharing and data protection to facilitate contact tracing to control COVID-19

The need for immediate and reliable information about COVID-19 has tested the systems in place for protecting data.

International and national laws recognize that, in extraordinary circumstances, certain fundamental rights, including the right to data protection, may be restricted, with the following conditions: basic democratic principles and safeguards are ensured, and the restriction is legitimate, time limited, and not arbitrary.[1]

Following the World Health Organization's declaration of a global pandemic in mid-March 2020,[2] governments around the world have adopted contact tracing strategies to track down any individual who might have come into contact with an infected person, so that they may be quarantined to prevent further spread of the disease.[3] Such contact tracing has historically been carried out manually by public health authorities.[4] However, it can be undertaken much more efficiently on a massive scale using digital technologies such as mobile applications, which can simultaneously deliver public health advice.

Despite these benefits, contact tracing raises several concerns. First, tools relying on location tracing may be construed as unwarranted surveillance and a threat to privacy, especially in jurisdictions with inadequate data protection frameworks[5] and given that location data are hard to anonymize fully. Second, personal data collected in contact tracing currently flow beyond trusted parties and organizations, reaching more third parties than accounted for in current governance models. Third, there is evidence that using geographic location in contact tracing may be inaccurate and inefficient because it does not provide all of the relevant facts. An empirical study of the Ebola outbreak found that those data are meaningful only when reidentified, touching on

the "purpose limitation" used in good-practice data protection laws.

While countries around the world have been developing contact tracing apps, two approaches have emerged: centralized and decentralized. Both approaches use Bluetooth signals to log when smartphone owners are in proximity to one another, sending alerts to users who may have been infected when someone develops COVID-19 symptoms.

Under the centralized model originally pursued by the UK government, anonymized data are gathered and uploaded to a remote server, where matches are made with other contacts when a person starts to experience COVID-19 symptoms.[6] The United Kingdom's proposed approach contains a persistent identifier that is shared with the National Health Service, allowing public authorities to receive infection data automatically. The central server then alerts other app users who have had significant contact with the infected person. Despite the public health merits of the centralized approach, the application was abandoned in mid-June 2020 in favor of a decentralized approach, due to low rates of phone recognition during its testing phase on the Isle of Wight.

In contrast, the decentralized model, promoted jointly by Apple and Google, aims to support contact tracing by health agencies, while integrating privacy and security into the design.[7] Users have more control over their information because it is stored in a decentralized manner on their phones, preventing the siphoning of data into central government servers. In this model, "The protocol excludes processing of any location data—unless the user opts in—applies 'Rolling Proximity Identifiers' that prevent identification of the user, processes proximity identifiers obtained from other devices exclusively on the device, [and] permits only users to decide whether to contribute to contact tracing by sharing Diagnosis Keys with the 'Diagnosis Server' if diagnosed with COVID-19, resulting in the alert to other users."[8]

A multistakeholder consortium, the Pan-European Privacy-Preserving Proximity Tracing (PEPP-PT) community, is developing contact tracing technologies that adhere to strong European privacy and data protection laws and principles.[9] The PEPP-PT technical mechanisms and standards fully protect privacy, while taking advantage of the possibilities of digital technology to maximize the speed and real-time capability of national pandemic responses. Initiatives under the umbrella of PEPP-PT aim to develop an open protocol for COVID- 19 proximity tracing using Bluetooth Low Energy on mobile devices and an architecture to ensure that personal data stay entirely on an individual's phone.

Notes

1. Access Now (2020).
2. WHO (2020).
3. Yan (2020).
4. eHealth Network (2020).
5. FPF (2020).
6. Economist (2020).
7. Google (2020); Sabbagh and Hern (2020).
8. eHealth Network (2020).
9. See Pan-European Privacy-Preserving Proximity Tracing (dashboard), n.d.

References

Access Now. 2020. "Recommendations on Privacy and Data Protection in the Fight against COVID-19." Access Now, Brooklyn, NY, March 2020. https://www.accessnow.org /cms/assets/uploads/2020/03/Access-Now-recommen dations-on-Covid-and-data-protection-and-privacy.pdf.

Economist. 2020. "Privacy Be Damned: Some Countries Want Central Databases for Contact-Tracing Apps." April 30, 2020. https://www.economist.com/europe/2020 /04/30/some-countries-want-central-databases-for -contact-tracing-apps.

eHealth Network. 2020. "Mobile Applications to Support Contact Tracing in the EU's Fight against COVID-19: Common EU Toolbox for Member States." Version 1.0, eHealth Network, Brussels, April 15, 2020. https:// ec.europa.eu/health/sites/health/files/ehealth/docs /covid-19_apps_en.pdf.

FPF (Future of Privacy Forum). 2020. "Privacy & Pandemics: The Role of Mobile Apps (Chart)." FPF, Washington, DC, April 2020. https://fpf.org/wp-content/uploads/2020/04 /editPrivacy-Pandemics_-The-Role-of-Mobile-Apps -Chart-11.pdf.

Google. 2020. "Apple and Google Partner on COVID-19 Contact Tracing Technology." *Company Announcements* (blog), April 10, 2020. https://blog.google/inside-google /company-announcements/apple-and-google-partner -covid-19-contact-tracing-technology/.

Pan-European Privacy-Preserving Proximity Tracing (dashboard). n.d. "PEPP-PT." GitHub. Accessed December 15, 2020. https://github.com/pepp-pt.

Sabbagh, Dan, and Alex Hern. 2020. "UK Abandons Contact-Tracing App for Apple and Google Model." *Guardian*, June 18, 2020. https://www.theguardian.com /world/2020/jun/18/uk-poised-to-abandon-coronavirus -app-in-favour-of-apple-and-google-models.

WHO (World Health Organization). 2020. "WHO Announces COVID-19 Outbreak a Pandemic." Media Release, March 12, 2020. WHO Regional Office for Europe, Copenhagen. https://www.euro.who.int/en/health-topics/health -emergencies/coronavirus-covid-19/news/news/2020/3 /who-announces-covid-19-outbreak-a-pandemic.

Yan, Holly. 2020. "Contact Tracing 101: How It Works, Who Could Get Hired, and Why It's So Critical in Fighting Coronavirus Now." *CNN Health* (blog), May 15, 2020. https://www.cnn.com/2020/04/27/health/contact-tracing -explainer-coronavirus/index.html.

Spotlight 6.2
The debate over ownership of personal data

Personal data "ownership" is incompatible with a rights-based approach to personal data protection.

The commercial value of personal data has prompted arguments that individuals should be allowed to commercialize their own data.[1] Granting individuals ownership rights over personal data is sometimes proposed to address data inequalities and to determine how such data can be used and by whom.[2] Yet "ownership" neither addresses these inequalities nor empowers individuals to control the use of data. Personal data "ownership" makes sense only if personal data are considered an "asset" with associated property rights.[3] If personal data are property, they can be used as collateral and for commercial exchange, with the potential implication that individuals could even trade away the data that contain their digital identity.

Some scholars suggest that concepts of property rights should apply to personal data.[4] Others suggest that market-based solutions should be used to protect data,[5] called the "personal data economy."[6] The economic literature is mixed on whether data ownership rights could solve market failures or improve social outcomes.[7] Some suggest that the optimal distribution of ownership rights would depend on factors including the investment required to create the data[8] and the ability to monetize data.[9] A regime based on property rights would likely increase the transaction costs involved in data sharing, by requiring negotiation of the terms of sale and use.

Ascribing data ownership rights to personal data also poses legal challenges. First, personal data often involve overlapping interests of different parties.[10] These interests are present in the collection, creation, and use of the data.[11] If ownership were allocated to the "party with the clearest interest or who could

make the most value out of it,"[12] it would be practically difficult to identify the party or parties meeting this definition.[13] It is also unclear how to compensate interested third parties if their rights are breached through downstream data uses.[14] Creating a data ownership right would require elaborating "necessary user" rights and rules to accommodate the public interest needs of such data,[15] such as those raised in the COVID-19 pandemic response.

Second, "owning" personal data might incentivize poor and more vulnerable people to sell their personal data, exacerbating existing inequities. Under a rights-based approach to personal data protection, individuals have fundamental rights regarding their data. Perhaps ironically, these rights—more than "ownership"—give individuals control over their data, enabling them to negotiate the use of these data.[16] These immutable rights—like due process under law—cannot be bargained away like chattel. Even current case law does not support ownership rights over personal data.

Notes

1. Start-ups providing personal data management services to internet users have appeared, ranging from companies that compensate users for their personal information to those that require users to pay fees to avoid the use of their personal information (Elvy 2017).
2. This spotlight deals only with issues concerning "ownership." Other theories include treating personal data as labor (see Posner and Weyl 2018, who posit that the individual's role in creating the data is recognized and compensated as labor) or allowing personal data to be shared through licensing arrangements (see Savona 2019, who suggests that data could be recognized as a

licensable asset owned by the individual who generates it); see also Fisher and Streinz 2021. A related aspect of this debate revolves around expanding the types of data available to creditors and other decision makers beyond traditional data, such as payments on loans. These nontraditional types of data could include utility payments, cash flow, and social media data. The reliability of such data and the ability to access and dispute the information are important issues. The analytics applied to such data may also fall in the nonpersonal category. Ownership of nonpersonal data, by contrast, is a more straightforward issue of intellectual property rights, which is addressed in chapter 6.

3. Castells (2010); Zuboff (2019).
4. Laudon (1996); Samuelson (2000).
5. See, for example, Carrascal et al. (2013) and Kerber (2016).
6. See, for example, Haupt (2016).
7. Duch-Brown, Martens, and Mueller-Langer (2017).
8. Tirole (2017); Zech (2016).
9. Dosis and Sand-Zantman (2019).
10. Scassa (2017).
11. Scassa (2017).
12. Wiebe (2016, 880).
13. See, for example, Farkas (2017).
14. Viljoen (2020)
15. Scassa (2017).
16. Scassa (2017).

References

Carrascal, Juan Pablo, Christopher Riederer, Vijay Erramilli, Mauro Cherubini, and Rodrigo de Oliveira. 2013. "Your Browsing Behavior for a Big Mac: Economics of Personal Information Online." In *WWW '13: Proceedings of the 22nd International Conference on World Wide Web*, 189–200. New York: Association for Computing Machinery. http://jpcarrascal.com/docs/publications/WWW2013 -Browsing_behavior_big_mac.pdf.

Castells, Manuel. 2010. *The Information Age: Economy, Society, and Culture*. Vol 1: *The Rise of the Network Society*, 2d ed. Malden, MA: Wiley-Blackwell.

Dosis, Anastasios, and Wilfried Sand-Zantman. 2019. "The Ownership of Data." TSE Working Paper 19-1025, Toulouse School of Economics, University of Toulouse, Toulouse, France, July 2019.

Duch-Brown, Nestor, Bertin Martens, and Frank Mueller-Langer. 2017. "The Economics of Ownership, Access, and Trade in Digital Data." JRC Digital Economy Working Paper 2017-01, Joint Research Center, European Commission, Seville, Spain.

Elvy, Stacy-Ann. 2017. "Paying for Privacy and the Personal Data Economy." *Colombia Law Review* 117 (6): 1369–459.

Farkas, Thomas J. 2017. "Data Created by the Internet of Things: The New Gold without Ownership?" *Revista la Propiedad Inmaterial* 23 (June): 5–17. https://revistas .uexternado.edu.co/index.php/propin/article/view/4975.

Fisher, Angelina, and Thomas Streinz. 2021. "Confronting Data Inequality." WDR 2021 background paper, World Bank, Washington, DC. https://papers.ssrn.com/sol3 /papers.cfm?abstract_id=3825724.

Haupt, Michael. 2016. "Introducing Personal Data Exchanges and the Personal Data Economy." *#ExitTheSystem* (blog), December 7, 2016. https://medium.com/project-2030 /what-is-a-personal-data-exchange-256bcd5bf447.

Kerber, Wolfgang. 2016. "Digital Markets, Data, and Privacy: Competition Law, Consumer Law, and Data Protection." MACIE Paper 2016/3, Marburg Centre for Institutional Economics, School of Business and Economics, Philipps-University Marburg, Marburg, Germany.

Laudon, Kenneth C. 1996. "Markets and Privacy." *Communications of the ACM* 39 (9): 92–104. https://doi.org/10.1145 /234215.234476.

Posner, Eric A., and E. Glen Weyl. 2018. *Radical Markets: Uprooting Capitalism and Democracy for a Just Society*. Princeton, NJ: Princeton University Press.

Samuelson, Pamela. 2000. "Privacy as Intellectual Property?" *Stanford Law Review* 52 (5): 1125–73. https://doi.org/10 .2307/1229511.

Savona, Maria. 2019. "The Value of Data: Towards a Framework to Redistribute It." SPRU Working Paper SWPS 2019-21, Science Policy Research Unit, Business School, University of Sussex, Brighton, UK, October 2019.

Scassa, Teresa. 2017. "Sharing Data in the Platform Economy: A Public Interest Argument for Access to Platform Data." *UBC Law Review* 54 (4): 1017–71.

Tirole, Jean. 2017. *Economics for the Common Good*. Princeton, NJ: Princeton University Press. https://press.princeton .edu/books/hardcover/9780691175164/economics-for-the -common-good.

Viljoen, Salomé. 2020. "Data as Property." *Phenomenal World*, October 16, 2020. https://phenomenalworld.org/analysis /data-as-property.

Wiebe, Andreas. 2016. "Protection of Industrial Data: A New Property Right for the Digital Economy?" *GRUR Int* 10/2016 (October): 877–83. http://www.grur.org/uploads /media/GRURInt_2016_10_Inhalt_fertig.pdf.

Zech, Herbert. 2016. "Data as a Tradeable Commodity." In *European Contract Law and the Digital Single Market: The Implications of the Digital Revolution*, edited by Alberto De Franceschi, 51–80. Cambridge, UK: Intersentia. https:// doi.org/10.1017/9781780685212.004.

Zuboff, Shoshana. 2019. *The Age of Surveillance Capitalism: The Fight for a Human Future at the New Frontier of Power*. New York: PublicAffairs.

CHAPTER

7

Creating value in the data economy: The role of competition, trade, and tax policy

Main messages

1. The expanding role of data in ubiquitous platform business models is reshaping competition, trade, and taxation in the real economy, posing important risks for low- and middle-income countries.

2. The way countries design safeguards and enablers for data will have knock-on effects for the real economy. For example, enabling data sharing among market players can play a valuable role in promoting competition. At the same time, the stringency of data safeguards will shape cross-border trading patterns for data-enabled services. Meanwhile, the intangible nature of digital value chains is posing major challenges for tax revenue mobilization.

3. Low- and middle-income countries too often lack the institutional capacity to manage the economic policy challenges posed by the data-driven economy. These challenges call for agile competition policies and modern trade and tax administrations. Complicating matters, policies on competition, trade, and taxation are significantly intertwined.

4. Internationally coordinated action—on antitrust enforcement, regulation of platform firms, data standards, trade agreements, and tax policy— is critical to ensuring efficient, equitable policies for the data economy that respond to countries' needs and interests.

Shaping data regulation to support competition, trade, and taxation

Rapid technological innovation and the associated explosive production of data are reshaping the business landscape (see chapter 3). New data-driven businesses—with their intangible assets such as data and algorithms—are rapidly gaining ground in markets worldwide. These include the global players that often make headlines, such as Alibaba, Amazon, Facebook, and Alphabet (Google), as well as more local platform businesses in lower-income countries, such as the Nigerian agricultural platform Hello Tractor, which matches smallholder farmers with underutilized tractors, and the Egyptian educational platform Tutorama, which matches students to high-quality tutors.

Data-driven businesses exhibit idiosyncrasies that distinguish them from more traditional firms—notably, their greater propensity for market dominance in some cases, their ability to achieve scale without mass, and the intangibility of their transactions (figure 7.1). Each of these characteristics poses important challenges for economic outcomes in competition, trade, and taxation, potentially offsetting some of their positive effects.

Using data as an input to the production process can give businesses a competitive advantage, which, because of economies of scale and scope associated with data and the strong network effects arising from platforms, enables them to entrench their market position and potentially exercise market power. Data-driven markets tend to exhibit economies of scale because of the large upfront fixed cost of technical infrastructure and the advantage large datasets offer for learning. By accumulating tremendous amounts of data through transactions and applying algorithms, businesses are able to provide their clients with customized services and products. For example, e-commerce platforms tailor product suggestions to their clients' shopping history, thereby enforcing the tendency of customers to stick with such platforms because they "understand" their customers better.

Figure 7.1 The unusual characteristics of data-driven businesses pose complex challenges for policy makers in the areas of competition, trade, and taxation

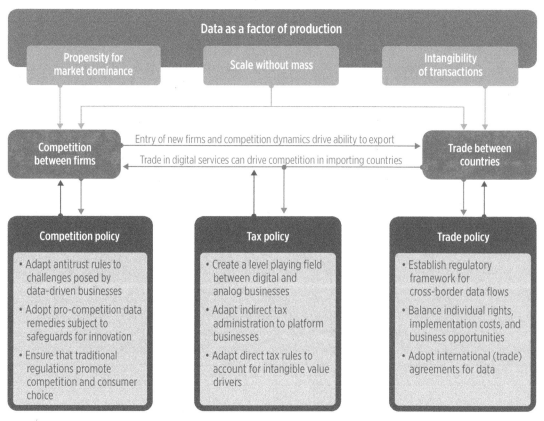

Source: WDR 2021 team.

Positive network effects further strengthen market positions because third-party suppliers prefer to display their products on more highly frequented platforms where the odds are higher they will make a sale. Customers, in turn, are more likely to visit such platforms because of the wider choice of third-party suppliers.

Because data-driven businesses rely on value drivers such as data and algorithms that can be infinitely replicated and instantly distributed around the world, they are able to achieve scale without mass. They can, then, be a major player in a market without having any brick-and-mortar facilities, local employees, or even domestic business registration. For example, Facebook has more than 2.6 billion active visitors each month spread over nearly every country in the world, but it maintains office locations in just 35 countries.[1] Similarly, AliExpress, a Chinese-based e-commerce platform launched in 2010, now has users in more than 230 countries and regions.[2] It, too, relies on data and algorithms rather than offline retail stores. Meanwhile, the cross-border trade in digital services is climbing. These services, largely intangible, include social media, big data analytics, cloud computing, and online services.

The changing nature of data-driven businesses challenges traditional economic policies, calling for adaptation and paradigm shifts (figure 7.1). In competition policy, it is important to address the tendency of data-driven businesses to tip toward concentrated market structures and entrenched market power. However, the complex and novel nature of data-driven business models can pose difficulties for traditional antitrust regulation in all countries. At the same time, the rapid growth of international trade in data-driven services is raising tensions between the need for data to flow across borders and the need to ensure that any personal data involved in such trade are adequately protected as they move into other jurisdictions. Taxation authorities are struggling to value, map, and track digital value chains in the data-driven sector. Administration of the value added tax (VAT) is complicated by third-party vendors operating through platform businesses. Meanwhile, the prevalence of scale without mass is challenging the long-standing taxation principle of permanent establishment and physical presence as a basis for establishing corporate tax liability.

Domestic policies relating to competition, trade, and taxation are significantly intertwined, requiring a coordinated approach to policy reform. Effective antitrust policies strengthen competition in the domestic market, thereby enhancing competitiveness

in international trade. Governance frameworks that support trade in data-enabled goods and services may at the same time intensify competitive pressures in the local economy. Nonetheless, for platform businesses, trade openness could lead instead to greater market concentration as the dominance of global firms is further reinforced by access to new markets and associated data. At the same time, the inability to tax platform businesses effectively may undermine competition between local and foreign firms, as well as between digital and analog businesses operating in the same sectors, affecting both competition in domestic markets and competitiveness in global markets.

All three of these policy areas call for internationally coordinated action. Antitrust measures in one country can affect the fortunes of globally active firms, with spillover effects for other jurisdictions. Trade agreements, as well as global harmonization of technical standards for data sharing, play an essential role in promoting international commerce for data-enabled goods and services. International tax policy regimes determine the allocation of taxation rights across countries, while cross-border cooperation on tax administration can help ensure that revenues are fully captured.

This chapter discusses the policy challenges and responses arising from competition, trade, and taxation. A central theme is how these policies interact with the broader legal and regulatory framework on data safeguards and enablers described in chapter 6. Policy makers should heed the two-way linkages between economic outcomes and data regulation and carefully weigh the trade-offs that may arise between safeguarding and enabling data sharing versus advancing wider economic goals such as productivity, competitiveness, and growth.

Competition policy

The rise of data-driven businesses can drive pro-development market opportunities, but data can also give firms a competitive advantage that may push markets into entrenched concentration and market power. This advantage increases the risk of excluding smaller firms and entrepreneurs and exploiting individual users of data (chapter 3). The key challenge for policy makers is to preserve the positive externalities that create value in data-driven markets, while ensuring that these externalities can be harnessed by all players in a competitive, vibrant ecosystem without violating the rights of individuals.

This chapter focuses on data-driven platform firms because of their pertinence across economies at different levels of development. The complex interactions between data protection concerns (outlined in chapter 6) and competition concerns (described in this chapter) are further explored in spotlight 7.1.

Governments have two complementary competition policy tools to safeguard against the risks of excluding smaller firms and exploiting individual users of data. The first tool is *enforcement of antitrust laws*, with adaptations to the context of data-driven businesses. Enforcement involves detecting and punishing anticompetitive practices (in which a firm abuses its dominant position or a group of firms enters into an anticompetitive agreement) or preventing anticompetitive mergers. The second tool is the *design of regulations* to allow data-driven firms to enter markets and compete on a level playing field, while also protecting users. These ex ante policies lay down ground rules for the market to promote competition and could include data governance regulations, regulations directed at large data-driven platforms, and traditional sector regulations. Because these two competition policy tools complement one another, they can be applied in parallel, depending on the institutional setting and the issues to be tackled.

Enforcing antitrust laws

Antitrust investigations in the data economy are not just a developed country phenomenon. Worldwide, as of January 2020 some 102 antitrust cases across 16 different sectors on abuse of dominance,

anticompetitive agreements, and mergers had been finalized.[3] European antitrust authorities have finalized the most cases (33 percent), followed by authorities in East Asia and the Pacific (18 percent) and Latin America (15 percent). The most active lower-middle-income countries included the Arab Republic of Egypt, India, and Kenya, with more cases still under investigation in Indonesia, Nigeria, and Zimbabwe. Low-income jurisdictions had not yet finalized any antitrust cases involving digital platforms, likely reflecting the absence of functional or well-resourced antitrust regimes and lower policy prioritization.[4]

Among landmark cases from the middle-income country group is the 2018 investigation by the Competition Commission of India finding that Google abused its dominant position in web search and advertising. Google favored its own services and partners through manual manipulation of its search algorithm, thereby putting smaller businesses at a disadvantage.[5] In another salient example, Mexico's Federal Economic Competition Commission (COFECE) blocked Walmart's proposed acquisition of the Cornershop app in 2019, because the new company would have access to data on the sales of competing retailers through the Cornershop platform, which was believed to prejudice smaller rivals.[6]

Antitrust cases related to the digital economy in e-commerce, passenger transport, and operating system application development account for more than half of cases globally (figure 7.2). E-commerce

Figure 7.2 In the digital economy, antitrust cases related to passenger transport are more prevalent in middle-income countries than in high-income countries

a. High-income countries (% of total cases)

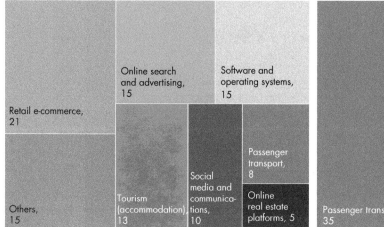

b. Middle-income countries (% of total cases)

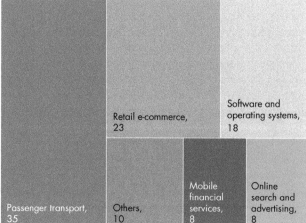

Source: Nyman and Barajas, forthcoming. Data at http://bit.do/WDR2021-Fig-7_2.

Note: Percentages are based on information for all antitrust cases involving digital platforms globally for which information was publicly available as of January 2020. Cases total 62 in high-income countries and 40 in middle-income countries. Panel a: "Others" includes digital music, e-books, educational materials, food delivery, online comparison platforms, dating platforms, and ticketing. Panel b: "Others" includes online delivery services, ticketing, and tourism. No cases were finalized in low-income countries, according to publicly available information.

cases account for about 20 percent of total cases sampled and are equally prevalent in middle- and high-income jurisdictions. Cases related to the passenger transport sector are the most prevalent in middle-income countries, where they make up one-third of all cases, reflecting in part a wave of mergers between ride-hailing firms in middle-income countries in recent years.

Abuse of dominance cases are more prevalent in middle-income countries, while cases on anticompetitive agreements are more common in high-income countries. The type of anticompetitive behavior by data-driven platforms in different sectors may depend on the nature of their business models. In the e-commerce and tourism sectors, cases of vertical restraints (agreements between firms at different levels of the value chain that constrain competition) predominate, potentially reflecting the reliance on small businesses to provide products and capacity in these sectors (figure 7.3). In online search and advertising and software and operating systems, cases of abuse of dominance are more common, likely because of their reliance on self-preferencing algorithms. In passenger transport, collusion cases (agreements to fix market parameters between firms at the same level of the value chain) have been the most frequent, which could stem from the scope for applying pricing algorithms in this sector.[7]

Adapting antitrust tools. New market dynamics arising from data-driven markets have spurred policy makers to rethink their approaches to antitrust enforcement, with jurisdictions around the world devising new strategies and articulating new guidance.[8] Debate and refinement continue, particularly when it comes to issues such as defining "relevant markets" and determining "dominance." For example, Kenya's competition authority recently published new Market Definition Guidelines to capture trends in data-driven markets. Such guidelines can be an effective way for authorities to begin to tackle these issues, while providing clarity to firms on the approach that will be taken to regulate their conduct and on the factors that will be assessed in antitrust cases.

The complexity of the data-driven economy for conventional antitrust reflects several departures from traditional markets. Salient challenges include how to assess consumer harm in markets in which goods and services are nominally provided for "free," how to address collusive algorithms (see chapter 3), and how to account for the nonprice dimensions of competition such as privacy.

The multisided nature of data-driven platforms also means that interactions among groups of users (including advertisers, in some cases) complicate the definition of markets and raises the possibility of cross-subsidization across different sides of the platform. This cross-subsidization includes advertising revenues effectively covering the cost of nominally "free" services provided to platform users. It is precisely the user data collected and processed by these

Figure 7.3 Among anticompetitive practices, abuse of dominance is more widespread worldwide across multiple sectors of the digital economy

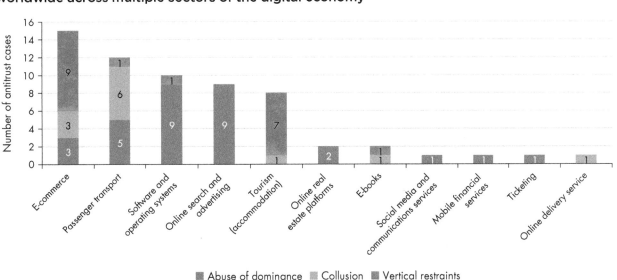

Source: Nyman and Barajas, forthcoming. Data at http://bit.do/WDR2021-Fig-7_3.

Note: Based on information for all antitrust cases involving digital platforms globally for which information was publicly available as of January 2020.

platforms that make advertising on these platforms so valuable because of better targeting (see chapter 3).

The multisided nature of platforms also means that, in addition to selling its own services, a platform acts as a buyer of services or even as a de facto employer of individuals in the gig economy such as drivers, household workers, or professionals who provide services. The potential imbalance in bargaining power between data-driven platform firms and individuals or small suppliers warrants the attention of policy makers. For example, in 2020 South Africa published regulations on protecting against abuse of buyer power that explicitly acknowledged the potential for such situations to arise in e-commerce markets and gig economy services.[9] Some competition authorities have also begun to consider adopting rules against abuse of a superior bargaining position.[10]

Platform firms typically exist in a digital ecosystem, where providers of complementary digital products interconnect and regularly exchange data to provide consumer products (such as the use of Google Maps by digital transport apps). To the extent that these complementor firms may also act as nascent competitors with larger platform firms, the effect of competition restrictions on these complementary products is an important consideration beyond the direct effect on the users of a platform. The potential for platforms to acquire potential competitors in complementary markets before they can become a competitive threat—and either shut them down or prevent further development of their products—has also become a topic of debate.[11] The potential for firms to engage in such "killer" or "zombie" acquisitions may merit consideration in merger reviews. Likewise, authorities should be increasingly alert to the possible harm to competition and innovation from mergers driven by the desire to acquire new data or data-relevant intellectual property such as algorithms.[12]

Under traditional antitrust regimes, mergers involving data-driven firms may be less likely to trigger a review by the antitrust authority because such firms typically do not have sufficient tangible assets or revenues to meet the traditional thresholds for merger notification.[13] Although the urgency of these concerns for developing countries will depend on the start-up environment in a country, thresholds for merger notification could be revamped to allow antitrust authorities to review potentially anticompetitive mergers involving data-driven firms that may appear small but could rapidly become market challengers through exponential growth. This has already occurred in Austria, Germany, and Japan, which have adopted complementary thresholds for

digital markets based on transaction values. Another option for triggering reviews would be requiring notification before mergers of any planned acquisition by dominant firms or shifting presumptions for future mergers so that an acquisition by a dominant platform would be presumed anticompetitive unless the merging parties are able to show otherwise.[14]

Creating institutional capacity to assess cases in the data economy. Views vary as to whether specialized digital market authorities should be established to oversee competition in the digital economy (as formally proposed in the United Kingdom[15] and informally discussed in the United States[16]). An increasing number of antitrust authorities in high-income economies have established teams specializing in the digital economy, but authorities in low- and middle-income countries lack the same capacity. A recent World Bank survey of eight competition authorities across developing regions found that none had specialized staff dedicated to cases in the digital economy, and almost all cited limited staffing as a key constraint in their ability to pursue competition issues in digital markets. Moreover, half the authorities surveyed acknowledged their lack of understanding of platform business models.[17] The shortage of capacity and resources among recently formed competition authorities contrasts with the abundant resources of large global digital firms. This imbalance must be taken into account by policy makers when considering the resourcing and institutional setup required to combat competition issues in the data-driven economy. It further strengthens the case for international cooperation as well as for ex ante measures to prevent harm from occurring in the first place (covered later in this section).

As for the substance of investigations, antitrust investigations of platform businesses are increasingly considering features specific to data-driven markets. But the most frequently assessed factors in antitrust cases involving platforms tend to be more traditional: assessment of competition from other platforms and the prices of goods and services. Although these factors often remain relevant, other, more novel issues posed by these markets appeared to be less systematically assessed by agencies. Network effects and multihoming behavior by consumers (use of multiple platforms for the same service) are explicitly mentioned in about 40 percent of cases across all jurisdictions. The issue of whether lack of access to data constitutes a barrier to entry or an essential input is present in 27 percent of all cases, but issues with algorithms are covered in only 13 percent. Data protection and privacy factors were raised as issues in only 6 percent of cases overall. Building capacity within regulatory authorities would help further address these challenges.

Some antitrust authorities may use data analytics to enhance their capability to detect competition issues in online markets. For example, the Russian Federation's antitrust authority has created an automated system to screen for bid rigging by analyzing data from public tenders to identify signs of collusion. Similarly, Brazil's competition authority has created a cartel screening unit to collect and analyze data, including through web scraping. In the context of COVID-19, competition authorities have encouraged e-commerce platform firms to monitor for excessive pricing practices by their sellers. For example, Amazon suspended thousands of sellers in the United States alone,[18] and Jumia delisted hundreds of products in Nigeria whose prices had been raised in response to the pandemic.[19]

Remedying harm caused by anticompetitive firm behavior. A consensus is growing that simply ending such behavior and imposing fines are insufficient. Antitrust authorities are moving toward designing remedies that can help restore competition in the market. Ordering the end of practices such as anticompetitive exclusivity clauses and the anticompetitive tying or bundling of products can, by encouraging multihoming by consumers, facilitate access to data by a broader range of competitors. Elsewhere, further measures specifically targeting data and algorithms may be necessary. But these remedies can be difficult to design and monitor, especially when the algorithms being used by the firm are not discernible.

In the Uber-Careem merger in Egypt, for example, Uber was obliged to grant future competitors access to Careem's "points of interest map data" on a onetime basis; to grant current competitors access to trip data (including rider and driver information), subject to data protection laws; and to give riders access to their own data. Uber also committed to removing exclusivity requirements in contracts with drivers to prevent them from being locked in the merged platform. A different approach was taken in the Uber-Grab merger in Singapore. There, the competition authority considered mandating transferability of driver data between apps before abandoning the idea after a survey of potential entrants suggested this was not an impediment to their entry.[20] This case reinforces the need to design remedies case by case and to link them clearly to a theory of harm in order to safeguard against remedies that are detrimental to innovation without significantly improving competition.

Cooperating across borders. Because of the global nature of many platform businesses, antitrust decisions taken in one jurisdiction often have spillover effects in other countries. For example, in Germany, as part of a remedy to respond to competition concerns from third-party sellers, Amazon agreed to amend its terms of business for sellers on Amazon's online marketplaces across Europe, North America, and Asia. Among the changes was a reduction in Amazon's (previously extensive) rights to use data on the products of third parties.[21] Such cross-country benefits could be further leveraged by promoting international cooperation among antitrust authorities, thereby creating a more predictable regulatory environment for firms.

To date, the European Union (EU) is alone in having a substantial track record in competition enforcement in digital markets at the regional level. However, several regional competition authorities are becoming more active—such as the Competition Commission of the Common Market for Eastern and Southern Africa (COMESA) free trade area—although they have yet to take on a digital markets case. More informal collaboration is also occurring among competition authorities. For example, the BRICS countries (Brazil, Russia, India, China, and South Africa) released a joint report on the digital economy that calls for increased cooperation among the authorities.[22] Antitrust agencies in the Group of Seven (G-7) also released a "common understanding of the challenges posed by the digital economy" in 2019, addressing the need for international cooperation.[23] Emerging free trade agreements—such as the African Continental Free Trade Agreement, which is likely to have a digital focus—could also foster harmonization on competition policy for the data-driven economy through their competition policy protocols.

Promoting competition through regulation ex ante

Ex ante market regulations that promote competition by enabling data use may be just as important as antitrust remedies. Indeed, given the durable nature of market power in data-driven markets and the challenges of designing antitrust remedies, ensuring that markets do not slip into entrenched market power in the first place may be even more important than enforcing antitrust rules ex post. In countries without a developed antitrust regime, including many low-income countries, this is the only line of policy response to foster competitive data-driven markets.

Adopting mandatory and voluntary schemes to improve access to data. Governments are considering various regulatory options to ease access to data in digital ecosystems. However, such options remain relatively untested, and evidence on their efficacy is still scarce. Options include facilitating multihoming; extending the right to portability of personal data (in essence, the right to move personal data between different controllers); facilitating data interoperability (the ability for different systems to share and use data in a coordinated, timely manner); and encouraging data sharing or pooling schemes (when two or more firms agree to merge their data for access by themselves and possibly third parties).

Relatively few jurisdictions have put mandatory portability and interoperability schemes into practice, although a few instructive models are emerging. The European Union has been at the forefront of this push, although an ability to enforce these schemes is not yet clear. The right to portability of personal data is contained in the European Union's General Data Protection Regulation (GDPR), whereas its 2019 regulation on the free flow of nonpersonal data should be important for firms that rely on machine data.[24] Kenya, Mexico, Nigeria, the Philippines, and Thailand are some other jurisdictions that have also put in place rights to portability, although—as with the GDPR—these regimes have yet to be tested.

Measures to mandate interoperability go beyond portability rights; they also aim to ease the sharing of data from a technical perspective. Ease is important where continual access to data is required.[25] An example is the implementation of "open banking" regimes whereby financial service providers are mandated to share data on user accounts to third parties through open application programming interfaces (APIs). Banking data are well suited to data sharing initiatives because they are relatively homogeneous and standardized, and the concept of open banking is now well established in Europe.

The United Kingdom's open banking initiative seems to have been particularly successful in spurring market entry and innovation, with 134 third-party providers currently registered and supplying services.[26] At least nine other jurisdictions also have emerging open banking regimes in place.[27] In Brazil, the central bank published a draft regulation on open banking in 2019. In India, although there is no mandatory open banking regime, policy measures to encourage data sharing have been introduced. These include safeguards such as the creation of "account aggregators" to ensure that individuals consent to use of their financial data and that data are not used beyond the agreed terms.[28] Beyond the realm of open banking, in Mexico several revisions of the Fintech Law have been adopted to enable data sharing, including facilitation of access to user data and regulation of the fees banks can charge for sharing user data.[29]

Voluntary industry data access schemes are also operating around the world. The Open Ag Data Alliance, an industrywide project, aims to standardize the way in which farmers' data are shared with larger firms (such as those developing precision agriculture models).[30] In Kenya, the One Million Farmer Platform connects agtech players across 14 value chains to take advantage of large-scale shared data collection and digitized farmer profiles.[31] In Nigeria, financial industry players have voluntarily formed an alliance to develop open banking APIs.[32] The Solid project, launched in 2018, aims to provide open-source software that allows users to fully own their data and allows developers to create decentralized apps that run on that data. Meanwhile, Apple, Facebook, Microsoft, and Twitter are developing the Data Transfer Project, an open-source initiative to enable portability of some types of user data among participating platforms, although its impact on competition has yet to be seen.

When jurisdictions seek to impose mandatory data sharing regulations, they must design such schemes carefully to avoid distortive effects such as stifling incentives to innovate, facilitating collusion through excessive transparency of firms' strategic variables such as prices, and unduly raising the cost of doing business. The immediate benefits of mandating data sharing need to be balanced with the possibility that it would reduce incentives for those sharing data to invest in data collection and for competitors receiving data to build their own collection capacity.

To safeguard incentives for innovation, it may be useful to examine whether the data to be shared have the features of an "essential facility" (akin to the "essential facilities doctrine" framework used to regulate sharing of infrastructure). Such an examination would require careful economic analysis of whether the data in question are an essential input that competitors cannot replicate or substitute. Because data, unlike physical infrastructure, are nonrivalrous, there should in theory be a stronger argument in favor of granting access requirements. Nonetheless, design of such requirements would still have to carefully consider future market dynamics, including incentives for innovation; whether the remedy should be timebound and limited to markets where a competition issue has been identified; and whether different firms should have different obligations according to their market position. Regulators should also ensure that shared data are kept secure, and that, when personal data are involved, the exchange is carried out in compliance with data protection laws.

Regulating the structure and behavior of data-driven platform firms. Calls to regulate large data-driven firms ex ante are gaining ground and merit consideration. Moves in this direction must be targeted at remedying specific competition bottlenecks and should be grounded in sound economic analysis (for example, remedies around data sharing should be based on a finding that a lack of data is indeed prohibiting firms from competing). The possibility of regulating large platforms as essential facilities (akin to telecom regulation) may be promising. However, it should be conditional on a platform or its data constituting a bottleneck or an unavoidable trading partner for other firms, and on the data in question being an essential, nonreplicable input to potential competitors.

Another area of discussion has been the possibility of breaking up large data-driven platform firms.[33] Because of the highly interventionist nature of this solution, it should be considered only when the firm in question holds market power believed to be entrenched and durable. It is also important to consider that the network effects that initially led to the firm's dominance may persist in each of the individual market segments after the firm is broken up. There is no guarantee that simply separating a firm's segments will overcome these network effects and allow expansion by others.

Nonetheless, structural solutions may be relevant to solve some issues typically seen with platform firms. Preventing firms from operating in multiple markets would mitigate the risk of firms leveraging economies of scope from data insights across multiple markets. It would also address the risk of vertically integrated firms providing preferences for their own products. All this needs to be weighed against the benefits consumers may experience from economies of scale and scope that arise when service providers participate in multiple markets.

Other ex ante regulations could target the "quality" dimensions of services provided by data-driven firms—particularly the protections afforded to individuals on the collection and use of their data (if not already adequately covered by the data protection regime). They could also look at the terms applied to the (often small) suppliers that participate in these platforms. In this vein, regulators could consider providing smaller firms with access to platforms or prominence in their rankings on a fair, consistent, and transparent basis. For example, the European Union enacted a platform-to-business regulation in 2019 that requires a platform to make its terms and conditions easily available to businesses that trade on the platform, including disclosure of conditions under which either party may access data generated by or provided to the platform, as well as explanations of the ranking algorithms employed.[34]

Leveraging offline regulation. For some data-driven businesses, the key to being able to enter and compete does not lie so much in data remedies as in other aspects of regulation, including "offline" regulation. In some countries, new regulations are being imposed to protect traditional or incumbent players. In Morocco and Tunisia, state-owned enterprises are not subject to the same data protection obligations that are binding for the private sector.[35] New e-commerce rules in India that prohibit foreign firms from selling their own products on their platforms are intended to protect domestic retailers against risks of exclusion (reflecting the line of regulatory reasoning on preventing self-preferencing noted earlier). However, the fact that these regulations target only foreign firms and are not predicated on the firm holding a dominant position may mean that such regulations could be creating an unlevel playing field beyond what is needed to prevent adverse outcomes.

Regulations that ban entry of data-driven business models are an obvious example of offline regulatory restrictions. Spurred by protests from incumbent players, Uber was blocked from entering a range of countries, including Bulgaria (for a time), Italy, and Spain.[36] In response, the competition authorities of at least 24 countries have advocated against disproportionate restrictions for transport platforms, including those in Brazil, Colombia, Indonesia, Kenya, Mexico, and Peru. In China, the government helped to resolve uncertainty by legalizing ridesharing apps and establishing procedures to formally license drivers.[37] In Mexico, the competition authority recommended that local governments recognize transportation services provided by platforms, leading to new regulations allowing them to operate fully in Mexico City and other localities.[38]

Still other regulations can raise the costs of data-driven firms to compete. For example, ridesharing regulations in Jordan specify that fares charged by ridesharing companies must be 15 percent higher than those of taxis, and discounts may not go below the tariff stipulated for taxis.[39] In Egypt, drivers and vehicles working with ridesharing platforms are required to pay 25 percent higher registration fees and taxes than traditional taxis.[40]

Fintech is another sector in which the conditions favoring incumbents are gradually being dismantled. Some regulations have focused on unstructured supplementary service data (USSD) channels, which establish a real-time session between a mobile handset and an application to generate a financial service and are considered an "essential facility" for many fintech providers. Regulators in Bangladesh, Colombia, Kenya, and Peru have promulgated regulations to open up third-party access to mobile network operators' USSD channels after some providers strategically restricted access to those channels to dampen competition from potential rivals.[41] Banks can also unfairly exclude non-bank rivals from payment settlement infrastructure, which is often owned or controlled by incumbent bank consortiums. In response to this issue, the People's Bank of China created a separate clearinghouse for nonbank payment providers in 2018, in part to create a more level playing field.

Recommended reforms of competition policy

The recommendations for competition policy that follow are grouped according to a maturity model designed to reflect a country's stage in the development process.

Establishing fundamentals

In low-income countries with limited institutional capacity, a pragmatic approach to competition policy focusing on the essentials is warranted. It should build on related instruments that may already be in place, while developing institutional capacity for the future.

Create a level playing field for data-driven businesses. The first priority is to ensure that traditional regulations and policies do not hinder entry by data-driven firms or create an unlevel playing field between firms. This could include harmonizing standards and requirements for entry and operation of data-driven firms with standards and requirements for traditional firms in competing markets (for example, ride-hailing platforms and regular taxis).

Build on existing sectoral regulations. In regulated sectors with institutional capacity—such as telecom, energy, and banking—more targeted regulatory approaches to encouraging data access could be considered, building on international experience such as with open banking.

Develop capacity for dealing with data-driven businesses. Governments should also invest in building an understanding of data-driven business models and data ecosystems in selected agencies, such as sector regulators, and by industry-related policy makers. As part of sectoral initiatives or industrial policies, policy makers could consult with the private sector—particularly start-ups—to understand data needs and data

bottlenecks for firms and broker industry-led solutions for data sharing.

Accelerating data flows

In addition to the preceding recommendations, countries with more capable institutions could encourage or mandate data sharing for markets or circumstances where it would be pro-competitive on balance and in compliance with data protection policies for personal data.

Develop guidelines for portability and interoperability. Where portability is possible, consumers should be trained to exercise these rights. Where data sharing may be mandated under existing legal tools (such as the competition law, market regulations, or license terms), policy makers could define an essential facilities–style framework and build the institutional skills needed to assess when data sharing might be appropriate. Policy makers could also work with international bodies to promote harmonization of concepts and standards for interoperability and data sharing between countries.

Apply ex ante regulations for data-driven markets. Governments may consider establishing an economy-wide ex ante regulatory regime governing data-driven markets in the longer term. Any regulatory remedies imposed should be based on a case-by-case analysis. They also should be carefully designed to avoid raising firm costs beyond the level necessary to remedy the competition issue; stifling incentives for firms to invest or innovate by mandating them to share proprietary data with competitors; or providing excessive transparency in firms' strategic variables such as prices, thereby facilitating collusion. These remedies should be limited to data that have been identified as a bottleneck to competition and should ideally be timebound.

Carefully assess the merits of ex ante regulation of platforms case by case. Overall, calls to regulate ex ante large data-driven platforms—or the use and sharing of data by these firms—may have merit but require careful targeting where a firm or its data pose a bottleneck to competition. Regulators may also find it helpful to provide smaller firms with access to platforms, or prominence within their display rankings, on a fair, consistent, and transparent basis.

Consider the impacts of competition when choosing between data protection regimes. Subject to ensuring the data rights of individuals over their personal data, policy makers could aim to design data protection policies in a way that minimizes potential distortions to competition as much as possible. If no generally applicable data protection regime is in place, these considerations could be embedded in sectoral approaches.

Create markets for data intermediaries. In cases in which personal data may be shared, regulators should ensure that sharing is carried out in compliance with data protection regulations. In the longer term, it may also be valuable to facilitate markets for personal information management systems so that intermediaries can streamline steps to obtain and monitor consent (see chapter 6). Such streamlining would be particularly useful when continual access to data is required. Regulators should ensure that all sharing complies with data protection regulations.

Establish data repositories. In some sectors, there may be merit in considering data repositories established by the government or through public-private partnerships. For example, in agriculture centrally curated data on farmers' identities or profiles, locations, and other parameters could aid the entry of players in agtech markets.

Optimizing the system

In addition to the preceding recommendations, in jurisdictions with a functioning antitrust enforcement regime, the following actions would be valuable. Several steps could be taken in the short term to better tailor existing antitrust regimes to data-driven markets.

Adapt the framework for reviewing antitrust cases involving data-driven firms. A good first step would be to reevaluate merger review frameworks to account for the characteristics of data-driven businesses. Such a review would include updating thresholds for notification of planned merger activity to enable authorities to review potentially anticompetitive mergers in the digital economy. Competition authorities could also publish guidelines to clarify their assessment approach for both mergers and anticompetitive practices cases, particularly when defining markets and assessing dominance, efficiencies, and theories of harm.

Publish guidelines for regulatory remedies. Guidelines for designing regulatory remedies for data-driven markets would also be valuable. In the shorter term, authorities could review the fines imposed on firms to increase their deterrent effect. Over time, competition authorities may work toward lessening their reliance on fines and move toward remedies aimed at restoring competition. Where remedies are imposed, sufficient resources should be available to cover the associated regulatory burden, as well as monitor and build evidence on the efficacy of remedies to feed back into their design.

Develop capacity in antitrust agencies. It is critical to build the capacity of antitrust authorities to understand the economics of data-driven markets. Such economic analysis should be tailored to the context of specific countries. To develop capacity and greater expertise in these areas, larger authorities may consider moving toward specialized staff or dedicated units in the longer term. Newer authorities with less capacity can leverage the analysis of competition issues in data-driven markets in developed jurisdictions, adapting it to their specific context.

Harness data tools for antitrust regulation. Better-resourced authorities operating in more advanced online economies may consider building the capacity to web scrape data on online markets and e-procurement bids to help screen for collusion and other competition issues.

Encourage domestic cooperation among regulators. Governments should encourage cooperation between competition authorities and data protection authorities, as well as other relevant sector regulators, where these institutions exist.

Promote international cooperation on antitrust. Governments could also promote international cooperation and exchange of knowledge between antitrust authorities in data-driven markets, including harmonization of the approaches to antitrust regulation and the digital economy.

Trade policy

Cross-border data flows are becoming one of the hallmarks of international trade in the twenty-first century. Although trade in goods has remained relatively stable over the last decade, the global trade in data-driven services has grown exponentially. Global data flows multiplied more than twentyfold between 2007 and 2017 (figure 7.4). They are expected to nearly quadruple from 2017 levels by 2022.[42] Such data flows were valued at US$7.8 trillion in 2014.[43] By contrast, global merchandise exports fluctuated at around US$20 trillion between 2007 and 2019.

By facilitating intangible transactions, new technologies have expanded global trade in services from its traditional focus on transport and travel services to modern, data-driven services such as telecommunications, finance, and a myriad of other business and professional activities. Trade in all kinds of services has grown sixfold over the past two decades, doubling its share of the global gross

Figure 7.4 Since 1990, the global trade in data-driven services has grown exponentially and now constitutes half of trade in services

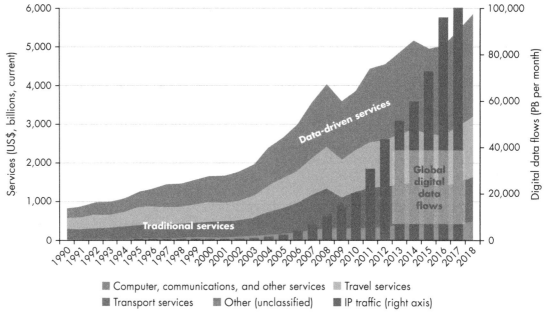

■ Computer, communications, and other services ■ Travel services
■ Transport services ■ Other (unclassified) ■ IP traffic (right axis)

Source: WDR team calculations, based on World Bank, WITS (World Integrated Trade Solution) database, http://wits.worldbank.org/WITS/. Data at http://bit.do/WDR2021-Fig-7_4.

Note: IP = Internet Protocol; PB = petabyte.

domestic product (GDP). Data-driven services have increased from about one-quarter to almost half of total service exports (figure 7.4).

Regulating data flows for digital trade

Digital trade—and in particular the regulation of cross-border data flows—has risen rapidly on the global governance agenda. Accordingly, it has been taken up in a variety of multilateral, regional, and bilateral forums—notably, the Group of Twenty (G-20) Osaka principles on "Data Free Flow with Trust"[44] and the World Trade Organization's Joint Statement on Electronic Commerce.[45] In light of these developments, countries should carefully design regulatory frameworks for cross-border data transfers that enable trade in digital goods and services while adequately addressing data protection and security concerns. The wide range of approaches across the globe highlights the various policy priorities as well as the perceptions of opportunities and risks.

Regulation of data flows, especially of personal data, lies at the heart of ongoing discussions of international trade governance. Domestic data regulation can either enable or hinder cross-border digital trade. A strong regulatory framework for privacy, security, and consumer protection is critical to supporting digital transactions.[46] At the same time, burdensome

regulations on the cross-border transfer and use of data can impose substantial costs on businesses, especially micro, small, and medium enterprises (MSMEs), deterring international exchanges. More than 40 percent of US firms surveyed by the US International Trade Commission (USITC) consider data localization requirements and market access regulations to be obstacles to trade, particularly larger firms and those in the digital communications, content, and retail services sectors.[47] Data localization means that at least one copy of the data is stored locally or the data are kept in domestic servers during processing.

Restrictions on global data flows can also burden the production of goods and the productivity of local companies using digital technologies, particularly in the context of global value chains.[48] Swedish manufacturing firms recently reported that data localization requirements and restrictions on cross-border data flows, including for outward transfers, adversely affect the setup and operation of their global production networks.[49]

The challenge for policy makers is promoting the sharing and transfer of data in a manner that supports the economic benefits of digital trade, while ensuring that sensitive information remains secure and the relevant regulations on personal data protection are respected. Data governance regimes for cross-border data flows are seldom fully open or closed, but they can be placed on a spectrum of three broad models (figure 7.5). These range from an open transfers approach allowing free movement of data based on private standards, to a conditional transfers approach based on conformity with established regulatory safeguards, to a limited transfers approach entailing government approval for cross-border movements as well as compliance with localization requirements for local storage or processing of data. In addition, the way in which the rules are implemented may make any one of these stylized models more or less open than the letter of the regulation may suggest.

"Open transfers" model. This model is defined by the general absence of government restrictions on cross-border transfers of personal data and reliance on voluntary private sector standards and practices, as opposed to statutory requirements set out in laws or regulations. The government's role is exercising ex post accountability by launching enforcement actions, such as fines, for misleading data subjects in the treatment of their data or for failing to abide by the voluntary standards the firm itself has adopted. This approach ensures the greatest flexibility in the movement of data because it does not impose any mandatory requirements or conditions for data transfers. The Cross-Border Privacy Rules adopted by the Asia-Pacific Economic Cooperation (APEC) provide for self-certification by organizations or audit by third-party accountability agents rather than requiring the prior approval of a data protection authority. A general concern about approaches based on voluntary private norms without overarching regulatory guidance from government or international agreements is the risk of proliferation of standards across firms and jurisdictions, raising costs for data sharing as well as regulatory oversight, without guaranteeing any minimum standard for personal data protection.

The "open transfers" model adopted by the United States features no general comprehensive framework for data protection at the national level, and it provides data subjects with only limited statutory rights. It relies instead on the US Federal Trade Commission to monitor the compliance of private companies with

Figure 7.5 Three distinct approaches to handling cross-border data flows

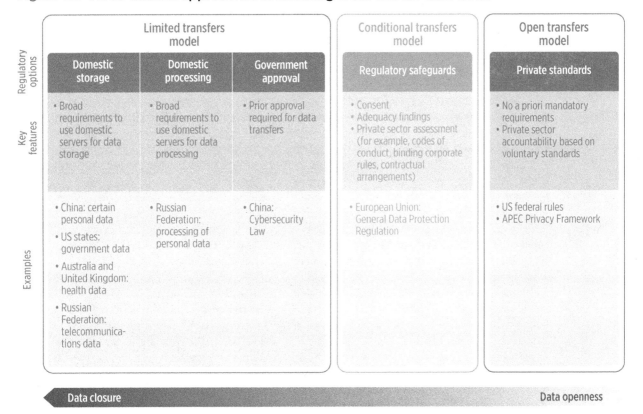

Sources: WDR 2021 team, based on Casalini and López González (2019); Cory (2017).

Note: APEC = Asia-Pacific Economic Cooperation.

their own data protection practices. Under this overarching framework, stricter data protection rules can nonetheless be incorporated in sectoral regulations, as indeed happens in highly regulated industries such as finance and health, or in a particular subnational jurisdiction, such as the state of California.[50]

"Conditional transfers" model. This model seeks to strike a balance between imperatives to protect data and the need for openness of data transfers. It sets out a series of mandatory regulatory safeguards that, once met, allow for the free flow of cross-border data. Such safeguards can restrict data sharing to jurisdictions that meet certain adequacy standards for data protection or to firms that have adopted mandatory data protection protocols, such as binding corporate rules or contractual terms.

The European Union's 1995 Data Protection Directive, and subsequent General Data Protection Regulation, pioneered this kind of model. A similar approach has since been adopted by many countries, including Argentina, Colombia, Estonia, Malaysia, the Republic of Korea, Senegal, and South Africa. The European Union limits the transfer of personal data to only those jurisdictions that have enacted "adequate" data protection rules in line with EU standards, which must be confirmed in advance by a national regulatory authority. This process can take a long time, creating bottlenecks in cross-border trade.[51] Alternatively, firms or institutions may be bound to comply with such standards through contractual clauses or binding corporate policies, including self-certification schemes such as the EU-US Privacy Shield.[52]

"Limited transfers" model. A more restrictive approach to cross-border data flows entails explicit regulatory approval for international data transfers and may sometimes also require data localization. Under this model, governments apply stringent regulatory requirements over personal data, including government access to data to protect national security and public order. Although such regulatory approvals do not formally preclude cross-border data flows, much depends on how a system of this kind is implemented. A broad strict approval regime that conditions data transfers on prior regulatory approval is likely to greatly limit cross-border data sharing and heavily restrict digital trade flows, akin to formal localization requirements.

As noted, data localization entails storing at least one copy of the data locally or keeping the data in domestic servers during processing. Mandatory storage entails placing the servers where the data are stored within the jurisdiction, and processing requirements obligate use of local entities. Mandatory localization can be even more stringent by requiring that both the main servers and the backup (or "recovery") servers be located within the jurisdiction. Localization requirements may technically allow for cross-border transfers as long as the data are stored or processed or backed up in the original jurisdiction, but at the risk of adding significant costs to management of the data, thereby disrupting cross-border businesses models.[53]

Countries fully adopting this model have enacted broad mandatory localization requirements.[54] Yet because of the burdensome nature of these measures, mandatory localization requirements are more commonly limited to certain specific and sensitive types of data, such as those related to finance and health care.[55] Australia, for example, prohibits the transfer of health data overseas in certain circumstances.[56] Korea restricts transfers related to financial data.

In China, mandatory localization requirements affect certain types of data considered "critical information infrastructure," including financial information, personal data, health and medical data, mapping services, online publishing, and telecom. Operators of such critical information infrastructure are required to store certain personal and business information in China,[57] and foreign companies may have to apply for permission before transferring data out of China. In Russia, the Personal Data Law mandates that all personal data about Russian citizens must be stored and processed using databases physically located in Russia, while allowing for cross-border transfer once this requirement is met.[58] In Nigeria, government data must be hosted within the country's borders.[59] In Vietnam, private sector internet service providers must retain a copy of their data in Vietnam for possible government inspection.[60]

Government control over data flows is sometimes confused and conflated with the broader concept of *data sovereignty.* From a narrow perspective, this can mean merely that data in a country are subject to the laws of that country. Increasingly, however, this concept is understood to refer to efforts by a country to exert national control over data as well as digital infrastructure and service providers in response to the perceived imbalances in the global data economy.

A review of the distribution of these regulatory models globally suggests growing adoption of the conditional transfers model for cross-border data flows (map 7.1). Of the 116 countries surveyed for this Report worldwide (including all EU members individually), about 57 percent have adopted this approach—often reflecting the EU's data protection framework.[61] Thirty-four percent feature an open

Map 7.1 Uptake of regulatory models to cross-border data flows

Limited transfers model
Conditional transfers model
Open transfers model
No data

IBRD WLD45649 | MARCH 2021

Source: WDR 2021 team, based on World Bank, Global Data Regulation Survey, https://microdata.worldbank.org/index.php/catalog/3866. Data at http://bit.do /WDR2021-Map-7_1.

transfers model, many of them simply because they have not yet adopted any data protection regime. More than half of low-income countries do not have any restrictions on cross-border transfers of personal data. The remaining 9 percent operate regulatory arrangements similar to the limited transfers model, such as China and Russia, as well as several large middle-income countries, including Indonesia, Nigeria, and Vietnam.[62]

Understanding the economic effects of data protection regimes

The treatment of cross-border flows of personal data stands out as a core difference in the data protection regimes of countries, reflecting the differences in importance given to various wider public policy goals (table 7.1).[63] As data flows become an increasingly important component of international trade, the choice of one data protection regime over another raises significant economic considerations and poses challenges in striking the right balance between promoting economic development and providing adequate data safeguards. The open transfers model minimizes the regulatory burden on service providers at both ends of a data transfer, maximizing the freedom businesses can enjoy in their data partnerships as well as their own business models, but providing few safeguards to boost trust in such data transfers. The limited transfers model is directed at the security of the domestic digital market, restricting its links with foreign suppliers and consumers. The conditional transfers model is a halfway house of sorts, allowing international transfers while requiring additional guarantees for the protection of personal data in destination markets, thereby adding somewhat to trading costs.

Table 7.1 Policy bases for regulating cross-border personal data

Model	Policy goal	Regulatory costs	Digital trade flows
Limited transfers	Cybersecurity and other security concerns	Higher	Limited by transfer approval or data localization requirements
Conditional transfers	Protection of personal data	Medium	Subject to regulatory conditions
Open transfers	Business freedom	Lower	Largely open

Source: WDR 2021 team.

Stronger restrictions on cross-border data flows, such as those found in the limited transfers model, can be particularly detrimental to international trade. Because trade in services relies on the global movement of data, including personal data, regulations that require the maintenance or processing of data within a country or a particular region can be a costly impediment. Restrictive data policies—especially mandatory localization requirements—reduce imports of data-intensive services in the countries imposing them, which, in turn, limits cross-border digital trade flows.[64] Depending on how the restrictions are cast, mandatory localization requirements can result in discrimination against firms without a physical presence in a country or even in abuses of human rights or the rule of law.[65] The burden associated with mandatory localization requirements is greater for small and developing economies because the cost of the infrastructure investment weighs more heavily. At the same time, the opportunity cost of restricting trade in services may be higher in countries that do not have a large domestic market of their own. By contrast, in larger countries with significant domestic markets, localization policies may be adopted to protect domestic infant industries from globally dominant competitors.

Although limitations on cross-border data flows are often justified on several policy grounds—notably, data protection, national security, economic development, or law enforcement—their effectiveness on each of these counts has been debated.[66]

National security is often invoked to justify restricting data flows. Under its Cybersecurity Law, China requires a security assessment for data transfers related to critical infrastructure. In the United States, domestic storage requirements are imposed for cloud computing services procured by the Department of Defense. Yet security experts argue that data localization may render information less, not more, secure by concentrating all such data for the country in one place.[67]

In developing countries, policy makers frequently cite economic considerations—technology transfers and job creation—as a reason for introducing data localization requirements. Nigeria's guidelines for information and communication technology (ICT) companies require them to host all consumer and government data locally within the country to fight a "negative trade balance" in the ICT sector.[68] Yet data storage requirements per se offer little in terms of jobs or innovation. Data centers do not rely on large numbers of staff to operate, and they can even be monitored and maintained remotely, whereas data storage requirements can hamper the digital trade and reduce overall competitiveness.

Some policy makers worry that access to data for law enforcement purposes may be hampered when the data are not stored domestically. Although tech firms largely cooperate with courts everywhere in their requests for data, there have indeed been cases that confirm this concern. They highlight the need for greater international cooperation for sharing digital data in the context of law enforcement, possibly updating and elaborating on the existing network of mutual legal assistance treaties (see chapter 6). In addition, governments may require firms offering online services to comply with court orders even if not established locally, as pioneered in the US CLOUD Act.[69]

Low- and middle-income countries have much to lose from data restrictions. Flexible regimes for cross-border data flows allow businesses from these countries not only to benefit from the services offered on the global market, but also to provide data-intensive services in return. For example, the Bangladeshi firm Augmedix offers remote assistance to medical doctors in the United States. The doctors wear smart glasses that allow their Bangladesh-based assistants to "witness" patient consultations and create associated medical records. This two-way exchange of data, and the high value-added services that they entail, is possible only because both countries—the United States and Bangladesh—allow for such sensitive data to move across borders. Restrictions on cross-border data flows are especially damaging to small economies that are likely to lack the domestic market size to justify the costs of developing the necessary determinants for a modern digital market, including skills and infrastructure such as data centers.[70]

Data rules incorporating strong data protection, complemented by a flexible regime for cross-border data flows, can help boost digital trade. New analysis conducted for this Report reveals how trade flows of digital services (such as telecommunications, computer, and information services) in 116 countries vary based on the data policy models adopted—limited transfers, conditional transfers, and open transfers—for both cross-border and associated domestic data regimes.[71] When it comes to cross-border regulations, the research finds that country pairs that adopt an open transfers model achieve higher volumes of trade in digital services than those operating under the conditional transfers or limited transfers models. However, domestic data regulations are also found to have a significant effect on trade in digital services. In this case, having a strong domestic data protection regime for personal data is positively associated with trade flows in digital services, compared with regimes that exercise little government regulation over personal data protection and those that apply tight government controls on domestic use of personal data.[72]

Although personal data protection regimes can help digital trade, they can also be costly, both for the government agencies tasked with their enforcement and for private operators that must comply with those regulations. For example, monitoring and enforcing the US Health Insurance Portability and Accountability Act (HIPAA) regulation that governs personal data sharing, among other things, require an annual budget of more than US$50 million for an agency employing roughly 150 employees. In a survey of relatively large firms, compliance with the EU's GDPR has been estimated to cost from US$250,000 to almost US$2 million a year.[73] Policy makers should avoid replicating foreign regulations that may prove costly for the domestic public administration or private sector. Instead, they should strive to protect data using solutions tailored to their own context.

Regulatory concerns about cross-border flows of personal data do not carry over to nonpersonal data (see chapter 6). Data that cannot be linked to an identified or identifiable person are an essential and significant component of international trade and are expected to grow dramatically with the advent of data from the Internet of Things. Free flows should be the general guiding principle for trade in nonpersonal data, subject to adequate cybersecurity safeguards. Although national security issues may arise in some cases—such as data related to national defense or critical infrastructure—the bulk of nonpersonal information may be treated with a higher degree of deference to data producers because it more rarely relates to the public interest. For example, the EU Non-Personal Data Regulation (NPDR) strengthens the principle of free circulation of nonpersonal data by banning data localization among EU members, unless such restrictions are justified on grounds of national security.[74]

Incorporating data regulation in international trade agreements

Trade agreements, which have been at the forefront of international data governance, have incorporated the first binding international rules on data flows. The General Agreement on Trade in Services (GATS), concluded in 1995 under the framework of the World Trade Organization (WTO), applies to 164 countries, including 36 least-developed countries.[75] GATS governs any type of government measure affecting trade in services, including measures related to cross-border data transfers. GATS does not prohibit restrictions on cross-border data flows per se. However, subject to the sectoral commitments adopted by each WTO member, mandatory localization and other limitations on cross-border data flows could be considered violations of the agreement's "non-discrimination" disciplines.[76] In addition to rules on cross-border services, WTO members have provisionally agreed not to impose customs duties on digital products (see section on tax policy at the end of this chapter).

Countries have built on such disciplines in a growing number of bilateral and regional preferential trade agreements (PTAs). At latest count, at least 89 countries are members of trade agreements that feature either a stand-alone chapter or specific provisions covering aspects of digital trade.[77]

Some of the latest generation of PTAs feature substantial disciplines supporting cross-border data flows. This is notably the case for the 2018 Comprehensive and Progressive Agreement for Trans-Pacific Partnership (CPTPP) among 11 countries bordering on the Pacific Ocean.[78] It seeks to guarantee cross-border data flows, prohibiting mandatory localization measures as a precondition for conducting business in the territories of the parties.[79]

Agreements focusing exclusively on digital trade are a new trend in regulation of data flows. The Digital Trade Agreement (DTA)[80] between Japan and the United States, concluded in 2019, parallels the United States–Mexico–Canada Agreement (USMCA)[81] in its rules and obligations. Among its features, the DTA includes prohibition of customs duties on digital products, prohibition of data localization measures, nondiscriminatory treatment of digital products, and electronic authentication and signatures, as well as protection of consumers' and businesses' confidential information. Chile, New Zealand, and Singapore signed (electronically) their Digital Economy Partnership Agreement (DEPA) in June 2020, featuring rules similar to those of the CPTPP (table 7.2).

Agreements at the regional level have also become increasingly popular. The ASEAN (Association of Southeast Asian Nations) Agreement on Electronic Commerce, adopted in 2019, is the only digital trade agreement to count low-income countries among its signatories. It addresses matters similar to those addressed by the CPTPP, though mostly in nonbinding language. Other regional groups have adopted instruments that, though not focused on trade, are meant to facilitate data flows. In 2014 the African Union adopted the Convention on Cyber Security and Personal Data Protection (Malabo Convention),

Table 7.2 Key provisions on digital trade in recent trade agreements

Provision	US–Singapore FTA (2004)	Canada–EU CETA (2014)	ChAFTA (2015)	CPTPP (2018)	ASEAN (2019)	USMCA (2020)	DEPA (2020)	RCEP (2020)
Nondiscrimination of digital products	■			■		■	■	▦
E-documents and e-signatures			■	■	■	■	■	■
Paperless trading			■	▦	■	■	▦	■
Online consumer protection				■	■	■	■	■
Privacy protection		▦		■	■	■	■	■
Cybersecurity				▦	▦	■	■	
Unrestricted cross-border data flows				■	■	■	■	▦
Prohibition of data localization				■	■	■	■	■
Customs duties	■			■		■	■	■

Source: WDR 2021 team.

Note: ■ indicates a binding provision; ▦ indicates a soft law provision; empty cell indicates no provision. ASEAN = Association of Southeast Asian Nations; CETA = Comprehensive Economic and Trade Agreement; ChAFTA = China-Australia Free Trade Agreement; CPTPP = Comprehensive and Progressive Agreement for Trans-Pacific Partnership; DEPA = Digital Economy Partnership Agreement; EU = European Union; FTA = Free Trade Agreement; RCEP = Regional Comprehensive Economic Partnership; US = United States; USMCA = United States–Mexico–Canada Agreement.

an international treaty seeking to protect data across Africa, but it has yet to enter into force.[82] APEC promulgated the APEC Privacy Framework for the Asia-Pacific region,[83] directed at facilitating information flows within the APEC community, while ensuring basic principles of data protection and providing ample flexibility to its member economies on the regulatory approach they follow. The recent Regional Comprehensive Economic Partnership (RCEP) among 15 nations in the Asia-Pacific region features rules on cross-border data flows and against data localization requirements, subject to a broad exception for national security. Notwithstanding, these arrangements, with their disparate objectives and instrumentalities, betray a hodgepodge approach that could result in the emergence of regional data silos, each with its own set of rules.

Despite these somewhat exceptional initiatives, the future of global trade rules on data flows remains uncertain, particularly at the global level. Most trade agreements addressing cross-border data flows, including some recent ones, simply feature soft law provisions that lack enforcement power or are aimed at promoting regulatory cooperation on this issue (table 7.2).[84] Discussions on digital trade are under way among a group of 85 WTO members, which account for nearly 90 percent of digital trade under the Joint Statement on Electronic Commerce.[85]

Possible disciplines on cross-border data flows are among the most contentious issues, and it is still unclear whether standard provisions will emerge for worldwide use, or whether such provisions will remain a distinctive feature of selected agreements.[86] An ambitious proposal to establish a data governance framework under the aegis of the WTO was proposed by Japan during its presidency of the G-20 in 2019. Yet data rules continue to be debated in trade circles.

Low-income countries remain underrepresented in digital trade talks. Only one low-income country, Burkina Faso, has so far joined the Joint Statement discussions on rules for digital trade under the WTO, compared with 52 high-income countries. This uneven representation hampers the inclusiveness of the potential rules under discussion and risks leading to a one-size-fits-all approach on global rules driven by the more advanced players. Although no WTO rules may ultimately be imposed on members without their explicit approval, the lack of voice of low-income countries means that legitimate development concerns may be overlooked. These concerns include both the difficulty in applying rules that require heavy investment in regulatory institutions or are costly for MSMEs and the need for capacity building and technical assistance.

Trade negotiations have traditionally focused on removing restrictions to international trade, but they are not suitable for addressing issues of regulatory convergence. Progress toward harmonization around the necessary regulatory safeguards for data rights, or common data standards and architectures that enable the exchange of information, could benefit from the more cooperative, and perhaps nonbinding, approaches offered by other international instruments. Relevant examples are the modernized Convention 108 of the Council of Europe on data protection and the Budapest Convention on Cybercrime. Because these instruments lack the binding nature (Convention 108) or enforcement mechanisms (Cybercrime Convention) found in the WTO and in PTAs, they may offer a less demanding channel for countries to incorporate key principles on data governance. Model laws, such as those developed by the United Nations Commission on International Trade Law (UNCITRAL) on electronic signatures, can also offer softer approaches that encourage and facilitate regulatory harmonization.

Recommended reforms of digital trade policy

The variety of policy recommendations arising from this discussion can be grouped according to a data maturity model designed to reflect a country's stage in the development process.

Establishing fundamentals

Develop a conducive regulatory framework for digital goods and services. A modern regulatory framework for digital trade can provide essential guidance for remote transactions—such as electronic documents, electronic signatures, and electronic payments—and set out clear rules for digital businesses. It can also foster trust in digital markets by ensuring that users' data are safe and remain private and by providing consumer protections for online transactions.

Strengthen the capacity of customs to tackle e-commerce flows. Some specific facilitation measures can improve the efficiency of e-commerce transactions, such as the use of de minimis thresholds, prearrival processing, and online procedures for customs clearance. Similarly, having a simplified declarations regime for low-value shipments can help e-commerce vendors and small traders move goods faster.

Accelerating data flows

Ensure comprehensive protection of personal data, while providing for flexible cross-border data transfers. A solid framework for data protection and individual rights promotes digital trade by boosting trust in digital markets, including across borders. These necessary

safeguards must also be supplemented with adequate enablers for data sharing, including across borders. Protection of personal data should facilitate cross-border data flows and allow free choice of storage location, while providing strong, clear-cut safeguards for data rights. Mandatory localization requirements should be reserved for exceptional circumstances and limited to specific, and narrow, types of data.

Ensure the free flow of nonpersonal data. For nonpersonal data, the principle of free movement should be the rule, subject to suitable, technically sound cybersecurity measures. Justification for any limited exceptions to this rule should be grounded in an objective assessment of risks to national security and other public interests.

Establish mechanisms for government access to critical data domestically and internationally. Facilitating safe and equitable cross-border data flows also entails incorporating mechanisms for government access to data, particularly on legitimate policy grounds such as law enforcement, regardless of where the data are physically stored. Similarly, mutual legal assistance treaties or similar instruments should be revamped for the digital world, fast-tracking procedures for cross-border data requests from foreign jurisdictions.

Improve availability of data on data trade. The collection of data on fast-growing cross-border services transactions, especially in digital services, is badly lacking and should be remedied. Strengthening data collection for cross-border services in the context of digital trade requires a multipronged approach at both the international and domestic levels. International cooperation should be expanded to set out collective guidelines for data collection on digital services transacted across borders, including shared definitions, standardized typologies, common deidentification and other data protection requirements, and harmonized reporting periods. In addition to strengthening traditional balance of payments data under the aegis of the International Monetary Fund (IMF), complementary approaches can be used that leverage big data from firms engaged in such trade.[87]

Optimizing the system

Advance global rules on digital trade. Global rules should expand to provide a solid framework for cross-border data flows in both setting principles and promoting standards. Multilateral trade agreements, especially under the umbrella of the WTO, should be at the forefront of rules on digital trade. The current Joint Statement talks on digital trade is a valuable initiative that warrants serious attention from WTO members at all levels of development. Such negotiations should be based on inclusive representation spanning all regions and income levels. Global trade rules should center on promoting cross-border data flows and free choice of data storage locations, grounded in adequate data protection standards. However, an inclusive agreement must also recognize that policy priorities for data flows may diverge across jurisdictions, and countries may also differ widely in their capability to implement data policies, as well as in their capacity to reap the economic benefits of data trade. To this end, multilateral negotiations should not be limited to replicating existing models or be bound by fictitious deadlines. Instead, they should strive to adopt an innovative, forward-looking framework for global data flows, affording adequate technical assistance and time to those least able to implement the agreed-on rules.

Promote international standards for cross-border data sharing and digital transactions. Cross-border data sharing requires cooperation on standard setting and regulatory harmonization that lies beyond the scope of trade agreements. International efforts to promote technical standards for data protection and cybersecurity are essential to ensure interoperability and must align with global trade rules on data flows. Further international instruments should promote common principles and rules for other important key aspects of digital trade, including regulation of online consumer protection, electronic payments, remote contracts, and intermediary liability rules (see chapter 6).

Tax policy

As data and digitalization change the business landscape, they are creating opportunities and challenges for tax policy and administration.

Data-driven value chains, with their basis in intangible assets, are difficult for tax administrators to map and track, facilitating aggressive tax avoidance by companies. The rules determining taxation rights and profit allocation tend to emphasize the tangible features of businesses, including the location of people and assets. Data service providers, however, are often nonresident, and sometimes virtual—with little or no physical presence in the country in which consumption occurs or value is created.[88]

Although progress has been made in adapting indirect taxation policies for platform businesses, such as those on the value added tax (VAT), lagging administrative capabilities in low- and middle-income countries prevent these approaches from being fully implemented. As for direct taxation of corporate profits, international efforts to coordinate direct tax policy responses are ongoing, and the outcomes are uncertain.

Addressing such shortfalls in taxation is important to ensure a level playing field for competition between digital and nondigital businesses, as well as foreign and domestic firms. And yet taxation in the data economy is a delicate matter. Poorly designed and misdirected taxes can blunt business growth and revenues, cutting off the potential development benefits of data-driven businesses.[89]

This section focuses on two key tax instruments: the value added tax (or similar consumption taxes) and the corporate income tax. The VAT holds the most immediate promise for mobilizing additional revenues for developing economies. Overall, analysis finds that the revenue potential from extending the VAT to the digital economy will likely be small at first in many of those economies, but that this potential will grow as digitalization expands.

Capturing value added taxes from data-driven businesses

The VAT is a type of indirect taxation that tends to be particularly important for revenue mobilization in developing economies.[90] Fortunately, there is an international consensus on how to assess the VAT liability and capture tax revenues from data-driven platform businesses.

Taxing rights under a VAT or general sales tax (GST) tend to be allocated to the jurisdiction where the final consumption occurs.[91] More than 80 countries already require nonresident providers of digital services to register and collect the VAT.[92] The *International VAT/GST Guidelines* of the Organisation for Economic Co-operation and Development (OECD) have served as a blueprint for many of these reforms.[93]

Many low- and middle-income economies, however, have not made the administrative adaptations needed to capture the VAT from third-party sellers through platform businesses. To collect the tax, countries must require foreign suppliers to register and account for the tax due on sales to consumers in their territories. They also should introduce a process for simplified registration, filing, and payment, usually through an online interface.[94] To leverage the system, countries will have to invest in an enhanced business registry to cross-check whether transactions taking place are business to business (B2B) or business to consumer (B2C). More than US$3.3 billion in taxes have been raised in the European Union through general application of these rules.[95] Australia adopted a similar approach in July 2017, requiring foreign suppliers that exceed a turnover threshold above approximately US$58,000 to account for the GST on digital and professional services. An online portal was set up to administer this tax.[96]

Effective compliance also requires investments—in particular, in the extensive use of third-party data combined with tax and customs data collected by the government. Third-party data sources might include internet service providers; banks and credit card companies; business registries; and tax treaty partners. To use these data effectively, countries should have technological solutions in place within the tax administration. Common tasks would include collecting, merging, and cross-checking data for compliance management purposes. These tasks should be automated, and safeguards should be in place to ensure data security and privacy.

Resource constraints and the needed upfront investments in information technology (IT) systems are sometimes to blame for the slow pace of adoption of these administrative reforms in low- and middle-income countries. But financing constraints are often less of a challenge than the organizational transformations that revenue authorities must undergo to enable successful implementation. These include streamlining business processes to enable seamless data sharing and appropriate staffing for IT management, analytics, and compliance.

To improve domestic revenue mobilization, tax administrations should collect more information from the digital platforms themselves. Governments could require such marketplaces to provide information about the income of both domestic and foreign vendors and rely on platforms to enforce tax compliance by, for example, verifying VAT registration. When combined with other third-party data, data on digital transactions can shed light on the VAT and wider tax compliance of numerous economic actors. A consistent approach to such reporting obligations across countries should help minimize compliance costs for platform businesses and facilitate cooperation. Model rules recently issued by OECD provide guidance for countries to follow in this area.[97] It recommends that platforms collect financial information on those entities with whom they transact, building on the existing experience of Australia, Denmark, France, and Spain with imposing such obligations.

Croatia's experience is an example of the importance of international cooperation among tax administrations. A compliance management campaign launched in 2018 drew on a comparison of domestic tax returns with third-country platform data on hotel and lodging accommodations sold on behalf of Croatian suppliers. Croatia accessed information from countries where platforms are resident for tax purposes, following a multilateral effort encompassing seven other economies with strong tourism sectors. Almost 40 percent of Croatian vendors that operated through the platform were not registered for the VAT in Croatia. When the administration asked Croatian vendors to explain nonregistration or major discrepancies in the income obtained from platform transactions and the income declared for tax purposes, 85 percent changed their tax return "voluntarily."[98]

For many developing countries, the revenue at stake from administrative failures to apply the current VAT rules is not insignificant even in the short term. Moreover, it could become substantial because of the rapid expansion of data-driven platforms, especially following the shift in demand toward platform businesses during the COVID-19 crisis. Evidence from East Asia indicates that the rapid growth of B2C e-commerce has resulted in equally significant growth in the tax potential of the sector, with the indirect tax potential growing some eightfold, rising from US$0.46 billion in 2015 to US$3.7 billion in 2019 (figure 7.6).[99] Other aspects of the digital economy, including online media and food delivery, have seen similar rapid growth in sales and indirect tax potential, whereas online travel has suffered because of the COVID-19 pandemic but is expected to recover over the medium term. In Indonesia, the gross VAT revenue potential of the B2C digital economy is estimated to be about 0.39 percent of GDP in 2021, and it is projected to grow to around 0.65 percent of GDP in 2025.[100] Assuming only half the amount of this estimated potential is collected (allowing for policy and administrative gaps),[101] this would still translate into gross VAT revenues of some US$2.3 billion in 2021, increasing to US$4.6 billion by 2025.[102]

The tax potential of the digital economy may also be constrained by antiquated tax rules. One example is the VAT registration threshold, which is designed to balance having a broad tax base to maximize revenue mobilization, while keeping administrative and compliance costs reasonable. In an increasingly digitalized world, the lower transaction costs associated with paperless tax collection may make it more feasible to include smaller actors. Tax rules on imports should be revised as well, particularly those for low-value shipments. The digital economy has enabled a huge increase in the volume of such shipments, turning simplification and trade facilitation via de minimis thresholds for VAT into a problematic source of base erosion for import duties, the VAT, and other taxes.[103] Following the example of EU member

Figure 7.6 East Asian countries are losing a substantial volume of tax revenue by failing to apply current VAT rules to digital services

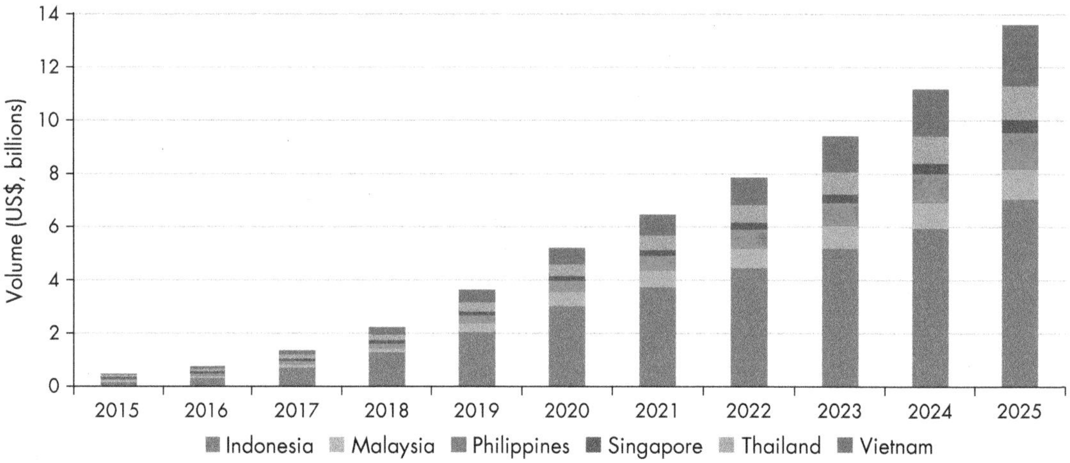

Legend: Indonesia ▪ Malaysia ▪ Philippines ▪ Singapore ▪ Thailand ▪ Vietnam

Source: Al-Rikabi and Loeprick, forthcoming. Data at http://bit.do/WDR2021-Fig-7_6.

Note: Figure shows the indirect tax potential of business-to-consumer e-commerce. VAT = value added tax.

states, many countries have thus begun to reduce or remove de minimis thresholds to ensure that duties are paid on most purchases. They are also exploring the role platforms can play in directly facilitating compliance with the rules governing the cross-border trade of tangible goods.

A more general question has arisen about customs duties. WTO members have exempted electronic transmissions from import duties since 1998—albeit not on a permanent basis. However, the WTO is under growing pressure to consider the revenue losses for developing economies in view of the rapid growth of digital trade.[104] The annual revenue losses of those economies from a moratorium on import duties on electronic transmissions have been estimated at US$5 billion–US$10 billion, and it may be a reason for avoiding a permanent moratorium.[105] However, considering the incidence of tariffs, consumer welfare, implications for export competitiveness, and the option to capture revenues through economically neutral value added taxes, the benefits of the moratorium may well outweigh the costs incurred.[106] Moreover, the application of reciprocal tariffs could make the application of tariffs on electronic transmissions fiscally counterproductive.[107]

Reforming international agreements on direct taxation rights

Intangible assets, such as user networks, are central to many data-driven business models and are closely linked to firm performance. Value generated by users and their data are a critical driver of the expansion of many digital service providers. Thus a case can be made for countries to try to capture this value.[108] Intangible assets are difficult to value, however, thereby worsening information asymmetries between taxpayers and administrators and making it more challenging to both collect taxes and design efficient and balanced tax policies. Firm-level analysis suggests that intangible assets are an important driver of corporate profit shifting across entities within a multinational enterprise (MNE).[109] The growth of digital business models therefore exacerbates the risks of the erosion of tax bases and the shifting of business profits to escape taxes,[110] creating an unlevel playing field.[111] It places additional pressure on the existing international tax consensus rules, which are already poorly adapted to developing country needs and priorities.[112]

The de facto standard setting body for international tax issues is the OECD/G20 Inclusive Framework on Base Erosion and Profit Shifting (BEPS).[113] It is currently finalizing a policy proposal aimed at addressing challenges arising from digitalization.[114] This proposal, which consists of two related "Pillars," embraces new concepts, but it falls short of calls for a fundamental overhaul of the international tax rules.[115]

Proposals for the first pillar were developed with the primary objective of ensuring that countries where users/consumers reside, but where an MNE does not have enough physical presence to become taxable under the current rules, are able to tax a share of the profits of the company. The BEPS's Unified Approach is a compromise drawing on elements of various proposals made by India and the Group of Twenty-Four (G-24), the United Kingdom, and the United States, among others.[116]

The second pillar is also known as the global anti-base erosion proposal (GLoBE). The current proposal seeks to ensure that the profits of MNEs are subject to a minimum rate of taxation. This arrangement is intended to reduce incentives for profit shifting across MNE entities and to establish a floor for tax competition among jurisdictions.[117]

Preliminary estimates by OECD suggest that global corporate income tax revenues could increase by up to 4 percent, equaling US$100 billion annually, if the reform proposals under the two pillars are agreed to and adopted.[118] The G-20 timeline initially aimed at reaching agreement by the end of 2020, but it has since been postponed.[119]

Failure to reach a new consensus risks triggering a proliferation of unilateral action, with important potential spillovers on global trade and growth. More than 30 countries, developed and developing, have already unilaterally exercised, or announced their intention to exercise, their right to impose taxation on the digital economy using interim measures.[120] They include Austria, France, Hungary, India, Indonesia, Italy, Kenya, Malaysia, Mexico, Pakistan, Poland, Singapore, Spain, Turkey, the United Kingdom, Uruguay, Vietnam, and Zimbabwe. Such measures are usually justified by citing the uncertainty about possible reforms of the global tax system and a determination to tax digital businesses on the value they derive from users in the country.

Measures tend to target the larger MNEs in the digital economy. When India introduced a 6 percent charge on digital services linked to online advertising in 2016, it branded the instrument an "equalization levy"—that is, a proxy for a corporate income tax on foreign suppliers that did not have a permanent establishment in the country. Several low- and middle-income economies also adopted new rules during the COVID-19 crisis. Kenya's 2020 Finance Bill proposed a 1.5 percent digital services tax, payable on revenue deemed to be derived or accrued in Kenya through a digital marketplace. In Indonesia, the April 2020 package of fiscal responses to the COVID-19 crisis included a commitment to implement an interim measure that would seek to tax the digital economy. In Brazil, a proposed digital services tax was submitted to the House of Representatives in May 2020. All these rules would be implemented either by extending the scope of existing income taxes or by introducing a new stand-alone tax.

Almost all countries are relying on a simple measure of gross revenue as the tax base, such as the gross revenue arising from the sale of advertising or data or the amounts collected from users for provision of a service.[121] The presumptive nature of these instruments tends to lead to either undertaxation or overtaxation, thereby limiting the effectiveness of the instrument to capture large economic rents[122] and reducing returns to the politically costly adoption of digital service taxes. The United States has reacted strongly to unilateral measures, threatening to subject French exports to tariffs if France proceeds with its digital services tax and announcing a review of similar measures introduced elsewhere.[123] Therefore, a potentially costly trade war over taxing the digital economy looms. Meanwhile, developing economies aiming to capture tax revenue from the sector are left with few palatable short-term choices. Regional coordination of measures, as considered by the African Tax Administration Forum (ATAF),[124] could help minimize administrative and compliance costs, as well as competitive dynamics between countries. Ultimately, however, a global agreement would be the safest route to a sustainable long-term solution.

Recommended reforms of tax policy

In considering proposals to tax the digital economy, policy makers in all countries should seek those that ensure equitable taxation of data-driven businesses, unlocking a potential revenue source for flattening the debt curve after the COVID-19 pandemic. They should also ensure that those sectors that have gained the most from the crisis are contributing their fair share. The recommendations that follow are organized according to a maturity model based on a country's level of development and data governance capacity.

Establishing fundamentals

Strengthen the capacity to collect indirect taxes. This entails adopting the existing international guidelines for VAT collection and making the necessary investments in administrative capacity to ensure that the VAT is collected on physical goods purchased online and on digital goods and services from both resident and nonresident companies.

Collect financial information from online marketplaces on the income/sales of sellers on their platforms. This information should be combined with other third-party data to strengthen the management of tax compliance across the economy.

Accelerating data flows

Seek a global agreement on direct taxation. The existing international tax principles on direct taxation were developed for a predigital age. There is a pressing need for updated principles to be agreed on in the relevant global forums. The best-case scenario is a last-minute global consensus on new rules that align with developing economy priorities and administrative capacity.

Minimize the impact of ad hoc taxation. In a second-best world, a trade war must be avoided. Compromise solutions entailing further interim taxation measures seem inevitable. Regional collaboration to build consensus around these solutions, share knowledge, and develop the capacity of low-income countries may help in part to fill the policy vacuum until a global solution can be reached.

Optimizing the system

Leverage data-driven tax administration. Policy makers should adopt the policies and make the investments needed to support data-driven tax administration, leveraging opportunities for improving its efficiency, effectiveness, and transparency. One step in that direction is creation of a data sharing ecosystem that for businesses and individuals minimizes the burden of paying taxes, while enabling compliance management to operate in the background through tax prefilling,[125] automatic checks of errors, and so on. New sources of data would also be required, including platform information on the income of sellers and the consumption of buyers, which would help to bring informal enterprises into the purview of tax authorities.

Ensure access to international sources of accounting data. Policy makers should seek to ensure that new international data sources are available to developing countries. One example is aggregate data on the global allocation of income, profit, and taxes paid by the largest MNEs as reported in the Country-by-Country Reports.[126] Such data, in addition to their relevance for domestic tax administration, could help fill the information gaps in international trade statistics (see earlier section on trade policy). In many countries, tax administration data are the most complete information source on private sector activity. Administrators should explore options to make aggregate or reliably anonymized tax data available to the wider public as a source of information on the effects of tax policy, on the performance of revenue administration, and for broader research purposes. As accounting data become accessible, it will be important to ensure that the data are protected (see chapter 6).

Conclusion

As this chapter has shown, sound competition, trade, and tax policy for the digital economy are essential to ensure that data create value for development. Devising and implementing good policies in each area are complex. Such efforts are even more difficult because all three areas are intertwined and present both domestic and international challenges. And yet meeting this challenge is more urgent than ever against the backdrop of COVID-19, which is further expanding the digital economy. Spotlight 7.2 discusses the role of regional and international cooperation in helping to meet some of these challenges.

Notes

1. Facebook, "Who We Are" (company information), https://about.fb.com/company-info/.
2. Information provided by the Alibaba Group during WDR 2021 private sector consultations. See the AliExpress website, at https://www.aliexpress.com/.
3. Several more cases remain under investigation or are being appealed. Of those finalized, contraventions of the law were found in 55 percent of abuse of dominance cases and 77 percent of anticompetitive agreement cases. Ninety-three percent of mergers were approved, about a quarter of which with conditions.
4. Nyman and Barajas (forthcoming).
5. Nyman and Barajas (forthcoming).
6. Nyman and Barajas (forthcoming).
7. For example, the Competition Commission of India investigated Uber for collusive practices facilitated through its pricing algorithm. Ultimately, however, it did not make a finding of collusion. It concluded that the algorithmically determined pricing for each rider and each trip tends to differ due to the interplay of large datasets. A case of collusion through pricing algorithms was also brought against Uber in the United States. Ultimately, Uber won a bid to move the case to arbitration.
8. Reports and papers commissioned by expert groups on addressing competition policy in the digital economy have been released by Australia, the BRICS (Brazil, Russian Federation, India, China, and South Africa), Canada, the European Union, Germany, Japan, Mexico, the Netherlands, Portugal, the United Kingdom, and the United States, among others.
9. See "Competition Act, 1998 (Act no. 89 of 1998): Regulations on Buyer Power Made by the Minister under Competition Act, 1998." Government Notice 168, *Government Gazette*, February 13, 2020, Government Printing Works, Pretoria, South Africa. https://www.gov.za/sites/default/files/gcis_document/202002/43018gon168.pdf.
10. BRICS Competition Centre (2019).
11. Argentesi et al. (2020); Motta and Peitz (2020).
12. Gautier and Lamesch (2020).
13. In some jurisdictions such as the United States, the antitrust authority may have the power to trigger a

review on its own initiative even when the authority is not automatically notified. Such self-initiated reviews presuppose significant technical capacity on the part of the authority to engage proactively in market monitoring, which is not always present in low-income countries.

14. This approach was recently suggested by the US House Judiciary Committee's Subcommittee on Antitrust, Commercial, and Administrative Law in its report *Investigation of Competition in Digital Markets* (House Committee on the Judiciary 2020).

15. HM Treasury (2019).

16. Stigler Center (2019).

17. Nyman and Carreras (forthcoming). The competition authorities surveyed were in Colombia, Egypt, Indonesia, Kenya, Malaysia, Peru, the Philippines, and Zimbabwe.

18. Amazon (2020).

19. Emejo (2020).

20. Lee (2018). The authority did, however, mandate that Grab should maintain its premerger pricing algorithm and driver commissions to protect riders and drivers. Since the authority's decision, there have been two new entries to the Singaporean market.

21. Bundeskartellamt (2019).

22. BRICS Competition Centre (2019).

23. DOJ (2019).

24. EU (2016).

25. Instead of the onetime transfer of data often envisaged under portability schemes.

26. The number of third-party providers is as of August 2020. See Open Banking (2020).

27. Gilbert + Tobin (2018).

28. RBI (2019).

29. Valdez, Branch, and Gallo Mainero (2020).

30. See Open Ag Data Alliance (2020).

31. Kim et al. (2020).

32. See Open Banking (2020).

33. This can be accomplished either through structural separation of their existing organization or by prohibiting them from operating in adjacent lines of business. This approach was recently suggested by the US House Judiciary Committee's Subcommittee on Antitrust, Commercial, and Administrative Law in its report *Investigation of Competition in Digital Markets* (House Committee on the Judiciary 2020).

34. EU (2019).

35. Examples are taken from World Bank (2020).

36. Markova (2016); Zampano and Hirst (2017).

37. Evans (2016).

38. See International Competition Network and World Bank, "The 2015–2016 Competition Advocacy Contest: How to Build a Culture of Competition for Private Sector Development and Economic Growth," https:// www.worldbank.org/en/events/2015/10/30/the-2015 ---2016-competition-advocacy-contest-how-to-build-a -culture-of-competition-for-private-sector-development -and-economic-growth#5.

39. Article 10 of the Regulations on Transportation Services through the Use of Smartphone Applications. This example was taken from World Bank, Deep Trade

Agreements: Data, Tools, and Analysis (dashboard), https://datatopics.worldbank.org/dta/table.html.

40. Articles 3 and 4 of Law 87 of 2018. Examples are taken from World Bank, Deep Trade Agreements: Data, Tools, and Analysis (dashboard), https://datatopics.worldbank .org/dta/table.html.

41. Soursourian and Plaitakis (2019).

42. Cisco (2018).

43. Cisco (2018). This figure appears to reflect the value of transactions pertaining directly to data flows, as well as the estimated value of data embedded in transactions of other goods and services.

44. The G-20 leaders assembled in Osaka in 2019 called for creation of a new international order based on "Data Free Flow with Trust," a collective term for global governance processes needed to unleash the benefits of cross-border data flows. This proposal is taken up in the World Economic Forum's 2020 white paper "Data Free Flow with Trust (DFFT): Paths Towards Free and Trusted Data Flows" (WEF 2020).

45. WTO (2017).

46. Daza Jaller, Gaillard, and Molinuevo (2020); OECD (2014).

47. USITC (2014).

48. World Bank (2020).

49. NBT (2015).

50. See Office of the Attorney General, Department of Justice, State of California, California Consumer Privacy Act (CCPA) (dashboard), https://oag.ca.gov/privacy/ccpa.

51. Cory (2017).

52. In July 2020, the Court of Justice of the European Union (CJEU) issued a decision in a case now known as *Schrems II* that effectively suspended the EU-US Privacy Shield. The Privacy Shield was an agreement between the European Union and the United States—a kind of negotiated adequacy determination—that enabled personal data to be transferred from the European Union to the United States on the grounds that protections against unauthorized access to personal data (such as by US intelligence agencies) could not be guaranteed by US companies such as Facebook that received the personal data of European citizens. The CJEU's decision cast doubt on whether data could still be transferred under what are known as "standard contractual clauses" (SCCs) without also taking into account the legal environment of the destination country. Maximillian Schrems, an Austrian national, brought the case, saying that Facebook did not have adequate measures in place to ensure that his data, if transferred to the United States, would be afforded treatment similar to that under the GDPR. The Privacy Shield, a post-GDPR solution, followed a previous EU-US agreement, the Safe Harbor, which was also struck down in a case brought by Schrems. The precise impact of the decision in *Schrems II* is at present unknown, as is the reliance on SCCs in the absence of the Privacy Shield agreement as a basis for transatlantic data transfers.

53. Chander et al. (2021).

54. All governments, regardless of their policy approach to cross-border data flows, retain some level of access

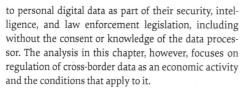

to personal digital data as part of their security, intelligence, and law enforcement legislation, including without the consent or knowledge of the data processor. The analysis in this chapter, however, focuses on regulation of cross-border data as an economic activity and the conditions that apply to it.

55. Bauer, Ferracane, and van der Marel (2016).

56. Cory (2017).

57. Cory (2017).

58. See "Russia's 'Big Brother' Law Enters into Force," with reporting by Anton Muratov, *Moscow Times*, July 1, 2018, https://www.themoscowtimes.com/2018/07/01/russias -big-brother-law-enters-into-force-a62066. See also the following two laws of the Russian Federation: **Федеральный закон от** 06.07.2016 г. № 374-ФЗ [Federal Law, July 6, 2016, No. 374-FZ] [in Russian], http:// kremlin.ru/acts/bank/41108; **Федеральный закон от** 06.07.2016 г. № 375-ФЗ [Federal Law, July 6, 2016, No. 375-FZ] [in Russian], http://kremlin.ru/acts/bank/41113.

59. Chander and Lê (2015).

60. Chander and Lê (2015).

61. To access the World Bank's Global Data Regulation Survey and its results, see https://microdata.worldbank .org/index.php/catalog/3866.

62. Ferracane and van der Marel (2019).

63. Biancotti (2019); Hillman (2018).

64. Ferracane and van der Marel (2019).

65. See Article 19 (2020). See also Case of OOO Flavus and Others v. Russia, Application no. 12468/15, Final Judgment (November 16, 2020), Third Section, European Court of Human Rights, Strasbourg, https://hudoc .echr.coe.int/eng#{%22itemid%22:[%22001-203178%22.

66. Baur-Yazbeck (2018).

67. Chander and Lê (2015); Spaulding, Falvey, and Merchant (2013).

68. Chander and Lê (2015).

69. Liu (2019); Molinuevo and Gaillard (2018).

70. On a related point, see Deardorff (2017).

71. To access the World Bank's Global Data Regulation Survey and its results, see https://microdata.worldbank .org/index.php/catalog/3866.

72. Ferracane and van der Marel (2021).

73. Chander et al. (2021).

74. EU (2018).

75. The WTO had 164 members, including countries and independent custom unions, at the time of writing.

76. Crosby (2016).

77. Burri (2017); World Bank, Deep Trade Agreements: Data, Tools, and Analysis (dashboard), https://data topics.worldbank.org/dta/table.html; Wu (2017).

78. Parties to the agreement are Australia, Brunei Darussalam, Canada, Chile, Japan, Malaysia, Mexico, New Zealand, Peru, Singapore, and Vietnam. The CPTPP built on the Trans-Pacific Partnership (TPP), which never entered into force because the United States withdrew.

79. Article 14.11 of the Comprehensive and Progressive Agreement for Trans-Pacific Partnership states: "Each Party shall allow the cross-border transfer of information by electronic means, including personal information, when this activity is for the conduct of the business of a covered person." See Government of Canada, "Consolidated TPP Text, Chapter 14: Electronic Commerce," last modified November 30, 2016, https://www.international.gc.ca/trade-commerce/trade -agreements-accords-commerciaux/agr-acc/tpp-ptp /text-texte/14.aspx?lang=eng.

80. See Office of the United States Trade Representative, U.S.–Japan Digital Trade Agreement Text (dashboard), https://ustr.gov/countries-regions/japan-korea-apec /japan/us-japan-trade-agreement-negotiations/us -japan-digital-trade-agreement-text.

81. The United States–Mexico–Canada Agreement (USMCA) provides that "no Party shall prohibit or restrict the cross-border transfer of information, including personal information, by electronic means if this activity is for the conduct of the business of a covered person" (USTR 2020a, 19-6).

82. African Union (2014).

83. APEC (2017).

84. Wu (2017).

85. WTO (2017).

86. Hufbauer and Lu (2019).

87. Ideally, improved trade policy data should be collected at the transaction level, leveraging information reported by cross-border services providers for fiscal purposes—duly deidentified and aggregated. The result would be much richer than what is typically reported for balance of payment purposes. Such information can be derived from customs declarations or submissions from foreign service providers.

88. Facebook opened its sole office in Africa in 2015 in Johannesburg, South Africa (BBC 2015). It serves more than 200 million African users (Rukundo 2020).

89. Digital services taxes are particularly controversial. Part of the challenge is related to their design because they appear to ringfence a small number of companies and are thus subject to the charge that they are discriminatory. Kennedy (2019) and the CCIA (2020) provide such a critique.

90. World Bank (2019).

91. OECD (2017).

92. Ahanchian et al. (2021).

93. OECD (2017, 2018a).

94. In the European Union, an online portal allows nonresident suppliers of telecommunications, broadcasting, and electronic services to register, submit quarterly returns, and pay the tax due (EC 2020).

95. The reported gains were more than €3 billion at a 2017 exchange rate of €1 to US$1.13, average closing price (OECD 2018b).

96. Australia's threshold was set at $A75,000 at a 2017 exchange rate of $A1 to US$0.77, average closing price (ATO 2020). Digital services include streaming or downloading music, movies, applications, games, and e-books. Professional services include architectural and legal services.

97. OECD (2020a).

98. Burić (2020).

99. Al-Rikabi and Loeprick (forthcoming). These preliminary figures are based on gross revenue estimates that were derived in 2019 before the COVID-19 crisis. They refer to estimates of the VAT potential of e-commerce,

online media and advertising, online travel, and the gig economy (food delivery and ride hailing). Estimates are being updated drawing on updated sales data (different sources) and tax data from government sources. To a degree, online and offline purchases are substitutes (for example, an additional TV bought online would be one less TV bought offline), so the growth of online commerce implies slower growth of offline commerce. Accordingly, revenue forecasts should not simply add estimated revenue gain from taxing the digital economy to forecasts of the VAT because that would lead to an overestimate of the growth in the VAT. A comprehensive forecast would disaggregate online and offline consumption so that the bases used in an elasticity-based forecast could vary accordingly.

Revenue authorities have for some time documented the problem of the "missing trader" fraud scheme, whereby business entities minimize their tax liability by establishing multiple companies to issue fictitious invoices. Several factors drive the missing trader scheme, but the rise of e-commerce has certainly been a major one, according to analysis conducted by revenue authorities. See KRA (2020).

100. Al-Rikabi and Loeprick (forthcoming). The estimates for Indonesia are preliminary and were derived before the COVID-19 crisis.

101. The largest policy gaps stem from the high VAT threshold (merchants with annual sales of less than Rp 4.8 billion do not have to charge the VAT), as well as exemptions and other preferential treatment in the VAT system for some sectors and types of economic activity. The administrative gap reflects challenges in compliance, which is generally low in Indonesia. For example, VAT compliance was estimated at 56.6 percent using 2013 data (Sugana and Hidayat 2014). Countries with more efficient revenue authorities and more limited tax thresholds and exemptions will have a narrower gap between tax collection and tax potential. Singapore is a good example.

102. This revenue gain could increase if broader VAT reforms are pursued, including lowering the VAT threshold, reducing exemptions, and implementing administrative measures to improve compliance.

103. The de minimis is a valuation ceiling for goods, including documents and trade samples, below which no duty or tax is charged and clearance procedures, including data requirements, are minimal. Apart from customs duties, the customs administration typically collects import VAT (a portion of the VAT tied to imports), excise taxes, and sometimes even withholding taxes on income (a form of advance payment of income taxes linked to imports used by many developing countries in a bid to include the informal sector in the tax base) (Keen 2008). In many jurisdictions, charging these additional taxes is linked to charging import duties, and thus shipments that fall below the de minimis often end up avoiding all the other taxes as well.

104. The scope of what is covered by the moratorium is subject to different interpretations by WTO member states. Several emerging market countries have signaled their unwillingness to extend the moratorium

further, feeding into broader tensions related to global taxation of the digital economy. India and Indonesia have openly criticized the moratorium and have signaled that they may opt out of any further extension.

105. Banga (2019).

106. Andrenelli and López González (2019).

107. Makiyama and Narayanan (2019).

108. See Aslam and Shah (2020).

109. Because intangibles can easily be moved, so, too, can the associated returns. This is a contributing factor to profit shifting to low-tax countries or regimes. See Beer and Loeprick (2015).

110. IMF (2019); OECD (2018a).

111. The European Commission suggested that companies with digital business models have, on average, half the effective tax rate of companies with traditional business models (see European Commission, Taxation and Customs Union, Fair Taxation of the Digital Economy [dashboard], https://ec.europa.eu/taxation_customs /business/company-tax/fair-taxation-digital-economy _en). However, these results have been challenged because they were not derived from industry data. Other studies suggest that digital businesses have similar, or slightly higher, effective tax rates than traditional businesses. See Bauer (2018). From an equity perspective more broadly, the evidence is clear that tax evasion is highly concentrated among the rich. See Alstadsæter, Johannesen, and Zucman (2019).

112. Clavey et al. (2019).

113. BEPS has 130 country members (including all OECD members) and is housed at OECD. International organizations such as the World Bank Group have an observer role.

114. Although harmonization of international taxation practices goes beyond the digital sector, the discussion in this chapter is necessarily limited to digital taxation.

115. Devereux et al. (2021) assess a more radical set of reform options in allocating taxing rights, including a full move to basing taxing rights on destination, or where sales are made, and options for adopting a variant of wide-reaching formulary apportionment for nonroutine profits in the form of residual profit allocation by income. To read BEPS's summary of progress and outline of key proposals it has developed, see OECD (2020b). For a summary of the development of BEPS's proposals and a discussion of an alternative departing from the arm's-length standard by embracing the apportionment of an MNE's taxable income based on its sales to unrelated customers in each country, see Avi-Yonah and Clausing (2019). An alternative view is set out by Romer (2019), who argues that taxation can be used to encourage platform companies to make changes in their business models. Another alternative to BEPS's Unified Approach involves a new tax based on internet bandwidth (Lucas-Mas and Junquera-Varela 2021).

116. The Unified Approach differentiates three elements of the returns on MNE activity within the scope of the measure. First, a portion of the deemed residual profit is to be allocated to all market jurisdictions, irrespective of whether the MNE has a physical presence.

This envisaged formulaic allocation represents a new taxing right. Second, a baseline or routine return will be established for distribution activities and marketing based on fixed ratios in jurisdictions with a physical presence. And, third, the existing transfer pricing methods are used to determine the nonroutine profit not captured under the first step. In addition, a form of mandatory arbitration is envisaged.

117. Four main technical mechanisms would be at work here: an income inclusion rule, an undertaxed payment rule, a switchover rule, and a subject-to-tax test. The idea is to implement residence-based taxation when the source tax is too low and impose source-based taxation when the residence-based taxation is too low.

118. OECD (2020b).

119. In addition to the COVID-19 crisis shifting priorities and attention, important disagreements persist about controversial design features of the proposal, including about the rule order, which will affect the extent to which developing countries can expect to benefit directly from the proposed minimum tax measures. Clavey et al. (2019) provide a summary of these differences. The call by the United States in June 2020 to suspend discussions on the first component stalled progress toward a consensus solution. See Fleming et al. (2020).

120. KPMG (2021).

121. Similarly, a draft provision and commentary prepared following the 20th session of the United Nations Committee of Experts on International Cooperation in Tax Matters, outlined a proposed targeted blueprint focused on taxing the automated digital services of providers either by taxing a share of gross revenue or by a simplified determination of the share of profits that would be subject to regular income taxation. See UN DESA (2020).

122. One alternative proposal is to target global excess profits directly. See Christians and Magalhães (2020).

123. USTR (2020b).

124. ATAF (2020).

125. The revenue authority can use information collected about taxpayers (such as from previously submitted tax forms; electronic invoices submitted; and third-party data from banks, land registries, and other sources) to "prefill" large parts of the tax forms taxpayers are required to submit. In this way, tax form prefilling reduces the time to file and submit taxes, lowering the burden of paying taxes and improving overall tax compliance.

126. Country-by-Country Reports (CbCRs) are part of the OECD's Base Erosion and Profit Shifting Action Plan 13. MNEs with a combined revenue of €750 million or more are required to provide an annual report—the CbCR—that breaks down key elements of their financial statement by jurisdiction. In this way, local jurisdictions gain greater insight into MNE activities in their jurisdiction, including revenue, income, tax paid and accrued, employment, capital, retained earnings, and tangible assets and activities. See Organisation for Economic Co-operation and Development, Action 13 Country-by-Country Reporting (dashboard), https://

www.oecd.org/tax/beps/beps-actions/action13/. For an illustration of the process, see PCT (2020). The European Parliament called for public disclosure of Country-by-Country Reports, but a consensus could not be reached in the Council of Ministers. See EC (2016).

References

African Union. 2014. "African Union Convention on Cyber Security and Personal Data Protection." Document EX.CL/846(XXV), June 27 (adopted), African Union, Addis Ababa, Ethiopia. https://www.opennetafrica.org/?wpfb_dl=4.

Ahanchian, Amie, Donald Hok, Philippe Stephanny, and Elizabeth Shingler. 2021. "Digital Services Tax: Why the World Is Watching." *Bloomberg Tax*, January 6, Bloomberg Industry Group, Arlington, VA. https://tax.kpmg.us/content/dam/tax/en/pdfs/2021/bloomberg-tax-kpmg-digital-services-tax-1.6.21.pdf.

Al-Rikabi, Jaffar, and Jan Loeprick. Forthcoming. "Direct and Indirect VAT Revenue Potential from Taxing the Digital Economy in Indonesia." WDR 2021 background paper, World Bank, Washington, DC.

Alstadsæter, Annette, Niels Johannesen, and Gabriel Zucman. 2019. "Tax Evasion and Inequality." *American Economic Review* 109 (6): 2073–2103.

Amazon. 2020. "Price Gouging Has No Place in Our Stores." *Company News* (blog), March 23, 2020. https://www.aboutamazon.com/news/company-news/price-gouging-has-no-place-in-our-stores.

Andrenelli, Andrea, and Javier López González. 2019. "Electronic Transmissions and International Trade: Shedding New Light on the Moratorium Debate." OECD Trade Policy Paper 233, Organisation for Economic Co-operation and Development, Paris. https://doi.org/10.1787/57b50a4b-en.

APEC (Asia-Pacific Economic Cooperation). 2017. "APEC Privacy Framework (2015)." Report APEC#217-CT-01.9, APEC, Singapore. https://www.apec.org/Publications/2017/08/APEC-Privacy-Framework-(2015).

Argentesi, Elena, Paolo Buccirossi, Emilio Calvano, Tomaso Duso, Alessia Marrazzo, and Salvatore Nava. 2020. "Merger Policy in Digital Markets: An Ex Post Assessment." *Journal of Competition Law and Economics*. Published ahead of print, July 21. https://doi.org/10.1093/joclec/nhaa020.

Article 19. 2020. "Russia: European Court Judgment Is Victory for Freedom of Expression." Article 19, London. https://www.article19.org/resources/russia-european-court-judgment-is-victory-for-freedom-of-expression/.

Aslam, Aqib, and Alpa Shah. 2020. "Tec(h)tonic Shifts: Taxing the 'Digital Economy.'" IMF Working Paper 20/76, International Monetary Fund, Washington, DC. https://www.imf.org/en/Publications/WP/Issues/2020/05/29/Tec-h-tonic-Shifts-Taxing-the-Digital-Economy-49363.

ATAF (African Tax Administration Forum). 2020. "Domestic Resource Mobilisation: Digital Services Taxation in Africa." Policy Brief 01, ATAF, Pretoria, South Africa. https://events.ataftax.org/index.php?page=documents&

func=view&https://events.ataftax.org/index.php?page=documents&func=view&document_id=61#=61#.

ATO (Australian Taxation Office). 2020. "GST on Imported Services and Digital Products." April 23, ATO, Canberra, Australia. https://www.ato.gov.au/Business/International-tax-for-business/GST-on-imported-services-and-digital-products/?default.

Avi-Yonah, Reuven S., and Kimberly A. Clausing. 2019. "Problems with Destination-Based Corporate Taxes and the Ryan Blueprint." *Columbia Journal of Tax Law* 8 (2): 229–56.

Banga, Rashmi. 2019. "Growing Trade in Electronic Transmissions: Implications for the South." UNCTAD Research Paper 29, UNCTAD/SER.RP/2019/1, United Nations Conference on Trade and Development, Geneva. https://unctad.org/system/files/official-document/ser-rp-2019d1_en.pdf.

Bauer, Matthias. 2018. "Digital Companies and Their Fair Share of Taxes: Myths and Misconceptions." ECIPE Occasional Paper 3/2018, European Center for International Political Economy, Brussels. https://ecipe.org/publications/digital-companies-and-their-fair-share-of-taxes/.

Bauer, Matthias, Martina Francesca Ferracane, and Erik van der Marel. 2016. "Tracing the Economic Impact of Regulations on the Free Flow of Data and Data Localization." CIGI Paper Series 30, Global Commission on Internet Governance, Center for International Governance Innovation, Waterloo, Ontario, Canada; Chatham House, London. https://www.cigionline.org/sites/default/files/gcig_no30web_2.pdf.

Baur-Yazbeck, Silvia. 2018. "3 Myths About Data Localization." *CGAP* (blog), August 21, 2018, Consultative Group to Assist the Poor, Washington, DC. https://www.cgap.org/blog/3-myths-about-data-localization.

BBC News. 2015. "Facebook Opens Its First Africa Office in Johannesburg." *BBC News*, June 29, 2015. https://www.bbc.com/news/world-africa-33310739.

Beer, Sebastian, and Jan Loeprick. 2015. "Profit Shifting: Drivers of Transfer (Mis)Pricing and the Potential of Countermeasures." *International Tax and Public Finance* 22 (3): 426–51. https://doi.org/10.1007/s10797-014-9323-2.

Biancotti, Claudia. 2019. "Reasonable Data Restrictions." Presentation, Peterson Institute for International Economics, Washington, DC, April 11, 2019. https://www.piie.com/system/files/documents/biancotti20190411ppt.pdf.

BRICS Competition Centre 2019. *Digital Era Competition: A BRICS View.* BRICS Report, version 1.0. Moscow: BRICS Competition Innovation Law and Policy Center, Skolkovo Institute for Law and Development, Faculty of Law, Higher School of Economics, HSE University. http://bricscompetition.org/materials/news/digital-era-competition-brics-report/.

Bundeskartellamt. 2019. "Bundeskartellamt Obtains Far-Reaching Improvements in the Terms of Business for Sellers on Amazon's Online Marketplaces." Press release, July 17, 2019, Bundeskartellamt, Bonn, Germany. https://www.bundeskartellamt.de/SharedDocs/Publikation/EN/Pressemitteilungen/2019/17_07_2019_Amazon.html;jsessionid=F840FC421918D688C3791E8B3C57DBCB.1_cid381?nn=3600108.

Burić, Davor. 2020. "Taxation of the Digital Economy." Presentation to the World Bank. Taxes and Audit Support Department, Tax Administration Central Office, Republic of Croatia.

Burri, Mira. 2017. "The Regulation of Data Flows through Trade Agreements." *Georgetown Journal of International Law* 48 (1): 407–48.

Casalini, Francesca, and Javier López González. 2019. "Trade and Cross-Border Data Flows." OECD Trade Policy Paper 220, Organisation for Economic Co-operation and Development, Paris. https://doi.org/10.1787/b2023a47-en.

CCIA (Computer and Communications Industry Association). 2020. "Comments of the Computer and Communications Industry Association (CCIA)." *In re Initiation of Section 301 Investigations of Digital Services Taxes*, Docket USTR-2020-0022, Office of the United States Trade Representative, Washington, DC. https://www.ccianet.org/wp-content/uploads/2020/07/Comments-of-CCIA-USTR-2020-0022-Section-301-Digital-Services-Taxes-.pdf.

Chander, Anupam, Meaza Abraham, Sandeep Chandy, Yuan Fang, Dayoung Park, and Isabel Yu. 2021. "Achieving Privacy: Costs of Compliance and Enforcement of Data Protection Regulation." Policy Research Working Paper 9594, World Bank, Washington, DC. http://documents.worldbank.org/curated/en/890791616529630648/Achieving-Privacy-Costs-of-Compliance-and-Enforcement-of-Data-Protection-Regulation.

Chander, Anupam, and Uyên P. Lê. 2015. "Data Nationalism." *Emory Law Journal* 64 (3): 677–739. https://scholarlycommons.law.emory.edu/elj/vol64/iss3/2/.

Christians, Allison, and Tarcísio Diniz Magalhães. 2020. "It's Time for Pillar 3: A Global Excess Profits Tax for COVID-19 and Beyond." *Tax Notes* (blog), May 1, 2020. https://www.taxnotes.com/featured-analysis/its-time-pillar-3-global-excess-profits-tax-covid-19-and-beyond/2020/05/01/2cg34.

Cisco. 2018. "Cisco Visual Networking Index: Forecast and Trends, 2017–2022." White paper, Cisco Systems, San Jose, CA. https://cloud.report/Resources/Whitepapers/eea79d9b-9fe3-4018-86c6-3d1df813d3b8_white-paper-c11-741490.pdf.

Clavey, Colin John, Jonathan Leigh Pemberton, Jan Loeprick, and Marinus Verhoeven. 2019. "International Tax Reform, Digitalization, and Developing Economies." MTI Discussion Paper 16, Macroeconomics, Trade, and Investment Global Practice, World Bank, Washington, DC. http://documents.worldbank.org/curated/en/735001569857911590/International-Tax-Reform-Digitalization-and-Developing-Economies.

Cory, Nigel. 2017. "Cross-Border Data Flows: Where Are the Barriers, and What Do They Cost?" Information Technology and Innovation Foundation, Washington, DC. https://itif.org/publications/2017/05/01/cross-border-data-flows-where-are-barriers-and-what-do-they-cost.

Crosby, Daniel. 2016. "Analysis of Data Localization Measures under WTO Services Trade Rules and Commitments." E15Initiative Policy Brief, International Centre for Trade and Sustainable Development and World Economic Forum, Geneva. http://e15initiative.org/publications/analysis-of-data-localization-measures-under-wto-services-trade-rules-and-commitments/.

Daza Jaller, Lillyana, Simon Jean Henri Gaillard, and Martín Molinuevo. 2020. "The Regulation of Digital Trade: Key Policies and International Trends." World Bank, Washington, DC. https://doi.org/10.1596/33164.

Deardorff, Alan V. 2017. "Comparative Advantage in Digital Trade." In *Cloth for Wine? The Relevance of Ricardo's Comparative Advantage in the 21st Century*, edited by Simon J. Evenett, 35–44. London: CEPR Press. https://voxeu.org/content/cloth-wine-relevance-ricardo-s-comparative-advantage-21st-century.

Devereux, Michael P., Alan J. Auerbach, Michael Keen, Paul Oosterhuis, Wolfgang Schön, and John Vella. 2021. *Taxing Profit in a Global Economy*. New York: Oxford University Press. https://global.oup.com/academic/product/taxing-profit-in-a-global-economy-9780198808077?cc=id&lang=en&#.

DOJ (United States Department of Justice). 2019. "G7 Announces Common Understanding of G7 Competition Authorities on Competition and the Digital Economy." Press Release 19–777, July 18, 2019, Office of Public Affairs, DOJ, Washington, DC. https://www.justice.gov/opa/pr/g7-announces-common-understanding-g7-competition-authorities-competition-and-digital-economy.

EC (European Commission). 2016. "Proposal for a Directive of the European Parliament and of the Council Amending Directive 2013/34/EU as Regards Disclosure of Income Tax Information by Certain Undertakings and Branches." Document COM(2016) 198 final, European Commission, Strasbourg. https://eur-lex.europa.eu/legal-content/EN/TXT/?uri=CELEX%3A52016PC0198.

EC (European Commission). 2020. "Explanatory Notes on VAT e-Commerce Rules." Directorate-General for Taxation and Customs Union, EC, Brussels. https://ec.europa.eu/taxation_customs/sites/taxation/files/vatecommerce explanatory_notes_30092020.pdf.

Emejo, James. 2020. "COVID-19: Jumia Delists 390 Products over Price Manipulations." *This Day*, March 12, 2020. https://www.thisdaylive.com/index.php/2020/03/12/covid-19-jumia-delists-390-products-over-price-manipulations/.

EU (European Union). 2016. "Regulation (EU) 2016/679 of the European Parliament and of the Council of 27 April 2016 on the Protection of Natural Persons with Regard to the Processing of Personal Data and on the Free Movement of Such Data, and Repealing Directive 95/46/EC (General Data Protection Regulation)." *Official Journal of the European Union* L 119/1 (May 4). https://eur-lex.europa.eu/eli/reg/2016/679/oj.

EU (European Union). 2018. "Regulation (EU) 2018/1807 of the European Parliament and of the Council of 14 November 2018 on a Framework for the Free Flow of Non-personal Data in the European Union." *Official Journal of the European Union* L 303, vol. 61 (November 10): 78–68. https://eur-lex.europa.eu/legal-content/EN/TXT/PDF/?uri=OJ:L:2018:303:FULL&from=EN.

EU (European Union). 2019. "Regulation (EU) 2019/1150 of the European Parliament and of the Council of 20 June 2019 on Promoting Fairness and Transparency for Business Users of Online Intermediation Services." *Official Journal of the European Union* L 186/57 (July 11). https://eur-lex.europa.eu/eli/reg/2019/1150/oj.

Evans, Peter C. 2016. "The Rise of Asian Platforms: A Regional Survey." Emerging Platform Economy Series 3, Center for Global Enterprise, New York. https://www.thecge.net/web/viewer.html?file=/app/uploads/2016/11/FINALAsianPlatformPaper.pdf.

Ferracane, Martina Francesca, and Erik van der Marel. 2019. "Do Data Policy Restrictions Inhibit Trade in Services?" EUI Working Paper RSCAS 2019/29, Global Governance Programme 342, Robert Schuman Centre for Advanced Studies, European University Institute, San Domenico di Fiesole, Italy. http://cadmus.eui.eu//handle/1814/62325.

Ferracane, Martina Francesca, and Erik Leendert van der Marel. 2021. "Regulating Personal Data: Data Models and Digital Services Trade." Policy Research Working Paper 9596, World Bank, Washington, DC. http://documents.worldbank.org/curated/en/890741616533448170/Regulating-Personal-Data-Data-Models-and-Digital-Services-Trade.

Fleming, Sam, Jim Brunsden, Chris Giles, and James Politi. 2020. "US Upends Global Digital Tax Plans after Pulling Out of Talks with Europe." *Financial Times*, June 17, 2020. https://www.ft.com/content/1ac26225-c5dc-48fa-84bd-b61e1f4a3d94.

Gautier, Axel, and Joe Lamesch. 2020. "Mergers in the Digital Economy." *Information Economics and Policy*. Published ahead of print, September 2. https://doi.org/10.1016/j.infoecopol.2020.100890.

Gilbert + Tobin. 2018. "Open Banking Regimes across the Globe." *Digital Domain: Knowledge*. Gilbert + Tobin, Sydney, Australia. https://www.gtlaw.com.au/insights/open-banking-regimes-across-globe.

Hillman, Jonathan E. 2018. "The Global Battle for Digital Trade." *The Future of Digital Trade Policy and the Role of the US and UK* (blog), April 13, 2018, Center for Strategic and International Studies, Washington, DC. https://www.csis.org/blogs/future-digital-trade-policy-and-role-us-and-uk/global-battle-digital-trade.

HM Treasury. 2019. *Unlocking Digital Competition: Report of the Digital Competition Expert Panel*. London: HM Treasury. https://assets.publishing.service.gov.uk/government/uploads/system/uploads/attachment_data/file/785547/unlocking_digital_competition_furman_review_web.pdf.

House Committee on the Judiciary. 2020. *Investigation of Competition in Digital Markets: Majority Staff Report and Recommendations*. Washington, DC: Subcommittee on Antitrust, Commercial and Administrative Law of the Committee on the Judiciary, US House of Representatives. https://judiciary.house.gov/uploadedfiles/competition_in_digital_markets.pdf.

Hufbauer, Gary Clyde, and Zhiyao (Lucy) Lu. 2019. "Global E-Commerce Talks Stumble on Data Issues, Privacy, and More." Policy Brief 19-14, Peterson Institute for International Economics, Washington, DC. https://www.piie.com/sites/default/files/documents/pb19-14.pdf.

IMF (International Monetary Fund). 2019. "Corporate Taxation in the Global Economy." IMF Policy Paper 19/007, IMF, Washington, DC. https://www.imf.org/en/Publications/Policy-Papers/Issues/2019/03/08/Corporate-Taxation-in-the-Global-Economy-46650.

Keen, Michael. 2008. "VAT, Tariffs, and Withholding: Border Taxes and Informality in Developing Countries." *Journal of Public Economics* 92 (10–11): 1892–1906.

Kennedy, Joe. 2019. "Digital Services Taxes: A Bad Idea Whose Time Should Never Come." Information Technology and Innovation Foundation, Washington, DC. https://itif.org/publications/2019/05/13/digital-services-taxes-bad-idea-whose-time-should-never-come.

Kim, Jeehye, Parmesh Shah, Joanne Catherine Gaskell, Ashesh Prasann, and Akanksha Luthra. 2020. *Scaling Up Disruptive Agricultural Technologies in Africa.* International Development in Focus Series. Washington, DC: World Bank. http://hdl.handle.net/10986/33961.

KPMG. 2021. "Taxation of the Digitalized Economy: Developments Summary." Updated February 3, 2021, KPMG, Amstelveen, the Netherlands. https://tax.kpmg.us/content/dam/tax/en/pdfs/2021/digitalized-economy-taxation-developments-summary.pdf.

KRA (Kenya Revenue Authority). 2020. "Missing Trader." *Tax Matters* 1 (August 21): 4–6, KRA, Nairobi, Kenya. https://kra.go.ke/images/publications/TaxMatters-Bulletin-Tax-Evasion-Edition.pdf.

Lee, Yoolim. 2018. "Go-Jek to Enter Singapore This Week in Challenge to Grab." *Bloomberg Technology*, November 28, 2018. https://www.bloomberg.com/news/articles/2018-11-28/go-jek-is-said-to-enter-singapore-this-week-in-challenge-to-grab.

Liu, Han-Wei. 2019. "Data Localization and Digital Trade Barriers: ASEAN in Megaregionalism." In *ASEAN Law in the New Regional Economic Order: Global Trends and Shifting Paradigms*, edited by Pasha L. Hsieh and Bryan Mercurio, 371–91. Cambridge, UK: Cambridge University Press. https://doi.org/10.1017/9781108563208.019.

Lucas-Mas, Cristian Oliver, and Raul Felix Junquera-Varela. 2021. *Tax Theory Applied to Taxing the Digital Economy.* Washington, DC: World Bank.

Makiyama, Hosuk-Lee, and Badri Narayanan. 2019. "The Economic Losses from Ending the WTO Moratorium on Electronic Transmissions." ECIPE Policy Brief 3/2019, European Center for International Political Economy, Brussels. https://ecipe.org/wp-content/uploads/2019/08/ECI_19_PolicyBrief_3_2019_LY04.pdf.

Markova, Ekaterina. 2016. "Bulgaria: Supreme Court Shuts Down Smartphone Car Service Uber." *Eurofound*, European Foundation for the Improvement of Living and Working Conditions, Dublin. https://www.eurofound.europa.eu/publications/article/2016/bulgaria-supreme-court-shuts-down-smartphone-car-service-uber.

Molinuevo, Martín, and Simon Jean Henri Gaillard. 2018. "Trade, Cross-Border Data, and the Next Regulatory Frontier: Law Enforcement and Data Localization Requirements." MTI Practice Notes 3, World Bank, Washington, DC. http://documents.worldbank.org/curated/en/903261543589829872/Trade-Cross-Border-Data-and-the-Next-Regulatory-Frontier-Law-Enforcement-and-Data-Localization-Requirements.

Motta, Massimo, and Martin Peitz. 2020. "Big Tech Mergers." *Information Economics and Policy.* Published ahead of print, May 26. https://doi.org/10.1016/j.infoecopol.2020.100868.

NBT (National Board of Trade). 2015. "No Transfer, No Production: A Report on Cross-Border Data Transfers, Global Value Chains, and the Production of Goods."

Kommerskollegium Report 2015:4, Kommerskollegium (National Board of Trade), Stockholm. https://ec.europa.eu/futurium/en/system/files/ged/publ-no-transfer-no-production.pdf.

Nyman, Sara, and Rodrigo Barajas. Forthcoming. "Antitrust in the Digital Economy: A Global Perspective." World Bank, Washington, DC.

Nyman, Sara, and Noelia Carreras. Forthcoming. "Young Competition Authorities and the Digital Economy: Selected Examples of Approaches to Tackling Emerging Competition Issues in Digital Markets." WDR 2021 background paper, World Bank, Washington, DC.

OECD (Organisation for Economic Co-operation and Development). 2014. *Measuring the Digital Economy: A New Perspective.* Paris: OECD. https://dx.doi.org/10.1787/9789264221796-en.

OECD (Organisation for Economic Co-operation and Development). 2017. *International VAT/GST Guidelines.* Paris: OECD. https://www.oecd-ilibrary.org/taxation/international-vat-gst-guidelines_9789264271401-en.

OECD (Organisation for Economic Co-operation and Development). 2018a. *Tax Challenges Arising from Digitalisation: Interim Report 2018, Inclusive Framework on BEPS.* OECD/G20 Base Erosion and Profit Shifting Project. Paris: OECD. https://doi.org/10.1787/9789264293083-en.

OECD (Organisation for Economic Co-operation and Development). 2018b. "Tax Challenges Arising from Digitalisation: More than 110 Countries Agree to Work towards a Consensus-Based Solution." *Topics*, March 16, OECD, Paris. http://www.oecd.org/tax/beps/tax-challenges-arising-from-digitalisation-more-than-110-countries-agree-to-work-towards-a-consensus-basedsolution.htm.

OECD (Organisation for Economic Co-operation and Development). 2020a. "Model Rules for Reporting by Platform Operators with Respect to Sellers in the Sharing and Gig Economy." OECD, Paris. https://www.oecd.org/tax/exchange-of-tax-information/model-rules-for-reporting-by-platform-operators-with-respect-to-sellers-in-the-sharing-and-gig-economy.htm.

OECD (Organisation for Economic Co-operation and Development). 2020b. "Statement by the OECD/G20 Inclusive Framework on BEPS on the Two-Pillar Approach to Address the Tax Challenges Arising from the Digitalisation of the Economy." OECD/G20 Inclusive Framework on BEPS, OECD, Paris. www.oecd.org/tax/beps/statement-by-the-oecd-g20-inclusive-framework-on-beps-january-2020.pdf.

Open Ag Data Alliance. 2020. "To Help Farmers Access and Control Their Data." http://openag.io/about-us/.

Open Banking. 2020. "Open Banking February Highlights." Open Banking Limited, London. https://www.openbanking.org.uk/about-us/latest-news/open-banking-february-highlights-2020/.

PCT (Platform for Collaboration on Tax). 2020. "PCT Progress Report 2020." International Monetary Fund; Center for Tax Policy and Administration, Organisation for Economic Co-operation and Development; United Nations; and World Bank, Washington, DC.

RBI (Reserve Bank of India). 2019. "Master Direction–Non-Banking Financial Company–Account Aggregator (Reserve Bank) Directions." Document RBI/DNBR/2016-17/46, Master Direction DNBR.PD.009/03.10.119

/2016-17, RBI, Mumbai. https://www.rbi.org.in/Scripts/BS_ViewMasDirections.aspx?id=10598.

Romer, Paul. 2019. "A Tax That Could Fix Big Tech." *New York Times*, May 6, 2019. https://www.nytimes.com/2019/05/06/opinion/tax-facebook-google.html.

Rukundo, Solomon. 2020. "Addressing the Challenges of Taxation of the Digital Economy: Lessons for African Countries." ICTD Working Paper 105, International Center for Tax and Development, Institute of Development Studies, Brighton, UK. https://media.africaportal.org/documents/Addressing_the_challenges.pdf.

Soursourian, Matthew, and Ariadne Plaitakis. 2019. "Fair Play: Ensuring Competition in Digital Financial Services." CGAP Working Paper, Consultative Group to Assist the Poor, Washington, DC. https://www.cgap.org/sites/default/files/publications/2019_11_Working_Paper_FairPlay.pdf.

Spaulding, Patrick, Sarah Falvey, and Ronak Merchant. 2013. "When the Cloud Goes Local: The Global Problem with Data Localization." *Computer Law and Security Review* 46 (12): 54–59.

Stigler Center. 2019. "Final Report of the Stigler Committee on Digital Platforms." Stigler Center for the Study of the Economy and the State, Booth School of Business, University of Chicago. https://www.chicagobooth.edu/-/media/research/stigler/pdfs/digital-platforms---committee-report---stigler-center.pdf.

Sugana, Rubino, and Asrul Hidayat. 2014. "Analysis of VAT Revenue Potential and Gaps in Indonesia 2013." *Journal of Indonesian Economy and Development* 15 (1): 1–40.

UN DESA (United Nations Department of Economic and Social Affairs). 2020. "Tax Treatment of Payments for Digital Services." United Nations, New York. https://www.un.org/development/desa/financing/document/tax-treatment-payments-digital-services.

USITC (United States International Trade Commission). 2014. *Digital Trade in the U.S. and Global Economies, Part 2.* Publication 4485, Investigation 332–540. Washington, DC: USITC. https://www.usitc.gov/publications/332/pub4485.pdf.

USTR (Office of the United States Trade Representative). 2020a. "Agreement between the United States of America, the United Mexican States, and Canada 7/1/20 Text." USTR, Washington, DC. https://ustr.gov/trade-agreements/free-trade-agreements/united-states-mexico-canada-agreement/agreement-between.

USTR (Office of the United States Trade Representative). 2020b. "Initiation of Section 301 Investigations of Digital Services Taxes." Docket USTR-2020-0022, USTR, Washington, DC. https://ustr.gov/sites/default/files/assets/frn/FRN.pdf.

Valdez, Yvette D., Roderick O. Branch, and Daniel Gallo Mainero. 2020. "Mexico Issues First License under New FinTech Law." *Global FinTech and Payments* (blog). February 24, 2020. Lexology, Law Business Research, London. https://www.lexology.com/library/detail.aspx?g=e54d449f-c4fa-4408-b1a5-5326f3a1cdd0.

WEF (World Economic Forum). 2020. "Data Free Flow with Trust (DFFT): Paths towards Free and Trusted Data Flows." White Paper, WEF, Geneva. http://www3.weforum.org/docs/WEF_Paths_Towards_Free_and_Trusted_Data%20_Flows_2020.pdf.

World Bank. 2019. *World Development Report 2019: The Changing Nature of Work.* Washington, DC: World Bank. https://www.worldbank.org/en/publication/wdr2019.

World Bank. 2020. *World Development Report 2020: Trading for Development in the Age of Global Value Chains.* Washington, DC: World Bank. https://www.worldbank.org/en/publication/wdr2020.

WTO (World Trade Organization). 2017. "Joint Statement on Electronic Commerce." Ministerial Conference, Eleventh Session, Buenos Aires, December 10–13, 2017. https://docs.wto.org/dol2fe/Pages/SS/directdoc.aspx?filename=q:/WT/MIN17/60.pdf&Open=True.

Wu, Mark. 2017. "Digital Trade-Related Provisions in Regional Trade Agreements: Existing Models and Lessons for the Multilateral Trade System." Overview paper, RTA Exchange, Geneva. https://e15initiative.org/wp-content/uploads/2015/09/RTA-Exchange-Digital-Trade-Mark-Wu-Final-2.pdf.

Zampano, Giada, and Nicholas Hirst. 2017. "Uber Wins Appeal against Ban in Italy." *Politico*, May 26. https://www.politico.eu/article/uber-wins-appeal-against-ban-in-italy/.

Spotlight 7.1
Understanding the interface between data protection and competition policy

While respecting the prime objective of protecting individuals' data rights, data protection provisions can be designed to minimize the effects on competition and innovation.

Data protection regulations are essential for safeguarding individual welfare and building trust. Yet complying with data protection obligations can also raise the costs of entry and operation for firms—especially smaller firms.[1] Data protection policies that reduce the incentives to share personal data or restrict the use of personal data that a firm has not collected can further entrench incumbent positions and reduce opportunities for innovation.[2] This is not to say that concerns about competition should override the need to safeguard individuals' data rights; rather, there is scope to review the design of data protection regimes to minimize the adverse impacts on competition while continuing to respect data rights.

Evidence from a study of 27,000 top websites found that the General Data Protection Regulation (GDPR) had the unintended consequence of increasing concentration in the web technology sector, with small web technology vendors losing the most market share. This also had the effect of making personal data collection more concentrated after the GDPR was instituted.[3] In these settings, differentiating regulatory treatment between firms according to their size or age may be an option to consider, subject to taking steps to maintain the data rights of individuals.[4]

On the other side of the coin, there is growing agreement that a firm's offering on protection of user data has value to consumers and could be considered a nonprice outcome of competition. Understanding the extent to which firms voluntarily provide enhanced data protection in order to compete becomes important for an accurate analysis of market dynamics.

In the first abuse-of-dominance case relating specifically to data protection lodged by the German competition authority against Facebook in 2019, one question raised during the appeal process was users' willingness to pay for enhanced data protection.[5] However, evidence on the valuation that individuals attach to data protection in different markets is mixed. Some evidence suggests that individuals' stated preferences for data protection often do not match their revealed preferences in practice.[6] Rather than implying a lower valuation of privacy, the issue may be that data subjects (and even the firm collecting the data) do not fully understand how data collected may be used in the future, given the complexity of big datasets and firms' data protection policies.

Moreover, data spillovers may complicate matters. If a platform holds sufficient data on a group of people to allow inferences to be drawn about individuals who have not yet contributed data, those individuals may perceive that they have already lost the power to protect themselves and therefore volunteer data despite their privacy concerns. Such issues may be exacerbated in low- and middle-income countries, where literacy rates, exposure to digital business models, and choice between firms are lower.

Only scarce evidence exists about data protection preferences in lower-income countries. The Data Confidence Index indicates that concerns about the impact of the internet on "personal privacy" appear strongest in Africa, Asia, and the Middle East, while respondents in Latin America generally express higher levels of concern about how companies are using their personal data.[7] Results from experiments in India and Kenya found that customers prefer digital loan products with more "data privacy" features.[8] However, low-income groups who are price sensitive may be more willing to obtain "zero" price products or services by relinquishing their data.

Overall, there is room for improved cooperation between competition authorities and data protection authorities. Collaboration between regulatory agencies can help policy makers to understand which type of ex ante data protection policies minimize distortions to competition; how to develop appropriate data-focused competition remedies while ensuring data protection; and which antitrust cases to pursue where there may be a link to excessive data collection or exploitation of consumers.

Notes

1. Gal and Aviv (2020).
2. Examples include requiring firms to monitor compliance with the data policy of firms with which they have shared data or limiting the use of data to the purposes for which they were originally collected.
3. Batikas et al. (2020). This increase likely occurred because, after the GDPR became effective, in order to reduce compliance risks, websites (including those that served citizens outside the European Union) reduced their connections to technology providers, especially regarding requests involving personal data. See Johnson, Shriver, and Goldberg (2021).
4. For example, the GDPR allows businesses with fewer than 250 employees to have a limited number of exemptions for recordkeeping (EU 2018). Likewise, in the United States, the Privacy Rule of the Health Information Privacy and Accountability Act does not apply to health plans with fewer than 50 participants that are administered solely by a single employer. See Health Information Privacy, US Department of Health and Human Services, Summary of the HIPAA Privacy Rule (dashboard), https://www.hhs.gov/hipaa/for-professionals/privacy/laws-regulations/index.html.
5. Colangelo (2019).
6. However, this evidence typically comes from experiments that apply to specific types of personal data in specific contexts and thus makes extrapolations to other settings difficult. See Gerber, Gerber, and Volkamer (2018) and OECD (2020).
7. The Data Confidence Index is constructed from the privacy-related concerns expressed by 391,130 respondents ages 16–64 during the Q1–Q4 waves of research conducted by GlobalWebIndex in 41 countries in 2018 (Datum Future and GWI 2019). Respondents are representative of the online populations of the markets covered.
8. Fernandez Vidal and Medine (2019).

References

Batikas, Michail, Stefan Bechtold, Tobias Kretschmer, and Christian Peukert. 2020. "European Privacy Law and Global Markets for Data." CEPR Discussion Paper 14475, Centre for Economic Policy Research, London, March 2020. https://cepr.org/active/publications/discussion_papers/dp.php?dpno=14475.

Colangelo, Giuseppe. 2019. "Facebook and Bundeskartellamt's Winter of Discontent." *CPI EU News* (blog), September 23, 2019. Competition Policy International, eSapience Center for Competition Policy, Cambridge, MA. https://www.competitionpolicyinternational.com/facebook-and-bundeskartellamts-winter-of-discontent/.

Datum Future and GWI (GlobalWebIndex). 2019. "The Data Confidence Index." Report, Datum Future, London. https://www.datumfuture.org/wp-content/uploads/2019/09/Data-Confidence-Index-Datum-Future-and-GWI-2019.pdf.

EU (European Union). 2018. "Recital 13: Taking Account of Micro, Small, and Medium-Sized Enterprises." *GDPR.EU*, November 14, 2018. Proton Technologies, Calgary, Canada. https://gdpr.eu/recital-13-taking-account-of-micro-small-and-medium-sized-enterprises/.

Fernandez Vidal, Maria, and David Medine. 2019. "Is Data Privacy Good for Business?" CGAP Focus Note, Consultative Group to Assist the Poor, Washington, DC, December 2019. https://www.cgap.org/sites/default/files/publications/2019_12_Focus_Note_Is_Data_Privacy_Good_for_Business_1.pdf.

Gal, Michal S., and Oshrit Aviv. 2020. "The Competitive Effects of the GDPR." *Journal of Competition Law and Economics* 16 (3): 349–91. https://doi.org/10.1093/joclec/nhaa012.

Gerber, Nina, Paul Gerber, and Melanie Volkamer. 2018. "Explaining the Privacy Paradox: A Systematic Review of Literature Investigating Privacy Attitude and Behavior." *Computers and Security* 77 (August): 226–61. https://doi.org/10.1016/j.cose.2018.04.002.

Johnson, Garrett A., Scott K. Shriver, and Samuel G. Goldberg. 2021. "Privacy and Market Concentration: Intended and Unintended Consequences of the GDPR." Paper presented at the American Economic Association and Allied Social Science Associations 2021 Virtual Annual Meeting, January 3–5, 2021.

OECD (Organisation for Economic Co-operation and Development). 2020. "Consumer Data Rights and Competition: Background Note." Document DAF/COMP(2020)1, Competition Committee, Directorate for Financial and Enterprise Affairs, OECD, Paris, April 29, 2020. https://one.oecd.org/document/DAF/COMP(2020)1/en/pdf.

Spotlight 7.2
The role of regional and international cooperation in addressing data governance challenges

Closer international cooperation across a wide range of areas is needed to settle many of the fundamental issues in the new social contract on data.

Many data governance challenges either cannot be fully resolved at the national level or could be addressed more efficiently or equitably through international cooperation. Specifically, international cooperation is needed at multiple levels, beginning with bilateral regulatory and administrative collaboration between individual countries and progressing to regional collaboration and wider international cooperation and global agreements as well as donor support.

Bilateral cooperation

Managing the data economy calls for increasing bilateral cooperation between governments, especially with regard to accessing critical data domestically and internationally. For example, having access to corporate financial data from corresponding third-country tax authorities would facilitate the capture of fiscal revenues from indirect taxes (value added taxes) levied on third-country companies trading across digital platforms. Tax administrations in low- and middle-income countries need to have secure access to aggregate data on the global allocation of income and profit taxes paid by the largest multinational enterprises. Such data are available from home-country tax administrations. Another critical area for bilateral cooperation across borders is in matters of law enforcement related to cybercrime (see chapter 6).

With the market for data-driven platforms dominated by a handful of global players, decisions taken by antitrust authorities in one jurisdiction have spillover effects in many others (see spotlight 7.1).[1] Going forward, there is scope for closer cooperation among

antitrust authorities, particularly on anticompetitive practices that affect several countries simultaneously or where the practice has a cross-border dimension. A regional competition regime is already in place in the European Union. Competition authorities from the BRICS countries (Brazil, the Russian Federation, India, China, South Africa) have begun to work together on platform businesses, looking to exchange experiences and achieve a more harmonized approach.[2]

Regional collaboration

Regional collaboration is one way to amplify the voice of smaller low- and middle-income countries, while making progress on the challenging goal of reaching global agreements on data governance. For example, regional coordination of ad hoc digital taxation measures, as considered by the African Tax Administration Forum,[3] could help to minimize administrative and compliance costs as well as to manage competitive dynamics among countries (such as tax and regulatory arbitrage or a race to the bottom).

Regional collaboration can also play a valuable role in the development of data infrastructure, such as internet exchange points and colocation data centers, which may lie beyond the reach of smaller or lower-income economies (see chapter 5). Countries with well-developed international gateways and competitive information and communication technology sectors can aggregate regional demand to support shared facilities, as long as there are strong fiber-optic links between neighboring countries and the regulatory framework for cross-border data flows is harmonized.

International cooperation and global agreements

Certain policy issues, particularly international rules governing cross-border trade in data-enabled services and associated tax rights, need to be tackled through multilateral cooperation and preferably at the global scale.

The current Joint Statement talks on e-commerce and digital trade warrant serious attention from World Trade Organization (WTO) members. In addition, although the WTO's General Agreement on Trade in Services (GATS) does not prohibit restrictions on cross-border data flows per se, limitations on cross-border data flows could be considered in violation of the GATS rules on nondiscrimination in those sectors where WTO members have undertaken specific commitments.[4] In addition to rules on cross-border services, WTO members have provisionally agreed not to impose customs duties on digital products.

Tackling the loss of direct tax revenue that results from cross-border profit shifting by multinational platform businesses calls for replacing the current rules on the allocation of taxation rights across countries. The de facto standard setting body for international tax issues, the Inclusive Framework on Base Erosion and Profit Shifting (BEPS), is in the process of finalizing policy proposals aimed at addressing these challenges.[5] If no global consensus is reached, low- and middle-income economies aiming to capture direct tax revenue from the sector will have few palatable short-term choices.

The limited participation of low-income countries in such international negotiations on taxation and trade is a cause for concern. For example, among the 85 countries involved in negotiating the data governance framework for cross-border data flows at the WTO, there is only one low-income country—Burkina Faso.[6] Similarly, only G-24 nations are participating in current negotiations for overhauling the international tax rules regarding rights to levy corporate tax on data-driven businesses that participate in a market without a physical presence. This lack of representation hampers the inclusiveness of the potential rules under discussion and risks leading to a "one-size-fits-all approach" on global rules that is driven by more advanced players.

Furthermore, cross-border data sharing requires cooperation on standard setting and regulatory harmonization. International treaties and model laws provide valuable frameworks for voluntary cooperation in these spheres. For example, in the case of cybersecurity, the Budapest Convention on Cybercrime and the modernized Convention 108 of the Council of Europe on data protection have played a pivotal role in achieving international convergence of standards. Another critical area for harmonization is interoperability of data and data systems, which is a technical prerequisite for the smooth flow of data across borders. Open standards can be determined by sectoral or international standard setting organizations at the level of specific sectors (such as banking), with strong leadership from leading industry participants.[7]

Donor support

Finally, the donor community can help to redress the underlying causes of inequity in the data-driven economy and society by supporting investments to fill gaps in physical and institutional systems as well as by helping governments to build the necessary human capital. A key role for donors is to provide technical assistance and support for policy reforms to improve the enabling environment for data, especially in critical areas such as statistical capacity building (see spotlight 2.2), data protection, cybersecurity, cross-border data flows, and the sharing of public intent and private intent data. Equally important is support for improving the investment climate for private actors, including efforts to strengthen the legal and regulatory framework for private investment in broadband networks and data infrastructure. Such indirect support is generally preferable to donors' direct investment in infrastructure (see chapter 5).

Notes

1. Bundeskartellamt (2019).
2. BRICS Competition Centre (2019).
3. ATAF (2020).
4. Under the GATS, the obligation on nondiscrimination applies only to those services sectors where each WTO member has explicitly recognized the obligation in its country-specific "schedule of specific commitments," subject to any conditions set out therein. See World Trade Organization, GATS (General Agreement on Trade in Services) (dashboard), https://www.wto.org/english/tratop _e/serv_e/gatsqa_e.htm.
5. The Inclusive Framework on BEPS has 130 country members (including all Organisation for Economic Co-operation and Development [OECD] members) and is housed at the OECD. International organizations such as the World Bank Group have an observer role. For a summary of the development of the Inclusive Framework proposals and a discussion of an alternative that departs from the arm's-length standard by embracing the apportionment of the taxable income of a multinational enterprise based on its sales to unrelated customers in each country, see Avi-Yonah and Clausing (2019).
6. Hufbauer and Lu (2019).
7. Ragavan, Murphy, and Davé (2016).

References

ATAF (African Tax Administration Forum). 2020. "Domestic Resource Mobilisation: Digital Services Taxation in Africa." Policy Brief 01, ATAF, Pretoria, South Africa, June 2020. https://events.ataftax.org/index.php?page= documents&func=view&https://events.ataftax.org /index.php?page=documents&func=view&document _id=61#=61#.

Avi-Yonah, Reuven S., and Kimberly A. Clausing. 2019. "Toward a 21st-Century International Tax Regime." *Tax Notes International* 95 (9): 839–49.

BRICS Competition Centre. 2019. *Digital Era Competition: A BRICS View*. BRICS Report, Version 1.0. Moscow: BRICS Competition Innovation Law and Policy Centre, Skolkovo Institute for Law and Development, Faculty of Law, Higher School of Economics, HSE University, September 18, 2019. http://bricscompetition.org/materials /news/digital-era-competition-brics-report/.

Bundeskartellamt. 2019. "Bundeskartellamt Obtains Far-Reaching Improvements in the Terms of Business for Sellers on Amazon's Online Marketplaces." Press Release, July 17, 2019. https://www.bundeskartellamt .de/SharedDocs/Publikation/EN/Pressemitteilungen /2019/17_07_2019_Amazon.html;jsessionid=F840FC 421918D688C3791E8B3C57DBCB.1_cid381?nn=3600108.

Hufbauer, Gary Clyde, and Zhiyao (Lucy) Lu. 2019. "Global E-Commerce Talks Stumble on Data Issues, Privacy, and More." Policy Brief 19-14, Peterson Institute for International Economics, Washington, DC, October 2019. https://www.piie.com/sites/default/files/documents /pb19-14.pdf.

Ragavan, Srividhya, Brendan Murphy, and Raj Davé. 2016. "FRAND v. Compulsory Licensing: The Lesser of the Two Evils." *Duke Law and Technology Review* 14 (1): 83–120.

Institutions for data governance: Building trust through collective action

Main messages

1. The institutions required to govern data fill four main functions: strategic planning; developing rules and standards; compliance and enforcement; and generating the learning and evidence needed to gain insights and address emerging challenges.

2. Nongovernmental institutions and mechanisms such as data intermediaries can help governments and other actors safely share and use data to capture greater value, while promoting equitable access to data and the value they create.

3. Public institutions must have sufficient resources, adequate autonomy, and technical capacity, including data literacy, to fulfill their mandates efficiently. Political champions in positions of power are critical to leading data management reforms that create incentives and a culture of data use, dissemination, and transparency.

4. A multistakeholder, purpose-driven approach to data management and governance can help institutions keep pace with an ever-evolving data ecosystem and enhance their legitimacy, transparency, and accountability.

How can institutions help govern data for development?

As described in part I of this Report, capturing greater value from data requires sharing and using more data. This chapter describes how institutions can help facilitate the secure flow of data, while ensuring their confidentiality and protection in alignment with principles of the social contract for data.

Formed by state and nonstate institutions, *a data governance ecosystem*[1] provides structure and incentives for the trusted creation, storage, processing, sharing, use, and destruction of data throughout their life cycle. It does so by means of implementation of policies, laws, platforms,[2] systems, and standards. Three building blocks contribute to an effective and inclusive data governance ecosystem: the data governance functions carried out by institutions and

actors; the role fulfilled by data intermediaries; and the performance-enhancing features of institutions.

Data governance functions include developing overarching data strategies and policies; elaborating legal frameworks and guidance on how rules should apply and be enforced if violated; undertaking arbitration in case of conflict; and maintaining monitoring, evaluation, and constant feedback loops to promote engagement, learning, and improvements.

These functions are performed by data governance institutions, whose roles and relations are specific to the context. This chapter highlights patterns in institutional mandates in the public sector and in the roles of nongovernmental institutions and actors across countries. Examples are provided of commonly used institutions, while recognizing that both the actual and optimal allocation of data governance functions across institutions will vary, depending on local conditions (see box 8.1).

Box 8.1 Uruguay's whole-of-government approach to data governance

Implementation of data governance reforms across the whole of government is complex. Some countries have opted to first build the foundational hard and soft infrastructure. This Report interprets soft infrastructure broadly to include software platforms (sometimes called data and information management systems[a]) supported by technical interoperability standards, data integration methods, and people accountable for the functioning of these systems. Siloed approaches, bespoke technical architecture, and disparate database taxonomies are often indicative of outdated soft infrastructure, preventing data from being used more widely.

Because of the disparate nature of existing platforms and the complex web of data management architecture, the initial stages of soft infrastructure reforms usually focus on digitizing, classifying, and sharing data within the public sector. The first step in the process should be identifying the data to which the government has access, how these data are classified (open, restricted, or personal), and who produces or uses the data, along with other information such as limitations and provenance. Desirable platforms and standards enable secure data flows across a wide variety of institutions and actors. This foundation of modern data infrastructure (both soft and hard) is meant to ensure that, for example, data produced in one ministry in the public sector can be easily shared with other ministries or users so that

programs and policies are informed by multiple sources of data. More generally, well-designed, user-centric data infrastructure will encourage the repurposing and reuse of data, thereby increasing the value of data otherwise trapped in siloed infrastructure.

Along with infrastructure, countries must invest in the "analog complements," including adopting enabling legislation and regulations and institutionalizing governance arrangements to ensure the sustainability of reform efforts.[b]

One example of an institution-focused approach to data-driven digital transformation is that taken by Uruguay. Its Agency for Electronic Government and Information and Knowledge Society (Agesic), launched in 2007, has driven the country's successful e-government reforms. Because of its proximity to the Office of the President, Agesic has benefited from the high-level strategic leadership required to drive the country's digital agenda in a multistakeholder manner. A central factor in the success of Uruguay's digital transformation has been the integration of a well-developed domestic information and communication technology (ICT) industry that provides access to quality platforms and services with local technical knowledge to inform design and implementation efforts and avoid reliance on infrastructure built by the public sector.[c] The country's interoperability platform, the Integrated Government Architecture,

(Box continues next page)

---

and its supporting Enterprise Architecture Framework (TOGAF), are the technical foundation on which a robust data governance framework has been built.

Uruguay's Digital Transformation Agenda 2020 exemplifies how countries can take a whole-of-government and multistakeholder approach to guaranteeing that the various layers of the data governance ecosystem (platforms, systems, policies, laws, standards,

and institutions) are designed and implemented in a coordinated, inclusive manner to enable better use of data for decision-making and user-centric service delivery.[d]

a. World Bank (2016).
b. OECD (2019a).
c. Porrúa (2013).
d. Agesic (2019).

After de jure governance arrangements are in place, actors may still not have strong incentives to create, share, and use data productively.[3] They may find these actions too costly, or they may try to free ride on the efforts of others.[4] Incentives to hoard data in siloes may arise from perceptions that control of data is tantamount to power over government decision-making. Other challenges to data sharing may be linked to autonomy or capacity constraints.

Data intermediaries and a user-centric design of digital platforms can lower the costs of sharing data, thereby reducing incentives for free riding. They also can support inclusion in data use by increasing the usability of information for nontechnical experts. This chapter explores how these new types of institutions and mechanisms facilitate data sharing and reuse between diverse actors and increase access to otherwise siloed datasets.

Free riding of data can occur in both the private and public sectors.[5] This chapter discusses three *features of institutions* that could improve incentives for collecting, sharing, and using data: (1) the technical capacity, including sound data literacy, to discharge their functions effectively; (2) a culture of performance and rewards and incentives for staff that support a transition to data-driven government; and (3) the institutional accountability and independence that help establish public trust in the integrity of institutions, particularly those tasked with rule making and compliance, which may otherwise be vulnerable to undue political or commercial influence.

Adopting an inclusive, multistakeholder approach to data governance can help ensure that the right challenges around data use are identified and addressed, keeping in mind the diverse needs of end users, including traditionally marginalized groups. Moreover, collaboration by a wide range of stakeholders

from the private sector, academia, civil society, and international organizations can help governments strengthen the social contract around data by enhancing perceptions of procedural fairness and legitimacy. Finally, coordination among institutions in the public sector and nongovernmental stakeholders can avoid data and process duplication and facilitate secure data sharing, leading to gains in efficiency. Transparency and opportunities for scrutiny and accountability can be built into decision-making processes to increase their legitimacy.

The final section of this chapter uses the maturity model introduced in chapter 1 to illustrate how countries can best develop a solid institutional foundation to support their data governance ecosystem.

Data management across the data life cycle

The data life cycle starts when a government, private sector firm, civil society organization (CSO), nongovernmental organization (NGO), or academic institution (including think tanks and researchers) collect data (see figure 1.2 in chapter 1). These data are then validated, stored, and processed, and then possibly shared with others. After using the data, the actor may archive them or destroy them. If the data are retained, they can be reused. The life cycle begins again when data are reused, potentially for a completely new purpose. Engaging in outcome-oriented and user-centric data management at each step of the data life cycle can promote greater value creation from data (for examples, see table 8.1).

Some data management decisions lower the costs of data sharing across actors, thereby facilitating reuse. For example, as data are being processed they should be coded using standardized units or

Table 8.1 Data management decisions along the data life cycle

Stage of life cycle	Area in which data management is needed
Create/receive	• Determine lawful use (such as obtaining consent for data collection and sharing). • Collect identifications that allow data to be merged with other datasets.
Process	• Standardize units and categories (such as industry classifications). • Use data formats that are widely compatible and accessible. • Validate the quality (accuracy), relevance, and integrity of data.
Store	• Encrypt data; use secure servers; back up and archive data.
Transfer/share	• Verify whether consent allows for data to be shared. • Deidentify data, if appropriate.^a • Sign confidentiality agreements for use of identified data. • Publish data via bulk downloads or APIs.
Analyze and use	• Ensure reproducibility; publish code or algorithms. • Do not publish identifiable data. • Visualize and communicate insights from data.
Archive and preserve	• Classify and catalog data systematically so they can be found easily. • Include data dictionaries and notes on how data were created. • Maintain access to data and their security and integrity over time.
Destroy or reuse	• Keep records of destruction processes. • Verify that consent for use is still valid.

Source: WDR 2021 team.

Note: APIs = application programming interfaces.

a. See Elliot et al. (2016); Polonetsky, Tene, and Finch (2016).

categories, such as common industry classifications, and converted to a format widely compatible with various types of software. Adopting common classifications and formats requires an upfront investment, but it will allow actors to share and combine data more easily. In Mexico, states and local municipalities collect and share data via the central government's open data network, Red México Abierto, in accordance with centralized data quality standards.[6]

The decisions at every stage of the data life cycle will vary, depending on the type of data and their proximity to features of public goods.[7] To guide and structure decisions, data management needs to rely on a data governance framework. In a mature data system, data governance and data management work together to create value from data use in a manner consistent with the values of the social contract (figure 8.1). The data governance framework can

Figure 8.1 Data governance and data management, working seamlessly together in support of the social contract

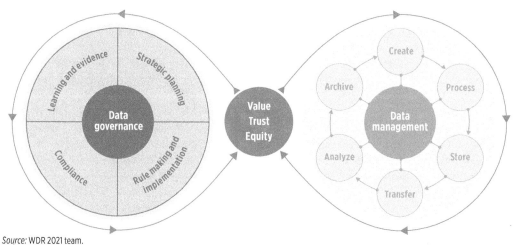

Source: WDR 2021 team.

Note: The data management life cycle at right appears in figure 1.2 in chapter 1.

stipulate rules about the use and reuse of data, including consent, and also set standards for processing and classifying data. Together, clearly defined data management standards and a robust data governance framework can help users better harness the value from data in a safe and equitable manner.

Data governance functions

Traditionally, scholars studying how data governance frameworks can improve data management have concentrated on private sector firms.[8] However, recognition is growing that data governance frameworks are also needed to guide countries' public sectors and multilateral organizations seeking to enhance the value of data to improve lives.[9] Box 8.2 illustrates why such a framework is important to the functioning of a data economy—and how intricate it can be—using the example of digital IDs.

This chapter draws on the literature and experiences of public sector management worldwide and the body of work on corporate data governance to

---

Box 8.2 The importance and complexity of data governance institutions: The example of digital identification (ID) systems

Verifying identity attributes or authenticating an identity—particularly using an official trusted source—can be an essential step in determining whether a person is who he or she claims to be and is authorized to apply for or receive the requested service or benefit. The application of digital identity verification and authentication mechanisms in conjunction with trusted and inclusive ID systems can increase access to services, reduce fraud and administrative costs, and create opportunities for innovation, such as through the automation, integration, and remote delivery of services. However, these mechanisms also process sensitive data, sometimes including biometric data, and therefore must be subject to strong governance and accountability frameworks.

An ID system's purpose—how personal data will be used—is typically set by law or regulation. These rules govern the system's design and operation, as well as the technical specifications, standards, and procedures to be adopted to ensure that the system delivers the level of assurance needed for identification and verification. These rules also protect security and personal data and mitigate risks of surveillance and discrimination.[a] Such rules may limit the collection and use of personal data to the minimum necessary to achieve the specific processing purpose, or require deidentification or encryption. The rules may state as well that certain data—such as biographical data and biometric data—should be processed separately to prevent any attempt to assemble complete profiles of individuals.[b] Whether data localization requirements will apply to the data will depend on the risks, opportunities, and costs involved, and whether third-party databases, processors, or cloud providers can provide assurances about security and data protection requirements.

Administrative rules aimed at mitigating risks of human error and misuse of personal data may require that identification and authentication functions be separated in the system or that administrators be authorized with the "least privilege" powers necessary to perform their delegated functions.[c] If the system outsources critical functions to others, such as enrollment agents, registrars, or credential providers, these parties may be subject to certification and obligations. Third parties using the system, such as hospitals, banks, universities, and public agencies, must be subject to rules on the basis by which they can access the ID system, standards on the form of data they exchange, and controls on how they can use the data they handle. Rules will govern how such interactions must be logged to create records of an individual's activities and relationships with numerous bodies.

Other institutions and actors may also be involved. For example, an independent digital identification agency may be responsible for managing the system. A civil registration agency may need to interoperate with it. A data protection authority (DPA) may exercise general oversight to ensure implementation of the appropriate governance principles[d] and compliance with the law. A foundational ID system may be considered critical infrastructure, requiring monitoring by the DPA, a Computer Security Incident Response Team (CSIRT), or other body responsible for cybersecurity. If the ID system is part of a regional mutual recognition arrangement[e]—such as the European Union's electronic IDentification, Authentication and trust Services (eIDAS) framework[f]—interoperability and use of common standards with foreign agencies that issue IDs and credentials may be required.

a. Cavoukian (2011).
b. Danezis et al. (2014).
c. For example, the Unique Identification Authority of India (UIDAI) operates clearance levels for accessing the Aadhaar identification database. See UIDAI, Aadhaar (dashboard), https://uidai.gov.in/.
d. The development of data strategy, policy, and regulations should be informed by a principles-based approach (Floridi and Taddeo 2016).
e. The African Union (AU), Economic Community of West African States (ECOWAS), East African Community (EAC), and Association of Southeast Asian Nations (ASEAN) are considering introducing mutual recognition of identification credentials across borders.
f. EC (2020); EU (2014).

Figure 8.2 Functions of data governance

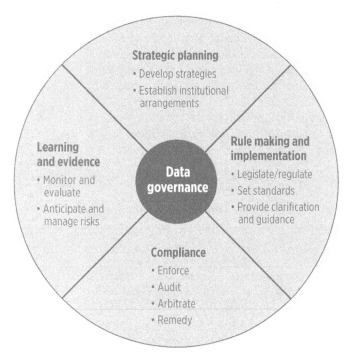

Source: WDR 2021 team.

take a broad view of data governance. Its functions are divided into four thematic clusters: strategic planning; rule making and implementation; compliance; and learning and evidence to provide insights and improve policy making (figure 8.2). Within each thematic cluster are several functions.[10] The next major section maps the governance functions described here to specific institutions and actors both inside and outside government.

Strategic planning

Developing strategies and establishing institutional arrangements. The overall objective of data institutions and governance frameworks is to safely realize greater social value from data. Finding the appropriate balance between encouraging greater use of data while maintaining safeguards against misuse is ultimately the role played by each country's social contract for data. Achieving this balance in practice requires that institutions and actors work together to transform the general principles[11] of the social contract into strategies, policies, and integrated data systems (chapter 9). This transformation must go beyond protecting personal data to include strategies for responsible and ethical data use (chapter 6). This step is particularly warranted because of the rapidly changing data landscape and incentives to collect vast amounts of data, creating opportunities for data

use and misuse (chapter 3). At the country level, the first step is to develop a national data strategy in line with the country's priorities (chapter 9). To facilitate implementation, strategies should be devolved into action plans with clear targets.[12] Strategies should also include identifying institutional arrangements and mapping governance functions to existing or new institutions.

Rule making and implementation

Legislating and regulating. Laws and regulations are the critical safeguards and enablers needed to standardize and organize data throughout the data life cycle. They stipulate how sharing, pooling, or granting of access will be carried out, including limits on certain uses of data to promote trust (see the detailed discussion in chapter 6). Rule-making functions include creating new public sector data governance institutions whose mandate, criteria for appointing managers, and funding arrangements are stipulated by regulation or decree.

Setting standards. Systems should be designed around recognized harmonized formats and protocols for data production, storage, transfer, access, protection, and security, thereby supporting interoperability, increasing data quality, and improving the usability and integrity of data.

Providing clarification and guidance. Institutions can reduce barriers to compliance with laws and regulations (say because of lack of information about obligations) by providing stakeholders with clear, practical, easily accessible, and user-friendly guidance.[13] The more complex the data and the actors involved, the greater may be the need to clarify and guide participants to ensure a shared understanding of how the data are governed.

Compliance

Enforcing. Enforcement is the day-to-day work of ensuring compliance with laws and regulations, standards, and norms.

Auditing. Enforcement is supplemented with regular and occasional audits to identify areas of noncompliance that may require remedies or improvements in the rules.

Arbitrating. When rules do not answer all the questions, arbitration may be helpful. For example, if there is doubt about whether the combination or association of certain data renders the data sensitive (such as by revealing religion), a decision may be required on whether the data processing falls within the scope of the data protection law.

Remedying. Faults in compliance require remedies to correct or compensate for any breaches or damage from the use of data. For example, if data have been obtained or manipulated without authority, thereby breaching data protection or security requirements, it may be necessary to notify the data subjects or cancel an identity credential.

Learning and evidence

Backward-looking monitoring and evaluation (M&E). M&E can serve at least two purposes. First, it can help supervisors track the performance of their own staff and organizations, allowing them to make better management decisions.[14] Second, M&E can assess how a program or policy delivers on identified objectives. Disseminating M&E frameworks and results in user-friendly formats can foster accountability and promote trust in data governance institutions.

Forward-looking learning and risk management. Complex areas of data governance can benefit from horizon scanning and scenario planning, as well as from anticipatory governance.[15] These tools and approaches can be used to identify and respond to emerging or unforeseen issues before they become acute societal challenges and to inform planning and policy-making activities. For example, the growing use of artificial intelligence (AI) and big data technologies in some sectors (such as the utilities market) or for emergency uses (such as contact tracing during the COVID-19 pandemic) may require policy makers to adapt existing data governance regimes before any misuse of that data occurs.

Innovation. Both M&E and risk management can be helpful in responding to the rapid technological changes reshaping the possibilities and risks in how data management systems are designed and used. In response to the rapidly changing environment, institutions can play an important role in facilitating timely assessments of what works in the newly evolving data environment and offer guidance on how to quickly adapt to change and promote knowledge sharing. Institutions can also play an important role in rolling out lessons and capacity building both within the nation and internationally. Once a new approach has been shown to succeed in one region, country, or locality, existing mechanisms should enable it to be tested in others, especially those with limited internal resources.

Mapping data governance functions to illustrative institutions

The governance functions described in the preceding section may be performed by *entities within government,* at the center of government, and at the technical level. They also may fall to sector-specific agencies, the judiciary, independent regulators and watchdogs, or subnational government bodies.[16]

These functions may be performed as well by *nongovernmental institutions,* including individual citizens; CSOs; NGOs; the private sector (such as industry associations and standard setting organizations); the news media; academic institutions, think tanks, or researchers; and bilateral and multilateral organizations.[17]

Nongovernmental institutions and actors play an important role in performing or informing data governance functions. Deliberation and consensus building between these actors promote trust and responsive policy making, thereby strengthening the social contract on data (see discussion later in this chapter). These processes have become more important over the last 20 years.[18] Nongovernmental institutions can also impose checks on governments in states with weak or limited formal institutions where elite capture may impede data governance and hinder outcomes in the public interest.[19]

Table 8.2 maps institutions and actors to the governance functions they typically perform, according to the most prominent function of each institution. This mapping does not imply that certain institutions do not also perform other functions that may fall in other thematic clusters. The institutions and actors discussed here are not meant to be prescriptive or exhaustive. Rather, they illustrate how these functions and processes can be performed in different contexts.

The institutional arrangements adopted should consider preferences about the data at issue, the existing structure of the public sector and society, technical capacity, and available technologies. Institutions that perform well in certain contexts may fail in others. As the 2002 *World Development Report* on building institutions for markets stated, "Much of the important work in building institutions lies in modifying those that already exist to complement better other institutions and in recognizing what not to build."[20]

Strategic planning institutions

Government entities. Many countries—especially higher-income countries—have taken a *centralized approach* by adopting a national data governance entity that provides strategic direction, makes policy decisions, and sets institutional arrangements. Countries either establish a separate data governance agency or opt for a dedicated data governance unit embedded in an existing institution. Fifty-three percent of high-income countries have a data governance entity in place, compared with only 18 percent of upper-middle-income

Table 8.2 Candidate institutions and actors to perform or inform data governance functions

Thematic clusters and functions	Indicative institutions and actors
Strategic planning • Developing strategies and policies in line with the social contract for data • Establishing institutional arrangements	*Data governance arrangement* • Centralized approach: data governance agency/unit embedded in an existing institution (such as NSO, digital economy ministry) • Decentralized approach: data governance units and responsibilities embedded across government • CSOs • Universities • Research institutions
Rule making and implementation • Legislating/regulating • Setting standards • Providing clarification and guidance	*National legislature and sector-specific regulators* • Telecom regulator • Banking and financial securities market regulator • Industry associations • CSOs • Institutional Review Boards *International institutions* • Sector-specific SSOs • International organizations (World Bank, IMF, UN, WTO)
Compliance • Enforcing • Auditing • Arbitrating • Remedying	*Watchdog and umpire* • Data protection authority • Access to information agency • Antitrust authority • Consumer protection agency • Audit body • Courts • Ombudsperson • CSIRT
Learning and evidence • Engaging in backward-looking monitoring and evaluation • Engaging in forward-looking learning and risk management	*Knowledge community* • M&E unit within entity or independent M&E body • CSOs and NGOs, multilateral development institutions, international development banks • Academic institutions • Think tanks, policy institutes, research institutions • News media • Training bodies • Professional associations

Source: WDR 2021 team, based on a functional approach to governance and public sector management.

Note: CSIRT = Computer Security Incident Response Team; CSO = civil society organization; IMF = International Monetary Fund; M&E = monitoring and evaluation; NGO = nongovernmental organization; NSO = national statistical office; SSO = standard setting organization; UN = United Nations; WTO = World Trade Organization.

countries and 10 percent of lower-middle-income countries (figure 8.3, panel a).[21] To date, no low-income country has established a data governance entity. For the most part, countries that do not have a data governance entity also do not have a stand-alone national data strategy in place. Only 3 percent of low-income countries have such a strategy, compared with 6 percent of lower-middle-income countries, 18 percent of upper-middle-income countries, and 52 percent of high-income countries (see chapter 9 for a discussion

of development of a national data system in support of a national data strategy).[22]

Lower-middle-income countries and upper-middle-income countries are more likely to embed the strategic planning function in an existing government institution (figure 8.3, panel b). One reason for doing so is that creating stand-alone institutions can be costly and inefficient, requiring sufficient resources and technical capacities to be productive.[23] Embedding new functions in existing institutions

Figure 8.3 No low-income and few lower-middle-income countries have a separate data governance entity; most embed them in another government institution

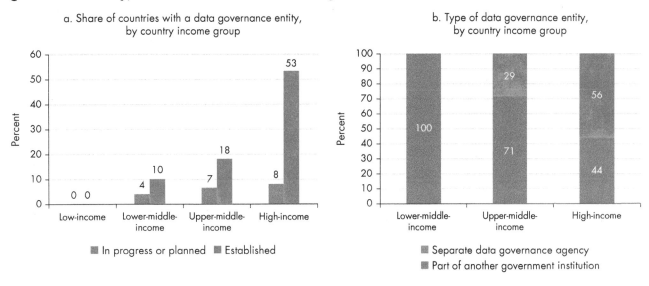

a. Share of countries with a data governance entity, by country income group

b. Type of data governance entity, by country income group

In progress or planned ■ Established

Separate data governance agency
Part of another government institution

Source: WDR 2021 team calculations, based on World Bank, DGSS (Digital Government/GovTech Systems and Services) (dataset), https://datacatalog.world bank.org/dataset/digital-governmentgovtech-systems-and-services-dgss-dataset. Data at http://bit.do/WDR2021-Fig-8_3.

Note: Panel a: data are for 198 economies. Data governance entities include both separate agencies and units that are part of another institution. Panel b: data are for 58 countries. Data are only for countries that have a data governance entity established or in process. Low-income countries are not included in the figure because none has a data governance entity.

or creating an interinstitutional body such as a data governance council may give governments greater flexibility in the early stages of establishing a data governance framework. This approach also enables governments to draw on expertise from relevant institutions and, by incorporating more stakeholders in the process, to increase the inclusivity of strategy setting and policy design.

In Jordan, the strategic planning function is assigned to an existing government institution. The Policies and Strategies Directorate of the Ministry of Digital Economy and Entrepreneurship (former Ministry of Information and Communications Technology) is responsible for developing relevant strategies and policies. The directorate has drafted the country's Digital Transformation Strategy for Government Services (2019–22), as well as technical policies related to various elements of data governance, including the government's policies on data classification and cybersecurity. Similarly, the government of Thailand assigned the strategic planning function to previously existing agencies by fully replacing its Ministry of Information and Communication Technology with the Ministry of Digital Economy and Society in 2016. Several agencies responsible for cross-cutting data and digital technology functions were consolidated under this new centralized structure.[24]

Brazil is one of the few upper-middle-income countries with a separate data governance entity. Established in 2019, the Central Data Governance Committee is tasked with steering Brazil's transition to a data-driven public sector by promoting data sharing among federal agencies and integrating citizens' information in a single platform (the Citizen Base Register).[25] The committee was created as a separate entity by presidential decree to ensure high-level collaboration and coordination of data governance activities.

Other countries have followed a more *decentralized approach*, whereby a network of ministries, departments, and agencies share responsibilities for implementing data governance functions. For example, national statistical offices (NSOs) often serve as the focal point for development of National Strategies for the Development of Statistics (NSDSs), a component of a country's data strategies (see chapters 2 and 9).[26]

The entity responsible for strategic planning must be placed at the highest level in government, where it can exercise the appropriate leverage. In some countries, this location is at the center of government, such as the Prime Minister's Office or President's Office, in coordination with the NSO.

Nongovernmental institutions. Institutions outside of government, including *civil society actors, academic institutions, think tanks, and nongovernmental research institutions,* also play a key role in developing strategies and policies.[27] Some initiatives are almost entirely driven by civil society, such as in the open data space. For example, nongovernmental actors established the Open Definition in 2012, standards for open data licensing in 2013, and the Open Data Charter in 2015.[28] Civil society actors can also add value by advising on how strategies and policies can build on and be responsive to local dynamics and address problems in a manner suited to the local context.

Strategic planning functions may also be performed by international or regional organizations. In 2018 the Association of Southeast Asian Nations (ASEAN) adopted the ASEAN Framework on Digital Data Governance, which guides members seeking to strengthen and coordinate their policy and regulatory regimes and institutional arrangements for data governance and to achieve interoperable data governance systems. The framework is aimed at bolstering the region's digital economy and enhancing cross-border data flows in a manner consistent with the data regulatory thresholds of partners. Similarly, the African Union's Digital Transformation Strategy for Africa (2020–30) is aimed at increasing data interoperability (to spur greater use of data and transform the digital economy) and improving standards for data protection.[29]

Rule making, standard setting, and implementing institutions

Rule making and implementation functions are performed across the three branches of government. *National legislatures* typically make laws, while executive bodies develop implementing regulations. Enforcement of legal frameworks is undertaken by independent regulators (such as data protection authorities) and the judiciary. Nongovernmental actors could support enforcement by means of monitoring, advocacy, advice, and legal aid. In addition, *sector-specific regulators*—such as telecommunications, banking, and financial securities market regulators— could support sectoral rule making. For example, a banking sector regulator could require banks to submit credit information to credit reference bureaus, which, in turn, could increase access to finance for those who may not be able to obtain bank credit in the absence of credit reference bureaus.[30] Similarly, securities markets regulators could compel listed companies to disclose financial data to assist investors in their decision-making and thus improve the allocation of resources across the economy (see chapter 6).

Sector-specific standard setting organizations, such as the Extractive Industries Transparency Initiative (EITI), the Open Government Partnership (OGP), and the United Nations' International Telecommunication Union (ITU), establish common sets of principles, rules, and procedures that help support interoperability and portability of data within a sector. Transaction costs then fall and the prospects rise for productive data flows between data suppliers, data intermediaries, and data users.

Private sector industry participants also have an important role to play in setting standards because they can facilitate market access, increase efficiency, reduce costs, and manage labor and environmental standards to achieve responsible productivity.[31] Although private standards are voluntary, they may become de facto industry norms if they are widely adopted. They can be especially appropriate when informed by public sentiments; industry actors may be moved by pressure related to ethical behavior, fair labor practices, their environmental footprint, and more. Voluntary industry standards can also potentially avoid the rigid qualities of government standard setting.[32] For example, *industry associations* develop standards and provide guidance at the industry level. The foremost example is the International Organization for Standardization (ISO),[33] an independent global organization with a membership of 165 national standards bodies composed of domain experts who develop market relevant standards based on an international consensus. On the other hand, market asymmetries may lead to a lack of inclusivity in the development of standards, with dominant companies having a first-mover advantage to determine industry specifications (see chapter 6).

Institutional Review Boards (IRBs) monitor research involving human subjects, including impact evaluations and other M&E efforts. They have the power to approve, require modifications in (to secure approval), or disapprove research. IRBs are mostly found in high-income countries and are not yet a critical data governance institution in low-income countries. Yet their reviews have an important role in ensuring responsible data use in research and protecting the rights and welfare of human research subjects, including those from low- and middle-income countries.

International organizations, academic institutions, and CSOs can also help transform the principles of the social contract into actionable guidelines for ethical data use. For example, they can help data science professionals and practitioners create ethical codes of conduct that are specific to their organization or stakeholder community. In 2017 the United Nations Sustainable Development Group—a consortium of 36 United Nations (UN) agencies, departments, and programs—convened to develop a set of ethical guiding principles to protect data privacy and to use big data in development and humanitarian contexts.[34] Likewise, the NGO DataEthics.eu, a collaborative effort across academia and civil society, has developed a series of data ethics principles designed using a European legal and value-based framework for voluntary adaptation and use by European Union (EU) data providers, data intermediaries, and data users.

Institutions that enforce compliance

Compliance can be enforced internally—that is, by parties governed or affected by the rules at issue—or externally by a third party. It can also be enforced informally[35] through peer pressure or shaming or formally through official investigations, rulings, and sanctions.

Informal institutional arrangements rely on commitment-based and opt-in approaches whereby parties are not obliged to undertake specific actions. For example, the United Nations Fundamental Principles of Official Statistics guide national statistical systems that self-govern according to these principles.[36]

Institutions with internal enforcement mechanisms can be effective because they typically feature a recognized system of incentives and penalties to encourage desired behaviors. For example, EITI and OGP have sanctioned or expelled member countries when it was determined that these countries did not adhere to articulated standards.[37] Both institutions sanctioned Azerbaijan (EITI in 2015 and OGP in 2016), and EITI delisted Equatorial Guinea and São Tomé and Príncipe in 2010 for insufficient progress against agreed-on deadlines. In the latter two countries, this delisting catalyzed the expected action.[38]

Public pressure can also be brought to bear by NGOs that assess the quality of data governance and monitor compliance with standards through public indexes or scorecards. An example is the Global Data Barometer, which assesses the quality and scope of countries' data governance, availability of key datasets, and capacity for responsible data use.[39]

Transnational institutional arrangements have a formal constitutional setup, such as Articles of Agreement, that obliges members to abide by specific standards or rules. They typically stipulate internal compliance requirements and articulate what sanctions apply to noncompliance. Censure is a typical enforcement mechanism. An example of a transnational institution is the International Monetary Fund (IMF). In 2011 it found Argentina to be in breach of its obligations under the IMF's Articles of Agreement because it was providing inaccurate consumer price

index and gross domestic product data. After reforms by Argentina's NSO to address the methodological and data quality issues in question, the IMF lifted the censure on the country in 2016.

At the national level, *data protection authorities (DPAs)* oversee and enforce compliance with data protection legislation by investigating data breaches and issuing monetary penalties, enforcement notices, or other punitive measures when an organization is found to have breached its data processing obligations.[40]

Some DPAs have adopted a more principle-based approach to compliance by encouraging data processing organizations to embed accountability practices into their operations. For example, Singapore's data protection commission, Infocomm Media Development Authority (IMDA), has adopted an enforcement framework that rewards good accountability practices such as adopting data protection by design and encouraging the use of data protection impact assessments through capacity building, change management, and organizational restructuring.[41] This approach can be helpful in instances in which existing data protection laws do not yet require such practices, in parallel to strengthening the legal framework. Other DPAs, such as the French National Commission for Informatics and Liberties (CNIL), provide incentives for compliance by developing certification schemes for data protection officers in order to standardize competencies within this compliance role.[42]

The presence of a DPA increases with country income level (figure 8.4). Although 81 percent of high-income countries have a DPA, only 45 percent of upper-middle-income countries, 38 percent of lower-middle-income countries, and 24 percent of low-income countries have such an authority.

In certain contexts, an existing institution, such as an *access to information agency* or related *ICT agency*, may be tasked with compliance responsibilities. For example, Argentina's DPA falls under the country's Agency of Access to Public Information—a 2018 presidential decree modified the then-newly adopted Access to Information Law.

An *antitrust authority* may find certain data practices anticompetitive (see chapter 7). It may break up an existing organization or its datasets when the organization has accumulated levels of control that give it an unacceptable level of market power. For example, a decision by Germany's Federal Cartel Office (Bundeskartellamt) prevented efforts by Facebook to combine data from Facebook, Instagram, and programming interfaces integrated into websites producing social plug-ins.[43] Antitrust authorities are

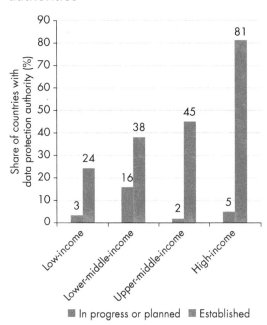

Figure 8.4 The lower the country income level, the fewer are the countries with data protection authorities

Share of countries with data protection authority (%)

	In progress or planned	Established
Low-income	3	24
Lower-middle-income	16	38
Upper-middle-income	2	45
High-income	5	81

■ In progress or planned   ■ Established

Source: WDR 2021 team calculations, based on World Bank, DGSS (Digital Government/GovTech Systems and Services) (dataset), https://datacatalog.worldbank.org/dataset/digital-governmentgovtech-systems-and-services-dgss-dataset. Data at http://bit.do/WDR2021-Fig-8_4.

Note: Data are for 198 economies.

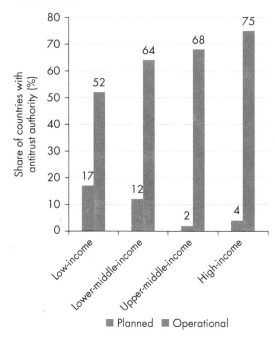

Figure 8.5 More than half of countries across all income groups have antitrust authorities

Share of countries with antitrust authority (%)

	Planned	Operational
Low-income	17	52
Lower-middle-income	12	64
Upper-middle-income	2	68
High-income	4	75

■ Planned   ■ Operational

Source: WDR 2021 team calculations, based on data from World Bank. Data at http://bit.do/WDR2021-Fig-8_5.

Note: Data are for 218 economies.

operational in more than half of countries across all income groups (figure 8.5).

Formal independent audits—or the possibility of one—can also be an effective mechanism to hold institutions to account and drive performance improvements. Audits are typically performed by an *audit body*, whether an independent Supreme Audit Institution, a committee (such as a parliamentary Public Accounts Committee), or a specialized subnational department (such as a city audit office).[44]

Likewise, *courts* provide a venue for independent redress and enforcement, and they can also facilitate informal settlement. A centralized or decentralized *ombudsperson* may be able to collect complaints and provide redress for grievances. In some countries, data protection legislation explicitly provides for grievance redress.[45] In countries with no such legislation or where existing legislation makes no such provision, service providers may set up specific grievance redress mechanisms to collect and address complaints internally.

Oversight is also needed to minimize risks to data platforms, data systems, and data per se. A *Computer*

Security Incident Response Team (CSIRT) is a designated team of information security experts. It protects data management architecture and detects and resolves any computer, network, or cybersecurity incidents, such as data breaches and denial of service attacks.[46] CSIRTs and related institutions are also typically responsible for running public awareness campaigns aimed at data intermediaries and users to help ensure adherence to data security protocols. Cybersecurity agencies are relatively widespread in middle- and high-income countries, but are present in only 24 percent of low-income countries (figure 8.6).[47]

Institutions that promote learning and evidence-based policy making

M&E functions, as well as anticipatory governance, can be embedded in dedicated units in ministries and agencies involved in data management and governance functions. Some countries may have a *national-level M&E agency*, such as the US Government Accountability Office (GAO), which is responsible for auditing and evaluating US federal government activities. Other countries may locate their *M&E unit within an executive office* responsible for tracking strategic key performance indicators.

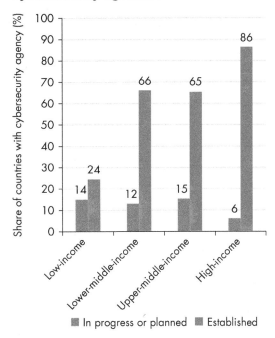

Figure 8.6 Only about one-quarter of low-income countries have cybersecurity agencies

Share of countries with cybersecurity agency (%)

In progress or planned   ■ Established

Source: WDR 2021 team calculations, based on World Bank, DGSS (Digital Government/GovTech Systems and Services) (dataset), https://datacatalóg.worldbank.org/dataset/digital-governmentgovtech-systems-and-services-dgss-dataset. Data at http://bit.do/WDR2021-Fig-8_6.

Note: Data are for 198 economies.

Outside of government, *CSOs, specialty NGOs, universities, think tanks, research organizations, the news media, and even individual citizens* play an important M&E role. Nongovernmental monitoring of issues of public concern can be useful in assessing government performance, as well as signaling accountability failures, such as corruption or inefficiencies or gaps in public service delivery. For example, during the COVID-19 pandemic Johns Hopkins University in the United States recognized and filled a gap by creating and launching a transparent, reliable data collection mechanism and dashboard for tracking virus cases globally. The mechanism was then used by policy makers and the public worldwide to better understand the spread of the virus and come up with ways to combat it. Such nongovernmental, independent actors can provide convenient and consistent access to accurate data and reduce data governance and management inefficiencies, while offering a host of actionable perspectives and advice. For example, the Data Governance Network is India's first policy-oriented research network on data governance, bringing together several leading think tanks. It was founded to inform

policy making.[48] In 2017 the UK's British Academy and Royal Society published a series of reports entitled "Data Management and Use: Governance in the 21st Century," based on consultations with stakeholders from civil society, the private sector, and academia.[49] Nongovernmental institutions can also help generate learning and evidence on potential opportunities and harms when developing social contracts on data in different contexts. Some institutions are devoted to understanding the ethical implications of new methodologies and uses of data.[50] Others focus on sharing knowledge and acting as a catalyst for learning.[51]

To undertake learning and evidence activities, government institutions and other actors must rely on a workforce with the appropriate skills, which requires, in turn, more *public or private institutions specializing in skills development and certification* (see chapter 4). This need grows more pressing as data governance and management become increasingly sophisticated and the number and range of technicians and skills required increase.

Data intermediation and collaboration

Another way to enable better data use, reuse, and sharing is through data intermediation. An entity (data intermediary) or simply a contractual arrangement facilitates the collection, validation, and aggregation of data from data contributors and makes data understandable, usable, and accessible to data users.[52] Data intermediaries can facilitate data sharing in a trusted, more efficient manner between government institutions or between government and nongovernment actors as part of the broader national data system (table 8.3).

Data intermediaries (sometimes called infomediaries) can be important enablers in low- and middle-income economies that may have gaps in their data management frameworks or weak enforcement. Where the potential of otherwise siloed data would remain unrealized,[53] they can mediate data flows between data producers and individuals or communities for research and evidence-based policy making,[54] or they can provide public sector institutions with feedback.[55] Grassroots-based data intermediaries could also help individuals better understand and enforce their rights over their personal data. Other intermediaries create commercial opportunities through data markets.

Data intermediation in the private sector. Exclusively commercial, for-profit data intermediaries are relatively commonplace, functioning primarily as data

Table 8.3 Snapshot of common data intermediary structures

Purposes	Objectives	Types	Examples
Create commercial value and data markets.	Transform raw data into more consumable information.	Data aggregators, data brokers	Acxiom, Experian
Exchange data to solve public problems through collaborative structures.	Increase incentives for competitors to share and combine data resources for common use within sectors.	Data pools	Global Data Synchronization Network (GDSN)
	Create and manage shared and interoperable data assets and computing infrastructure for research.	Data commons, data clubs	The Open Commons Consortium (OCC), UK Biobank
	Contribute data in exchange for collective benefits.	Data cooperatives	LunaDNA (community-owned platform for health research)
Enable trusted sharing and use of sensitive data through enhanced accountability mechanisms.	Facilitate sharing of sensitive data and provide collective bargaining power to individuals.	Data trusts	Platform Info Exchange, UK (Mozilla Data Futures Lab pilot)

Source: WDR 2021 team.

aggregators. These intermediaries collect raw, disaggregated data that are difficult to work with, systematize and sometimes analyze them, and then repackage them for sale to others. Many commercially driven data aggregators are familiar features of society, including credit reference bureaus. More broadly, data brokers scrape public records and buy or license private data to build profiles of individuals that can be sold for a profit—often for marketing purposes, risk mitigation (including for identification verification and fraud detection), and people search pages.[56] Some 4,000 data brokers operate worldwide in an industry valued at US$250 billion.[57]

Data markets are passive digital platforms through which data owners can offer their datasets for sale. When structured well, data markets can enable crowdsourcing of data (including from data subjects), support interoperability, create a central point of discoverability, and enforce minimum data quality standards.[58] Rising concerns about the use (and abuse) of personal data by profit-driven data intermediaries—particularly given the rise in locational data and the ultimate anonymity of data, as well as data subjects' lack of control—have increased public scrutiny and led to new rules on their operations (box 8.3).

Data intermediation for public or common goods. New types of intermediaries oriented toward public or common goods are emerging. Data collaboratives facilitate and promote data sharing between diverse actors by ensuring compliance with minimum data protection and security rules, as well as quality standards and rules to make data interoperable.

Data collaboratives can involve a diverse array of actors—such as government institutions, private companies, research institutions, or CSOs—that come together to exchange data with a view toward solving public problems.[59] Data sharing arrangements[60] could, but need not, involve the creation of a separate entity tasked with managing data, including ensuring safe and ethical usage.

Some data collaboratives function primarily to increase participants' access to data in order to solve collective action issues and use insights from analyzing aggregated, nonrivalrous data. *Data pools* are usually contract-based mechanisms in the private sector that create a centralized repository of data. Participants can obtain, maintain, and exchange information in a standard format.[61] The Global Data Synchronization Network (GDSN),[62] an internet-based, interconnected network of interoperable data pools, facilitates product-related data sharing across companies in sectors such as retail, health care, and transport and logistics. In the private sector, data pools create unique opportunities for market insight, gains in efficiency, and innovation because of their tailored analytical function, although they also present competition risks (see chapters 6 and 7).[63] In the public sector, data pools can be used to safeguard centralized data stores. Mauritius has built trusted digital data repositories using unique digital identities, federated authentication, and a set of key digital services that can be embedded in wider public or private sector applications when data sharing is required.[64]

Data commons and data clubs, broadly inspired by data pools, may help entities or people create, curate, maintain, and analyze shared data assets to create an evolving, interoperable resource for the research

Box 8.3 Increased scrutiny of and constraints on private data intermediaries

Although for-profit data intermediaries have historically operated with little public awareness of their practices or even existence, society's growing unease with the private collection and sale of personal data, often without the consent of data subjects, has led to greater regulatory scrutiny in recent years.[a] The vast amount of locational data being collected by companies via smartphone apps and then repackaged for sale to advertisers, financial institutions, geospatial analysis companies, and real estate investment firms, among many others, raises additional concerns about the ultimate anonymity of data.[b] Locational data become especially valuable when they are combined with a mobile advertising ID, which allows advertisers and other businesses to integrate activity across apps.

The United States issued a high-level government report in 2014 recommending federal legislation that would subject data brokers to heightened governance rules around data security, transparency, and the degree of control held by data subjects.[c] Although no federal legislation has been passed, the state governments of California and Vermont have adopted laws requiring data brokers that collect and sell information about the residents of these states to register annually with the state government. Neither state has gone so far as to give data subjects the right to opt out of data collection and trading (although the Vermont law does require detailed disclosure of such procedures), nor has either required data brokers to disclose what data they collect

and to whom they are selling data.[d] Both states require data brokers to abide by certain minimum data security standards.

In Europe, Privacy International, a European civil society organization (CSO), filed complaints in 2018 with the data protection agencies of France, Ireland, and the United Kingdom alleging that seven data brokers, credit bureaus, and ad-tech companies were violating individuals' privacy rights under the European Union's General Data Protection Regulation (GDPR).[e] The complaints claim that the companies in question build intricate, potentially inaccurate profiles of peoples' lives based in part on derived, inferred, and predicted data used as personal data, inconsistent with protections provided under the GDPR's Data Protection Principles. CSOs and governments are likely to increase their scrutiny with the spread of data broker activity, particularly if governments are perceived as failing to respond to citizens' concerns through stronger regulation and enforcement.

a. Ram and Murgia (2019).
b. Thompson and Warzel (2019).
c. FTC (2014).
d. For California, see Assembly Bill No. 1202, An Act to Add Title 1.81.48 (Commencing with Section 1798.99.80) to Part 4 of Division 3 of the Civil Code, Relating to Privacy (*Legislative Counsel's Digest*, October 14, 2019). See also Attorney General's Office, California Department of Justice, "Data Broker Registry," Sacramento, https://oag.ca.gov/data-brokers. For Vermont, see Vermont Office of the Attorney General (2018). See also Vermont Secretary of State, "Data Brokers," Montpelier, https://sos .vermont.gov/corporations/other-services/data-brokers/.
e. PI (2018).

community.[65] The Open Commons Consortium (OCC), a US nonprofit, operates data commons and cloud computing infrastructure to support research related to scientific, environmental, medical, and health care issues.[66] Since 2009, the OCC has managed the Open Science Data Cloud (OSDC), a membership-based, multipetabyte science cloud that colocates scientific data with cloud-based computing, high-performance data transport services, and common analytical tools. UK Biobank aggregates the health data of more than 500,000 individuals from the United Kingdom and makes it available to any "bona fide researcher" in the world.[67] Making public intent data available in a similar manner across government, and between government and the private sector and civil society, can promote evaluation and learning activities around

existing public policy and service delivery, especially where the technical capacity to run the required statistical analyses is lacking.

Somewhat similarly, *data cooperatives* usually involve individuals who choose to contribute their personal data (while retaining ownership) in exchange for collective social and personal benefits, such as research using larger common data that would otherwise be siloed or inaccessible.[68] The objectives are generally nonmonetary. For example, patients with specific health conditions might contribute their health records to a cooperative that makes them available for medical research. LunaDNA is a community-owned platform for health research that anyone can join, share their health data, and in exchange receive ownership shares in the organization.[69]

Data intermediaries with built-in accountability mechanisms can facilitate sharing of sensitive data, including between the public and private sectors.[70] The role of these intermediaries can be played by individuals or legal structures that are positioned between data contributors and users and provide independent third-party stewardship of data.[71] In the context of public-private partnerships, they may be more effective if they are located outside government. But they can also be governed by public institutions tasked with safeguarding and facilitating data sharing across government. For example, India's 2020 "Report by the Committee of Experts on Non-Personal Data Governance Framework" identifies the Ministry of Health and Family Welfare as the appropriate trustee for data on diabetes among Indian citizens.[72]

Certain forms of these intermediaries are emerging in some jurisdictions, to support the protection of transactions involving personal data. In India, pursuant to draft legislation similar to the European Union's General Data Protection Regulation, third-party consent managers ensure that individuals are consenting to every instance of data sharing rather than "preauthorizing" data processing and sharing at the point of collection. The Reserve Bank of India has already introduced these standards across the entire financial sector. A data trust, a unique type of accountability-based data intermediary, is based on the legal structure of a "trust," and as such imposes a fiduciary duty on trustees.[73] Trustees are legally required to steward data with impartiality, prudence, transparency, and undivided loyalty toward the trust's beneficiaries, and in accordance with the trust's internal rules of governance.[74] Depending on the context, additional rules governing data access and use, as well as internal liability mechanisms for data breaches or misuse, can be tailored accordingly through contractual agreement. One of the alleged benefits of data trusts is that they offer individuals and groups a means of restoring "bottom-up" control over personal data: individuals can pool the legal rights they have over their personal data within the framework of the trust and negotiate with larger data "controllers" from there.[75]

Data trusts may be particularly useful in managing personal health data in the context of COVID-19 contact tracing in which deidentified data on test results can be shared (with data protection safeguards) and used to alert other individuals if they are at risk of infection.[76] Data trusts can also support the responsible collection and reuse of sensitive health data to support academic research or public health monitoring. Data trusts are still largely theoretical constructs.

However, examples are beginning to be piloted,[77] given growing interest in such mechanisms to promote accountability and rebalance collective bargaining powers between data providers and users. In countries with an enabling legal system, data trusts can create unique opportunities in low-capacity contexts, and especially in countries with weak data protection legislation and enforcement. Certain countries and organizations have taken a broader definition of data trusts (which creates an accountability role without necessarily imposing a strict fiduciary duty) to pilot their effectiveness in practice. Such structures have been explored for use in the fight against illegal wildlife poaching in lower-middle-income countries by the UK government. WILDLABS is a community working to discover and implement technology-enabled solutions to conservation challenges, and the Open Data Institute (ODI), a London-based nonprofit organization, is creating more open and trustworthy data ecosystems. These arrangements are a low-cost, secure means for the conservation community to collect and share data, while overcoming shortcomings in local laws and enforcement, as well as limited resources.[78] Data trusts or other contractual data sharing structures can also facilitate cross-border data transfers, especially where international data sharing agreements do not exist. The Microsoft Intelligent Network for Eyecare (MINE), a collaboration between Microsoft India and India's L V Prasad Eye Institute, facilitates the transfer of patient data from a diverse range of countries to the United States, where participating research institutes then use advanced analytics and machine learning to inform the development of strategies to prevent avoidable blindness and scale delivery of eye care services worldwide.[79]

Making data governance institutions effective

No matter the country context, institutions can only carry out their roles effectively if their staff are capable of and willing to use good data to undertake their core operations, inform policies, and deliver services (figure 8.7). Countries that have made great strides in improving data governance implementation across the whole of government have typically benefited from the leadership of a strong political champion of the importance of data.

Increasing technical capacity, resources, and data literacy for civil servants

The cognitive challenges posed by data are unlike those of most other commodities in terms of

Figure 8.7 Features of well-functioning institutions for effective data governance

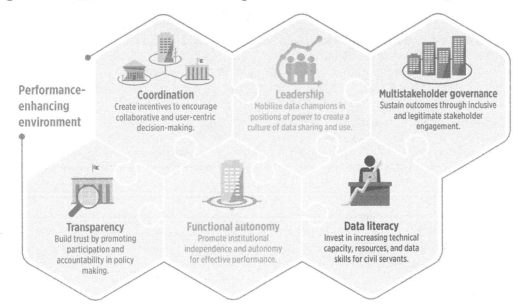

Performance-enhancing environment

Coordination
Create incentives to encourage collaborative and user-centric decision-making.

Leadership
Mobilize data champions in positions of power to create a culture of data sharing and use.

Multistakeholder governance
Sustain outcomes through inclusive and legitimate stakeholder engagement.

Transparency
Build trust by promoting participation and accountability in policy making.

Functional autonomy
Promote institutional independence and autonomy for effective performance.

Data literacy
Invest in increasing technical capacity, resources, and data skills for civil servants.

Source: WDR 2021 team.

understanding the scale and complexities of (potential) use. Governing data thus requires a strong technical capacity and investments in human capital development for those who collect, process, analyze, and use data to support evidence-based policy making, core government operations, and service delivery.[80] Investing in technical capacity is also essential when regulating data-driven businesses (see chapter 7). The public sector will need resources to meet the increasing demand for data analytics and information technology (IT) skills (see chapters 4 and 5), especially with the shift to digital government.

Data literacy, which refers to an individual's capacity to "read, work with, analyze, and argue with data," is particularly weak in government institutions in low- and middle-income countries.[81] Skilled staff may be concentrated in ministries of finance or planning, as well as in entities responsible for the production and quality of statistics, such as NSOs. Strict salary scales and wage caps within most public sector entities affect their ability to compete with the private sector in recruiting specialized staff.

Building data literacy requires investing in training to develop a range of technical competencies in data collection, management, and interpretation across the data life cycle, including data protection and security.[82] Training also should empower civil servants to examine data for inaccuracy and bias and to contextualize data, including through effective visualization and communication techniques.[83] These tasks require cooperation between data specialists (such as data officers and IT staff) and technical staff in sectoral or cross-cutting entities.

Public sector training institutions may have the requisite organizational role and resources to support the development of specialized training courses.[84] Where local resources are lacking, or to further bolster domestic capacity, international nonprofit institutions could provide up-to-date, standardized training programs in collaboration with entities that traditionally train civil servants. These programs could be specific to certain areas or sectors, such as the multijurisdictional training and certification on data protection of the International Association of Privacy Professionals (IAPP) or the Open Data Institute's training to support open government data. Other organizations provide more tailored training to meet user needs, such as that by the GovLab Academy[85] or Apolitical.[86] Certification schemes can help support compliance by harmonizing training requirements.

Institutions should also ensure that human resources and staffing needs are planned for and managed through national capabilities plans or other instruments. Institutional mandates and staff terms of reference should be redefined to incorporate data governance functions and prescribe standardized guidelines for handling data properly.

Chapter 9 discusses how, beyond the public sector, governments should invest in programs to build data literacy within the broader population to reduce the digital divide and empower people to use data to improve their lives.

Creating a culture of performance that supports a data-driven public sector

Even when institutions have the necessary technical infrastructure and de jure frameworks, shifting policy makers away from traditional and often siloed decision-making toward data-driven and coordinated policy design and implementation depends on creating the right incentives. These incentives are a combination of institutional management practices and cultural norms that are especially relevant to low- and middle-income countries, where reform efforts are often stymied by "implementation gaps" resulting from behavioral and political economy constraints. Research conducted in Ghana finds that innovation in public agencies with fixed hierarchies may partly constrain innovation by impeding the acceptance of ideas from subordinate civil servants.[87] At the organizational level, institutional fragmentation, the large transaction costs of information sharing, and budgetary allocations can create incentives to restrict access to data or keep data siloed.[88]

Investments in change management and other techniques are essential to increasing the buy-in to and impact of data governance reforms.[89] These tools should be deployed within a strategy of change management that is adapted to the organizational culture of an institution[90] and broader political economy considerations.[91]

Mobilizing "data smart" political champions who view data as foundational. Strong political champions or a political culture that appreciates and understands the value of data are critical to ensuring the effectiveness of change management reforms. Countries at the forefront of leveraging greater value from data through better data governance frequently have strong advocates of the value of data in positions of power. Estonia, with its decades-long history of leadership by data advocates, has invested in improving the data science skills of the general public.[92] As a result, it is the first country to allow online voting in its general elections, and essentially all public services are available online.

Adopting a collaborative leadership approach to decision-making. Collaborative leadership is a central feature of effective change management. Leaders seek a diversity of opinions and ideas among teammates in building strategies and solving problems.[93] Governments can benefit from collaborating with the relevant entities across the public sector and with nongovernmental stakeholders such as civil society and private sector organizations to identify challenges and prioritize key drivers of change.[94] In Tunisia, the government's decision to adopt a collaborative leadership approach to drafting its latest open data decree was an important shift from its previously unsuccessful efforts that had resulted in siloed and fragmented initiatives and limited results. By convening more than 50 officials from across the Tunisian public administration and several CSOs, the government was able to gather diverse views on the best-fit options to include in the decree.[95] This collaborative process was led by a unit in the Prime Minister's Office, thereby endowing the effort with high-level support and ownership.[96]

Deploying effective communication and dissemination strategies to increase actual and perceived transparency and promote trust in the process. In environments characterized by low levels of trust, effective collaboration may have to begin by addressing underlying conflicts. Such a process can generate creative solutions and important trade-offs.[97] Perceived increases in transparency and accountability, including diverse representation in stakeholder groups, are key to fostering trust.[98] Communication is also essential to support enforcement of rules in novel situations. For example, during the COVID-19 pandemic guidance from the European Commission and the European Data Protection Board[99] helped national data protection authorities, governments, businesses, and civil society stakeholders understand how to build interoperable data sharing efforts and technologies (such as privacy-preserving contact tracing applications) for health monitoring and policy making while complying with the GDPR.[100]

Creating incentives and reward mechanisms that encourage innovation and coordinated decision-making in the public sector.[101] Salaries and bonuses can be effective incentives or rewards, but in low-capacity environments where funds are restricted, awarding prizes or other monetary incentives can incentivize collaboration and performance in the public sector.[102] In Morocco, since 2015 the Ministry of Economy, Finance and Administrative Reform has awarded the annual e-mtiaz prize to support competition between public sector entities and service providers in adopting innovative tools and services that improve the quality of public service delivery through e-administration, including the development and use of e-services.[103]

A data-driven culture can also be supported through "hackathon" initiatives and competitions in which data users are encouraged to collaborate for a short period of time on a project. In 2019 the Tunisian Court of Accounts organized a "Hack 4 Transparency" event to support objectives that included collecting, processing, exchanging, mining, and analyzing public financial data; improving communication with external stakeholders; and improving transparency, accountability, and participation in the use of public funds. The winners of the five regional hackathons and the subsequent national final received cash prizes offered by the private sector.[104]

Promoting institutional independence and autonomy for better performance

De facto autonomy—defined as the actual scope of independent decision-making powers and influence over (and protection from) other institutions in the governance system[105]—is critical to institutional performance and successful implementation of policies or legal frameworks.

Within institutions, performance depends on staff having sufficient autonomy to make informed, innovative decisions.[106] Independence may also be important to ensure the integrity of the data processed by an institution. Identification agencies that process personal data, including potentially sensitive data, about the population and the various services and benefits they receive should be able to resist undue access to this data by those who might misuse it. Similarly, NSOs that produce reliable, objective data for public policy making and administration must not be swayed by political interests that may wish to downplay, distort, or conceal inconvenient statistics. Beyond incentivizing performance, institutional independence and autonomy can strengthen accountability mechanisms in the data ecosystem. Performance reporting and audits are more trustworthy when they are conducted by impartial institutions.

An institution may operate with significant de facto (actual) independence regardless of its de jure (formal) status.[107] Nonetheless, public sector institutions often require de jure independence so they can undertake the activities falling within their mandate. The need for institutional independence is critical when both government and nongovernment entities are regulated within the same framework and competitive neutrality is required. It is also critical when decisions can have a significant impact on interests and actual and perceived impartiality in the execution of governance functions is needed.[108] Entities playing a rule-making or compliance function, such as DPAs, regulators, audit institutions, and courts or independent ombudspersons, need to be formally independent in order to effectively oversee compliance of other entities and to provide an impartial venue for redress and remedy.

Formal independence has legal, financial, and administrative dimensions. Legislation can define roles and responsibilities and establish formal protections. It may be necessary to establish a legally autonomous institution with formally delegated authority, especially for regulators, oversight institutions, and NSOs.[109]

Financial independence relies on institutional funding free from day-to-day political or private influence. Such independence can be supported by putting in place the appropriate procedures for proposing and approving budgets. In Ethiopia, the Philippines, and Rwanda, NSOs are authorized to formulate their own budgets flexibly, based on the demands made on them through national development plans and other routine activities in the statistical system, such as periodic censuses. Providing funding on a multiyear basis rather than every year can increase stability and protect institutions from short-term political change. Institutions may also be able to raise funds directly through licensing fees, enforcement penalties, and administrative charges.[110]

Administratively, key positions may be politicized by the executive or be vulnerable to state capture and corruption. Independence may be enhanced by establishing precise, transparent criteria for selecting and appointing qualified leaders. Candidates should be required to disclose conflicts of interest.[111]

Achieving better coordination across institutions for better data governance

Coordinating for better data governance. Coordination across institutions helps prevent siloed or uneven application of data governance functions based on opportunities and capacity. Coordination can ensure that data governance processes, such as technical standards, rules and means of audit, remedies in case of noncompliance, and M&E frameworks, are consistently applied and, where relevant, can identify emerging areas for action. Useful outputs could include guidance notes or technical manuals that provide detailed instructions on how to harmonize knowledge and implementation efforts across institutions.

Successful coordination depends at the outset on clearly allocating and delineating the roles and responsibilities of data governance institutions. Institutions or individuals tasked with coordination should then create robust processes to guide and govern their interactions and track their efficacy. Coordinating entities should also be sufficiently empowered by high-level leadership to effectively undertake this role. The structure and formality of coordination mechanisms will vary. Some countries have chosen to designate a central coordinating institution or individual located within the executive. In Albania, the Albanian National Agency for Information Society is under the direct supervision of the Prime Minister's Office. France has taken a similar vertical approach. The chief data officer (*administrateur général des données*) works directly under the authority of the prime minister. Centralizing coordination responsibilities and oversight in this way facilitates a strong hierarchy with direct supervision entities that review, revise, and approve plans and initiatives from subordinates and oversee their implementation.[112]

In other contexts, horizontal coordination mechanisms may involve networks of "peers" at the same functional or hierarchical level.[113] These types of coordination are often carried out by interagency committees or working groups. In the United States, 24 government agencies are required to designate an employee (civil servant) who is not a political appointee as their chief data officer. The officer is charged with convening and coordinating agency data governance and interagency coordination.[114] Chief data officers coordinate with one another through the Chief Data Officers Council. They also coordinate with other government councils that conduct data-related activities.[115]

Because of the cross-cutting nature of data governance and the scale of the challenge, stakeholders would benefit from a range of coordination mechanisms to leverage their relative strengths and reinforce one another. Centralized coordination can reduce transaction costs, compared with the more horizontal approaches to coordination, although consolidating too much power in a single entity can heighten the risk of mismanagement and abuse.

Coordinating for better data use. Ministries and government agencies collect, manage, and use data, whether in the form of tax returns, the outcomes of social or business programs, research, fuel consumption statistics, health data, immigration flows, geospatial maps, land management results, or crop inventories. However, data management platforms across ministries are often limited and lack unified interoperability standards, leading to duplication in data production and IT procurement. These issues may be compounded by a broader culture of rivalries and lack of collaboration within the public sector. As a result, data generated in the public sector may be consigned to data wastelands, captured in siloed repositories and platforms. Adherence to established norms and standards and efficient use of shared digital platforms to integrate and share data can improve government efficiency and public service delivery through administrative simplification and shared services.

Ensuring the transparency and accountability of public sector institutions

To encourage the transparency and accountability of data governance institutions, policy makers should offer opportunities for scrutiny and input. Public consultation and inputs on the design of policies and laws and regulations can support transparency and stakeholder engagement.[116] Institutions should be required to publish and review their objectives and performance indicators during regular planning cycles. Peer-to-peer scrutiny can be enhanced through formal processes or technical working groups, depending on the institutional culture and needs.[117]

In addition to regular review procedures, institutions could open their records and reports for review. In some cases, audit by independent third parties, including NGOs, using international standards and benchmarks with a view toward identifying areas of underperformance or noncompliance, may incentivize institutional accountability. The transparency of such processes is enhanced if the results of the audit are shared with the public through either publications or public hearings. Public knowledge and review of the performance of institutions are critical to building and maintaining confidence and trust in data governance institutions. Civil society's role in supporting trusted data use and reuse is also reflected in newer forms of community-led data governance and oversight mechanisms. For example, the UK's Connected Health Cities project in Manchester convenes a "citizens' jury" to hear expert evidence before approving an approach for the project.[118]

When institutions prioritize datasets for publication on an open data platform, stakeholder input in the process can ensure that priorities are based on user demand rather than on government preferences or judgment alone. Greater transparency and collaboration could increase the use of open data by nongovernmental actors, which, in turn, could increase research and advocacy opportunities, as well as innovation and private sector development.

Sustainable outcomes through inclusive multistakeholder governance

As the digital economy has expanded globally, an increasingly complex, geographically diverse group of stakeholders has become active in the data ecosystem. However, traditional concepts of governance based on national sovereignty or strict multilateralism do not take into account these dynamics. A multistakeholder approach to data governance is better equipped to govern the complex data ecosystem in a transparent, inclusive, and distributed way, which reflects the interests of all key stakeholders. This approach is aligned conceptually with the successful application of multistakeholder processes designed to govern the internet.[119] And it is an essential component of the "trust framework" that strengthens the social contract around data use. It will be especially important as data governance shifts toward international harmonization of policies, rules, and standards.

"Multistakeholderism" is an approach to data governance, not an end in itself. It is intended to facilitate better, more sustainable outcomes by enabling all stakeholders to undertake their roles in a coordinated manner.[120] These outcomes include ensuring more robust and flexible data governance frameworks that respond to the pace of technological change[121] and improving the transparency and legitimacy of and buy-in to the process (see box 8.4).[122] More broadly, this approach can contribute to achieving a more equitable distribution of the value of data, as well as protection from any harm arising from data misuse.[123] More equitable distribution emerges when traditionally excluded groups—including lower-middle-income countries, small and medium enterprises (SMEs), CSOs, and indigenous peoples—are able to participate and benefit from the technical expertise in these forums (see spotlight 8.2).

A continuum of multistakeholder arrangements.[124] Although some areas of data governance (such as setting standards for interoperability) may accommodate or even require a more deliberative, consensus-based approach dominated by technical experts, the development of policies and laws and regulations will inevitably involve some form of top-down, final decision-making by a government agency or a regulator (such as developing mechanisms to ensure data security, which may need to be centralized).[125] In such cases, nongovernmental actors may play more of a nonbinding consultative role, providing inputs in the policy-making or rule-making process.[126] These actors will have an important role to play in developing "soft law" mechanisms (chapter 6), research, training, and advocacy.

Leading successful examples of multistakeholder initiatives that develop technical standards for internet (and increasingly data) governance include the World Wide Web Consortium (W3C) and Internet Corporation for Assigned Names and Numbers

(ICANN). Although they differ in structure, both organizations are constituent-driven, developing their governance processes and outputs using a bottom-up, participative approach. Meaningful participation of civil society and other nongovernmental groups is assured through their inclusion in formal decision-making structures.[127]

Like stakeholder roles, the type of forum designed to host multistakeholder governance processes should be purpose-driven. Concerns about restricting access to commercially sensitive or confidential data and processes may at times limit participation to members. Other issues, particularly those of societal importance such as the use of facial recognition in the public sector, may require unrestricted forums for debate.[128]

For all its advantages, the multistakeholder approach poses various challenges. Self-regulation frameworks, including voluntary codes of conduct, developed through multistakeholder processes are effective only if strong domestic enforcement mechanisms are in place.[129] Even for a consensus-based and stakeholder-driven rule-making process, weak enforcement and outcomes may reduce stakeholder buy-in. In addition, legitimacy and buy-in may suffer if the process is merely consultative rather than using stakeholders' inputs to shape outcomes. Meaningful participation of underrepresented or marginalized groups can be difficult, particularly for new market entrants such as start-ups or SMEs, smaller CSOs and NGOs, or indigenous peoples.[130] Barriers to effective multistakeholder participation can also be found in international data governance arenas. Lower-middle-income countries may find it difficult to participate as co-designers or "standard setters" and find themselves limited to being "standard-takers" (see chapter 7).[131]

Finally, stakeholders need to guard against use of the multistakeholder approach by government and others to legitimize top-down decision-making that leads to an accumulation of power. Where accountability mechanisms are lacking, the multistakeholder approach can be misused to exclude other parties (whether in the public or private sector or civil society).[132] Designing inclusive forums and accountable processes and earmarking resources to enable the participation of traditionally underrepresented stakeholders will be key to the success of such processes. Creating bottom-up approaches to data governance designed around multistakeholder engagement can help realign power asymmetries and improve contestability in the current social contract on data (see box 8.4).

Box 8.4 Building multistakeholder data governance into smart city initiatives through "digital democracy"

Smart cities combine sensors and other technologies with physical infrastructure and services to enhance the lives of their residents.[a] Investments usually target sectors and services such as transportation, utilities, and law enforcement. Meanwhile, public-private partnerships are often used to leverage the technical and innovation capability of the private sector by outsourcing infrastructure and data management.[b] Because these initiatives involve the continual collection of personal or nonpersonal data from embedded sensors,[c] governance structures are needed to ensure that the data collected from citizens are used responsibly for public intent rather than commercial use and that residents retain control over their data. The need for robust data governance in this area will become more acute as the uptake of smart cities increases against a backdrop of growing urbanization worldwide.[d]

More inclusive decision-making about data collection and use is being facilitated by bottom-up models of collaboration. Barcelona was one of the first cities to leverage the analytical opportunities of the Internet of Things (IoT) and combine datasets to improve evidence-based policy making and service delivery. And it was one of the pilots for the European Union's DECODE initiative. DECODE is exploring how to build data-centric digital economies in which data generated and gathered by individuals, the IoT, and sensor networks are made available for collective use, while making sure that individuals

retain control over their data and their personal data are safeguarded.[e] Barcelona's City Council partnered with the city's digital democracy platform to publish data collected by sensors and other means on the Decidim platform[f] to promote transparency and accountability in decision-making.

In Belgium, Ghent has developed a collective governance model. In its "City of People," citizens can create online profiles on the platform Mijn Ghent (My Ghent), which they can use to access public services such as libraries and child care.[g]

Such digital democracy platforms have been replicated in lower- and middle-income countries. For example, Morocco's Fikra e-participation platform collects citizen feedback and generates community-driven ideas to improve public service delivery.[h]

a. Maddox (2015).
b. Copenhagen has created a public-private partnership with Hitachi to assess how to monetize datasets. Abu Dhabi has partnered with a Swiss telemedicine company to improve health care. And Singapore's Smart-Nation initiative is relying on a network of start-ups to provide the government with technology and data-driven services. See MGI (2019).
c. Scassa and Vilain (2019).
d. According to Cisco Systems, more than 60 percent of the world's population will live in cities by 2050. See Mitchell et al. (2013).
e. See DECODE, "Giving People Ownership of Their Personal Data," Barcelona, https://decodeproject.eu/.
f. See "Construïm la Barcelona que volem!" decidim.barcelona, Barcelona, https://www.decidim.barcelona/.
g. Tannam (2018).
h. See e-Government Program, Kingdom of Morocco, "e-Participation Platform: FIKRA," http://www.egov.ma/en/e-participation-platform-fikra.

Assessing the institutional foundation through the lens of a maturity model

Recommendations for improving the institutional foundations of data governance at the national level can be tailored to a country's current level of institutional development. Based on the maturity model introduced in chapter 1, recommendations for assessing and improving institutions are presented in the sections that follow.

Establishing fundamentals

Any gaps and weak links in a country's institutional arrangement for data governance will be revealed by first taking stock. In many countries, especially lower-income ones, infrastructure, data collection

and processing, and technical capabilities in the public sector are generally uneven. At best, certain "islands of excellence" may be using data effectively for decision-making or service delivery on an ad hoc basis, but without a clear strategic orientation or executive-level leadership of the data governance agenda. As a result, duplication of data is common, interoperability infrastructures are lacking, and the institutions needed to ensure the security, integrity, quality, and protection of data are minimal.

Countries should begin by establishing a baseline for assessing the capabilities of the existing institutions to facilitate the secure generation and flow of data among all data producers and users (recognizing that many actors are both producers and users of data). This analysis should be purpose-driven, with a view toward understanding the activities already taking place—either inside or outside of government—that may be development opportunities, along with the risks. The analysis should distinguish between the stated function of institutions and what they actually deliver. As one example, the African Union Commission's Malabo Convention supported the harmonization of the regional policy and legal framework for cybersecurity and data protection across Africa,[133] but institutions working in support of the convention have often come up short, in part because of the underrepresentation of local DPAs to enforce agreements of the convention.[134]

This stocktaking should examine institutional relationships as they interact with the private sector and civil society. It would then serve as a springboard to developing institutional arrangements that promote the production and flow of data between these actors. These institutions and initiatives can provide market participants with the confidence in and certainty about the rules of the game, reduce risk, and increase capacity and the incentives for firms to use data for economically and socially productive purposes.

Initiating data flows

Once it is clear how well the existing institutions are promoting the secure production and flow of data, work can begin to fill in gaps and strengthen their capabilities. Not all gaps have to be filled by public institutions. Domestic or international academic institutions, CSOs, international organizations, and research institutions could help fill capacity gaps in government. Depending on the local context, a government agency or unit (new or existing) could be given responsibility for establishing a strategic plan to promote greater use of data to improve public policy, the efficiency of the private sector, and the informational awareness of the population—all within the agreed-on parameters of the social contract for data. This entity should have sufficient leverage across the public sector agencies that govern or manage data and should reside at the center of government under high-level executive leadership.

Institutions should coordinate the development of standards to ensure data quality and data integration capabilities across government. This effort would include developing an integrated data management architecture for public intent data that curates, maintains, and facilitates secure data sharing and reuse across government. Data trusts or other contract-based mechanisms could continue to play an important role in promoting access to private intent data in areas in which public institutions, rules, and

enforcement remain weak and fail to address the concerns of data owners and data subjects. At the same time, institutional arrangements should be developed to encourage and enforce compliance with rules established to promote the dissemination and safe use of data.

Signs of a maturing system will include adequate technical capacity, sufficient resources, clear roles and responsibilities, and a high level of data literacy. Extensive training—for both civil servants and citizens—to overcome digital literacy barriers and enable data management and use will also be part of the maturation process.[135] To engender trust and increase their transparency and accountability, institutions should also be required to publish annual plans and reports on their activities. Furthermore, certain institutions, such as regulators, NSOs, and data protection authorities, must be protected from undue political and commercial influences.

Optimizing the system

To maximize the value of data, institutions need to support a whole-of-government approach to the management of data. Capacity-building and communication efforts should be directed at training civil servants to use data for results, including better decision-making, performance monitoring, and service delivery. To strengthen a data-driven culture in the public sector, reward mechanisms such as prizes and performance-related pay can incentivize civil servants to pursue innovations and engage in collaborative decision-making. With sufficient investments in data institutions and the technical skills of civil servants, critical processes and service delivery channels can become automated and interconnected.

Establishing processes for data quality assurance, data integration, and data synchronization should be integral parts of data management at this stage. Institutions should similarly fully integrate stakeholder feedback mechanisms into data flows, thereby helping to increase the transparency and quality of processes. Ministries and agencies should share data via common platforms subject to robust data protection safeguards, which limit consolidated access to and control over large volumes of personal data.

Finally, institutions should be regularly monitored[136] and evaluated, with the results informing adjustments in resources and policies. Both should be adapted to cope with disruptive technologies and services as data generation (and use) continues to grow in both volume and variety.

To meet the challenges from cross-border data transfers associated with safeguarding and enabling the use of both personal and nonpersonal data, institutions should coordinate at the regional or international level.[137] Such global efforts toward data governance should be recognized and promoted[138] and should enable convergence in the development of high-level principles to guide the design and implementation of national-level data governance frameworks (see spotlight 8.1).[139] These efforts should protect the interests of poorer nations in international negotiations on data issues in which they may have a limited voice.

No one-size-fits-all approach can be prescribed for every context. The maturity model is dynamic, and institutions will need to continually learn and improve to move to the next level. This approach can be applied equally to countries with low maturity and low resources and those with high maturity and high resources.

Notes

1. Harrison, Pardo, and Cook (2012).
2. One class of platforms is software infrastructure, which can include civil registration and vital statistics systems, digital identification systems, population registries, sectoral information management systems, data catalogs, data architecture (one of the pillars of enterprise architecture), Government Service Bus, interoperability frameworks, data lakes and warehouses, webservices and application programming interfaces, eTrust services, cybersecurity solutions, and privacy-enhancing technologies. These platforms are essential components of soft infrastructure.
3. Aghion and Tirole (1997).
4. Bergstrom, Blume, and Varian (1986).
5. Arraiz et al. (2019); Brown et al. (2019).
6. Government of Mexico, Datos Abiertos de México (database), https://www.datos.gob.mx/.
7. See Shapiro and Varian (1998).
8. See Abraham, Schneider, and vom Brocke (2019) for a review of this literature.
9. ASEAN (2012); OECD (2019b).
10. Many of the data governance functions included here coincide with those proposed by the British Academy and the Royal Society (2017b). Their report "Data Management and Use: Governance in the 21st Century" distills three groups of essential data governance functions: (1) anticipate, monitor, and evaluate; (2) build practices and set standards; and (3) clarify, enforce, and remedy. The report also argues for a single body to act as steward of the data governance landscape.
11. Principles—such as certainty, transparency, accountability, nondiscrimination, fairness, inclusiveness, openness, necessity, proportionality, and security—need to be developed to link data management practices to positive uses and behaviors to improve lives (see chapter 6). They also help identify practical steps for a data strategy along the data life cycle and ensure that data are valued as a strategic asset. An example is the US Federal Data Strategy. See Office of Management and Budget, "Federal Data Strategy: Leveraging Data as a Strategic Asset," Washington, DC, https://strategy.data.gov/.
12. The targets also include intermediate milestones and measurable key performance indicators (KPIs) to support monitoring and evaluation activities.
13. OECD (2018).
14. Brown et al. (2019).
15. Quay (2010).
16. Blair (2011).
17. Cheruiyot, Baack, and Ferrer-Conill (2019); Deloitte (2012); Garcia (2007); Gopal Jayal (2007); Grandvoinnet, Aslam, and Raha (2015); Hanna (2012); Hjalmarsson, Johansson, and Rudmark (2015); Malena (2004); Paul (2011); Peruzzotti and Smulovitz (2006).
18. Carson and Hartz-Karp (2005); He (2011).
19. Kpundeh (2000); World Bank (2017).
20. World Bank (2002, 4).
21. The DGSS data on which figure 8.3 is based were collected by visiting government, CSO, and other relevant websites. Most governments have a substantial web presence, and information on data governance is visible on their websites. However, the data do not capture institutions without a web presence. See World Bank, DGSS (Digital Government/GovTech Systems and Services) (dataset), https://datacatalog.worldbank.org/dataset/digital-governmentgovtech-systems-and-services-dgss-dataset.
22. These statistics are based on Data Governance System and Services (DGSS) data for 198 economies. See World Bank, DGSS (Digital Government/GovTech Systems and Services) (dataset), https://datacatalog.worldbank.org/dataset/digital-governmentgovtech-systems-and-services-dgss-dataset.
23. Bertelli et al. (2020).
24. The national statistics office of Thailand, the Electronic Transactions Development Agency, and CAT Telecom Public Company Limited (a state-owned enterprise that runs the country's international telecommunications infrastructure), among other agencies, were consolidated under the Ministry of Digital Economy and Society.
25. SGD (2020).
26. PARIS21 (2017).
27. See, for example, Fölscher and Gay (2012); Sjoberg, Mellon, and Peixoto (2017).
28. Wilson (2019).
29. African Union (2020).
30. Martinez Pería and Singh (2014).
31. Gunningham and Rees (1997); Gupta and Lad (1983).
32. Gunningham and Rees (1997); Gupta and Lad (1983).
33. See the website of the International Organization for Standardization, https://www.iso.org/about-us.html.
34. UNSDG (2017).
35. Informal or internal mechanisms may be especially effective if combined to provide multiple avenues for incentivizing compliance. This is one of the strengths of a multistakeholder approach to data governance.
36. United Nations (2014).

37. Turianskyi et al. (2018).

38. This delistment was accompanied by an invitation to return to EITI when implementation obstacles had been removed (which as of this writing has occurred).

39. See Latin American Open Data Initiative (Iniciativa Latinoamericana de Datos Abiertos), GDB (Global Data Barometer) (dashboard), https://globaldatabarometer.org/.

40. The Moroccan Data Protection Law of 2009 provides for fines of up to DH 300,000, depending on the severity of the violations. In certain cases, prison sentences can be issued for between three months and two years (Kettani 2017).

41. Kin (2020).

42. See Commission Nationale de l'Informatique et des Libertés, "What You Should Know about Our Standard on Data Protection Training Programmes," https://www.cnil.fr/en/what-you-should-know-about-our-standard-data-protection-training-programmes.

43. Bundeskartellamt (2019). A plug-in is a piece of add-on software that helps make the base software do what it does not normally do by itself. Plug-ins (also known as extensions or add-ons) are downloaded and installed to make the software being used more feature-rich (O'Neill 2020).

44. Richardson, Hendrickson, and Boussina (2018).

45. Gauri (2011).

46. A CSIRT is known, among other designations, as a Computer Emergency Response Team (CERT); Incident Response Team (IRT); Computer Security Incident Response Capability or Center (CSIRC); Computer Incident Response Capability or Center (CIRC); Computer Incident Response Team (CIRT); Incident Handling Team (IHT); Incident Response Center or Incident Response Capability (IRC); Security Emergency Response Team (SERT); or Security Incident Response Team (SIRT).

47. See chapter 6 for data on cybersecurity legislation collected through the Global Data Regulation Survey.

48. See Data Governance Network, IDFC Institute, Research (document and data repository), Mumbai, India, https://datagovernance.org/research.

49. British Academy and Royal Society (2017a).

50. Examples are the Centre for Data Ethics and Innovation in the United Kingdom; the Ethics of AI Lab at the University of Toronto in Canada; and the Ethics and Governance of Artificial Intelligence Initiative at the Massachusetts Institute of Technology and Harvard University in the United States.

51. Examples are the Global Partnership for Sustainable Development Data and the World Data Forum.

52. O'Donnell and Keller (2020).

53. Wylie and McDonald (2018).

54. Hill, Stein, and Williams (2020).

55. Shkabatur (2012).

56. FTC (2014).

57. WebFX Team (2020).

58. Deichmann et al. (2016).

59. See Governance Lab, Tandon School of Engineering, New York University, "Data Collaboratives," Brooklyn, NY, https://datacollaboratives.org/.

60. Bernholz (2016).

61. Rodian (2018).

62. GS1, "How GDSN Works," Ewing Township, NJ, https://www.gs1.org/services/gdsn/how-gdsn-works.

63. Lundqvist (2018).

64. World Bank (2021).

65. Grossman (2019); Grossman et al. (2016); Hardinges and Tennison (2020).

66. See the Open Commons Consortium website, https://www.occ-data.org/.

67. See the UK Biobank website, https://www.ukbiobank.ac.uk/learn-more-about-uk-biobank.

68. Pentland and Hardjono (2020).

69. See the LunaDNA website, https://www.lunadna.com/about/.

70. Wylie and McDonald (2018).

71. Bernholz (2016); Hardinges (2018).

72. MeitY (2020).

73. Delacroix and Lawrence (2019).

74. Hardinges (2020).

75. Delacroix and Lawrence (2019); ODI (2019).

76. Bengio (2020).

77. Platform Info Exchange is a UK-based nonprofit trade union for rideshare drivers such as Uber. The organization helps these "gig workers" access, analyze, and inform decisions using the personal data collected about them while they are working, through class action data requests. This work is designed to create a worker-led data trust downstream. Platform Info Exchange is funding this pilot through a fellowship received in January 2021 by Mozilla's Data Futures Lab. See https://foundation.mozilla.org/en/blog/announcing-3-new-awards-to-fuel-better-data-stewardship/.

78. WiredGov (2019).

79. Microsoft News Center India (2016).

80. OECD (2019b).

81. Bhargava and D'Ignazio (2015).

82. Skills should be developed to support the collection or acquisition of data (purpose-driven data collection), the management and curation of data (managing the data life cycle and promoting interoperability), and the analysis, visualization, and other uses of data across their life cycle.

83. Egle and Zahuranec (2020); OECD (1997).

84. OECD (1997).

85. See Governance Lab, Tandon School of Engineering, New York University, "Solving Public Problems with Data," Brooklyn, NY, http://sppd.thegovlab.org/.

86. Apolitical has a number of resources and courses on using data better in the public sector. See the Apolitical website, https://apolitical.co/home.

87. Williams and Yecalo-Tecle (2020).

88. Brown et al. (2019).

89. Management Concepts (2016).

90. Campbell and Sandino (2019).

91. See, for example, Nauheimer (2015); UNDP (2006).

92. *Economist* (2013).

93. Ibarra and Hansen (2011).

94. CL4D (2016).

95. See Open Government Partnership program, "A Workshop for Representatives of Public Structures on the

Open Data Order Project," Tunis, Tunisia, http://www
.ogptunisie.gov.tn/?p=226.

96. These efforts were supported closely by the World Bank as part of technical assistance under the Moussanada Multi-Donor Trust Fund.

97. Weiss and Hughes (2005).

98. Carr and Walton (2014). Social accountability committees can be a helpful vehicle to promote legitimacy and impact through multistakeholder decision-making (World Bank 2020).

99. For example, see EDPB (2020).

100. eHealth Network (2020); EU (2020).

101. Mazzucato (2018).

102. Camera, Casari, and Bigoni (2013).

103. Recent applications or services that have won awards include the geoportal for the Urban Agency of Errachidia-Midelt, the e-upgrade for Royal Air Maroc (the national airline), and the online portal for the Moroccan pension fund (Caisse Marocaine des Retraites). See Ministry of Economy, Finance, and Administrative Reform, "Prix National de l'Administration Electronique e-mtiaz," Rabat, Morocco, https://www.mmsp.gov.ma/fr/decline.aspx?m=4&r=218.

104. The hackathon was supported by the World Bank through the Moussanada Multi-Donor Trust Fund. In addition to the main competition, teams that did not proceed to the final still had an opportunity to present their solutions to the Court of Accounts for the following challenges: decentralization and local governance; citizen participation in the audit process; and simplification of, disclosure of, and follow-up on audit recommendations.

105. Bach (2016).

106. For a useful definition of autonomy in the public sector, see the autonomy index developed by Rasul, Rogger, and Williams (2018). It captures "the extent to which bureaucrats of all levels are empowered to make meaningful contributions into policy formulation and implementation processes, and the flexibility with [which] bureaucrats can use their discretion in responding to project peculiarities and introducing innovations" (Rasul, Rogger, and Williams 2018, 3).

107. Gilardi and Maggetti (2011); World Bank (2017).

108. OECD (2012).

109. OECD (2017).

110. Blackman and Srivastava (2011).

111. OECD (2017).

112. Peters (2018).

113. Peters (2018).

114. See the Foundations for Evidence-Based Policymaking Act of 2018, Pub L. No. 115–435, 132 STAT. 5529 (2019), which applies to 24 agencies identified in the Chief Financial Officers Act of 1990 (CFO Act) in 31 U.S.C. §901(b). For more information, see DOJ (2020).

115. See OMB (2020).

116. Johns and Saltane (2016).

117. Arizti et al. (2020).

118. NHSA (2020).

119. WGIG (2005).

120. DeNardis and Raymond (2013).

121. Effective multistakeholder approaches to policy design and implementation can increase the responsiveness of government, compared with the traditional top-down approaches or rule making that tend to lag behind the pace of technological change and may become obsolete by the time the legislative process is completed and regulations are adopted.

122. Multistakeholder approaches can also increase buy-in among stakeholders, so long as they are adequately represented, their interests are considered, and their preferences are reflected (to the extent possible) in policy setting, design, and implementation.

123. In bringing divergent interest groups together, multistakeholder approaches to data governance can balance differing priorities to broker agreement on the systems to be adopted for the use, reuse, and sharing of data for development. For example, the multistakeholder approach can facilitate convergence on (1) the principles, norms, and standards for data collection and use; (2) the tools and mechanisms (technical, legal, and procedural) to enable responsible and trustworthy data use and sharing; and (3) the types of institutions or functions required to effectively implement these principles, norms, standards, tools, and mechanisms. For example, stakeholders may differ in their views of data minimization (that is, acquiring only the data necessary to achieve the limited and disclosed purpose for which those data are necessary); protecting data; or creating or identifying the institutions tasked with extracting the maximum public value from data.

124. Strickling and Hill (2017).

125. Dutton (2015).

126. WGIG (2005).

127. At ICANN, civil society is represented in the at-large mechanisms for participation in decision-making; in management and address registries; and in the Internet Architecture Board. It also participates in the selection of board members. Business representatives participate in their own business constituency group. More broadly, ICANN supports transparent and inclusive decision-making by providing unrestricted access to its meetings and encourages public debate through public forums, including representation from low- and middle-income countries. See WGIG (2005).

128. Dutton (2015); Strickling and Hill (2017).

129. Rubinstein (2018).

130. Strickling and Hill (2017).

131. WGIG (2005).

132. For example, a study by Maurer and Morgus (2014) found that two-thirds of the countries that favored intergovernmental (multilateral) control over the internet regulate political, social, or religious content on the internet within their borders, constraining freedom of expression. The study analyzed state voting records at the ITU's World Conference on International Telecommunications (WCIT) in Dubai, Saudi Arabia, in 2012.

133. African Union (2014).

134. Information communicated during the World Bank and German Federal Ministry of Economic

Cooperation and Development's Online Consultation, "Data for Better Lives: Enablers and Safeguards," June 9–10, 2020.

135. Bruhn, Lara Ibarra, and McKenzie (2014); Bruhn et al. (2016); Frisancho (2020); Lührmann, Serra-Garcia, and Winter (2018).

136. For example, the CSO Privacy International tracks extraordinary measures adopted by governments, international organizations, and technology companies in response to COVID-19 to ensure these measures do not lead to data exploitation and violate human rights. See Privacy International, "Tracking the Global Response to COVID-19," London, https://privacyinternational.org /examples/tracking-global-response-covid-19.

137. OECD (2013).

138. According to a survey conducted by the Pathways to Prosperity Commission in 2019, policy makers in lower-income countries emphasized that the areas in which "global efforts" were most needed were taxation; cybercrime and cybersecurity; privacy and data protection; market competition; intellectual property; and data sharing and interoperability. Within these priority areas, international cooperation and coordination were considered the most needed to support the development of regulatory and technical standards. International regulatory cooperation in these six areas can have positive externalities, including improving regulatory predictability, reducing compliance burdens and the risks of regulatory arbitrage, and potentially encouraging investment flows. See Pathways for Prosperity Commission (2019).

139. Carter and Yayboke (2019).

References

Abraham, Rene, Johannes Schneider, and Jan vom Brocke. 2019. "Data Governance: A Conceptual Framework, Structured Review, and Research Agenda." *International Journal of Information Management* 49 (December): 424–38.

African Union. 2014. "African Union Convention on Cyber Security and Personal Data Protection." Document EX. CL/846(XXV), June 27, 2014 (adopted), African Union, Addis Ababa, Ethiopia. https://www.opennetafrica.org /?wpfb_dl=4.

African Union. 2020. "The Digital Transformation Strategy for Africa (2020–2030)." African Union, Addis Ababa, Ethiopia. https://au.int/sites/default/files/documents /38507-doc-dts-english.pdf.

Agesic (Agencia de Gobierno Electrónico y Sociedad de la Información y del Conocimiento, Agency for Electronic Government and Information and Knowledge Society, Uruguay). 2019. "Agenda Uruguay Digital 2020: Transforming with Equity." Agesic, Office of the President of the Republic, Montevideo, Uruguay.

Aghion, Philippe, and Jean Tirole. 1997. "Formal and Real Authority in Organizations." *Journal of Political Economy* 105 (1): 1–29.

Arizti, Pedro, Daniel J. Boyce, Natalia Manuilova, Carlos Sabatino, Roby Senderowitsch, and Ermal Vila. 2020. *Building Effective, Accountable, and Inclusive Institutions in Europe and Central Asia: Lessons from the Region*. With contributions of William Gallagher and Patricia Rogers. Washington, DC: World Bank.

Arraiz, Irani, Miriam Bruhn, Benjamin N. Roth, Claudia Ruiz Ortega, and Rodolfo Mario Stucchi. 2019. "Free Riding in Loan Approvals: Evidence from SME Lending in Peru." Policy Research Working Paper 9072, World Bank, Washington, DC.

ASEAN (Association of Southeast Asian Nations). 2012. "Framework on Digital Data Science." Document endorsed at 12th ASEAN Telecommunications and Information Technology Ministers Meeting (TELMIN), Cebu, the Philippines, November 15–16, 2012. https://asean.org /storage/2012/05/6B-ASEAN-Framework-on-Digital-Data -Governance_Endorsed.pdf.

Bach, Tobias. 2016. "Administrative Autonomy of Public Organizations." In *Global Encyclopedia of Public Administration, Public Policy, and Governance*, edited by Ali Farazmand, 171–79. Cham, Switzerland: Springer.

Bengio, Yoshua. 2020. "Peer-to-Peer AI-Tracing of COVID-19." *Yoshua Bengio* (blog), March 23, 2020. https://yoshua bengio.org/2020/03/23/peer-to-peer-ai-tracing-of-covid-19/.

Bergstrom, Theodore, Lawrence Blume, and Hal Varian. 1986. "On the Private Provision of Public Goods." *Journal of Public Economics* 29 (1): 25–49.

Bernholz, Lucy. 2016. "Workshop Summary: Trusted Data Intermediaries." Stanford Center on Philanthropy and Civil Society, Stanford University, Stanford, CA. https:// pacscenter.stanford.edu/wp-content/uploads/2018/05 /TDI-Workshop-Summary.pdf.

Bertelli, Anthony M., Mai Hassan, Dan Honig, Daniel Rogger, and Martin J. Williams. 2020. "An Agenda for the Study of Public Administration in Developing Countries." *Governance* 33 (4): 735–48.

Bhargava, Rahul, and Catherine D'Ignazio. 2015. "Designing Tools and Activities for Data Literacy Learners." Paper presented at Workshop on Data Literacy, Web Science 2015 Conference, Oxford, UK, June 30, 2015.

Blackman, Colin, and Lara Srivastava, eds. 2011. *Telecommunications Regulation Handbook*. Washington, DC: World Bank, InfoDev, and International Telecommunication Union.

Blair, Harry. 2011. "Gaining State Support for Social Accountability." In *Accountability through Public Opinion: From Inertia to Public Action*, edited by Sina Odugbemi and Taeku Lee, 37–51. Washington, DC: World Bank. https://elibrary .worldbank.org/doi/10.1596/9780821385050_CH04.

British Academy and Royal Society. 2017a. "Data Governance: Public Engagement Review." British Academy and Royal Society, London. https://royalsociety.org/-/media/policy /projects/data-governance/data-governance-public -engagement-review.pdf.

British Academy and Royal Society. 2017b. "Data Management and Use: Governance in the 21st Century; A Joint Report by the British Academy and the Royal Society." British Academy and Royal Society, London. https://royal society.org/topics-policy/projects/data-governance/.

Brown, Walter, Daniel Rogger, Ella Spencer, and Martin Williams. 2019. "Information and Innovation in the Public Sector." IGC Growth Brief 019, International

Growth Center, London. https://www.theigc.org/wp-content/uploads/2019/10/Brown-et-al-2019-Growth-Brief_Web.pdf.

Bruhn, Miriam, Luciana de Souza Leão, Arianna Legovini, Rogelio Marchetti, and Bilal Zia. 2016. "The Impact of High School Financial Education: Evidence from a Large-Scale Evaluation in Brazil." *American Economic Journal: Applied Economics* 8 (4): 256–95.

Bruhn, Miriam, Gabriel Lara Ibarra, and David McKenzie. 2014. "The Minimal Impact of a Large-Scale Financial Education Program in Mexico City." *Journal of Development Economics* 108 (May): 184–89.

Bundeskartellamt. 2019. "Bundeskartellamt Prohibits Facebook from Combining User Data from Different Sources." *News*, February 7, 2019, Bundeskartellamt, Bonn, Germany. https://www.bundeskartellamt.de/SharedDocs/Meldung/EN/Pressemitteilungen/2019/07_02_2019_Facebook.html.

Camera, Gabriele, Marco Casari, and Maria Bigoni. 2013. "Money and Trust among Strangers." *PNAS, Proceedings of the National Academy of Sciences* 110 (37): 14889–93.

Campbell, Dennis, and Tatiana Sandino. 2019. "Sustaining Corporate Culture in a Growing Organization." Harvard Business School Technical Note 119–109, Harvard Business School, Boston, MA.

Carr, Priyanka B., and Gregory M. Walton. 2014. "Cues of Working Together Fuel Intrinsic Motivation." *Journal of Experimental Social Psychology* 53 (July): 169–84.

Carson, Lyn, and Janette Hartz-Karp. 2005. "Adapting and Combining Deliberative Designs: Juries, Polls, and Forums." In *The Deliberative Democracy Handbook: Strategies for Effective Civic Engagement in the Twenty-First Century*, edited by John Gastil and Peter Levine, 120–38. San Francisco: Jossey-Bass.

Carter, William A., and Erol Yayboke. 2019. "Data Governance Principles for the Global Digital Economy." Report, Center for Strategic and International Studies, Washington, DC. https://www.csis.org/analysis/data-governance-principles-global-digital-economy.

Cavoukian, Ann. 2011. "PbD, Privacy by Design, the 7 Foundational Principles: Implementation and Mapping of Fair Information Practices." Information and Privacy Commissioner of Ontario, Toronto. https://iapp.org/resources/article/privacy-by-design-the-7-foundational-principles/.

Cheruiyot, David, Stefan Baack, and Raul Ferrer-Conill. 2019. "Data Journalism beyond Legacy Media: The Case of African and European Civic Technology Organizations." *Digital Journalism* 7 (9): 1215–29.

CL4D (Collaborative Leadership for Development). 2016. "CL4D Portfolio of Unblocking Project Implementation Challenges and Accelerating Progress." World Bank, Washington, DC. https://www.leadfordev.org/Data/gpl4d/files/field/documents/cl4d_portfolio_brochuresoftcopyversion.pdf.

Danezis, George, Josep Domingo-Ferrer, Marit Hansen, Jaap-Henk Hoepman, Daniel Le Métayer, Rodica Tirtea, and Stefan Schiffner. 2014. "Privacy and Data Protection by Design." European Union Agency for Network and Information Security, Heraklion, Greece. https://www.enisa.europa.eu/publications/privacy-and-data-protection-by-design.

Deichmann, Johannes, Kersten Heineke, Thomas Reinbacher, and Dominik Wee. 2016. "Creating a Successful Internet of Things Data Marketplace." *Our Insights* (blog), October 7, 2016, McKinsey and Company, New York. https://www.mckinsey.com/business-functions/mckinsey-digital/our-insights/creating-a-successful-internet-of-things-data-marketplace.

Delacroix, Sylvie, and Neil D. Lawrence. 2019. "Bottom-Up Data Trusts: Disturbing the 'One Size Fits All' Approach to Data Governance." *International Data Privacy Law* 9 (4): 236–52.

Deloitte. 2012. "Open Growth: Stimulating Demand for Open Data in the UK." Briefing note, Deloitte Analytics, London. https://www2.deloitte.com/content/dam/Deloitte/uk/Documents/deloitte-analytics/open-growth.pdf.

DeNardis, Laura, and Mark Raymond. 2013. "Thinking Clearly about Multistakeholder Internet Governance." Paper presented at GigaNet, the Eighth Annual Global Internet Governance Academic Network Symposium, Bali, Indonesia, October 21, 2013.

DOJ (Department of Justice, United States). 2020. "Roles and Responsibilities under the Foundations for Evidence-Based Policymaking Act." Open Government. https://www.justice.gov/open/roles-and-responsibilities-under-foundations-evidence-based-policymaking-act.

Dutton, William H. 2015. "Multistakeholder Internet Governance?" Background paper, *World Development Report 2016: Digital Dividends*, World Bank, Washington, DC.

EC (European Commission). 2020. "Trust Services and Electronic Identification (eID)." *Shaping Europe's Digital Future: Policy.* https://ec.europa.eu/digital-single-market/en/policies/trust-services-and-eidentification.

Economist. 2013. "How Did Estonia Become a Leader in Technology?" *The Economist Explains*, July 31, 2013. https://www.economist.com/the-economist-explains/2013/07/30/how-did-estonia-become-a-leader-in-technology.

EDPB (European Data Protection Board). 2020. "Guidelines 03/2020 on the Processing of Data Concerning Health for the Purpose of Scientific Research in the Context of the COVID-19 Outbreak." *Guidelines*, EDPB, Brussels. https://edpb.europa.eu/our-work-tools/our-documents/ohjeet/guidelines-032020-processing-data-concerning-health-purpose_en.

Egle, Danuta, and Andrew J. Zahuranec. 2020. "How to Build the Data Skills Toolkit Public Employees Need." *Data Stewards* (blog), June 24, 2020. https://medium.com/data-stewards-network/how-to-build-the-data-skills-toolkit-public-employees-need-6af3af43e627.

eHealth Network. 2020. "Mobile Applications to Support Contact Tracing in the EU's Fight against COVID-19: Common EU Toolbox for Member States." Version 1.0, eHealth Network, Brussels. https://ec.europa.eu/health/sites/health/files/ehealth/docs/covid-19_apps_en.pdf.

Elliot, Mark James, Elaine Mackey, Kieron O'Hara, and Caroline Tudor. 2016. *The Anonymisation Decision-Making Framework.* Manchester, UK: UKAN Publications.

EU (European Union). 2014. "Regulation (EU) No 910/2014 of the European Parliament and of the Council of 23 July 2014 on Electronic Identification and Trust Services for Electronic Transactions in the Internal Market and Repealing Directive 1999/93/EC." *Official Journal of the*

European Union L 257/73. https://ec.europa.eu/futurium /en/system/files/ged/eidas_regulation.pdf.

EU (European Union). 2020. "Communication from the Commission: Guidance on Apps Supporting the Fight against COVID 19 Pandemic in Relation to Data Protection." *Official Journal of the European Union* C 124 I/1. https://eur-lex.europa.eu/legal-content/EN/TXT/PDF /?uri=CELEX:52020XC0417(08)&from=EN.

Floridi, Luciano, and Mariarosaria Taddeo. 2016. "What Is Data Ethics?" *Philosophical Transactions of the Royal Society A: Mathematical, Physical, and Engineering Sciences* 374 (2083): 20160360. https://doi.org/10.1098/rsta.2016.0360.

Fölscher, Alta, and Emilie Gay. 2012. "Fiscal Transparency and Participation in Africa: A Status Report." Collaborative Africa Budget Reform Initiative, National Treasury, Pretoria, South Africa.

Frisancho, Verónica C. 2020. "The Impact of School-Based Financial Education on High School Students and Their Teachers: Experimental Evidence from Peru." IDB Working Paper IDP-WP-871, Inter-American Development Bank, Washington, DC.

FTC (Federal Trade Commission, United States). 2014. *Data Brokers: A Call for Transparency and Accountability.* Washington, DC: FTC. https://www.ftc.gov/reports/data -brokers-call-transparency-accountability-report-federal -trade-commission-may-2014.

Garcia, Helen R. 2007. "Perspectives on Communication and Social Accountability: A Qualitative Survey of World Bank Practitioners." Paper presented at World Bank's Communication for Governance and Accountability Program Workshop, "Generating Genuine Demand with Social Accountability Mechanisms," World Bank Office, Paris, November 1–2, 2007.

Gauri, Varun. 2011. "Redressing Grievances and Complaints Regarding Basic Service Delivery." Policy Research Working Paper 5699, World Bank, Washington, DC.

Gilardi, Fabrizio, and Martino Maggetti. 2011. "The Independence of Regulatory Authorities." In *Handbook on the Politics of Regulation,* edited by David Levi-Faur, 201–14. Cheltenham, UK: Edward Elgar Publishing.

Gopal Jayal, Niraja. 2007. "New Directions in Theorising Social Accountability?" *IDS Bulletin* 38 (6): 105–10.

Grandvoinnet, Helene, Ghazia Aslam, and Shomikho Raha. 2015. *Opening the Black Box: The Contextual Drivers of Social Accountability.* New Frontiers of Social Policy Series. Washington, DC: World Bank.

Grossman, Robert L. 2019. "Data Lakes, Clouds, and Commons: A Review of Platforms for Analyzing and Sharing Genomic Data." *Trends in Genetics* 35 (3): 223–34.

Grossman, Robert L., Allison Heath, Mark Murphy, Maria Patterson, and Walt Wells. 2016. "A Case for Data Commons: Toward Data Science as a Service." *Computing in Science and Engineering* 18 (5): 10–20.

Gunningham, Neil, and Joseph Rees. 1997. "Industry Self-Regulation: An Institutional Perspective." *Law and Policy* 19 (4): 363–414.

Gupta, Anil K., and Lawrence J. Lad. 1983. "Industry Self-Regulation: An Economic, Organizational, and Political Analysis." *Academy of Management Review* 8 (3): 416–25.

Hanna, Nagy K. 2012. "Open Development: ICT for Governance in Africa." World Bank, Washington, DC.

Hardinges, Jack. 2018. "Defining a 'Data Trust.'" *Knowledge and Opinion* (blog), October 19, 2018, Open Data Institute, London. https://theodi.org/article/defining-a-data-trust/.

Hardinges, Jack. 2020. "Data Trusts in 2020." *Knowledge and Opinion* (blog), March 17, 2020, Open Data Institute, London. https://theodi.org/article/data-trusts-in-2020/.

Hardinges, Jack, and Jeni Tennison. 2020. "What Do We Mean by Data Institutions?" *Knowledge and Opinion* (blog), February 10, 2020, Open Data Institute, London. https://theodi.org/article/what-do-we-mean-by-data -institutions/.

Harrison, Teresa M., Theresa A. Pardo, and Meghan Cook. 2012. "Creating Open Government Ecosystems: A Research and Development Agenda." *Future Internet* 4 (4): 900–28.

He, Baogang. 2011. "Deliberation and Institutional Mechanisms for Shaping Public Opinion." In *Accountability through Public Opinion: From Inertia to Public Action,* edited by Sina Odugbemi and Taeku Lee, 203–14. Washington, DC: World Bank. https://elibrary.worldbank.org /doi/10.1596/9780821385050_CH14.

Hill, Ryan, Carolyn Stein, and Heidi Williams. 2020. "Internalizing Externalities: Designing Effective Data Policies." *AEA Papers and Proceedings* 110 (May): 49–54. https://doi .org/10.1257/pandp.20201060.

Hjalmarsson, Anders, Niklas Johansson, and Daniel Rudmark. 2015. "Mind the Gap: Exploring Stakeholders' Value with Open Data Assessment." In *Proceedings of the 48th Annual Hawaii International Conference on System Sciences, HICSS 2015,* edited by Tung X. Bui and Ralph H. Sprague, Jr., 1314–23. Los Alamitos, CA: Institute of Electrical and Electronics Engineers. https://doi.org/10.1109 /HICSS.2015.160.

Ibarra, Herminia, and Morten T. Hansen. 2011. "Are You a Collaborative Leader?" *Harvard Business Review* 89 (7–8): 68–74.

Johns, Melissa, and Valentina Saltane. 2016. "Citizen Engagement in Rulemaking: Evidence on Regulatory Practices in 185 Countries." Policy Research Working Paper 7840, World Bank, Washington, DC.

Kettani, Mehdi. 2017. "Régime Juridique de la Protection des Données Personnelles." Client Brief, DLA Piper, New York.

Kin, Yeong Zee. 2020. "Enabling Data Innovation through Accountability: Singapore's Approach." Paper presented at seminar organized in Singapore by the Office of the Chief Economist, Middle East and North Africa Region, World Bank, April 7, 2020.

Kpundeh, Sahr J. 2000. "Corruption and Corruption Control in Africa." Paper prepared for Gulbenkian Foundation workshop, "Democracy and Development in Africa," Lisbon, June 23–24, 2000. http://citeseerx.ist.psu.edu/viewdoc /download?doi=10.1.1.595.4791&rep=rep1&type=pdf.

Lührmann, Melanie, Marta Serra-Garcia, and Joachim Winter. 2018. "The Impact of Financial Education on Adolescents' Intertemporal Choices." *American Economic Journal: Economic Policy* 10 (3): 309–32.

Lundqvist, Björn. 2018. "Data Collaboration, Pooling, and Hoarding under Competition Law." Stockholm Faculty of Law Research Paper 61, Stockholm University, Stockholm.

Maddox, Teena. 2015. "The World's Smartest Cities: What IoT and Smart Governments Will Mean for You." *TechRepublic*, November 10, 2015. https://www.techrepublic.com/article/smart-cities/.

Malena, Carmen. 2004. "Social Accountability: An Introduction to the Concept and Emerging Practice." With Reiner Forster and Janmejay Singh. Social Development Paper: Participation and Civic Engagement, World Bank. Washington, DC.

Management Concepts. 2016. "Successful Change Management Practices in the Public Sector: How Governmental Agencies Implement Organizational Change Management." Management Concepts, Tysons Corner, VA.

Martínez Pería, María Soledad, and Sandeep Singh. 2014. "The Impact of Credit Information Sharing Reforms on Firm Financing." Policy Research Working Paper 7013, World Bank, Washington, DC.

Maurer, Tim, and Robert Morgus. 2014. "Tipping the Scale: An Analysis of Global Swing States in the Internet Governance Debate." Internet Governance Paper 7, Center for International Governance Innovation, Waterloo, Ontario, Canada.

Mazzucato, Mariana. 2018. "Mission-Oriented Research and Innovation in the European Union: A Problem-Solving Approach to Fuel Innovation-Led Growth." European Commission, Brussels. https://ec.europa.eu/info/sites/info/files/mazzucato_report_2018.pdf.

MeitY (Ministry of Electronics and Information Technology). 2020. "Report by the Committee of Experts on Non-Personal Data Governance Framework." Report 111972/2020/CL&ES, MeitY, New Delhi. https://www.huntonprivacyblog.com/wp-content/uploads/sites/28/2020/08/mygov_159453381955063671.pdf.

MGI (McKinsey Global Institute). 2019. "How Can the Private and Public Sectors Work Together to Create Smart Cities?" McKinsey, New York.

Microsoft News Center India. 2016. "Microsoft, L V Prasad Eye Institute, and Global Experts Collaborate to Launch Microsoft Intelligent Network for Eyecare." *Microsoft Stories India*, December 19, 2016. https://news.microsoft.com/en-in/microsoft-l-v-prasad-eye-institute-and-global-experts-collaborate-to-launch-microsoft-intelligent-network-for-eyecare/.

Mitchell, Shane, Nicola Villa, Martin Stewart-Weeks, and Anne Lange. 2013. "The Internet of Everything for Cities: Connecting People, Process, Data, and Things to Improve the 'Livability' of Cities and Communities." Point of View, Cisco Systems, San Jose, CA. https://www.cisco.com/c/dam/en_us/solutions/industries/docs/gov/everything-for-cities.pdf.

Nauheimer, Holger. 2015. *The Change Management Toolbook: A Collection of Tools, Methods, and Strategies.* Stellenbosch, South Africa: ChangeWright Consulting.

NHSA (Northern Health Science Alliance). 2020. "Connected Health Cities: Impact Summary 2016–2020." NHSA, Manchester, UK. https://www.thenhsa.co.uk/app/uploads/2020/03/Connected-Health-Cities-Impact-Report-Summary.pdf.

ODI (Open Data Institute). 2019. "Huge Appetite for Data Trusts, According to New ODI Research." *Knowledge and Opinion* (blog), April 15, 2019, Open Data Institute, London. https://theodi.org/article/huge-appetite-for-data-trusts-according-to-new-odi-research/.

O'Donnell, Fionntán, and Jared Robert Keller. 2020. "Building Trust in Alternative Data Ecosystems." *Knowledge and Opinion* (blog), April 16, 2020, Open Data Institute, London. https://theodi.org/article/building-trust-in-alternative-data-ecosystems/.

OECD (Organisation for Economic Co-operation and Development). 1997. "Public Service Training in OECD Countries." SIGMA Paper 16, OECD, Paris. https://doi.org/10.1787/5kml619ljzzn-en.

OECD (Organisation for Economic Co-operation and Development). 2012. "Recommendation of the Council on Regulatory Policy and Governance." Council on Regulatory Policy and Governance, OECD, Paris. https://www.oecd.org/governance/regulatory-policy/49990817.pdf.

OECD (Organisation for Economic Co-operation and Development). 2013. *The OECD Privacy Framework.* Paris: OECD. http://www.oecd.org/sti/ieconomy/oecd_privacy_framework.pdf.

OECD (Organisation for Economic Co-operation and Development). 2017. "Creating a Culture of Independence: Practical Guidance against Undue Influence." OECD, Paris. https://www.oecd.org/gov/creating-a-culture-of-independence-9789264274198-en.htm.

OECD (Organisation for Economic Co-operation and Development). 2018. "OECD Regulatory Enforcement and Inspections Toolkit." OECD, Paris. https://doi.org/10.1787/9789264303959-en.

OECD (Organisation for Economic Co-operation and Development). 2019a. *Digital Government Review of Argentina: Accelerating the Digitalisation of the Public Sector.* OECD Digital Government Studies Series. Paris: OECD. https://www.oecd-ilibrary.org/governance/digital-government-review-of-argentina_354732cc-en.

OECD (Organisation for Economic Co-operation and Development). 2019b. *The Path to Becoming a Data-Driven Public Sector.* OECD Digital Government Studies Series, November 28. Paris: OECD. https://doi.org/10.1787/059814a7-en.

OMB (Office of Management and Budget). 2020. "Federal Chief Data Officers Council Holds Inaugural Meeting." OMB, Washington, DC. https://strategy.data.gov/news/2020/01/31/federal-chief-data-officers-council-holds-inaugural-meeting/.

O'Neill, Mark. 2020. "What Is a Plugin?" *Technology Trends* (blog). January 7, 2020 (updated). https://smallbiztrends.com/2014/07/what-is-a-plugin.html.

PARIS21 (Partnership in Statistics for Development in the 21st Century). 2017. "National Strategies for the Development of Statistics." PARIS21 Consortium, Paris. https://paris21.org/national-strategy-development-statistics-nsds.

Pathways for Prosperity Commission. 2019. "Digital Diplomacy: Technology Governance for Developing Countries." Pathways for Prosperity Commission, Oxford, UK. https://pathwayscommission.bsg.ox.ac.uk/sites/default/files/2019-10/Digital-Diplomacy.pdf.

Paul, Samuel. 2011. "Stimulating Activism through Champions of Change." In *Accountability through Public Opinion:*

From Inertia to Public Action, edited by Sina Odugbemi and Taeku Lee, 347–57. Washington, DC: World Bank. https://doi.org/10.1596/9780821385050_CH23.

Pentland, Alex, and Thomas Hardjono. 2020. "Data Cooperatives." In *Building the New Economy: Data as Capital*, edited by Alex Pentland, Alexander Lipton, and Thomas Hardjono, chap. 2. Cambridge, MA: MIT Press. Published ahead of print, April 30, 2020. https://wip.mitpress.mit.edu/pub/pnxgvubq/release/2.

Peruzzotti, Enrique, and Catalina Smulovitz, eds. 2006. *Enforcing the Rule of Law: Social Accountability in the New Latin American Democracies*. Pitt Latin American Studies Series. Pittsburgh: University of Pittsburgh Press.

Peters, B. Guy. 2018. "The Challenge of Policy Coordination." *Policy Design and Practice* 1 (1): 1–11.

PI (Privacy International). 2018. "Why We've Filed Complaints against Companies That Most People Have Never Heard of, and What Needs to Happen Next." *Advocacy*, November 8, 2018, PI, London. http://privacyinternational.org/advocacy/2434/why-weve-filed-complaints-against-companies-most-people-have-never-heard-and-what.

Polonetsky, Jules, Omer Tene, and Kelsey Finch. 2016. "Shades of Gray: Seeing the Full Spectrum of Practical Data De-Identification." *Santa Clara Law Review* 56 (3): 593–629.

Porrúa, Miguel A. 2013. "E-Government in Latin America: A Review of the Success in Colombia, Uruguay, and Panama." In *The Global Information Technology Report 2013: Growth and Jobs in a Hyperconnected World*, edited by Beñat Bilbao-Osorio, Soumitra Dutta, and Bruno Lanvin, 127–36. Insight Report. Geneva: World Economic Forum. http://www3.weforum.org/docs/WEF_GITR_Report_2013.pdf.

Quay, Ray. 2010. "Anticipatory Governance: A Tool for Climate Change Adaptation." *Journal of the American Planning Association* 76 (4): 496–511. https://doi.org/10.1080/01944363.2010.508428.

Ram, Aliya, and Madhumita Murgia. 2019. "Data Brokers: Regulators Try to Rein In the 'Privacy Deathstars.'" *Financial Times*, January 7, 2019. https://www.ft.com/content/f1590694-fe68-11e8-aebf-99e208d3e521.

Rasul, Imran, Daniel Rogger, and Martin J. Williams. 2018. "Management of Bureaucrats and Public Service Delivery: Evidence from the Nigerian Civil Service." Policy Research Working Paper 8595, World Bank, Washington, DC.

Richardson, Harriet, Steve Hendrickson, and Houman Boussina. 2018. "ERP Planning: Information Technology and Data Governance." Audit Report (rev.), Office of the City Auditor, Palo Alto, CA. https://www.cityofpaloalto.org/civicax/filebank/documents/66250.

Rodian, Justine. 2018. "Master Data Management Definitions: The Complete A-Z of MDM." *Master Data Management* (blog), April 19, 2018. https://blog.stibosystems.com/the-complete-a-z-of-master-data-management.

Rubinstein, Ira S. 2018. "The Future of Self-Regulation Is Co-Regulation." In *The Cambridge Handbook of Consumer Privacy*, edited by Evan Selinger, Jules Polonetsky, and Omer Tene, 503–23. Cambridge Law Handbooks Series. Cambridge, UK: Cambridge University Press.

Scassa, Teresa, and Merlynda Vilain. 2019. "Governing Smart Data in the Public Interest: Lessons from Ontario's Smart Metering Entity." CIGI Paper 221, Center for International Governance Innovation, Waterloo, Ontario, Canada. https://www.cigionline.org/publications/governing-smart-data-public-interest-lessons-ontarios-smart-metering-entity.

SGD (Digital Government Secretariat, Brazil). 2020. "Central Data Governance Committee." *Digital Government*, June 22, 2020, SGD, Brasília. https://www.gov.br/governodigital/pt-br/governanca-de-dados/comite-central-de-governanca-de-dados.

Shapiro, Carl, and Hal R. Varian. 1998. *Information Rules: A Strategic Guide to the Network Economy*. Brighton, MA: Harvard Business Review Press.

Shkabatur, Jennifer. 2012. "Check My School: A Case Study on Citizens' Monitoring of the Education Sector in the Philippines." World Bank Institute, Washington, DC.

Sjoberg, Fredrik M., Jonathan Mellon, and Tiago Peixoto. 2017. "The Effect of Bureaucratic Responsiveness on Citizen Participation." *Public Administration Review* 77 (3): 340–51.

Strickling, Lawrence E., and Jonah Force Hill. 2017. "Multi-Stakeholder Internet Governance: Successes and Opportunities." *Journal of Cyber Policy* 2 (3): 296–317.

Tannam, Ellen. 2018. "How Can Smart Cities Make Data a Public Good before Time Runs Out?" *Silicon Republic*, July 26, 2018. https://www.siliconrepublic.com/enterprise/decode-nesta-smart-cities.

Thompson, Stuart A., and Charlie Warzel. 2019. "Twelve Million Phones, One Dataset, Zero Privacy." *New York Times*, December 19, 2019. https://www.nytimes.com/interactive/2019/12/19/opinion/location-tracking-cell-phone.html.

Turianskyi, Yarik, Terence Corrigan, Matebe Chisiza, and Alex Benkesnstein. 2018. "Multi-Stakeholder Initiatives: What Have We Learned? An Overview and Literature Review." United States Agency for International Development, Washington, DC. https://www.saiia.org.za/wp-content/uploads/2018/08/2018-MSI-overview-literature-review.pdf.

UNDP (United Nations Development Programme). 2006. "Institutional Reform and Change Management: Managing Change in Public Sector Organisations." Conference Paper 5, UNDP, New York.

United Nations. 2014. "Resolution Adopted by the General Assembly on 29 January 2014: Fundamental Principles of Official Statistics." Document A/RES/68/261, United Nations, New York. https://unstats.un.org/unsd/dnss/gp/FP-New-E.pdf.

UNSDG (United Nations Sustainable Development Group). 2017. "Data Privacy, Ethics, and Protection: Guidance Note on Big Data for Achievement of the 2030 Agenda." UNSDG, New York. https://unsdg.un.org/sites/default/files/UNDG_BigData_final_web.pdf.

Vermont Office of the Attorney General. 2018. "Guidance on Vermont's Act 171 of 2018: Data Broker Regulation." Office of the Attorney General, Montpelier, VT. https://ago.vermont.gov/wp-content/uploads/2018/12/2018-12-11-VT-Data-Broker-Regulation-Guidance.pdf.

WebFX Team. 2020. "What Are Data Brokers, and What Is Your Data Worth? [Infographic]." *Internet* (blog). March 16, 2020. https://www.webfx.com/blog/internet/what-are -data-brokers-and-what-is-your-data-worth-infographic/.

Weiss, Jeff, and Jonathan Hughes. 2005. "Want Collaboration? Accept and Actively Manage Conflict." *Harvard Business Review* 83 (3): 92–101.

WGIG (Working Group on Internet Governance, United Nations). 2005. "Background Report." Château de Bossey, Bogis-Bossey, Switzerland. https://www.itu.int/net/wsis /wgig/docs/wgig-background-report.pdf.

Williams, Martin J., and Liah Yecalo-Tecle. 2020. "Innovation, Voice, and Hierarchy in the Public Sector: Evidence from Ghana's Civil Service." *Governance* 33 (4): 789–807.

Wilson, Christopher. 2019. "Civil Society." In *The State of Open Data: Histories and Horizons*, edited by Tim Davies, Stephen B. Walker, Mor Rubinstein, and Fernando Perini, 355–66. Ottawa, Canada: International Development Research Center; Cape Town, South Africa: African Minds.

WiredGov. 2019. "Digital Revolution to Use the Power of Data to Combat Illegal Wildlife Trade and Reduce Food Waste." Press release, January 31, 2019, WiredGov, Stockport, UK. https://www.wired-gov.net/wg/news.nsf /articles/Digital+revolution+to+use+the+power+of +data+to+combat+illegal+wildlife+trade+and+reduce +food+waste+01022019081000?open.

World Bank. 2002. *World Development Report 2002: Building Institutions for Markets*. Washington, DC: World Bank; New York: Oxford University Press.

World Bank. 2016. *World Development Report 2016: Digital Dividends*. Washington, DC: World Bank.

World Bank. 2017. *World Development Report 2017: Governance and the Law*. Washington, DC: World Bank.

World Bank. 2020. *Enhancing Government Effectiveness and Transparency: The Fight against Corruption*. Global Report (revised October 3). Washington, DC: World Bank.

World Bank. 2021. *Unraveling Data's Gordian Knot: Enablers and Safeguards for Trusted Data Sharing in the New Economy*. Washington, DC: World Bank.

Wylie, Bianca, and Sean McDonald. 2018. "What Is a Data Trust?" *Big Data, Platform Governance* (blog). October 9, 2018. https://www.cigionline.org/articles/what-data -trust.

Spotlight 8.1

The need for a new global consensus on data: A call to action

A global consensus is needed to ensure that data are safeguarded as a global public good and as a resource to achieve equitable and sustainable development.

Many stakeholders around the world have concluded that some sort of global charter or convention is now required to realize the benefits of data in a safe and secure way and to avoid destructive beggar-thy-neighbor strategies. The World Economic Forum is hosting a Global Future Council on Data Policy to examine data architecture and models that promote an appropriate balance of creativity, innovation, responsible use, and efficiency. The Rockefeller Foundation has posited that institutions may be needed to help to manage artificial intelligence (AI) responsibly and has called for a Bretton Woods for AI. Microsoft has called for a Digital Geneva Convention. These efforts parallel similar efforts to reach a global consensus in other contexts,[1] particularly natural resources management and cultural protection.[2]

A global consensus would give individuals and enterprises confidence that data relevant to them carry similar protections and obligations no matter where they are collected or used. It would effectively establish a social contract that would strike a balance between the use of data for development and the protection of data in terms of security, privacy, and

human rights of the individual. It would also establish ground rules for the exchange of data between commercial use and the public good.

The consensus would constitute an integrated set of data values, principles, and standards that define the elements of responsible and ethical handling and sharing of data and that unite national governments, public institutions, the private sector, civil society organizations, and academia. A global mechanism is needed to provide incentives for applying these principles and overseeing their consistent application across different communities.

The global data consensus might build on some of the following ideas to go beyond principles and create an architecture of standards, incentives, and institutions that can implement them.

- International human rights and other areas of law already provide a good starting point, with many of the necessary values and principles for thinking about the impacts of data on people and commerce. These laws should be augmented.
- Learning from existing conventions and treaties can help to define effective mechanisms that encourage communities to respect common data values and principles, while discouraging noncompliance.[3]
- The way in which data are collected, used, and reused changes quickly, as do societal attitudes and practices regarding data. Thus, principles should be supported by clear and precise expectations.

This spotlight was written by the Committee for the Coordination of Statistical Activities (CCSA). The CCSA is composed of international and supranational organizations whose mandate includes the provision of international official statistics in the context of the United Nations Statistical Commission Principles Governing International Statistical Activities (see https://unstats.un.org/unsd/ccsa/).

- To maintain and update these data standards and expectations, global institutions are needed to embrace the broad global community of data providers and users, including national governments, the private sector, and civil society as well as stakeholders from not only the traditional data ecosystems but also from the new ones of AI and digital and information technology services. Such institutions can oversee accountability frameworks and support mechanisms to facilitate the exchange and responsible use of data.
- There will be value in establishing universal values, principles, standards, and expectations for data use and reuse, regardless of sector or type of data. However, it will be necessary to address specific sectors or types of data. Opportunities are currently present to build on ethical principles and standards that already exist in many specific data communities.
- National legislation could be complemented and inspired by a voluntary international governance framework to which all stakeholders could become signatories. Such an architecture would ideally protect and encourage data exchange and facilitate trade mechanisms between entities that adhere to the same standards.

A global consensus could provide the basis for promoting open data and data exchange, helping to address public health crises and other development goals, deal with the weaponization of data, and think about the trusted use and reuse of data.

A series of high-level dialogues is necessary to test and build this idea in 2021 and beyond. To be effective, the consensus will need to embrace the broadest global community of data providers and users, including national governments, the private sector, and civil society as well as stakeholders from every community that collects and uses data.

Notes

1. See https://www.cigionline.org/articles/digital-platforms-require-global-governance-framework.
2. Examples include the Convention on International Trade in Endangered Species of Wild Fauna and Flora, the Basel Convention on the Control of Transboundary Movements of Hazardous Wastes and Their Disposal, and the Convention for the Protection of Cultural Property in the Event of Armed Conflict.
3. These conventions establish a mutual commitment of parties to (1) protect a certain resource; (2) facilitate regulated use and trade among parties; (3) establish sanctions if the principles of the conventions are not followed (typically, national laws defining administrative or criminal sanctions are needed); (4) make each party accountable to the principles of the convention and sanction parties that do not follow the principles (for example, parties can stop trading the commodity with those that do not follow the provisions of the conventions); and (5) report to a monitoring system.

Spotlight 8.2
Promoting citizen science in the Amazon basin

A wide-ranging regional initiative is pooling indigenous, local, and international knowledge and efforts to study and protect Amazon freshwater systems.

For people living in the basin of the Amazon River—an area the size of the continental United States and home to 30 million people—fish are the most important source of animal protein, and fishing is the most important source of income. Yet the Amazon's aquatic ecosystems are being threatened by the expansion of agriculture, cattle pastures, infrastructure, logging, mining, and overfishing.[1] Managing fish populations is critical to sustaining these ecosystems and the human communities dependent on them. In turn, collecting, monitoring, and sharing data are critical to managing sustainable fisheries.

Citizen Science for the Amazon, created in 2017, is a network of multiple stakeholders, including more than 100 groups of citizen scientists (fishermen, indigenous peoples, local communities, and students) from across the Amazon basin and more than 25 academic, conservation, and grassroots organizations from seven countries.[2] These citizen scientists regularly monitor fish migrations and water quality, registering and sharing their observations via a common app and a platform. This platform is designed to guide data management decisions by connecting local efforts, using interoperable standards, aggregating data, and making the information open, safe, and accessible.[3] The result is the first database of the entire Amazon basin that is available for researchers, practitioners, and decision-makers.

Participants jointly define a large-scale question that is general enough to attract multiple stakeholders, but simple enough to encompass questions at smaller scales (see figure S8.2.1). Local partners work with citizen scientists to identify what local questions to answer, how to analyze and use the data, what decisions to inform, and what audiences to target.

Citizen Science for the Amazon jointly designs, tests, and adapts innovative solutions to the Amazon context. Over time, partners have agreed on elements of the data governance framework, including guiding principles, variables, protocols, terms of use, credit, and protection of privacy. Citizen science is supplanting traditional, prohibitively expensive, scientific survey methods and helping to bridge indigenous, local knowledge and mainstream, professional science.

Public engagement fosters the sustainable use and management of fish and natural resources, conserves key rivers, lakes, and wetlands, and improves livelihoods. It also empowers local communities to negotiate with government agencies and other stakeholders on issues such as securing fishing permits, selling sustainably caught fish in niche markets with higher prices, using evidence in grievance cases against hydroelectric dams for their impact on reducing fish stocks, and requesting supplemental social security income during no-fishing seasons. Leaders of the United Nations Environment Programme have recognized the significant contribution that citizen science is making to achievement of the Sustainable Development Goals.[4]

Information in this spotlight was supplied by Libby Hepburn, co-chair of the Sustainable Development Goals and Citizen Science Maximisation Group and co-chair of the Open Science and Citizen Science Council of Parties; Mariana Varese of the Wildlife Conservation Society; and Lea Shanley, senior fellow, Nelson Institute for Environmental Studies, University of Wisconsin–Madison.

Figure S8.2.1 Using a diverse set of open science and citizen science tools and technologies in the Amazon basin

Where and when do fish migrate in the Amazon basin and what environmental factors influence those migrations?

Network partners use diverse technologies to answer the question and
• gather, share and use data,
• collaborate in generating information for multiple purposes and audiences

Community-based, participatory and Indigenous and local knowledge methods, tools and protocols (e.g., journals, printed survey forms, community maps) facilitate engagement of diverse audiences.

Ictio.org is an application and open & safe database to collect and share information on Amazonian migratory fish.

Data is safely transferred and stored in servers. Then, open data is accessible to multiple audiences with diverse levels of access and in user-friendly formats.

Collaboration is enabled through carefully designed methodologies, in-person and virtual meetings, social media, Google platform and tools.

Source: Ciencia Ciudadana para la Amazonía (Citizen Science for the Amazon), Lima, Peru, https://www.amazoniacienciaciudadana.org/english/. Website screenshot © Citizen Science for the Amazon Network, Wildlife Conservation Society (WCS). Used with permission; further permission required for reuse.

Photo credits (clockwise, from top left): © G. Da Roit/WCS; © J. Becerra/WCS; © V. Eyng/Instituto de Desenvolvimento Sustentável Mamirauá; © Julio Araújo/ Centro de Innovación Científica Amazónica. All images used with permission; further permission required for reuse.

Notes

1. Alho, Reis, and Aquino (2015, 412).
2. See Ciencia Ciudadana para la Amazonía (Citizen Science for the Amazon), at https://www.amazoniaciencia ciudadana.org/english/.
3. See Citizen Science for the Amazon, Ictio (dashboard), https://ictio.org/.
4. See UNEP (2019). In addition, citizen science is a core component of open science (for example, see OECD 2015). The United Nations Educational, Scientific, and Cultural Organization (UNESCO) is developing a global policy and regulatory agenda on open science. As part of this effort, UNESCO launched a global consultation on open science, which has included consultation through the Citizen Science Global Partnership. (See the website, at http://citizenscienceglobal.org.) UNESCO "is expected to define shared values and principles for Open Science and identify concrete measures on Open Access and Open Data with proposals to bring citizens closer to science and commitments to facilitate the production and dissemination of scientific knowledge around the world." (See "UNESCO Recommendation on Open Science," United Nations Educational, Scientific, and Cultural Organization, Paris, https://en.uunesco.org/science -sustainable-future/open-science/recommendation.) Such recommendations are legal instruments with the aim of influencing the development of national laws and practices that UNESCO member states will be asked to report on. They represent a major opportunity for influencing the uptake of citizen science around the world.

References

Alho, Cleber J. R., Roberto E. Reis, and Pedro P. U. Aquino. 2015. "Amazonian Freshwater Habitats Experiencing Environmental and Socioeconomic Threats Affecting Subsistence Fisheries." *Ambio* 44 (5): 412–25. doi: 10.1007 /s13280-014-0610-z.

OECD (Organisation for Economic Co-operation and Development). 2015. *Making Open Science a Reality.* OECD Science, Technology, and Industry Policy Paper 25 (October 15). Paris: OECD. https://doi.org/10.1787/5jrs2f963zs1-en.

UNEP (United Nations Environment Programme). 2019. "United Nations Environment Programme Contributions to Secretary-General's Background Note for the Preparatory Meeting of the 2020 United Nations Conference to Support the Implementation of Sustainable Development Goal 14." Nairobi, Kenya, October 31, 2019. https://www.un.org/sites/un2.un.org/files/unep.pdf.

PART III

Moving toward an integrated national data system

9. Creating an integrated national data system

CHAPTER

9

Creating an integrated national data system

Main messages

1. By building an integrated national data system, countries can realize the full value of data for development. The system should provide a framework for the trustworthy, equitable production, flow, and use of data.

2. An integrated data system is built on an approach to data governance that is intentional, whole-of-government, and multistakeholder. The steps needed to implement such a system depend on a country's data maturity. What works in one context may not work in another.

3. To be sustainable, an integrated national data system must be continually improved. This will depend on having highly skilled human resources in government, civil society, academia, and the private sector.

4. Robust data protection is critical to building an integrated national data system. As the scope of such a system expands, the economic, social, and development returns increase, as do the data protection requirements.

Toward an integrated national data system

This chapter describes how to create an integrated national data system designed to realize the potential of data for development. Such a system relies on an approach to data governance that is intentional, whole-of-government, multistakeholder, and collaborative. It explicitly builds data production, protection, exchange, and use into planning and decision-making and integrates participants from civil society and the public and private sectors into the data life cycle and into the governance structures of the system. Although such a system is related to a national statistical system, it differs in key areas (box 9.1).

An integrated national data system is all about people. A well-functioning system requires people to produce, process, and manage high-quality data; people to populate the institutions that safeguard and protect the data from misuse; and people to draft, oversee, and implement data strategies, policies, and regulations. A well-functioning system also requires people to use data as a factor of production in both the public sector—for policy design and implementation—and the private sector—for decision-making and innovations in products and services. People are also needed to hold the public and private sectors accountable. All this requires robust data literacy.[1] Meanwhile, at the end of the day, it is people who will benefit from an integrated national data system. They will see better public policies, programs, and service delivery; more business opportunities and jobs; higher market efficiency; and greater accountability.

It is vital that the public trusts that data are being safely stored, exchanged, and used to create value equitably, while protecting against misuse. Thus the social contract for data is built into a well-functioning national data system and should be recognized in national development strategies.

When the foundation of an integrated national data system is in place and a variety of participants are included in the data life cycle, it can yield vast benefits for development. In fact, the more integrated the system and the more participants involved, the higher is the potential return. If two participants safely exchange data with each other, data can flow in two directions. If three participants exchange data, data can flow in six directions, and with four participants, in 12 directions. If data are reused and repurposed, these connections can increase exponentially. When government agencies, civil society, academia, and the private sector securely take part in a national data system, the potential uses of data expand and so does the potential development impact. As the scope of the system expands, so do the data protection requirements and the needs for safeguards against misuse.

An integrated national data system implies that all participants and stakeholders collaborate in a system in which data are safely produced, exchanged, and used. It does not mean that all data are stored in an integrated national database. And while such collaboration requires close coordination and shared governance between the participants, it does not necessarily require a centralized governance structure.

For many countries, a system in which high-quality data flow and are used safely among various participants remains a distant vision. A low-income country suffering from high levels of poverty, fragility, and poor governance may struggle to produce even the most fundamental data, let alone set up a whole-of-government, multistakeholder approach to data governance. Yet keeping sight of this vision matters for all countries, even those struggling the most with data, because it can serve as a guide in making decisions on how to develop their data systems.

Box 9.1 Relationship between an integrated national data system and a national statistical system

A national statistical system is an ensemble of units within a country that jointly collect, protect, process, and disseminate official statistics.[a] As such, a national statistical system is a core part of the more expansive integrated national data system. The scope of the integrated national data system goes beyond official statistics to encompass the data produced, exchanged, and used by participants from civil society and the public and private sectors for a variety of purposes. The blueprint for building an integrated national data system is a national data strategy, which is a country's plan for capturing greater economic and social value from data in line with the principles of a social contract for data. By contrast, the blueprint for building a national statistical system is a national statistical development strategy, which focuses on official statistics.

a. See the definition of a national statistical system proposed by the Organisation for Economic Co-operation and Development (OECD 2002, 220).

After envisioning what a well-functioning national data system might look like in a frictionless world, this chapter extends the use of the data maturity model of the last four chapters to discuss how countries can move closer to realizing this vision, depending on their context and their level of data maturity. One size will not fit all. Concrete steps to move closer to the vision will critically depend on local factors, many of which are related to political economy issues, such as the strength of institutions and key decision-makers. Another important aspect is the structure of the government: the system will look different in a centralized government structure than in a federal one, for example. But even for countries that remain far from the frontier of good data governance, if their policies address lack of human capital, trust, proper incentives, funding, and a culture of data use, the potential of data for development can be better realized.

The vision of an integrated national data system

An integrated national data system serves a number of important functions; it incorporates various participants from government, civil society, and the private sector; and it is built on the pillars discussed in part II. These pillars rest on a foundation of human capital, trust, funding, incentives, and data demand (figure 9.1).

Figure 9.1 What happens in an integrated national data system?

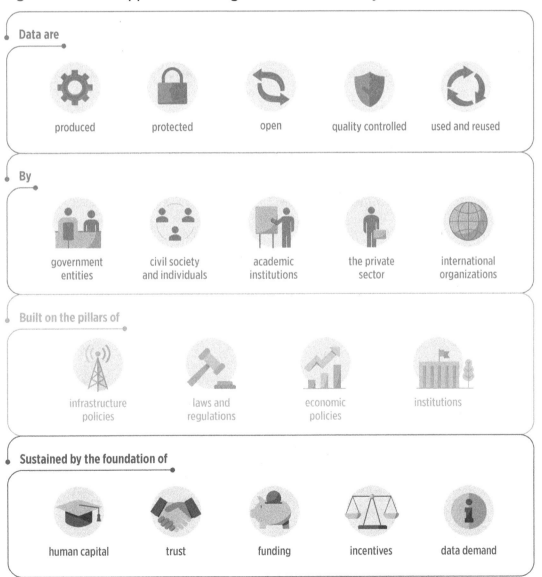

Data are
- produced
- protected
- open
- quality controlled
- used and reused

By
- government entities
- civil society and individuals
- academic institutions
- the private sector
- international organizations

Built on the pillars of
- infrastructure policies
- laws and regulations
- economic policies
- institutions

Sustained by the foundation of
- human capital
- trust
- funding
- incentives
- data demand

Source: WDR 2021 team.

Functions of an integrated national data system

An integrated national data system enables the production of data relevant to development; the equitable and safe flow of data among the participants in the system; and their ability to use and reuse the data while safeguarding against misuse.

Data production. A well-functioning national data system produces data relevant to policy planning, decision-making, and the national discourse. The data meet the needs of the various participants and cover and represent the population of interest. In line with a multistakeholder approach to data production, data produced by private sector entities, civil society organizations, and academia, as well as by citizens, are incorporated where appropriate into the national data system to fill in gaps and enable synergies with government data.

Data protection. To ensure rigorous protection of data and sensitive information, secure storage and transfer of data and safeguards against misuse are in place. This arrangement works as a catalyst for trust and participation in the system. As the types and volume of data expand, the producers and users of data increase, and their interoperability improves, data protection becomes increasingly important for safeguarding the integrity of the system. To the extent possible, robust data protection is achieved by legal and technological solutions before restricting access to data, which is a measure of last resort in an integrated national data system.

Data openness and flow. Open data and interoperability foster the flow of data within government and between the participants in the national data system. Common standards enable the exchange of data across government agencies to improve planning and decision-making as well as to enable cross-border data flows and collaboration.

Data quality control. To safeguard the integrity and quality of the data produced, sound methodological foundations in data production and stringent standards for quality control are adopted. Such foundations also improve the interoperability and comparability of data from different sources. To function well in this regard, the quality control processes must have a high degree of political independence.

Data use and reuse. The frequent and widespread use and reuse of data propel a successful national data system. A critical aspect is the routine use of data in planning and decision-making across government entities and the use and reuse of data beyond their original purpose, including in business models of data-driven companies, in academic research, in policy making and policy reform, and in informing media content and coverage.

Participants in an integrated national data system

The integrated national data system incorporates participants from the three development pathways—government and international organizations, individuals and civil society, and the private sector. This chapter discusses in more detail five groups of participants: government entities, civil society, academia, the private sector, and international and regional organizations. Although all five groups both produce and use data, each plays a different role in the national data system, which merits separate treatment.

Government entities. Government entities are the primary producers of public intent data for policy and government functions, such as by collecting admin- istrative data through censuses and surveys and through the national statistical system at large. But the role of government entities in the national data system extends beyond producing data for reporting and monitoring to exchanging data across entities and with other participants and using data for policy design and decision-making. Government entities also act as data stewards, setting out the rules that govern data use and ensuring data accessibility and protection. And they act as data managers, laying out and enforcing quality standards and ensuring secure data transactions.

Civil society and individuals. Civil society organizations (CSOs), national and international nongovernmental organizations (NGOs), the media, and individ- uals play a critical role as the producers and users of data that hold governments and the private sector accountable and highlight issues of public concern. This accountability function also applies to the production of citizen-generated data that act as a check on official government data if they are in doubt, fill gaps in coverage, or otherwise complement public intent and private intent data. The data produced by civil society are valuable beyond their primary functions, and their value increases through wider use and reuse by other participants in the national data system.

Academia. Academic institutions, think tanks, and research organizations both produce and use data in their research to guide and evaluate policy reforms through impact evaluations and forecasting, for example, and to inform and influence media and the public debate. Academic institutions also provide important education and training for data users and producers in government, the private sector, and civil society, as well as perform data research and development functions in the national data system.

The private sector. Firms in the private sector are prolific producers of data for their business processes, needs, and decisions. Some of these data are very valuable to those making public policy and to the public interest (see chapter 3). Thus the private sector is an important contributor to data production in the national data system, whose data are subject to common standards and quality control. In an integrated national data system, businesses gain from a data-driven culture in terms of competitiveness and profitability, and the national data system facilitates the transition to such a data-driven culture. Businesses also routinely rely on public intent data to improve business decisions and processes or to create new products and services.

International and regional organizations. These groups are de facto players in the national data system. Many international organizations require their members to engage in various types of reporting, such as progress in meeting the United Nations' Sustainable Development Goals (SDGs), which affects national data production.[2] International organizations develop methods and tools that cannot be produced efficiently at the national level. They also commonly act as standard setters. Best practice standards and methods are central to the international comparability of the data produced in the national data system (see spotlight 2.2). In low- and middle-income countries, international organizations also frequently act as donors to support data production. Furthermore, given economies of scale, some goals for a national data system may best be tackled at the supranational level (see spotlight 8.1). Regional organizations can be effective mechanisms for data governance and creating economies of scale in data and statistical capacity.

Pillars of an integrated national data system

An integrated national data system builds on the infrastructure policies, laws and regulations, economic policies, and institutions outlined in part II of this Report.

Infrastructure policies. In a well-functioning integrated national data system, hard and soft infrastructure policies are designed to enable the equitable and trustworthy production, processing, flow, and use of data (see chapter 5). People have access to the internet and can use it properly, consuming an adequate volume of data. Gaps in access—in terms of coverage, usage, and consumption—are addressed. These policies enable countries to improve access to international connectivity, favoring competition along the entire infrastructure supply chain. A proper competitive environment facilitates development of the more complex elements of data infrastructure. The establishment of internet exchange points (IXPs), which requires a competitive market for internet providers, helps create a vibrant digital ecosystem. Well-functioning IXPs attract content providers locally and from abroad. The consequent growth of data consumption generates investments from colocation data centers and cloud providers.

Laws and regulations. In an integrated national data system, laws and regulations guiding data openness, usage, and protection are in place (see chapter 6). Open data laws and access to information legislation complement one another by requiring public institutions to disclose data by default while granting individuals the right to compel disclosure. The rights of individuals on the use of their personal data are recognized and reserved, and an independent data protection authority safeguards those rights. Data controllers and processors are held accountable to ensure cybersecurity. Governments play a stewardship role by incorporating soft law around data use that reflects societal values, including standards, terms and conditions of use, norms, codes of conduct, and other voluntary frameworks. Both state and nonstate participants adhere to this body of soft law (see chapter 6).

Economic policies. Executive-level decision-makers in both the public and private sectors view data as foundational for creating value and are committed to implementing policies to maximize the value of data while ensuring that the proper safeguards are in place. In the whole-of-government strategy for data governance, policies set out norms, objectives, and tools. Antitrust tools are adapted to data-driven markets, and antitrust authorities tackle anticompetitive behavior by data-driven firms. Data can flow securely across borders and facilitate cross-border services transactions, such as in the financial services or telecommunications sectors. Tax loopholes for data-driven businesses are addressed (see chapter 7).

Institutions. The institutions required to effectively govern data are in place (see chapter 8). They include those that enact overarching strategic and policy objectives, such as an executive-level cross-functional group of key stakeholders that makes policy decisions, provides strategic direction, and mobilizes the necessary resources. To execute the strategy and manage the national data system, a repurposed existing institution or a newly created data governance office is fully operational. A national statistical office with sufficient financing, independence, and capacity to fulfill its role is in place. Institutions that monitor compliance, such as a data protection authority and an antitrust authority, are operating. Institutions that monitor and evaluate the system as a whole are created—such as oversight agencies that effectively monitor the accountability of data producers and users and nongovernment watchdogs that monitor public and private sector compliance with rules and standards.

Foundations of an integrated national data system

Putting these pillars in place for the national data system is not easy. They need to be anchored in a solid foundation of human capital, trust, funding, incentives, and data demand. Trust in particular plays a critical role in facilitating the integration of participants and their data. It is essential to binding the national data system to the social contract on data (see chapter 8).

Human capital. Human capital underpins a well-functioning national data system. Data producers have the skills needed to produce high-quality data that measure up to best practices and international standards for processing, storing, and ensuring the interoperability of data. The institutions that safeguard data, perform quality checks, and ensure that data flow among participants are staffed with skilled workers, as are the institutions that lay out the policies, laws, and regulations governing data flows. Individuals have the data literacy needed to ensure that data can be used effectively and equitably, to be empowered, and to hold governments accountable. Data literacy should be understood in a broad sense to include understanding basic statistical and numerical concepts; understanding how to analyze, interpret, and communicate data using digital tools; understanding the place of data in decision-making; and understanding data rights and data governance essentials. Finally, the next generation of data users is trained in data literacy through educational curricula, and the next generation of data scientists and statisticians is trained through higher education, ensuring the sustainability of the national data system.

Trust. For data to flow securely within the national data system, participants in the system trust that the data will be protected, that the information inherent in the data will not be misused, and that the value created from the data will be shared equitably. People trust the ability of government, academia, and the private sector to collect, protect, and safely share data gathered from them. Firms trust that their data will be used properly when those data are shared with third parties. And, in general, participants trust that the public sector enforcement systems are robust and that appropriate measures will be taken in the event of data misuse.

Funding. A well-functioning national data system is sufficiently funded. Government agencies have the resources to hire and pay highly skilled data sci- entists, statisticians, and data collectors at competitive levels, as well as the resources to purchase the technical infrastructure needed to collect, process, and manage data. Likewise, government agencies have the funding needed to achieve the goals set out in the national data strategy and to sufficiently staff the safeguarding and enabling institutions. Academia has funding to create, access, and analyze data. Civil society and individuals have the financial resources needed to acquire the technology often needed to monitor government data, produce data themselves, and use data from other participants.

Incentives. The right incentives and power balances conducive to the equitable production, exchange, and use of data are in place. To overcome the reluctance of government entities to share data openly because it could expose poor performance, risk data protection breaches with little return, or shrink their power, data exchanges are mandated or encouraged through incentives, where relevant. Incentives are similarly in place for the private sector, encouraging, and where relevant mandating, businesses to exchange data. In the private sector, such incentives deal appropriately with situations in which corporations may have invested capital in systems to accumulate data and wish to earn a return on the investment, keep data out of the hands of competitors, or both.

Data demand. An integrated national data system has a high demand for data and a culture of valuing and prioritizing data use. Data are viewed as foundational for creating public value through improved policy making, particularly by high-level management in both the public and private sectors. In the public sector, central analytical units and technical staff in ministries gather and analyze data tailored to the needs of decision-makers. In the private sector, companies view data as a valuable asset. For individuals and civil society at large, data are viewed as a tool for empowerment and for holding governments accountable. Programs to improve the data literacy of individuals, journalists, and other stakeholders are in place, ensuring future demand and the long-term sustainability of the national data system. Fact-checking is also well established to challenge the misuse of data.

Realizing the vision

For a country suffering from fragility, poverty, and poor governance, this vision of an integrated national data system may seem unattainable. As discussed in chapter 2, for many governments, just producing high-quality data is a challenge. Thus data exchanges and integration among various partners may not seem feasible. Yet any country can take steps toward fulfilling the vision of an integrated national data system. Using the data maturity model, this section describes the concrete steps countries can take to

move closer to the system envisioned here, focusing on how to integrate in the national data system the various participants: government agencies, civil society, academia, the private sector, and international and regional organizations.

Integrating these participants depends not only on a country's data maturity level, but also on other context-specific factors such as the relative strengths and weaknesses of the current institutions and actors. Where relevant, this discussion explores how local contexts might affect progress toward attaining the vision.

The data maturity model is used as an organizing framework to help determine the strengths and weaknesses of the existing data system and identify the sequential steps that can be taken to establish an integrated national data system. The model differentiates three stages. At low levels of data maturity, countries should prioritize establishing the fundamentals of a national data system. Once the fundamentals are in place, countries should seek to initiate data flows. At advanced levels of data maturity, the goal is to optimize the system (figure 9.2).

Figure 9.2 A data maturity model for a hypothetical national data system

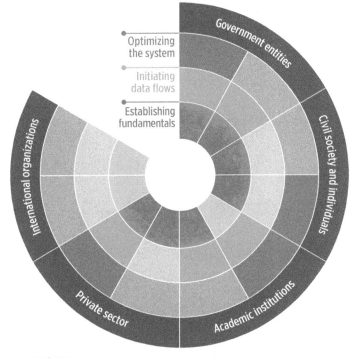

Source: WDR 2021 team.

Note: The figure shows steps in a data maturity model for a hypothetical national data system. The inner circle is the first stage of maturity, the second the middle stage, and so forth. Darker colors indicate steps accomplished; lighter colors indicate steps not accomplished. Thus for each participant, segments may be dark or light. In this way, the figure illustrates that countries may be at different data maturity stages at the same time and that some participants may be more integrated than others.

In practice, deviations from these steps are likely to occur as countries adapt them to their specific circumstances and exigencies. Early steps will likely need to be revisited, refined, and adjusted at later stages. Some countries will be more advanced in some domains but lacking in others—that is, elements identified as fundamentals may not be present in some mostly advanced systems. In a few circumstances, it may be appropriate for a country to change the sequencing of steps in certain domains.

Some countries may not have an intentional whole-of-government approach to data governance but still be advanced in data maturity. Although these countries can have much to gain from taking an intentional whole-of-government approach, an integrated national data system does not call for discarding what has been established, but rather building on its strengths. Regardless of where a country's current data maturity stands, building an integrated national data system will not happen overnight. It is a long-term process of ongoing steps, refinements, and improvements.

Integrating government

Government entities play a central role in the national data system as the main producers of public intent data. To contribute to and sustain a strong national data system, these entities must meet several objectives. They must address shortcomings in the coverage, quality, and usability of public intent data. They need to ensure the effective coordination of public sector data producers and data exchanges and the interoperability of data from various sources. And they must make data available and accessible to stakeholders across the system to promote use, reuse, and repurposing (see figure 9.3).

Data strategy formulation. Recognizing the importance of an integrated national data system in a high-level strategic document, such as a national data strategy, is central to accomplishing these objectives and to garnering the necessary political commitment and resources. The formulation of a national data strategy should be a transparent, collaborative process and include stakeholders from across the government, civil society, academia, and the private

Figure 9.3 Steps to integrating the public sector into the national data system

Establishing fundamentals

- **Policies:** Recognize the importance of an integrated national data system in a high-level strategic document.
- **Laws and regulations:** Put in place robust data protection regulations.
- **Human capital and funding:** Strengthen the technical capacity and financing of NSOs.
- **Institutions:** Create technical units in ministries to strengthen administrative data and coordinate data efforts across ministries.
- **Incentives:** Ensure that data scientists and statisticians in the public sector are appropriately remunerated.

Initiating data flows

- **Data demand:** Establish a culture of data use in ministries and among policy makers and legislators.
- **Incentives:** Prioritize open data for development and use of common standards throughout the data life cycle.
- **Infrastructure policies:** Establish a secure, integrated digital platform for storing and providing access to deidentified public intent data.

Optimizing the system

- **Institutions:** Charge an existing or new government unit with responsibility for overseeing and reporting on implementation of a national data strategy.
- **Incentives:** Empower the NSO to take an active role in the national data system.
- **Policies:** Define clear institutional mandates for the various government institutions.

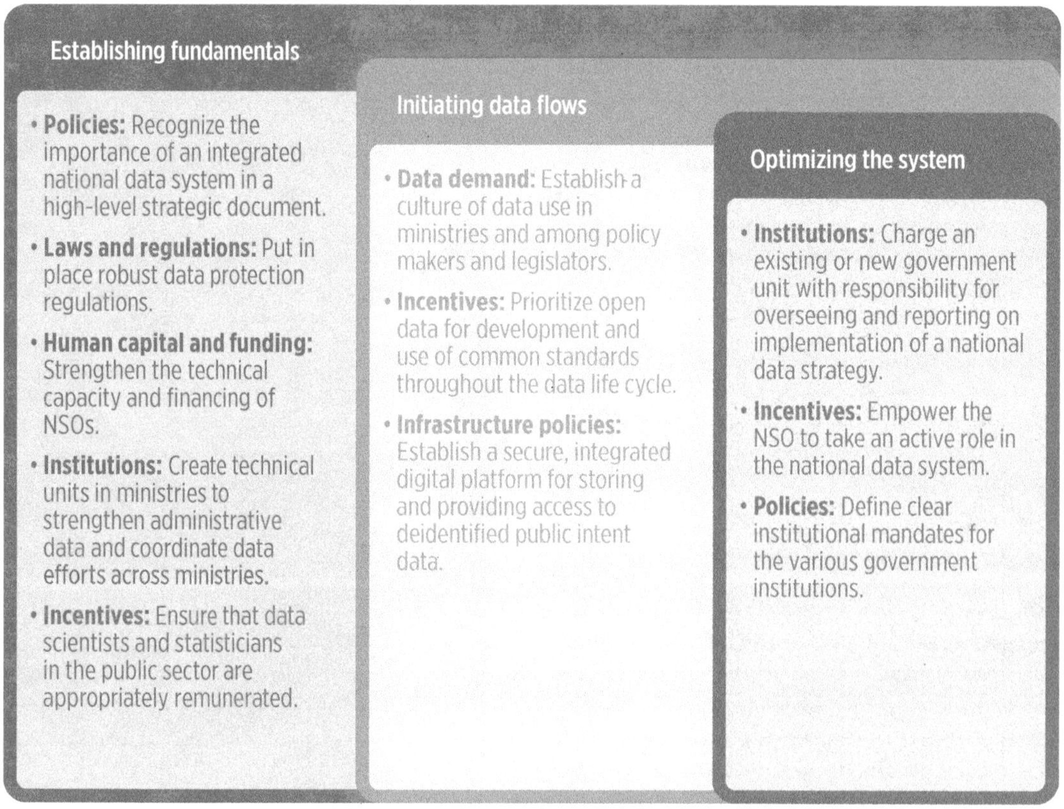

Source: WDR 2021 team.

Note: Categories overlap and are meant to be illustrative. NSO = national statistical office.

sector to encourage broad-based buy-in. To address shortcomings in public intent data, the national data strategy should reflect the priorities discussed in previous chapters: robust data protection, political commitments to the independence of data producers, adequate and sustained financing, investments in human capital, and efforts to strengthen the data literacy of the general populace, policy makers, legislators, and civil society. This process should also establish a common framework for accountability in and independent oversight of the national data system. To achieve these priorities, the national data strategy should include concrete policy steps, such as the ones that follow, and it should be reflected in the national development plans. For example, in Colombia, National Development Plan 2014–18 was used as a vehicle to formally assign its National Statistical Administrative Department (DANE) the role of coordinator and regulator of the national statistical system.[3]

Data protection regulations. Putting in place robust data and privacy protection regulations is an early priority in establishing an integrated national data system. These regulations should be backed by independent oversight of compliance with them, a function that a data protection authority may serve (see chapter 8). An example of independent oversight is the United Kingdom's Information Commissioner's Office, a nondepartmental body tasked with upholding "information rights in the public interest." Reporting directly to Parliament, it oversees the Data Protection Act, Freedom of Information Act, Privacy and Electronic Communications Regulations (PECR), Environmental Information Regulations, INSPIRE Regulations, and Re-use of Public Sector Information (RPSI) regulations.[4] Although these regulatory steps need to be taken early, they remain relevant for advanced data systems. Legal and institutional arrangements will require adjustment as the data and policy landscapes change.

NSO capacity. Because the NSO fulfills the core function of producing official statistics, it is fundamental that the office be integrated into the national data system. This requires strengthening the technical capacity and financing of NSOs to fill data gaps and produce high-quality official statistics (see chapter 2).

Technical data units. Within government ministries and agencies, the foundations of administrative data should be strengthened. Creating and staffing technical units dedicated to the production and management of administrative data are vital for the participation of ministries in the national data system. Administrative data should be based on common standards promoted across the national data system for their production, processing, management, and protection. In addition, ensuring the interoperability and accessibility of administrative data must be a priority of administrative data systems. For example, Argentina connects data registers through its data interoperability platform for the public sector (INTEROPER.AR).[5] Statistical units at ministries should centralize cataloging and storage of datasets, including of existing datasets. This will require continually modernizing the technological and data infrastructure for the production, management, safe exchange, and secure storage of data.

Remuneration of data scientists. To ensure a functional integration of government institutions in the national data system, civil servants need the incentives and capabilities to produce, safeguard, and use data. To this end, governments could pursue civil service reforms to ensure that data scientists and statisticians in the public sector are appropriately remunerated. These steps are needed to attract and retain the human capital required to build and sustain a successful national data system. Lack of competitive salaries and career opportunities is a frequently cited barrier to greater institutional performance and the capacity of data producers, for instance in El Salvador, Guatemala, and Peru.[6]

Culture of data use. To initiate data flows, it is vital to establish a culture of data use in ministries and among policy makers and legislators. Institutionalizing data-intensive management practices can jump-start this process (see chapter 2). This effort should be accompanied by ongoing investments in the data literacy of policy makers and legislators. Technical units should be required to periodically deliver knowledge products based on administrative data and disseminated in accordance with a public release calendar. Such products should become an integral part of monitoring, evaluation, and citizen engagement efforts.

Common standards. Open access to public intent data is central to realizing the broad benefits of widespread data use, reuse, and repurposing. On the political front, it is critical that governments prioritize open data for development and use common standards throughout the data life cycle. Government entities should view data stewardship as a strategic function needed for the effective management and use of internal data assets, as well as for seamless data exchanges among entities. To undertake this function, each entity should receive the required financial and human resources and should use common standards for the production, management, quality assurance, and interoperability of public intent data.

Integrated digital platforms. On the technical front, establishing a secure, integrated digital platform for storing and providing access to deidentified public intent data deposited on the platform by producers from across the public sector can initiate data flows and spur further demands for data. The creation of a unified platform should be conditional on putting in place common technological, legal, and institutional standards for safeguarding confidential and sensitive information. An example is Open Data Philippines (ODPH). ODPH was launched in January 2014 as part of the multilateral Open Government Partnership initiative, which also includes Brazil, Indonesia, Mexico, Norway, South Africa, the United Kingdom, and the United States.[7] The ODPH repository works as a core government program ensuring citizens' rights of transparency and access to information. The platform collects more than 1,237 datasets from 99 government agencies and organizations, which allows the disclosure of specific data from different sectors. ODPH acts as an intermediary between the national government and its constituents. It also removes barriers limiting data sharing between agencies.

Data strategy oversight unit. A national data strategy is key to optimizing the national data system. Central to this process is charging an existing or new government unit with overseeing and reporting on implementation of the national data strategy. The unit will play an important coordinating and integrating role in optimizing data flows among participants in the national data system. This role will include acting as liaison with the technical data production teams in ministries and the NSO to support the development and use of common standards for activities across the data life cycle. Of particular importance is ensuring a common and robust approach to the protection of personal data and sensitive information across the system. The institutional home and reporting lines for such a unit will likely differ, depending on the country context. To be effective, the unit should have both the political power to oversee the data agenda of other government institutions and the technical and legal know-how to understand the complexities of data governance.

Many NSOs have the most extensive experience of government agencies in dealing with important data issues. To the extent that a strong and capable NSO exists or that reforms can be readily undertaken to shore up its independence, financial resources, and technical capabilities in line with the recommendations put forth in chapter 2, the NSO may be well placed to co-lead formulation of the national data strategy and possibly to oversee its implementation.[8]

In New Zealand, the NSO is branded as a data agency, and the head of the NSO was appointed Government Chief Data Steward by the State Services Commissioner in July 2017. A cabinet mandate empowers the Chief Data Steward to facilitate and enable "an inclusive, joined-up approach across government to set standards and establish common capabilities, including developing data policy, infrastructure, strategy, and planning."[9]

Estonia has opted for another institutional home for the unit overseeing implementation of the national data agenda. The steering body for implementing the government's digital strategy, which includes overseeing its national data system, is the e-Estonia Council.[10] The council is chaired by the prime minister and organized by the Strategy Unit of Government Office, a public entity charged with assisting the government in designing and implementing policy.[11] Estonia's national data system centers around X-Road, an open-source data exchange layer solution that allows linked public and private databases to automatically exchange information, ensuring confidentiality, integrity, and interoperability among the parties exchanging data.[12] X-Road's cryptography protocols enhance transparency because they log entries into the system and give individuals detailed insights into who is sharing their data and for what purposes.

Similar to Estonia, Argentina has adopted a federated data sharing model that connects data registers and has enabled the development of public services through its data interoperability platform for the public sector. This system includes the Smart Judicial Investigation tool and the National Tax and Social Identification System (SINTyS), which coordinates database exchanges and single data requests at the national, provincial, and municipal levels to support better targeting and monitoring of social programs.[13]

NSO empowerment. Regardless of whether the NSO houses the oversight unit, as the data system matures the NSO should be empowered to take on an active role (see chapter 2). In Estonia, although the NSO does not oversee the national data system, it has been elevated to national data agency status—"a center of excellence for public sector data administration and research, which would support the making of data-based decisions nationwide, integrating data administration and analytics."[14] In line with this recommendation, NSOs could take on a bigger role in many ways, including conducting data literacy training for stakeholders in government, CSOs, the media, academia, and the private sector, as well as by providing specialized technical assistance to government departments aimed at improving methods for the production, processing, management, deidentification, and dissemination of public intent datasets. As part of an expanded role in training, NSOs could also develop (or hire) staff to engage in research on new methods for data collection and test the validity of experimental statistics. In addition, NSOs could offer independent quality assurance of the administrative data products and related official statistics produced outside of the NSO.

Institutional mandates. National data strategies should be revisited periodically as the national data system matures in light of evolving data needs and technological improvements. The process of formulating a national data strategy is an opportunity to define clear institutional mandates for the NSO, ministries, and specialized government agencies for the production, quality assurance, exchange, and protection of public intent data. Such mandates can minimize overlapping and duplicated data production, thereby making the whole system more efficient. Defining clear institutional mandates also helps identify the comparative advantages and expected contributions of each institution and simplifies the task of securing financial and human resources commensurate with the mandates of each institution.

Integrating civil society and individuals

Civil society and individuals should be empowered to participate in the national data system as users of data and as data producers in their own right, whether citizen-generated or collected by CSOs (figure 9.4). A key function of CSOs, national and international NGOs, individual citizens, and journalists and the media is to hold the government and private sector accountable. But the national data system also stands to gain from the systematic incorporation of citizen-generated data for use by other participants. This effort requires collaboration and shared governance arrangements between government and civil society. Because of the importance of civil society's accountability function, these governance arrangements must be set up to reinforce the unconditional independence of civil society data producers and users.

For civil society and individuals to be an integral part of a national data system, several prerequisites must be met.

Legal rights to data production. Laws and regulatory frameworks are needed to protect people's rights to produce, use, and disseminate data. Laws should be amended to support individuals' role in, as well as their accountability function for, the data system. At the same time, laws and regulatory frameworks need to credibly protect data and sensitive information on people so they will trust they can safely participate in the national data system. Instituting civil society watchdogs to monitor public and private sector compliance with the rules and regulations of the data system can act as additional safeguards for independence and data protection.

Figure 9.4 Steps to integrating civil society into the national data system

Establishing fundamentals

- **Laws and regulations:** Institute laws protecting people's rights to produce, use, and disseminate data.
- **Incentives:** Create civil society watchdogs to monitor compliance with the rules of the system.
- **Funding:** Ensure that civil society has sufficient funding and resources for data production and use.

Initiating data flows

- **Human capital:** Improve data literacy through joint projects, training, and secondments and through the education system.
- **Infrastructure policies:** Ensure adoption of common standards that improve data quality and interoperability.
- **Trust:** Promote trust through establishment of an independent scientific quality control unit.

Optimizing the system

- **Institutions:** Institutionalize collaboration for the systematic use of citizen-generated data in decision-making.
- **Incentives:** Include civil society in planning, high-level decisions, and strategy setting for the national data system.

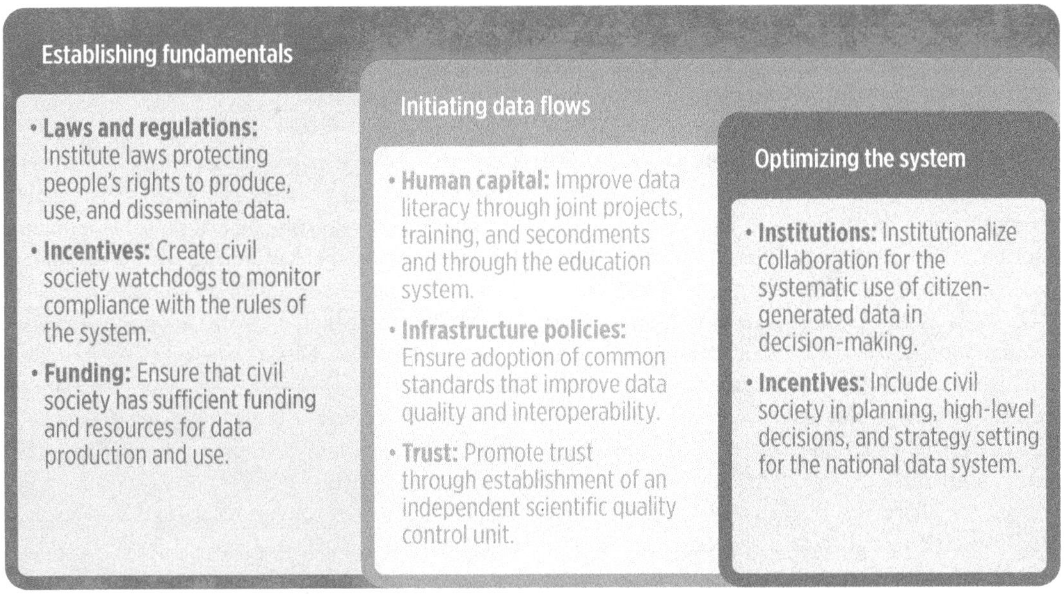

Source: WDR 2021 team.

Note: Categories overlap and are meant to be illustrative.

Funding and resources. Civil society also needs sufficient funding and resources for data production and use. Interviews with representatives of NGOs in Argentina, Kenya, and Nepal revealed that lack of funding can constrain citizen-generated data.[15] Both international donors and national funders could improve funding by including specific budgets for citizen data production alongside funding for institutional data collection.[16] General funds for citizen data collection akin to those for funding of scientific research could also be created. When civil society has limited access to data collection resources, such as smartphones for computer-assisted interviewing or collection of satellite-based global positioning system (GPS) data, such resources could be directly distributed by funders or loaned through organizations dedicated to providing communities with technological tools and training.[17] Open-source software for data collection, such as ODK, as well as free-of-charge software for data collection, such as Survey Solutions and CSPro, could be supported.[18] CSOs also need technical support in adopting and operating such resources and software to ensure they have the capability to produce high-quality data.

Data literacy. Lack of data literacy in civil society is a major barrier to the demand for high-quality, accessible data, and it limits the accountability role that civil society can play. It also leads to low levels of trust in citizen-generated data by other participants, which, in turn, hinders data flows from civil society to the national data system. Improving data literacy through project partnerships, training, and secondments can help address these skill gaps and trust deficits. For example, the Ugandan Bureau of Statistics and Ministry of Education supported the CSO Twaweza in survey and sampling design for a numeracy and literacy survey. Twaweza then independently carried out the data collection and processing, improving the quality of and trust in citizen-generated data. The data were later used by the Ministry of Education.[19] In addition to training, joint projects, fellowships, and secondments of staff from CSOs to data-driven institutions can increase the technical capacities of CSOs.[20] One private sector–led initiative to increase digital literacy in civil society, StoryLab Academy, uses online webinars and face-to-face training to improve digital literacy among African journalists.[21] The academy is a joint initiative of Code for Africa, the World Bank's Global Media Development Program, and Google News Lab.

Data literacy should also be reinforced across society more broadly. One aspect is incorporating data literacy in primary and secondary education curricula (chapter 2). Empirical studies on financial literacy suggest that integrating data literacy into school curricula may ultimately be more effective than targeted adult education.[22] Because of the relatively young populations of lower- and middle-income countries, incorporating data literacy programs in school curricula could reap valuable returns. For example, Rwanda has supported initiatives to build digital skills through its multistakeholder Digital Ambassador Program.[23] In addition to general programs, targeted data literacy efforts to reach traditionally marginalized groups such as women and indigenous communities may be needed to reduce the digital divide.

Common standards. Data flows between civil society and other actors can also be promoted by adopting common standards that improve data quality and interoperability. The efforts to promote adoption of these standards should be augmented by efforts aimed at strengthening analytical capacity to ensure their proper implementation. For example, the collaboration between Twaweza and public institutions helped ensure that data on literacy and numeracy were collected in accordance with official educational standards.[24] Similarly, in Mozambique the standardization of community scorecards used by several NGOs to assess school and health care services at the local level allowed the data to be aggregated to the national level, where they were used in research and advocacy campaigns.[25]

Quality control unit. For citizen-generated data to be reused—such as to inform policy decisions—their quality and representativeness need to be guaranteed. One specific concern is advocacy bias in cases in which the primary purpose of the data produced by civil society is to advocate for certain issues. To this end, the relevant government agencies and CSOs could together establish an independent scientific quality control unit to assess the methodological soundness and representativeness of citizen-generated data for possible use in national data portals and in SDG reporting.[26] Closer collaboration and the adoption of common standards do not mean that civil society ceases to play its critical role of holding other actors accountable by challenging their data, views, or priorities. Methodological rigor and common standards may in fact empower civil society to play an accountability role by increasing the credibility and interoperability of citizen-generated and CSO data. At the same time, not all CSOs may opt for their data to be used for policy purposes or SDG reporting if advocacy is their primary concern. In any case, data should flow to civil society to empower and inform decisions of communities and individuals and ensure that benefits from an integrated data system are broadly shared.

Institutionalized collaboration. To optimize data flows, the relationship between civil society and other participants should evolve from a stage of ad hoc collaboration to institutionalized collaboration for the production and use of data. From the perspective of the government, this means that citizen data production and use are by default integrated into policy-making and administrative processes.[27] An example is the framework developed by South Africa's Department of Planning, Monitoring and Evaluation on how to include citizen-based monitoring in planning, budgeting, and evaluation systems.[28] Institutionalized collaboration allows the government to leverage civil society's unique perspectives, local expertise, and motivation, whereas civil society can influence policies and services, highlighting problems that may otherwise go unnoticed or be ignored. With institutionalized collaboration, civil society could have a designated role of collecting data that would otherwise be too expensive or difficult to collect, such as wildlife counts. Institutionalized collaboration on data would also serve as an incentive for relying on data for policy making more broadly, and thus would bolster demand for data.

Joint planning and strategy setting. Finally, governments should take steps to include civil society in planning, high-level decisions, and strategy setting for the national data system. In Chile, where civil society participation is mandated by the national Law on Associations and Citizen Participation in Public Management, the NSO has put in place a civil society council.[29] Once included in multistakeholder governance forums, civil society can progress from being a standard-taker to a standard-maker. Including citizens in the planning, production, and use of data can also help empower individuals and enhance trust between citizens and their governments.[30]

Integrating academia

In a well-functioning national data system, academia (including universities, think tanks, and research organizations) generates data and insights, advances the methodological frontier, and trains other participants in data production and use (figure 9.5).

For academia to realize this potential, several conditions must be in place.

Technological infrastructure. Academics must have adequate financial support and access to key information and communication technology (ICT) infrastructure. Higher education funding should prioritize and include designated budgets for data infrastructure. Where limited, access to ICT infrastructure required for any work involving large datasets should be expanded.

Data awareness. Any form of cooperation and data exchange between academia and other participants in the national data system requires awareness of which databases are maintained by participants. A survey of policy makers in 126 low- and middle-income countries found that they learn about domestic data sources primarily through consultations and informal communications, highlighting the important

Figure 9.5 Steps to integrating academia into the national data system

Establishing fundamentals

- **Infrastructure policies:** Ensure that academics have adequate financial support and access to key ICT infrastructure.
- **Data demand:** Promote awareness of the datasets of participants by building relationships among partners in academia and government.

Initiating data flows

- **Data demand:** Set up data sharing agreements, commission data production by academics, and support the repurposing of academic data.
- **Human capital:** Promote data literacy through quantitative degree programs, workshops, and secondments.

Optimizing the system

- **Infrastructure policies:** Institutionalize access to data through data portals and data enclaves.
- **Data demand:** Support and adopt data innovations by academia.
- **Incentives:** Support initiatives that provide legal access to scientific journals.

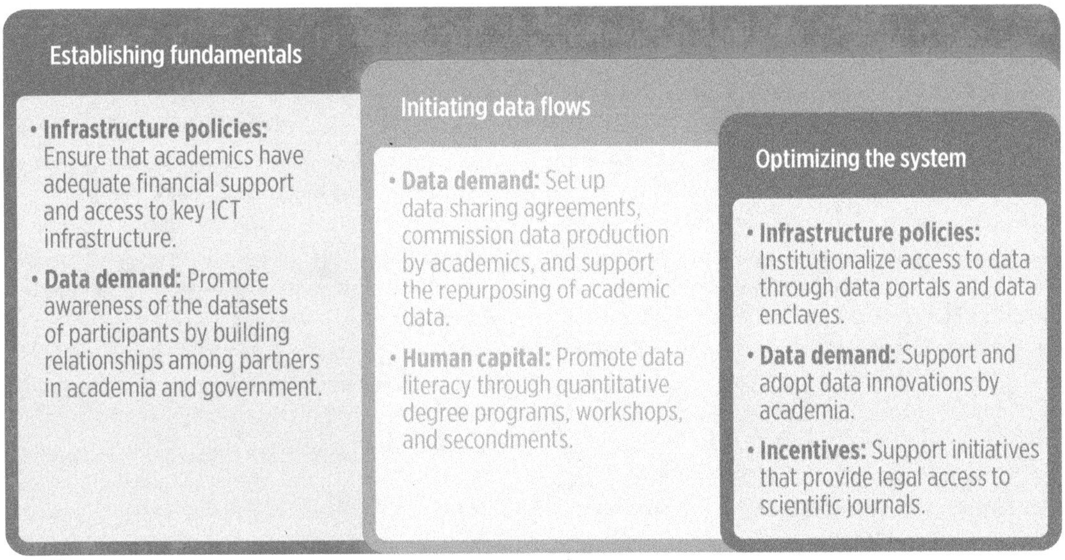

Source: WDR 2021 team.

Note: Categories overlap and are meant to be illustrative. ICT = information and communication technology.

role of personal interactions and social capital.[31] At low data maturity levels, promoting awareness of the datasets of participants by building relationships between partners in government and academia, such as through workshops, is therefore a priority. As in civil society, laws and regulations need to protect academics' rights to collect and share data.

Data exchange agreements. To initiate data flows, researchers can leverage relationships with other participants in the national data system and set up project-based data exchange agreements—for example, to access administrative data collected by the government. Other participants may take advantage of academia's expertise and commission the generation of data for their needs. Data generated by academics as part of their research could be repurposed by other participants in the national data system, from government policy makers to students pursuing higher education. An example of how researchers can make their data available for repurposing is the Datahub for Field Experiments in Economics and Public Policy, a public searchable database that researchers affiliated with Innovations for Poverty Action (IPA) and the Abdul Latif Jameel Poverty Action Lab (J-PAL) use to publish their data from impact evaluations.[32] It is critical to ensure that the data made available for downstream use are sufficiently documented, not only to confirm replicability of past findings but also to properly inform future use.

Data literacy. Academia also plays an important role in the flow of human capital and the promotion of data literacy. Tertiary education programs should be geared toward training professionals skilled in using data who are prepared to join institutions in the data system. At lower data maturity levels, any programs providing skills in quantitative fields, such as statistics, economics, or computer science, will be useful. Beyond formal tertiary education, academia can train participants from government agencies, the private sector, or civil society by means of training courses, workshops, and seminars. For example, the Data Literacy pillar of the Data-Pop Alliance—an alliance created by the Harvard Humanitarian Initiative, MIT Connection Science, and Overseas Development Institute—has developed a framework and tools to establish core competencies toward becoming data literate.[33] The Nepal Data Literacy Program, established in 2019 through a partnership between the Nepalese government, the World Bank, and the United Kingdom's Department for International Development (since incorporated into the Foreign, Commonwealth and Development Office), comprises a 100-hour modular, customizable pedagogy to support both building technical skills and efforts to enhance a culture of data use among Nepalis.[34] The program is now partnering with the Kathmandu University School of Management to incorporate data literacy toolkits into university programs and develop a data-driven course that will be free to other institutions and thousands of students as a result.

Embedding a team of researchers in public institutions is another effective way of transferring skills. In Peru, IPA and J-PAL partnered with the Ministry of Education to embed a team of researchers in the ministry. They then worked with public officials to conduct several impact evaluations using administrative data. The ministry subsequently scaled up three programs based on the evaluation results, and the unit is now government-run.[35]

Data portals and enclaves. To optimize data flows to academia, academia's access to public intent data could be institutionalized by establishing data portals and data enclaves. The latter enable researchers to use confidential microdata from surveys and government censuses behind secure firewalls. For example, Mexico's National Institute of Statistics and Geography (INEGI) offers researchers data access through its Microdata Laboratory, which is located in secure enclaves on its premises, provided they undergo an application and training process.[36] Similar institutions have been set up in other countries, such as DataFirst in South Africa[37] and the Scientific Research Center at the Palestinian Central Bureau of Statistics in the West Bank and Gaza.[38] Implementing these models requires a secure infrastructure, skills in the deidentification of data, trust, and sanctions for misuse and attempts to reidentify individuals. When public intent data are made accessible to researchers, data producers should require that insights gained from the data flow back to them such as in the form of technical briefs or open-access journal articles. This requirement helps ensure that data exchanges serve broader development objectives. Microdata access should also extend to metadata and syntax files to increase ease of use and transparency.

Data innovations. Finally, innovations emanating from academia should be supported and, where relevant, adopted. Academia can play a role in transferring and applying global knowledge to local contexts. For example, randomized experiments in international development research were originally pioneered by academics at elite universities, but since then they have proliferated and been adopted as a decision-making tool by many governments, including those in low- and middle-income countries.[39] A prominent example is Mexico's National Council for the Evaluation of Social Development Policy (CONEVAL), which was set up in 2004 with the mandate to coordinate evaluation exercises of the National Social Development Policy, as well as to provide guidelines to define, identify, and measure poverty.[40] The agency, endowed by the government of Mexico with budgetary, technical, and management autonomy, implements or commissions evaluations of the social policies developed by the Mexican government.

Access to scientific journals. Local research institutions, partnering with governments, have acted as important knowledge brokers in this process. Domestic researchers can also push the methodological frontier and develop methods tailored to the specific country contexts. For academia to play this role, it needs not only sufficient funding and academic freedom, but also access to international journals, databases, and exchange opportunities. For example, in light of high access fees, especially for scholars and institutions in low- and middle-income countries, initiatives that provide legal access to scientific journals should be supported and scaled. One example of such initiatives is Research4Life.[41] Similarly, researchers from high-income countries should be more responsive to requests for full-text publications from other researchers on platforms such as ResearchGate or LinkedIn.

Integrating the private sector

Targeted policies, initiatives, and incentives are needed to support businesses through the transition to a data-driven culture and enable them to become active participants in the national data system (figure 9.6).

High-speed wireless broadband. Establishing reliable, efficient physical infrastructure is foundational to the production and use of data and is an obvious prerequisite to integrating the private sector into a national data system. As data traffic expands globally in volume and velocity, businesses can participate in national and international data systems only if they have access to reliable, affordable high-speed wireless broadband.[42] Notwithstanding the high investment costs involved in the construction and operation of the national transmission networks (backbones) connected via fiber-optic cable and satellite to international links, governments need to find ways to support this vital infrastructure (see chapter 5).[43] Incentives, including subsidies, can be used to encourage existing or new operators to invest in less lucrative geographical areas. And there may be opportunities to leverage fiber-optic infrastructure in other sectors such as utilities and railways. Fiber can also be installed cost effectively in conjunction with new road construction.[44]

Data literacy. Another priority in the early stages of the integrated national data system is to equip workers and businesses with the skills and appliances needed to produce and use data, including having access to mobile devices and computing and data management infrastructure. Data systems

Figure 9.6 Steps to integrating the private sector into the national data system

Establishing fundamentals

- **Infrastructure policies:** Construct national transmission networks for high-speed wireless broadband access.
- **Human capital:** Equip workers and businesses with the skills and appliances needed to produce and use data.

Initiating data flows

- **Infrastructure policies:** Increase IXPs and data centers to improve the efficiency of data transfers.
- **Incentives:** Adopt compensation and noncompensation schemes to promote data exchanges.
- **Data demand:** Promote the role of data stewards in business.

Optimizing the system

- **Incentives:** Increase data interoperability through the adoption of stringent data quality and privacy standards that are also pro-business.
- **Infrastructure policies:** Promote the expansion of and access to colocation data centers.
- **Trust:** Engage business through trusted data intermediaries.

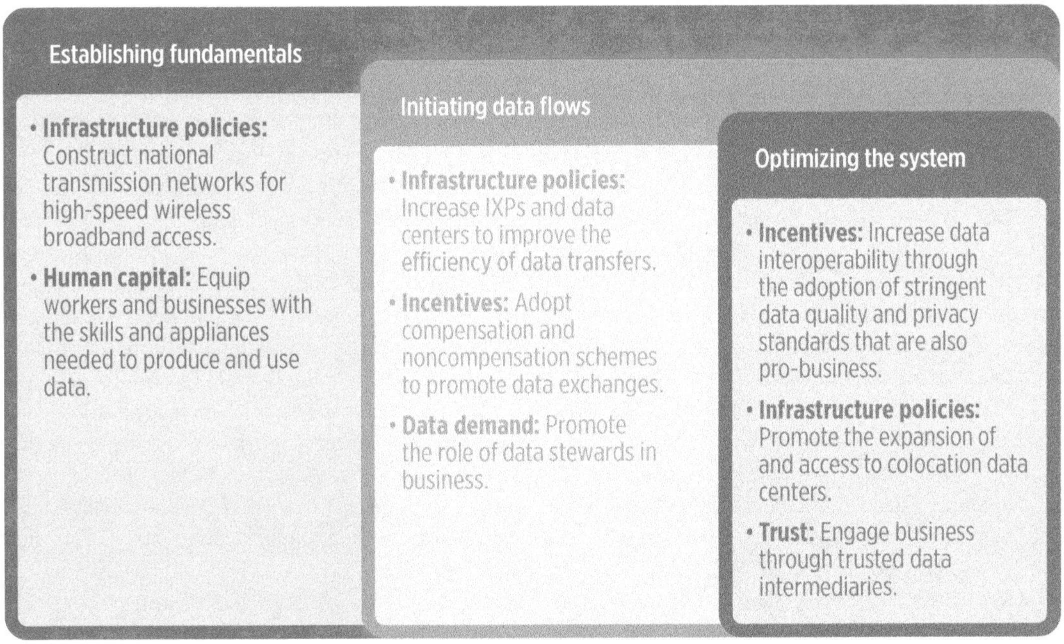

Source: WDR 2021 team.

Note: Categories overlap and are meant to be illustrative. IXPs = internet exchange points.

require workers with specialized skills in statistics, economics, computer science, geographic information systems, and data science to allow businesses to collect, store, and process data in the first place. Government-led or -funded training initiatives on data literacy for the current labor force are essential to equip workers with the skills required in today's labor markets and create the necessary data literacy and demand for data. In particular, much more needs to be done to scale up the availability—and gradually the sophistication—of public data literacy programs for the workforce outside of formal secondary or tertiary education systems. Government-funded examples include the Nepal Data Literacy Program and the Sudan Evidence-Base and Data Literacy Capacity Development Program, which has developed an introductory data literacy course and an intermediate-level "data storytelling" curriculum.[45]

Installation of IXPs. Increasing the efficiency of data transfers is central to initiating data flows within the private sector and across the integrated national data system. Governments can take steps to encourage private-led investment in the installation of IXPs, which reduce internet access costs and improve performance for users. For example, it is estimated that the absence of an IXP regional interconnection infrastructure forced Latin America to pay nearly US$2 billion in international traffic costs in 2014; increasing IXPs in the region could reduce overall traffic costs by one-third.[46] At the technical level, building an IXP is relatively simple and inexpensive, but establishing and maintaining the necessary level of trust and collaboration between stakeholders can be a challenge.[47] To establish an IXP, internet service providers (ISPs) and other actors (many of whom are competitors) must agree on IXP location, mode of operation, and management structure—all of which should be neutral to ensure buy-in.[48] For example, when the first IXP, KIXP, was established in Kenya in 2000, a legal challenge filed by the incumbent telecom operator led to its immediate closure. Only after a year of appeals and persistent lobbying was KIXP allowed to reopen.[49] In Mexico, the first IXP was not established until 2014 because of problems around trust and a lack of collaboration between ISPs. The second was installed in 2018.

Compensation and noncompensation schemes. To initiate and maintain flows, proactive compensation and noncompensation schemes to encourage private sector data exchanges are critical. Business-to-government (B2G) data exchanges are generally based on voluntary contractual agreements. The government should typically take a somewhat restrained approach to measures that force the private sector to exchange data (see chapters 6 and 7). Although data are a nonrival good and the reasons in favor of data sharing are compelling, the private sector does not necessarily have to provide the government with access to its data for free. The European Commission has suggested that compensation schemes could be in the public interest. Options include free data; free of charge plus tax incentives; marginal cost pricing; marginal cost pricing plus a return on investment markup; or market price.[50] The Contracts for Data Collaboration (C4DC) initiative has created an analytical framework and an online library of key elements of data sharing agreements to reduce the transaction costs of negotiating data sharing between the private sector and policy makers.[51]

Other types of incentives to increase B2G data exchanges without compensation include public recognition programs that showcase engagement. Such a program could enhance the reputations of companies and reduce the amount of compensation expected (if any). By increasing the transparency of B2G data exchange arrangements, societal expectations about the utility of private intent data for public policy, as well as expectations about B2G engagement, could gradually shift, thereby encouraging other businesses to join. Governments could also consider marketing mechanisms such as labeling schemes that could be used to highlight B2G data exchanges undertaken to pursue public policy goals.[52]

Companies could be incentivized to share their data through corporate social responsibility programs. For example, Facebook's Data for Good initiative is offering innovative datasets intended to aid public policy decisions. Other private companies may be encouraged to share their data at a reduced cost for public initiatives, with special grants for researchers or tax breaks for the data provider. If the private sector considers the risks of data exchanges to be too great, data intermediaries can facilitate arrangements in which the relevant algorithms are sent to companies directly for local data analysis. For example, OPAL (Open Algorithms), which describes itself as a "non-profit socio-technological innovation," provides a platform that allows researchers to send companies certified open-source algorithms that are then run on big data behind companies' firewalls.[53] This arrangement allows governments and others to analyze and gain insight from granular datasets collected by private companies that otherwise would be unavailable for legal, commercial, or ethical reasons.

Data stewards. Data exchanges can be advanced by businesses designating data stewards within their organizations to oversee internal data governance and engage with others. Data stewards play a vital role in establishing good data management in the private sector and in pursuing and facilitating sustainable data exchange arrangements.[54] Alongside their business-led functions, data stewards could be tasked with identifying data that could be shared to promote the public interest and identifying and nurturing potential collaboration with the government or others, such as data collaboratives. Data stewards can also lead efforts to ensure that any insights gained from exchanges are acted on. Although primary oversight of data protection issues should be assigned to a chief privacy officer, in the context of data exchange and reuse data stewards should be responsible for protecting potentially sensitive information and ensuring the protection of data when reused.[55]

Common standards. Transitioning to high data maturity levels requires facilitating the interoperability of public and private data through the adoption of stringent data quality and privacy standards that are also pro-business. Like all participants in the national data system, businesses must be incentivized to adopt stringent standards for data quality and interoperability to facilitate integration with public systems. Businesses' adoption of such standards could be promoted through some of the incentive mechanisms discussed earlier in this chapter and rolled out through advanced training programs. Uptake by businesses can also be increased as countries adopt international standards that improve the cross-border interoperability of data in the commercial sphere—such as the International Organization for Standardization (ISO) standard for electronic data interchange between financial institutions (ISO 20022).[56] For private sector data to be safely integrated in the national data system, businesses further need to comply with the data protection and privacy regulations put in place as a fundamental step in moving toward an integrated national data system.

Colocation data centers. As firms become more reliant on data systems, they will need access to colocation data centers to help manage their data processing and storage needs and to reduce the costs associated with running and certifying internal data centers.[57] Access to data centers in lower-income countries remains poor, in part because of these countries' fragile business environments and low demand for data (see chapter 5).[58] Appropriate measures to promote the expansion of data centers and increase access will depend on the context. In high-capacity, high-demand contexts, data centers may need to be located relatively close to users to maximize cost savings and speed, and changes to the local business climate

may be sufficient to encourage the necessary investments. Where local capacity and demand are low, however, regional efforts to promote investment in regional data centers and other digital infrastructure may be more appropriate. Governments might also explore opportunities to work with large businesses in-country that already have in-house data storage systems and that could, if aggregated, create the necessary scale for colocation data centers to meet local needs. So long as the business of running carrier-neutral colocation data centers proves profitable in a particular context, securing private investment should be straightforward.[59] In Africa, at least 20 new private sector data centers are expected to come online by 2021, which will bring the total to more than 100 across the continent.[60]

Data intermediaries. Trusted data intermediaries can be used to optimize B2G data flows in more mature data systems (see chapter 8). Data intermediaries can provide sophisticated, data-driven businesses with the assurances they need about the security of their data, combined with strong accountability and transparency mechanisms that grant them more control over and visibility of data use.[61] For example, the Reserve Bank of India (RBI), in response to national guidelines introduced by the Ministry of Electronics and Information Technology (MEITy) for standardizing consent for data sharing, is institutionally separating the collection of customer consent from data processing to enhance trust in their data management processes and use.[62]

Integrating international and regional organizations and collaborating across borders

International and regional organizations, donors, as well as international NGOs are important participants in the national data system by collecting their own data, funding country-level data collection, setting international standards, and using country data for monitoring and analysis. International and regional organizations are also forums for cross-border collaboration on data production and exchange as well as data governance.

Although national governments have rather limited control over international organizations and their agendas, they can take steps to integrate these institutions into the national data system in a beneficial fashion (figure 9.7).

Technical assistance. At low levels of data maturity, countries often struggle with limited resources for setting up a national data system, but they could utilize funding, technical assistance, and global public

Figure 9.7 Steps to integrating international and regional organizations into the national data system and collaborating across borders

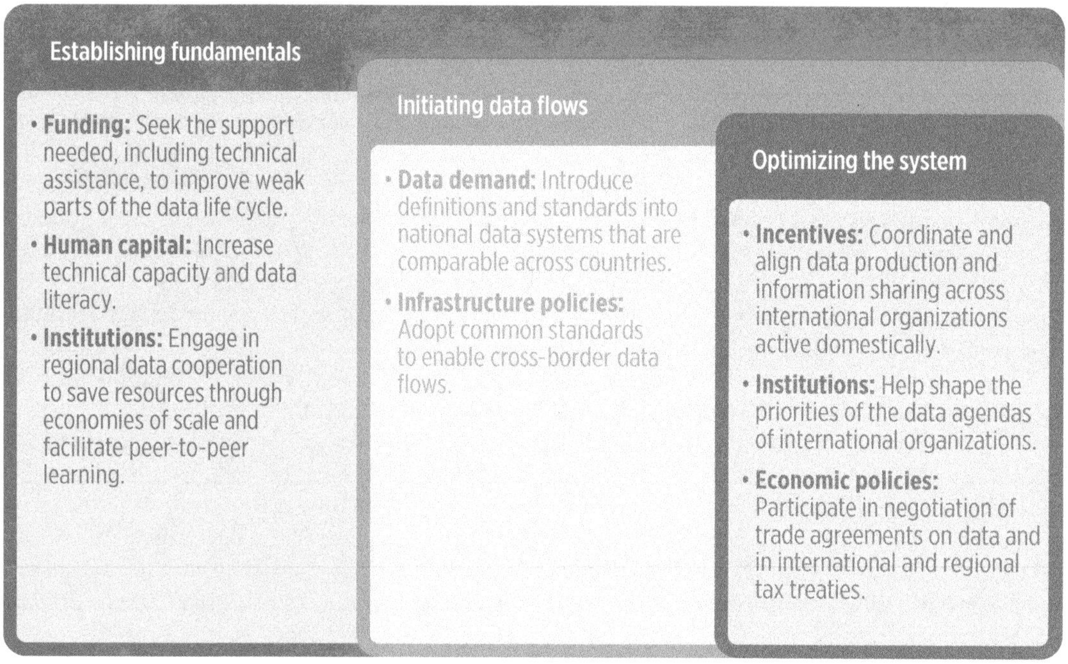

Establishing fundamentals

- **Funding:** Seek the support needed, including technical assistance, to improve weak parts of the data life cycle.
- **Human capital:** Increase technical capacity and data literacy.
- **Institutions:** Engage in regional data cooperation to save resources through economies of scale and facilitate peer-to-peer learning.

Initiating data flows

- **Data demand:** Introduce definitions and standards into national data systems that are comparable across countries.
- **Infrastructure policies:** Adopt common standards to enable cross-border data flows.

Optimizing the system

- **Incentives:** Coordinate and align data production and information sharing across international organizations active domestically.
- **Institutions:** Help shape the priorities of the data agendas of international organizations.
- **Economic policies:** Participate in negotiation of trade agreements on data and in international and regional tax treaties.

Source: WDR 2021 team.

Note: Categories overlap and are meant to be illustrative.

goods from international organizations to address weak spots in the data life cycle. International and regional organizations are well placed to level the playing field by putting in place the conditions that would enable countries with the least data maturity to begin catching up to their more data mature peers. For some countries, this may mean obtaining funding for core data production. For others, it may be seeking assistance with data storage and management. For still others, international organizations can help deidentify datasets, assist in the adoption of improved methods and tools for data production, and suggest modernization of statistical laws and regulations to ensure they are conducive to safe data exchanges. For these steps to be effective, governments need to assess where in the data life cycle they might need support.

Data literacy. At the early stages of data maturity, governments may also rely on international organizations and development partners for programs aimed at improving technical capacity and data literacy. The former could include short-term training, such as the World Bank's C4D2 Training Initiative, which provides statisticians in low- and middle-income countries with specialized training in the collection, analysis, and use of microdata. It could also

include twinning arrangements between statistical agencies that could create opportunities for on-the-job or postgraduate training and staff exchanges or secondments, such as those carried by Statistics Norway.[63] One example of a regional institution created to address data literacy, among other things, is the African Union Institute for Statistics.[64] It is important to keep long-term sustainability in mind for such programs. Training a handful of staff in an agency is of little value if the retention rate of these staff is low. Through the Data for Policy Initiative, the World Bank has committed to sustainable technical support of national statistical systems in at least 30 low-income countries.[65] Long-term institutional relationships with such agencies increase the ease with which they can adopt demanding international best practices.

Regional cooperation. Starting in the early stages of data maturity, countries can use cross-border collaboration to save resources through economies of scale. Countries can cooperate in setting up certain functions of the national data system at a supranational level when trying to perform these functions in each country individually would be inefficient and could precipitate balkanization. For example, through the Statistics for Development Division of the Secretariat of the Pacific Community, nations are working together on data collection, analysis, dissemination, and methodology, thereby reducing costs across the data life cycle.[66] Regional collaboration in data-related regulatory matters can also be beneficial. The African Tax Administration Forum (ATAF) is one example (see spotlight 7.2).[67]

Most countries are members of a regional network where peer-to-peer learning can facilitate the adoption of best practices. In these networks, countries can learn from peers that are one step further down the road. This learning can spur innovation and help countries move up the data maturity model. For example, experienced member countries of the Programme for International Student Assessment (PISA), a benchmarking initiative of the Organisation for Economic Co-operation and Development (OECD), have shared their experiences with new program members, facilitating comparable measurement of educational outcomes internationally.[68] In the area of competition, international exchanges of knowledge would be particularly useful in improving understanding of antitrust issues in data-driven markets.

Common standards. After the resource limitations are addressed, data should flow from international organizations to domestic participants and vice versa, as well as across borders. To successfully and securely initiate data flows to and from international organizations, data must be internationally comparable and anchored in common standards. National decision-makers could insist on introducing cross-country comparable definitions and measures into project monitoring, evaluation, and high-level strategic documents. Working closely with international standard setting organizations is instrumental to this end. For example, the System of National Accounts (SNA), the international standard for measuring economic activity, includes a set of internationally agreed-on concepts, definitions, classifications, and accounting rules. The SNA has facilitated the comparability of macroeconomic statistics internationally, with 90 percent of countries using at least the 1993 SNA standard.[69] Common standards also facilitate comparisons across countries, allowing international organizations to better prioritize resources.

Similarly, international organizations can play an important role in coordinating and supporting the development of national statistical systems that are comparable and compatible across countries. For example, the Cape Town Global Action Plan for Sustainable Development Data, adopted by the UN Statistical Commission, provides a roadmap for the funding and modernization of national statistical systems needed around the world to monitor the Sustainable Development Goals.

Coordination. To integrate international organizations into the national data system and to avoid overlapping and conflicting initiatives, domestic actors need to ensure that the data roles and responsibilities of international agencies within a country are coordinated. In India, this challenge was solved by creating sectoral committees in which the country offices of various United Nations (UN) organizations, ministries, and research institutions participated. Through these committees, the SDG-related activities and technical support of the various international agencies were divided across regions and domains in a nonoverlapping manner, anchored in the UN Resident Coordinator's office.[70] A similar model could be replicated or refined to ensure the efforts of international agencies are coordinated. Although this step is needed to optimize flows, such coordination is crucial in countries with less developed national data systems where many donors are active.

Data agendas of international organizations. As countries build their capacity and obtain more resources, their scope for influencing the data agenda of international organizations increases. Countries can work to ensure that the agendas of international organizations are guided by country needs and priorities. Such an effort can minimize competing agendas and better align data needs and data gaps between national and international agencies, maximizing, in turn, the relevance of data and thus data exchanges among participants.

Trade agreements. At this stage, countries can also seek to leverage international and regional organizations to participate in the negotiation of trade agreements on data aimed at facilitating cross-border trade in data. This may be tackled bilaterally—such as the Digital Trade Agreement between Japan and the United States[71]—or attempted through the World Trade Organization (see chapter 7 and spotlight 7.2). To capture tax revenues from the multinational digital economy, an international tax treaty will be necessary. Similarly, countries should seek to coordinate their antitrust authorities' regulatory actions on data-driven businesses across borders (see spotlight 7.2).

Integrating the national data system

A successful national data system creates an environment in which the value of data for development can be maximized. The impact of data on development increases with the number of participants safely producing, exchanging, using, reusing, and repurposing the data. Incorporating the various participants in the national data system is a central task in building an integrated system. This chapter has laid out steps for how to approach this task. Some cross-cutting themes that have emerged from this discussion have the potential to tie together and strengthen the entire system:

- *Data literacy and data education* are prerequisites for people's participation in the national data system. Better data literacy improves policy-making and business decisions and strengthens efforts to hold governments and the private sector accountable. Data literacy also boosts trust in data.
- *Stringent and shared approaches to data protection* are necessary for participants to trust the integrity of data production and use and initiate data exchanges.
- *Data interoperability, comparability, and reliability through common standards and quality control* allow data to be integrated from different sources and boost their usefulness. These standards and quality controls may need to be developed. Data stewards can play an important role in ensuring quality and interoperability.
- *Data openness and accessibility* through means such as digital platforms make widespread data use and reuse possible.

Investing in these cross-cutting steps can have wide-ranging benefits for all participants in the national data system and for development, but they will require commensurate financial and political commitments.

Meanwhile, countries are already constructing national data systems, whether intentionally or not. Some of this is happening through day-to-day government activities, such as service delivery and monitoring of programs. Some of this is happening because events such as the COVID-19 pandemic are accelerating change. And some of this is happening because technological advances are ushering in sweeping transformations on an unprecedented scale. As the country examples in this Report show, pushes and pulls across the economy and society are shaping the construction of national data systems implicitly or explicitly.

This *World Development Report* on data for development advocates an intentional, comprehensive, multistakeholder, collaborative approach to constructing an integrated national data system that aims to maximize the development benefits of data while minimizing the risks. This approach takes into account those now left out of or marginalized in the data economy.

It prescribes a data-driven culture that can creatively and constructively use, reuse, and repurpose data. It calls on countries to shape their system based on their own circumstances, including their own capabilities, values, and political economy. It recognizes the complexity of this endeavor but recommends a phased approach to make it happen. It moves away from reactive steps to proactive ones. It calls on the international community to help countries take these steps and to provide the standardization, harmonization, and tools necessary to make it work. And, not least, it is the considered aim of this Report to foster a global discussion that can truly help data improve lives.

Notes

1. A similar argument is made in MacFeely (2020).
2. International and regional organizations are also key producers of data. One important role they have is producing transnational data—flows, interactions, and links between countries or phenomena that are difficult or impossible for a country itself to record. For example, the United Nations Office on Drugs and Crime collects data on illicit activities between countries, such as trafficking in drugs, that one country alone cannot collect because the object of interest leaves the country of origin without being detected.
3. Dargent et al. (2020).
4. British Academy and Royal Society (2017).
5. OECD (2019a).
6. Dargent et al. (2020).
7. See Department of Information and Communications Technology, ODPH (Open Data Philippines) (dashboard), https://data.gov.ph/. See also Aceron (2018), Warwick (2017), and an example of open government data in Australia at Digital Transformation Agency, Search for Data (dashboard), https://data.gov.au/.
8. United Nations Statistical Commission (2021) contains case studies of the role of national statistical offices in national data systems.
9. Stats NZ (2018).
10. MKM (2018).
11. See Government Office, Government of Estonia, "E-Estonia Council," https://www.riigikantselei.ee/en/supporting-government/e-estonia-council.
12. Kivimäki (2018); World Bank (2021).
13. OECD (2019a).
14. MKM (2018, 22).
15. Piovesan (2015).
16. Gray, Lämmerhirt, and Bounegru (2016); Lämmerhirt et al. (2018).
17. Lämmerhirt et al. (2018).
18. See ODK (dashboard), https://getodk.org/. See also US Census Bureau, Census and Survey Processing System (CSPro) version 7.5.0 (dashboard), https://www.census.gov/data/software/cspro.html; World Bank, Survey Solutions version 21.01 (dashboard), https://mysurvey.solutions/en/.

19. Carranza (2018); Gray, Lämmerhirt, and Bounegru (2016).

20. Wilson and Rahman (2015).

21. For more information, see Code for Africa, Academy Africa: Courses (dashboard), https://academy.africa/courses.

22. Bruhn, Lara Ibarra, and McKenzie (2014); Bruhn et al. (2016); Frisancho (2018); Lührmann, Serra-Garcia, and Winter (2018). However, the long-term effects are not yet known (Entorf and Hou 2018).

23. Bizimungu (2017).

24. Gray, Lämmerhirt, and Bounegru (2016).

25. Lämmerhirt et al. (2018).

26. Cázarez-Grageda et al. (2020) and MacFeely and Nastav (2019) present more elaborate proposals for how data from civil society can be used for tracking SDGs and in official reporting, and they establish quality frameworks enabling NSOs to engage with CSOs.

27. Lämmerhirt et al. (2018).

28. Lämmerhirt et al. (2018).

29. Carranza (2018).

30. Misra and Schmidt (2020).

31. Masaki et al. (2017).

32. Harvard Dataverse, Datahub for Field Experiments in Economics and Public Policy (data repository), https://dataverse.harvard.edu/dataverse/DFEEP?q=&types=dataverses%3Adatasets%3Afiles&sort=dateSort&order=desc&page=1.

33. Data-Pop Alliance brings together researchers, experts, practitioners, and activists to change the world with data through three pillars of work: diagnosing local realities and human problems with data and artificial intelligence (AI); mobilizing capacities, communities, and ideas toward more data-literate societies; and transforming the systems and processes that underpin societies and countries. In 2016 Flowminder Foundation joined as the fourth Core Member. For more information, see ThoughtWorks, Data-Pop Alliance (dashboard), https://datapopalliance.org/.

34. See Nepal Data Literacy Program, Data Literacy for Prosperous Nepal (data literacy portal), https://dataliteracy.github.io/.

35. Ministry of Education, MineduLAB (dashboard), http://www.minedu.gob.pe/minedulab/.

36. Volkow (2019).

37. University of Cape Town, DataFirst (data repository), https://www.datafirst.uct.ac.za/.

38. Palestinian Central Bureau of Statistics, "Research Center," West Bank and Gaza, http://www.pcbs.gov.ps/site/lang__en/598/default.aspx.

39. Many governments have established dedicated monitoring and evaluation agencies or even ministries. For Spain, see "Building a Monitoring and Evaluation Framework for Open Government," chapter 4, pages 117–40, in OECD (2019b).

40. See Consejo Nacional de Evaluación de la Política de Desarrollo Social (National Council for the Evaluation of Social Development Policy), "About Us? Features" (¿Quiénes Somos? Funciones), Mexico City, https://www.coneval.org.mx/quienessomos/Conocenos/Paginas/Funciones.aspx.

41. Bohannon (2016). For information on Research4Life, see https://www.research4life.org/about/.

42. Katz and Callorda (2018).

43. Vertically integrated operators have constructed most national transmission networks. As long as there is strong competition among several players, final consumer prices can be affordable and networks can be resilient. Where private investment is lacking, a government could construct a state-owned transmission network, although the implications for public debt could be severe. Alternatively, a government could take on a coordinating role among operators to create a heterogenous backbone, requiring open access to and cost-based pricing for operator fiber routes.

44. An example is landlocked Mongolia's north-south fiber-optic backbone connecting it to China and the Russian Federation runs along the railway (Tsolmondelger 2019).

45. For a description of the Sudanese program, see Moscoso (2016). For elements of the training course, see "Welcome to the Sudan Evidence Base Programme–Data Literacy Training," https://sudanebp.tuvalabs.com/.

46. Agudelo et al. (2014).

47. Rosa (2018).

48. Kenya's IXP, launched in 2000, was Africa's first IXP. It was established and is run by the local ISP industry association, the Telecommunication Service Providers of Kenya. See Jensen (2012); Technology Service Providers of Kenya, "KIXP Background," https://www.tespok.co.ke/?page_id=11651.

49. Jensen (2012).

50. High-Level Expert Group on Business-to-Government Data Sharing (2020).

51. Dahmm (2020). Contracts for Data Collaboration (C4DC) is a joint initiative of SDSN TReNDS, New York University's GovLab, the World Economic Forum, and the University of Washington.

52. High-Level Expert Group on Business-to-Government Data Sharing (2020).

53. OPAL was created by groups at MIT Media Lab, Imperial College London, Orange, the World Economic Forum, and Data-Pop Alliance. For more information, see the OPAL website, https://www.opalproject.org/home-en.

54. High-Level Expert Group on Business-to-Government Data Sharing (2020).

55. GovLab (2020).

56. See International Organization for Standardization, About ISO 20022: Governance (dashboard), https://www.iso20022.org/about-iso-20022/governance.

57. A colocation data center is a facility equipped with networked computers providing remote storage, processing, and distribution of data where multiple data service providers may colocate. They are mainly operated by global information technology (IT) companies, governments, and enterprises that host other companies' data (known as colocation). For the relevant standard of the International Organization for Standardization (ISO), see ISO, "ISO/IEC 27001:2013(en)," at OBP (Online Browsing Platform) (database), https://www.iso.org/obp/ui/#iso:std:iso-iec:27001:ed-2:v1:en.

58. This is often attributed to a lack of demand, as well as aversion to a country's perceived high risk of natural disasters, unpredictable political environment, barriers to doing business, and unreliable energy and internet infrastructure (C&W 2016).

59. Munshi (2020).

60. ADCA (2020).

61. World Bank (2021).

62. RBI (2019).

63. SSB (2020).

64. More broadly, the Global Network of Institutions for Statistical Training works to build sustainable statistical capacities through efficient and harmonized training programs.

65. Dabalen, Himelein, and Rodríguez-Castelán (2020).

66. Statistics for Development Division, Pacific Community, "Pacific Statistics Methods Board (PSMB)," Nouméa, New Caledonia, https://sdd.spc.int/pacific -statistics-methods-board-psmb.

67. ATAF (2020).

68. OECD (2018).

69. Fifty percent of countries are using the latest—the 2008 SNA standard. See Statistics Division, Department of Economic and Social Affairs, United Nations, National Accounts (database), https://unstats.un.org/unsd /nationalaccount/; World Bank, Statistical Performance Indicators (database), http://www.worldbank.org/spi.

70. Recently, a coordination forum was instituted in which key stakeholders collaborate on issues related to support for statistical monitoring of SDG goals and targets, including the use of new technologies and capacity development to track SDG-related outcomes.

71. Office of the United States Trade Representative, U.S.–Japan Digital Trade Agreement Text (dashboard), https://ustr.gov/countries-regions/japan-korea-apec /japan/us-japan-trade-agreement-negotiations/us-japan -digital-trade-agreement-text.

References

Aceron, Joy. 2018. "Independent Reporting Mechanism (IRM): Philippines End of Term Report 2015–2017." Open Government Partnership, Washington, DC. https://www .opengovpartnership.org/wp-content/uploads/2018/10 /Philippines_End-of-Term_Report_2015-2017.pdf.

ADCA (Africa Data Centres Association). 2020. "State of the African Data Centre Market 2020." ADCA, Abidjan, Côte d'Ivoire. http://africadca.org/en/state-of-the-african-data -centre-market-2020.

Agudelo, Mauricio, Raúl Katz, Ernesto Flores-Roux, María Cristina Duarte Botero, Fernando Callorda, and Taylor Berry. 2014. Expansión de Infraestructura Regional para la Interconexión de Tráfico de Internet en América Latina. Infraestructura Series. Caracas, República Bolivariana de Venezuela: Development Bank of Latin America. http:// scioteca.caf.com/handle/123456789/522.

ATAF (African Tax Administration Forum). 2020. "Domestic Resource Mobilisation: Digital Services Taxation in Africa." Policy Brief 01, ATAF, Pretoria, South Africa.

https://events.ataftax.org/index.php?page=documents& func=view&document_id=61.

Bizimungu, Julius. 2017. "New Initiatives to Drive Digital Literacy and Use of Tech Services." New Times, September 30, 2017. https://www.newtimes.co.rw/section /read/220887.

Bohannon, John. 2016. "Who's Downloading Pirated Papers? Everyone." Science (blog), April 28, 2016. https://www .sciencemag.org/news/2016/04/whos-downloading -pirated-papers-everyone.

British Academy and Royal Society. 2017. "Data Management and Use: Governance in the 21st Century: A Joint Report by the British Academy and the Royal Society." British Academy and Royal Society, London. https://royalsociety .org/topics-policy/projects/data-governance/.

Bruhn, Miriam, Gabriel Lara Ibarra, and David McKenzie. 2014. "The Minimal Impact of a Large-Scale Financial Education Program in Mexico City." Journal of Development Economics 108 (May): 184–89. https://doi.org/10.1016 /j.jdeveco.2014.02.009.

Bruhn, Miriam, Luciana de Souza Leão, Arianna Legovini, Rogelio Marchetti, and Bilal Zia. 2016. "The Impact of High School Financial Education: Evidence from a Large-Scale Evaluation in Brazil." American Economic Journal: Applied Economics 8 (4): 256–95. https://doi.org/10.1257 /app.20150149.

C&W (Cushman and Wakefield). 2016. "Data Centre Risk Index." C&W, London. https://verne-global-lackey.s3 .amazonaws.com/uploads%2F2017%2F1%2Fb5e0a0da -5ad2-01b3-1eb8-8f782f22a534%2FC%26W_Data _Centre+Risk_Index_Report_2016.pdf.

Carranza, Javier. 2018. "Citizen to Government Data Partnerships: What Can We Learn from and Recommend to Civil Society Groups Working in the Official Statistics Domain?" Eurostat Statistical Working Paper KS-TC-18-007-EN-N, European Union, Luxembourg. https://doi .org/10.2785/728477.

Cázarez-Grageda, Karina, Julia Schmidt, and Rajiv Ranjan. 2020. "Reusing Citizen-Generated Data for Official Reporting: A Quality Framework for National Statistical Office–Civil Society Organization Engagement." PARIS21 working paper, PARIS21 Consortium, Paris.

Dabalen, Andrew L., Kristen Himelein, and Carlos Rodríguez-Castelán. 2020. "Data for Policy (D4P) Initiative." Poverty and Equity Note 23, World Bank, Washington, DC. https://openknowledge.worldbank.org/handle /10986/33857.

Dahmm, Hayden. 2020. "Laying the Foundation for Effective Partnerships: An Examination of Data Sharing Agreements." UN Sustainable Development Solutions Network's Thematic Research Network on Data and Statistics (SDSN TReNDS) on behalf of Contracts for Data Collaboration (C4DC).

Dargent, Eduardo, Gabriela Lotta, José Antonio Mejía-Guerra, and Gilberto Moncada. 2020. "Who Wants to Know? The Political Economy of Statistical Capacity in Latin America." Inter-American Development Bank, Washington, DC.

Entorf, Horst, and Jia Hou. 2018. "Financial Education for the Disadvantaged? A Review." IZA Discussion Paper 11515, Institute of Labor Economics, Bonn, Germany.

Frisancho, Verónica. 2018. "The Impact of School-Based Financial Education on High School Students and Their Teachers: Experimental Evidence from Peru." IDB Working Paper IDB-WP-871, Inter-American Development Bank, Washington, DC. https://doi.org/10.18235/0001056.

GovLab (Governance Lab). 2020. "Wanted: Data Stewards; (Re-)Defining the Roles and Responsibilities of Data Stewards for an Age of Data Collaboration." GovLab, Tandon School of Engineering, New York University, Brooklyn, NY. http://www.thegovlab.org/static/files /publications/wanted-data-stewards.pdf.

Gray, Jonathan, Danny Lämmerhirt, and Liliana Bounegru. 2016. "Changing What Counts: How Can Citizen-Generated and Civil Society Data Be Used as an Advocacy Tool to Change Official Data Collection?" DataShift, Civicus, Johannesburg. http://civicus.org /thedatashift/wp-content/uploads/2016/03/changing -what-counts-2.pdf.

High-Level Expert Group on Business-to-Government Data Sharing. 2020. *Towards a European Strategy on Business-to-Government Data Sharing for the Public Interest.* Luxembourg: European Union. https://www.euractiv.com /wp-content/uploads/sites/2/2020/02/B2GDataSharing ExpertGroupReport-1.pdf.

Jensen, Mike. 2012. "Promoting the Use of Internet Exchange Points: A Guide to Policy, Management, and Technical Issues." Internet Society Report, Internet Society, Reston, VA. https://www.internetsociety.org/wp-content /uploads/2012/12/promote-ixp-guide.pdf.

Katz, Raul, and Fernando Callorda. 2018. "The Economic Contribution of Broadband, Digitization, and ICT Regulation." Thematic Report: Regulatory and Market Environment Series, International Telecommunication Union, Geneva. https://www.itu.int/pub/D-PREF-EF .BDR-2018.

Kivimäki, Petteri. 2018. "X-Road as a Platform to Exchange MyData." Nordic Institute for Interoperability Solutions, Tallinn, Estonia. https://www.niis.org/blog/2019/10/30/x -road-as-a-platform-to-exchange-mydata.

Lämmerhirt, Danny, Jonathan Gray, Tommaso Venturini, and Axel Meunier. 2018. "Advancing Sustainability Together? Citizen-Generated Data and the Sustainable Development Goals." Global Partnership for Sustainable Development Data, United Nations, New York. http://www.data4sdgs.org/resources/advancing -sustainability-together-citizen-generated-data-and -sustainable-development.

Lührmann, Melanie, Marta Serra-Garcia, and Joachim Winter. 2018. "The Impact of Financial Education on Adolescents' Intertemporal Choices." *American Economic Journal: Economic Policy* 10 (3): 309–32. https://doi.org/10.1257 /pol.20170012.

MacFeely, Steve. 2020. "In Search of the Data Revolution: Has the Official Statistics Paradigm Shifted?" *Statistical Journal of the IAOS* 36 (4): 1075–94.

MacFeely, Steve, and Bojan Nastav. 2019. "You Say You Want a [Data] Revolution: A Proposal to Use Unofficial Statistics for the SDG Global Indicator Framework." *Statistical Journal of the IAOS* 35 (3): 309–27.

Masaki, Takaaki, Samantha Custer, Agustina Eskenazi, Alena Stern, and Rebecca Latourell. 2017. "Decoding Data Use: How Do Leaders Use Data and Use It to Accelerate Development?" AidData, Global Research Institute, College of William and Mary, Williamsburg, VA.

Misra, Archita, and Julia Schmidt. 2020. "Enhancing Trust in Data—Participatory Data Ecosystems for the Post-COVID Society." In *Shaping the COVID-19 Recovery: Ideas from OECD's Generation Y and Z.* Paris: Organisation for Economic Co-operation and Development.

MKM (Ministry of Economic Affairs and Communications, Estonia). 2018. "Digital Agenda 2020 for Estonia." MKM, Tallinn, Estonia. https://www.mkm.ee/sites/default/files /digital_agenda_2020_web_eng_04.06.19.pdf.

Moscoso, Sandra. 2016. "Increasing Data Literacy to Improve Policy-Making in Sudan." *Governance for Development* (blog), March 15, 2016. https://blogs.worldbank.org /governance/increasing-data-literacy-improve-policy -making-sudan#.

Munshi, Neil. 2020. "Africa's Cloud Computing Boom Creates Data Centre Gold Rush." *Technology Sector* (blog), March 2, 2020. https://www.ft.com/content/402a18c8 -5a32-11ea-abe5-8e03987b7b20.

OECD (Organisation for Economic Co-operation and Development). 2002. *Measuring the Non-Observed Economy: A Handbook.* Paris: OECD. http://www.oecd.org/sdd/na /1963116.pdf.

OECD (Organisation for Economic Co-operation and Development). 2018. "Peer-to-Peer Learning to Strengthen Dissemination of PISA for Development Results." PISA for Development Brief 27, OECD, Paris. https://www .oecd.org/pisa/pisa-for-development/27_Peer_learning _results_dissemination.pdf.

OECD (Organisation for Economic Co-operation and Development). 2019a. *Digital Government Review of Argentina: Accelerating the Digitalisation of the Public Sector.* OECD Digital Government Studies Series. Paris: OECD. https://www.oecd-ilibrary.org/governance/digital -government-review-of-argentina_354732cc-en.

OECD (Organisation for Economic Co-operation and Development). 2019b. *Open Government in Biscay.* OECD Public Governance Reviews Series. Paris: OECD. https://doi .org/10.1787/a70e8be3-en.

Piovesan, Federico. 2015. "Statistical Perspectives on Citizen-Generated Data." DataShift, Civicus, Johannesburg, South Africa. http://civicus.org/thedatashift/wp-content /uploads/2015/07/statistical-perspectives-on-cgd_web _single-page.pdf.

RBI (Reserve Bank of India). 2019. "Master Direction–Non-Banking Financial Company–Account Aggregator (Reserve Bank) Directions." Document RBI/DNBR/2016-17/46, Master Direction DNBR.PD.009/03.10.119/2016-17, RBI, Mumbai. https://www.rbi.org.in/Scripts/BS_View MasDirections.aspx?id=10598.

Rosa, Fernanda R. 2018. "Internet Node as a Network of Relationships: Sociotechnical Aspects of an Internet Exchange Point." Paper presented at TPRC46: Research Conference on Communications, Information, and Internet Policy, Washington College of Law, American University, Washington, DC, September 21–22, 2018.

SSB (Statistisk sentralbyrå, Statistics Norway). 2020. "Annual Report 2019: International Development Cooperation in Statistics Norway." Plans and Reports 2020/1,

SSB, Oslo. https://www.ssb.no/en/omssb/om-oss/vaar
-virksomhet/planer-og-meldinger/_attachment/416480?
_ts=1711b58ce28.

Stats NZ (Statistics New Zealand). 2018. "Data Strategy and
Roadmap." Fact Sheet, Wellington, New Zealand. https://
www.data.govt.nz/assets/Uploads/fact-sheet-data-road
map-12422-oct-18.pdf.

Tsolmondelger, Odkhuu. 2019. "ICT Infrastructure along
Transport Network." Presentation, Information Communications Network LLC, Ulaanbaatar, Mongolia, November 20, 2019. https://www.unescap.org/sites/default
/files/ICT%20Infrastructure%20Along%20Transport
%20Network%2C%20Mongolia%20NetCom.pdf.

United Nations Statistical Commission. 2021. "Approaches
to Data Stewardship." Paper prepared for the High-Level
Group for Partnership, Coordination and Capacity-
Building for Statistics for the 2030 Agenda for Sustainable Development. https://unstats.un.org/unsd/statcom
/52nd-session/documents/BG-3a-DataStewardship-E.pdf.

Volkow, Natalia. 2019. "Harnessing the Potentiality of
Microdata Access Risk Management Model." Paper
presented at Joint UNECE/Eurostat Work Session on
Statistical Data Confidentiality, Session 1.1, Conference
of European Statisticians, The Hague, Netherlands,
October 29–31, 2019.

Warwick, Mara. 2017. "Philippines: Open Data Launch."
Speeches and Transcripts, World Bank, Washington, DC.
https://www.worldbank.org/en/news/speech/2017
/03/02/open-data-launch.

Wilson, Christopher, and Zara Rahman. 2015. "Citizen-
Generated Data and Governments: Towards a Collaborative Model." DataShift, Civicus, Johannesburg, South
Africa. http://civicus.org/images/citizen-generated%20
data%20and%20governments.pdf.

World Bank. 2021. *Unraveling Data's Gordian Knot: Enablers
and Safeguards for Trusted Data Sharing in the New Economy.*
Washington, DC: World Bank.